T0306502

UNRELIABLE WATCHDOG

TED GALEN CARPENTER

UNRELIABLE WATCHDOG

THE NEWS MEDIA AND U.S. FOREIGN POLICY

Print ISBN: 978-1-952223-33-4
eBook ISBN: 978-1-952223-34-1

Cover design: Jon Meyers

Library of Congress Cataloging-in-Publication Data

Carpenter, Ted Galen, author.
    Unreliable watchdog : the news media and U.S. foreign policy / Ted
    Galen Carpenter.
            pages   cm
    Washington : Cato Institute, [2022]
    Includes bibliographical references and index.
    ISBN 9781952223334 (hardcover) | ISBN 9781952223341 (ebook)   1. Press and politics—
    United States History—20th century. 2. Press and politics—United States—History—21st century.
    3. Government and the press—United States—History—20th century. 4. Government and the press—
    United States—History—21st century. 5. United States—Foreign relations—20th century. 6. United
    States—Foreign relations—21st century.
    PN4888.P6 C375 2022
    071.309—dc23   2022000815

Printed in the United States of America.

CATO INSTITUTE
1000 Massachusetts Ave. NW
Washington, DC 20001
www.cato.org

Unreliable Watchdog is dedicated to the memory of my two mentors, Professor David F. Healy and Professor Robert A. Divine.

CONTENTS

INTRODUCTION
An Ambiguous Press Legacy on Foreign Policy

Veteran media analysts Seth Ackerman and Jim Naureckas observe that "in times of war, there is always intense pressure for reporters to serve as propagandists rather than journalists." Such pressure must be resisted, they emphasize. "While the role of the journalist is to present the world in all its complexity, giving the public as much information as possible in order to facilitate a democratic debate, the propagandist simplifies the world in order to mobilize the public behind a common goal."[1] Those two missions are inherently incompatible.

Yet too many journalists seem unable to make that crucial distinction. Ackerman and Naureckas actually understate the scope and severity of corrupting influences on the coverage of foreign policy issues: although the problem has tended to be more pervasive and blatant during times of war, it is not confined to such periods. Since World War II, the corrosive impact on journalism has become significantly more pronounced, even during periods when the republic is technically at peace. As America has become a truly global power with commitments around the world, and a garrison state always prepared for armed conflict, the conflating of journalism and propaganda has grown more extensive and intensive, even with respect to situations that do not involve actual combat. Indeed, the news media's support for a highly activist U.S. role increasingly constrains, if not distorts, public debate about numerous aspects of the nation's foreign policy.

Throughout the history of the American republic, ambitious officials have sought to enlist journalists and other opinion shapers to promote their version of events and policy choices. When enticement proves insufficient, those same officials are not above harassing, vilifying, and attempting to intimidate members of the news profession who insist on raising troublesome questions or criticizing government actions and justifications. Such behavior became increasingly evident as Washington's global role blossomed during the 20th century, and the trend has both deepened and accelerated in the new millennium.

A global interventionist foreign policy depends on unity of purpose, credibility of commitments, and speed of execution. Those requirements run directly counter to the objectives of an unrestricted press and vigorous public debate. Advocates of effective U.S. "global leadership" tend to regard outside criticism as an annoyance at best and a menace at worst. From the perspective of officials committed to an activist foreign policy, a critical press is inconvenient, even dangerous. Investigative journalism may expose cherry-picked evidence, half-truths, or outright lies that underlie official policy justifications. The public's awareness or ignorance of such factors can greatly influence the level of support for an initiative. Critical coverage also can cast doubt on the wisdom or effectiveness of existing policies, leading to an erosion of public confidence in both the policies and their architects.

As a result, government agencies tend to maintain a love-hate relationship with the news media. Although officials profess that a free press is essential to the health of a democratic political system, they tend to regard the fourth estate as a necessary evil at best. Consequently, they seek to restrict it, manipulate it, or seduce it. Officials tasked with responsibility for managing the nation's foreign policy prefer to formulate and execute decisions away from the prying eyes of inquisitive journalists. At the same time, political leaders and their appointees recognize that the press can be an effective, indeed invaluable, conduit for disseminating government propaganda and manipulating public opinion. Therefore, from the government's standpoint, journalists can be either menacing adversaries or useful tools.

Members of the news media likewise have exhibited a love-hate relationship with national security practitioners. However, that relationship has shifted increasingly toward love over the decades since World War II and seemingly has even deepened during the post–Cold War period. Journalists have a pronounced bias in favor of a highly activist U.S. foreign policy—especially if officials can invoke a plausible national security or humanitarian justification for Washington to intervene in a foreign conflict. The tools for such an intervention include economic sanctions, covert operations, and even direct military action. The national security rationale played the leading role throughout the Cold War, when policymakers routinely cited the Soviet threat or the more amorphous menace of international communism to justify Washington's growing network of military alliances, as well as largely unilateral military actions in such places as Korea, Lebanon, the Dominican Republic, and Vietnam.

The Vietnam debacle made at least some journalists more skeptical of the national security rationale, especially for missions in the Third World. That greater caution manifested itself in frequently hostile media scrutiny of the Reagan administration's case for undermining left-wing political factions in Central America and Angola. Overall press treatments of Washington's official justifications were decidedly more diverse and wary than they had been pre-Vietnam. Such skepticism even carried over to some extent in the lead-up to the 1991 Persian Gulf War under President George H. W. Bush. Officials throughout the Reagan and Bush administrations derided negative, or even wary, press coverage as just another manifestation of the "Vietnam Syndrome"—what they considered to be a public overreaction to the humiliating failure of U.S. policy in that country.

The unexpectedly low cost of the Persian Gulf War in American blood and treasure seemed to vindicate a highly assertive U.S. policy and banished the Vietnam Syndrome of greater skepticism and caution. The democratic West's definitive triumph in the Cold War with the collapse of the Soviet Union's East European satellite empire, and ultimately the dissolution of the USSR itself, reinforced the perception that an assertive, globalist strategy for the United States was normally successful and beneficial, despite the Vietnam setback. A strong pro-activist pattern emerged with a vengeance again and again with respect to both U.S. policy and media coverage of that policy throughout the post–Cold War era.

That revived activist bias among journalists played a prominent role in generating public support for the Somalia intervention during the early 1990s and the two Balkan wars (in Bosnia and Kosovo) later that decade. Indeed, media enthusiasm for military intervention in the Balkans significantly exceeded that among officials in Bill Clinton's administration. In both cases, the press corps became a passionate lobbyist for military action—a role it had not played so enthusiastically since the yellow journalism campaign in the late 1890s helped push the United States into the Spanish-American War. Advocacy journalism surged in strength and prominence, and the concept of journalistic objectivity—or even reasonable balance and fairness—faded.

Most media proponents of these military interventions, though, did not rely on national security justifications. Few credible foreign policy experts believed that the United States had meaningful, tangible *security* interests at stake in either Somalia or the Balkans. Instead, pro-intervention journalists relied on "humanitarian" justifications. The essence of their argument was that brutal aggressors (warlords in Somalia and Serb nationalists in Bosnia and Kosovo) were inflicting enormous suffering on innocent civilian populations, and that the United States, both because of its national values and vast power, had a moral obligation to lead international military missions to stop the tragedies.

A handful of journalists attempted to sell the argument that an intervention also would benefit U.S. security interests, but most did not even bother trying to make that flimsy case. Instead, they based their arguments overwhelmingly on humanitarian grounds and appeals to emotion. In doing so, they oversimplified the issues at stake in those conflicts as well as the nature of the contending parties—especially by sanitizing the record of the faction they wanted Washington to support. Instead of receiving nuanced press treatments of murky, complex quarrels, news consumers were treated to a barrage of melodramatic accounts pitting one-dimensional villains against equally one-dimensional freedom-seeking victims. Worse, the selling of the Balkan wars through such mythology became a template for media treatments of subsequent intra-state conflicts, especially in the Middle East.

A growing number of journalists explicitly or implicitly signed onto the Responsibility to Protect (R2P) doctrine, which insisted that America's global leadership role required the United States to use its overwhelming military power to defend innocent civilians from evil rulers. R2P not only became the midwife for humanitarian wars, but it served the same function for a corollary objective: regime-change wars to oust tyrants that U.S. leaders disliked—even if those regimes did not pose a credible threat to the United States or even U.S. security partners. The bulk of the media increasingly cheered on new interventions on behalf of either goal, with little reflection or caution.

This bias became evident again in the media's treatment of the Iraq War, at least during its early stages. Part of the enthusiasm for military action reflected the pervasive national mood in the wake of the 9/11 terrorist attacks—and members of the press both reflected and amplified that mood. In doing so, they helped foment and exacerbate public alarm with far-reaching consequences. Very few journalists raised questions about, much less criticized, President George W. Bush's push for an extraordinarily broad authorization for the use of military force to wage the new "War on Terror." Not many even suggested caution when the administration and its congressional allies enacted the so-called Patriot Act, despite its vast grants of power to intelligence and law enforcement agencies and the menace such changes posed to fundamental rights under the First, Fourth, and Fifth Amendments. Instead, media watchdogs went along with the emotional tide and largely supported the Iraq War without question.

Unlike the Balkan conflicts, when the media were significantly ahead of U.S. officialdom in pushing for military action, the prelude to the Iraq War epitomized a toxic, equal partnership between a pro-war administration and pro-war journalists. Indeed, some of the most prominent media titans, including the *New York Times*, the *Washington Post*, and CNN, were the most egregious violators of basic journalistic standards. They circulated administration propaganda, as well as the dubious "intelligence" generated by the Iraqi National Congress (INC)—the pro-intervention exile group headed by Ahmed Chalabi—with little or no skepticism.

Two bogus narratives were especially crucial in generating public support for launching a war to overthrow Iraqi dictator Saddam Hussein. One stream featured allegations that Saddam's regime had extensive ties to al Qaeda, including reported clandestine meetings between Iraqi officials and leaders of the terrorist organization. The implication was that the Iraqi strongman was involved, at least indirectly, in the 9/11 attacks that had killed nearly 3,000 Americans. In reality, the evidence for such an association was thin to nonexistent. Yet most media outlets did not note the lack of evidence, did not question the credibility of the INC as a source, and did not seek independent corroboration of a de facto Baghdad–al Qaeda alliance.

The mainstream media's treatment of the other big allegation— that Saddam already had built or acquired an arsenal of chemical and biological weapons and was working feverishly on obtaining a nuclear capability—was even more negligent and irresponsible. Almost all the information about this weapons program was spoon-fed to credulous journalists by a supposed defector, helpfully provided by the INC. The circulation of those stories by mainstream media outlets with a strong record of credibility convinced the public that the Iraqi regime posed an existential threat to the United States. The media thus helped generate far more public support for a U.S.-led military intervention to topple Saddam than likely would have existed otherwise.

Worse, the bulk of the mainstream media systematically excluded experts who disputed the dominant narrative even mildly. Pro-war voices utterly dominated the airwaves, op-ed pages, and even supposedly straight news stories. As a result, there was little meaningful debate about either the necessity or the wisdom of going to war against Iraq. The predictable destabilizing consequences throughout the Middle East of a U.S.-led war, which dissenting analysts had tried to highlight, thus blindsided most Americans.

When Western military forces occupying Iraq failed to find evidence of a Baghdad–al Qaeda connection or discover an arsenal of weapons of mass destruction (WMD), a few journalists, especially *New York Times* reporter Judith Miller, did suffer damage to their reputations—and in her case, even the loss of her position. But most offenders emerged unscathed. Indeed, the prominent analysts—who had distorted the Iraq coverage, helped along by the leading talking heads on CNN and other television networks—were usually the same ones providing distorted commentary on Washington's later foreign policy escapades in Libya, Syria, and elsewhere.

Any caution that the press may have taken away from the Iraq experience was short-lived. When Barack Obama's administration joined with insurgents to overthrow Libyan dictator Muammar Qaddafi in 2011, media enthusiasm for another regime-change war seemed uninhibited. The same emotional, pro-intervention clichés that had dominated coverage of the Balkan conflicts and the Iraq War were evident once again. So was the pervasive media optimism that Libya would be much better off once the dictator was gone. However, the opposite outcome proved to be the case. Libya descended into chaos, with multiple armed militias, some of which were strongly Islamist, squaring off in turf fights. The result was a massive humanitarian crisis with thousands of fatalities and more than a million civilians turned into beleaguered refugees. Shockingly, even slave markets featuring black African captives made a reappearance. Ultimately, the fighting coalesced into a struggle between a warlord (who was an estranged CIA asset) and a corrupt government that had received both United Nations (UN) and Western recognition. The ongoing conflict also became a proxy war featuring Russia and several Middle East powers backing their respective clients.

Press coverage of Libya's post-Qaddafi tragedy was minimal and grudging. One striking feature was the pervasive unwillingness to acknowledge that policy blunders by the United States and the North Atlantic Treaty Organization (NATO) had led to the chaos. Media outlets assiduously avoided mentioning any connection, even when they published otherwise informative accounts of the ongoing power struggles or the tragic conditions Libyan civilians were enduring.

Coverage of the campaign by the United States and its Western allies to unseat Syria's Bashar al-Assad followed a similar pattern. Once again, most news coverage prodded the American people to support a dubious regime-change war with little thought about the possible adverse consequences if the targeted tyrant was overthrown. And once again, U.S. policy proceeded to worsen an internal conflict that had complex historical and religious roots. The result was a slaughter that consumed approximately 500,000 Syrian lives by 2021 and created more than 6 million refugees—many of whom flowed into Europe, exacerbating social tensions there.

An abundance of news stories idealized the rebels who were attempting to expel Assad, and supposedly knowledgeable accounts merely echoed Obama administration propaganda on that issue. Too many journalists minimized or even ignored the extreme Islamist credentials of several insurgent factions in Syria. The reality was that most of those groups were not "moderates," even given a very generous definition of the term. They certainly were not advocates of Western-style secular democracy. Yet some reporters seemed to go out of their way to deny that reality and conceal the ideological pedigrees of the insurgents Washington was supporting. That tendency among leading media outlets was especially pronounced during Obama's presidency, but in some quarters it persisted throughout Donald Trump's as well.

The media turned in an equally defective performance with respect to U.S.-Russia relations and allegations that President Trump was colluding with Moscow. Members of America's news media were tasked with addressing several interlocking issues. One set was relatively narrow, involving three key questions: (a) did the Russian government attempt to interfere in the 2016 U.S. election, and if it did, what degree of success did it have; (b) was such an effort designed to benefit Donald Trump's political prospects, or was it simply aimed at causing dissension and division in American public opinion; and (c) most important, did the Trump campaign collaborate in any interference? The media paid extensive attention to all three questions. Indeed, one could make the case that the degree of attention was excessive and eventually became an obsession. Worse, there was a pronounced anti-Trump and anti-Russia bias from the outset, and the attitude persisted during the initial stages of Joe Biden's administration.

Coverage of the broader issue of U.S. policy toward Russia was even worse. Most reporters and analysts paid little attention to the wider geopolitical context—especially the poisonous deterioration in bilateral relations that took place long before the 2016 election cycle.

That so much of the media succumbed to both Russophobia and partisanship in their treatment of allegations of election interference and collusion was bad enough. But their inflammatory, one-sided coverage had wider and more serious implications than just advancing the preferred narrative of one political party and its hawkish allies in the national security agencies. It helped promote a public image of Russia that contributed to the intensification of a new cold war. Once again, journalists signed on as advocates of a confrontational and potentially very dangerous foreign policy.

Indeed, some mainstream journalists were in tacit alliance with key figures in the national security apparatus who viewed Russia as an existential threat to America's security and who lobbied for an uncompromising, confrontational stance toward that country. In the process, those portions of the press fostered the rise of what amounted to neo-McCarthyism. That narrative not only vilified Trump and his supporters, but it impugned the motives and integrity of other critics who opposed or even questioned the hardline approach. The result was to stifle debate about policy toward a major power and one of the key members of the international system—an unhealthy development in any vibrant democracy.

The media's handling of the important and sensitive issue of Russia policy does not bode well for journalism's role in the 21st century. The mission of informing the public is not advanced when journalists create and circulate one-dimensional portrayals of a foreign country as a villainous, existential threat, ignoring crucial context and nuances to do so. Even worse are press outlets that collaborate with hawkish advocates and partisan political figures within the government to promote hostile U.S. policies against one of the most powerful countries in the world and denigrate any initiatives that move even modestly in the opposite direction.

Yet the bulk of America's news media repeatedly committed all those offenses with respect to their coverage of Russia policy. Some members of the fourth estate acted as though the Cold War had never ended and noncommunist Russia was little different from the totalitarian Soviet Union. Throughout, mainstream journalists and government advocates of a hard-line policy toward Moscow were consistently on the same page.

Coverage of policy regarding another major power, China, was less monolithic. Since the establishment of the People's Republic of China (PRC) in 1949, there have been major swings in U.S. news outlets' views of the country. At most times, a herd mentality has been evident, with an overwhelming percentage of news stories portraying China in one particular fashion. During some periods, the prevailing view has been extremely hostile, with nearly all accounts describing the PRC as an oppressor domestically and a dire security threat to the United States. That was the case during the first two decades following the communist revolution.

In 1971–1972, Richard Nixon suddenly altered U.S. policy, and Washington no longer treated the PRC as a rogue state. The press largely went along. For the next three decades, most of the media, except for a handful of right-wing holdouts, portrayed China in more benign terms, as a constructive diplomatic player and an increasingly important trading partner. Hopes for China's greater internal political liberalization also soared in U.S. press coverage. Not even the PRC government's June 1989 bloody crackdown on pro–democracy demonstrators in Tiananmen Square undermined the dominant narrative for long.

That favorable image gradually eroded over the past decade or so, as concerns rose about the PRC's brass-knuckles competitive style in the economic arena. The Communist Party's reversal of liberalization at home and Beijing's greater assertiveness on an array of security issues throughout East Asia also affected the American public's perspective. Media negativity toward the PRC jumped in 2020 in response to China's crackdown on Hong Kong and lack of transparency regarding the outbreak of the COVID-19 pandemic.

A sizable, mostly conservative faction in the media is now promoting a strongly confrontational U.S. policy toward the PRC. Although a considerable number of journalists still advocate a policy of maximum U.S. engagement with China, those ranks are shrinking. The media narrative regarding relations with China shifted along with the Trump administration's more confrontational policy. Widespread expectations that Joe Biden would embrace the status quo ante failed to materialize during the initial months of the new administration, as officials largely continued the Trump administration's policies—especially those regarding Taiwan and other security issues. Even if a milder strategy ultimately emerges and is reflected in a more accommodating media stance generally, a significant portion of the press will likely continue to align with the anti-PRC perspective among Biden's political adversaries in the Republican Party.

Overall, the media treatment of foreign policy issues has followed a fairly consistent and frustrating pattern throughout the post–Cold War era. Too many journalists embraced the most aggressive, hyper-activist factions in the administrations of Bill Clinton, George W. Bush, and Barack Obama. When Donald Trump indicated that he might break with the policy of U.S. global interventionism, the press reaction was strikingly hostile. Even when Trump's actions did not match his rhetoric of greater restraint, media opposition to his foreign policy remained intense. Indeed, many of the most influential figures in the press made common cause with high-level players in the military and intelligence communities who worked to undermine Trump's tepid changes and thwart any reduction in Washington's global activism. With few exceptions, the press moved from being a watchdog—albeit inconsistent and frequently ineffective—with respect to ill-considered or unsavory policies to being an apologist for or accomplice in such policies.

Journalists with the increasingly dominant activist ideological perspective can find numerous causes to highlight, and a set of powerful social and career incentives encourages them to embrace that approach. Correspondents, pundits, editors, and publishers who work for major media outlets—nearly all based in the "Acela corridor" between Boston and Washington, DC—see themselves as members of an opinion-shaping elite dedicated to guiding a less enlightened general public to endorse foreign policies that will not only improve America's position in the world, but also benefit the global community as a whole. To the extent that officials pursue policies that appear to advance those same objectives, prominent media types are inclined to sympathize and cooperate with those officials, rather than criticize them and impede their work. Such cooperation is a relatively subtle but important manifestation of groupthink—a herd mentality.

Indeed, neither groupthink nor the willingness of media figures to collaborate with favored policymakers first developed during the post–Cold War era. In some respects, both tendencies were even stronger during the initial decades of the Cold War. Presidential administrations openly appealed to the patriotism of journalists and their corporate employers to get them to enlist in the struggle against the Soviet Union and international communism. The intelligence community even recruited hundreds of reporters to be outright CIA assets and assist the agency in its global operations.[2] Journalists who engaged in such collusion seriously compromised their independence and integrity, but officials so successfully made the case that the USSR was an existential threat that the appeals to patriotic duty apparently overwhelmed any qualms the recruits may have harbored.

In subsequent decades, the collaboration became more subtle and informal, but it never went away entirely. Congenial reporters and editors still cleared stories with officials in the Pentagon and the intelligence agencies. They also acted as willing conduits for perspectives on world developments that elements of the national security state wished to see disseminated.

To this day, officials continue to employ decidedly unsubtle measures to discourage maverick journalists who might be inclined to dispute the government's foreign affairs narrative or, worse, reveal deceptions and other abuses. The Espionage Act of 1917 still hangs like a Sword of Damocles over the necks of press members who engage in such behavior. An out-of-control classification system stymies reporters and their sources who seek to unmask the national security bureaucracy's misdeeds without leaking classified documents. Yet using such documents exposes the sources—and potentially the journalists—to criminal prosecution. The risk level for enterprising reporters has risen over the past two decades, and the government's crusade against WikiLeaks founder Julian Assange highlights the danger.[3] Members of the press are much safer if they remain on good terms with the mandarins directing U.S. foreign policy. Whether for that reason or other motives, most portions of the establishment press were surprisingly unsympathetic to Assange's plight and even implicitly cheered on the government's prosecution efforts.[4]

Other, more subtle factors reinforce the tendency of the news media to treat foreign policy officials as allies rather than adversaries. Many leading journalists and policymakers come from similar socioeconomic and educational backgrounds (a disproportionate percentage in both camps attended Ivy League universities). They also tend to congregate and circulate at the same social and political gatherings. For the DC cluster, that often means being a member of the "Georgetown cocktail circuit."

Another important career incentive is that most portions of the press exist to report on governmental activities. If the federal government were substantially smaller and played a lesser, more focused, role in the nation's affairs, the news media's role likewise would become less prominent. The careers of journalists based in Washington and devoted to covering foreign policy and national security developments would especially be at risk. That realization creates a powerful incentive to hype the importance of those topics and favor an extremely vigorous U.S. role in the world. The incentive to do so is strengthened because most Americans normally show little interest in foreign affairs. Only when the perception of a crisis exists—and especially if American military personnel are at risk—does the public perk up and pay attention.

Media economics reinforce the preference of journalists for an activist U.S. foreign policy. During the Cold War—and especially during shooting wars, such as those in Korea and Vietnam—overseas correspondents occupied a prominent niche in the hierarchy of news coverage. Most major publications maintained full-time overseas bureaus in several foreign capitals. When the Cold War abruptly ended, severe cutbacks in coverage ensued. The number of overseas news bureaus shrank dramatically, as did the number of journalists with expertise in a particular region of the world. Even the periodic crises during the first post–Cold War decade were much smaller in scale and involved few U.S. troops in theaters of combat, so public interest and press coverage remained modest.

The 9/11 attacks altered the media landscape, since the subsequent War on Terror led to military interventions with U.S. troops on the ground in Afghanistan and Iraq. But even those conflicts were relatively small-scale compared with the two world wars, the Korean War, or the Vietnam War. The shrinkage of overseas news bureaus meant that far more often than before, elite newspapers and the television networks would dispatch U.S.-based reporters to cover developments rather than relying on correspondents based in the region. Not only did that reduce the experience and expertise of the reporters on the scene, but it meant that journalists covering a conflict or evolving crisis were more likely to have been thoroughly marinated in the foreign policy groupthink of the Washington–New York corridor.

All of those factors combine to strengthen a journalistic herd mentality on foreign policy. Most elite journalists and policymakers view world developments and the "proper" U.S. response to such developments in roughly similar ways. That's not to say there are no significant differences in policy views and no mavericks within those two communities. Examples of both can be identified without too much difficulty, and purely partisan considerations reinforce differences—at least within a limited range. But staunch critics of the general, global activist foreign policy the United States has pursued since World War II are very much in the minority.

In addition to these career incentives, another specific incentive encourages news personnel to go along with the dominant foreign policy perspective of government officials and media titans. In the corporate world of modern journalism, outspoken iconoclasts are not likely to be rewarded. Being a conventional thinker—or at most a very mild, occasional dissenter—is far safer and more conducive to career preservation and advancement.

Foreign policy journalists are especially vulnerable to pressure not to challenge the conventional wisdom. The competition for limited column space, airtime, or number of clicks is ferocious and creates an inherent incentive to hype the importance of one's subject. Also, a reporter is more likely to get newsworthy information from important sources (usually government officials) if those sources are pleased with the journalist's previous treatments—and with how consistently "friendly" the media outlet has been.

Henry Kissinger described the mechanics of that symbiotic relationship with surprising candor. "Much as the journalist may resent it, he performs a partly governmental function. . . . Officials seek him out to bring their pet projects to general attention, to settle scores, or to reverse a decision that went against them. Whatever the official's motive, it cannot be disinterested. At a minimum, he seeks to put himself in his best light. The journalist has comparably interested motives in his contacts with the official. He must woo and flatter the official, because without his goodwill he will be deprived of information."[5]

Such factors exist on every press beat, but they are especially relevant to defense and foreign policy. Because of the pervasive classification system and the overall shroud of secrecy surrounding the formulation and execution of policies in those two areas, journalists are exceptionally dependent on inside sources. Officials are likely to feed selective information to cooperative reporters who publish stories that advance those officials' policy and personal agendas. Conversely, they are most unlikely to feed useful information (much less cherished "exclusives") to reporters or pundits who have a habit of criticizing government policies. That situation gives officials powerful leverage because it may be extremely difficult to gain alternative access to the needed information.[6]

Given those incentives, an anti-interventionist perspective antagonizes policymakers, drying up vital, covert sources of information, and usually becomes a quick route to obscurity for iconoclastic journalists. Conversely, media members who show themselves to be friendly allies with respect to Washington's foreign policy agenda maximize their career prospects. The price in terms of integrity can be high though. Government functionaries are eager to use such "cooperative" journalists as outright propaganda conduits. Even the cynical Kissinger warned of that danger. A journalist who woos an official for concealed information and seeks an exclusive, he cautioned, "cannot let himself be seduced—the secret dream of most officials—or he will lose his objectivity."[7] The balance is not easy to maintain, and many contemporary foreign affairs journalists don't even seem to make the attempt.

Criticism from the news media of Washington's global agenda and specific foreign policy undertakings normally is constrained and tepid. The one major exception is when a prominent policy split occurs within the political elite. Such a division is then reflected within the media

establishment as well. The most prominent example is the disenchantment with the Vietnam War that grew among some members of both
elites in the late 1960s and early 1970s. The unity of purpose and overall
media and public optimism about the prospects for success that marked
the initial escalation of America's military commitment in 1964 and
1965 faded badly within a few years. A surge of anti-war demonstrations
swept the country, rattling political leaders and their media allies. Following the stunning Tet Offensive in early 1968, only the most incorri-
gibly optimistic types still believed that the United States could "win"
the Vietnam conflict at anything resembling a reasonable cost in blood
and treasure.

Media outlets, especially the most prominent ones in the northeastern
corridor—which had been uniformly supportive of the war effort a few
years earlier—now became significantly more negative, as did major
political figures in Washington. To some extent, that greater skepticism carried over to coverage of other aspects of U.S. foreign policy
in the 1970s and 1980s. An uptick also occurred in the willingness of
major media players to view some behaviors of the CIA and other intelligence actors with a more critical eye. Again, a split in the political
elite facilitated the shift in media coverage, as congressional committees,
especially the special Senate committee chaired by Sen. Frank Church
(D-ID), uncovered and publicized some of the misdeeds those agencies
had committed.

An abundance of critical news stories and opinion pieces with respect
to Washington's support for anti-communist factions in such places as
Central America and Angola also appeared. The coverage of these cases,
however, took on a noticeable partisan split. Liberal outlets scrutinized
the policies of the Reagan administration in those regions with considerable hostility, warning of the danger of another Vietnam. Right-wing
outlets passionately defended both the administration and the foreign
clients it backed.

As noted previously, the revitalized inclination of the press to be
a watchdog with respect to U.S. foreign policy did not last past the
Persian Gulf War and the demise of the Soviet Union. Both developments fed an attitude of national superiority, and that arrogance soon

became evident in the news media as it did in other societal and political sectors. A troubling number of journalists became lobbyists for activist measures, as advocacy journalism displaced the more detached variety. Many of these individuals implicitly embraced Secretary of State Madeleine Albright's expression of American narcissism that the United States was "the indispensable nation" because "we stand tall and we see further than other nations into the future."[8] That tendency toward national hubris—with a brief, partial interruption following the widespread public disillusionment with the Iraq War—has persisted in most of the journalistic community to the present day in its coverage of foreign affairs.

A crucial 21st-century development whose impact on coverage of foreign affairs remains uncertain is the exponential rise of social media. That phenomenon has facilitated the growth of alternate sites that already were diluting the dominance of the legacy media—the principal metropolitan dailies, news magazines, big commercial networks, and earliest news channels, especially CNN. The explosive growth of social media undoubtedly has led to a much wider range of views being available to consumers in the United States and around the world. However, the change has been a mixed blessing, since the quality of the information is at least as varied as the range of perspectives. News consumers face a major challenge in sifting poorly supported accounts—and in some cases flagrant disinformation and "fake news"—from good-quality information, whether it reflects conventional or unorthodox perspectives.

Moreover, attempts by Facebook, Twitter, and other social media giants to police the content on their sites have produced mixed results and even outright abuses. The social media sector is no more immune from toxic ideological and partisan political bias than any other portion of the media. A troubling example of the danger was the attempts by both Facebook and Twitter to suppress news stories during the final weeks of the 2020 presidential campaign regarding evidence that Joe Biden and other members of his family may have had questionable financial entanglements with Ukraine, China, and other foreign powers.

Perhaps even worse, powerful government agencies and individuals have demonstrated that they wish to use social media to propagandize the public and to stifle critics. That menace is not confined to defense and foreign policy. During the Trump years, centrist and left-of-center members of Congress demanded that social media companies bar vaguely defined "hate speech"—with the implicit threat that if they failed to do so, Congress would preempt them and take the requisite action. Governmental pressure was evident on another nonsecurity issue. Officials insisted that social media companies exclude dissenting views, even from highly reputable scientists, regarding measures that agencies at the federal, state, and local level adopted in response to the outbreak of the coronavirus in 2020. With few exceptions, social media executives complied with such "requests."

Those firms also appeared to silence dissenters in the aftermath of the January 6, 2021, riot that saw demonstrators storm the U.S. Capitol. Not only did the social media giants close the accounts of individuals arrested for involvement in the assault, but they even closed the accounts of President Trump and some of his closest advisers. Other individuals who continued to allege voter fraud and dispute the 2020 election results, or who rejected the continuing narrative that Russia was an existential cyber threat extensively circulating "disinformation," received similar treatment.

Even before the January 6 episode, the national security apparatus was insisting that social media companies freeze or eliminate the accounts of sites, especially foreign-linked sites, that officials accuse of disseminating propaganda or disinformation. In too many instances, the government's case was questionable and could easily become a vehicle for suppressing views that challenge Washington's overseas policies or expose misconduct associated with those policies. China's comprehensively repressive approach confirms that independent social media platforms can be effectively curbed and even turned into another tool for government propaganda. U.S. policies have not gone nearly that far yet, but just as the legacy media have long been vulnerable to being used as a de facto ally of the national security state, especially during periods of crisis, social media can succumb to a similar process.

Another worrisome development emanating from the January 6 turmoil was a surge in calls for new domestic terrorism laws and dusting off hoary sedition statutes. The widespread willingness of press outlets to label the violence an "insurrection" created ideal conditions for such an overreaction. Given the history of abuse associated with sedition laws, especially the Alien and Sedition Acts of 1798, and the 1918 amendments to the 1917 Espionage Act (amendments popularly referred to as the Sedition Act), one might expect intense resistance to going down that path, especially from members of the media. But the extent of public and congressional alarm in early 2021 pointed to a different, more worrisome outcome. The opinion-shaping elite seemed even more receptive to giving the government broad additional powers to combat vaguely defined domestic terrorism than they had been to the Patriot Act and other measures that were hastily approved in the name of fighting international terrorism.

Alarmingly, portions of the news media are willing to advocate (or at least flirt with) that strategy, despite its potential to pose a serious threat to their own professed mission. The *Washington Post* prominently featured a laudatory op-ed about the 1798 Sedition Act and how it represented a worthy attempt to suppress "misinformation." The author argued that there was at least some applicability to the situation Americans currently faced.[9] The harassment inflicted on dissenters (especially foreign policy dissenters) during and immediately following World War I and throughout the period of McCarthyism in the 1950s demonstrates the risks associated with encouraging surveillance, investigations, and prosecutions for sedition. Major media players like the *Washington Post* certainly should know better than to embrace this behavior.

Unfortunately, the overall record of the news media with respect to defense and foreign policy issues since the 1890s has been mixed at best. Far too often, journalists have not played the role of watchdogs who alert the public to potential abuses or dangerous miscalculations on the part of officials. Instead, they've served as public relations conduits for those officials, failing to scrutinize, much less question or dispute, the justifications for proposed policies or the efficacy of existing policies. On some occasions, the press has become an integral part of the national security apparatus itself, obediently disseminating government propaganda as though it were legitimate news and even assisting intelligence and military operations. In the most egregious cases, journalists have played the role of the national security establishment's allies, engaging in distorted, hawkish lobbying while seeking to discredit and smear media colleagues who dare question the dominant narrative on an important foreign policy issue.

It is imperative that the news media improve their performance. Otherwise, the dismal spectacle of the United States embracing a seemingly endless series of morally questionable, impractical, or disastrous foreign policy initiatives will continue. The public's watchdog has been asleep—or worse—and the results have been most unpleasant.

CHAPTER 1
A Century of Hawkish Sentiments

A tension has long existed in the United States between the media's watchdog role and the government's national security claims and overall agenda. It was no accident that the first serious attempt to restrict freedom of the press, the Alien and Sedition Acts of 1798, occurred during a period of acute tension between the United States and France that culminated in an undeclared naval war. John Adams's administration regarded any criticism of its foreign policy as bordering on treason and sought to squelch it.

The Alien and Sedition Acts set the pattern for the subsequent relationship between the government and the press. Especially in times of crisis, real or contrived, political leaders have sought to enlist journalists as allies in selling the government's version of events and the issues at stake. If government officials encounter resistance to their campaign of seduction, they are quite willing to smear or even attempt to suppress critics. Maverick journalists working for smaller, less politically connected publications are especially vulnerable to intimidation, legal harassment, and even outright persecution. The government's campaign against WikiLeaks editor Julian Assange is only the most recent example of such treatment.

Political leaders generally view the press as either a useful propaganda tool to promote U.S. foreign policy or a dangerous adversary that must be curbed. That attitude became especially apparent during the two world wars. Even the courts offered little vindication of freedom of the press at the time. Instead of resisting the executive branch's assault on the First Amendment, the federal judiciary more often aided and abetted it. One crucial blow came in the Supreme Court's 1919 landmark case *Schenk v. United States.* The Court unanimously upheld the Espionage Act of 1917, and the law became a permanent menace to a free press.

Two aspects of the *Schenk* decision were especially destructive. First, the ruling came down after the war ended; by then, any claimed national security justification based on supposedly extraordinary wartime needs had become moot. Second, the logic underlying the ruling was alarmingly vague and expansive. Speaking for the Court, Justice Oliver Wendell Holmes expressed the view that First Amendment freedoms must give way to the exigencies of national security "when a nation is at war." Holmes argued that many views that might be printed or spoken in times of peace "are such a hindrance" to the war effort "that their utterance will not be endured so long as men fight, and no Court would regard them as protected by any constitutional right."[1]

He then gave an example that attained notoriety in both legal scholarship and popular culture: falsely shouting "fire" in a theater was not protected speech. But Schenk's supposed offense was circulating pamphlets and giving speeches criticizing the new law that imposed military conscription. Equating such peaceful dissent with creating a sudden, needless panic was a ludicrous comparison, but the consequences of the *Schenk* decision have been far-reaching, long-lasting, and corrosive.[2]

Moreover, those effects have not been limited to periods of declared war. Congress has issued no declaration of war against any adversary since December 1941. Yet, the overuse of the power to classify and conceal documents from public view, vindictive prosecutions of whistleblowers, and threats to do the same to journalists who collaborate with them have become ever present. The Espionage Act and its underlying logic still menace First Amendment rights more than a century later. Perhaps even worse, this mentality—which says the press is either a useful tool to promote U.S. foreign policy or a threat that must be neutralized—has been an ongoing feature of the government-media relationship since the United States seized the global leadership mantle after World War II.

During both global conflicts, the vast majority of journalists were quite willing to embrace and market Washington's war aims. That cozy relationship persisted after World War II, and it seemed just as strong during the Korean "police action" and the initial phase of the Vietnam War. Indeed, the phenomenon of journalists acting as sales personnel marketing a U.S. military crusade was evident even earlier—during the Spanish-American War of 1898.

YELLOW JOURNALISM AND THE SPANISH-AMERICAN WAR

In the prelude to the Spanish-American War, journalists did not merely reflect the pro-war sentiments of some officials in William McKinley's administration; key reporters and their employers were adamant lobbyists for war with Spain. Their behavior demonstrated that the press sometimes whips up public sentiment in favor of military actions that subsequent evidence indicated were unnecessary and even immoral. Historians have long recognized that jingoistic "yellow journalism," epitomized by the newspaper chains owned by William Randolph Hearst and Joseph Pulitzer, played a significant role as a catalyst for war on that occasion. Months before the outbreak of the war, one of Hearst's reporters wished to return home from Cuba because there was no sign of a worsening crisis. Hearst instructed him to stay, adding, "You furnish the pictures and I'll furnish the war."[3]

Hearst's boast was hyperbole, but the Hearst and Pulitzer papers did repeatedly hype the Spanish "threat" and beat the drums for war against Spain. They featured stories that not only focused on but exaggerated the uglier features of Madrid's treatment of its colonial subjects in Cuba. Those outlets also exploited the mysterious explosion that destroyed the U.S. battleship *Maine* in Havana's harbor.[4] To this day, the identity of the perpetrator is not known for certain, but the yellow press expressed no doubts whatever. According to their accounts, it was an outrageous attack on America by the villainous Spanish regime. And that questionable

conclusion soon characterized most of the coverage—even in newspapers that had previously taken a more measured stance on issues in Cuba.

Such journalistic pressure was not the only factor that impelled
McKinley's administration to push for a declaration of war against
Spain or for Congress to approve that declaration. A rising generation of
American imperialists wanted to emulate the European great powers and
build a colonial empire. That underlying motive became evident when
the first U.S. attack following the declaration of war came not in Cuba,
but in the Philippines, Spain's colony on the other side of the Pacific.

Nevertheless, it would be naïve to assume that the jingoist press did
not play a significant role in fomenting the war against Spain. Indeed,
the corrupt role of yellow journalism in creating public support for that
conflict is not a particularly controversial proposition among historians.

WORLD WAR I:
THE PRESS AS AN ORGAN OF WAR PROPAGANDA

The role of the press in the lead up to America's entry into World
War I was somewhat different and more complex. Americans were subjected to a barrage of propaganda from both Britain and Germany once
the conflict erupted in August 1914. Author and historian Stewart Halsey
Ross aptly describes that campaign as "the first of two great propaganda
wars on American soil" for the hearts and minds of Americans. "The
British worked diligently to involve the United States as an active belligerent on its side, while Germany sought vainly to maintain a precarious
American neutrality. Both countries flooded America with war 'news,'
pamphlets, books, speakers, movies, all presenting one-sided versions of
the origins of the war and the righteousness of their cause."[5]

Some portions of the press echoed President Woodrow Wilson's
official position, emphasizing U.S. neutrality with respect to the
European conflict. On September 9, 1914, the *New York Times* noted
that concerted, competing propaganda campaigns already were underway, and that the desire of those countries "to have American favor
is perfectly natural." However, the editors of the *Times* were unper-
turbed by that development, predicting that no harm should come

from the rival propaganda offensives, because "the good sense of the American people will compel the preservation of strict neutrality to the end." Ross notes sardonically that "the *Times* proved to be far off the mark."[6]

Moreover, the news media in general did not play a neutral role regarding the European war. Most publications—especially the big metropolitan daily newspapers and the principal news magazines—increasingly sided with Britain and its allies. They also printed British-generated stories about alleged German atrocities on the western front, especially the offensive through neutral Belgium, with little to no skepticism. By early 1917, although major pockets of strong neutralist sentiment remained in portions of the United States (especially among German-Americans, Irish Americans, and committed socialists), much of the public had been conditioned to support the Allied cause.

In contrast to the Spanish-American War when yellow journalists were the principal lobbyists for war, dragging along a reluctant McKinley administration, this time the British propaganda machine was the chief culprit for generating war fever in the United States. The role of Woodrow Wilson's administration was murkier. Wilson officially and repeatedly proclaimed U.S. neutrality, but his personal sympathies and those of key advisers were clearly pro-British. Moreover, Washington's biased policies on such matters as the Allied blockade of Germany and Berlin's use of submarine warfare inexorably pushed the United States toward becoming a belligerent in the war.

Whatever its earlier stance, Wilson's administration became the driving force in whipping up public enthusiasm for Washington's new crusade once he secured a declaration of war against Germany from a divided Congress in April 1917. As Ross observes, upon Washington's entry into the war, "a second propaganda onslaught was directed at Americans, this time by their own leaders."[7] Thereafter, the press played a compliant and subordinate, albeit extremely crucial, role. Even the concept of a truly independent press became inapplicable; the government enlisted the news media, and most journalists obediently carried out their assignment—as much as did the soldiers fighting in France.

War correspondents had little real choice in the matter. Military authorities required correspondents to take an oath to "convey the truth to the people of the United States" but refrain from disclosing information that might aid the enemy. Not surprisingly, the field commanders believed that any information, no matter how factual, that placed their efforts in an unfavorable light aided the enemy and therefore should not appear in print. Since each journalist had to put up a $10,000 bond to ensure that he conducted himself as "a gentleman of the press," there was a powerful disincentive to publish anything other than laudatory accounts.[8] The military authorities had unfettered discretion to decide whether a correspondent had violated their vacuous standard; if they concluded that a particular dispatch constituted a violation, the bond was forfeited without appeal. Needless to say, the vast majority of publications and their reporters felt compelled to tread carefully, whatever their private opinions might have been about specific military decisions or the overall war effort.

Beyond the battlefield restrictions, the Wilson government enlisted journalists to enforce censorship measures against their colleagues— much as prison officials use trustee inmates to keep other prisoners in line. In one striking example, commanders of the American Expeditionary Force gave the job of monitoring and managing the release of newspaper dispatches from the western front in France to Frederick Palmer, a former reporter for the *New York Herald* and the Associated Press (AP). His appointment was not random. Palmer had been the only American reporter accredited to the British army before the U.S. entry into the war. He did not disappoint the officials who had granted him that unique status. Palmer produced one gushing dispatch after another about the British war effort.

U.S. military leaders expected him to be an enthusiastic booster for the Wilson administration's war policy, and like the British, they were not disappointed. Some of Palmer's former colleagues, though, chafed at his restrictions as they became ever more stifling. To address that problem, the U.S. Army commissioned Palmer a major, and his behavior quickly became that of a typical officer, exhibiting rote obedience to the military and its mission. As time went on, his news releases became increasingly sparse and less informative. When reporters submitted their dispatches, he and his staff approved only the ones that praised the war effort and celebrated victories, real or fictional.[9]

Frederick Palmer was the quintessential willing journalistic tool for the government and its military policies. But he was hardly the only journalist during World War I deserving that label. Another was George Creel, the man Wilson appointed to head the Committee on Public Information (CPI), an agency that the president created by executive order just seven days after Congress approved the declaration of war. Creel began his career as a reporter for the *Kansas City World* in 1894 and started his own competing newspaper, the *Kansas City Independent*, in 1899. After that venture sputtered, he began writing for the *Denver Post* in 1909 and subsequently became editor of the *Rocky Mountain News* in 1911. During his career, Creel had established a reputation as a capable investigative reporter and a journalist with integrity.

He also was a staunch Wilson loyalist. Indeed, he played a crucial role in promoting Wilson's 1916 campaign for reelection—ironically emphasizing the president's role in keeping America out of the war that was causing such carnage in Europe. Just months later, Creel would, with equal passion, make the case that America's involvement in that war was both necessary and noble. Historian Alan Axelrod asks, "How could Creel shift his rhetoric so completely and effortlessly? As he saw it, there was no shift. To Creel, it was the policy of Woodrow Wilson that mattered, whether that policy happened to be the absolute neutrality of 1916 or the absolute commitment to war of 1917. Devoted to Wilson, Creel based his public relations campaigns on the same principles employing the same techniques, whether the object promoted was peace or war."[10]

Creel made the CPI the enthusiastic instrument of the government's shrill, pro-war propaganda. One of his first steps was to enlist 150,000 journalists, writers, scholars, and other communications personnel in the administration's concerted campaign to promote the war effort. Few in the vast number of journalists that the CPI recruited seemed to have any more difficulty than Creel did in making the mental transition from being independent gatherers of news to being disseminators of propaganda that the government created.[11] Frank Cobb, editor of the *New York World*, later described the CPI's mission: "Government conscripted public opinion as they conscripted men and money and materials. Having conscripted it, they dealt with it as they dealt with other raw materials. They mobilized it. They put it in the charge of drill sergeants. They goose-stepped it. They taught it to stand at attention and salute."[12]

The CPI's effectiveness was impressive. Axelrod notes that the committee "controlled virtually every scrap of information America and much of rest of the world received concerning the war. It did not rely on censorship so much as the total monopolization of information, shaping news, shaping images, shaping emotions to create a reality in which President Wilson's war emerged as not merely desirable but inevitable."[13] In reality, to fulfill its mission the CPI relied on both strict censorship *and* all those other techniques. Still, there is no disputing the organization's effectiveness.

A mission based on those techniques is incompatible with journalistic integrity. Yet thousands of newspaper reporters, columnists, and editors willingly and even eagerly became instruments of Washington's propaganda campaign. Creel's strategy stressed two related messages. One was the depiction of Germany as an odious, extremely dangerous threat to America's security and the American way of life. It was a caricature that portrayed the bumbling, often clueless Kaiser Wilhelm II as the "Beast of Berlin." CPI propagandists wildly exaggerated German wartime atrocities or circulated outright fiction.[14] The notion that Germany plotted and had the capability to extend its dominion to the Western Hemisphere was preposterous. Yet supposedly sober, reputable journalists disseminated such misinformation with no apparent sense of chagrin.

The overall message to the American people was that they must fear and hate Germany and everything for which that country supposedly stood. The objective of the propaganda campaign was to whip up pro-war sentiment to a frenzy. One component of that campaign was even directed at children, prodding them to assist the war effort in whatever modest way they could.[15] An especially ugly theme was that they should report "slackers"—anyone who seemed insufficiently dedicated to the war effort—to parents, police, teachers, and other trusted authority figures. The attempt to enlist children for that task was a subset of the larger message that good, loyal, patriotic children—like their adult counterparts—should obey the authorities and support the war without hesitation or doubt. The tactics used, and the objectives pursued, in America's wartime propaganda offensive bore more than a small resemblance to the mechanisms that fascist and communist regimes would put into operation around the world in subsequent decades.

The other main CPI theme was the glorification of the U.S. and Allied war effort as a crusade to protect and advance the cause of democracy throughout the world. That image may have had some tenuous connection to reality with respect to the agenda of the idealistic Woodrow Wilson. But such a depiction was absurd regarding the policy goals of the imperialists in London, Paris, and St. Petersburg. As the Versailles peace conference confirmed, their objectives were vastly more substantive, mundane, and cynical. Stripping Germany of its overseas colonies, imposing onerous reparations on Berlin, and placing restrictions on the size and capabilities of democratic Germany's armed forces were provisions that all highlighted practical geostrategic objectives. Notions of reconciliation and international idealism were in short supply among Washington's European allies.

The CPI's propaganda was crude even by the standards of the day, and it is laughably crude by 21st-century standards. But it succeeded admirably in heightening war consciousness and jingoism. Indeed, the CPI's stable of journalists helped foster a wave of hysterical intolerance among the American people toward even mild dissenters or people who were unfortunate enough to have German ancestry. That intolerance would resurface in equally virulent forms during future crises. The internment of Japanese Americans in World War II, the onset of McCarthyism during the 1950s, the smearing of people who opposed the U.S. intervention in Iraq, and the Russophobia that characterized the second decade of the 21st century all had some of their origins in the systematically generated hysteria of World War I. And a distressing number of supposedly professional journalists played roles in all of those episodes.

The media's pro-war propaganda offensive was strikingly successful. Stanford University Professor David M. Kennedy contends that the ability of so many thoughtful people "to pass so swiftly from favoring peace to embracing war" had less to do with the weakness of their previous convictions than it did with the effectiveness of the Wilson administration's campaign of persuasion. The appeal reflected "Wilson's remarkable adroitness in figuring the war in terms congenial to the American mind, and particularly appealing to the progressives: a war for democracy, a war to end wars, a war to protect liberalism, a war against militarism, a war to redeem barbarous Europe, a crusade."[16]

It was a message based on either dangerously utopian idealism or cynical, bogus idealism, but it got the job done—at least through the end of the war. And the press was an essential, perhaps the most essential, mechanism for selling that message and generating public support for a war whose negative consequences continue to plague America and the international system a century later. Both the appeal (sincere or insincere) to idealistic objectives and the media's role in selling wars partially or entirely on that basis also has persisted to the present day.

During the 1920s and most of the 1930s, though, most of the press reflected the public's disillusionment with the "war to end all wars." It became painfully clear that Wilson's crusade to protect and expand democracy in Europe and elsewhere had not succeeded. Instead, Europe had become an arena featuring petty autocracies—especially in the newly minted countries of Central and Eastern Europe, but also in some Western European countries, such as Italy and Portugal. Benito Mussolini's fascist model was especially unsettling, particularly when an even more virulent form came to power with Adolf Hitler in Germany. Farther east was the equally alarming specter of totalitarian communism in the Soviet Union.

The widespread perception that the war had been a costly, bloody folly became the dominant narrative in the United States during the interwar period. A few internationalist papers, primarily in the Northeast, attempted to make the case that had the United States joined the League of Nations as Wilson had recommended, matters might have turned out better in Europe. But that was decidedly a minority view among both the press and the public. Not until a new war broke out in Europe in September 1939—and generally not until Nazi Germany's stunning military victory over France in June 1940—did American public, and especially media, opinion begin to shift. Even then, majorities continued to favor U.S. neutrality. Only when Japan launched the surprise attack on the U.S. fleet at Pearl Harbor did a pro-war consensus emerge. Then, as in World War I, a government-press partnership utterly controlled the message the American people received.

COOPERATIVE JOURNALISTS: STILL ON A LEASH IN WORLD WAR II

Government mastery of the press in World War II was more sophisticated but at least as comprehensive as it had been in World War I. The suppression of dissent was less blatant, and far fewer maverick journalistic dissenters were prosecuted for sedition. But that more benign record was largely due to the dearth of opposition to the war after Pearl Harbor. Before that seminal event, President Franklin D. Roosevelt personally expressed loathing for advocates of continued U.S. neutrality, especially as he moved U.S. policy toward open support for the Allied powers after the fall of France to Nazi forces.

It was not just personal animus. Acting on Roosevelt's instructions, the FBI became an instrument to surveil and impede members of the America First Committee and other organizations that opposed U.S. involvement in the European war.[17] FBI agents even investigated anti-interventionist members of Congress, including Senators Gerald P. Nye (R-ND) and Burton K. Wheeler (D-MT), as well as the *Chicago Tribune*.[18] Government harassment of journalists opposed to U.S. entry into the war was considerable long before the United States formally entered the global conflict.[19] Both before and after Pearl Harbor, Roosevelt himself habitually derided "isolationist" critics in the press and elsewhere as "happy idiots" at best and fascist sympathizers at worst.[20]

Roosevelt's administration was eager to impose restraints on journalists if gentle persuasion failed. On December 30, 1940, Secretary of the Navy Frank Knox asked the news media to refrain from publishing information about a variety of topics, including the program to construct new warships. Although his action took the form of a "request," Knox and other administration officials hinted that the restraints might become mandatory if full cooperation was not forthcoming. When the Japanese attack took place, the government responded immediately with a thorough censorship system.

As Wilson had done, Roosevelt placed a compliant journalist in charge of restricting information and policing colleagues. He appointed Byron Price, an Associated Press editor, to head the new Office of Censorship. In addition to monitoring (and limiting) all communications between the United States and other countries, Price's agency issued the Code of Wartime Practices and "requested" that publishers and broadcasters abide by it. Price's deputy, Theodore F. Koop, stated that no one "can remain aloof as a more-or-less interested spectator." Newspapers and radio stations, he said, "must be as actively behind the war effort as merchants or manufacturers."[21] His comment succinctly summarized the Roosevelt administration's attitude about the proper role of the press.

The Code of Wartime Practices applied to articles generated on the home front as well as dispatches coming from the theaters of war. The latter, though, were subject to additional constraints that the relevant military commanders imposed. Censorship was especially strict in the Pacific Theater under Gen. Douglas MacArthur and Adm. Ernest King. Both men did their utmost to make certain that reporters portrayed U.S. forces and their top commanders in the most favorable light possible. Conversely, they suppressed any dispatches that fostered a different image, even when correspondents uncovered outright abuses or military blunders. Restrictions were less brazen in the European theater, but the coverage was still far short of independent reporting. When war correspondents were allowed to publish critical accounts, they invariably were expected to pair them with stories of battlefield successes.[22]

Even though military and civilian officials had every reason to trust members of the press to publish accounts that did not undercut the war effort, they hedged their bets with censorship measures or other manipulative procedures. One favorite tactic was to delay the release of insufficiently flattering stories for days, or sometimes even weeks, while they conducted a "security review." Meanwhile, the military's official but often misleading version of events went forward speedily and had the opportunity to shape public opinion before contradictory information could challenge the official account.

In contrast to World War I, when the CPI was in charge of both censorship and propaganda, the Roosevelt administration divided those missions between two agencies. The president signed an executive order in June 1942, establishing the Office of War Information to oversee propaganda. In reality, though, Roosevelt had created components of a pro-war propaganda apparatus months before the United States formally entered the war.

One significant component was the Foreign Information Service (FIS). Col. William "Wild Bill" Donovan, who would soon gain fame as the director of the Office of Strategic Services (the Central Intelligence Agency's predecessor), nominally headed the FIS; but playwright and presidential speechwriter Robert Sherwood led day-to-day operations. Sherwood was a close Roosevelt confidant, and he gathered around him an array of reporters, pundits, and broadcasters to present Washington's (or more accurately, Roosevelt's) perspective on the world crisis. Almost all of Sherwood's recruits were staunch advocates of U.S. entry into the war, and the "information" the FIS provided was often flagrant pro-war propaganda, paid for by U.S. taxpayers.

After the attack on Pearl Harbor, the FIS promptly created a radio broadcast service, the Voice of America, to disseminate U.S. news and views to the rest of the world. The independence and objectivity of both agencies can be gauged by a comment from Sherwood: "all U.S. information to the world should be considered as though it were a continuous speech by the President."[23] Despite this narrow, partisan focus, several dozen members of the journalistic community lent their talents to the effort, willingly acting as conduits of White House propaganda, just as their predecessors had done a generation earlier.

The twin tools of censorship and propaganda worked effectively throughout the war. Rigorous censorship during World War II was probably superfluous. Virtually all reporters were enthusiastic supporters of the war and willingly responded to official requests to sanitize or omit unpleasant information. Stories of Allied atrocities were notably absent, even though such incidents did occur.[24] Likewise, accounts of dubious policies or even outright military blunders seldom appeared. Some battlefield correspondents, such as the famed Ernie Pyle, did convey the gritty nature of modern warfare. Even those accounts, however, were unmistakably favorable not only to the GIs but to their missions.

American journalists regarded themselves as members of the team prosecuting the war, not as anything even faintly resembling detached observers reporting on the conflict. In an interview decades later, John Hersey emphasized that point and lamented the change in attitude of the subsequent generation of journalists. He recalled that what impressed him the most when he arrived in the Pacific theater during World War II "was the degree to which I was trusted by the military." He added that the assumption of military commanders "in their dealings with us was that 'we're all in this together.'"[25]

What Hersey failed to comprehend is that the overwhelming majority of Americans, including those in the news media, embraced the view that World War II was a monumental struggle between good and evil—not only America's security but its very existence and freedoms were endangered by an existential threat. Later U.S. military interventions were more limited, and many of the conflicts were strategically and morally ambiguous. It is unsurprising that as the number of murky conflicts proliferated, uneasiness, skepticism, and even some outright opposition would increase among both the general public and the journalistic community.

Censorship and manipulation aside, the American media's overall portrayal of World War II was one of a heroic, victorious crusade that an alliance of noble democracies was waging against odious totalitarian aggressors. That image was true in some respects, but it ignored, minimized, or rationalized abuses that the Allied powers, including the United States and Britain, routinely committed—especially the saturation bombing of civilian population centers. The propaganda campaign also conveniently ignored or sanitized the troublesome detail that

Joseph Stalin's Soviet Union was part of that grand, freedom-loving alliance.

Encouraged by the Office of War Information, some publications went to extraordinary lengths to whitewash the real nature of the totalitarian USSR. An especially egregious example was a huge, multi-article spread in the March 29, 1943, issue of *Life* magazine. One article informed its readers that the Russians were "one hell of a people," who "think like Americans." Another article described the Soviet interior ministry, or "NKVD" (predecessor to the Committee for State Security, or KGB) as "a national police force similar to the FBI."[26] Even taking into account that most of the FBI's numerous abuses were not known to the public at the time, it was a strained, offensive comparison. The *Life* accounts gave virtually no indications that Stalin presided over a horrid totalitarian regime that held hundreds of thousands of political and religious prisoners in a network of forced labor camps that would later become notorious as the Gulag Archipelago. Worse, they gave no hint that America's ally already had murdered millions of Soviet citizens.

Life's fawning treatment of the USSR was hardly unique in the U.S. news media. Many of the American war correspondents reporting from the Eastern front also served as prolific disseminators of pro-Soviet propaganda. Their accounts not only glorified Soviet combat exploits but portrayed the Soviet system as generally benign—certainly one that was far less repressive, brutal, and odious than the fascist powers. Again, the image that such so-called journalists fostered bore little resemblance to the actual situation.

In contrast to the media's kid-glove treatment of the USSR throughout the war, their portrayals of the Axis countries were even worse than the horrible reality warranted. American media outlets not only, justifiably, vilified the fascist regimes, but they also demonized the German, Italian, and Japanese populations. The crude, racist approach was especially pronounced with respect to the Japanese—and the media showed little inclination to distinguish between Japanese nationals living in Japan and those living in the United States. Indeed, they made virtually no distinction between Japanese aliens and American citizens of Japanese descent.

In their 2012 book, *News for All the People: The Epic Story of Race and the American Media*, authors Juan Gonzalez and Joseph Torres provide some examples of the news media's behavior:

> The day after Pearl Harbor, the *Los Angeles Times* reported that some Japanese could very well be upstanding good citizens, but "what the rest may be we do not know, nor can we take a chance in the light of yesterday's demonstration that treachery and double-dealing are major Japanese weapons." Later, the *Times* called for the removal of the Japanese, declaring, "A viper is nonetheless a viper wherever the egg is hatched—so a Japanese American, born of Japanese parents, grows up to be a Japanese, not an American."
>
> Scripps-Howard columnist Westbrook Peglar advocated executing a hundred detained Japanese for every American killed in the war, suspending habeas corpus for all Japanese, and placing them under government surveillance. While a few papers initially defended the Japanese minority, even those papers changed their tone after government officials warned of possible spies among the immigrants. [27]

Some of the racism was stunning even by the standards of the day, much less the standards of the 21st century.[28] Propaganda posters and cartoons featured caricatures of subhuman Japanese that were even more absurd and vicious than the "Beast of Berlin" images directed against Germans in World War I. Respected media sources stoked the frenzy. *Life* magazine, on December 22, 1941, published an article titled "How to Tell Japs from the Chinese," which included a variety of preposterous visual stereotypes.[29]

As the war continued, the ugly, racist nature of the stereotypes intensified. The depictions of Japanese soldiers and civilians alike became more evil and rat-like—showing them as alien, utterly inhuman enemies, hell-bent on world domination—in both government propaganda and mass media accounts.

The media also served as a loyal messenger in justifying President Roosevelt's executive order forcibly relocating Japanese and Japanese Americans residing in the three west coast states. The messaging was a curious, contradictory muddle, however. Some press accounts stressed what a lethal threat to national security leaving those disloyal "fifth columnists" in place would pose. A parallel, somewhat less common, message was that given the societal tensions on the west coast, the decision to send people of Japanese ancestry to "relocation centers" actually was done for their own safety. One *Washington Post* editorial cartoon made the latter argument explicitly.[30] Virtually none of the media stories mentioned that the relocation centers bore a striking resemblance to concentration camps, surrounded by barbed wire and featuring manned guard towers bristling with machine guns.

Nor did the articles discuss the awkward point that Japanese residents of Hawaii, where they made up a much larger portion of the population and were much closer to the war zone, were not expelled from their homes. Such an observation might have raised questions about the actual motives, on the part of both white West Coast residents and the Roosevelt administration, for applying such a draconian measure in that region. The compliant press, though, exhibited no inclination whatever to discomfit the president and his associates by bringing up such inconvenient issues.

Press images and messaging changed in fundamental ways once the war ended. Just as the focus shifted from the "Hun" to the Bolshevik menace (triggering the panic and civil liberties abuses of the "Red Scare") once World War I ended, a similar process occurred after World War II. That change was most evident with respect to the media's perspective on the Soviet Union. The prevailing press narrative went almost seamlessly from favorable to extremely hostile when relations between Washington and Moscow began to sour in the immediate post–World War II period. The allied governments likewise anticipated the possibility of war with the USSR; the United Kingdom's highly secret Operation Unthinkable, a plan to invade the Soviet Union, had been developed before World War II was even concluded.[31]

Policymakers promptly sought to enlist the media in the Cold War crusade against communism in general and the USSR in particular—much as they had for the crusades against the Kaiser and the fascists. As in those earlier episodes, the bulk of the opinion-shaping sector responded willingly. With rare exceptions, those journalists who were not seduced were at least cowed. Members of the press viewed their proper role much as they did during the world wars, even though the country was technically at peace. They certainly appeared more concerned about promoting U.S. policy objectives than they did about any abstract quest for the truth.

Indeed, journalists tended to be exceedingly deferential to U.S. officials in the national security arena—meaning the White House, the State Department, the Defense Department, and the new intelligence agencies. Political scientist Dan Nimmo notes that in the 1950s and 1960s, there was an implicit agreement between the government and press leaders that "certain matters can be publicized in the 'national interest' while others must remain unrevealed, hidden, or overlooked."[32]

A lengthy memo from David Sarnoff, the founder and initial president of CBS, to President Dwight D. Eisenhower in 1955 epitomizes the incestuous relationship between government and the media during the early years of the Cold War—and the potential for corrupt enforcement of ideological conformity. Sarnoff not only envisioned an extensive use of radio, television, and other communications outlets to disseminate U.S. government propaganda, but he railed against (mostly left-wing) media outlets that he believed would not cooperate in such an effort.[33]

The outcome of the de facto media-government partnership was a dearth of critical scrutiny in the press of the government's stewardship of foreign affairs. Media historian J. Fred MacDonald describes the corrosive consequences, noting even the language that news personnel used. "Reporters clearly identified with the United States. They spoke consistently of 'our bloc,' 'our side,' 'our power,' and 'our policy.' Reporters spoke as partisans, and viewers were hard-pressed not to support 'our position' on any given issue."[34]

Officials used a variety of methods to try to control or at least manipulate the media. During both world wars and the first two decades of the Cold War, their dominant technique was to co-opt journalists. That approach took several forms. At the top of the list were appeals to patriotism. One element of that appeal insisted that helping the government keep classified information secret was essential to prevent the designated enemy from threatening America's liberty and safety.

Another component argued that publishing stories highlighting the alleged nobility and successes of U.S. foreign policy initiatives helped boost national unity and morale. A final element of the appeal to patriotism contended that the willingness of the press to echo and amplify official warnings about dire threats from abroad helped keep the republic strong and united against dangerous foreign adversaries.

Sometimes they appealed subtly (or not so subtly) to snobbery and elitism. The underlying message that top policymakers conveyed to media figures is that they both were part of a knowledgeable and responsible elite tasked with keeping America safe. Such elite membership meant, among other obligations, keeping "sensitive" information out of the public domain, since ordinary Americans were incapable of evaluating that information accurately and reaching intelligent conclusions about the best policy options.

Lurking in the background, though, was the explicit or implied threat that it was both unhelpful and unwise for members of the media to express opposition to, or even skepticism about, any element of U.S. foreign policy—much less suggest that Washington's overall approach to global affairs was needlessly expensive, confrontational, or dangerous. Officials conveyed the message to would-be journalistic mavericks and iconoclasts that, at a minimum, they would be frozen out of crucial sources of information, while their more cooperative competitors would have extensive access.

Usually appeals to patriotism and snobbery were sufficient to ensure a compliant media without resorting to the less subtle methods. Indeed, many journalists were eager collaborators. Some even became outright assets of the CIA—especially during the first few decades of the Cold War. *Washington Post* reporter Carl Bernstein's October 1977, 25,000-word article in *Rolling Stone* provided an extraordinarily detailed account of cooperation between the CIA and members of the press, and it provided key insights into that relationship.[35] In some cases, the "journalists" were actually full-time CIA employees masquerading as members of the fourth estate. However, Bernstein also confirmed that some 400 bona fide American journalists had secretly carried out assignments for the Central Intelligence Agency during the previous 25 years.

As noted in Chapter 11, there is credible evidence that a *New York Times* correspondent actually played an active role in helping the CIA overthrow Iran's democratically elected prime minister, Mohammad Mossadegh, and restore the Shah to power in 1953.

Such activities created a serious conflict of interest. Journalists are supposed to monitor, scrutinize, and when necessary, criticize government policy. Collaborating with policymakers, much less going on the government payroll, was a profound betrayal of that mission and of basic journalistic ethics. It was little wonder that even some of the most ill-advised or unsavory aspects of U.S. foreign policy during the first three decades of the Cold War went largely unexamined in the news media. The supposed watchdog was busy taking treats from the burglars.

The government's velvet-glove approach worked well as a seduction technique until developments during the Vietnam War led to widespread, albeit belated, disillusionment throughout much of the news media. As that conflict wore on, and it became obvious that official predictions of imminent success were either delusional or dishonest, negative news stories became more frequent. Critical stories proliferated when evidence surfaced of U.S. atrocities and blatant war crimes in Southeast Asia. Daniel Ellsberg's leak of the Pentagon Papers was the capstone to the process of disillusionment, since it provided extensive, irrefutable evidence that U.S. officials had systematically lied to the news media and the American people about the Vietnam War for years.

The bonds of trust between the mainstream media and the foreign policy elite were not severed, but they were severely frayed. Greater skepticism about official pronouncements became the norm during the 1970s and 1980s. It was not until the Persian Gulf War that the trust was largely restored and most of the media again actively cooperated to promote Washington's agenda and official foreign policy line.

CHAPTER 2
A (Belated) Vietnam Wakeup Call and Its Aftermath

Historian William Hammond asks, "What went wrong between the military and the news media in Vietnam?" He observes that "no one could have anticipated when the war began, the corrosive animosity that developed between the two as the conflict evolved. Neither could anyone have predicted that the controversies the war sparked would continue to fester for more than a generation following its end. . . ."[1] Hammond describes the situation well, but his focus was a little too narrow. The estrangement that evolved was not just between the press and the military, but between much of the press and the political elites that directed U.S. foreign and military policy. That estrangement would indeed last for more than a generation.

The American news media was overwhelmingly supportive of the U.S. military intervention in Vietnam during its early stages, to the extent that the conflict received much attention at all. President Dwight D. Eisenhower's 1955 decision to dispatch 700 military "advisers" to the Republic of Vietnam (South Vietnam) largely flew under the radar as far as the press was concerned. The same was true when President John F. Kennedy not only continued Eisenhower's program but added another 500 advisers in May 1961.

It wasn't until 1962 and early 1963, when the number of U.S. military personnel in South Vietnam climbed well into the thousands, that news stories on the topic became more frequent. Some of those analyses began to note that the "advisers" were entrenched with South Vietnamese combat units and that their role was increasingly difficult to distinguish from outright combat. As Americans began to be wounded and killed, press and public interest mounted. By the end of 1962, approximately 11,000 military advisers were stationed in South Vietnam, and in that year alone 53 of them had been killed. Kennedy would soon send even more personnel to Vietnam. By the end of 1963, the numbers had risen to 16,000, and casualties also were rising rapidly.[2]

The growing press attention, however, usually did not translate into probing questions about the nature of the U.S. mission or potential pitfalls. Journalists, like most other Americans, were firmly caught up in the 1930s (or Munich) syndrome. The pervasive belief was that the lack of action by Western powers, including the United States, to stop the rise of the fascist powers during that decade had led inexorably to the catastrophe of World War II. The corollary was that aggression from any source must be confronted early and decisively.

The Munich syndrome produced the perverse caricature in which the emergence of a nationalist communist regime in North Vietnam was equated with the rampages of Nazi Germany and Imperial Japan. Advocates of U.S. intervention in Vietnam saw communist leader Ho Chi Minh as merely an obedient servant of the Soviet Union and/or Communist China—serving the same function that puppet rulers like Manchukuo's Aisin-Gioro Puyi, China's last Qing emperor, or Norway's Vidkun Quisling did for the fascists. As Eisenhower argued in presenting his domino theory, a communist triumph in Vietnam would not only lead to the loss of the other Southeast Asian countries, but it would be the first stage of a red tide that would prevail from India to Japan.[3]

There were many problems with the Munich syndrome's arguments and conclusions, but the worst was the simplistic belief in a monolithic, global communist threat. That line of reasoning minimized, if not ignored, the role of nationalism. Unfortunately, communists did dominate the insurgency that overthrew French colonial rule in Vietnam and the rest of Indochina in the mid-1950s. Nevertheless, Ho Chi Minh and his compatriots also were fierce nationalists who had no desire to see their country become a tool of Soviet or Chinese ambitions. Ho was especially worried about a possible Chinese bid for domination, which explains why he reached out to the Truman administration to ask for U.S. support. Hanoi wanted a counterweight to Beijing's influence. Unfortunately, not only were U.S. officials oblivious to such important geopolitical dynamics in Southeast Asia, but the American press corps was as well.

Consequently, most of the press and public initially saw U.S. military support for South Vietnam's noncommunist government as a necessary step to strangle aggression in its cradle, thereby avoiding the mistakes of the 1930s that ultimately produced a cataclysmic global war. Very few journalists questioned the narrative, even when U.S. military involvement spiked under President Lyndon B. Johnson following the Gulf of Tonkin incident on August 2, 1964. According to administration officials, North Vietnamese ships allegedly fired on two U.S. naval vessels—an "attack" that most experts have since concluded probably never occurred.[4]

Johnson promptly used the incident to launch previously contemplated air strikes on targets in North Vietnam[5] and received overwhelming support in the press for his decision. In its August 7, 1964, edition, the *New York Times* published excerpts from 27 editorials about the administration's response. The extent of media enthusiasm was breathtaking; 24 of the editorials endorsed the bombing campaign without reservation, 2 expressed minor reservations, and 1 was noncommittal.[6] Similarly, when Johnson dispatched tens of thousands of American combat personnel to the increasingly hot war zone in 1965, there was little dispute in the press that the step was prudent and necessary. Optimism was widespread that the mission to repel Ho's bid to overthrow South Vietnam's government and unify Vietnam under communist rule would be successful in a relatively short period of time and at a manageable cost in American blood and treasure.

The earliest cracks in the news media's support for the war were the result of concerns, morphing eventually into revulsion, about the nature of the South Vietnamese government the United States was supporting. One consequence of the influx of American journalists into South Vietnam to cover the war was increased scrutiny of President Ngo Dinh Diem's regime. A substantial number of correspondents were troubled by what they saw. The Diem government's rampant nepotism and corruption was all too apparent. News accounts began to note that as a Catholic in a majority Buddhist country, Diem automatically had a somewhat fragile political base. The tendency of Diem and his inner circle to keep influential Buddhist figures at arm's length, and even display disdain for them on some occasions, made the problem worse.

The nepotism, corruption, and growing repression proved hard to defend in American news accounts. The president's closest advisers by far were his brother, Ngo Dinh Nhu, and his sister-in-law, Tran Le Xuan (better known as Madame Nhu), who served as South Vietnam's de facto first lady. Such insularity led to ever greater public discontent. Reporters also took note of the regime's civil liberties abuses, including the routine jailing and torture of Diem's critics. When Buddhist monks began leading major street protests in late 1962 and early 1963, those demonstrations received growing coverage in news accounts—including television film footage—going back to the United States.

Several incidents beginning in June 1963 intensified that coverage when Buddhist monks, willing to become martyrs, set themselves ablaze in the streets of Saigon. Those horrifying television images began to turn American public opinion sharply against the Diem government. Madame Nhu made the already volatile situation much worse. On one occasion when a monk lit himself on fire, she flippantly said that he had been "barbecued" with "imported gasoline," and offered to supply more fuel for others so inclined to duplicate the spectacle. She even stated that she would stand by "and clap."[7] Such shockingly callous comments did not play well with American news consumers, and public support for continued U.S. backing of Diem's regime eroded further.

Despite such episodes, the Diem government still had its defenders in the American press. In a late September 1963 op-ed, syndicated columnist Joseph Alsop asserted that Diem was "a courageous, quite viable leader."[8] Alsop was part of a delegation of "friendly" news personnel based in the United States that the Kennedy administration had organized, funded, and dispatched to Vietnam to write favorable accounts, hoping to counter some of the more critical stories that had begun to emerge from U.S. reporters based in South Vietnam. The Alsop column illustrated the success of the effort.

Moreover, the growing media discontent with and criticism of the Diem government did not usually translate into criticism of the U.S. military effort to defeat the communist Viet Cong and its backers in North Vietnam. Most accounts still portrayed the Viet Cong, not unreasonably, as an extension of Hanoi's effort to unify the country under communist rule. Only gradually—and much later—did elements of the media question the corollary assumption that North Vietnam was nothing more than a component of an international communist offensive directed from Moscow or Beijing. In the meantime, pressure mounted on the Kennedy administration to find new, more palatable political leadership in the country the United States was trying to save from a communist takeover.

When the South Vietnamese military (with strong encouragement from Washington) overthrew Diem in early November 1963, killing him and his brother, the prevailing assumption in the American press seemed to be that now the mission to keep South Vietnam out of the communist orbit could get back on track with new, more enlightened leadership in Saigon. That assumption proved to be a cruel illusion. South Vietnamese politics instead entered a period of turbulence as one would-be candidate for supremacy after another briefly attained power. The governmental chaos in Saigon was one important factor inducing the Johnson administration to deepen America's own military role, lest the entire mission to prevent a communist takeover of the country unravel. By late 1964, the early post-Diem optimism in the U.S. press also had faded.[9] The assumption grew that if Washington did not make major changes in its approach, South Vietnam might well succumb to a communist takeover.

PRESS SUPPORT FOR WASHINGTON'S ESCALATION OF THE WAR

Beginning in 1965, the U.S. role in direct combat became an ever-greater component of the overall war effort. Yet even with that change, most media portrayals of the conflict remained positive. That perspective finally began to change as U.S. casualties mounted and a definitive victory proved elusive. Unease within the news media about the worthiness of the mission began to set in. Reporters began to ask harder, more pointed, questions of the military spokesmen in Saigon who provided briefings to the press.

One of the more puzzling aspects of the U.S. military's policy toward media coverage was the absence of formal censorship.[10] Initially, that lackadaisical approach might have been attributable to overconfidence that the war correspondents of the Vietnam era were, like their predecessors in the two world wars and Korea, loyal advocates of U.S. policy who saw themselves as members of the policy "team." Yet even in those earlier conflicts, the government had maintained a rigorous censorship system. In Vietnam, the authorities did not. The lack of censorship did not cause many headaches during the early years of the U.S. intervention because, as noted previously, reporters tended not to criticize the fundamental worthiness of the mission. Criticisms of specific features might have been annoying at times, but military leaders did not find such behavior sufficiently worrisome to impose censorship.

They may have regretted that decision when coverage of the war effort became increasingly negative. Yet they still refrained from censoring the press. Censorship had developed a distinctly negative connotation in American culture, so perhaps they were intimidated by that change. And initially, officials may have sought to maintain the fiction that the U.S. role in Vietnam was to assist the Saigon government repel an insurgency, not wage a full-scale war. Whatever the reason, the absence of censorship continued. That restraint enabled the American people to see ugly features of the Vietnam War and read critical, even caustic, accounts of the U.S. mission that would have been unthinkable in previous wars.

The process of disillusionment was gradual. *New York Times* reporter David Halberstam went to South Vietnam in 1962 and quickly gained a reputation for viewing glowing, disingenuous official accounts of successful missions with skepticism bordering on disdain, but even he was slow to reach the conclusion that the rationale for the war itself was fatally flawed. Halberstam would ultimately eviscerate most of the justifications and puncture the pretentions of renowned members of America's political and policy elites in his best-selling book *The Best and the Brightest*, but he was surprisingly supportive of the war as late as 1964. He insisted that as a "strategic country in a key area [Vietnam] is perhaps one of only five or six nations in the world that is truly vital to U.S. interests."[11]

Halberstam was adamantly opposed to terminating the mission, despite the rising toll of U.S. casualties and the political chaos in Saigon. U.S. withdrawal, he asserted, would consign the people of South Vietnam to a "drab, lifeless, and controlled society," and they deserved a better fate. Withdrawal would also mean "that the United States' prestige will be lowered throughout the world, and it means that the pressure of Communism on the rest of Southeast Asia will intensify." And the negative strategic consequences would not be confined to that region. "Withdrawal means that throughout the world the enemies of the West will be encouraged to try insurgencies like the one in Vietnam." Conversely, "an anti-Communist victory in Vietnam would serve to discourage so-called wars of liberation."[12]

Such a defense of the U.S. mission could just as readily have been penned by a Johnson administration official. It contained all the standard justifications: terminating the intervention would betray the Vietnamese people, damage U.S. credibility globally, and encourage more communist insurgencies. It even contained an implicit endorsement of the domino theory: the ramifications of a communist triumph in South Vietnam would be felt far beyond the region.

The reality is that while Halberstam and other members of the Saigon press corps frequently criticized specific aspects of the war effort (especially examples of military dishonesty or incompetence) as early as 1962 and 1963, most did not truly turn against the war and advocate U.S. disengagement until it started to become glaringly apparent in 1966 and 1967 that the mission was failing and had few prospects of revival.[13] As the leaked Pentagon Papers showed in 1971, key U.S. officials had reached similar conclusions by that time—although they were not about to share such information and insights with Congress or the American people. Efforts to portray the (mostly young) reporters on the scene as perceptive and outspoken early opponents of a disastrous foreign policy blunder are unduly creative historical revisionism.

Like Halberstam, most other news personnel in the Saigon press corps initially did not question the wisdom, morality, or necessity of the U.S. intervention, they merely questioned whether it was being waged in an effective manner. Their disagreements with U.S. officials were over tactics and strategy, not the substance of the mission itself. *Time's* Charles Mohr, for example, was chagrined when anti-war groups in the late 1960s cited his 1963 resignation from the magazine as an early example of a courageous protest against an immoral war—a war that *Time* had repeatedly supported in its editorials. "Everyone thought I left because I was against the war," Mohr recalled. But that wasn't the reason at all; he was angry that *Time's* editorial management team had criticized the coverage by reporters in Saigon (including, by implication, its own correspondent, Mohr) as defeatist and even disloyal. As for the war itself, Mohr stated candidly, "I just thought it wasn't working. I didn't come to think of it as immoral until the very end."[14]

Support for the war was even more evident in the editorial offices back home. A typical example was a news series, "Vietnam Perspectives," that CBS television aired in August 1965—at the very time Washington was ramping-up the U.S. military presence in Vietnam. The series featured interviews with numerous administration officials, including Secretary of State Dean Rusk, Secretary of Defense Robert McNamara, National Security Advisor McGeorge Bundy, and Gen. Maxwell Taylor, the adviser who had been the principal lobbyist within the administration for sending U.S. combat units. Episodes also incorporated the views of nongovernmental experts who justified escalating the war. Yet not a single critic of the war was given airtime.[15] Worse, the network allowed the officials to review and edit tapes of their comments before the relevant episodes aired. CBS was not playing the role of an independent observer of a government policy; it was serving as a government mouthpiece for that policy.

Unfortunately, CBS's accommodating posture was all too typical of the media's coverage of the Vietnam War before 1967–1968. J. Fred MacDonald, a historian of television's role during the Cold War, notes that in the early stages of the conflict, television journalists failed to offer their viewers "informed rebuttal or even healthy doubt" when the government provided official justifications for the U.S. military campaign in Southeast Asia. "There were no opposing voices" calling for a wide-ranging discussion of all the issues associated with the Vietnam conflict, MacDonald concluded, much less voices calling for "a national debate on the advisability of the U.S. actions."[16]

Expressions of doubt about prospects for success gradually increased during 1966 and 1967 as U.S. casualties mounted. Even staunch media supporters of the war found it increasingly hard to ignore that the predictions of a decisive victory in the near future were less and less credible. Critical accounts of the autocratic regime of Nguyen Van Thieu proliferated; Thieu had emerged from the post-Diem chaos to lead South Vietnam, first as the leader of a military coup in 1965 and then as president following a highly suspect election in September 1967. Reporters ridiculed the U.S. military's daily briefings to reporters in Saigon as "the 5 o'clock follies" and regarded the "information" those briefings presented as exercises in fiction.[17]

Still, at that point, most mainstream press accounts did not challenge the Johnson administration's confident predictions about the war's progress. The headline of an article by columnist Orr Kelly in the *Washington Star* asserted flatly, "In a Military Sense, the War Is Just about Won."[18] The *Philadelphia Inquirer*'s Bob Considine admonished critics of the war to "stop griping." "We're winning this lousy war," he concluded. "It is not, repeat not, a stalemate."[19] In early 1968, though, the media narrative about Vietnam took a sharp turn toward the negative.

DISILLUSIONMENT

Two major events in the first quarter of 1968 were the catalysts for change. The first blow came in January and directly undermined the Johnson administration's continuing assurances that victory was at hand with just a little more time and effort. On January 30, coinciding with the Tet lunar new year, communist forces initiated a massive, multifront offensive throughout South Vietnam. They launched attacks on 36 of 44 provincial capitals, five of the six largest cities, and more than one-fourth of the district capitals. The initial successes of the offensive,

including the seizure of major portions of the old imperial city of Hue in
northern South Vietnam, stunned observers. The television visuals were
especially disheartening; they confirmed that, despite the massive U.S.
combat role, now entering its fourth year, Washington's adversary was
surprisingly strong and capable. Television footage of Vietcong sappers
penetrating the U.S. embassy compound in Saigon graphically conveyed
the point.

Media outlets seemed disillusioned and bitter about the turn of
events. Coverage of the fighting was extensive, and much of it was far
from upbeat.[20] The *New Republic*'s reaction was typical. "A year before,
President Johnson had said that the enemy was losing his grip on South
Vietnam. With Tet, that prophecy seemed as broken as the policy it
served." The title of the editorial fully conveyed the surging cynicism in
the journalistic community: "Misled. In Every Sense."[21]

Over the next several weeks, U.S. and South Vietnamese troops
repelled the offensive, inflicting extensive casualties on regular North
Vietnamese units and damaging the Viet Cong so badly that it could
no longer conduct significant independent operations. Reports to that
effect were true, but they missed the fundamental point: according to
U.S. leaders—and generally reported in the same vein by the American
press—the communists were supposed to be on the brink of defeat and
utterly incapable of waging an offensive on the scale of Tet.[22] The principal casualty of the Tet Offensive may well have been the credibility
of U.S. officials and their closest allies in the media. After Tet, far more
reporters and their home publications and television networks viewed
official assurances about the Vietnam War with undisguised skepticism.
In fact, debunking those accounts appeared to have become a favorite
pastime. That attitude would persist long past the January 1973 Paris
Peace Accords that formally ended U.S. involvement in the war; it would
continue until Saigon fell to North Vietnamese forces in April 1975.

CBS Evening News anchor Walter Cronkite epitomized the new
perspective. Reportedly, his response when seeing the bulletins coming out of Saigon about the Tet Offensive was, "What the hell is
going on? I thought we were winning the war!"[23] Cronkite made his
own fact-finding tour of South Vietnam in February. In an hour-long,

prime-time broadcast upon his return to the United States, he expressed his candid conclusion about the war. "We've been too often disappointed by the optimism of the American leaders both in Vietnam and Washington to have faith any longer in the silver linings they find in the darkest clouds. For it seems now more certain than ever, that the bloody experience of Vietnam is to end in a stalemate. To say that we are closer to victory today is to believe in the face of the evidence, the optimists who have been wrong in the past." He added, "It is increasingly clear to this reporter that the only rational way out then will be to negotiate, not as victors, but as an honorable people who lived up to their pledge to defend democracy, and did the best they could."[24]

"Uncle Walter's" pessimistic assessment did not immediately cause a dramatic drop in public support for the war effort, but the longer-term impact was considerable.[25] Whatever remained of optimism about the war among the American people began to evaporate. Among an increasingly divided public, most saw the war as, at best, a thankless slog that had to be endured until an honorable peace could be negotiated. Outright opponents of the war became more vocal and assertive. For the first time, rumbles of criticism in Congress came from sources other than the small flock of doves. And with that growing division among America's political elite, critics in the media had both more sources of negative information and more latitude to express their views without imperiling their reputations and careers.

The Tet experience and Cronkite's high-profile broadcast had an especially significant impact on his journalistic colleagues, both in Vietnam and in the United States. Their mistrust of U.S. officials and their arguments came out in the open in an increasingly blunt fashion. By the time President Richard Nixon took office in January 1969, press views of the war effort were frequently, and sometimes intensely, hostile.

The second transformative event occurred on March 16, 1968, but wasn't reported until the following year. What was left of the media's partnership with the government in selling the Vietnam War shattered when news broke about an incident in the South Vietnamese village of My Lai. The military's official statement following the bloodshed on that day portrayed the carnage as an impressive victory over communist fighters, and most accounts in news outlets reflected that view.[26] But the cover story unraveled in November 1969 with the publication of an investigative report by a young freelance journalist named Seymour Hersh. His report uncovered what had really taken place, and the revelation caused widespread revulsion in the United States.[27] A U.S. Army company under the command of Lt. William Calley had massacred at least 347 unarmed civilians in the South Vietnamese hamlet.

As the months passed, evidence emerged that—while My Lai was the worst—other war crimes had taken place but gone largely unreported. The proliferation of such news accounts raised doubts not only about the U.S. mission's prospects for success, but about its moral foundation. William Hammond noted that the press was especially angry about the delay in the release of official information about My Lai. "Editorial writers across the country asked again and again why it had taken almost two years for the facts in the case to become known."[28]

There was, in fact, solid evidence of military indifference (at best) to civilian suffering much earlier in the war, but the mainstream media turned a blind eye to such evidence. When independent reporter Martha Gellhorn returned from a lengthy trip to Vietnam in September 1966, she pitched a series of articles to various outlets about the impact of U.S. napalm strikes on Vietnamese civilians, especially children. Christian G. Appy, a professor of history at the University of Massachusetts, notes that "her articles were rejected by almost every U.S. publisher, which is why one of her most penetrating exposés appeared in the most unlikely source imaginable—the *Ladies' Home Journal*."[29] That article, "Suffer the Little Children," documented the horrifying effects of napalm burns on scores of Vietnamese children and appeared in the January 1967 issue. One could certainly ask where were such top-tier publications as the *New York Times, Washington Post, Newsweek, Time,* and others when that article could have appeared in their pages? At the time, those media paladins were still fully supportive of Washington's war effort and showed little inclination to raise uncomfortable questions.

Before Tet, the press-government relationship had showed signs of becoming testy. After, it was often openly combative. An incident during a February 1968 press conference with Secretary of State Dean

Rusk highlighted the growing animosity. Rusk presented the Johnson administration's official line that Tet had been a major victory for U.S. and South Vietnamese forces and a corresponding debacle for communist units. ABC reporter John Scali disputed the secretary's optimistic assessment. Rusk, who had already been subjected to skeptical if not derisive questioning from the press corps blew up. "There gets to be a point," he fumed, "when the question is, whose side are you on?"[30] Scali later recalled his reaction to that innuendo. "I got angry. I got out of my chair. I was going to hit him in the nose. But two reporters restrained me."[31] An episode in which the secretary of state implied that a prominent establishment journalist was a traitor and the journalist responded by trying to punch the secretary of state in the nose was emblematic of the rapidly deteriorating relationship between press and government with respect to the Vietnam War.

The posture became even more openly adversarial once Richard Nixon became president. Most journalists had never been fond of Nixon, and they had even less incentive to accord him or his policies friendly treatment than they had with Johnson during his final year in office. Once the My Lai revelations surfaced, the media's hostile relationship with the Nixon White House was undeniable. From that point until the end of U.S. involvement in the war, the government and a growing portion of the press behaved as adversaries, each questioning both the judgment and the motives of the other.

That attitude hardened when U.S. military action expanded into Cambodia and Laos in 1970 and 1971. In addition to presenting Washington's conduct in an unflattering light, reporters routinely disclosed details of officially top-secret operations, such as the bombing of Cambodia, which had commenced in the spring of 1969.[32]

Such behavior from the mainstream media would have been unthinkable during America's previous wars or, up to this point, the Cold War. And not surprisingly, U.S. officials did not react well. The Nixon administration railed against such revelations, contending that irresponsible journalists were aiding the enemy cause and jeopardizing the lives of American military personnel.[33] It was a feeble claim. The Cambodians certainly knew that they were being bombed, and North Vietnamese units operating in the country knew they were being targeted. The only parties whose awareness of such missions seemed lacking were Congress and the American people. And as when whistleblowers such as Julian Assange and Edward Snowden disclosed unsavory U.S. covert conduct a half century later, U.S. leaders did not dispute the truth of the revelations; they were angry because the news stories were inconvenient and embarrassing.

Backlash: Blaming the Press for the U.S. Defeat

Press-government relations continued their downhill slide during the final phases of U.S. involvement in the Vietnam War. The shift in the dominant media narrative toward "defeatism" both shaped and reflected the changes in congressional and public opinion. Disillusionment in those arenas was widespread on two different levels. One involved the psychological trauma of failure—the realization that for the first time, the vaunted U.S. military was losing a war. True, the War of 1812 was objectively a draw, but Andrew Jackson's decisive triumph at New Orleans (albeit after the peace treaty had been signed on the other side of the Atlantic) fostered the impression of victory. The Korean War, too, could be spun as a U.S. success since South Korea remained out of the clutches of international communism. But as the United States completed the withdrawal of its forces from Vietnam and signed the Paris Peace Accords in January 1973, the perception of failure was difficult to avoid.

Moreover, the United States had been unable to prevail over what was by all military measures a qualitatively inferior adversary. The battlefield failure was accompanied by an equally humbling policy failure, although the latter point was not fully driven home until the South Vietnamese government and army collapsed in the spring of 1975 and communist forces occupied Saigon. The television images of the panicky evacuation by helicopter from the roof of the U.S. embassy in April 1975 was a searing sight that underscored the extent of the blow to America's pride and prestige.

The Vietnam mission also struck a severe blow to the national self-image of America as an icon of goodness and morality in the world.[34]

Most Americans had held that belief with a fervor. Even when the United States "had to" wage war, as in the two world wars, Americans had little doubt the country was fighting for a righteous cause. A subsidiary belief was that, while other counties and their militaries might commit horrifying atrocities and war crimes, America and its soldiers did not do so. A sober look at the country's history, including the brutal wars against the various Native American nations and the suppression of the insurrection in the Philippines following the Spanish-American War would have debunked such notions, but both the news media and the historical profession had consistently sustained the comforting national myth.

My Lai and other episodes in Vietnam compelled Americans to face the ugly truth that "American boys" serving in the military had committed unspeakable acts. News stories about rampant drug use, the "fragging" of unpopular officers by their own troops, and other troubling revelations further shook America's sense of moral superiority. The news media, serving as the messenger of such unwelcome tidings, attracted substantial resentment in official circles and among some, primarily conservative, segments of the rattled public.

How great a role negative media accounts of the Vietnam War played in galvanizing public opposition to U.S. policy was a matter of conjecture at the time. Subsequent assessments continue to reach various conclusions. A 1967 *Newsweek* survey found that graphic images of the war actually tended to make viewers *more* supportive of the war effort.[35] At least that was the case until the war dragged on with mounting casualties and no prospect of victory in sight. War weariness resulting from those factors seemed to spur the growth of public alienation toward the policies of the Johnson and Nixon administrations.[36] William J. Small, director of CBS television in Washington, noted that "when television covered its first war in Vietnam, it showed a terrible truth of war in a manner new to mass audiences." He concluded the case could be made that such imagery "was cardinal to the disillusionment of Americans with this war, the cynicism of many young people toward America, and the destruction of Lyndon Johnson's tenure of office."[37]

There certainly was disillusionment and greater wariness throughout the journalistic community about both the war and the credibility of political and military leaders. Journalist, editor, and author Bill Katovsky succinctly captured how the relationship between the news media and the government had soured as the war dragged on and evidence of the military command's duplicity and human-rights violations mounted: "The Pentagon started blaming the press for standing in the way of victory, while the press accused the government of lying about the war."[38]

In his memoirs, Lyndon Johnson strongly implied that the media had stabbed America in the back. Referring to the Tet Offensive, Johnson asserted that "there was a great deal of emotional and exaggerated reporting . . . in our press and on television." Indeed, "the media seemed to be in competition as to who could provide the most lurid and depressing accounts. Columnists unsympathetic to American involvement in Southeast Asia jumped on the bandwagon." As a result, the American people "subjected to this daily barrage of bleakness and near panic, began to think that we had suffered a defeat."[39]

One of the main architects of Washington's Vietnam policy, Gen. Maxwell Taylor, epitomized the attitude of many of his colleagues that the war could have been won if the prying eyes of the press had been kept away. Although he gave a perfunctory acknowledgment that the American people had a right to know what U.S. forces were doing in combat situations, he asserted that information about military operations should be given "not today, not tomorrow, but at the appropriate time." When asked who should decide when the time was right for the press to inform the public about a military intervention, Taylor replied without hesitation that it "should be the President of the United States."[40]

The extent of his bitterness and animosity toward the post–Vietnam War press came through clearly. "In World War II," Taylor stated, "the press was admirable, because they felt they were American citizens and that their country was sacred. In Vietnam there was the feeling on the part of some of the press that their task was to destroy the American command and to work against what was being done." He added ominously, "That kind of thing should not be tolerated."[41]

Gen. Dwight Eisenhower, Supreme Allied Commander in World War II, had expressed the same view as Taylor about the role of the press in that earlier conflict. Eisenhower declared that "public opinion wins wars, and I have always considered as quasi-staff officers [the] correspondents accredited to my headquarters.'[42] Most journalists viewed their role in a similar fashion during World War II and for the first two decades of the Cold War, but clearly the latest generation no longer did so.

MEDIA SKEPTICISM BEYOND VIETNAM—WITH AN IDEOLOGICAL SPLIT

By and large, members of the press did not seem to be intimidated by attempts to blame them for Washington's debacle in Vietnam. In fact, the mainstream media's greater skepticism and wariness about U.S. policy became apparent on an array of other international issues. The growth of more robust skepticism influenced analyses of U.S. policy initiatives in Central America and other parts of the Third World. It also led to often concerted (even hostile) scrutiny of the activities of the Central Intelligence Agency—dovetailing with congressional hearings, especially the Senate hearings chaired by Sen. Frank Church (D-ID) in the mid-1970s that uncovered multiple abuses that occurred over several decades. During this era, much of the news media came closer to playing the role of foreign policy watchdog—a role it frequently failed to play during earlier or later periods.

Journalists had greater latitude as well. In a sign of the changing *zeitgeist*, two congressional committees, the House Committee on Un-American Activities and the Senate Internal Security Subcommittee, which had harassed journalists and other foreign policy dissenters for decades, were both abolished during this period. The House committee was terminated in 1975, and its Senate counterpart shut down two years later.

Coverage of several international issues, however, was marked by an ideological, or even a partisan, split. Liberal and left-wing journalists tended to openly oppose most of Washington's security initiatives in the developing world, especially during Ronald Reagan's presidency. Conservative journalists, admittedly a minority within the press community, remained supportive of assertive, including outright interventionist, policies. Indeed, some became increasingly vocal in their support.

The split was apparent in coverage of the so-called Reagan Doctrine, which supported insurgent movements in the Third World that professed to be anti-communist, especially anti-Soviet. The most detailed exposition of the policy came from Reagan's second secretary of state, George Shultz, during a crucial speech to the Commonwealth Club in San Francisco on February 22, 1985. The title of his talk was "America and the Struggle for Freedom."[43]

"A revolution is sweeping the world today," Shultz proclaimed, "a democratic revolution."[44] He emphasized that the United States was now determined to wrest the initiative from Moscow in the West's global ideological struggle with the Soviet Union. "For many years we saw our adversaries act without restraint to back insurgencies around the world to spread communist dictatorships." Moreover, "any victory of communism was held to be irreversible," the infamous Brezhnev Doctrine. But those days were over, Shultz emphasized. "In recent years, Soviet activities and pretensions have run head-on into the democratic revolution. People are insisting on their right to independence, on their right to choose their government free of outside control."[45]

Shultz and other administration officials casually identified America's interests and values with those of foreign insurgent groups. The new revolutionary trend "we are witnessing around the world—popular insurgencies against communist domination—is not an American creation," Shultz assured his audience. He did give the administration a little wiggle room, stating that "the nature and extent of our support—whether moral support or something more—necessarily varies from case to case." Nevertheless, "there should be no doubt where our sympathies lie."[46]

In reality, the United States was already providing financial, logistical, and military aid to insurgents in several countries—most notably Nicaragua, Angola, and Afghanistan—long before the secretary of state outlined an explicit doctrine.[47] The bulk of the assistance went to the Afghan mujahideen who were resisting the Soviet army of occupation. This effort received wide bipartisan support and drew little criticism in the media.[48] The overwhelming majority of journalists embraced the narrative that the Soviet Union had committed egregious aggression and that the Afghans were fully justified in mounting and sustaining a ferocious resistance. Reporters and columnists argued that Washington's material support for that armed resistance was justified both on moral grounds (aiding the victims of aggression) and on the grounds of realpolitik. With respect to the latter, helping Afghan fighters tie down Soviet troops and cause a major geopolitical headache for the Kremlin benefited overall U.S. Cold War strategy to contain Moscow's power.

Modest differences did emerge in press treatments of the Afghan war, with conservative and libertarian outlets more inclined to portray the insurgents as true freedom fighters, not just anti-Soviet rebels. Among the most enthusiastic proponents of that thesis were writers for the libertarian *Reason* magazine. During a June 1987 *Reason* symposium, one of those writers, Jack Wheeler, stated flatly that supporting "these freedom fighter organizations is the most cost-effective way that I can possibly think of to defend the interests of the U.S." But it would "also do something which I would consider to be moral, and that is to make an effort to bring freedom to these peoples under Soviet colonial sway."[49]

Articles from centrist and liberal outlets were somewhat less credulous and laudatory about the mujahideen's alleged commitment to freedom and focused more on the supposed moral imperative for the United States to help insurgents resist blatant outside aggression. One aspect of accounts across the political spectrum, though, was rather consistent: they ignored or glossed over evidence that misogynistic Islamic extremists dominated the mujahideen coalition.[50] That pervasive failure to comprehend the real ideological orientation of the factions Washington was helping caused Americans to be horrified when the individuals leading those factions formed the core of the Taliban regime in the 1990s. Worse, some of the "Arab volunteers" in the ranks of the mujahideen, including a young Saudi named Osama bin Laden, subsequently formed al Qaeda—the organization that conducted the terrorist attacks on September 11, 2001.

In contrast to the general acceptance of military aid to the Afghan rebels, the Nicaraguan and Angolan programs were intensely controversial. Press coverage mirrored the deep, bitter ideological and partisan split in the political arena about those policies.

To conservatives, the Nicaraguan Contras were noble freedom fighters struggling against the latest Kremlin puppet, the Sandinista government of Daniel Ortega. Leaving aside other considerations, conservatives deemed the geographic proximity of Nicaragua to the United States sufficient reason to support the Contras. That security consideration, along with the moral obligation to oppose dehumanizing communist tyranny wherever it appeared, meant that Washington had both a strategic and moral imperative to aid the anti-Sandinista insurgents in their fight. Doing so also would help prevent the spread of the communist virus to the rest of Central America. Some or all of those arguments appeared frequently in such publications as the *Wall Street Journal* and *National Review.*

To liberals in Congress and the media, however, the Contras were little more than armed remnants of former Nicaraguan dictator Anastasio Somoza's regime. They were not freedom fighters, but autocratic thugs who routinely committed human rights violations. According to this view, the U.S. government was engaging in shameful behavior by supporting them. Opponents in Congress, along with their allies in most of the mainstream media, fought relentlessly to prevent the Reagan administration from continuing to assist the Contras.

Despite the geographic factor, administration officials sensed a problem in trying to justify assistance to anti-Sandinista forces solely on pragmatic, strategic grounds. Both the public and Congress, severely scarred by the war in Vietnam, were doubly wary of arguments that another small nation was crucial to America's security and warranted significant U.S. intervention. Portraying the Sandinistas as odious Soviet puppets and their opponents as freedom fighters became an important way to broaden the appeal of providing U.S. support to the Contras. This portrayal was especially necessary to gain support among people who might not respond well to arguments based on cold calculations of realpolitik.

Consequently, Reagan heaped praise on anti-Sandinista fighters, asserting that they were nothing less than the "moral equal of our founding fathers," and that "we owe them our help" in their efforts to topple Ortega's regime.[51] Nearly a decade later, in his memoirs, the former president still described the anti-Sandinista rebels as "freedom fighters."[52] He also railed against most American journalists, contending that they were too favorable to Ortega's government and far too negative toward the Contras. "Perhaps after Vietnam when many reporters had cast Uncle Sam in the role of the villain," Reagan speculated, "they didn't want to put white hats on the Contra freedom fighters because the U.S. government was supporting them."[53] He implicitly rejected the possibility that critical journalists had good reason to conclude that many of the Contras weren't wearing metaphorical white hats.

Attempting to cast the Contras as democratic freedom fighters seemed to work only with conservative true believers in the media and their appreciative readers and viewers. Most others remained skeptical if not scornful of that interpretation. And given the reality that most top Contra leaders indeed had been officers in Somoza's corrupt, brutal National Guard, such a negative view among much of the American press was hardly surprising. Important outlets, including the *New York Times*, highlighted reliable reports of frequent and serious human rights abuses by Contra forces.[54] Such accounts added to the already heavily negative coverage.

The Contras' actions, which belied the benign image their U.S. sponsors sought to foster, caused one media relations problem for the Reagan administration. But administration officials undermined their own credibility in another way as well. Policymakers asserted that the U.S. goal was not to forcibly overthrow the Sandinista regime but only to pressure it to sever its ties with Moscow and negotiate with the Contras to create a more broad-based government. Most members of the media treated that official rationale with a combination of astonishment and disdain. *New York Times* correspondent Tim Weiner, for example, expressed surprise that "President Reagan stuck with the cover story maintaining the fiction that the United States was not seeking to topple the Sandinista regime."[55] Indeed, if the Sandinistas were truly as evil as administration officials alleged, why wasn't the explicit objective to oust them, not just pressure them to establish a coalition government? The administration's own professed pragmatism in this case undercut its rhetorical moral absolutism.

Nevertheless, conservative journalists joined with their ideological compatriots in Congress to condemn efforts to scale back, much less end, U.S. assistance to the Contras. When the House of Representatives passed the so-called Boland Amendment to prohibit efforts to overthrow the Sandinista government, syndicated columnist George Will was livid. "The Brezhnev doctrine asserts that the process of becoming a Soviet satellite is irreversible. The Boland amendment forbids support to freedom fighters attempting to liberate Nicaragua from a satellite regime. Republican Representative Don Ritter of Pennsylvania rightly says that the amendment makes the United States the enforcer of the Brezhnev doctrine."[56]

As controversial and ideologically driven as the press coverage was of Washington's relationship with the Contras, it paled in comparison with the treatment of U.S. support for Angolan rebel leader Jonas Savimbi. As the head of the insurgent National Union for the Total Independence of Angola (known by its Portuguese acronym UNITA), Savimbi waged a bloody struggle for power against newly independent Angola's far-left government from 1975 to the early 1990s. That government received important backing from both the Soviet Union and Cuba—including the deployment of several thousand Cuban troops. Such meddling by Moscow and Havana enraged conservatives in the United States and made them push for strong U.S. support for UNITA.

The enthusiasm of conservative journalists for Savimbi reached impressive heights. Various publications—including *Human Events, National Review, American Spectator,* and the *Wall Street Journal*—amplified the pro-Savimbi case. Those publications and other backers even arranged a major speaking tour for the Angolan leader in 1979 and facilitated his meetings in Washington with congressional leaders and high-ranking executive branch officials in 1981, 1986, and 1989.

Their admiration for Savimbi remained intact despite troubling indications early on of UNITA's harsh, autocratic internal practices and the organization's collaboration with South Africa's apartheid government. In the view of conservative journalists, Angola was the latest arena in the Cold War, and Jonas Savimbi was an effective leader capable of scoring important victories. In a subsequent analysis, Johns Hopkins University Professor Piero Gleijeses contended that "Savimbi's champions—in the press and in Congress—did not care" about his rumored character flaws. "They knew what mattered to them: there were thousands of Cuban soldiers in Angola, and Savimbi had promised to defeat them." Gleijeses added that "the pro-Savimbi forces seized the high ground; they argued in terms of both U.S. interests and morality."[57]

Glowing accounts of the Angolan rebel appeared throughout right-wing publications. An article in *National Review* by William F. Buckley Jr. was typical. He argued that for years "Savimbi fought for independence against Portugal," to secure "democratic government and civil liberties." When the Marxist People's Movement for the Liberation of Angola hijacked the independence movement, Buckley insisted that Savimbi began battling against Soviet-Cuban imperialism to achieve those same values.[58] Some Savimbi admirers in the media even implied that a failure to support UNITA reflected, if not outright racism, at least insensitivity to the aspirations for liberty on the part of black Africans.

Washington Times correspondents Arnaud de Borchgrave and Roger Fontaine were noticeably upbeat about Savimbi after visiting his headquarters in rural Angola in May 1984. They described him as "the world's most successful anti-Marxist guerrilla fighter and one of Africa's most impressive leaders."[59] They also favorably relayed his boast in interviews with them that if the Cuban troops left, the Marxist government would collapse within 3 months, and that even if those forces stayed, the regime would be finished in 12 to 18 months. Here was an early example of American media observers vastly overrating the internal popular support and military prowess of supposedly democratic insurgents. A similar pattern would occur decades later in such places as Iraq and Syria.

Gleijeses highlighted the principal difference in the cases that supporters and opponents of aid to Savimbi presented. UNITA's advocates insisted that helping the insurgent movement was both in America's strategic interests and justified on moral principles. Aid opponents made narrower arguments. They contended that increasing U.S. involvement in Angola's struggle risked snaring America in another military quagmire like Vietnam. They also typically expressed worries about UNITA's relationship to South Africa and what Washington's indirect collaboration with that racist pariah state might do to America's reputation in sub-Saharan Africa and the rest of the Third World. According to Gleijeses, UNITA's critics, especially media critics, "did not, however, challenge the heroic portrait of Savimbi drawn by his admirers, or they did so only fleetingly." Most did not even highlight the group's human rights record, although "UNITA's atrocities provided sufficient cause to oppose Savimbi's ambitions."[60] Such timidity conceded a major advantage in the debate to pro-Savimbi factions.

Media conservatives were impatient with the pace and extent of the Reagan administration's aid to Savimbi. Norman Podhoretz, the neoconservative editor of *Commentary*, echoed UN Ambassador Jeane Kirkpatrick's demand for "real assistance" to UNITA, not merely "empty expressions of pious support."[61] According to Podhoretz, providing such aid was an eminently worthy cause. Savimbi, Podhoretz stated, "has done nothing to forfeit his claim to good faith when he speaks of democracy and freedom."[62]

Some passionate backers went to great lengths to explain away blatantly troubling signs regarding UNITA's conduct. Peter Worthington, a conservative journalist who had visited the UNITA headquarters near the city of Jamba, exhibited that tendency. He noted that Savimbi "has 'political officers' throughout his army," and admitted that initially he found that aspect "disquieting." But his uneasiness persisted only "until I sat in on lectures." Why? Because those lectures "concentrated on the virtues of democracy, of multiple political choices, of free movement, of self-reliance, individual initiative, private property, free enterprise, fiscal accountability, balanced budgets, democracy, human rights, a humane and just judicial system, democratic institutions, rule by law and constitution," and other Western values.[63] Even a cursory examination, though, of UNITA's internal governance and how it actually ruled the portion of Angola it controlled should have caused Worthington to doubt all of his benign assertions.

One of the more embarrassing episodes in the conservative media campaign to lionize Savimbi was the appearance of an op-ed under his byline (though major portions of it apparently were written by an American right-wing ghostwriter) in the June 2, 1986, edition of the *Wall Street Journal.* It hailed the virtues of capitalism and democracy and pledged to make Angola a model of both values if the United States helped UNITA oust the pro-communist government in Luanda.

Savimbi's article told conservatives exactly what they wanted to hear. Angolans, he wrote, had discovered that "there was something worse than [traditional] colonialism: Soviet colonial exploitation and imposition of socialism." He then outlined his movement's supposed objectives. "UNITA's first goal is win the independence of Angola—to drive the Cuban and Soviet troops and 'advisers' from our shore." But that was only the start; the larger goal was to build a new, democratic country. Nor was that all. "In addition to UNITA's commitment to a democratic, multiparty Angola with religious tolerance and freedom of speech, it is vital that we recognize the importance of economic liberties."[64] Savimbi proceeded to express support for a "completely free market" in agriculture and the elimination of all trade barriers. It was as though Milton Friedman's intellectual disciple had shown up in southern Africa. *National Review* gushed about his "astonishing defense of freedom."[65]

What is so striking about the *Wall Street Journal* piece was that UNITA did not practice any of those political or economic principles in the Angolan territory it controlled. There was certainly no evidence of democracy, multiparty or otherwise; UNITA maintained a ruthless monopoly of power. Despite the pledge in the article to exempt farmers from all taxes (a rather difficult commitment in a heavily rural country in any case), UNITA imposed heavy taxes on the agricultural sector. And trade was a nearly exclusive province of Savimbi and his close associates—a textbook example of crony capitalism. At least some of that information already was available when the *Wall Street Journal* published the op-ed. Moreover, none of those damaging revelations would have surprised centrist and liberal journalists who had long been extremely critical of Jonas Savimbi and U.S. support for him.

Indeed, as the decade drew to a close the *Wall Street Journal* became somewhat of an outlier with respect to conservative media attitudes regarding Savimbi. Other media conservatives were beginning to express doubts about their onetime Angolan hero. *National Review* even began to break ranks openly with Savimbi's supporters. The magazine's roving correspondent, Radosław "Radek" Sikorski, spent three months in Jamba and elsewhere in UNITA-controlled territory in early 1989. While there, he amassed information from defectors and his own observations that led him to conclude that the evidence of abuses was too extensive and persistent to ignore.[66] By the early 1990s, conservative disenchantment with Savimbi seemed nearly complete.[67]

The diversity in press accounts about the Contras and UNITA mirrored the dissension within America's political and policy elites. Attitudes about both movements split sharply along ideological and partisan lines. Conservatives supported both the Contras and UNITA—to the point of being laudatory. That position was as firm a feature in right-wing publications as it was among Reagan administration officials and Republicans in Congress. Conversely, most liberal journalists, along with Democrats in Congress, were unrelentingly critical of the so-called freedom fighters who had won the hearts of conservatives.

Criticisms of both the Contras and UNITA were warranted— although with respect to the former, liberal critiques sometimes went too far, bordering on caricature. But the press response to the "liberation movement" in Afghanistan suggests that negative assessments had little to do with the intrinsic characteristics of those movements. Media portrayals of the Afghan mujahideen guerillas who were trying to expel Soviet occupation forces were overwhelmingly favorable. Yet most factions within the mujahideen were dominated by religious zealots who treated women and ethnic minorities in a shameful, brutal fashion and did not share an iota of Western values.[68]

Support within America's political establishment for the Afghan insurgency was overwhelming and solidly bipartisan. Accounts in the press likewise were overwhelmingly positive. Without a policy split in the American political hierarchy, media figures seldom raised questions about the wisdom of helping empower authoritarian religious fanatics in the name of opposing the rival superpower—and still less did they openly oppose that course.

That pattern helps explain why the "Vietnam syndrome" of wariness and skepticism about aspects of U.S. foreign policy did not endure in the news media beyond the 1980s. The divisions among politicians and in public opinion that fuel dissent in the media faded. Moreover, even during the 1980s, government officials worked very hard to tame a recalcitrant media with respect to at least the more militarized aspects of foreign policy. By the time of the Persian Gulf War, such restraints were in place and quite effective—especially with conditioned and relatively receptive journalists.

CHAPTER 3
New Restraints and Enticements: Grenada, the Gulf War, and Somalia

Following the Vietnam War, much of the U.S. political and military elite believed that negative press coverage had stoked domestic public opposition to the conflict. Members of the media generally shared that perspective, although in contrast to current and former officials, they considered that coverage to have been necessary and honorable. Indeed, for left-of-center anti-war journalists, the perception that the media helped end a bloody, unnecessary war was a source of personal and institutional pride. Although the conclusion that the media was crucial seemed intuitively sound, as noted in Chapter 2, some evidence suggests that the thesis was exaggerated.

Whatever the truth about the extent and impact of negative media portrayals of the Vietnam War, the prevailing assumption among supporters of the war was that hostile, sensationalistic, and unfair media coverage had been a major cause of the U.S. defeat. That belief and the accompanying resentment festered throughout the 1970s and early 1980s. The attitude was especially prevalent among civilian policymakers and top military leaders in President Ronald Reagan's administration. They were determined that "never again" would journalists undermine a U.S. war effort.

The new policy became evident in October 1983 when U.S. troops, along with token paramilitary units from the obscure Organization of

Eastern Caribbean States, launched an invasion of the small island nation of Grenada to oust the country's new, ultra-leftist government. When the intervening forces went ashore to execute Operation Urgent Fury on the morning of October 25, there was no press coverage whatsoever. The comprehensive blackout ordered by military commanders exceeded anything imposed during previous American conflicts—even the two world wars. A 1985 Twentieth Century Fund report on the military and the media stressed that the government's "failure, at the outset, to allow an independent flow of information to the public was unprecedented in modern American history."[1]

Thus, the situation had changed 180 degrees in a little more than a decade—from the total absence of formal censorship during the Vietnam War to a blanket prohibition of news coverage during the Grenada intervention. Not only did Washington exclude reporters from covering the initial stages of the landing, but it prevented news organizations from coming to the island for more than 48 hours. Television crews were barred for an additional two days. Measures that the military used to enforce the blackout and prevent eyewitness coverage also were unprecedented. On several occasions, Navy patrols intercepted and turned away enterprising journalists who chartered private boats from nearby islands. Military personnel emphasized that they would use force against members of the press to maintain the exclusion zone. Reporters refrained from testing whether that warning was a bluff. Their restraint probably was prudent, although it might seem improbable (and horrifying) that U.S. troops would fire on unarmed journalists—especially their fellow citizens.

The treatment meted out to persistent reporters sailing to Grenada ranged from harassment to outright threats. One example of the former occurred when *Washington Post* correspondent Edward Cody and three other reporters successfully landed in Grenada after chartering a fishing boat. Military personnel immediately placed them in custody and took them to the USS *Guam*. The reporters' attempts to file their stories were firmly rebuffed. Indeed, the Navy held them under constant surveillance aboard the *Guam* for nearly two days while refusing even to let them contact their home offices.[2]

However annoying, that response was mild compared to another incident in which the possibility that the Navy would use lethal force to preserve the news blackout did not appear far-fetched. Navy planes intercepted an ABC News radio and television crew traveling on a vessel they had chartered in Barbados to take them to Grenada. A U.S. jet dropped a buoy with a message warning them to go back to Barbados. When they failed to respond and instead continued on course, the jet made mock strafing runs with its bomb doors open.[3]

The Navy's attitude seemed chillingly clear. During one press briefing, Rear Admiral Joseph Metcalf, commander of the U.S. naval task force coordinating the military operations in Grenada, warned reporters against continuing their independent quests for access to the island. "Any of you guys coming in on press boats? Well I know how to stop those press boats," Metcalf sneered. "We've been shooting at them. We haven't sunk any yet, but who are we to know who's on them."[4] Reporters who attempted to get to Grenada by air did not fare any better than their colleagues who sought to do so by sea. A group of journalists who chartered a plane and landed it at Pearls airport on Grenada immediately found themselves taken into custody by U.S. military police and ordered to fly back to Barbados.

Only after the majority of fighting was concluded did the military allow the press on the island, and even then, reporters could only venture out with escorted press pools. Complete, unsupervised press access did not occur until a week after the fighting ended.[5] A news blackout of that length had the inherent potential to allow military authorities to sanitize or cover up blunders or misdeeds that troops might have committed.

The press pool was another innovation that the government created to "manage" the press and reduce the prospect that hostile stories would become a problem. Reporters from various news outlets were assigned to a pool; then the military granted the pool special access to areas it deemed relevant. In exchange for that special access, the work product of any pool member became the property of any accredited news organization covering the war.[6] Reporters not included in the approved pools were barred from the theater of operations unless and until the military commander issued the order to allow unrestricted press access. Although not evident in the Grenada operation, it became apparent in later wars that the Pentagon had a propensity to exclude from the pools reporters considered unfriendly to the military and its objectives.

Grenada offered a hint of how much latitude even the press pools would have in gathering information the military command didn't approve. Pool reporters could access only those areas of the island that military leaders authorized. When a *Newsweek* photographer, J. Ross Baughman, left his pool group to take shots in other areas, the authorities not only expelled him but also barred all personnel from the magazine from making press trips to Grenada.[7]

Military commanders clearly were not acting on their own in imposing such draconian restrictions on the news media. Reagan administration officials back in Washington, especially Secretary of Defense Caspar Weinberger and other civilian leaders at the Pentagon, gave their unflinching support. More important, the pronouncements from the White House enthusiastically supported curbing press coverage of the Grenada operation. The implicit message was that if reporters were not going to behave as loyal Americans supporting the U.S. mission but might instead behave as their predecessors did in Vietnam, then the government would treat them as adversaries and squelch all independent coverage.

Leaders of print publications and the television networks reacted with shock, anger, and dismay at the restrictions and the government's disingenuous justifications for imposing them.[8] Officials argued that allowing press coverage of the initial invasion would have risked leaks that could have alerted the Grenadian junta that an attack was coming and jeopardized the mission. Journalists scoffed at that rationale, pointing out that Soviet spy satellites undoubtedly spotted the invasion fleet sailing toward Grenada at least two days before the landing. It was highly improbable that the Kremlin would have withheld such information from the latest communist government in the Western hemisphere. In his autobiography, President Reagan was more candid about the reason for the extraordinary secrecy, which applied even to Congress. "I suspected that, if we told the leaders of Congress about the operation, even under terms of strictest confidentiality, there would be some who would leak it to the press together with the prediction that Grenada was going to become 'another Vietnam.'"[9]

The second justification annoyed reporters and their editors even more. The Pentagon emphasized that without the delayed access and the use of the press pool system, the military could not guarantee the safety of reporters and photographers working in Grenada. Press representatives countered that war correspondents in previous conflicts had not asked the military for safety guarantees, and reporters assigned to cover Operation Urgent Fury had not made such a request either. Professional journalists operating in war zones understood that an elevated risk was inherent in their profession.[10]

Even some staunchly conservative journalists were upset at the administration's excuses for suppressing coverage of the Grenada invasion. *New York Times* columnist William Safire flatly rejected both official rationales for excluding and then constraining the media. "The President dictated that coverage of his Grenada invasion would be handled exclusively by Pentagon press agents. He not only barred the traditional access, but in effect kidnapped and whisked away the American reporters on the scene. The excuses given for this communications power grab were false."[11] Indeed, the military command's apparent contempt for the press accurately reflected the attitude in the White House. In an October 30 diary entry, the president wrote, "They [journalists] are still whining because we didn't give them a guided tour the 1st day we were on Grenada."[12]

Interestingly, despite the government's assumption that the press was riddled with radical members of a "blame America first" crowd, coverage of the Grenada episode did not reflect that belief. When ABC News reporters in Barbados began to see evidence of large-scale movements of U.S. ships and planes in the Caribbean, they held off publishing any stories about that activity once Pentagon sources assured them nothing significant was afoot. That assurance, of course, turned out to be false.

Most of the accounts of the invasion itself also were favorable to Washington's perspective and critical of the Grenadian revolutionary regime. The bulk of the criticism in the U.S. press about the intervention focused on the administration's official justification that the military action was to secure the safety of students and the medical school on the island. With good reason, journalists considered that rationale disingenuous. Relatively little criticism was leveled at the United States for trying to prevent "another Cuba" in the Western Hemisphere. The Reagan administration's war on the press was directed against a target that was not really a policy adversary.

The public's assessment of the government's exclusion of the press seemed ambivalent. Initially, the views were generally supportive. A *Los Angeles Times* poll conducted three weeks after the invasion showed that that public approved the policy of "denying unrestricted press access" by a margin of 52 percent to 41 percent. Other surveys showed even wider levels of support.[13] After time for some sober reflection, though, American public opinion seemed decidedly less supportive. A Louis Harris poll taken in February 1984 found that respondents opposed the press ban 65 percent to 32 percent.[14]

Nevertheless, the government had discovered that it could restrict or even bar press coverage of a military action launched by Washington. The Grenada operation set a dangerous precedent, and a *San Francisco News* editorial captured the scope of the underlying danger. "If the American news media can be excluded by their own government from direct coverage of events of great importance to the American people, the whole character of the relationship between governors and the governed is affected."[15]

A *New York Times* story published more than 24 hours after the Grenada invasion began illustrated a key feature of that danger. The *Times* noted that because its correspondents could not gain access to the theater of operations, the stories were written by reporters in Washington "based on information given to them by State Department and other government sources."[16] When news about an important international event—especially one involving a U.S. military action—consists entirely of material that national security bureaucrats deign to spoon-feed cooperative journalists, the credibility of such "news" is severely undermined. So is the public's ability to get an accurate picture of developments. Media bias either for or against a mission can endanger accuracy too, but this new arrangement was far worse. The system that the

Reagan administration deployed in Grenada amounted to a suffocating form of news management.

Indeed, the administration was able to manipulate the media into giving a false portrayal of one very important facet of the Grenada conflict. Administration officials charged that Grenada had been in danger of imminent domination by Fidel Castro's communist regime, backed by the Soviet Union. The implication was that Washington was responding to a serious threat to America's security that would emerge if Moscow was able to establish another client state—a second Cuba—in the Western Hemisphere. Reagan still made that assertion in his memoirs seven years later. He asserted that documents seized on the island proved "that the Soviet Union and Cuba had been bankrolling the Marxists on Grenada as part of a scheme to bring Communism to the entire region." The president stated that the trove of documents was taken to a warehouse at Andrews Air Force Base and the press was invited to examine it. "Reporters would have found evidence of everything we were saying." But, he added sarcastically, "very few" bothered to examine the trove.[17]

Reagan's implication that the press casually dismissed Washington's allegations was untrue. Indeed, with the news blackout, the administration's estimate that more than a thousand Cuban troops were already on the island went largely unchallenged. Later, it became apparent that only about half that number of Cuban nationals were there—and many of them were construction workers laboring to expand the island's airport. Even if some or most of those workers had received military training (a plausible assumption), the Cuban presence constituted something less than a new strategic bastion for the USSR and its allies.

But the first impressions that media accounts provide invariably prove to be crucial. They tend to persist in the minds of the American people, even when contrary, well-established facts emerge later. Indeed, more than a decade after the end of the Iraq War a sizable percentage of Americans still believed that Saddam Hussein had possessed an arsenal of weapons of mass destruction, although that allegation had been thoroughly debunked. A January 2015 "Public Mind" poll taken by Farleigh Dickinson University found that 32 percent of Democrats, 46 percent of independents, and 52 percent of Republicans believed the WMD story.[18]

So too, a significant percentage of Americans still believe that Donald Trump's 2016 presidential campaign illegally colluded with Russia's government, even though lengthy investigations by both the FBI and Special Counsel Robert Mueller failed to find credible evidence to support that accusation. A March 2019 Reuters/Ipsos poll, taken at the end of Mueller's inquiry, showed that 48 percent of respondents—and more than three-quarters of Democrats—still assumed that Trump and his associates cooperated with Russian efforts to interfere in the presidential election.[19] A *Just the Polls* survey conducted by pollster Scott Rasmussen in October 2020 discovered that 45 percent of likely voters still embraced the view that the Trump campaign had colluded with Russia.[20]

Those results confirm that the initial impressions the media help create on any issue matter a lot. Beliefs become entrenched in the public mind, and even when erroneous, they are difficult to dislodge. That is especially true with regard to issues impacting U.S. foreign policy. People typically know less about those issues than they do about domestic topics, and their ability to obtain information independently is far lower. Moreover, in both of the cases mentioned previously (WMD in Iraq and collusion with Russia), a one-sided media narrative led people to believe not only that the false allegations were valid, but that they were indisputable and only fools or disreputable types ("terrorist sympathizers" or "Russian assets") would challenge the veracity of those accounts. The barrage of misinformation made news consumers resistant if not impervious to later (far more credible) counterevidence.

That tendency becomes even more ingrained when partisan allegiances are involved. Loyal Republicans were especially inclined to believe the pro-intervention case that the Bush administration put forth. It was no coincidence that previously pro-intervention Democrats were the first to pull away from supporting the Iraq War once the WMD story unraveled, while many Republicans stubbornly continued to defend both the mission and the debunked allegations. Similarly, staunch Democrats were far more likely to believe the canard that Trump was a Russian agent, and they continued to believe it despite the results of the Mueller inquiry and the absence of any credible evidence.

The misleading impression about the extent of the Cuban military presence in Grenada reflected a similar, albeit less sustained, erroneous media narrative. Consequently, the mistaken public perception persisted for years, and to some extent the false version of events continues to be believed. Several years after the invasion *Los Angeles Times* bureau chief Jack Nelson noted, "There are still people who think that the place was crawling with Cubans. It doesn't matter how many times you go back and say that the fact was there were only five or six hundred Cubans."[21]

The government manipulated some publications into tamely reporting other misleading or exaggerated stories about the Grenada operation as well. At times, journalists became little more than stenographers for the military command. In one case, the Pentagon contended that there had been a raging battle between Allied (U.S. and Canadian) troops and Cuban forces for control of Fort Rupert, an installation atop Richmond Hill, one of the highest points on the island. *Newsweek* subsequently published an article based on the military's account. The article provided a vivid picture to readers of an intense battle. From behind the fort's limestone walls "Cuban and Grenadian defenders showered small-arms fire on the U.S. attack squads. Grenadian soldiers fired their AK-47s straight up at dive bombing U.S. jets and helicopters. . . . Eventually the American air attack reduced Fort Rupert to a smoldering shell, with only one full wall left standing."[22]

There was just one problem with the *Newsweek* story. No such major battle had taken place. At most, there had been a minor skirmish, and the bulk of the evidence that enterprising reporters uncovered much later indicated that the defenders had surrendered Fort Rupert with scarcely a shot fired. The fort definitely retained its full complement of walls and was not reduced "to a smoldering shell."[23] The episode was a prime example of what can happen when media personnel do not (or cannot) independently examine government claims—and do so in a timely fashion. Heavily slanted government propaganda, and even outright fiction, then passes for genuine news.

The Reagan administration's treatment of the news media during the Grenada invasion set a variety of destructive precedents regarding freedom of the press. U.S. officials managed to restrict press access to a relatively minor military operation to a greater extent than they did even during the two massive world wars. And while media representatives complained loudly, with a divided public opinion and a determined military command, they discovered that they could do little about the restrictions and the precedents those restraints established.

Over the next three decades, national security officials demonstrated that they had thoroughly absorbed the lessons of what was possible in terms of limiting press coverage of U.S. military interventions and thereby controlling the message that the American people would receive. However, they also gradually learned more subtle and effective ways of manipulating press battlefield access and the resulting images and message. Unfortunately, much of the journalistic community became increasingly accommodating in response to the government's system of news management.

The Media's Ineffectual Pushback after the Grenada Restrictions

After the Grenada invasion, press–government relations were at least as testy as they had been during the latter stages of the Vietnam War and the years that immediately followed. Media anger at the restrictions the military had imposed on the coverage of Operation Urgent Fury neared the boiling point. And distrust of the Reagan administration and its policies reinforced the already-evident skepticism.

The leading media power brokers pressured the government to agree to guidelines and procedures that would guarantee far greater press access to future military theaters of operations. But political leaders had learned a crucial lesson from the Grenada mission: waging war was far easier without press coverage. Even coverage of military operations by friendly correspondents who generally subscribed to Washington's policy objectives was certain to contain some inconvenient, if not devastating, revelations. Officials were not about to return to the freewheeling system that characterized journalism during the Vietnam era. If official Washington had to compromise after the Grenada conflict, it was determined at least to limit the access of reporters who were unwilling to regurgitate the official versions of events.

Policymakers no longer viewed even returning to the status quo ante of the two world wars and the Korean War as a viable option. Reagan administration leaders, as well as top military personnel, saw the current generation of journalists as far less loyal and patriotic than their predecessors. Secretary of State George Shultz stated on one occasion that reporters could go along on operations with the troops in World War II because they "were on our side." The obvious implication was that journalists were no longer loyal to America's objectives. President Reagan offered a similar perspective during his December 20, 1983, press conference when ABC News reporter Sam Donaldson asked him to clarify Shultz's comment. Reagan replied that "certainly in Vietnam," the media were "no longer on our side militarily."[24] His underlying bitterness and suspicion regarding press coverage of any current or future U.S. wars was apparent. About the only area of ambiguity was whether Reagan believed that American journalists were ambivalent, unreliable neutrals or outright treasonous adversaries.

During the second half of the 1980s, a prolonged diplomatic dance took place between the government and the media about coverage of future U.S. military missions. In response to the complaints from the highest level of the establishment media hierarchy, the Department of Defense commissioned retired Major General Winant Sidle to review the military's press policy. The Sidle commission released its report and recommendations in 1984. Those recommendations ultimately led to the creation of the first national media pool in 1985. The idea was to identify a small, preselected group of reporters who could be "activated" to cover rapidly evolving operations that were planned and initially launched in secret. In theory, the pool system would allow some press access while safeguarding the operational security of the military operations.[25]

Predictably, negotiations between press and government representatives produced a compromise on this and other issues. But the result was a less than healthy outcome for press freedoms and the ability of journalists to scrutinize U.S. armed conflicts and their implications. The eventual guidelines theoretically provided more access than existed during the Grenada invasion, but it remained a far cry from open access of the Vietnam era. Press pools were now a mandatory feature for reporting on at least the initial phases of military operations. And the military retained the authority to delay or even quash dispatches that, in the military's opinion, might jeopardize ongoing operations. The danger of an outright news blackout had been reduced, but the new conditions were hardly conducive to robust, independent media scrutiny.

Even holding government officials to the terms of the post–Grenada compromise proved extremely difficult. In late 1989, George H. W. Bush's administration launched a military invasion of Panama to overthrow the country's dictator and former CIA asset Manuel Noriega. Bill Katovsky described the fate of reporters during that conflict. Most were "left stranded on airport tarmacs in Miami or San Jose, Costa Rica, or sequestered in a Panama City warehouse throughout most of the fighting."[26]

Once again, the government largely decided what the public would see with respect to a major U.S. military incursion into a foreign country to overthrow a head of state who had incurred Washington's disfavor. Such control did not eliminate negative press treatments of both the strategic rationale and the moral justifications given for the intervention, but it did inhibit reporters' ability to obtain the supporting evidence. And once again, the restrictions seemed to be a case of overkill and chasing phantom press adversaries. Manuel Noriega had few friends in the U.S. news media or among the American public. Meager tears were shed at his ouster and subsequent imprisonment in the United States on drug trafficking charges. The most influential media players opted to defend the invasion, but with some tones of reluctance and uneasiness.

A December 21, 1989, *New York Times* editorial epitomized that approach.[27] The *Times*'s analysis actually began by ridiculing some of President Bush's official explanations. Noting that Bush had offered four reasons for the operations, the editors contended that "two of them [were] so inflated that they evaporate on inspection. 'To defend democracy in Panama,' he said. Yes? Well, who appointed America the world's political policeman? 'To combat drug trafficking,' he said. Yes? Well, when did it become the mission of America's armed forces to chase after Manuel Noriega like an operetta Foreign Legion pursuing the Red Shadow?"

Nevertheless, the *Times* argued that "impatience with puffed-up reasons should not detract from solid ones. The President also said he acted to safeguard the lives of Americans and to protect the integrity of the Panama Canal treaties. Those are sound reasons, and taken together they support the intervention." The editorial acknowledged that "some important friends and allies have already voiced misgivings. And the invasion has fueled enduring Latin suspicions about Washington's selective respect for sovereignty." It then added an observation that ignored numerous episodes in America's past and would become even less credible over the next three decades: "Civilized countries, with the U.S. usually in the vanguard," the editorial writers proclaimed, "oppose foreign intervention in the affairs of sovereign states."

A few members of the press questioned more emphatically the legality and propriety of overthrowing the government of another independent country in the Western Hemisphere, even if the leader in question was odious. The vast majority, though, portrayed the invasion as not only necessary but desirable and even noble. Mark Cook and Jeff Cohen, analysts for Fairness and Accuracy in Reporting, noted that "there was a mix of opinion inside Panama"—including a fair amount of hostility—"but it was virtually unreported on television, the dominant medium shaping U.S. attitudes about the invasion. Panamanian opposition to the U.S. was dismissed as nothing more than 'DigBat [Dignity Battalion] thugs' who'd been given jobs by Noriega." Cook and Cohen observed further that the coverage had a nationalistic, parochial orientation: "In the first days of the invasion, TV journalists had one overriding obsession: How many American soldiers have died? The question, repeated with drumbeat regularity, tended to drown out the other issues: Panamanian casualties, international law, foreign reaction."[28]

Foreign media outlets were noticeably less inclined to echo the patriotic, anti-Noriega fervor that U.S. publications and television networks exuded. The *Toronto Globe and Mail,* one of Canada's leading newspapers, ran a front-page article analyzing the impact of the Panama invasion and criticizing the U.S. government and the American media for "the peculiar jingoism . . . so evident to foreigners but almost invisible for most Americans."[29]

Cook and Cohen likewise took the U.S. media to task for flagrant nationalistic bias. In a section of their report sarcastically titled "The 'Objective' Reporter's Lexicon: We, Us, Ours," they wrote:

> In covering the invasion, many TV journalists abandoned even the pretense of operating in a neutral, independent mode. Television anchors used pronouns like "we" and "us" in describing the mission into Panama, as if they themselves were members of the invasion force, or at least helpful advisors. *NBC*'s [Tom] Brokaw exclaimed, on day one: "We haven't got [Noriega] yet." *CNN* anchor Mary Anne Loughlin asked a former CIA official (12/21/89): "Noriega has stayed one step ahead of us. Do you think we'll be able to find him?" After eagerly quizzing a panel of U.S. military experts on "MacNeil/ Lehrer" (12/21/89) about whether "we" had wiped out the Panamanian Defense Forces (PDF), Judy Woodruff concluded, "So not only have we done away with the PDF, we've also done away with the police force." So much for the separation of press and state.[30]

The coverage of Washington's invasion of Panama certainly was not a stellar example of media balance or even modest distancing from U.S. policy and U.S. military operations. A few press accounts did ponder whether the Grenada and Panama precedents might lead to similar, perhaps even larger, U.S. military ventures elsewhere. The answer was not long in coming.

DEMISE OF THE "VIETNAM SYNDROME": LAUDATORY COVERAGE OF THE GULF WAR

When Saddam Hussein's forces invaded Kuwait on August 2, 1990, most journalists and editorial writers responded by echoing the outrage that officials in Washington and other Western capitals expressed. The coverage evinced a widespread reversion to the collective pre-Vietnam Cold War mindset. With rare exceptions, most American journalists accepted the administration's policy assumptions. Those assumptions included (1) Iraq's invasion and occupation of its neighbor constituted a dangerous precedent—especially as it was the first such move in the new, post–Cold War world; (2) Iraq's aggression against Kuwait was likely just the prelude to a similar campaign against Saudi Arabia and its Gulf allies—a move that would make Saddam the dominant player in the Middle East, thereby giving him control of the world's oil supply and a stranglehold over the economies of the United States and the other Western countries; and (3) if the United States did not lead an international effort to expel Iraqi forces and restore the political status quo, no other nation or combination of nations was willing and able to do so. Underlying those assumptions was the assertion that Saddam was a "new Hitler" and that a failure to reverse Baghdad's aggression would risk a repetition of the 1930s, eventually culminating in a much larger, more destructive war.

Each of those assumptions warranted tough media scrutiny. Experts had already raised serious questions about the oil stranglehold thesis, and it was fast on its way to being debunked entirely.[31] The contention that Iraq's annexation was a precedent that the United States and other democracies could not tolerate in a "rules-based international system" ignored several embarrassing examples to the contrary. Indonesia's annexation of East Timor, India's amputation of Pakistan's eastern provinces to form the new client state of Bangladesh, Israel's seizure of the West Bank and the Golan Heights, and NATO ally Turkey's invasion and occupation of northern Cyprus were all episodes that did not impel the United States to threaten and eventually launch a major war to restore the status quo. Bush administration officials never clearly explained why Kuwait was so different.[32] And the vast majority of journalists never mentioned, much less explored, the discrepancy.

Even the administration's core allegation—that Iraq planned to commit a broader, more serious disruption by attacking Saudi Arabia—was flimsy and warranted far more media skepticism. That was especially true since it was the primary justification administration officials used for Operation Desert Shield, the dispatch of U.S. troops to the Saudi-Iraqi border, which set the stage for Operation Desert Storm. Media outlets also failed to explore the underlying assumption that Iraq had a powerful military capable of posing an expansionist threat throughout the Middle East.

Instead, the August 13, 1990, issue of *U.S. News & World Report* declared that Iraq's huge tank army, operating in open desert suited for tank warfare, would be a very dangerous opponent for U.S. forces; and this sentiment came to pervade the media narrative.[33] Articles in other publications routinely referred to Saddam's "battle-hardened" army of a million troops and warned that it was capable of achieving regional domination for Baghdad.

Such accounts habitually ignored contrary evidence or knowledge-able analyses. University of Chicago Professor John J. Mearsheimer, a leading expert on military strategy, concluded that even by Third World standards, the Iraqi army was "a below-average fighting force." Indeed, it did not "even measure up well to the Egyptian and Syrian armies," much less the far more capable militaries of the United States and other Western powers.[34] Tom Marks, an analyst who had studied the Iraqi military for U.S. intelligence agencies, determined that Saddam's force was "a giant with feet of clay."[35]

Those assessments proved to be impressively accurate. Numeri-cally, Iraq's military seemed impressive, but it was largely a collection of ill-trained, ill-fed, ill-equipped, and poorly motivated conscripts. Unfortunately, skeptical accounts, such as those by Mearsheimer and Marks, rarely made their way into media coverage of the lead-up to the Persian Gulf War. Instead, account after account repeated White House and Pentagon talking points.

Most journalists covering the crisis did not even address the glaring discrepancy between the Bush administration's portrayal of Baghdad's supposed dire threat to its neighbors and regional stability and the real-ity of Iraq's anemic performance in its long war against Iran during the previous decade. Saddam had all the advantages when he launched the invasion of his eastern neighbor in September 1980. Iran was in revolu-tionary turmoil following the overthrow of the shah the previous year. The new clerical regime had purged the country's military of officers even suspected of being loyal to the shah or secular rule, leaving major gaps in the capabilities of its officer corps. Iran also was under severe international sanctions, which created shortages in key military goods. Perhaps most damaging, Washington had cut off Tehran's access to the

spare parts essential to maintain the weapons systems that it had pur-
chased from the United States during the shah's rule.

Despite those advantages, Iraq was not able to achieve a definitive
victory over Iran in eight years of warfare. Baghdad failed to attain its
goal even though the United States and several major Arab powers provided it extensive (albeit covert) financial assistance and sophisticated
weaponry. Yet it was now supposedly a military juggernaut that posed a
threat to the peace and independence of the entire Middle East following
its annexation of Kuwait. One might have thought that media outlets
would explore such a blatant contradiction—especially since it undermined the Bush administration's case for war. But very few did so even
in a cursory fashion.

The failure to scrutinize Iraq's military capability was symptomatic
of a larger defect in the media coverage of Desert Shield and the looming
prospect of war. Instead of examining and dissecting the key rationales
for U.S. military intervention, the media placidly accepted the administration's interpretation of historical and contemporary developments in
the Persian Gulf region. Most of the press fed the public a steady diet of
simplistic images and analyses that bore little resemblance to the complex
reality.[36] That treatment dovetailed perfectly with the Bush administration's agenda. Journalists focused on two questions: Would the United
States go to war, and would it win? As Marie Gottschalk, associate editor
at *World Policy Journal*, pointed out, other important questions, especially
"whether the United States *should* go to war," received little attention.[37]

The extent of the imbalance in media coverage and perspective was
stunning. A survey of editorials in the nation's 25 leading newspapers
from August to mid-November 1990 found that only one, the *Rocky
Mountain News*, consistently argued against U.S. military action to expel
Iraqi forces from Kuwait. That paper's editorial page editor, Vincent
Carroll, considered it both remarkable and disturbing that a looming
conflict of such serious magnitude generated so little editorial debate
in the press.[38] Other experts also lamented the overwhelming jingoism.
Veteran journalist Gene Ruffini observed that "the healthy, feisty skepticism of government hoopla that is supposed to characterize a free press
never came into play."[39]

Media analyst Mark Hertsgaard described the coverage during the initial months of the crisis as strikingly bellicose. "President Bush had no sooner drawn his line in the sand than the nation's leading news organizations snapped to attention like a line of buck privates."[40] Indeed, the overall impression that the bulk of the news stories, op-eds, and house editorials conveyed was a veritable international melodrama. According to the media-generated image, a brutal modern-day Hitler had wantonly attacked innocent, freedom-loving Kuwait and overthrown what President Bush later termed that country's "legitimate rulers."[41] The proper role of the United States and other free world countries was to rescue Kuwait from the clutches of the monstrously evil aggressor.

That image bore little resemblance to reality. Kuwait's rulers were an interlocking network of corrupt royals, and there was not even a semblance of democratic governance. But very few news stories or editorials mentioned that detail or disputed the Bush administration's official line. To the contrary, the media promoted both the demonization of Saddam and the whitewashing of Kuwait's autocratic system. Johns Hopkins University Professor Mark Crispin Miller accused *Time* and other leading publications of recycling "the same trite plot that had played so well the year before, when Manuel Noriega stood in as the tropical menace of the month."[42]

The media's propensity to portray complex geopolitical quarrels as stark melodramas pitting good and evil factions against each other did not begin in Panama, nor would it end in the Persian Gulf. In fact, the tendency would become even more pronounced in conflicts during the decades after the Gulf War. It would decisively shape the imagery and public perceptions of the internecine conflicts in the Balkans, the prelude to the Iraq War, and the U.S.-orchestrated military interventions in Libya and Syria.

Developments that contradicted the Bush administration's portrayal of Kuwait as a freedom-loving ally suffering under an oppressive foreign occupation received little attention. Most news outlets also ignored or minimized evidence that the Kuwaiti aristocracy viewed U.S. and allied troops as little more than mercenaries they had hired to restore them to power. Members of the Kuwaiti elite relaxed in resorts on the

Mediterranean while the military buildup took place and fighting eventually erupted.

An especially appalling aspect of the press coverage of the Gulf crisis was the media's credulity about atrocities that Saddam's forces supposedly committed in Kuwait. In the process, prominent press outlets became little more than conduits for crude propaganda that the Kuwaiti government (through a new front group, the Committee for a Free Kuwait) generated. The centerpiece of the atrocity charges was that Iraq soldiers had forced maternity ward nurses at three Kuwaiti hospitals to remove newborns from their incubators. That action supposedly resulted in the deaths of 312 infants.

Rumors about the incidents began to circulate in the United States and Britain in early September 1990, but they gained new traction on October 10 when the Congressional Human Rights Caucus held a hearing featuring alleged eyewitnesses. The featured witness was a tearful 15-year-old girl that Caucus chairman Rep. Tom Lantos (D-CA) introduced only as "Nayirah." A more detailed identification, Lantos cautioned, would endanger her friends and relatives in Kuwait. Nayirah described herself as a volunteer at one of the hospitals who personally witnessed Iraqi soldiers commit the shockingly brutal acts.

The story was reminiscent of Allied propaganda in 1914 that German troops had bayonetted babies and raped nuns in Belgium. The incidents had two other features in common. One was that they were part of a sophisticated disinformation campaign designed to whip American public opinion into a frenzied willingness to endorse going to war. The other was that both incidents were utterly fictional. As would eventually be discovered, "Nayirah" was not a hospital volunteer at all.

In the meantime, though, Bush administration officials quickly incorporated the alleged atrocities in their propaganda offensive against Iraq, and the media devoured the story like hungry predators being given fresh meat. A striking feature of the press coverage of the "baby killers" story was the marked lack of skepticism and the pervasive failure of reporters to ask probing follow-up questions. It was sloppy, unduly credulous, and unprofessional journalism by almost any reasonable standard.

Granted, such a terrible alleged atrocity had some superficial credibility given the Iraqi regime's odious track record. Human rights organizations had documented numerous war crimes during the Iraq-Iran war, including Baghdad's use of poison gas against Iraqi Kurds whom Saddam suspected were aiding Iran. The worst incident was an attack on the village of Halabja, which killed perhaps as many as 5,000 people (estimates vary greatly). With that record, even the accusation that Saddam's troops might have murdered innocent babies in Kuwait did not seem outlandish.

Nevertheless, there was important counterevidence from the outset. A Palestinian doctor and an Icelandic doctor who were in Kuwait City hospitals at the time of the alleged incidents disputed the incubator story. Mainstream American media outlets, however, ignored their statements or buried them on the back pages. An interview with the Palestinian doctor appeared in only one newspaper, the *Seattle Times*, in an article on page 13. A brief story including comments by Icelandic physician Dr. Gisli Sigurdsson ran on page 7 of *USA Today* on December 10, two months after the caucus hearing. No other major metropolitan dailies, news magazines, or television networks mentioned either account.[43]

Gradually, the "babies pulled from incubators" story began to unravel. Determined digging by John R. MacArthur, the publisher of *Harper's,* as well as belated investigations by Middle East Watch and other human rights organizations, cast doubt on the account and the overall propaganda offensive.[44] Most of the witnesses who testified before the congressional caucus and a UN session turned out to be Kuwaiti government operatives. Hill and Knowlton, a leading Washington consulting and public relations firm working for the Kuwaiti government, supplied and carefully coached those witnesses. Eventually, the falsity of the incubator atrocity story became indisputable, especially when information confirmed that "Nayirah" was not a hospital volunteer but the daughter of Kuwait's ambassador to the United States.[45]

Unfortunately, much of the information debunking the allegation did not emerge until months later—long after Washington and its allies had waged their war. The false atrocity story undoubtedly strengthened the administration's campaign to condition the American public to support a war against Iraq.[46] As Phillip Knightley commented about the British government's use of phony inflammatory incidents in World War I, "By the time the atrocity story was discredited, it had served its role."[47]

The media's faulty performance contributed to the success of the Bush administration's propaganda campaign, with the incubator story as the centerpiece. Even rudimentary efforts to check and gain independent verification of the explosive allegation were lacking. Journalists made little attempt to evaluate the credibility of Nayirah and other accusers by uncovering their real identities and backgrounds. The revelation that she was an ambassador's daughter, and that the others were government employees, would certainly have raised questions about how much trust and confidence could be given to their accounts.

Other aspects of the press coverage showed laxity and sloppiness as well. Most news stories implied that the "witnesses" had testified under oath in a formal hearing before a congressional committee. That simply was not true; the statements were part of an "informational" session conducted by a special-interest caucus, and none of the statements were under oath. The failure to disclose and emphasize such a key difference constituted a major journalistic lapse.

More generally, the extent of the mainstream media's credulity was surprising and unsettling. Despite Baghdad's track record of atrocities, the willingness of professional journalists to accept the incubator story and other elements of the administration's anti-Iraq propaganda without verification reflected both laziness and gullibility. Receptive reporters seemed to believe the account because they wanted to believe it. The atrocity allegation fit perfectly into the already dominant narrative that Saddam's regime was monstrous, with no moral scruples whatever. Nevertheless, such negligence was indefensible given the knowledge that false reports of atrocities were a staple of previous conflicts. That indisputable history should have made reporters covering the ongoing Gulf crisis doubly wary of similar, highly inflammatory, accusations.

In its coverage of the events leading up to the Persian Gulf War, America's news media was little more than a useful mechanism to sell the Bush administration's case for a highly questionable war. Even before

Washington launched its own combat operations and the war quickly became a U.S. military triumph, it was apparent that the skepticism that had built up during the latter stages of the Vietnam conflict and persisted in many media quarters for years afterward had faded badly.

SYCOPHANTIC BATTLEFIELD COVERAGE

Once combat operations commenced in January 1991, the media's performance did not improve to any significant extent. The Pentagon's restrictions of battlefield coverage in Grenada and Panama, crude and mean-spirited as they were, had weakened the journalistic community's resistance to governmental control and manipulation. Bill Katovsky concluded that by the time of the Gulf War, "the media practically begged for access." The administration and the military commanders in the Persian Gulf relented a little, but only a little. They were still "determined to call the shots, maintaining tight control over the flow of information through censorship, pool reporting, and press conferences bleached of meaningful content." And as in the case of Grenada, that system "led to the reporting of false or misleading information, such as the highly exaggerated success rate of Patriot missiles downing Scuds."[48]

Once again, elements of the press had allowed themselves to be maneuvered into circulating government propaganda rather than independent news. Outlets that played along with the system the government mandated prospered from extensive access and exposure. Those that were less cooperative and insisted on greater accuracy found themselves frozen out of the juiciest stories.

Seduction began to balance restrictions in the government's strategy for dealing with the news media during the Gulf War. Both the logistical challenges and the opportunities for Pentagon battlefield news management had increased markedly since the Vietnam War. Only about 200 reporters were in Vietnam at any one time; the number was several times greater in the Gulf War. (Notably, by the time of U.S. invasion of Iraq in 2003, the total number of journalists in theater to cover the war would approach 3,000). Moreover, during the Vietnam era, journalists were still using film that had to be flown out of the war zone for developing—a procedure that took at least 48 hours to complete. There was no instantaneous coverage.[49] By the time of the Gulf War, videotape and the ability to upload images via satellite were a reality. For the first time, audiences could see live television coverage of an armed conflict. That change heightened the incentive for senior military commanders to ensure that news reports portraying the U.S. war effort in anything other than a favorable light were impeded, if not suppressed.

Gradually, most portions of the press became more and more compliant with the government's restrictions and underlying policy agendas. Some of the mainstream press even exhibited the characteristics of Stockholm syndrome, ultimately making common cause with the institution placing the restraints on their profession. The pattern would become more apparent in the battlefield coverage of the Iraq War, but signs of an accommodating, even supplicant attitude emerged during the earlier Gulf conflict.

Overall, the media's coverage of the Gulf War epitomized a return to the uncritical, pro-war portrayals that had characterized the profession's behavior before the belated disillusionment of Vietnam. Once again, a majority of journalists did not treat the U.S. case for war, or the military action itself, as an issue to be analyzed and discussed dispassionately. Instead, they became de facto, and in many cases explicit, proponents of the government policy. Marie Gottschalk's conclusion was on the mark. She emphasized that "the problem was not simply that the Pentagon and the president misled the media, but that the media generally swallowed without questions whatever the military and president dished out."[50]

To some extent, the media's narrative and priorities in their treatment of the Gulf War reflected as well as shaped public opinion. American viewers and readers were most concerned about how the conflict would affect them and their loved ones—especially their fellow citizens at risk on the battlefield. They wanted a maximum of information on such matters, and the press increasingly stressed the topics, perspectives, and images that seemed to have greatest resonance with their news consumers.[51] However, that priority usually had the short-term effect of reinforcing the "patriotic" messages that the government wanted emphasized.

Thus, a significant result of the Gulf War was the noticeable weakening of the so-called Vietnam Syndrome. The media were again on board for a more assertive U.S. role, especially a military role, in world affairs. Public resistance to such a role also had eroded. However, uneasiness remained throughout much of the population if a clear security "threat" could not be identified as a justification for action. U.S. leaders still could not count on public support for future military ventures, particularly if the Gulf War's scenario of surprisingly few American casualties could not be replicated. Indeed, the public's reaction to even a small number of fatalities during the subsequent Somalia intervention (see the following section) confirmed that significant resistance to a cost in blood remained, and the threshold for triggering an adverse public response continued to be fairly low.

The demise of the Soviet Union as Washington's only credible strategic rival eliminated any significant international barrier to more robust U.S. strategic ambitions. Most notably, the absence of a powerful adversary greatly reduced the risk that future U.S. military interventions might lead to a highly destructive great power war resulting in mass casualties and a domestic public backlash. U.S. leaders were ready to exploit what *Washington Post* columnist Charles Krauthammer labeled the "unipolar moment," in which Washington's power was unchallenged and unchecked. And like U.S. officials, most members of the news media were ready to bury the Vietnam Syndrome and cheer on the renewal of a hyper-activist global policy, including one with a very strong military component.

MORE OF THE SAME: UNCRITICAL COVERAGE OF THE SOMALIA "HUMANITARIAN" MISSION

An early example of the activist, global approach came during the waning weeks of George H. W. Bush's administration, when the United States commenced a militarized "humanitarian" mission in Somalia. Although the effort ostensibly operated under the auspices of the United Nations, Washington was firmly in command. The multisided conflict in Somalia among rival militias had spawned a serious famine, which the U.S. and Western press increasingly highlighted (and hyped). Bush himself stressed that the motive for the military intervention was purely to help restore some semblance of order so that food and medical supplies could flow to badly suffering Somali civilians.

Interestingly, when Washington initiated Operation Restore Hope with amphibious troop landings near Somalia's nominal capital, Mogadishu, the Pentagon granted reporters generous access. That openness, despite the plethora of armed militias in the vicinity and the generalized disorder afflicting the country, cast serious doubts on the justifications that had been used for restricting press access in Grenada and Panama. But this time U.S. officials were trying to market a humanitarian/military mission that they were confident would be popular with the public.

The media showed every willingness to be allies in that marketing campaign. The headline in the *Los Angeles Times* about the White House's announcement of the mission—"Bush Sending Troops to Help Somalia's Hungry Millions"—was typical of the uncritical, if not outright laudatory, coverage.[52] No one seemed willing to question whether the administration might have other policy or institutional motives for initiating an ostensibly humanitarian operation in Somalia.

However, the humanitarian mission quickly morphed into a counterinsurgency mission primarily directed against the forces of one factional leader, Mohamed Farah Aideed (or Mohamed Farrah Aidid). The U.S. military command's cooperation with the media then noticeably began to fade. The Bush administration and the Pentagon welcomed reports (especially television images) of U.S. troops distributing food to hungry Somali children; coverage of Cobra helicopter gunships obliterating human targets were decidedly less welcome, but the latter increasingly reflected the reality of the Somalia intervention.

Most journalists, though, stayed with the administration's portrayal of the security situation in Somalia and the underlying issues. Media outlets invariably described leaders of the feuding political factions as "warlords" and the various militias as "bandits" or "gangs." By ignoring or glossing over the deeper underlying societal divisions based on irreconcilable tribal and clan differences, they could promote the image of the United States as a purely humanitarian rescuer, not an outside power forcibly trying to shape Somalia's future political and security orientation. Journalists had a professional and moral obligation to ask questions about those matters, but most of them did not.

The oversimplified treatment of Somalia's fragmented political struggles was epitomized by the shifting, one-dimensional portrayals of Aideed. When the first clash between U.S./UN forces and Aideed's fighters occurred in June 1993, media outlets quickly made him the personification of evil, echoing the assessment of Bill Clinton's administration. Some news reports might have led readers and viewers to assume that Aideed's middle names were "fugitive" and "warlord." This phase continued as the fighting escalated during the summer and fall of 1993. It culminated in the infamous "Black Hawk down" episode on October 3 and 4 in Mogadishu, in which 18 U.S. troops were killed and 75 more were wounded.[53]

At that point, the Clinton administration decided to bring the U.S. mission to an end before the fighting spiraled out of control and entangled the United States in an unpopular Vietnam-style quagmire. The original intervention had been sold as a humanitarian mission, so repackaging it as necessary for the security of the American people would have been extremely difficult.

However, the mainstream media's narrative did shift in concert with the administration's new policy. Press accounts of the onetime odious dictator, Aideed, now referred to him in more favorable terms. Princeton University Professor Richard Falk described the transformation: "When the focus was on his opposition [to U.S. policy], he was portrayed as a hated warlord, but as soon as the United States negotiated with his representatives to achieve a cease-fire, Aidid was immediately described far more benignly as a respected 'clan leader.' Flattering pictures of a smiling Aidid were suddenly being shown on TV and in newspapers, which described his position as that of a relevant, even if not sympathetic, political leader."[54]

The news media largely lost interest in Somalia once the United States completed its troop withdrawal. Despite America's bruising experience, few journalists seemed to learn any lasting lessons from the intervention. In particular, they failed to consider whether the United States could become involved militarily in Somalia for humanitarian reasons without being caught up in the soon-dominant U.S./UN goal of (somehow) unifying the country politically. And just as in the Gulf War, the media failed to convey any sense of historical context or provide worthwhile information about the complex roots of the conflict in Somalia.[55] Instead, the press provided overwrought accounts of a morally stark struggle between the United States and cartoonish warlords. Such defective analyses would become even more pronounced with respect to U.S. missions in several other countries over the next quarter century.

A new and bigger opportunity for the media not only to act as cheerleaders for a U.S. "rescue mission" but to lobby avidly for a militarized approach soon surfaced in the Balkans. And much of the press adopted the pro-intervention lobbyist role with undisguised enthusiasm.

CHAPTER 4
Advocacy Journalism and Propaganda: Press Coverage of the Balkan Wars

With the collapse of the Soviet Union and the surprisingly easy U.S. victory in the Persian Gulf War, America's press corps saw nearly unlimited potential for the United States to shape world affairs. Media personnel soon had an especially favored ideological cause—military interventions based on humanitarian objectives—that they believed would express, in concrete terms, America's global status and proper role. That attitude revealed an even more worrisome lack of professionalism and detachment than the usual endorsement of Washington's wars. In the past those wars had rested heavily on national security justifications, whether valid or bogus. Now the reasoning was less clear-cut. Reporters covering the ethnic fighting that broke out in the Balkans during the 1990s leapt in and took advocacy journalism to an extreme. They avidly lobbied for the United States and its NATO allies to intervene in those complex, messy conflicts.

Yugoslavia's slow-motion disintegration produced adverse consequences that affected nearly every part of the country, including Slovenia, Croatia, and Bosnia-Herzegovina.[1] The turmoil and human tragedy was especially pronounced in Bosnia. Three major ethno-religious groups—Catholic Croats, Eastern Orthodox Serbs, and Bosnian Muslims (Bosniaks)—all maneuvered for advantage there in a brass-knuckles political, and ultimately military, struggle. For a brief period, Croats and Muslims maintained a fragile alliance against the Serbs for the objective of securing Bosnia's independence from Belgrade. That alliance barely outlasted the onset of formal independence, however. Instead, both Croats and Serbs rebelled against the new Muslim-controlled Bosnian national government. Croats sought the right to join their ethnic brethren across the border in newly independent Croatia. Bosnian Serbs declared their own independent state, the Republika Srpska. Whether their ultimate goal was to merge with Serbia itself or to maintain an independent status was not clear.

The fighting soon became fierce, and all three factions engaged in ethnic cleansing—attempting to expel all ethnic groups other than their own—whenever they established control over a chunk of territory. Fighters in all three armies also committed atrocities and other war crimes. Serb forces seemed somewhat more inclined to engage in such brutal conduct, but the scope of their offenses, both in numbers and severity, was not hugely disproportionate.

The picture that most Western news media (as well as U.S. and NATO officials) painted was decidedly more skewed than that reality, however. In the dominant media narrative, Bosnia's murky, multisided struggle became a straightforward Serbian war of aggression aimed at innocent Croat, and especially Muslim, civilians. The supposed architect of the plot against Bosnia was Slobodan Milosevic, the leader of neighboring Serbia, one of the other successor states of the disintegrating Yugoslavia. We now have credible evidence that this thesis was an oversimplification. Nearly two decades after the Balkan wars ended, the International Criminal Tribunal for the Former Yugoslavia issued a surprise ruling that Milosevic was not responsible for war crimes committed during the 1992–1995 Bosnian civil war. Indeed, the tribunal found that Milosevic tried to restrain Bosnian Serb leader Radovan Karadzic's efforts to split Bosnia and establish the independent Republika Srpska.[2]

Pervasive Media Bias and Bosnia's Civil War

Western coverage of the civil war in Bosnia became a textbook example of advocacy journalism, with reporters often not making even a pretense of objectivity. Indeed, many of them showed no detachment from a staunchly anti-Serb agenda. When correspondents on the scene did not follow that line, their editors back home often did. The pattern of demonizing the Serbs already was evident at the beginning of 1993, during the war's early stages. Laura Silber, an American correspondent for the *Financial Times*, described one frustrating incident: "I was shocked when a relative read a story to me over the telephone. My byline was on top of the story, but I couldn't recognize anything else." She voiced a complaint that some other, generally older, journalists expressed about the growing insistence on presenting the Bosnian conflict in stark, moralistic terms. Desk editors thousands of miles away, she said, wanted all articles about the war "kept in black and white. There was no room for nuance."[3] Unfortunately, Silber was part of a shrinking minority that sought more balanced and detached coverage; a troubling number of the reporters in the Balkan theater did not seem to value those standards.

In most of America's wars during the 20th and 21st centuries, U.S. officials initiated and worked hard to shape their preferred narrative. Much of the media then echoed the official accounts with little dissent or skepticism. But the Balkan wars of the 1990s produced a somewhat different pattern. For the first time since the 1939–1941 period, a sizable faction in the press ranks was ahead of government policy in the thirst for military action. Eager, pro-intervention journalists sought to push reluctant NATO governments, especially President Bill Clinton's administration, to overcome any qualms and launch armed interventions on behalf of the media's favored factions in Bosnia and Kosovo.

In some ways, the process was a throwback to the yellow journalism that marked the period leading to the Spanish-American War in 1898. However, the motive this time seemed to be more a misguided, overly enthusiastic humanitarian impulse than a cynical search for journalistic fame and profits that might accrue from hyping emotional incidents— although there did appear to be some of the latter. Careerist incentives typically rise up in wartime settings. It is not unreasonable to conclude that some of the reporters covering the Balkans may have thought that this conflict was an opportunity for them to make their mark—much as Halberstam, Sheehan, and others did in Vietnam. Still, ideological fervor seemed to play the primary role.

Whatever the mix of motives, the effect of pro-war journalism regarding the Balkans was similar to the journalism preceding the Spanish-American War; the press campaigned successfully to push the United States into war. This time, in both Bosnia and Kosovo, the intervention was confined to the use of air power, which reflected the preferred style of U.S. warfare in the post–Cold War era. Bombing strikes from 20,000 feet limited U.S. risk exposure and, hence, the danger of public pushback against Washington's policies that American military casualties might engender. U.S. leaders would violate that principle in Afghanistan and Iraq, but they adhered to it in Libya and (for the most part) in Syria.

Mick Hume, editor of Britain's *LM* magazine and later a columnist for the *Times*, highlighted the stunningly biased coverage of the Bosnia war. "In Bosnia, a generation of crusading journalists set the pattern for seeing the complex conflicts in the Balkans as a simple morality play, to be understood and reported in terms of Good against Evil. These war reporters urged Western governments to intervene forcefully against the Serbs at a time when none was keen to do so."[4] A minority of astute media observers cautioned against the growing tendency to present the Bosnia conflict in a rigid moralistic framework. BBC reporter Andrew Thompson described the trend as the "regular presentation of one side as bad (the Serbs) and one side as good (everyone else)."[5]

When a February 1993 report from the European Community (the earlier name of today's European Union) asserted that Serb forces had raped more than 20,000 Muslim and Croat women, the story became the lead in most major metropolitan dailies. However, when a subsequent UN commission report concluded that no reliable estimate could be made about the number of victims—and that while Serb units had committed a majority of rapes, all sides in the civil war were guilty of the same offense—the information was buried on the back pages or ignored entirely. The *Washington Post*, for example, merely printed a brief Reuters dispatch on page 16.[6]

Veteran journalist Peter Brock, an editor at the *El Paso Herald-Post*, was an early critic of the way his journalist colleagues were reporting on the Bosnian war. In 2005, Brock would present a detailed examination of the press coverage of the conflict in his book, *Media Cleansing: Dirty Reporting—Journalism and Tragedy in Yugoslavia*. His article in the winter 1993–94 issue of *Foreign Policy* describes some of the misinformation that was already becoming too common. "Among wounded 'Muslim toddlers and infants' aboard a Sarajevo bus hit by sniper fire were a number of Serb children—a fact revealed much later. One of the children who died in the incident was identified at the funeral as Muslim by television reporters. But the unmistakable Serbian Orthodox funeral ritual told a different story."

According to Brock, that was not the only episode that mischaracterized the ethnicity of civilian war victims. "In its January 4, 1993 issue, *Newsweek* published a photo of several bodies with an accompanying story that began: 'Is there any way to stop Serbian atrocities in Bosnia?' The photo was actually of Serb victims." CNN aired reports in March and May 1993 "from the scenes of massacres of 14 Muslims and 10 Muslims who were supposedly killed by Serbs. The victims later turned out to be Serbs." Nevertheless, Brock noted, "There was no correction."[7] Brock's own statements about the numbers and ethnicity of some of the victims came under skeptical scrutiny as well.[8] The entire truth may never be known, but there is little question that Western press treatments tended to give the most anti-Serb spin possible, especially with respect to wartime atrocities.

An especially prominent case of the Western press hyping a story for maximum emotional impact with the goal of generating greater anti-Serb sentiment in the West was an August 1992 photo shoot of prisoners being held in Trnopolje, a Serb-run detention facility in Bosnia. U.S. and Western media outlets spun those images into articles warning that this was the start of a new Holocaust. *Newsweek*'s cover package went on for 12 pages, including headlines and photos. *Time*'s coverage was nearly as extensive and shrill.[9] Reporters focused like a laser on one unusually emaciated prisoner named Fikret Alić. Other individuals who appeared to be at least reasonably well-fed were not included in the widely circulated photos.

One idealistic young American who epitomized the commitment to extreme advocacy journalism in Bosnia was Samantha Power; in a few more years she would achieve fame covering the genocide in Rwanda and publishing a Pulitzer Prize–winning book on the episode. Power also was a rising political and policy star who would later serve as a high-level foreign policy adviser, culminating with her service as U.S. ambassador to the United Nations in Barack Obama's administration.

Power showed notable tenacity in seizing the opportunity to go to Bosnia to cover the burgeoning armed conflict. At the time she was employed as an intern at the Carnegie Endowment for International Peace, where she had established ties with Mort Abramowitz, the head of the think tank and an outspoken advocate of Western military intervention in Bosnia. Power lacked press credentials from any recognized news organization, but as she describes in her memoirs, she solved that problem. "I waited until the *Foreign Policy* editorial staff had headed home and the cleaners had completed their nighttime rounds on the floor. Once the suite was completely deserted, I walked into the office of Charles William Maynes, the journal's editor, picked up several sheets of his stationery and then hurried back to my desk. Hands shaking, I began typing a letter impersonating the unwitting Maynes." She acknowledges twinges of guilt "all these years later" for having violated the trust of the people at Carnegie. "But determined to get to Bosnia, I went ahead and wrote to the head of the UN Press Office, asking that the UN provide Samantha Power, *Foreign Policy's* 'Balkan correspondent,' with 'all necessary access.'"[10]

Such conduct said volumes both about her determination to cover the Bosnian war and her sense of ethics. Her overwhelming bias about the Bosnian conflict itself also was evident, and she remains surprisingly candid about it. "I had never been without opinions, but my certitude previously had to do with seemingly trivial issues like an umpire's bad call in a baseball game. Now, as I researched and reflected on real-world events, I seemed unable to contain my emotions or modulate my judgments. If the subject of Bosnia came up and someone innocently described the conflict as a civil war, I would erupt: It is genocide!" Individuals with that mentality are not news reporters. At best, they're editorialists or de facto opinion columnists; at worst, they're propagandists. Power and too many of her media colleagues in Bosnia seemed to belong in that final category.

Power's coverage of the Bosnia conflict reflected her extreme bias. She insisted, "The Bosnian Serb paramilitaries had first introduced the chilling term 'ethnic cleansing' in places like Banja Luka [a city in northern Bosnia] to describe how they sought to 'purify' the land they controlled of its Muslim and Croat residents."[11] That statement is factually wrong. Albanian nationalists in Kosovo used the same term and similar rhetoric as early as 1982 to describe their goal of driving out the Serb minority and making that province "ethnically pure." Seth Ackerman, a media analyst for Fairness and Accuracy in Reporting (FAIR), and veteran investigative journalist Jim Naureckas, noted that "all of the half-dozen references in Nexis to 'ethnically clean' or 'ethnic cleansing' over the next seven years attribute the term to Albanian nationalists." Yet, "despite being easily available on Nexis, virtually none of that material found its way into contemporary U.S. coverage" of the Bosnia or Kosovo conflicts.[12]

Power exhibited no shyness about engaging in blatant advocacy journalism. "Mort [Abramowitz] had convinced me that the only way President Clinton would intervene to break the siege of Sarajevo was if he felt domestic pressure to do so. As a journalist, therefore, I believed that I had a critical role to play. I wanted not only to inform members of Congress and other decision-makers, but to try to make everyday readers care about what was happening to people thousands of miles away. Many journalists in Bosnia brought a similar focus to their work." They wanted "our governments' actions to change." Power acknowledged that "this aspiration was more reminiscent of an editorial writer's ambitions than that of a traditional reporter, whose job it was to document what she saw."[13] She fretted, though, that "if I did not make the stakes clear and compelling, most people would not read past the first paragraph."[14]

Indeed, she was frustrated that the advocacy journalism she and her press associates in Sarajevo generated was slow to have a meaningful impact on U.S. policy, and it seemed to have even less effect on general U.S. public opinion. Until the summer of 1995, Power recalled, "I had believed that if my colleagues and I conveyed the suffering around us to decision-makers in Washington, our journalism might move President Clinton to stage a rescue mission. This had not happened. The words, the photographs, the videos, nothing had changed the President's mind. While Sarajevans had once thought of Western journalists as messengers on their behalf, they now began to see us as ambassadors of idle nations."[15]

Such language indicates that Power had lost any semblance of detachment and was identifying entirely with one faction in the internecine conflict that she was covering. In her memoirs, Power conceded that she had an "all-consuming focus" on Bosnia. When the war ended and she returned to the United States, "I sometimes acted as if I had suffered the losses of war."[16] Such an emotional entanglement made a credible journalistic treatment of a complex armed conflict impossible.

Her frustration with Western policy rose sharply in the spring and summer of 1995. "No matter how many massacres we covered, Western governments seemed determined to steer clear of the conflict," she recalled. Her concern was not entirely about humanitarian issues. Power's analysis of the Bosnia conflict displayed much of the overwrought perspective that would characterize her later positions on the Libyan and Syrian civil wars. "Even if Clinton and his advisers did not think it reasonable to get involved to prevent atrocities, I thought they should have seen how failing to shore up a fragmenting part of Europe would impact traditional U.S. security interests. The occurrence of such a conflict *in the heart of Europe* made NATO look feckless."[17]

Considering any portion of the Balkan Peninsula to be "the heart of Europe" was simplistic thinking even on the part of a newly minted journalist. Such significant economic and strategic players as Germany, France, and Italy constitute Europe's heart. The Balkans historically have been more like Europe's occasionally infected hangnail, not its heart. Nineteenth-century German chancellor Otto von Bismarck put the matter bluntly when he asserted that the Balkans were "not worth the bones of a single Pomeranian grenadier." Given a post–Cold War strategic environment in which the Soviet threat had evaporated, the Balkans were even less important than they had been during that period.

Power seems blissfully unaware of, or indifferent to, the danger that she might have presented oversimplified and unfair accounts. One subtle but important indicator of her bias, both in her accounts at the time and in her memoirs a quarter century later, was that she typically used "Bosnians" as a synonym for the country's Muslim population.[18] Power implicitly treated Serbs and Croats as foreign interlopers, even though they lived in Bosnia, and in most instances their families had done so for generations. In sum, Samantha Power's coverage of the Bosnian war was a textbook example of toxic advocacy journalism.

Too many Western journalists in Bosnia exhibited similar attitudes.[19] CNN's Christiane Amanpour was one of the most avid practitioners of a blatant double standard regarding several aspects of the war. Charles G. Boyd, deputy commander-in-chief of the U.S. European Command during the early and mid-1990s, noted that Muslim and Croat civilians were hardly the only victims of the fighting. "Serbian people have suffered when hostile forces have advanced, with little interest or condemnation by Washington or *CNN* correspondent Christiane Amanpour."[20]

Amanpour was easily the most frequent and recognizable television analyst regarding the Bosnian civil war, so her influence on public opinion in the United States and throughout the West was considerable. However, there was scarcely a trace of balance, much less objectivity, in her reports. Peter Brock later charged that Amanpour "eventually became CNN's 'foreign ministry' in Sarajevo, where her news 'reporting' at least rivaled the rhetoric and bias coming from the information specialists on the payroll of the Bosnian Muslim government."[21]

New York Times reporter Stephen Kinzer gave Amanpour credit for pushing early on to cover the Balkan turmoil when others showed little interest in the topic. But he was nearly as harsh as Brock in his assessment of her performance. "I have winced at some of what she's done, at what used to be called advocacy journalism." Referring to the shelling of Markale Marketplace in Sarajevo on February 5, 1994, Kinzer observed that Amanpour "was sitting in Belgrade" when the incident occurred. Yet she "went on the air to say that the Serbs had probably done it. There was no way she could have known that. She was assuming an omniscience which no journalist had."[22]

The Markale Market explosion illustrates how overall media bias shaped the public's perception of the Bosnian war and steadily built the case for Western military intervention. The explosion in that crowded market caused great carnage, ultimately killing 68 people and wounding 144.[23] Media accounts immediately accused the insurgent Republika Srpska army of callously shelling innocent civilians. The available evidence at least should have raised serious questions about that assumption. Indeed, a significant body of evidence pointed to Bosnian government (Muslim) forces as the more likely perpetrators. Serb units had already commenced a withdrawal from areas near the market in the days before the incident.

Moreover, the direction of the shelling indicated that it likely originated from positions that government forces controlled very close to the market. Brock later summarized a key piece of evidence pointing to that conclusion. "A UN observation post was set up inside an armored personnel carrier atop a summit overlooking Sarajevo five months earlier . . . and the vehicle used artillery-tracking sensors to pinpoint the source of mortars and heavier shells." The mortar shell that fell on the marketplace "had a nearly vertical trajectory, meaning that it had been launched very close to the vendors and their customers. Also the 'flower pattern' signature of the mortar when it detonated on the pavement showed its source was no more than a couple of streets away."[24] Reports leaked from the Pentagon indicated that even U.S. military analysts believed that the explosion "came from the Muslims, who fired on their own people to provoke Western air strikes."[25]

The overwhelming majority of print publications as well as radio and television outlets ignored evidence that contradicted the narrative they had adopted. This herd mentality, combined with a pervasive rush to judgment about alleged Serb responsibility for the bloodshed, was bad enough, but another aspect was worse. Some publications went out of their way to suppress contrary views. For example, the editors at the *New York Times* squelched an analysis that the publication's longtime Balkans correspondent, David Binder, submitted. Binder had concluded that evidence pointed to Bosnian government forces as the likely culprits of the Markale shelling. Binder's story eventually appeared in the Swiss news weekly *Die Weltwoche*, and his more detailed analysis appeared later in *Foreign Policy*.[26] While useful, such belated, limited exposures had only a tiny fraction of the impact that a timely story in the *New York Times* would have had.

The multitude of questions and doubts surrounding the February 1994 shelling incident should have generated even greater caution and skepticism when the market was shelled again on August 28, 1995, killing 43 shoppers. Once again, the evidence, murky as it was, tended to implicate the Bosnian government and army more than Serb insurgents. At a war crimes trial in The Hague in 2015, former UN military observer Paul Conway testified that on August 28, 1995, he was stationed at a checkpoint south of Sarajevo, between Bosnian army and Bosnian Serb positions, when he heard several muted detonations and saw smoke rising near the Markale Market soon afterward. "I couldn't establish where the fire came from," Conway conceded. However, Conway noted that in December 1995, he had discovered a mortar position of the Bosnian Army south of Sarajevo, with at least four mortars directed toward the city. The mortar position was approximately one kilometer from the Markale Market. Most significant, Conway testified that on the morning of the attack, he and his colleagues didn't register any shelling from the Bosnian Serb side.[27]

Instead of approaching the incident without prejudging the evidence, the Western media seemed utterly certain of Serb guilt. U.S. and European political leaders adopted the same attitude, and the second shelling incident led promptly to NATO's military intervention. Air strikes were directed at Bosnian Serb targets throughout the country.[28] That action led in turn to the Dayton peace agreement in December 1995, which compelled the warring parties to maintain Bosnia as one state. The NATO powers continued to insist on that arrangement despite its dysfunctional nature over the subsequent quarter century. With few exceptions, the press portrayed the Dayton Accords as a great diplomatic achievement at the time; that narrative persists decades later despite ample evidence that Bosnia remains a bitterly divided country in which the UN's High Representative—a de facto international viceroy—makes most of the substantive decisions.[29] In 2018 and 2019, the country's feuding ethnic factions endured a 14-month deadlock before they could form even a nominally functioning central government.[30] And that "achievement" appeared to do little to resolve Bosnia's chronic lack of effective governance.[31] Yet another political crisis erupted in the autumn of 2021, with frustrated Serb leaders threatening again to seek independence for the territories they controlled.[32]

Throughout the nearly three-year period leading up to NATO's August 1995 intervention, much of the media acted like determined lobbyists for war rather than independent news-gathering professionals. That was certainly true of most of the correspondents in Bosnia. A caustic assessment of their coverage came from a UN official who insisted on anonymity. Although personally sympathizing with the plight of Bosnian refugees and extremely critical of the conduct of Serb forces, the official noted the pervasive media bias about which Binder, Brock, and other critics had complained. "The press corps [in Sarajevo] developed its own momentum and esprit. Much of it set out to invoke international intervention against the Serb aggressors—a principal strategy of the Bosnian government. That induced in some a personal commitment—indeed crusade—that lay uneasily with the maintenance of true professional standards." The official added that the "collective political fury of the Sarajevo press corps became legendary among all who had to deal with them."[33]

Another defective aspect of the media coverage was its implicit portrayal of the strife in Bosnia as a two-sided fight pitting Serbs against Muslims. Indeed, the rupture of the early Croat-Muslim alliance caught most Balkan correspondents by surprise, and they never effectively came to grips with that leg of the triangular power struggle. Ironically, some of the most intense fighting took place between Muslim and Croat forces, especially in the southwest part of the country near the city of Mostar. The destruction of a UNESCO World Heritage Site (and a treasure of Ottoman architecture)—the 16th-century bridge in the heart of Mostar—generated abundant outrage throughout the West. Croatian forces engaging Muslim defenders had perpetrated the shelling, but some Western television accounts were so vague about which faction was responsible that viewers could easily have come away with the impression that the villainous Serbs did it.

The anonymous UN official mentioned previously berated the media's sparse coverage of fighting between Croat and Muslim forces—and especially the minimal focus on the questionable conduct of Croatian military units. "One of the major mysteries," according to that official "is how the Croats have gotten off so lightly in the Western press." The media routinely excoriated the government in Serbia for interference in Bosnia, including the involvement of the Serbian army in Bosnia's fighting. But while the Croatian army's "presence in Bosnia has been evident and notorious," U.S. and European press accounts of it were minimal. Moreover, Croatian army forces were "committing atrocities" both in Bosnia and in the predominantly Serb Krajina region of Croatia itself. The omission of such stories in the press, the official stated, "has been especially bizarre and certainly requires explanation."[34]

The editors and columnists back home were as strident and biased as their correspondents in the Balkans. The *New York Times* was especially hawkish. Three of the *Times'* regular columnists—Leslie Gelb, Anthony Lewis, and William Safire—repeatedly beat the drums for Western military intervention. Their efforts were matched by a steady stream of pro-war house editorials. Adding to that imbalance, the overwhelming majority of guest op-eds dealing with Bosnia also advocated some form of U.S. or NATO military action.

Condemning the "pack journalism" that he believed characterized much of the coverage of the Bosnian war, David Binder charged that journalistic transgressions included "outright fabrications, widespread use of dubious secondhand sources, and blatantly one-sided accounts of strife involving at least two and sometimes three sets of combatants."[35] Binder endorsed Peter Brock's conclusion that the media served as "a 'co-belligerent' clearly taking one side" in the Balkan turmoil.[36] Considerable evidence supported that assessment. Time and time again, journalists openly promoted the case that Bosnian Muslims and advocates of military intervention within the U.S. government were pushing.

In addition to obsessively focusing on ethnic cleansing and war crimes by Serb forces while minimizing or ignoring the actions of the other two factions, Western journalists were far too cozy with officials in Bosnia's Muslim-dominated government. Some stories did little more than regurgitate that regime's official statements; journalists repeated the government's wartime casualty figures without caveats or reservations. Brock noted several examples:[37] *New York Times* correspondent

John F. Burns was the first to circulate the wildly inflated figure of 200,000 Bosnian Muslim deaths by July 1993. (The UN's figure in late 1993 for all three ethnic factions was only 130,000.) The supposed tally of innocent Muslim victims continued to climb in subsequent media accounts, with *Los Angeles Times* reporter Carol Williams and others alleging in early 1994 that the correct estimate was 250,000. That figure seemed to stick throughout the rest of the war, and President Clinton cited it as one of the justifications when he sent U.S. peacekeeping troops to Bosnia in December 1995. Brock reserved special scorn for Burns, whom he contended "ventured less and less outside of Sarajevo [and] consistently reported the government's inflated casualty counts during the war."

Very few media accounts disputed the 200,000 or even the 250,000 estimate. One of the rare exceptions was an April 23, 1995, *New York Times* article by George Kenney, a former State Department official and onetime avid supporter of Western military intervention. Reflecting his growing skepticism about the standard narrative of the conflict, Kenney stated that "by my count, the number of fatalities in Bosnia's war isn't 200,000 but 25,000 to 60,000—total, from all sides. What surprises me is not that the popular figure is so inflated—informed people can and will argue about it for some time to come—but that it has been so widely and uncritically accepted."[38]

Whatever the motives of Burns, Williams, and other reporters who circulated the inflated fatality figures, their calculations were badly off the mark. Although there were only modest differences among the numbers cited at the time, multiple investigations after the war confirmed that the actual numbers were far lower than those featured in wartime news stories. One investigation by the Research and Documentation Center in Sarajevo, funded primarily by Norway's government in 2007, concluded that the total number of deaths in Bosnia's civil war was 97,207, with 25 percent of the fatalities being Serbs and 8 percent Croats.[39] Further investigations by the same organization, whose lead investigator was a Bosnian Muslim, concluded that roughly half of that number consisted of military personnel. Of the civilian fatalities, some 82 percent appeared to be Muslims.[40]

Despite being responsible for much of the misleading information, the Balkan press corps of advocacy journalists finally got the U.S.-led military intervention in Bosnia for which they had lobbied. That "achievement" set the stage for similar media campaigns pushing for humanitarian or regime-change wars in such places as Iraq, Libya, and Syria. One other aspect of the mainstream media's behavior in the Balkans also would show up in subsequent policy debates: impugning the motives and character of critics who dared dispute the dominant, pro-war narrative. Both Brock and Binder were prominent targets of such attacks during the Balkan conflicts.[41] The roster of similar recipients of such treatment grew steadily over the next quarter century. Indeed, the episodes frequently bore an unsettling resemblance to the environment of intolerance that marked the period when Sen. Joseph McCarthy was ascendant in the 1950s.

WESTERN MEDIA BIAS REDUX: THE KOSOVO INSURGENCY

Compared with the Bosnia conflict, the internecine struggle in Kosovo had even more complex, morally ambiguous roots and misdeeds by all parties. Kosovo had both historical and cultural importance to the people of Serbia; indeed, Serbs often referred to the area as the cradle of their civilization—their "Jerusalem." As late as the mid-1930s, Kosovo's population was about 38 percent Serb and about 45 percent Albanian, with an assortment of other ethnicities making up the remainder. Over the next five decades, that ethnic composition changed dramatically. After German and Italian forces defeated and occupied Yugoslavia in April 1941, the victorious Axis powers handed Kosovo over to neighboring Albania. Tens of thousands of Serbs then fled and were replaced by an influx of new Albanian residents. Some Serbs returned after the war, but many did not. During the following decades, Kosovo's ethnic composition continued to change—so much so that by the end of the 1980s the province was nearly 90 percent Albanian.[42]

Some of the shift resulted from a substantially higher birthrate among Albanian families. Other causes were less savory, including the effects of the Axis occupation and the Albanian majority's discriminatory rule (sometimes outright harassment) in the post–World War II era.[43] After the war, Yugoslav dictator Josip Broz Tito authorized the Albanian provincial authorities in Pristina to exercise considerable autonomy. That was especially true after the implementation of a new Yugoslav constitution in 1974, which allowed Kosovo to establish its own parliament, school system, and other institutions. The Albanian Kosovars used that power as part of a campaign to eradicate Kosovo's Serbian heritage and to discriminate against and harass Serb inhabitants, pressuring them to leave the province. To some extent, those practices occurred even before 1974, but the problems of discrimination and insidious ethnic cleansing against Kosovo's shrinking Serb population grew far worse under the new constitution.

Once Tito died in May 1980, ethnic nationalist sentiments steadily grew throughout the decade in all of Yugoslavia's constituent republics. Albanian Kosovars no longer had a monopoly on intolerance or the ability to implement it. Serb nationalism produced an especially outspoken leader in Slobodan Milosevic, who gained control of Serbia's government in 1989. One of his first acts was to curtail Kosovo's political autonomy and exert greater control over the province's affairs from Belgrade. That move intensified tensions in the province and ignited an Albanian Kosovar bid for outright independence.

Soon, the militant Kosovo Liberation Army (KLA) displaced more moderate elements and gained control of the insurgency. The KLA launched attacks on Serbian security forces throughout the province, and a low-intensity civil war developed. KLA assaults were not confined to military and police targets; the insurgents also kidnapped, tortured, and killed Serb and other ethnic civilians.[44] Belgrade's security forces also became increasingly brutal and indiscriminate in their campaign to suppress the mounting insurgency.

The Kosovo conflict was a classic instance in which there were villains as well as innocent parties on both sides. Unfortunately, the dominant narrative that drove U.S. and European policy—and which mainstream media figures enthusiastically promoted—was a simplistic, Manichean one, as it had been in Bosnia.[45] Analyst James George Jatras accurately summarized the one-sided narrative:

> Prior to 1989, the NATO mythology goes, Kosovo was at peace under a system of autonomy that allowed the ethnic Albanian majority a large degree of self-rule. That status quo was disturbed when the Serbs revoked Kosovo's autonomy and initiated an apartheid system of ethnic discrimination. After a decade of oppression by the Serbs, the ethnic Albanians of Kosovo were ultimately faced with a pre-planned program of genocide, similar to that undertaken by the Serbs in Bosnia. The rise of the KLA was an inevitable response to that threat.[46]

Secretary of State Madeleine Albright and other State Department officials pushed this view. Jatras contended that Washington's Kosovo policy, which pointed toward a NATO military intervention at some point, could not be justified "without recasting a frightfully complex conflict, with plenty of blame to go around, as a caricature: a morality play in which one side is completely innocent and the other entirely villainous."[47] U.S. and European news media were crucial players in advancing that narrative.

Media accounts virtually ignored the larger historical context of the Kosovo conflict that came to a boil in the late 1990s. In particular, they neglected the turbulent events of the 1970s and early 1980s before Milosevic came to power. In their analysis of media bias, Ackerman and Naureckas observed that what was notable about the oversimplified State Department narrative was how faithfully the American press corps followed it. "When attempting to provide background to the Kosovo story, the U.S. media followed Albright's lead" in dating the start of the Kosovo conflict to the late 1980s and the rise of Milosevic. Crucially, "the strife of the 1970s and 1980s was effectively erased from the historical record."[48]

Yet that period was highly relevant to the internecine war that broke out in the 1990s. A handful of maverick journalists had even documented the turbulence at the time. Writing in November 1982, David Binder described the bitter, enduring legacy of a key incident.

"In violence growing out of the Pristina University riots of March 1981, a score of people have been killed and hundreds injured. There have been almost weekly incidents of rape, arson, pillage, and industrial sabotage, most seemingly designed to drive Kosovo's remaining indigenous Slavs—Serbs and Montenegrins—out of the province." Binder noted that the authorities in Belgrade estimated that "some 20,000 Serbs and Montenegrins had fled Kosovo in 18 months following those riots."[49] That figure amounted to approximately 10 percent of the province's pre-riot Slavic population.

In 1987, Binder documented various components of the intensifying Albanian campaign to cleanse Kosovo of its dwindling Serb population. Ethnic Albanians in Kosovo's provincial government, he reported, "have manipulated public funds and regulations to take over land belonging to Serbs. And politicians have exchanged vicious insults. Slavic Orthodox churches have been attacked, and flags have been torn down. Wells have been poisoned and crops burned. Slavic boys have been knifed, and some young ethnic Albanians have been told by their elders to rape Serbian girls." Binder correctly assessed the implications of such trends: "As Slavs flee the protracted violence, Kosovo is becoming what ethnic Albanian nationalists have been demanding for years . . . an 'ethnically pure' Albanian region, a 'Republic of Kosovo' in all but name." [50]

Such contemporary accounts undercut the Clinton administration's contention during the Kosovo War in the late 1990s that the two ethnic groups had lived in harmony until Milosevic rescinded the province's political autonomy. Serious trouble was brewing long before that action, and Serbs were the principal victims—not the perpetrators—of discrimination and violence. If Western reporters and analysts had exercised even modest due diligence instead of casually repeating the U.S. government's flawed narrative, they would have provided more accurate, balanced accounts. But few journalists or the outlets they worked for bothered to make the effort. Worse, the handful of journalists who were inquisitive found themselves increasingly ostracized. Even Binder, who had provided some of the best, most in-depth coverage of Balkan affairs for more than two decades, discovered that his analyses were usually no longer welcomed at the *Times* or other major publications.

Media treatments of the underlying issues in the late 1990s were scarcely better than their performance regarding the historical context. Instead, renderings of emotionally evocative scenes became the usual fare. Ackerman and Naureckas noted that "this tendency was most pronounced on U.S. television, which focused primarily on images of huddled [Kosovar] refugees and atrocities stories, rather than reporting on the political and military situation inside Kosovo." Even when Kosovo "took up most of the evening news broadcasts, it was not uncommon for entire broadcasts to go by without any reference to the Kosovo guerrillas or the war on the ground."[51]

Once the U.S.-led NATO air war against Serbia commenced in March 1999, many journalists became unabashed proponents of maximum military punishment with little apparent thought about the suffering inflicted on Serb civilians. *New York Times* columnist Thomas L. Friedman typified that attitude. An April 6 column exhibited a troubling bloodlust: "Twelve days of surgical bombing was never going to turn Serbia around. Let's see what 12 weeks of less than surgical bombing does. Give war a chance."[52]

A later column made clear that Friedman wanted war waged against the Serbian people, not just the Milosevic regime. "Let's at least have a real air war. The idea that people are still holding rock concerts in Belgrade or going out for Sunday merry-go-round rides while their fellow Serbs are 'cleansing' Kosovo is outrageous. It should be lights out in Belgrade; every power grid, water pipe, bridge, road, and war-related factory has to be targeted." If any flickering doubt remained that Friedman was calling for unrestricted warfare against Serb civilians, his subsequent comments extinguished that doubt. "Like it or not we are at war with the Serbian nation," Friedman emphasized, "and the stakes have to be very clear: Every week you ravage Kosovo, is another decade we will set your country back by pulverizing you. You want 1950? We can do 1950. You want 1389? We can do 1389, too."[53]

When he expressed such sentiments, Friedman was no longer even remotely acting as a journalist. He was an unabashed lobbyist for a U.S. war to benefit one faction in a foreign conflict. Indeed, he was advocating the commission of U.S. war crimes against civilian members of the faction he opposed. Especially troubling was that such destructive advocacy was coming from a writer for America's leading newspaper—a publication that had long had considerable influence on policymakers in Washington.

Other members of the media seemed equally ready to embrace the doctrine of collective guilt to justify attacks on civilian targets. Strangely, as Ackerman and Naureckas noted, "U.S. media saw no contradiction between calling Milosevic a 'dictator' and holding the people of Yugoslavia morally responsible for his actions."[54] *New York Times* columnist Blaine Harden went so far as to assert that Milosevic had won three elections that were "more or less fair"—a statement that was patently false. Harden argued further that such (imaginary) electoral triumphs "along with the Serb leader's soaring popularity in the wake of NATO bombing, support an argument that what ails Serbia goes far deeper than one man." Harden went on to posit a solution for the Serbian population's monumental sins, although he doubted the NATO governments would embrace it: treat Serbia the same way the Allies treated Germany and Japan. "To follow that model, Serbia's military would have to be destroyed, and Mr. Milosevic crushed, by an invasion that almost certainly would cost the lives of hundreds of American soldiers. After unconditional surrender, the political, social and economic fabric of Serbia would be remade under outside supervision so that the Serbs could take their place in a prosperous and democratic world." One could scarcely imagine a more striking embrace of the doctrine of collective guilt—or a more strained equating of Serbia with Nazi Germany.[55]

Unfortunately, such sentiments were not an aberration among members of the media. Mick Hume took both government officials and his media colleagues to task for their overwrought, distorted portrayals of the Bosnia and Kosovo conflicts. "The Serbs were not just the enemy, they were evil incarnate. In such an apocalyptic confrontation there could be no observers or innocent bystanders. If you were not on the side of the NATO angels, you were deemed to be in the camp of Slobodan Beelzebub." Hume was appalled at how authorities in the NATO countries "aided by too many in the media had demonized the Serbs."[56]

Hume was especially alarmed at the tendency of Western officials and journalists to equate Serbs with the Nazis and accuse them of "genocide" in both Bosnia and Kosovo. He believed that the behavior of reporters often was worse than that of Western government functionaries. "Where NATO politicians tended to imply that there were parallels between the Serbs and the Nazis, the newspapers insisted on it and added the dreaded "H" word."[57] He was not exaggerating. As early as the 1992 presidential election campaign, Bill Clinton began comparing the events in Bosnia to the Holocaust.[58] Major Western press outlets promoted the same theme even during the earliest years of the Bosnia conflict."[59] That perspective, including explicit—often crude and clumsy—comparisons to the Holocaust, became increasingly prominent as the fighting in Bosnia deepened and the number of war crimes grew.

A prominent example of that genre was Steve Coll's lengthy cover story in the September 25, 1994, issue of the *Washington Post Magazine*.[60] Coll's overall message was obvious from the title of the article, "In the Shadow of the Holocaust." In the unlikely event that a reader might somehow have missed the equation of Bosnia's ethnic armed conflict to Hitler's extermination campaign, a two-page photo shoot accompanied the article, showing a Nazi death camp and such Nazi leaders as Hermann Goering and Joachim von Ribbentrop being tried at Nuremberg for war crimes. Brock noted that Coll "peppered his article" with references to everything Nazi, including the SS, the Gestapo, *Schindler's List*, and Hitler.[61] What relevance any of that had to do with an internecine conflict in the Balkans a half century later was implied or asserted with very little accompanying evidence.

The July 1995 massacre of more than 8,000 military-age Muslim males by Bosnian Serb forces at Srebrenica gave a great boost to allegations of genocide and comparisons to the Holocaust.[62] There was no question that the slaughter at Srebrenica was an atrocity and a war crime. However, there were significant differences between that episode and indisputable historical cases of genocide. Perpetrators of those earlier campaigns sought to exterminate ethnic, racial, or political minorities. The murderers at Srebrenica sought to deplete the manpower of an opposing army; they exempted old men, women, and children.

Such groups were not spared in the Armenian genocide, the Holocaust, Stalin's systematic starvation of millions of Ukrainians, Pol Pot's orchestrated bloodbath in Cambodia, or the genocidal attacks on Tutsis that would occur in Rwanda at the end of the 1990s. Srebrenica was a horrifying war crime, but it did not fit the classic definition of genocide.

Nevertheless, by the time of the Kosovo conflict, the genocide theme had become nearly a cliché in most Western news media treatments of the Balkan wars. As Hume warned, though, terms like "genocide" and "Holocaust" invoke "modern moral absolutes." Using such inflammatory language, "with all the historical baggage that comes with it," Hume stated, was "automatically to suggest that the Milosevic regime should be put on a par with the Nazis." But those who made such a comparison risked "losing all sense of perspective and proportion."[63]

Without the pervasive allegations in the media that the Milosevic government was committing genocide, would the KLA's drive to secure Western military backing have succeeded? The notion that Milosevic's forces had buried thousands of innocent victims in numerous mass graves in Kosovo became—and remains—part of the Western lore about the conflict between Belgrade and Albanian Kosovars. In the prelude to NATO's military intervention in March 1999, American officials and journalists peddled even the most inflated atrocity allegations with little skepticism or reflection. Secretary of Defense William Cohen claimed that 100,000 Kosovar men may have been murdered by Serbian security forces; David Scheffer, the U.S. special envoy for war crimes, put the number of victims as high as 225,000.[64] Some media outlets reported these extreme exaggerations as though they were Gospel.[65]

Despite cries of genocide in the Western media, and repeated claims that tens of thousands of Albanian Kosovars had been killed, postwar investigators determined that only 2,000–3,000 people perished in the years of fighting between Serb forces and Kosovar insurgents preceding NATO's air war—many of them military fighters.[66] Carla Del Ponte, the chief prosecutor for the International Criminal Court for the Former Yugoslavia—and no friend of Serbia's—told the UN Security Council that investigators "had found 2,108 bodies" in some 195 sites.[67]

Moreover, that far more modest total included Serb victims, both military and civilian. British Defence Secretary George Robertson later conceded that until January 1999, "the KLA were responsible for more deaths in Kosovo than the Yugoslav authorities."[68] The actual number of Albanian noncombatants who died was probably under 1,000. If that level of violence constitutes genocide, virtually any conflict between two or more groups of different races, religions, or ethnic backgrounds qualifies. Using the term so promiscuously, however, dilutes the horror of true cases of genocide.[69]

Some staunch defenders of the Kosovo intervention later grudgingly conceded that the tales of mass slaughter were exaggerated. Brookings Institution scholars Ivo Daalder and Michael O'Hanlon admitted that the "levels of violence in Kosovo before March 23, 1999, were modest by the standards of civil conflict. . . . The violence had caused the deaths of 2,000 people in the previous year. This was not an attempted genocide of the ethnic Albanian people."[70] Such admissions were virtually nonexistent from intervention proponents, though, in the period leading up to NATO's air war or during the assault itself. Skeptical media accounts about the Kosovar civilian fatality figures that U.S. and other Western officials tossed about were equally rare—and most were in fairly obscure outlets.

Indeed, the United States and its NATO allies seemed intent on discouraging if not suppressing dissent. Hume contended that "throughout the war over Kosovo, journalists and others who tried to ask awkward questions were likely to find themselves treated like some kind of fascist fifth columnists by the authorities."[71] The problem of McCarthy-style intimidation would grow even worse during the Iraq War and, later, the new cold war with Russia.

The irony was that systematic efforts to denigrate dissenters were unnecessary. Mainstream media outlets already excluded them to such an extent that they were nearly invisible. Given how closely the major U.S. media identified with the perspective of Western governments, the dominant presence of NATO political and military leaders in interviews, discussions, and debates regarding Kosovo was not surprising. That imbalance was especially pronounced once the alliance began its

air war against Serbia. A FAIR study confirmed the extent of the bias.[72]
Looking at the coverage on two prominent public affairs programs
(ABC's *Nightline* and PBS's *NewsHour*) during the initial weeks of the
bombing campaign, FAIR found that of 291 sources who appeared on
those two shows, only 24 were critics of that strategy.

Worse, some of the "critics" (e.g., Kansas GOP Sen. Robert Dole)
advocated even more hardline policies. The bulk of discussions on both
programs focused on whether NATO should confine its intervention to
the use of airpower or invade Serbia with ground forces. Debates about
whether the intervention itself was necessary to American or Western
security, much less whether attacking Serbia violated international law
and the U.S. Constitution, were notable by their absence. Instead, the
programs aired a steady diet of assertions that the Milosevic government and frequently the Serbian people were irredeemably evil and that
NATO military action to prevent additional suffering by Kosovars was
a moral imperative.

Many of the guests were current or former U.S. government officials
or NATO representatives. These individuals made up 39 percent of the
interview subjects on the *NewsHour,* and their dominance on *Nightline*
was even more pronounced—55 percent. Genuine regional and foreign
policy experts (academic and think tank scholars) were extremely sparse.
They accounted for just 5 percent of the guests on *Nightline* and 2 percent
on *NewsHour.* Moreover, all of them were proponents of NATO's military action, thereby intensifying rather than reducing the bias in coverage. The pattern was strikingly similar to the imbalance that existed
during the Gulf War, suggesting that such imbalance was a systemic
problem, not one confined to coverage of a specific conflict.

The FAIR study's quantitative analysis regarding imbalanced coverage of the Kosovo War was confined to two high-profile news programs,
but its results were typical. There was no indication of more balanced
treatments of the conflict elsewhere. Data compiled by University of
Pennsylvania Professor Emeritus Edward S. Herman and his coau-
thor David Peterson on CNN's coverage over two multiweek periods
(in March and May 1999) showed a pattern strikingly similar to the
FAIR study. NATO bloc officials accounted for 37 percent of all guests

discussing Kosovo on CNN programs. Other U.S. and UK policy-makers and former NATO bloc officials made up another 24 percent. Critics of NATO's military intervention, in marked contrast, had only 0.7 percent of the guest spots.[73]

In late April 1999, Richard Holbrooke, Washington's Special Envoy for Yugoslavia and the architect of the Dayton Accords that ended the combat in Bosnia, heaped praise on the U.S. news media for their "extraordinary and exemplary" coverage of the Kosovo War.[74] He singled out CNN for special mention. Herman and Peterson noted that Holbrooke's enthusiasm for CNN's performance was entirely understandable. "CNN's anchors and reporters almost without exception took the justice of NATO's war as obvious and were completely unaware of or unconcerned with the first principle of objectivity—that you can't take sides and serve as a virtual promoter of 'your' side." The result, they contended, was highly unfortunate. "[I]n word usage, assumptions, and choice in issues and treatment of sources, CNN and its reporters on the Kosovo war followed NATO's lead and served as a *de facto* public-information partner" of the alliance. "Those reporters never questioned NATO's motives, explored any hidden agendas, challenged NATO's claims of fact, or followed investigatory leads that did not correspond to NATO propaganda requirements."[75]

According to Herman and Peterson, the numerical preponderance of pro-war sources and the failure of CNN reporters to direct challenging questions to NATO officials were not the full extent of the network's malfeasance. "CNN's journalists not only followed NATO's agenda and failed to ask critical questions, they served as salespersons and promoters for NATO's war." Indeed, they constantly prodded U.S. and NATO officials to escalate the war. "Wolf Blitzer pressed unrelentingly for an introduction of NATO ground troops, raising the issue a dozen times in a single program." Christiane Amanpour "complained bitterly that General Wesley Clark 'had to lobby hard to get his political masters to escalate the bombing.'"[76] As in the prelude to the U.S.-led intervention in Bosnia, some eager journalists were even more hawkish than Clinton administration military and foreign policy officials. They weren't just echoing government pro-war propaganda, they were out front in

creating pressure for military action. In the process, some of them sacrificed their commitment to the most basic journalistic standards.

WAR'S AFTERMATH: ANTI-SERB MEDIA BIAS

NATO's air war caused the Serbian government to capitulate
in early June 1999, relinquishing control of Kosovo to "international
authorities." Milosevic's decision spared Western leaders from making the difficult and controversial choice about whether to escalate the
intervention by sending in ground troops—a step that likely would have
caused NATO casualties to spike.[77] Even the air war was costly to Serb
civilians. A highly conservative estimate by Human Rights Watch put
the number of fatalities at between 489 and 528; the Serbian government
and some independent observers contended that the actual figure was
several times higher.[78]

The news media's anti-Serb spin continued after the war. Radio
Free Europe/Radio Liberty contended that evidence of mass slaughter or even lesser actions was not necessary to demonstrate the danger
of genocide; mere inflammatory rhetoric was sufficient. "Milosevic's
aggressive intentions were clear from the rhetoric in the 1980s, just as
Hitler's were in the 1930s. But it was not until Kosova [sic] in 1999 that
the Atlantic Alliance showed that the lessons of the previous decade had
been learned."[79] Radio Free Europe/Radio Liberty's ideological bias
was evident even in its decision to spell the name of the province as
"Kosova," an unconventional spelling favored only by the Kosovars and
their international supporters. Again, media defenders of the Western
intervention were fostering the image that the complex ethnic quarrel in
Kosovo was a rerun of the Nazis' horrific campaign of genocide, and that
the Kosovar insurgents were the moral equivalent of Jews and Hitler's
other victims.

Even when they were not conflating ethnic cleansing with genocide, journalists seemed eager to highlight Serb abuses. Yet they adopted
a very different attitude about the reverse ethnic cleansing that took
place in Kosovo following NATO's military victory. Despite a NATO
peacekeeping force occupying the province, the KLA proceeded to wage

campaigns of terror and intimidation against non-Albanian inhabitants with little interference from those forces—and even less criticism from the Western news media.

The media double standard about ethnic cleansing in the Balkans was nothing new—and it was not confined to the situation in Kosovo. Earlier, when Croatian government forces drove Serb inhabitants from Croatia's Krajina region, condemnations in the Western, especially American, press were both few and tepid. Krajina had a large Serb population going back many generations. When Yugoslavia began to unravel in 1991 and Croatia pursued secession and independence, the Krajina Serbs sought to create their own independent state, Serbian Krajina, much as their ethnic compatriots were doing next door in Bosnia. Croats living in Krajina fled or were driven away. In August 1995, Croatia's military launched a massive counteroffensive, Operation Storm, against Krajina's Serbs, driving out some 200,000 people in a matter of days.

Operation Storm was an exceptionally large case of ethnic cleansing, yet Western journalists gave it far less coverage than they did smaller, Serb-generated campaigns in either Bosnia or Kosovo. Moreover, the tone of most of the coverage was strikingly different. Many accounts avoided using the term "ethnic cleansing" to describe the mass expulsion, although the term clearly applied, and UN officials on the scene stated that it was an accurate description of what was taking place.[80] Some stories attached great weight to statements from Serbian Krajina officials urging residents to flee, with the implication that much of the exodus was voluntary, not a result of measures the Croatian army had taken. The British newspaper the *Independent* concluded that the reasons for the exodus constituted a "riddle."[81] Such descriptions were highly misleading and bordered on journalistic malpractice. The reasons that targeted civilians would flee massive shelling and the advancing troops of a hostile army were not a great mystery.

Even those articles acknowledging that ethnic cleansing was indeed taking place seemed insensitive to the plight of the Serb victims. Some of the accounts implicitly conveyed the impression that the Serbs had brought this development on themselves because of their actions in both Croatia and Bosnia. Serbian President Slobodan Milosevic was a special target for blame because of his goal of creating a "Greater Serbia."[82] One need only compare the analyses and images Western media provided of columns of refugees, including a large percentage of women and children fleeing Serb forces in Bosnia and Kosovo, with the meager and generally indifferent treatment of the Krajina ethnic cleansing to see a journalistic double standard on display.

Washington Post columnist Charles Krauthammer was a rare, principled voice of criticism about both the media and U.S. government reaction to the Krajina episode.[83]

> This week in four days of blitzkrieg by the Croatian army, 150,000 Serbs living in the Krajina region of Croatia were ethnically cleansed, sent running for their lives to Bosnia and Serbia. In the face of what U.N. observers in Croatia call the largest instance of ethnic cleansing in the entire Balkan wars, where were the moralists who for years have been so loudly decrying the ethnic cleansing of Bosnia's Muslims? Where were the cries for blood, the demand for arms, the call to action on behalf of today's pitiful victims? Where were the columnists, the senators, the other posturers who excoriate the West for standing by when Bosnian Muslims are victimized and are silent when the victim of the day is Serb?

His conclusion about the underlying reason for the silence was on target:

> The reason for the deathly silence is the unspoken feeling that, well, the Serbs had it coming: Look at what the Serbs have done to the Muslims in Bosnia. What goes around comes around.
>
> The Serbs? Which Serbs? Most Krajina Serbs had nothing to do with the war in Bosnia, let alone with the atrocities committed there by other Serbs. How, in particular, are the women and children and old people of Krajina—now terrorized, displaced and universally unlamented—responsible for the suffering of Sarajevo?

Given the media's track record, it was unsurprising that most portions of the American press reacted with either a shrug or barely disguised *schadenfreude* four years later when Kosovar Albanians expelled their Serb neighbors in a wave of ethnic cleansing. In the months following NATO's military intervention in Kosovo, some 240,000 people fled or were driven from that province. And the victims were not just Serbs, but members of other minority ethnic groups, including Bulgarians, Romanians, Greeks, Roma, and Jews.[84]

The Roma had an especially tough time, and the treatment of that minority at the hands of the KLA-led Kosovo regime did not improve much with the passage of time. Almost as soon as Milosevic's troops began their withdrawal in early June 1999, Kosovar military units and auxiliary mobs launched a series of revenge attacks on the Roma. Although most Roma had tried to remain neutral in the war between Belgrade and the KLA, Kosovars generally viewed them as Serb allies. As documented in a 2017 Al Jazeera investigation, such attacks "varied from harassment and theft to arson, rape and murder." As many as 1,000 Serbs and Roma were missing and unaccounted for in the months following the cessation of the war. "'Investigations, as far as I can remember were never done,' one Roma man, Hisen Gashnjani, who recalls the incidents, told Al Jazeera." Gashnjani also noted that "there weren't even any arrests."[85]

Western reporters presented a multitude of accounts of Serbian government abuses—real, exaggerated, and fictional—against Kosovo's Albanian population during the mid- and late 1990s. Yet they seemed strangely uninterested in the reverse ethnic cleansing story. News accounts and longer analyses of the persecution of non-Albanians were rare, and even when they appeared, most authors couched them in a way that suggested that those incidents, while regrettable, were the inevitable (and justifiable) reaction to previous Serb abuses.

Western news outlets were similarly uninterested in the systematic desecration of Christian monasteries and other religious sites—some of which were hundreds of years old and had historical as well as religious significance. In the first five years after NATO took over the province, more than 100 Serbian Orthodox churches and monasteries were destroyed, culminating in an orgy of violence by Kosovar Albanian mobs in early 2004. Witnesses stated that NATO troops, supposedly there to protect inhabitants and property, did little or nothing.[86]

The overwhelming media indifference to the abuses directed against Serbs and other non-Albanians was consonant with the policies that

Western governments adopted. The new KLA-dominated government in Pristina was clearly a U.S./NATO client, and even mildly negative scrutiny by reporters was not welcome. Indeed, Washington and most of its European allies maneuvered to bypass the UN Security Council and grant Kosovo full independence in 2008, setting a dangerous and disruptive international precedent. Media outlets expressed little criticism about that move either.[87]

Journalistic advocates of Washington's war on behalf of the Kosovo Liberation Army had reason to be ever more embarrassed as the years passed. An especially damaging blow to the media-cultivated myth of the insurgents' noble cause came in December 2010 with the release of an investigative report for the Council of Europe. The report confirmed longstanding rumors that the KLA was involved in the trafficking of human organs, including killing Serb prisoners of war to harvest their kidneys and other organs.[88] Two aspects of the report were especially damning. First, the author and lead investigator was Swiss Sen. Dick Marty, a highly respected champion of human rights; his authorship gave the document substantial credibility. Second, the report specifically named former guerrilla commander and later Kosovo Prime Minister Hashim Thaçi as an accomplice in the atrocities—as well as other criminal activities, including drug trafficking and politically motivated murders.

The mainstream media gave the Marty report minimal coverage, and even that scrutiny faded quickly. However, the scandal about human rights abuses on the part of KLA alumni did not go away. In June 2020, it erupted with full force. The prosecutor for the Kosovo Specialist Chambers, a war crimes court based in The Hague, indicted Thaçi and nine other former KLA military leaders for crimes against humanity and war crimes. The court had been probing their actions against ethnic Serbs and others during and after the 1998–1999 war for independence. The prosecutor stated that Thaçi and the nine others "are criminally responsible for nearly 100 murders" involving hundreds of Serb and Roma victims, as well as Kosovo Albanian political opponents.[89]

At the time of his indictment, Thaçi was about to depart on one of his many trips to Washington to consult with U.S. officials on Balkan affairs.

Much of the news coverage focused on the disruption of the diplomatic effort that Donald Trump's administration had been waging to mediate a settlement between Belgrade and Pristina on an array of issues as a vital step toward the full normalization of their bilateral relations.[90] Coverage of the alleged crimes themselves was extensive but secondary and mostly neutral in tone. There were few prejudgments either stating or implying that the Kosovo leaders were probably guilty of the charges. Nor did most stories dwell on the extent of the support that Washington had given to the KLA during the war or the KLA-dominated government in the two decades since the end of the war. The media's general neutrality stood in stark contrast to the usual treatment that journalists meted out to accused tyrants and war criminals that U.S. administrations did not support.

Interestingly, some news stories and opinion pieces mentioned the atrocity allegations only as a side point to push broader agendas—typically another opportunity to criticize the Trump administration's Balkan and overall European diplomacy.[91] What was singularly missing in the mainstream media that had once cheered on the KLA and demanded that the United States intervene militarily on behalf of Kosovo insurgents was any admission of error, much less any expression of contrition that American and other Western journalists might have been apologists for probable war criminals.

JOURNALISM AS PROPAGANDA: THE MEDIA'S RECORD IN THE BALKANS

The media's performance in covering the Balkan wars and their aftermath was disappointing and often unprofessional. Moreover, it strengthened a disturbing pattern of portraying complex quarrels as morality plays featuring a villainous faction and an innocent set of victims. The concerted campaign to demonize the Serbs as the second coming of the Nazis was especially pronounced and offensive.[92] Supposedly professional journalists consciously pursued a biased agenda, renouncing any effort to present American readers and viewers with a balanced, informative picture of the conflict they were covering. Instead, those journalists became hawkish lobbyists, prodding the United States and its NATO allies to launch military interventions against the media's designated villains.

A major journalistic scandal erupted in 2004, and it raised additional questions and concerns about the coverage of the Balkan wars in the 1990s. In January 2004, evidence surfaced that *USA Today* correspondent Jack Kelley appeared to have plagiarized some of the articles under his byline and fabricated others.[93] That revelation should have raised red flags about the dozens of stories Kelley had filed from the former Yugoslavia, including some 38 accounts between March and August 1999—during and immediately following the Kosovo war.[94]

After a detailed investigation confirmed most of the negative allegations, Kelley was forced to resign. But another aspect of *USA Today*'s resolution of the scandal was both curious and troubling. Investigators determined that only two of Kelley's many stories about supposed Croat and Muslim civilian war victims were factual. Regarding the others, the publication's editors stated, the passage of time and the difficulty of retracing events in that part of the world made verification impossible. Yet *USA Today* took no steps to label those articles in the archives—so that readers would be aware the author was tainted and could better evaluate the accuracy and credibility of the stories. Instead, Peter Brock noted, the outcome "unmistakably indicated that Kelley's remaining Yugoslav reports were being taken for granted," even though serious questions obviously existed about their veracity.[95]

One other feature of the Kelley scandal was unsettling. Media accounts lamented his misconduct and called for tighter monitoring of stories—especially those filed from foreign locales where developments often are unclear. But almost no calls came for a serious reconsideration of the accuracy and balance of the deluge of articles that had emerged from the Balkans during the 1990s. Brock raised perhaps the most troubling aspect the Kelley episode. "Strangest of all was the silence and absence of any efforts to interview others who were part of the pack-reporting in the coverage of the Yugoslav wars. The equally obvious question went unasked, profession-wide: Was Kelley alone?"[96] Given the emotional, one-sided treatment of the turmoil in the former Yugoslavia by so many journalists, the question was pertinent.

Overall, the Balkans coverage by Western and especially American reporters was sensationalist—advocacy journalism on steroids. The individuals who embraced that approach acted as though promoting so-called humanitarian wars constituted the journalistic profession's highest calling and moral obligation. Worse, the defective coverage of the messy conflicts in the Balkans was not an aberration. The self-righteous, hawkish arrogance it epitomized became an ever-stronger theme in the years after the Balkan wars. That attitude would show up with special virulence when Washington pursued its next crusade: the campaign to overthrow Iraqi leader Saddam Hussein.

CHAPTER 5
Recirculating Government Disinformation on Iraq

The media's treatment of the Balkan wars weaponized bias and emotionalism in an effort to push the Clinton administration to take military action on behalf of factions that journalists had designated as innocent victims. Unfortunately, the media's performance did not improve during the crucial prelude to the Iraq War. Most prominent outlets virtually excluded analyses or opinion pieces that even raised questions about, much less explicitly opposed, using force against Saddam Hussein. Similarly, advocates of restraint were rarely invited to appear on television talk shows or be interviewed for segments on major news programs. And many supposedly straight news stories seemed to be little more than rewritten statements or press releases from the White House, State Department, or Pentagon. In other words, they were thinly disguised pro-war editorials.

Much of that behavior was a carryover effect from the shock that the 9/11 terrorist attacks inflicted on both the American public and the journalistic community. Pervasive self-censorship was evident following that horrific event. No one, especially respectable reporters and pundits, wanted to be seen as "soft on terrorism," or worse, a "terrorist sympathizer." The result was knee-jerk support throughout the public, Congress, and the news media for the anti-terrorism policies emanating from George W. Bush's administration.

This attitude became clear almost immediately. Congressional approval of the Authorization for Use of Military Force (AUMF), which Congress passed barely a week after the 9/11 attacks, was nearly universal. The AUMF authorized the president to "use all necessary and appropriate force against those nations, organizations, or persons he determines planned, authorized, committed, or aided the terrorist attacks that occurred on September 11, 2001, or harbored such organizations or persons, in order to prevent any future acts of international terrorism against the United States by such nations, organizations or persons."[1] The Senate passed the measure by voice vote, and the House approved it 420 to 1; Rep. Barbara Lee (D-CA) was the only opponent.

In a subsequent op-ed in the *San Francisco Chronicle*, Lee explained the rationale for her vote. The measure, she warned, "was a blank check to the president to attack anyone involved in the September 11 events—anywhere, in any country, without regard to our nation's long-term foreign policy, economic and national security interests, and without time limit."[2] The consequences ultimately proved worse than she had feared. Not only did the legislation give the president a blank check to attack individuals and governments associated with the 9/11 attacks, but it soon would enable occupants of the Oval Office to go after parties *not* involved in those attacks. Saddam Hussein's Iraq would become the first target in that category.

The AUMF was insidious, eroding what was left of the congressional war power under the Constitution. That power had been fading for decades, beginning when President Harry Truman waged war in Korea without asking for a declaration of war or even a tepid "authorization" from Congress. The failure of Congress to push back on Truman's usurpation of the war power set in motion the rise of the imperial presidency. Truman's successors conducted an array of military interventions using vague, "blank check" congressional authorizations (such as the Gulf of Tonkin resolution). Sometimes they proceeded even without such legislative fig leaves—as with Ronald Reagan's military missions in Lebanon and Grenada and Bill Clinton's crusades in the Balkans.

The AUMF continued the process of presidential aggrandizement and perpetuated the executive branch's contempt for congressional prerogatives regarding issues of war and peace. Bush promptly used the AUMF to justify the U.S.-led invasion of Afghanistan to root out al Qaeda and the Taliban, but the measure had much broader and lasting effects that went well beyond Afghanistan. The AUMF would pave the way for Washington's burgeoning military adventures. It became the legal rationale for several operations—including some against organizations such as the Islamic State (ISIS), which didn't exist in 2001, and others against countries such as Syria that did not even arguably have a connection to the events on 9/11.

The Iraq intervention was based on a separate measure, the 2002 AUMF, which specifically authorized President Bush to take action against Saddam Hussein's government. In 2021, Congress, with the approval of Joe Biden's administration, finally moved to repeal that authorization, although even that effort faltered. The 2001 legislation remains firmly in place. As *Reason* magazine's Fiona Harrigan pointed out, the 2001 law "is a far more important framework to repeal." Presidents have justified "41 operations in 19 countries thanks to generous interpretations of the 2001 AUMF's phrasing." She emphasized, "The 2002 AUMF, meanwhile, has mostly been used to bolster the 2001 AUMF in conducting military engagements. Since the Iraq War ended in 2011, it has not been the sole authorization behind any military operations. In 2014, the Obama administration named it as an 'alternative statutory basis' for the U.S. campaign against the Islamic State in Iraq. The Trump administration also invoked it to justify its conflict with the Islamic State, but asserted authorization to address threats in 'Syria or elsewhere' as well."[3] In other words, the 2001 AUMF is by far the more dangerous of the two authorizations, and it remains in effect. Repeal of the 2002 legislation would be a significant symbolic step, but the actual impact would be relatively modest.

Notably, members of the press said virtually nothing against the 2001 AUMF when it became law; to the contrary, they expressed effusive praise for the legislation and directed vitriol against Barbara Lee for her lonely dissent. Critics in the press repeatedly vilified her as anti-American. Conservative outlets, especially the *Wall Street Journal* and the *Washington Times*, were especially angry, citing Lee's far-left background but skirting any discussion of the substantive arguments she raised against the AUMF.

The *Wall Street Journal*'s John Fund was one such detractor. He wrote that "one wishes Ms. Lee were just a clueless liberal, but her history leads me to conclude that she is the kind of 'San Francisco Democrat' that former United Nations Ambassador Jeane Kirkpatrick criticized in 1984: someone who 'always blames America first.'" He harped on the point of her alleged special aversion to America's role in the world: "America has been attacked, and while pacifism has an honorable tradition in this country, Ms. Lee seems to use it as a cloak for her belief that when it comes to the use of American power, her country can never do right." He noted her opposition to air strikes against Iraq in the late 1990s as another piece of evidence. Fund even compared Lee unfavorably to senators Wayne Morse and Ernest Gruening, two Democrats who cast the only votes against the 1964 Gulf of Tonkin Resolution. He credited those two senators with "suspecting correctly that LBJ wasn't being fully candid with Congress and would turn the authority to wage war into a blank check."[4] Fund's statement proved to be especially ironic because the AUMF that Lee opposed became precisely the same kind of blank check.

A September 18 *Washington Times* editorial adopted the same approach as Fund's piece. It asserted that "Ms. Lee is a long-practicing supporter of America's enemies—from Fidel Castro on down." The editorial added that "while most of the left-wing Democrats spent the week praising President Bush and trying to sound as moderate as possible, Barbara Lee continued to sail under her true colors."[5]

Congress approved further unwise legislation with lopsided votes in October 2001. The Uniting and Strengthening America by Providing Appropriate Tools Required to Intercept and Obstruct Terrorism Act (Patriot Act) unleashed the FBI and the intelligence agencies to conduct unprecedented levels of surveillance of the American people. Its passage confirmed both the extent of public fear and the degree of public unity in favor of measures granting vast new powers to the FBI and the intelligence agencies. That far-reaching, ominous measure passed the House 357–66 and the Senate 98–1, with Russ Feingold (D-WI) casting the lone dissenting vote in the upper chamber.

A *New York Times* article captured the panicky environment in which Congress enacted that legislation. "Passage of the bill . . . was the climax of a remarkable 18-hour period in which both the House and the Senate adopted complex, far-reaching antiterrorism legislation with little debate in an atmosphere of edgy alarm, as federal law enforcement officials warned that another attack could be imminent. Many lawmakers said it had been impossible to truly debate, or even read, the legislation that passed today."[6]

The Patriot Act was more controversial than the AUMF, but both the quantity and the severity of the criticism were still surprisingly limited. Articles by the handful of critics mostly appeared in obscure publications. Robert Levy, chairman of the libertarian Cato Institute, expressed the need for caution before lavishing the government with the powers embodied in the Patriot Act. "To be sure, the Constitution is not a suicide pact," Levy wrote. "Government is legitimately charged with defending life, liberty, and property against both domestic and foreign predators. First among those obligations is to protect life. With America under attack, and lives at risk, civil liberties cannot remain inviolable." But, he emphasized, "that's a far cry from asserting that they may be flouted to wage war against fanatics."[7]

Dissents in obscure outlets had no impact on the drive to approve the Patriot Act. In a sign of the extent to which alarm was gripping the country, no editorials in the major metropolitan dailies opposed either the AUMF or the Patriot Act.

Even months after passage of the Patriot Act, press scrutiny, much less outright criticism, remained sparse. One of the few skeptics was Frank Davies, a correspondent for Knight-Ridder newspapers. In a September 2002 analysis, Davies wrote, "The legislation, overwhelmingly approved by Congress after the White House demanded new tools to prevent the next terrorist assault, resulted in the largest expansion of police powers in decades. Yet Americans know little about it, Congress is having difficulty getting questions answered and Bush administration officials won't say how it has been used." He mentioned two of the most worrisome aspects: "The CIA and FBI for the first time ever are allowed to mix foreign intelligence with law enforcement on

U.S. soil. Citing the act, Attorney General John Ashcroft also authorized FBI agents to spy on domestic groups without having to show
evidence of a crime."[8]

A few more journalists on the left began to exhibit unease about
the vast grant of power that the act had given the FBI and the intelligence agencies. Even a handful of conservative reporters and pundits
expressed some criticisms—especially about the Bush administration's
shroud of secrecy regarding the specific measures that were being undertaken. Syndicated columnist Robert Novak, for example, complained
that Attorney General Ashcroft was unacceptably "intractable" in providing information to Congress.[9] But such voices of caution and concern
remained sparse and had little effect in the short term.

As the Bush administration commenced its "war on terror," it soon
became apparent that the only way to guard against "soft on terrorism"
charges and innuendoes was to be an outspoken advocate of an aggressive foreign policy to rid the world not just of al Qaeda, but of the global
terrorist threat. Many opinion leaders, especially on the political right,
even embraced President Bush's utopian goal to, as he put it, "rid the
world of evil." David Frum, a contributing editor at *National Review*,
and Richard Perle, a former assistant secretary of defense, published a
best-selling book in 2003 with the title *An End to Evil*, championing
such hubris.[10]

Dissent on any aspect of the administration's anti-terror strategy was
strongly discouraged. Michael Kinsley, editor of *Slate* and one of the
country's most prominent liberal pundits, admitted in 2002 that he had
been listening to his "inner Ashcroft" regarding the mugging of the Bill
of Rights and other features of the war on terror. "As a writer and editor,
I have been censoring myself and others quite a bit since September 11."
Kinsley also conceded that sometimes it was "simple cowardice" that
sparked the censorship.[11] For Kinsley and many other editors, the patriotic obligation to censor included maintaining an implicit blacklist
of writers who dared raise doubts about the increasingly strident calls
to target Iraq.

Given the crusading mentality that gripped the nation, opponents
of launching a regime-change war to remove Saddam Hussein never

stood a chance once the administration and its media enablers moved to tie Iraq to the horrors of 9/11. Key members of the administration's national security team worked assiduously to establish such linkage, and they began that process even when the ashes of the twin towers were still smoldering. The principal activists making the case for war against Iraq as a component of the broader war on terror included Secretary of Defense Donald Rumsfeld, his deputy secretary, Paul Wolfowitz, as well as Vice President Dick Cheney and several assistants, including his chief of staff, "Scooter" Libby. Major portions of the news media became important allies in that effort.

One tactic was to freeze out analysts who criticized the rush to war against Iraq. Another was to impugn the motives of the handful of critics who were able to gain some exposure. David Frum enthusiastically applied that tactic in his March 25, 2003, *National Review* article, "Unpatriotic Conservatives." Frum linked a wide array of conservative and libertarian critics of the new war to a few genuine anti-Semites, tarring all of them with that brush. He also accused skeptics of Washington's latest military venture of "having made common cause with left-wing and Islamist antiwar movements in this country and in Europe." Such anti-war types, Frum charged, "deny and excuse terror." Worse, "some of them explicitly yearn for the victory of their nation's enemies."[12]

Even before the war began Stephen F. Hayes, a senior writer at the *Weekly Standard*, leveled a similar imputation of disloyalty at Scott Ritter, a former member of the UN's weapons inspection team in Iraq. Hayes quoted Ritter disdainfully, citing Ritter's comment that "Iraq today represents a threat to no one." Hayes expressed shock at such a statement. "It's hard to imagine that argument coming these days from anyone other than Tariq Aziz, or another of Saddam Hussein's propagandists," he wrote. "But those are in fact the words of Scott Ritter, former chief U.N. weapons inspector in Iraq."[13]

Not surprisingly, conservatives in the media adopted the stance that a war against Baghdad was indisputably justified; endorsing military force to overthrow Saddam Hussein was consistent with their overall hawkish approach to U.S. foreign policy. Moreover, several right-wing publications, especially the *Wall Street Journal*, the *Washington Times*, and the *Weekly Standard*, had repeatedly served as platforms for activists who had been pushing for a regime change effort against Saddam Hussein since the early 1990s.[14] The post-9/11 propaganda offensive from that faction was merely the latest phase of an ongoing obsession. Such pro-war, conservative media outlets also were supporting the policy of a Republican president, a stance that was both consistent and predictable.

More surprising was the sight of moderate and liberal members of the press supporting the war with equal enthusiasm. Perhaps their willingness to push for humanitarian crusades in the Balkans should have served as a warning that this faction was increasingly receptive to U.S. military force. In any case, a near consensus emerged throughout the news media: not only was Saddam the epitome of evil, but Iraq posed an existential security threat both to its Middle East neighbors and to the United States.

Journalists Collaborate with Bush Administration Neoconservative Hawks

The most troubling aspect of the media's performance in the lead-up to the Iraq War was the willingness of so many journalists to be passive channels for the disinformation that the Bush administration and its ally, the Iraqi National Congress (INC), generated. The administration's usual right-wing supporters at the *Wall Street Journal*, Fox News, the *Washington Times*, *National Review*, and other outlets were outspoken proponents of war. But the liberal media factions that frequently criticized Bush and his associates on domestic issues and were at least wary about the civil liberties implications of the Patriot Act stood shoulder-to-shoulder with their right-wing colleagues when it came to Iraq policy. They were equally willing to believe and circulate even the most thinly supported allegations advancing the argument that Saddam was a menace that needed to be eliminated. Regardless of their ideology or partisan political allegiance, members of the press who did so became accomplices in deceiving the American people and creating support for an unnecessary war—one that produced catastrophic long-term consequences for the Middle East and America's best interests.

The INC, the collection of anti-Saddam Iraqi exiles headed by Ahmed Chalabi, superbly exploited the trust of key news outlets. The *New York Times* and its lead reporter, Judith Miller, became especially compliant in circulating the INC's pro-interventionist propaganda. The INC fed journalists bogus information about two developments that were certain to alarm the American people and generate public pressure for war.

The first intelligence stream highlighted Saddam's alleged ties to al Qaeda, including reported clandestine meetings between Iraqi officials and leaders of the terrorist organization. A *New York Times* story by Patrick E. Tyler and John Tagliabue gave great exposure to that allegation, contending that an Iraqi intelligence agent met with 9/11 hijacker Mohammed Atta and other al Qaeda operatives in Prague shortly before the attack.[15] When Miller met Chalabi at Washington's Reagan National Airport in November 2001, she gently prodded him about the apparent role he had played in generating that story and another piece in her paper.

> I mentioned to Chalabi two *Times* stories that seemed to have his finger-prints all over them. The more explosive was about a defector: an Iraqi general who had allegedly seen his officers train Arab fighters to hijack airplanes without weapons at a camp near Salman Pak in Iraq. The story suggested a link between Iraq and Al Qaeda—and, hence, between Iraq and 9/11. Had he been responsible for that story? Yes, Chalabi con-firmed that he had connected my *Times* colleagues and others to the general, as well as other defectors.[16]

This admission undercuts the assertion that Bush administration policymakers, their political allies, and cooperative members of the press put forth later that the intelligence they received about the sup-posed Iraq–al Qaeda connection and Saddam's alleged weapons of mass destruction did not come from Chalabi and the INC. In actuality, most of the information came from that source—and most of it turned out to be misleading or even fictional.

The *New York Times* was not the only major news player to publish stories alleging that Iraq and al Qaeda were close allies and had colluded in the 9/11 attacks. *Washington Post* columnist Jim Hoagland made the same allegation in an article on October 12, 2001, again relying heavily on information supplied by Iraqi defectors. The incestuous nature of the East Coast elite news community on this issue became apparent when *New York Times* columnist William Safire cited Hoagland's story as "evidence" of Baghdad's culpability in the terrorist assault. Al Jazeera analyst Muhammad Idrees Ahmad noted that "Safire would harp on this theme well into 2003, long after it had been discarded by others."[17] In November 2001, the PBS program *Frontline* gave a platform to prominent American advocates of war with Iraq (including former CIA director James Woolsey and former ambassador to Israel Dennis Ross), along with Chalabi and a bevy of INC-supplied Iraqi defectors to push the narrative of Saddam's assistance to al Qaeda.

British journalist David Rose joined the fray in December with a long article in *Vanity Fair* highlighting Iraq's alleged role in 9/11.[18] His article was based on testimony by a defector that the INC furnished. Rose showed no signs of skepticism about the accuracy of that information. Indeed, he appeared on CNN and NBC to repeat the unsupported allegations. At one point, he told NBC's Chris Matthews that 9/11 was a "joint operation between al Qaeda and Iraq." The thesis seemed to become an obsession with Rose. Ahmad points out that in the subsequent period leading up to the March 2003 U.S.-led invasion of Iraq, Rose "would produce three more equally fantastic reports, all referencing INC defectors."[19]

Other media figures explicitly or implicitly endorsed the narrative of a Baghdad–al Qaeda axis. In a lengthy piece in *New Yorker* magazine about the Iraqi military's 1988 chemical weapons attack on the Kurdish village of Halabja in northern Iraq, Jeffrey Goldberg incorporated arguments that Saddam could help al Qaeda do the same against targets in the West. "On the surface," Goldberg conceded, "a marriage of Saddam's secular Baath Party regime with the fundamentalist Al Qaeda seems unlikely." But he argued that Saddam's "relationship with secular Palestinian groups is well known; both Abu Nidal and Abul Abbas, two prominent Palestinian terrorists, are currently believed to be in Baghdad." Moreover, "about ten years ago Saddam underwent something of a battlefield conversion to a fundamentalist brand of Islam." Goldberg added, "This conversion, cynical though it may be, has opened doors to

Saddam in the fundamentalist world. He is now a prime supporter of the Palestinian Islamic Jihad and of Hamas, paying families of suicide bombers ten thousand dollars in exchange for their sons' martyrdom. This is part of Saddam's attempt to harness the power of Islamic extremism and direct it against his enemies."[20]

Goldberg approvingly cited comments from Kurdish officials and Arab prisoners held by the Kurdish separatist government in northern Iraq. Among the allegations they voiced were "that Ansar al-Islam has received funds directly from Al Qaeda; that the intelligence service of Saddam Hussein has joint control, with Al Qaeda operatives, over Ansar al-Islam; that Saddam Hussein hosted a senior leader of Al Qaeda in Baghdad in 1992; that a number of Al Qaeda members fleeing Afghanistan have been secretly brought into territory controlled by Ansar al-Islam; and that Iraqi intelligence agents smuggled conventional weapons, and possibly even chemical and biological weapons, into Afghanistan. If these charges are true, it would mean that the relationship between Saddam's regime and Al Qaeda is far closer than previously thought." To leave little doubt about the danger that Saddam Hussein posed to the United States and civilization in general, Goldberg linked the two key elements of the media narrative that was emerging with ever-greater prominence in America: the Iraqi leader's supposed ties to al Qaeda and other Islamic extremists, and Baghdad's capability and (as the Halabja episode demonstrated) willingness to use weapons of mass destruction (WMD).[21]

In addition to the allegations that Saddam's regime was collaborating with al Qaeda, another intelligence stream featured a supposed defector (code name "Curveball"), who charged that Saddam was indeed vigorously expanding a WMD arsenal—specifically, chemical and biological weapons. Even more worrisome were allegations that Baghdad was actively pursuing a nuclear weapons program and already had achieved substantial advances.[22] Chalabi also made certain that Judith Miller broke that story in a *New York Times* exclusive.[23] Investigative reporter and Chalabi biographer Aram Roston observed that Miller's account "splashed across the newspapers of the world like a can of paint. Reuters, the AP, and other wire services picked it up. Newspapers from Australia to Austin, Texas, ran the story. Network news anchors read terse accounts of it."[24]

As longtime national security writer James Bamford concluded about the reports of close ties between Baghdad and al Qaeda and the existence of an Iraqi WMD arsenal, "It was damning stuff—just the kind of evidence the Bush administration was looking for." If the charges were true, they would offer the White House a compelling reason to invade Iraq and depose Saddam. There was only one problem, Bamford noted: "It was all a lie."[25]

Pro-war members of the press scorned any attempts to raise caveats or questions regarding the credibility of those reports. The herd mentality in the media in this instance was pervasive, intense, and intolerant. Neoconservative luminaries William Kristol and Robert Kagan exemplified the efforts to push the case for war and denigrate any expressions of doubt. They also inadvertently confirmed the extent of the herd mentality on the Iraq issue and the dangers that such a mentality always creates. Writing in the *Washington Examiner* in January 2002, a few weeks after Miller's blockbuster article, they stated, "The amazing thing about the current 'debate' over Iraq is that no one disputes the nature of the threat. Everyone agrees that, as Al Gore's former national security adviser Leon Fuerth puts it, 'Saddam Hussein is dangerous and likely to become more so,' that he 'is a permanent menace to his region and to the vital interests of the United States.' No one questions, furthermore, the basic facts about Saddam Hussein's weapons programs."[26]

As if fomenting fear on that front was not sufficient, Kristol and Kagan also highlighted the allegations about the connections between Saddam and al Qaeda. The *Examiner* article continued, "Reliable reports from defectors and former U.N. weapons inspectors have confirmed the existence of a terrorist training camp in Iraq, complete with a Boeing 707 for practicing hijackings, and filled with non-Iraqi radical Muslims. We know, too, that Mohamed Atta, the ringleader of September 11, went out of his way to meet with an Iraqi intelligence official a few months before he flew a plane into the World Trade Center." Here again they insisted, "So there is no debate about the facts."

As in other articles, the incestuous, self-reinforcing media elite's take on the Iraq issue was apparent. Kristol and Kagan repeatedly cited Leon Fuerth, someone with impeccable Democratic Party credentials, to stress both the bipartisan nature of the case against Saddam and the lack of any dispute about his guilt. The corollary message was that there also should be no doubt—and certainly no debate—about the urgent need for a U.S. military intervention to overthrow the menacing Iraqi strongman.

Chalabi and his INC associates continued to peddle the allegation that Saddam was developing an arsenal of WMD that posed a grave danger to both regional peace and U.S. security. And the INC's propaganda was widely believed. Worries about an Iraqi nuclear weapons program had special resonance with the American people, and both the Bush administration and its media allies exploited that fear. National Security Advisor Condoleezza Rice was especially brazen in doing so. During a September 8, 2002, interview with CNN's Wolf Blitzer, she stated, "The problem here is that there will always be some uncertainty about how quickly he can acquire nuclear weapons. But we don't want the smoking gun to be a mushroom cloud."[27]

The INC-supplied information about weapons of mass destruction ultimately proved to be as bogus as the allegations about Baghdad's supposed alliance with al Qaeda. Unfortunately, in the crucial period before the start of the war, press scrutiny of the claims that Iraqi defectors and the Bush administration put forth about Saddam's quest for nuclear weapons was feeble at best.

Miller was an especially useful conduit for the INC's disinformation. She was a close confidant of White House aide Scooter Libby and other leading neoconservatives in the Bush administration, and she had been a trusted outlet for INC propaganda for years.[28] Instead of exercising caution, she published a series of articles beginning in December 2001, hyping the allegations of weapons of mass destruction. Bamford noted that "for months, hawks inside and outside the administration had been pressing for a pre-emptive attack on Iraq." Now, thanks to Miller's stories, "they could point to 'proof' of Saddam's 'nuclear threat.'"[29]

Miller and other journalists who circulated the INC's disinformation later went to great lengths to emulate Pontius Pilate and wash their hands of the policy disaster that ensued. In an April 2015 *Wall Street Journal* op-ed, Miller denied all responsibility for helping build a false case for war.[30] She protested that "relying on the mistakes of others and [making] errors of judgment are not the same as lying."

To some extent, she had a valid point: relying on faulty sources and making errors of judgment are not the equivalent of lying. But critics justifiably countered that Miller treated the information that INC operatives fed her with a credulity unworthy of a serious journalist—especially one writing for the most prestigious and influential newspaper in the United States, if not the world. One group of critics, Veteran Intelligence Professionals for Sanity, wrote, "It's almost as though she is saying that if Ahmed Chalabi told her that in Iraq the sun rises in the west, and she duly reported it, that would not be 'the same as lying.'" These intelligence experts had little patience for her excuses. Instead, the group argued, she should be judged "by her authoring studies for the 'newspaper of record' that were questionably sourced and very often misleading." Despite her post-facto denials, Miller "played a pivotal role in building the public case for an attack on Iraq based upon shoddy reporting that even her editor at the *New York Times* has since discredited—including over reliance on a single-source of easy virtue and questionable credibility—Ahmed Chalabi."[31]

Indeed, Miller's role was crucial. Media outlets throughout the country and around the world routinely cite or even reprint *New York Times* articles, thereby giving such stories much wider circulation. That was certainly the case regarding panicky accounts of Iraq's alleged weapons of mass destruction. To a great extent, the *New York Times* sets the news agenda for television, radio, and print coverage—especially on international issues. In her memoirs, Miller bristles at suggestions that she and other members of the media pushed America into a disastrous war, noting that none of them had the authority to set policy.[32] That argument is technically true but disingenuous. She and other pro-war journalists helped distort public opinion to support an armed crusade to depose Saddam. Miller was, therefore, an enabler of a disastrous, avoidable war.

One cannot overstate the impact that the INC-supplied disinformation about Saddam's allegedly cozy relationship with al Qaeda and Iraq's equally fictional WMD had on the direction of U.S. policy and the public's perception of the alleged danger that Iraq posed.[33] A CNN/*USA Today*/Gallup Poll conducted in mid-March 2003 found that 88 percent of respondents believed that Iraq was supporting terrorist groups and had plans to attack the United States. Moreover, 51 percent thought that Saddam Hussein was personally involved in the 9/11 attacks. Only 41 percent rejected the allegation that the Iraqi leader was an accomplice in 9/11.[34]

If prominent mainstream journalists had done their jobs properly, they would have treated the INC-suppled intelligence with far more caution and skepticism.[35] They would have posed penetrating questions about the alleged caches of WMD and the Baghdad regime's supposed collaboration with al Qaeda. They would have sought corroboration for the intelligence supplied by the INC-provided "defectors." Instead, far too many reporters and columnists simply regurgitated the inflammatory and outlandish allegations that Chalabi and his cohorts circulated.

The INC was not operating on its own, however. The pro-war campaign was a collaborative effort between that organization and key elements of the Bush administration. Secretary of Defense Rumsfeld and his chief subordinates, especially Paul Wolfowitz and Douglas Feith, undersecretary for policy, avidly promoted the INC's misinformation to the media. So, too, did Vice President Cheney and his aides. Indeed, both of those factions put pressure on the CIA and other intelligence agencies to tailor their reports so that they corresponded to the version of events that the INC was circulating.[36] It's uncertain whether Cheney, Rumsfeld, and company also were taken in by Chalabi and became unwitting conduits for lies, or whether they realized that the information was phony but chose to present it anyway to justify a regime-change war that they all wanted to launch.

Whatever the motivation of the Bush administration and its INC allies, such a potent propaganda alliance had a decisive effect on the media, producing the pro-war spin that the administration desired. Even when journalists thought that they were getting independent assessments of Iraq's intentions and capabilities from U.S. policymakers—as well as from supposedly professional intelligence experts—too often they were merely receiving the INC's laundered accounts passed along by an administration determined to build an impregnable case for war. Whether willingly or unwillingly, much of the press became a tool of hawks within the Bush administration.

Most editorial pages echoed President Bush's assertion that Saddam must go.[37] And that sentiment became pervasive long before the

March 2003 invasion. An editorial circulated nationwide by the *Chicago Tribune*'s syndicate in December 2002 appeared in several newspapers with the headline "Free Iraq, World from Saddam Hussein."[38] Some pro-interventionists urged the United States to take on the mission unilaterally if a supportive international coalition couldn't be assembled.[39]

Even the minority of dissenting editorials and op-eds rarely ruled out the use of force. They merely urged the Bush administration to let the international weapons inspectors continue to do their work and to persist in a coordinated campaign with allies and other nations to press Saddam to capitulate. For many of them, the choice seemed to come down to either going to war immediately or trying to buy some time and hoping that war might be avoided. If other options were exhausted, an overwhelming majority of commentators in the press favored the use of force. They opposed hasty or "preemptive" war, not war "as a last resort."[40] Analysts opposing war with Iraq unconditionally were rare and consisted almost entirely of staunch left-wing or libertarian anti-war activists. Such people received little exposure in the mass media.

In what was perhaps the most devious and astute move on the part of the administration's ardently pro-war faction, officials managed to persuade Secretary of State Colin Powell to make the administration's case to a session of the UN Security Council on February 5, 2003.[41] The choice of Powell was crucial. He had a longstanding reputation as a sober and cautious foreign policy realist. Consequently, when he delivered the detailed indictment of Iraq's supposed misconduct and the dire security threat it posed to the region and to the United States, Powell had a very high level of credibility. He also went out of his way to stress that he, with his vast experience in such matters, had carefully evaluated the evidence on his own and was not merely reporting the intelligence assessments that others had supplied him.

Given Powell's background, credentials, and demeanor, the American people and members of Congress reacted to the case he made with little skepticism.[42] The major news media seemed to have even less doubt. CNN passively repeated National Security Advisor Rice's assessment that Powell had made a "very compelling case."[43] Most other stories adopted a similar view.[44]

If Rumsfeld or some other notorious administration hawk had delivered the presentation, it likely would have been less credible and would
have generated at least some skepticism and dissent. "What makes the
speech persuasive is Colin Powell delivering it," said Kathleen Hall
Jamieson, dean of the Annenberg School of Communication at the University of Pennsylvania.[45] Powell's presentation turned out to be little
more than a recap of INC-supplied disinformation, but neither the public nor the incurious press realized that at the time. His speech, and the
news media's reaction to it, gave the momentum toward war a final,
decisive push, especially among members of Congress and the media.

The substantive justifications about thwarting a security threat that
Iraq supposedly posed were the most frequent rationales appearing in
media accounts, but they were not the only ones. Neoconservatives both
inside and outside the Bush administration used media platforms to artic-
ulate a more ambitious agenda. For them, the goal was not only the
removal of Saddam Hussein but the democratic transformation of Iraq
and, ultimately, the entire Middle East. Typical of that argument was an
October 15, 2001, opinion column by Max Boot, a contributing editor at
the *Washington Examiner* and soon-to-be senior fellow at the Council on
Foreign Relations. In a rather peculiar historical reference, Boot recalled:

> Long before British and American armies had returned to the conti-
> nent of Europe—even before America had entered the struggle against
> Germany and Japan—Winston Churchill and Franklin Roosevelt met
> on a battleship in the North Atlantic to plan the shape of the postwar
> world. The Atlantic Charter of August 14, 1941, pledged Britain and
> America to creating a liberal world order based on peace and national
> self-determination. The leaders of America, and of the West, should
> be making similar plans today. Once they do, they will see that ambi-
> tious goals—such as "regime change"—are also the most realistic.[46]

Boot's vision was of an enlightened, humanitarian U.S. imperialism applied to the Middle East. In the *Examiner* piece, he continued confidently, "Once we have deposed Saddam, we can impose an
American-led, international regency in Baghdad, to go along with the
one in Kabul. With American seriousness and credibility thus restored,

we will enjoy fruitful cooperation from the region's many opportunists, who will show a newfound eagerness to be helpful in our larger task of rolling up the international terror network that threatens us."

Such a step also would help make amends for Washington's long-standing policy of backing corrupt Middle East autocrats, Boot contended. In the process, it would afford an opportunity "to establish the first Arab democracy, and to show the Arab people that America is as committed to freedom for them as we were for the people of Eastern Europe. To turn Iraq into a beacon of hope for the oppressed peoples of the Middle East: Now that would be a historic war aim." Although Boot's position was a bit more grandiose than policy proposals by other pro-war advocates, it was not unusual. Other authors also combined realpolitik objectives (eliminating Iraq's supposed WMDs and breaking Baghdad's supposed ties with al Qaeda) with calls for an intervention to transform Iraq into a pro-Western democracy.

Also, like Boot, other intervention advocates casually compared the current situation in the Middle East with America's experience in Europe after World War II, when U.S. and allied forces were greeted as liberators, and again after the collapse of the Soviet Union, when Eastern Europeans embraced democracy and sought close ties with the United States. Knowledgeable experts on the Middle East likely winced at such gullibility. Europeans understandably cheered the United States as the country that liberated them from first Nazi and then communist oppression. In the Middle East, though, major portions of the populations viewed the United States and its allies, especially former colonial powers Britain and France, as their imperial oppressors. Expecting them to greet a Western military intervention as an act of liberation rather than just another round of imperial subjugation was unrealistic. Yet few media accounts appreciated the crucial differences between the historical experiences of the two regions. Such journalistic malpractice stifled a badly needed national debate about the wisdom or necessity of the impending war against Iraq.

Once the war began, media cheerleading for the overthrow of Saddam Hussein continued unabated. Members of the press portrayed the invasion as a righteous crusade that would eliminate a horrid tyrant and bring the blessings of freedom and democracy to Iraq. The rapid advance of U.S. and "coalition" forces to Baghdad reinforced the sense of optimism, especially the belief in a worthy, and surprisingly easy, triumph. An April 10, 2003, Pew Research Survey found that 60 percent of respondents believed that the war was going "very well," and 71 percent believed that launching the invasion had been the right decision.[47] A slim majority, though, subscribed to the belief that the war would not truly be won until Saddam was killed or captured.

The finding that large majorities believed the war was both justified and an impending triumph was not surprising. For well over a year, most portions of the press had been making the argument that military force was not only justified but imperative. If the Pew poll yielded a surprise, it was that one-fifth of respondents rejected the administration's massive propaganda offensive and the overwhelmingly supportive media narrative. Coverage of the invasion itself was unrelentingly upbeat, and the focus was narrow: a military victory would assure a stable, pro-Western, democratic Iraq. Few analyses in the media posed the broader questions about the likely impact of the underlying political, religious, and ethnic dynamics in Iraq and the rest of the region.

Yet long before the war began, plenty of signs pointed to potential trouble on all those fronts if Saddam was removed from power.[48] A few Middle East experts and foreign policy analysts did pose pertinent questions and express warnings. The *New Republic*'s John B. Judis, one of the rare critics of the drive to war in the mainstream media, found in his own inquiries that "the people who had the most familiarity with the Middle East and with the perils of war were dead set against the invasion."[49] One sign of that perspective was an ad that appeared on the op-ed page of the September 26, 2002, edition of the *New York Times* by 33 leading U.S. foreign policy academics, many with extensive backgrounds in Middle East affairs, opposing the option of war.[50]

But other members of the press largely ignored those individuals and the cases they made. That was especially true of the media's elite layer. In their 2009 study of the media's performance before and during the Iraq War, Leslie Gelb and Jeanne-Palma Zelmati contended that five print publications—the *New York Times*, the *Washington Post*, the *Wall*

Street Journal, Time, and *Newsweek*—along with the three major television networks and CNN overwhelmingly dominated the gathering and dissemination of news, especially with regard to military and foreign affairs.[51] That assessment was accurate, and none of those outlets exhibited a willingness to treat the Iraq war as a bona fide topic for debate.

Instead, their de facto stance was similar to the attitude that Kristol and Kagan expressed: there was no valid reason for debate, since all the pertinent facts were known and "everyone" (or at least every responsible person) agreed that military action was essential. Opponents of going to war, especially outspoken, unequivocal critics of that course, received few opportunities to express the need for caution before the United States barged into Iraq.[52] (The op-ed page of *USA Today,* under the direction of the page's editor, Sid Hurlburt, was a partial, refreshing exception to the pervasive exclusionary policy.)[53] To the extent that antiwar analysts managed to gain exposure at all, it was in the op-ed pages of maverick, second-tier publications, such as the *Orange County Register,* the *Rocky Mountain News,* and United Press International, or third-tier outlets like Antiwar.com and *Counterpunch.*[54]

The imbalance of featured views was even more pronounced among the television networks. Fairness and Accuracy in Reporting (FAIR) documented that point.[55] Looking at two weeks of coverage (January 30, 2003–February 12, 2003), FAIR examined the 393 on-camera sources who appeared in nightly news stories about Iraq on *ABC World News Tonight, CBS Evening News, NBC Nightly News,* and PBS's *NewsHour with Jim Lehrer.* The study began one week before and ended one week after Secretary of State Powell's crucial February 5 presentation at the UN. FAIR's analysis found several problems with the coverage. More than two-thirds (267 out of 393) of the guests featured were from the United States. Of those guests, some 75 percent (199) were either current or former government or military officials. Only one of those interview subjects—Sen. Edward Kennedy (D-MA)—expressed skepticism about or opposition to going to war. And as FAIR noted, even his comments were couched in vague and conditional terms.

The study added that the remaining 68 American sources—those without a current or former government connection—had slightly more balanced views; 26 percent of these nonofficial sources took a skeptical or critical position on the war. Yet FAIR concluded, "at a time when 61 percent of respondents in a CBS poll [February 5–6, 2003] were saying that they felt the U.S. should 'wait and give the United Nations and weapons inspectors more time,' only 16 of the 68 U.S. guests (24 percent) who were not officials represented such views." And many of the skeptics in the CBS poll were people captured in "man on the street" interviews who had no reputations for expertise and were unlikely to be taken seriously. Such a record suggested a pronounced pro-war bias in all the television outlets examined.

The coverage in Europe, however, was noticeably different from the coverage in the United States. Skepticism about the case for going to war was far greater among European media players, and outlets there featured a much wider variety of sources for comments and analyses.[56] That greater diversity was true even in the assessments of Powell's speech to the UN Security Council.[57] Whereas praise for his presentation was pervasive among American journalists, their counterparts across the Atlantic were considerably more restrained. Although Powell's presentation did move the needle toward greater support for using force among Europeans as it did with Americans, a sizable number of voices still urged continued caution, and some even asserted that Washington had not made an adequate case for using force.

Once the war began, the media in the United States remained both supportive of the military crusade and incurious about any possible drawbacks. The Bush administration's public relations offensive also carried on, unabated. Administration leaders were not even inclined to wait until Saddam was killed or captured before proclaiming victory. President Bush made a jet landing on the USS *Lincoln* on May 1, 2003, with the carrier displaying a giant "Mission Accomplished" banner in the background. The photo op would later become a subject of derision. But at the time, the American press corps featured it as an appropriate symbol of pride in a great U.S. military success, and journalists were generous in their praise of Bush's energy and leadership.[58] CNN described his remarks aboard the *Lincoln* as "a historic speech," with no hint that taking credit for a victory in that fashion might be premature or unwarranted. The sole, mildly negative comment in a long follow-up article the next day was that "the president's address about the success in Iraq comes as Bush's domestic agenda is under renewed fire by Democrats."[59] Again, there was no criticism of the substance of the victory proclamation itself.

Most members of the press had ignored or disregarded warnings by worried Middle East experts that Washington's actions would likely unleash instability in Iraq and beyond, especially by fomenting a bloody power struggle between Sunni and Shiite factions in Iraq and throughout the region. Optimistic journalists showed no inclination to reconsider that conclusion until the surging level of violence in post-Saddam Iraq finally compelled some rethinking. Gelb and Zelmati's conclusion on that point was brutally succinct. "Long after the Iraq War went south, when its failures could no longer be minimized, the elite newspapers and weeklies finally got around to offering sound analyses and asking the Bush Administration tough questions. It took them long enough—not until after December 2003, by which time the war was underway and its damage irreversible."[60] And for many leading members of the opinion-shaping sector, optimism prevailed long after December 2003.

EMBEDDED AND SEDUCED: THE AMERICAN MEDIA'S COVERAGE FROM IRAQ

A thoroughly pro-war, pro-administration perspective also was evident in the battlefield coverage—at least during the initial months of the war. Author Bill Katovsky noted that a "high-stakes media game unfolded" as the impending U.S. invasion drew near. The cable news networks and the big three commercial networks deployed hundreds of personnel and millions of dollars in the new technology that had developed over the previous decade to provide unprecedented coverage. The government also displayed a much friendlier attitude regarding press coverage of military operations than it had during the Grenada and Panama invasions, or even the Gulf War. The Pentagon "issued a Super Bowl's worth of media credentials—2,700 of them—to a worldwide army" of journalists, according to Katovsky.

He concluded that the government's attitude was "a significant turn-around" from the days when "a wary military, still trying to shake the Vietnam monkey off its back, micromanaged battlefield news by limiting press access." Instead, the Pentagon pushed "a full-blown version of the public relations strategy of embedding reporters directly into military units." This approach was based on logic similar to requiring press pools to operate under direct, ongoing military supervision, but it took that rationale one significant step further. "Embedded reporters ate, lived, traveled, and slept with the troops." Reporters were "going to have the coziest lovefest with the military since World War II."[61]

Writing in late 2003—after the initial U.S. military victory, but before Washington's Iraq policy began to unravel—Katovsky rightly worried about the price the media was paying for such up-close and personal access to combat operations. In his view, the "Fourth Estate was made an honorary member" of the "cobbled together" international coalition the Bush administration had assembled to wage the Iraq War. He noted that "skeptics questioned the underlying motives" for the Pentagon's extremely accommodating attitude. In this new era of embedded media, "a tension existed between freedom of expression and following the rules." That tension automatically raised questions about whether the embedded reporters would be able to provide independent news or would simply become propaganda agents. "Once embedded, ease of movement was drastically curtailed and unfettered mobility denied. The trade-off existed between generous access and narrow-aperture coverage."[62] In other words, embedded reporters, for the most part, were able to see and report only what the military allowed them to witness.

And military commanders did not hesitate to retaliate against cor-respondents who sought to evade the rules. Approximately two dozen reporters were "dis-embedded," supposedly for violating requirements about not revealing sensitive information or trying to wander away from their minders. Embedding was inherently a tool for weeding out poten-tial troublemakers. Mavericks and outspoken critics of the military were likely to be excluded from embedded billets in the first place. If they somehow got through the approval process and landed in Iraq, they were likely to be expelled at the first hint of a rules violation—and expelled not just from the military unit in question, but from the entire Iraq theater. Most who received that treatment were relatively obscure, iconoclastic figures, but a few were not, including Fox News correspondent Geraldo Rivera.

Beyond these arbitrary rules and heavy-handed restrictions lay a more subtle, insidious problem. For reporters, a clear line should always exist between being a detached observer and being an advocate. Too many journalists during the Balkan wars not only blurred that line, but they obliterated it, and the quality of coverage suffered accordingly. A similar problem developed with the battlefield coverage of the Iraq War, especially during the initial months of the conflict. Embedding war correspondents into combat units inevitably created powerful incentives to see the military personnel not as participants on one side of a nasty armed conflict, but as friends risking their lives.

Once that perspective takes hold, it is just a small step to see the cause that those "friends" are fighting for as important and worthy. The emotional bonds that developed between embedded reporters and soldiers could not help but influence the news stories emerging from Iraq. Katovsky pondered that point: "How critical can the press be when these troops are also, as ABC News correspondent John Donovan put it, 'my protectors'?" And, Katovsky wondered, "at what point did embeds become a marketing tool for the military, and less a countervailing force?"[63]

Embedding skewed Iraq coverage in ways both obvious and subtle. Even more than during the Gulf War, television was the principal lens through which the American people viewed and evaluated the conflict. Television, by its very nature, focuses on images that are graphic and emotionally evocative. Embeds were in an ideal position to send such footage back to their studios in the United States, and they did so quite successfully. But television is not a good mechanism for portraying complex issues, much less doing so in an in-depth fashion that facilitates greater understanding. Katovsky noted correctly that correspondents found moments of "truth and poignancy," but they did so "while failing to account for mounting civilian deaths or aggressively challenging the Bush administration's pretext about taking out those elusive weapons of mass destruction."[64] On balance, embedding was a devil's bargain for the press that inhibited candid coverage of the Iraq War and its many implications.

MEDIA DISILLUSIONMENT WITH THE IRAQ WAR

The initial accounts of military progress in Iraq were almost uniformly upbeat, and the visuals supported the narrative that the offensive was a great success. In one famous Baghdad scene, demonstrators tore down a huge statue of Saddam Hussein. The act seemed to symbolize not only the culmination of military victory, but Iraq's birth as a democratic country—though it later turned out that U.S. officials had staged the scene.[65] The relative ease of the invasion and occupation of the country implicitly undercut the administration's case that Iraq had posed a dire threat to the region and the United States, but few reporters mentioned that detail. Instead, they contended, America as a whole should celebrate the victory. Indeed, much of media coverage echoed Bush's boast of "mission accomplished."

A celebratory atmosphere was apparent throughout the news media during the early months of the intervention. Howard Kurtz, the *Washington Post*'s in-house media analyst, even chastised some of his colleagues for being too pessimistic. A subsequent FAIR analysis described Kurtz's reaction: "In the heady days of 'post-war' Iraq, Howard Kurtz went out of his way to criticize those journalists who didn't adopt Bush's short-sighted optimism about the 'success' of the invasion." Indeed, Kurtz portrayed the intervention as a major achievement, citing "the sheer joy of Baghdad residents hacking away at that Saddam statue." Such footage, he said, "sent the world a message more compelling than a thousand op-ed pieces or a million propaganda leaflets dropped from U.S. planes." In a column on April 14, 2003, Kurtz congratulated the press for its coverage of the just-concluded Iraq War. Kurtz's piece, FAIR countered, provided a useful insight into "the conventional wisdom that guides not just journalism, but also the profession's most powerful internal critics."[66]

Reporters on the scene and back in the United States expressed little doubt that the new army of occupation would soon discover definitive evidence of Baghdad's collusion with al Qaeda and would locate the weapons of mass destruction that the Bush administration had highlighted as the main justification for taking military action. But as time passed and no credible evidence emerged about either allegation, uneasiness began to grow. The doubts were especially apparent with respect to the elusive arsenal of WMD. By the end of 2003, everyone except the Bush administration's dead-ender defenders understood that no vast arsenal containing chemical or biological weapons, much less nuclear weapons, existed.

Some of the shift in perspective on the WMD issue occurred early on. Middle East analyst Jim Lobe noted that during a single week in late May and early June 2003, *Time*, *Newsweek*, and *U.S. News* all ran major features speculating about whether the administration had misled the public about WMDs. In addition, "when the two most important outlets of neoconservative opinion—*The Weekly Standard* and *The Wall Street Journal*—come out on the same day with lead editorials spluttering outrage about suggestions of government lying," one could bet that public skepticism about Washington's official rationale for the war was heating up.[67]

John B. Judis stated later that "most of the people I worked with [at the *New Republic*] began to doubt the war within about four months."[68] Kenneth M. Pollack, who had been an avid proponent of going to war, put the matter bluntly in his January–February 2004 *Atlantic* article. "Let's start with one truth: last March, when the United States and its coalition partners invaded Iraq, the American public and much of the rest of the world believed that after Saddam Hussein's regime sank, a vast flotsam of weapons of mass destruction would bob to the surface. That, of course, has not been the case." He added, "Many people are now asking very reasonable questions about why they were misled."[69]

Resentment at the administration's failure to find Iraq's alleged WMDs soon spread widely. Some portions of the press also criticized the administration's handling of the Iraq invasion and occupation—while trying to escape any blame themselves for the unraveling policy. A September 26, 2003, *New York Times* editorial, for example, asserted that "this page did not support the war in Iraq," which was technically true of the editorial page, but conveniently ignored the deluge of pro-war pieces that had appeared in its news stories and op-ed pages. After that perfunctory attempt at self-exoneration, the editorial went on to admit, "Like President Bush, we believed that Saddam Hussein was hiding potentially large quantities of chemical and biological weapons and aggressively pursuing nuclear arms. Like the president, we thought those weapons posed a grave danger to the United States and the rest of the world. Now it appears that premise was wrong." The editors added, however, that "we cannot in hindsight blame the administration for its original conclusions. They were based on the best intelligence available. . . ."

The *New York Times* editorial contended that Americans and other populations around the world were glad that Saddam was gone. But it made a major concession, noting that "it was the fear of weapons of mass destruction placed in the hands of enemy terrorists that made doing something about Iraq seem urgent. If it had seemed unlikely that Mr. Hussein had them, we doubt that Congress or the American people would have endorsed the war."[70]

Some members of the media were more critical than the *New York Times* of the Bush administration's conduct, and they exhibited greater distress about the apparent lack of diligence or candor about the WMD issue during the period before the war.[71] Others were vitriolic in their anger. One outraged writer in the University of Minnesota's student newspaper stated bluntly, "Bush lied to me, and I'm mad as hell."[72] Once again, though, foreign news outlets seemed more inclined than their American counterparts to express the categorical conclusion that the WMD threat had been an illusion all along.[73]

Ahmed Chalabi, the leader of the Iraqi National Congress, which had provided most of the bogus intelligence about the alleged arsenal, did not help soothe the rising discontent. In February 2004, he insisted that he and his compatriots had simply been "heroes in error."[74] Bush administration spokesmen who adopted a similar argument—that ridding Iraq and the world of Saddam Hussein was a great achievement, even if no WMDs were discovered—also failed to gain traction. More and more members of the press, as well as the public, concluded instead that the pro-war camp had engaged in a cynical campaign of deception and manipulation.

Unfortunately, the media showed little willingness, even after the fact, to address the question of whether war would have been justified if caches of WMD had existed. That implicit lack of faith in America's overwhelming deterrence capabilities, for which taxpayers were spending billions of dollars annually, was evident in both Congress and the news media. It was one of the more curious features of discussions about the war.

Even the administration's most tenacious defenders in the press, though, found it difficult to stay the course in the face of overwhelming evidence that no WMD arsenal existed. An especially harsh blow came in April 2005 when the CIA issued a final report with that conclusion.[75]

Greater press annoyance about the fallacious WMD menace also gradually led to a reassessment of the other arguments used to justify the war—at least among a growing number of centrist and liberal figures.[76] That review did not, however, necessarily translate into greater media scrutiny and criticism of other aspects of Washington's policy toward Iraq or the broader war on terror. Even the abuses that U.S. military personnel committed at the Abu Ghraib prison, which came to light in the spring of 2004, sparked only a limited amount of outrage.[77]

Perhaps most telling and frustrating, early critics of the Iraq intervention still received a chilly response to their work. It was almost as though their presence was an unpleasant reminder to the gatekeepers in the mainstream media of their own failures of judgment. That attitude tended to persist despite mounting evidence that opponents of going to war had been correct and the cheerleaders for intervention had been disastrously wrong. James Bovard recalled, "Even after the appalling Abu Ghraib photos and a 'presidential torture entitlement memo' leaked out, most publications shirked the issue or simply printed increasingly far-fetched official denials of barbaric interrogations."[78] Indeed, new converts to the anti-war cause seemed to get exposure more easily than did the longtime opponents of the Iraq intervention.

The disillusionment did grow, however, as American military casualties mounted. Attacks by resistance forces using improvised explosive devices against U.S. military vehicles and other targets were especially deadly. Bitter jokes began about the prewar prediction made by Bush adviser Kenneth Adelman that the Iraq War would be "a cakewalk."

Washington's successful invasion was proving to be merely the first stage of what threatened to become a long, bloody struggle with an uncertain outcome.

It was increasingly apparent that not all Iraqis viewed U.S. troops as liberators. The restless Kurds in the country's northern region did so, but the ousted (formerly ruling) Sunni Arab minority, which had been Saddam's base of support, saw matters differently. The long-subjugated Shiite Arabs, who amounted to slightly more than half of the country's population, were torn. They were pleased to be rid of Saddam and witness the end of Sunni domination, but many of them also shared the anti-U.S. perspectives of their coreligionists across the border in Iran. They tended to see the U.S.-led invasion and occupation not as a liberation but as a manifestation of Western imperialism. Relations between occupation troops and pro-Iranian Shiite militias were extremely tense, at best.

American news coverage of the occupation gradually turned more skeptical and worried. Nevertheless, the sea change to vehement criticism of the Iraq mission was slow to build. When Iraq held its first free election in January 2005, many media accounts praised that achievement and portrayed it as evidence of a successful U.S. policy despite the violence and other problems.[79] Television images and newspaper photos showed beaming Iraqi voters who emerged from polling places showing their thumbs stained with purple dye to confirm that they had voted. Many of those voters, though, were Shiites celebrating their faction's attainment of political dominance over the hated Sunnis. Internecine fighting, as well as attacks on U.S. forces, continued to grow. The deteriorating situation finally reached a point that NBC News began to refer to it as a full-fledged civil war.[80] NBC joined both the *Los Angeles Times* and the McClatchy newspaper chain, which had already been using the term.[81]

As the fighting grew, criticism in the American press of both the current mission and the original decision to invade Iraq expanded. It also took on an increasingly partisan flavor. The Bush administration's defenders in conservative publications and Fox News still insisted that the United States had made the right decision in going to war, and they remained confident that the mission to transform Iraq into a peaceful, democratic, pro-Western society would ultimately prove successful.

Journalists on the left, conversely, were noticeably harsh in their criticism, accusing the administration of having lied the country into war
and then bungling the execution. Democrats in Congress, sensing a great
political opportunity, made criticism of the bloody Iraq mission a major
point in the 2006 midterm elections. The outcome of that balloting—a
near landslide victory for the Democrats—confirmed the extent of the
public's discontent.

The partisan flavor of the media coverage became increasingly
prominent as bipartisan support for the war—in Congress and throughout the country—continued to erode. Conservatives in the press dug
in, though, as the fighting in Iraq subsided in 2007 and 2008. The Bush
administration and its allies took credit for that development, citing the
impact of the deployment of additional troops—the so-called surge.[82] A
Wall Street Journal writer, Omar Fadhil, conceded that Iraq "was going
through the worst times ever as we moved towards the end of 2006. . . .
Iraq was said to be on the verge of 'civil war,' if it wasn't actually there
already." But, he stated confidently, "the situation looks quite different
now."[83] The reliably pro-intervention Max Boot likewise asserted without hesitation that the surge was working and that Iraq would be able to
complete its transition to a stable democracy.[84]

Media accounts about the surge reflected the deep partisan and
ideological divide that had opened in the United States about the war.
An article in *Salon* cautioned some prominent Democrats who seemed
inclined to climb aboard the pro-surge bandwagon, typifying a more
skeptical view in left-of-center publications.[85] Skepticism was certainly
warranted. The lull in fighting proved to be limited and temporary.
Indeed, Washington's willingness to make generous payments to the
leaders of Sunni tribes in Anbar province and other portions of western
Iraq appeared to have at least as much to do with dampening the number
of violent military incidents as did the presence of more U.S. troops.[86]
The animosity between Sunnis and Shiites remained, and the power
struggle would resume in a few years, culminating with the rise of the
Sunni-dominated ISIS and the creation of the Islamic caliphate.

Whatever the cause or causes, the reduction in fighting from a full boil
to a simmer convinced Bush to accede to the Iraqi government's request

that Washington execute a gradual withdrawal of U.S. forces. In December 2008, he approved a Status of Forces Agreement (SOFA) with Baghdad to have all American troops out of the country by the end of 2011. Bush's successor, Barack Obama, announced on February 27, 2009, that most troops would be removed by August 2010 and U.S. combat operations would cease at that time.[87] As the remaining personnel were drawn down thereafter, they would perform only support functions for Iraq's military.

The withdrawal agreement became increasingly controversial as evidence grew that Iraq remained a violent, unstable place. Oddly, congressional Democrats and left-of-center members of the press became the principal defenders of Bush's diplomatic handiwork, while members of the former president's party implicitly disowned the SOFA and pressured U.S. officials not to abide by the withdrawal deadline. Cynical types implied that Obama was to blame for the deadline, though his signature did not appear on the agreement.[88]

As the withdrawal date drew closer, neoconservative critics excoriated Obama for not pressuring the Iraqi government to conclude a revised SOFA that would leave a sizable contingent of U.S. troops in the country indefinitely. Among the most vociferous proponents of that view were *Washington Post* columnist Jennifer Rubin and *Wall Street Journal* guest columnist Max Boot. Rubin fumed about the "irresponsibility of a complete withdrawal of U.S. forces in Iraq." She accused the Obama administration of bungling negotiations for a new SOFA and called for congressional investigations. A key witness she wanted called during such hearings was former commander of U.S. forces in Iraq, and principal architect of the surge, Gen. David Petraeus. "It might be interesting to get his assessment of the Iraqi security situation from his current vantage point at the CIA," Rubin wrote. "But the main reason for calling him would be to get a valuable assessment from the most knowlegeable [sic] person on the planet about the security requirements in Iraq, the level of troops required and the expectation of the military that we would have an ongoing presence. His great achievement, and America's victory, hang in the balance."[89]

Boot also accused Obama of mishandling negotiations for a new agreement to keep U.S. forces in the country. He charged that the president "undercut his own negotiating team by regularly bragging—in political speeches delivered while talks were ongoing—of his plans to 'end' the 'war in Iraq.' Even more damaging was his August decision to commit only 3,000 to 5,000 troops to a possible mission in Iraq post-2011. This was far below the number judged necessary by our military commanders." Boot concluded that "the end of the U.S. military mission in Iraq is a tragedy, not a triumph—and a self-inflicted one at that."[90]

National Review's editors echoed the argument of Rubin, Boot, and other neoconservatives that the withdrawal decision was a dangerous, strategic "gift" to America's implacable adversary: Iran. "It once seemed that Iraq could be a strategic ally and base for our influence in the Middle East; it now may become both those things for our foremost enemy in the region."[91] Writing for CNN, former Reagan administration cabinet member William J. Bennett asserted that "only very few of the loudest opponents of the Iraq war advocated complete withdrawal. The U.S. military commanders recommended that at least 15,000 troops remain. Obama once again ignored his generals, as he did with Afghanistan, and instead pressed ahead with a politically calculated decision."[92] Bennett neglected to mention that one of the "very few" who had approved a complete withdrawal was George W. Bush—and on roughly the same timeline that Obama implemented.

THE MEDIA'S DISMAL IRAQ PERFORMANCE

The media's performance in the run-up to the Iraq war was myopic and disturbingly hawkish. The dominant perspective during that period was blind enthusiasm about the prospect of a military crusade to eliminate Saddam Hussein's regime. Most journalists—and nearly all prominent figures in the elite press—ignored warning signs that the outcome might be far less benign than anticipated. Worse, most publications and television news programs systematically excluded the views of dissenting experts. The mainstream press fed the American people a steady diet of pro-war arguments that ultimately proved to be off the mark.

Several expectations were erroneous: finding and eliminating an Iraqi WMD arsenal, confirming a connection between Saddam's regime and al Qaeda, and seeing U.S. troops greeted as liberators by the Iraqi people. Among key media players, some evidence of reflection and chagrin did emerge. The *New York Times* acknowledged several major blunders and even pressed star reporter Judith Miller to leave. In its May 26, 2004, mea culpa, the editors conceded:

> We have found a number of instances of coverage that was not as rigorous as it should have been. In some cases, information that was controversial then, and seems questionable now, was insufficiently qualified or allowed to stand unchallenged. Looking back, we wish we had been more aggressive in re-examining the claims as new evidence emerged—or failed to emerge.
>
> The problematic articles varied in authorship and subject matter, but many shared a common feature. They depended at least in part on information from a circle of Iraqi informants, defectors and exiles bent on "regime change" in Iraq, people whose credibility has come under increasing public debate.[93]

The *Washington Post*'s self-inspection was less forthcoming, but the paper at least grudgingly admitted that its coverage may have exhibited some omissions and blind spots. Executive editor Leonard Downie Jr. specifically conceded that the paper "did not pay enough attention to voices raising questions about the war."[94] The willingness of other prominent pro-war media outlets, such as CNN and the *New Republic*, to admit error seemed more limited and reluctant.[95] Yet even those outlets conceded that their willingness to accept allegations about WMDs had been a bit too credulous.

Conservative factions in the press were far more reluctant to acknowledge any errors.[96] A widespread argument from the right-wing press was a bait-and-switch that echoed the administration's new emphasis: Per the Bush team's revised case, the failure to find WMD was not really that important, because that had never been Washington's sole, or even principal, objective. The main goal all along, administration officials insisted, was to transform Iraq into a stable, pro-Western democracy.

The administration and its right-wing media allies cited the country's first democratic elections as evidence of success. American Enterprise

Institute scholar Michael Rubin epitomized that perspective. "Yesterday, President Bush spoke of the success of the elections, saying 'Today the people of Iraq have spoken to the world, and the world is hearing the voice of freedom from the center of the Middle East.' That voice of freedom may still be young, but Iraqis yesterday determined that it cannot be silenced."[97] Conservatives in both government and the media clung to that justification even as violence and growing chaos convulsed Iraq.[98] Indeed, both *National Review* and the *Wall Street Journal* were still pushing the narrative of intrepid, resilient Iraqi voters embracing democracy years later.[99]

On the other side of the political spectrum, figures in politics and the press rapidly distanced themselves from the outcome of the Iraq policy they once embraced. A few maverick journalists on the left, though, denounced such efforts to evade responsibility, and those criticisms grew with the passage of time. In a March 22, 2019, retrospective in *Rolling Stone*, independent journalist Matt Taibbi went after his progressive colleagues for trying to shift all the blame for the media's role in the Iraq debacle onto the Bush administration and a handful of mostly right-wing journalists.[100]

> In the popular imagination, the case for war was driven by a bunch of Republicans and one over-caffeinated *New York Times* reporter named Judith Miller. Even the attempts to make comprehensive lists of Iraq cheerleaders post-invasion inevitably focus on usual suspects like [White House press secretary Ari] Fleischer, current Trump official John Bolton, neoconservatives like Max Boot, David Frum, and Bill Kristol, and winger goons like Sean Hannity, Rush Limbaugh and Ann Coulter. But we expect the worst from such people.

Taibbi made clear he had little patience for such self-serving, exculpatory attempts on the part of his left-of-center brethren:

> It's been forgotten this was actually a business-wide consensus, which included the enthusiastic participation of a blue-state intelligentsia. The *New Yorker* . . . was a source of many of the most ferocious pro-invasion pieces, including a pair written by current *Atlantic* editor Jeffrey Goldberg, one of a number of WMD hawks who failed up

after the war case fell apart. Other prominent Democrat voices like Ezra Klein, Jonathan Chait, and even quasi-skeptic Nick Kristof (who denounced war critics for calling Bush a liar) were on board.

Taibbi presented an impressive number of details to back up his case that progressive journalists and their corporate media employers had played crucial roles in trying to whip up public sentiment for a war to overthrow Saddam Hussein:

> The *Washington Post* and *New York Times* were key editorial-page drivers of the conflict; MSNBC unhired Phil Donahue and Jesse Ventura over their war skepticism; CNN flooded the airwaves with generals and ex-Pentagon stooges, and broadcast outlets ABC, CBS, NBC and PBS stacked the deck even worse. . . . Exactly one major news organization refused to pick up pom-poms, the Knight-Ridder newspaper chain. All the other major outlets, whether they ostensibly catered to Republican or Democratic audiences, sold the war lie.

A retrospective from John B. Judis on the 10th anniversary of the Iraq invasion made similar points about the extent of the pro-war herd mentality that establishment journalists had exhibited throughout 2002 and early 2003.[101] Judis stressed just how isolated he had felt as an opponent of military action. "When *The New Republic*'s editor-in-chief and editor proclaimed the need for a 'muscular' foreign policy, I was usually the only vocal dissenter, and the only people who agreed with me were the women on staff. . . . Both of the major national dailies—*The Washington Post* and *The New York Times* (featuring Judith Miller's reporting)—were beating the drums for war."

Judis recounted an incident at a December 2002 conference on political Islam held in Key West, Florida, featuring many of the country's best-known journalists. "The conversation invariably got around to Iraq, and I found myself one of the few attendees who outright opposed an invasion. Two of the speakers at the event—Christopher Hitchens, who was then writing for *Slate*, and Jeffrey Goldberg, who was then writing for *The New Yorker*—generously offered to school me on the errors of my way." Judis observed, "Some people in Washington still haven't recanted (unless I missed an editorial on Fred Hiatt's *Washington Post* op-ed page apologizing for the newspaper's leading role in stoking the flames of war)."

Judis's prudent skepticism about the pro-war case during the months before the invasion should be a model for journalistic conduct regarding emotional issues of war and peace in all settings. "I opposed the war, and didn't listen to those who claimed to have 'inside information' probably because I had come of age politically during the Vietnam War and had learned then not to trust government justifications for war," he wrote. Unfortunately, few of his colleagues adopted his approach. He related the belated awakening to reality by Lawrence Kaplan, normally one of the media's more insightful analysts of world affairs. "Lawrence had excellent contacts within neo-conservative circles, and told me that, to his astonishment, some people he talked to had already trained their sights on regime change in Iran and Syria. I think that was Lawrence's first inkling that he had gotten on a train to Baghdad with a lot of nutty people."

Little evidence emerged, though, that media leaders drew lasting, appropriate lessons from their profession's substandard performance with regard to the Iraq War. Major media players who had promoted pro-war policies and systematically excluded the analyses and warnings that dissenters expressed, either ignored their own role in the policy fiasco or placed all the blame at the feet of the Bush administration. Partisanship, more than any genuine reappraisal of the pro-war case, may have been the motivating factor.

Recent converts to the anti-war perspective seemed unlikely to apply any lessons of the Iraq War to their coverage of future foreign policy crises. Their conduct was reminiscent of the blinkered conclusions that too many prominent establishment figures adopted after the Vietnam War. One frustrated opponent of U.S. policy in Vietnam voiced the cynical assessment that the appropriate lesson of the Vietnam War for such people seemed to be "don't fight a war in a country named Vietnam."[102] When the United States intervened in such places as Libya and Syria, and returned to Iraq to combat ISIS, William Kristol and other hawks from the original lobbying campaign for war in Iraq frequently appeared on television news shows to discuss what policy Washington should pursue in those new arenas. And once again, proponents of U.S. military action dominated the op-ed pages of the nation's leading newspapers and online sites. American news consumers could be forgiven if they had an overpowering sense of déjà vu. However, once again, too many members of the public would respond favorably to the threat inflation of these media campaigns.

CHAPTER 6
Cheerleading for Humanitarian Crusades: Libya and Syria

Media perspectives during the Balkan wars and the prelude to the U.S.-led invasion of Iraq were characterized by pervasive bias, the promotion of emotional responses, and the framing of complex issues in stark moral terms. Despite the acute embarrassment and damage done to the reputations of some prominent media figures, a similar pattern of willing credulity reemerged with respect to press coverage of the conflicts in Libya and Syria during Barack Obama's administration. Once again, the vast majority of the press cheered, or at best stood by mute, as a U.S. administration misread the political dynamics in the two countries and launched new, ill-advised military interventions.

In time, it became abundantly clear that these policies had produced unexpectedly bad results, worsening the instability and bloodshed in both countries. Yet the media's performance did not appreciably improve. Instead, most reporters and commentators continued to minimize or ignore both the magnitude of the policy failures and Washington's culpability in the resulting debacles.

THE MEDIA DISTORT THE SITUATION IN LIBYA

Another in a long series of uprisings against Libyan dictator Muammar Qaddafi began in early 2011, centered, as were all previous ones, in eastern Libya near the country's second largest city, Benghazi. As the fighting began, American journalists largely echoed the arguments of pro-intervention figures in the U.S. and European governments. Qaddafi, they contended, was a brutal monster who had subjected the Libyan people to a nightmare of oppression and human rights abuses. If he managed to reconquer rebel-controlled regions in eastern Libya, they warned, a bloodbath would ensue; only a Western military intervention could prevent such a humanitarian tragedy.

Not surprisingly, the Libyan insurgents continuously hyped atrocity stories and provided a drumbeat of warnings that Qaddafi would conduct a mass slaughter if the United States and its allies did not intervene militarily. At one point early in the struggle, the insurgents made the wildly inflated claim that government forces had already killed 30,000 civilians.[1] Yet neither U.S. officials nor any prominent reporters bothered to ask how Qaddafi's relatively small, lackluster army, confronting an armed rebellion on multiple fronts, had managed to achieve such a feat in just a two-week period after fighting erupted.

The rebel political leadership issued other outlandish statements and received little or no media pushback. On March 10, 2011, an opposition leader, Mustafa Abdul Jalil, asserted that Qaddafi's regime would kill 500,000 people unless the UN or the Western powers promptly imposed a no-fly zone to ground the dictator's fleet of fighter planes and helicopters.[2] Western officials and media outlets accepted comments and predictions like this at face value and regurgitated them to a somnolent but generally credulous American public.

As they had in the lead-up to the U.S.-led crusades in Bosnia and Kosovo, Western activists assisted the insurgents by stoking speculation and hyperbole about the humanitarian stakes. Dennis Ross, a senior Obama administration adviser, warned that 100,000 people would be killed in Benghazi if Qaddafi succeeded in conquering the city.[3] Such a monstrous total would have been one-seventh of Benghazi's population. But as Professor Rajan Menon later pointed out in his book, *The Conceit of Humanitarian Intervention*, Ross made his allegation "without a shred of evidence."[4]

Very few journalists questioned the apocalyptic narrative, even though plenty of logic and evidence indicated that it greatly exaggerated the danger. Yale University Professor David Bromwich pointed out that "Qaddafi had marched from the west to the east of the country . . . without the occurrence of any such massacre, and the Pentagon and U.S. intelligence assigned low credibility to the threat."[5] Menon also observed that the regime had not killed civilians en masse throughout the multi-week military offensive that brought Qaddafi's forces to the outskirts of Benghazi.

Such evidence should at least have generated some media caution and skepticism about predictions of wholesale slaughter and possible genocide. Greater caution was especially appropriate given the track record of exaggerated, and in some cases utterly false, atrocity warnings and accounts during the Persian Gulf War and the Balkan wars. Yet such healthy wariness was once again in short supply throughout the U.S. and other Western news media.

Most of the mainstream press ignored evidence that Qaddafi had approached foreign intermediaries, including retired Rear Admiral Charles Kubic, retired General Wesley Clark, and even former British prime minister Tony Blair, about concluding a cease fire with insurgent forces and commencing negotiations on a political settlement. Stories on these initiatives appeared in both the *Washington Times* and the *New York Times*, but they gained surprisingly little traction with the rest of the mainstream media or with the Obama administration.[6]

When NATO launched its air strikes on Qaddafi's forces in mid-March 2011, the *New York Times* editorial board cheered.[7] The editors saw the military action as "an extraordinary moment in recent history. The United Nations, the United States and the Europeans dithered for an agonizingly long time and then—with the rebels' last redoubt, Benghazi, about to fall—acted with astonishing speed to endorse a robust mandate that goes far beyond a simple no-fly zone."

Key NATO allies and the American news media undertook a mutually supportive effort to pressure the Obama administration into being more pro-active against Qaddafi. In their respective memoirs, Secretary of State Hillary Clinton and Secretary of Defense Robert M. Gates reveal how those allies prodded the reluctant Obama administration into making the fateful decision to intervene militarily in Libya. Clinton described the promotional blitz by major U.S. allies, especially France. "When I met with French President Nicolas Sarkozy, he urged the United States to support international military intervention to stop Qaddafi's advance toward the rebel stronghold of Benghazi in eastern Libya. I was sympathetic," she recalled, "but not convinced."[8]

Members of the Arab League, who had long loathed the volatile, populist Qaddafi, also pressed for international intervention. The league included such close U.S. security partners as Saudi Arabia, Qatar, and the United Arab Emirates. But Clinton noted that at a meeting of the G-8 economic powers "the Europeans were even more gung ho. I got an earful about military intervention from Sarkozy." Pro-intervention lobbying from Britain impressed her even more. "When I saw British Foreign Secretary William Hague at dinner that night, he pressed the case for action." If Hague thought military action in Libya was necessary, "that counted for a lot."[9]

Gates also emphasized the impact of the calls for military action coming from key NATO allies on administration leaders. Arab League advocacy "and strong British and French pressure for NATO to act, I think, together persuaded the president that the United States would need to take the lead" in organizing "a military campaign to stop Qaddafi."[10]

Mainstream media accounts in the United States were friendly, bordering on laudatory regarding France's increasingly insistent calls for Western military action against Qaddafi. The *Washington Post*'s Edward Cody prominently included an emotional appeal by French Foreign Minister Alain Juppé, which implicitly evoked the 1930s. "This is urgent," Juppé declared on his blog, adding, "We have often seen in our contemporary history that the weakness of democracies leaves the field open to dictatorships. It is not too late to defy this rule."[11]

On the surface, the language of the resolution that finally cleared the UN Security Council authorized a limited mission, with the primary justification being the need to prevent civilian suffering. Indeed, the emphasis on protecting civilians was the reason that Russia and China withheld their vetoes, casting abstentions instead. The "protect civilians" provision soon proved to be nothing more than a cynical fig leaf. Once the intervention began, the press ignored evidence that Obama administration officials had misrepresented both the scope and purpose of the mission. Almost immediately, U.S. and other NATO planes, as well as cruise missiles, began to attack Qaddafi's air defenses and other targets that posed no threat to civilians but had everything to do with which side would win the war.

Secretary Gates later admitted as much in his memoir, noting that "as the list of bombing targets steadily grew, it became obvious that very few targets were off-limits," and that NATO was intent on getting rid of Qaddafi.[12] Yet U.S. leaders, from President Obama on down, still clung to the official humanitarian rationale, even when it became obvious that the goal was far broader.[13] Very few members of the press challenged the administration on the yawning gap between its official rationale and the facts on the ground. One looks in vain for accounts in the mainstream press at the time pointing out that the administration had misled Congress, the American people, and the international community about the real purpose of the "humanitarian" intervention. Such criticisms would only emerge much later, and even then, they were few and far between.[14]

Media coverage of Qaddafi's ouster and its immediate aftermath was even more emotional and one-sided than the treatment of NATO's military intervention itself. *New York Times* columnist Nicholas Kristof gushed about how the people he encountered in Libya loved America. "Americans are not often heroes in the Arab world, but as nonstop celebrations unfold here in the Libyan capital I keep running into ordinary people who learn where I'm from and then fervently repeat variants of the same phrase: 'Thank you, America!'" Unlike some supporters of the intervention, Kristof at least made the pro forma caveat that things could still go wrong, but he saw the Libya intervention as an attractive model for future regime-change missions. "[T]o me Libya is a reminder that sometimes it is possible to use military tools to advance humanitarian causes." The Libyans, Kristof contended, "overwhelmingly favored our multilateral military intervention."[15]

As usual, the *New York Times* became a reliable platform for government officials and their ideological allies to express pro-intervention views regarding a regime-change war. Ivo H. Daalder, U.S. ambassador to NATO, and Admiral James Stavridis were at least as euphoric in their op-ed as Kristof was about the outcome of the Libya mission. Describing the intervention as "an extraordinary job, well done," they termed it "an historic victory for the people of Libya who, with NATO's help, transformed their country from an international pariah into a nation with the potential to become a productive partner with the West."[16]

Only a few voices dissented from the media's chorus of celebration. Glenn Greenwald expressed his astonishment and dismay at the lack of realism or even minimal skepticism on the part of policymakers. Writing in *Salon* in early September, he stated, "One key applicable lesson from Iraq is that it's incredibly foolish and premature to declare victory upon the mere removal of the dictator; whether the war is a 'victory' or was wisely fought depends upon the resolution of an array of unanswered questions, particularly what follows. Indeed, disregarding this lesson due to the eagerness of war proponents to throw celebratory vindication parties for themselves is worse than foolish; it is downright destructive, as it causes the victory-drunk foreign power to think its job is done and thus ignore the vast destruction, chaos, serious uncertainties, ugliness and humanitarian suffering the war spawned."[17] On another occasion he lamented, "I'm genuinely astounded at the pervasive willingness to view what has happened in Libya as some sort of grand triumph even though virtually none of the information needed to make that assessment is known yet, including: how many civilians have died, how much more bloodshed will there be, what will be needed to stabilize that country and, most of all, what type of regime will replace (Moammar) Gadhafi?"[18]

As post-Qaddafi Libya descended into all-too-predictable dysfunction and chaos, Greenwald was again one of the few media figures to predict the likely outcome. He asked perceptively, "how much longer will it be before we hear that military intervention in Libya is (again) necessary, this time to control the anti-US extremists who are now armed and empowered by virtue of the first intervention? US military interventions are most adept at ensuring that future US military interventions will always be necessary."[19] That prediction couldn't have been more accurate. A little more than three years after Greenwald published his article, the United States initiated a campaign of airstrikes to prevent

ISIS from consolidating and expanding a beachhead that it had established in the Libyan city of Sirte the previous year.[20]

The Libya intervention came back to bite the United States even earlier. On September 11, 2012, extremist militias attacked the U.S. consulate in Benghazi, killing Ambassador Christopher Stevens and three other Americans (likely CIA operatives).[21] The GOP-controlled House of Representatives launched an array of investigations into the incident, focusing on apparent security lapses and aspects of the administration's initial explanation of the attack, which contained significant inconsistencies and contradictions. The investigations culminated in lengthy hearings by a Select Committee on Benghazi in 2014 and 2015 and a final report issued the following June.

Congressional Democrats condemned the decision to create the Select Committee, and they briefly threatened to boycott any hearings. Writing in May 2014, *Washington Post* columnist Charles Krauthammer wrote, "The Democrats are portraying the not-yet-even-constituted House Select Committee on Benghazi as nothing but a partisan exercise. They are even considering boycotting the hearings to delegitimize them." Krauthammer didn't think that a boycott would fatally impair the investigation, but he did contend that it "would give the Obama-protective media a further reason to ignore Benghazi."[22]

He was right. Whether because of media favoritism toward a Democratic administration or their all-too-common partiality toward the State Department, the CIA, and other national security agencies, most of the press dismissed the congressional inquiry as nothing more than petty partisanship on the part of Republicans.[23] When a fired GOP staffer asserted in 2015 that he was terminated because he had voiced complaints that the proceedings were partisan, media accounts eagerly embraced that allegation as definitive evidence.[24] The committee report ultimately issued in June 2016 was certainly underwhelming. Although it documented some failures of security protocols, it failed to establish evidence of wrongdoing or malfeasance on the part of Secretary Clinton or the State Department.[25]

Partisan motives were certainly a part of the GOP-led investigations.[26] By all appearances, the top priority of Republican legislators was to prove that Clinton had failed to provide adequate security for Stevens and the consulate staff and then tried to cover up the blunder. The Republican majority's underlying motive was not terribly subtle either: it was to injure her probable candidacy for president in 2016.

But such deficiencies did not mean that no investigation was warranted—the position that too many journalists adopted. Both Clinton's GOP critics and most of the news media failed to address broader and more important questions about the nature of the U.S. relationship with various militias in eastern Libya, including the Islamist militia that carried out the Benghazi attack. Those forces appeared to have been an integral part of the insurgency against Qaddafi that Washington had backed, funded, and equipped. And Chris Stevens had been the principal liaison between the U.S. government and the Benghazi-based insurgents in the months leading up to Qaddafi's overthrow.[27]

That background, in turn, raised several other questions. Did U.S. officials vet those groups to try to exclude extreme Islamist elements? If not, why not? If so, why did the process fail so spectacularly that the United States ended up with a burned-out consulate and a dead ambassador? That so few reporters bothered to investigate and demand answers from Obama administration policymakers was a dereliction of professional journalistic standards.

One reporter, Sharyl Attkisson at CBS, did express frustration at the passivity and lack of curiosity or skepticism on the part of her compatriots in the press.

> For months, the Obama administration had dismissed all questions as partisan witch-hunting. And why not? That approach has proven successful at least among some colleagues in the news media. They're apparently satisfied with the limited answers. They aren't curious about the gaping holes. The contradictions. They're part of the club that's decided that only agenda-driven Republicans would be curious about all of that. These journalists don't need to ask questions about Benghazi at the White House press briefings, at Attorney General Eric Holder's public appearances, or during President Obama's limited media availabilities. It might make the administration mad. It might even prompt [administration officials] to threaten the "access" of uncooperative journalists.[28]

Attkisson's lamentations about media passivity and negligence toward the Benghazi incident could just as easily serve as an indictment of so much of the journalistic community's performance concerning numerous aspects of U.S. foreign policy over the decades. The coverage of the Libyan military intervention and its aftermath certainly seemed to lack curiosity and diligence. Journalists allowed their ideological and partisan biases to determine their focus and priorities.

Long after the Benghazi episode, members of the media remained willfully blind about the damage that U.S. policy had caused in Libya. A February 2020 report from the United Nations bluntly conveys the extent of the continuing chaos in Libya and the suffering it had caused. Yacoub El Hillo, the UN humanitarian coordinator for Libya, is quoted as saying that the impact of the country's nine-year internecine war on civilians was "incalculable."[29]

Although Libya had experienced extensive internal strife since the United States and its NATO allies helped insurgents overthrow Qaddafi's regime in 2011, the UN report confirmed that matters had grown noticeably worse over the previous year. In the spring of 2019, the Benghazi-based Libyan National Army, led by one-time CIA asset Field Marshal Khalifa Haftar (sometimes spelled Hifter), launched a military offensive against the UN-recognized Government of National Accord based in Tripoli. Haftar's offensive initially seemed likely to prevail, but it soon bogged down, and a bloody stalemate ensued.

In addition to the rising violence, the Libya conflict increasingly became a proxy war involving various Middle East powers as well as Russia.[30] Haftar obtained weapons, funds, and other backing from several countries, most notably Egypt and the United Arab Emirates. The Government of National Accord, on the other hand, received diplomatic and financial support from the UN and most Western governments and enjoyed ever-stronger backing from Turkey. In early February 2020, Ankara significantly escalated its involvement in Libya's strife when the parliament authorized the deployment of Turkish forces to Libya.[31] Russian mercenaries were already fighting there on Haftar's behalf, so the international implications of the country's civil war grew.

There was little question that post-Qaddafi Libya was a chaotic mess. Once again, however, Western news outlets strained to portray a complex foreign conflict as a contest between good and evil factions. Journalists intensified their hostility to Haftar's cause and designated him as the villain in the latest phase of Libya's internal strife. The *New York Times* seized the lead in the media campaign to discredit Haftar. Several prominent stories in the newspaper's pages highlighted his authoritarianism and brutality.[32]

The problem is not that such accounts of Haftar's rule were inaccurate; most of the allegations against him were supported by credible evidence. But the implication that his villainy was unique in Libya is misleading. Competing militias also committed an assortment of crimes against civilians throughout the post-2011 period. In 2013, Andrew Engel, a scholar at the Washington Institute, documented the growing Libyan chaos, including the role of armed militias in committing extensive human rights abuses. Engel contended that "to make up for its weakness following the revolution, the nascent central government cultivated semiofficial militias" to "project state authority." Many rebel brigades joined one such militia, Libya Shield, as intact units, and "Libya Shield has become an army unto itself." The would-be government dispatched that force to the Kufra district in April 2012 to halt clashes between Zwai Arabs and the minority Tebu tribe. Numerous bloody incidents ensued, and the Tebu accused the militia of atrocities bordering on "an extermination policy."[33] Engel also noted a June 8, 2013, clash in Benghazi between Libya Shield and protestors demanding its dissolution. He emphasized that the protests targeted "an Islamist militia that, despite its semiofficial government imprimatur, largely oversees its own agenda and is led by figures with loose ties to al-Qaeda."[34]

The insurgents that the United States helped bring to power were equally unpleasant in their dealings with the Coptic Christian religious faction. Coptic leaders accused Libya Shield of running a torture center and targeting people with cross tattoos.[35] Apparently ISIS was not the only bane of the dwindling Christian community in Libya. All of these incidents occurred before Haftar became a key player in the country's internal fighting. The *New York Times*' and other media outlets' portrayal of him as the sole, or even primary, source of Libya's troubles was misleading.

Although they were slow to do so, Western journalists eventually did a tolerable job of covering human rights abuses inside Libya. Coverage of the massive number of refugees trying to flee the country, though, was spotty at best. By early 2020, an estimated 650,000 migrants and internally displaced refugees clogged detention centers in Libya.[36] Tens of thousands more had tried to flee across the Mediterranean—many in leaky, overcrowded boats.[37] No one was able to establish a reliable estimate for the number of victims who perished in those attempts. These tragedies received some attention in the mainstream U.S. press, but the number of stories in the leading publications was surprisingly sparse.

The overall scope of coverage regarding post-Qaddafi Libyan affairs also remained disturbingly limited, although it grew once Haftar mounted his offensive in 2019. The one thing that most members of the press establishment remained steadfastly unwilling to do was explain to readers and viewers how the widespread chaos in Libya began—much less who was responsible for the tragedy regarding human rights abuses, the plight of refugees, and a variety of other issues.

Reporters and commentators notably failed to make explicit connections between U.S. policy and those horrid developments. Writing in 2016, *New York Times* reporter Mark Landler pithily described how Libya "has descended into a state of *Mad Max*–like anarchy." Post-Qaddafi Libya is now "a seedbed for militancy that has spread west and south across Africa." Moreover, the country has "become the most important Islamic State stronghold outside of Syria and Iraq" and sends out "waves of desperate migrants across the Mediterranean, where they drown in capsized vessels."[38] But Landler held back from indicting U.S. policy for such an awful outcome.

Other analysts were even less inclined to fault Washington. A passage in a 2016 *New York Times* story by reporters Jo Becker and Scott Shane seemingly put the blame on Libyan insurgents for having misled U.S. officials. "Mrs. Clinton was won over" to the position of endorsing a U.S.-led military intervention, the reporters contended. "Opposition leaders 'said all the right things about supporting democracy and inclusivity and building Libyan institutions, providing some hope that we might be able to pull this off,' said Philip H. Gordon, one of her assistant secretaries. 'They gave us what we wanted to hear. And you do want to believe.'"[39]

A few refreshing analyses in the media were less accepting of the self-serving excuses. Daniel Larison, at the time a senior editor at *The American Conservative*, pointed out what was terribly wrong about such a defense.

> "Wanting to believe" in dubious or obviously bad causes in other countries is one of the biggest problems with ideologically-driven interventionists from both parties. They aren't just willing to take sides in foreign conflicts, but they are looking for an excuse to join them. As long as they can get representatives of the opposition to repeat the required phrases and pay lip service to the "right things," they will do their best to drag the U.S. into a conflict in which it has nothing at stake.[40]

David Bromwich likewise believed the negative results were directly attributable to Washington's regime-change war in Libya and was unsparing in his assessment. He stated that the U.S.-NATO action to overthrow Qaddafi with the hope of a democratic replacement "has turned out to be a catastrophe with strong resemblance to Iraq—a catastrophe smaller in degree but hardly less consequential in its ramifications, from North Africa to the Middle East to southern Europe."[41]

Such assessments were very much in the minority, however. Convenient amnesia characterized most of the mainstream media's postwar coverage of the Obama administration policy in Libya, and it bordered on being an outright whitewash. Indeed, such indulgent perspectives were a common feature in press treatments of the Obama administration's overall foreign policy.

One issue graphically illustrates the reluctance to assign appropriate responsibility for the Libya tragedy. In late 2017, Western reporters belatedly discovered that a slave trade in captured black Africans had become a feature of "liberated" post-Qaddafi Libya. A devastating November 28, 2017, account by FAIR's Ben Norton, however, documented the mainstream media's ongoing willingness to minimize

U.S. and NATO responsibility for the tragic outcome of the regime-change war in Libya. In particular, Western journalists largely ignored that war's connection to the resumption of slave trading in that country.[42] "The American and British media have awakened to the grim reality in Libya, where African refugees are for sale in open-air slave markets," Norton acknowledged. "Yet a crucial detail in this scandal has been downplayed or even ignored in many corporate media reports: the role of the North Atlantic Treaty Organization in bringing slavery to the North African nation."

NATO supported an array of rebel groups in Libya, Norton noted, "many of which were dominated by Islamist extremists and harbored violently racist views. Militants in the NATO-backed rebel stronghold of Misrata even referred to themselves in 2011 as 'the brigade for purging slaves, black skin'—an eerie foreshadowing of the horrors that were to come.'[43] Despite that background, too many Western journalists "have largely forgotten about the key role NATO played in destroying Libya's government, destabilizing the country and empowering human traffickers." Even the few news reports that acknowledged NATO's complicity in Libya's chaos since the 2011 intervention "do not go a step further and detail the well-documented, violent racism of the NATO-backed Libyan rebels who ushered in slavery after ethnically cleansing and committing brutal crimes against black Libyans."

Norton singled out a November 14, 2017, CNN report for criticism. Despite the flashy, multimedia features, he contended, "something was missing: The 1,000-word story made no mention of NATO, or the 2011 war that destroyed Libya's government, or Muammar Qadhafi, or any kind of historical and political context whatsoever." The same omission, Norton contended, occurred in a series of subsequent CNN news stories about human trafficking in Libya. "Reports by the *BBC* (11/18/17), the *New York Times* (11/20/17), *Deutsche Welle* (reprinted by *USA Today*, 11/23/17) and the *Associated Press* (reprinted by the *Washington Post*, 11/23/17) also failed to mention the 2011 war, let alone NATO's role in it."

Later news accounts about instability and repression in Libya exhibited a similar desire to avoid discussing the destructive impact that

NATO's policies had on Libyan society. The otherwise excellent article in the February 20, 2020, *New York Times*, documenting the oppression in the portion of Libya that Haftar's forces controlled, devoted only one sentence to NATO's role: "[Libya] has been in turmoil since an Arab Spring revolt and NATO's intervention toppled Colonel el-Qaddafi nine years ago."[44] That was the extent of any acknowledgment in a nearly 2,000-word article of the alliance's responsibility for Libya's persistent human tragedy.

When they participate in such a conspiracy of silence, journalists shirk their duty as watchdogs alerting the public to government incompetence or misconduct. Whatever the Obama administration's motives and goals in launching the military intervention that ousted Qaddafi, the results were indisputably catastrophic. Yet Obama, Secretary of State Clinton, and key advisers such as Susan Rice and Samantha Power steadfastly refused to acknowledge their blunders or apologize to the suffering Libyan people for those mistakes. Power subsequently offered the facile excuse, "We could hardly expect to have a crystal ball when it came to accurately predicting outcomes in places where the culture was not our own."[45] Dexter Filkins, who reviewed her memoir in the *New Yorker*, commented that "this sounds like an argument for not intervening at all."[46] His conclusion would certainly seem to make more sense than hers.

The attempts by Power and other Obama administration officials to exonerate themselves were bad enough; the media's continuing willingness to let them evade responsibility is worse. Articles in late 2020 and early 2021 about the ongoing turmoil in Libya still failed to provide a meaningful picture of Washington's culpability for the debacle that its supposedly humanitarian intervention created.

Even Deeper Bias in Coverage of the Syrian War

For most portions of the media, the Syrian civil war that erupted in 2011 was indisputably a fight between good and evil, just as they had seen and portrayed earlier conflicts in the Balkans, Iraq, and Libya. Their perception of the struggle in Syria often seemed akin to the characters and plot in the 1999 feature film *Dudley Do-Right* (based on the earlier animated television series). In the standard media narrative, Syrian dictator Bashar al-Assad was archvillain Snidely Whiplash, while Syrian insurgents were his innocent, democracy-seeking victims—the equivalent of sweet Nell being tied to the railroad tracks. The United States, of course, was supposed to be the noble, idealistic Dudley Do-Right, riding to the rescue.

Members of the media blandly accepted the Obama administration's portrayal of U.S. involvement as motivated by humanitarian concerns. That official rationale, though, could not hold up to serious scrutiny. Washington's motives for backing the insurgency were not primarily revulsion at Assad's treatment of his people. After all, the U.S. government has repeatedly sided with repressive regimes around the world when doing so appeared to benefit more tangible American economic and geostrategic interests.[47] Indeed, even as it sought Assad's ouster, the Obama administration continued to maintain a close relationship with Saudi Arabia and Riyadh's Gulf allies—some of the most brutal, autocratic governments on the planet.

Something more than humanitarian impulses impelled Washington to aid the rebellion seeking to overthrow Assad. A major reason why Washington backed the Turkish and Saudi-initiated policy of supporting the insurgents was to weaken Iran by depriving the clerical regime of a crucial ally. Some of the most avid advocates in the press for a U.S.-led regime-change campaign in Syria—including *Washington Post* columnist Max Boot, *The Atlantic*'s Jeffrey Goldberg, and former assistant secretary of state Jamie Rubin—pushed that argument repeatedly.[48]

All major Sunni powers and the United States shared an intense hostility toward Tehran, and Assad had run afoul of their desire to curb, if not fatally undermine, Iran's regional influence. But in supporting the anti-Assad insurgency, the United States helped destabilize yet another Middle East country and strengthen some highly questionable political and ideological forces. Unfortunately, the vast majority of mainstream press accounts missed or deliberately ignored that dimension.

Those accounts also ignored or minimized the crucial religious dimension of the Syria conflict. The insurgency was overwhelmingly Sunni, while Assad's supporters were a loose coalition of religious minorities

consisting mainly of Christians, Druze, and Assad's own Alawites—a
Shiite offshoot—who feared their likely fate under a Sunni-dominated
successor government.[49] What erupted in 2011 quickly became a largely
Sunni Arab bid to overthrow that "coalition of minorities" regime. Even
Hillary Clinton, a staunch supporter of the rebellion, conceded that "the
rebels were predominantly Sunnis."[50] The Sunni Arab hatred of the apos-
tate Alawites was especially virulent and had exploded into violence on
several occasions in the past.[51] Veteran U.S. diplomat Chas W. Freeman Jr.
captured a key reason why some Syrian factions rallied around Assad,
despite his many character flaws and ugly policies. Freeman believed that
"a lot of Syrians with no love for Mr. Assad had formed a well-founded
fear of who and what might succeed him."[52]

Very little of that important religious and political context appeared
in the American news media. Analysts denied or ignored the radical
Islamist orientation of several rebel factions; some went so far as to simply regurgitate Obama administration propaganda, which claimed that
the groups Washington backed were "moderates." American enthusiasts
about the Syrian rebellion exhibited great reluctance to acknowledge
rebel abuses and the extremist nature of some insurgent factions. Occasionally, especially during the siege of the northern city of Aleppo by
Syrian government forces, stories in the American press painted a picture
that almost reversed reality.

A small minority of more skeptical journalists sharply criticized
their colleagues for such naïve or biased conduct. The *Boston Globe*'s
Stephen Kinzer excoriated the prevailing coverage of the Syrian civil
war, especially the fighting around Aleppo. In early 2016, the Syrian
Army, backed by Russian air support, launched an offensive to push
the militants out of Aleppo. But according to Kinzer, "much of the
American press is reporting the opposite of what is actually happening.
Many news reports suggest that Aleppo has been a 'liberated zone' for
three years but is now being pulled back into misery." To the contrary,
Kinzer noted that "for three years, violent militias have run Aleppo.
Their rule began with a wave of repression. They posted notices warn-
ing residents: 'Don't send your children to school. If you do, we will get
the backpack and you will get the coffin.'"[53] Washington-based reporters

"used terminology that attempted to portray even the staunchly Islamist faction, Jabhat al-Nusra, as being composed "of 'rebels' or 'moderates,' not that it was the local al-Qaeda franchise."[54]

Georgetown University senior fellow Paul R. Pillar likewise was critical of much of the Aleppo coverage, finding it excessively emotional and one-sided.[55] British journalist Patrick Cockburn contended that far more propaganda than genuine news was coming out of Aleppo. Because it was extremely dangerous for Western news personnel to operate in the area, he noted, most outlets were relying on locals to provide information, a process that guaranteed blatant bias. "The foreign media has allowed—through naivety or self-interest—people who could only operate with the permission of al-Qaeda-type groups such as Jabhat al-Nusra and Ahrar al-Sham to dominate the news agenda."[56]

The reliance on rebel personnel both for access to key areas of Syria and as sources of information about the fighting was an insidious problem that went well beyond the situation in Aleppo. CBS *60 Minutes* correspondent Scott Pelley presented several major stories about the Assad regime's attacks on civilians. One aired on December 18, 2016, and focused on the rescue efforts of Syria's White Helmets (see subsequent section).[57] "The airstrikes, day and night, obliterate apartments and shatter the nerves. Often, the bombs are not aimed at military targets—they're not aimed at all—just a barrel of shrapnel and TNT, heaved from a helicopter, onto any neighborhood the Assad dictatorship does not control," Pelley intoned. Later in the segment, he asserted that "Syria has descended into murder on an industrial scale." The message was clear throughout: Assad is a genocidal monster slaughtering innocent civilians. People interviewed were identified simply as journalists, doctors, rescue workers, and so on. Nowhere was there even a hint about political affiliations or their stance on the civil war, although the segment was filmed in a city that had long been under rebel control.

Another *60 Minutes* program, which aired on August 5, 2018, highlighted Syrian government attacks on hospitals and the hellish difficulties medical personnel faced in trying to treat the victims.[58] The introduction was a less-than-balanced treatment of the complex Syrian civil war. "Bashar al-Assad destroyed Syria in order to remain its president. The dictator,

son of a dictator, has committed every war crime on the books; bombing civilians, gassing neighborhoods, torturing prisoners. An estimated
500,000 people have been killed in the civil war and 12 million have
been forced from their homes." Apparently, the rebels were responsible
for none of that suffering in Pelley's view, nor apparently had they committed any atrocities. As if those comments were not enough to make the
news coverage a morality play, Pelley added that "standing in Assad's way
are courageous doctors, many of them American volunteers, risking their
lives to heal the wounds of war." His closing sentence in the program
conveyed the message even more bluntly. "The war against the hospitals
is designed to break the will of the rebellion. But as long as some will
fight for mercy, there is reason for all to hope." There wasn't much doubt
about which side of the Syrian civil war Scott Pelley was on. Yet again,
a prominent American journalist served as a propagandist for one side in
a foreign conflict.

Still another *60 Minutes* episode, on August 19, 2018, updated a segment that originally aired in February and conveyed a similar message
about the Syrian government's beastly behavior. This time it focused on
the alleged use of chemical weapons, especially a 2017 incident in the
village of Khan Shaykhun.[59] That incident led Donald Trump's administration to launch missile strikes against a Syrian air force base in retaliation (see the following paragraph).

The images of burned and maimed people, including children, in
the *60 Minutes* segments were heartrending. But in all three programs,
Pelley ignored or quickly glossed over the point that he and his crew
were entirely dependent on rebel forces for access to the areas in which
those apparent atrocities took place. The closest he came to a meaningful disclosure was a brief statement in the program on chemical
weapons attacks: "We traveled into the province where Khan Shaykhun
is located. Idlib province, largely controlled by an Islamist extremist
group, Hai'yat Tahrir al-Sham." The programs on the White Helmets
and the hospital attacks didn't even give that pro forma notice; they
failed to inform viewers not only that an armed insurgent faction was
totally in charge of access, but that the group in question was one of the
extreme Islamist militias.

Such omissions were especially troubling because rebel personnel provided all the witnesses that Pelley interviewed—another key piece of information at which he barely hinted—and in most cases insurgent leaders carefully watched over the proceedings. Several of the interviews had a painfully staged quality to them. In one case, a young boy with an amputated leg, who had featured prominently in an earlier *60 Minutes* program, just happened to show up during filming of the follow-up episode more than two years later when Pelley and his camera crew were at a hospital in rebel-controlled territory to cover the hospital's treatment and rehabilitation efforts. One had to be incredibly trusting to believe that such a meeting was not carefully orchestrated. Yet Pelley never voiced the slightest skepticism at the time or in his subsequent voiceover about that scene, or about any of the other incidents, even those that were the most emotionally inflammatory. It was hard to escape the conclusion that Pelley and *60 Minutes* were willing conduits for Syrian rebel propaganda.

WHITEWASHING THE WHITE HELMETS?

Pelley's December 2016 program epitomized the media bias on a related issue in the Syrian civil war: the role of the Syria Civil Defense (SCD) organization, the so-called White Helmets. Officially, the SCD is a volunteer, charitable organization devoted to rescuing and treating victims of the fighting in Syria, and it certainly has played that role, saving numerous lives in the process. But the SCD is not like Doctors without Borders, which has a well-deserved, rigorously maintained reputation for not taking sides in the armed struggles occurring in the countries where it operates. The medical relief work of that group is not confined to alleviating the suffering of only one faction in an armed conflict.

The situation with White Helmets is more complicated. The organization has worked to save the lives of thousands of civilians caught up in Syria's bloody civil strife. But the White Helmets definitely do not embrace political neutrality; despite their official assertions, they openly back the insurgency against the Assad government. For example, the organization repeatedly called for the United Nations or the Western powers to impose a no-fly zone over portions of Syria. That demand is a longstanding political and military objective of insurgent leaders to neutralize the Assad government's principal military advantage: total air power dominance.[60]

In addition to their entanglement in Syria's civil war, the White Helmets have worked with rebel factions to guide Western news crews to scenes of carnage and provide access to witnesses to alleged atrocities by government forces, thus shaping the narrative given to Western news consumers. The White Helmets especially were key sources of disputed evidence that the Syrian government engaged in chemical weapons attacks on civilians, which will be discussed subsequently.

Independent investigative journalist Ben Swann, winner of two Emmys and the Edward R. Murrow Award, raised some pertinent questions about the origins of the White Helmets and the group's apparent political orientation. "Are they a legitimate organization," Swann asked, "or pawns, funded for the purpose of regime change?"[61] Although the SCD received significant contributions from private individuals, foundations, and charities, Western governments (including those in Washington, London, and Berlin) also provided generous funding. Perhaps by mere coincidence those same governments also were leading the effort to assist insurgent factions trying to overthrow Assad. Of special note, the United States released funds for the White Helmets in June 2018, though other U.S. humanitarian aid to Syria remained suspended.[62]

The background of the principal founder of the White Helmets, James Le Mesurier, and the group's origins should also have raised some questions among inquiring reporters. The organization's official website states that the group was founded in early 2014, though evidence indicates that it was operating months earlier. According to Scott Ritter, a former U.S. Marine Corps intelligence officer and a member of the UN weapons inspection team in Iraq in the years before the U.S.-led invasion of that country, "the organizational underpinnings of the White Helmets can be sourced to a March 2013 meeting in Istanbul."[63] There, Le Mesurier met with representatives of the Syrian National Council, the umbrella political organization for the rebel factions waging the war against Assad. Subsequent media stories about the organization should have paid more attention to the composition of that early meeting. Also worthy of attention was Le Mesurier's background, which was decidedly not in the field of humanitarian relief. He was a former British Army officer and military contractor with a long record of direct involvement in British and NATO covert and military interventions, including missions in Kenya, Yemen, Iraq, and Libya.[64]

As Swann noted, an especially important funder of the White Helmets was Mayday Rescue, "a Washington, D.C. based contractor that was awarded $128.5 million in January 2013 to support 'a peaceful transition to a democratic and stable Syria' as part of USAID's Syria regional program." At least $32 million in Mayday Rescue funding had been transferred to the White Helmets as of February 2018. Swann stated that the firm "has been funded by USAID for years, and carries a record of failures in supporting so-called humanitarian interventions, including in Libya."[65] At the least, that kind of long-standing, cozy association between ostensibly private, purely humanitarian organizations and a U.S. government agency that has facilitated questionable foreign policy objectives elsewhere in the world should have generated some press inquiries regarding both Mayday Rescue and the White Helmets.

Yet investigative reports such as Swann's that raised even the slightest questions about the White Helmets' parentage and apparent policy agenda were exceedingly rare. Stories in the leading mainstream outlets were overwhelmingly favorable. *The White Helmets*, a laudatory account of the organization and its work, even received the Academy Award for "best documentary, short subject" in 2017.[66]

BIAS PERVADES MEDIA ANALYSES OF SYRIAN AFFAIRS

Media treatments of the humanitarian issues in Syria's civil war showed a pronounced imbalance. In her role as moderator of the second debate in the 2016 presidential election campaign, Martha Raddatz, chief global affairs correspondent for ABC News, seemed to epitomize the defective model that Kinzer and Pillar highlighted. "Just days ago, the State Department called for a war crimes investigation of the Syrian regime of Bashar al-Assad and its ally, Russia, for their bombardment of

Aleppo," Raddatz began. "So this next question comes through social media through Facebook. Diane from Pennsylvania asks, if you were president, what would you do about Syria and the humanitarian crisis in Aleppo? Isn't it a lot like the Holocaust when the U.S. waited too long before we helped?"[67] Framing the Aleppo issue in that fashion implied that the rebels in eastern Aleppo were innocent victims of Russian and Syrian regime savagery and certainly did not encourage a balanced discussion.

A *Washington Post* op-ed by Brookings Institution fellow Leon Wieseltier provides an even more blatant example of the over-the-top treatment of the Aleppo situation that Kinzer and Pillar criticized. Wieseltier's piece begins with an allegation about "the extermination of Aleppo and its people." He invokes the teachings of Holocaust survivor and human rights activist Elie Wiesel, reminding us that standing by while a repetition of Auschwitz and Rwanda takes place is unacceptable.[68] As Pillar noted, the rest of the op-ed proceeds "in a comparably black-and-white and overwrought vein," with disparagements of President Obama mixed in for not taking more decisive action to back the anti-Assad forces. Yet the newspaper's editors apparently had no problem displaying such a simplistic piece on its pages. Giving prominence to Wieseltier's biased, inflammatory "analysis" in one of the world's elite newspapers did not contribute to meaningful public understanding of the Syrian civil war.

A July 2016 report from Amnesty International painted a far different picture than the pro-rebel versions of Raddatz, Wieseltier, and others in the media. The report also tended to validate many of Kinzer's assessments about Aleppo. Amnesty's findings confirmed that al-Nusra and allied "armed groups operating in Aleppo, Idleb and surrounding areas in the north of Syria have carried out a chilling wave of abductions, torture and summary killings."[69] Strangely, while Amnesty investigators were able to uncover a wave of such incidents, Western journalists operating in the same area apparently saw well-behaved insurgents simply trying to survive the brutal bombing and shelling campaign that Syrian government forces waged.

Incidents of rebel war crimes were hardly limited to Aleppo. Human Rights Watch documented another episode of rebel atrocities during the autumn of 2013 in another part of the country. A coalition of Islamist forces—including Jabhat al-Nusra, Ahrar al-Sham, and ISIS—launched an offensive into the Alawite heartland near the Mediterranean coast. At one point, the militias came within 20 kilometers of Assad's hometown, Qardaha, before loyalist forces drove them back. Human Rights Watch reported that some 190 civilians were killed, including at least 67 whom the rebels summarily executed.[70] Although the militant groups all denied responsibility, Human Rights Watch confirmed that they were the perpetrators. The credibility of the denials eroded badly when al-Nusra publicly executed a prominent Alawite sheik who had been captured by another Islamist faction, Harakat Sham al-Islam.[71]

In addition to such outright atrocities, extremist Sunni militias vigorously pursued the ethnic cleansing of Alawites as part of their agenda. In one province, Tartous, in western Syria's Alawite heartland, the population had been 90 percent Alawite before the war. That figure dropped to 75 percent by July 2012 following the initial rounds of combat. After intensified fighting later that year, the level was down to 60 percent.[72] News stories about those incidents, though, were few and far between in the mainstream media.

GOVERNMENT DISINFORMATION AND MISLEADING MEDIA ACCOUNTS ABOUT THE REBELS

Sanitized media accounts about the insurgent forces and their ideological orientation echoed the positions that Secretary of State John Kerry and other Obama administration officials adopted. Speaking in September 2013, Kerry stated that the armed opposition to Assad "has increasingly become more defined by its moderation, more defined by the breadth of its adherence to . . . democratic process and to an all-inclusive, minority-protecting constitution."[73] Reuters correspondents Mark Hosenball and Phil Stewart noted that Kerry's optimistic assessment about the moderate political composition of rebel forces was at odds with the emerging conclusions of U.S. intelligence agencies.[74] But their skeptical view was in the minority.

Scholarly treatments of the Syrian civil war differed markedly from the U.S. government and mainstream media versions. Chatham House and Queen Mary University of London scholar Christopher Phillips disputed the complacent view that Islamists were not significant players during the initial stages of Syria's civil war. He concluded that "there was an Islamist presence from the start." Moreover, "its influence and power grew substantially as the conflict progressed." The United States and other Western governments backed the Free Syrian Army (FSA) as the preferred umbrella group for the insurgent factions. But Phillips presented evidence that "by mid-2012, only half of the active militias had sworn allegiance to the FSA, and by the end of that year many disillusioned former FSA brigades had broken off to form independent bodies, mostly with an Islamist bent. By mid-2013 radicals who rejected the FSA controlled large swaths of Syrian territory."[75]

Evidence about the extent of Sunni (and often radical Sunni) domination of the Free Syrian Army was ample from the outset. Phillips emphasized that even the FSA "was never explicitly secular and, despite a spine of nationalist former military figures in its leadership, boasted a large number of Islamist militias within its fold." That finding was unsurprising, in his view. "Many of the rebels were already pious Sunnis and the life and death experience of combat further increased religiosity." Another factor was important as well—namely, "the search for external funds and weaponry offered further incentives to adopt Islamist identities."[76]

By early 2013, Islamists of various stripes had thoroughly eclipsed secular types as the leading players in the Syrian rebellion. Phillips identified three Islamist ideological strands within the insurgency—moderate, Salafist, and jihadist. Indicative of the political realities in Syria, though, his examples of "moderate" Islamists were militias affiliated with the Muslim Brotherhood—hardly a moderate organization in any normal context.[77] Whereas the so-called moderate Islamists were willing to accept at least a nominal separation of religion and state, the Salafists insisted on establishing an overtly religious state in Syria. That was to be expected since the Salafist beliefs coincided with those of Saudi Arabia and other conservative Sunni Gulf allies—their main foreign sponsors.

What separated the Salafist rebels from outright jihadists, according to Phillips, was that the former confined their agenda to Syria, while the latter pursued global jihad. The most militarily successful Salafist militia was Ahrar al-Sham. However, by 2014, Ahrar al-Sham was forming increasingly close ties with the virulently jihadist militia Jabhat al-Nusra (the Nusra Front).[78] And as noted previously, the Nusra Front was an especially important player in the battle for Aleppo.

A few media mavericks dared to dispute the prevailing government-media narrative about the insurgents' alleged commitment to moderation and cooperation with non-Sunnis. David Enders, a reporter for McClatchy newspapers, spent a month with rebel forces in northern and central Syria in the spring of 2012. He found that even during that initial phase of the armed rebellion, while the early anti-Assad street demonstrations were sometimes multiethnic and multireligious, "the armed rebels are Sunni to a man."[79] As in the case of the prelude to and early stages of the Iraq War, the McClatchy papers did better than most of their competitors in providing more restrained, balanced stories on the Syria insurgency.

The nature of the outside sponsors of the "democratic" insurgents should have raised numerous red flags in the American media. The main sponsors were Saudi Arabia, the United Arab Emirates, Qatar, and an increasingly autocratic Turkey. With the Obama administration's blessing, rebel forces were receiving extensive financial aid as well as weaponry from those leading Sunni powers. Such governments were not about to back non-Sunni forces, nor were they likely to back a campaign to plant secular democracy in Syria. By and large, though, American publications and television networks failed to note, much less discuss, this troubling factor.

Even the Obama administration did not seem to believe its own portrayal of the allegedly moderate Syrian rebels. It had good reason not to. Although the administration officially repudiated al-Nusra as a terrorist organization, some of the other factions the United States directly or indirectly supported were nearly as bad. Investigative journalist Gareth Porter emphasized that "a major recipient of Turkish funding and arms was Ahrar al-Sham, which shared its Al Qaeda ally al-Nusra Front's sectarian Sunni view of the Alawite minority. It considered the Alawites to be part of the Shiite enemy and therefore the object of a 'holy war.' Another favorite of the U.S. allies was Jaish al-Islam, the Salafist organization in the Damascus suburbs whose former leader Zahran Alloush talked openly about cleansing Damascus of the Shiites and Alawites, both of whom he lumped together as 'Majous'—the abusive term used for pre-Islamic non-Arabic people from Iran."[80] Still, very few news stories or analyses in the American press mentioned any of these details.

Faced with growing frustration regarding the existing rebel factions, the Obama administration adopted a new, parallel strategy: the United States would identify and train its own contingent of "moderate rebels." Although covert efforts to train and equip vetted moderate insurgents appear to have been already underway in 2013, the administration formally proclaimed that policy in June 2014, asking Congress to authorize $500 million.[81] Officials would spend all those funds over the next 14 months.

Writing in *Foreign Affairs*, Brookings Institution scholar Kenneth Pollack had in mind an even more extensive and robust effort to produce an insurgent army capable of achieving "a decisive victory" in the war. To do that, he emphasized, "the United States would have to commit itself to building a new Syrian army that could end the war and help establish stability when the fighting was over. The effort should carry the resources and credibility of the United States behind it and must not have the tentative and halfhearted support that has defined every prior U.S. initiative in Syria since 2011."[82]

The Obama administration's program proved to be a total flop. Contrary to administration expectations that the Pentagon's new "train and equip" venture would produce thousands of loyal fighters for a democratic Syria, only 54 graduates emerged to create a moderate bulwark within the anti-Assad rebellion. By September 2015, administration officials informed the Senate that only "four or five" remained actively in the field.[83] That failure did attract some negative media attention—especially among fiscal conservatives. Jonah Goldberg jeered, "The news that the Obama administration has spent $500 million to put 'four or five' fighters on the ground in Syria adds an almost comic irony to what is ultimately a tragic farce."[84]

Nevertheless, Washington refused to acknowledge that political moderates in Syria did not constitute a significant faction within the insurgency—especially within its fighting forces. Instead, U.S. officials clung to the official position that a viable moderate and secular alternative to the Assad regime existed. Few accounts in the mainstream media attempted to debunk the administration's rationale, despite mounting evidence that it was erroneous.

MEDIA COVERAGE OF ALLEGED CHEMICAL WEAPONS ATTACKS

Press performances were not materially better regarding another controversial aspect of the Syrian civil war: the Assad regime's alleged use of chemical weapons. In response to some small-scale incidents in 2012 that may have involved chemical agents, President Obama warned Assad's government that any further use of such weapons would cross a "bright red line" that could not be tolerated.[85] On August 21, 2013, Syrian government forces appeared to cross that line with a chemical attack in Ghouta, a rebel-controlled Damascus suburb. At least several hundred people—and perhaps more than 1,400—died from the effects of sarin gas.[86]

As Scott Ritter noted, though, "In August 2013, the OPCW [Organisation for the Prohibition of Chemical Weapons] dispatched an inspection team into Syria as part of a U.N.-led effort . . . to investigate allegations that sarin had been used in the attack on civilians in the town of Ghouta. While the mission found conclusive evidence that sarin nerve agent had been used, it did not assign blame for the attack. Despite the lack of causality, the U.S. and its NATO allies quickly assigned blame for the sarin attacks on the Syrian government."[87]

The Western news media did the same. The pattern persisted throughout subsequent chemical weapons incidents in 2017 and 2018. The February and August 2018 *60 Minutes* programs discussed earlier are textbook examples of how press treatments of such episodes accepted insurgents' allegations and the U.S. government's conclusions without hesitation or caveat. Mainstream media accounts that aimed for balance and expressed at least some reservation about the Obama administration's version of events in 2013 were rare.[88]

However, as the administration moved to make good on its threat for retaliation in 2013, and as most of the press embraced the calls for military action, interventionists discovered that both congressional and public opposition to U.S. entanglement in Syria's civil war was much stronger than anticipated. A September 3, 2013, survey by the Pew Research Center found that only 29 percent of respondents supported airstrikes in retaliation for the alleged chemical attack, while 48 percent were opposed. Worse, from the standpoint of the Obama administration's political considerations, even more Democrats and independents opposed a U.S. strike than did Republicans.[89] And backing from the Republican congressional delegation was both highly conditional and grudging. European allies also remained extremely hesitant.[90]

The Republican leadership in Congress insisted that Obama seek formal congressional authorization for conducting any military strikes. Unilateral presidential action appeared to be increasingly perilous, and the outcome of a vote on an authorization measure was highly uncertain. Faced with the growing convergence of adverse domestic and international factors, Obama backed away from the abyss associated with a full-scale U.S. military intervention in Syria, despite the Assad regime's alleged use of chemical weapons.

Deputy National Security Advisor Ben Rhodes described the situation the administration faced. He noted that "foreign policy luminaries" had endorsed a congressional authorization to use force in Syria. "Clinton announced her support, AIPAC lobbied in support of our position; so did the Saudi government—but none of it mattered. No wave of support materialized in Congress or in public polls."[91] Rhodes was chagrined, but neither the administration nor its pro-war media allies could do much about that situation.

The 2013 chemical weapons episode was a refreshing case in which an administration's desire to use military force and strong media support for that option were not sufficient to stampede the country into launching another ill-advised war. A Russian-sponsored agreement under which Assad was to give up his chemical weapons resolved the 2013 crisis, but, as discussed subsequently, later incidents revived allegations about the regime's use of such weapons.

As certainty about the Assad government's guilt in the 2013 episode withered, hints emerged of possible rebel complicity in the attack. Skeptics about the prevailing narrative, such as former CIA analyst Ray McGovern, suggested that the attack may have been a "false flag" operation—that a foreign government or a rebel faction conducted the attack for the explicit purpose of drawing the United States into the fighting as a full-fledged belligerent against Assad.[92] Writing in the April 2014 *London Review of Books*, veteran investigative journalist Seymour M. Hersh echoed that thesis and specifically implicated both extremist Syrian rebels and Turkey's intelligence service.[93] The evidence that McGovern, Hersh, and other dissenters presented raised troubling questions about the episode that the vast majority of journalists ignored.

Reports of a new chemical weapons attack in April 2017 on the village of Khan Sheikhoun repeated the pattern of media credulity that marked the earlier incident. Most outlets echoed Washington's assertion that the Syrian government had again committed another vicious war crime. The new Trump administration also reacted to the April incident as if there was no possible doubt of the culprit, launching cruise missile strikes against the Syrian air base that U.S. officials identified as the source. And unlike Obama, Trump never considered seeking official congressional approval for the action.

Even usually anti-Trump journalists cheered the attacks, although some of the compliments had a decidedly backhanded quality about them. *New York Times* columnist Nicholas Kristof stated that President Trump's attack on Syria was "of dubious legality," "hypocritical," and "impulsive." Nevertheless, he concluded that Trump "was right" to order the strikes.[94] Others were less restrained in their support of Trump's hawkishness. *Daily Beast* columnist Matt Lewis nearly gushed with enthusiasm following the missile salvo. "This seemed like a very different Donald Trump. More serious—and clearly moved emotionally."[95] Fareed Zakaria, the host of CNN's *Global Public Square*, asserted that "President Trump recognized that the President of the United States does have to act to enforce international norms, does have to have this broader moral and political purpose. . . . I think there has been an interesting morphing and education of Donald Trump." Indeed, he "became President of the United States last night."[96]

The response of MSNBC host (and former anchor of the *Nightly News* on the main NBC network) Brian Williams to the missile strikes on Syria set the benchmark, though, for militaristic enthusiasm. "We see these beautiful pictures at night from the decks of these two U.S. Navy vessels in the eastern Mediterranean. . . . I am tempted to quote the great Leonard Cohen: 'I am guided by the beauty of our weapons.'"[97] That kind of reaction suggested just how much the mainstream media had embraced the idea of U.S. military intervention in Syria.

Despite the journalistic community's overwhelming endorsement of Trump's action, knowledgeable critics, including Theodore Postol, a professor at the Massachusetts Institute of Technology and longtime distinguished expert on intelligence issues, raised major questions about the quality of Washington's intelligence assessment.[98] At least some skepticism about the Syrian government's guilt was warranted for another reason. Just days before the incident, U.S. Secretary of State Rex Tillerson and other officials stated that Washington would no longer demand that Assad leave office before a peace settlement could be negotiated.[99] That was a major change in the U.S. position and one that Assad's government had been seeking for years. Having just achieved such a diplomatic breakthrough, it would have been the height of folly for the Damascus government to commit the one act that was most likely to bring about harsh retaliation and possibly a full-scale U.S. military intervention.

On the other hand, the rebels were already reeling from several recent military defeats at the hands of government forces and their Russian allies following Moscow's 2015 decision to intervene in the Syrian conflict. The loss of Aleppo especially was a severe military and psychological blow. Now the insurgents confronted an adverse change in Washington's diplomatic stance regarding Assad's departure. They had every motive in the world to get the United States to escalate its military involvement. When assessing any incident (or policy), the first question wise investigators ask is "*cui bono?*" (Who benefits?). Unfortunately, neither the Trump administration nor most members of the news media bothered to ask that question.

It is certainly possible that the Assad regime, in a foolish, self-defeating move, ordered the attack—or that a trigger-happy military commander did so. A subsequent OPCW investigation concluded that the Syrian government was responsible, although some independent experts disputed that conclusion as well.[100] Even the OPCW report contained a significant revelation that should have raised doubts about the source of the chemical attack. In a brief passage that almost all media accounts ignored, the commission concluded that ISIS had used sulfur mustard gas in a September assault in northeast Syria.[101] Thus, ISIS clearly had access to some chemical weapons, leaving culpability for the Khan Shaykhoun episode murkier than ever.

Indeed, the overall credibility of the OPCW itself eroded as time went on. The organization's investigation into another chemical weapons incident—the April 7, 2018, attack on Douma, a Damascus suburb— was especially damaging to the OPCW's reputation. The United States and Britain responded to the Douma attack with a new round of airstrikes against Syrian government targets on April 12, once again assuming without definitive evidence that the Assad government was guilty. The OPCW released an interim report on the Douma attack in July 2018[102] and published its final report in March 2019.[103] Both the official interim report and the final report concluded that the weapon likely had been two cylinders of chlorine gas dropped from the air. The conclusion about the delivery method was important because insurgent forces lacked both fighter planes and helicopters, making aerial delivery of a chemical weapon from that faction highly unlikely. Ruling out possible manual placement of the cylinders thus made Assad's regime the obvious suspect for the atrocity. However, the July 2018 and March 2019 official reports omitted significant material that investigators had included in their initial draft of the interim report.[104]

In May 2019, an internal memo that Ian Henderson, a member of the OPCW fact-finding mission in Syria, had written to the organization's leaders leaked to the press. Henderson's memo expressed pointed complaints about aspects of the official interim report and implied that OPCW officials misled the public about the conclusions in that report. Specifically, the conclusion that an aerial attack had been responsible was only a majority view, not a consensus. As Henderson stressed, a minority assessment raised significant doubts about the Assad regime's culpability. Yet OPCW officials had kept the dissenting views under wraps for months, with no explanation or apparent justification.[105] Other doubts soon arose about the nature and scope of the Douma episode, including whether the casualties were caused by a gas attack, and, if so, which faction had been the perpetrator. Doubts were especially pertinent about the credibility of the sources in Syria (mainly insurgents along with pro-rebel, but supposedly independent, organizations such as the White Helmets) that OPCW investigators had relied on for information.[106]

The OPCW was strikingly defensive about the Henderson leak. OPCW officials insisted that the organization was focusing its investigation on "the unauthorized release" of the document questioning the official report, adding that "at this time, there is no further public information on this matter and the OPCW is unable to accommodate requests for interviews."[107] British journalist Peter Hitchens responded with a multipart query.[108] And fellow British journalist Robert Fisk observed, "Here is an institution investigating a war crime in a conflict which has cost hundreds of thousands of lives—yet its only response to an enquiry about the engineers' 'secret' assessment is to concentrate on its own witch-hunt for the source of the document it wished to keep secret from the world." Unfortunately, he contended, "It's a tactic that until now seems to have worked: not a single news media which reported the OPCW's official conclusions has followed up the story of the report which the OPCW suppressed."[109]

Questions about the OPCW's conduct became more pertinent in November 2019, when WikiLeaks began releasing other internal documents showing the existence of dissenting views and demonstrating that the team that wrote the OPCW's report on Douma apparently hadn't even gone to Syria.[110] U.S. media coverage of the whistleblowers and their complaints was remarkably sparse. What coverage did occur was openly sympathetic to the efforts of OPCW leaders and their allies in Western governments and the press to dismiss the objections as without merit. Some accounts even smeared challenges to the official account as echoing a "Russian disinformation campaign."[111]

Then, in early April 2020, the OPCW issued a new report insisting that the Syrian government's guilt in three other chemical weapons incidents in 2017 was beyond dispute.[112] This time, the press coverage was extensive, and it again placidly accepted the OPCW's conclusion. Dissenting OPCW insiders, though, expressed scathing criticisms of the new report as they had the earlier ones.[113] And once again, most of the Western (especially American) press ignored or casually dismissed the latest objections and presented Secretary of State Mike Pompeo's endorsement of the report's findings without indicating that anyone with expertise had disputed those findings.[114]

Writing at Antiwar.com, Belgian scholar Bas Spliet, who had been in Syria in 2017 and investigated at least one of the incidents, criticized the media's double standard. Referring to the earlier Douma investigation furor, Spliet noted that "four OPCW employees have blown the whistle on the manipulation of the investigation. Moreover, internal documents published by WikiLeaks indicate that many investigators of the OPCW's team on site leaned towards the conclusion that the rebels fabricated the incident," but those dissenters "were sidelined." The media, Spliet charged, "all but ignored the leaks. Yet, last week they were quick to report on a new OPCW report that for the first time directly accuses the Syrian air force of three different chemical weapons attacks in 2017."[115] The only publications to acknowledge that dissenters of the latest report even existed were the usual journalistic mavericks, such as Grayzone and Antiwar.com.

The unwillingness to challenge official accounts persisted even when more information surfaced about questionable aspects of the OPCW's Douma investigation. Little media interest in those revelations was evident in either the United States or other NATO countries.[116] Canadian writer Yves Engler chastised his colleagues for their behavior. "Journalists are supposed to seek the truth, not simply what their government says. In fact, according to what is taught in J-school, journalists have a special responsibility to question what their government claims to be true. No journalism program in Canada teaches that governments should always be believed, especially on military and foreign affairs. But that is how the dominant media has acted in the case of Syrian chemical weapons."[117]

The pervasive media indifference to the damaging revelations persisted. What modest coverage the new information did receive was confined largely to nonmainstream outlets such as *The Intercept*, Antiwar.com, the Grayzone, and *Counterpunch*. The Grayzone's Aaron Maté expressed disappointment bordering on disgust about the performance of the journalistic community: "as the suppressed findings come out via brave whistleblowers and Wikileaks, they are still being kept from the public. That is because the Western media—including top progressive, adversarial outlets—have ignored or whitewashed the story. And that media self-censorship has become a scandal in itself."[118]

The few mainstream journalists who did try to cover the embarrassing developments regarding the OPCW encountered ferocious resistance. One angry *Newsweek* writer, Tareq Haddad, resigned from that publication after editors repeatedly blocked his attempts to publish revelations about the leaked OPCW documents. One of the more disturbing aspects of his experience was that an editor making those decisions had previously worked for the European Council on Foreign Relations, an establishment think tank with extremely close ties to several NATO governments.[119]

Scott Ritter contended that Haddad's analysis had the potential to be a blockbuster scandal involving a widely respected UN agency because Haddad's investigative article "was not about Ian Henderson's report, but rather a series of new documents backed up by an inspector turned whistleblower known only as 'Alex,' that accused the OPCW leadership of ignoring the findings of its own inspectors in favor of a revisionist report prepared by another team of inspectors based out of Turkey."[120] The latter group allegedly relied heavily on data and witnesses provided by the White Helmets and another anti-Assad "humanitarian" organization. Perhaps the most unsettling aspect of the media's handling of the entire episode was that *Newsweek* not only blocked publication of Haddad's article in its own pages but allegedly threatened to sue Haddad if he published his analysis elsewhere.[121] Once again, the mainstream media were serving as cooperative conduits for the official explanations from Washington and other NATO governments and ignoring (or squashing) dissenting views.

There were credible reasons to question the OPCW's independence and insulation from U.S. pressure. Scott Ritter was especially harsh in his assessment, charging that the tenure of the organization's first director general, José Maurício Bustani, "was marred by controversy that saw the OPCW transition away from its intended role as an independent implementor of the Chemical Weapons Convention to that of a tool of unilateral U.S. policy, a role that continues to mar the OPCW's work in Syria today."[122]

The most reasonable conclusion about the various chemical incidents in Syria is that the evidence was mixed and inconclusive. Although the Assad government may well have been the guilty party, the possibility of false flag operations from ISIS should not have been dismissed. Even non-ISIS Sunni insurgent forces might have gained access to chemical weapons, perhaps from Syrian government stocks captured during the fighting. Obviously, ISIS obtained such weapons from somewhere, and to assume that Jabhat al-Nusra or another extremist group could not have done so was naïve. To consider the evidence of the 2013, 2017, and 2018 chemical attacks—much of which was provided by the White Helmets or other pro-rebel sources—as definitive virtually invited manipulation of media coverage. The sources that Western officials and most reporters relied on were Syrian insurgent factions (or allies of those factions) with their own sometimes unsavory political agendas. At the very least, journalists should have exhibited greater caution before accepting official conclusions from the United States and its NATO partners about responsibility for the chemical attacks. Instead, the vast majority repeated Washington's allegations as though they were established, indisputable facts.

A similar absence of caution in the coverage characterized the media's treatment of another aspect of the bloody Syrian civil strife: the rise of ISIS. The Obama administration's obsession with undermining Assad and his Iranian patron made it overly eager to back anti-Assad factions, especially those who were clients of Saudi Arabia and other Sunni powers. Unfortunately, some of those factions were even more radical than Jabhat al-Nusra and its allies. Those ultraradical factions eventually formed the core of ISIS.

A 2012 Defense Intelligence Agency report, declassified in June 2015, confirmed the extent and consequences of Washington's egregious policy blunder. Even more damning, the report confirmed that U.S. officials were already aware in 2012 that U.S. backing of insurgent forces would likely produce that result.[123] A few outlets did report on the startling information in the report; much of that reporting came from award-winning investigative journalist Nafeez Ahmed.[124] But the scope of the coverage fell far short of the issue's importance. Evidence that U.S. policy had helped establish the terrorist organization that U.S. officials later cited as the main reason to increase Washington's military involvement in both Syria and Iraq *should* have been a blockbuster news story. Yet coverage in mainstream media outlets ranged from sparse to nonexistent. The American press seemed uninterested in exploring the U.S. role in the emergence and strengthening of an exceptionally powerful terrorist group—a group that succeeded for a time in creating a caliphate that encompassed major portions of Syria and Iraq and even extended its tentacles into Libya and Afghanistan.

THE AMERICAN PRESS'S LOVE AFFAIR WITH SYRIA'S KURDS

The search for moderates (much less a pro-Western secular faction) in Syria was futile, with one partial exception: the Kurds and the Kurdish-dominated Syrian Democratic Forces. Moreover, the Kurds were effective fighters, defeating ISIS on several occasions in northern Syria. Nevertheless, the Kurds were not without some significant moral blemishes. Their commitment to democratic norms was superficially impressive, but their actual conduct, both in Syria and in Iraqi Kurdistan, was somewhat murkier. The Kurdish track record on democracy was better than other political factions in that part of the world, but it often still fell short of the ideal.[125] The behavior of Syrian Kurdish forces also included some disturbing evidence of human-rights abuses.[126]

Western journalists largely overlooked those problems. News and opinion pieces portrayed the Kurds as America's most worthy and effective allies in that part of the Middle East. The media's pro-Kurdish sentiment became especially evident when Washington's NATO ally, Turkey, took military action against the Kurds in northern Syria, and the Trump administration appeared to tilt toward Ankara's position.

Turkish President Recep Tayyip Erdogan's intense hostility toward the Kurds in both Iraq and Syria was not new, but his animosity spiked when the Syrian Kurds gained control of a large swath of Syrian territory along the border with Turkey. Erdogan and other Turkish leaders already were unhappy with the existence of a de facto independent Kurdish state in northern Iraq; they had no intention of tolerating a similar entity in Syria. They feared that the existence of such autonomous territories would be an irresistible model for Turkey's own discontented Kurdish population, which lived primarily in southeastern Turkey, adjacent to Iraq and Syria.

Matters came to a head in October 2019 when Erdogan informed Washington that Turkish military forces would move into northern Syria to clear out Kurdish "terrorists" and establish a security zone several miles wide along the border. President Trump then ordered the small contingent of U.S. troops that had been stationed in the area assisting the Syrian Democratic Forces to withdraw.

News accounts in the United States treated Trump's decision as though it was the worst betrayal of a democratic ally since Britain and France sold out Czechoslovakia to Adolf Hitler at the Munich Conference in 1938. *The Atlantic*'s Peter Wehner accused the president of shamefully "putting faithful American allies in harm's way," and asserted that "Trump betrayed the Kurds. He just couldn't help himself," apparently because he was inherently a duplicitous, amoral character.[127] The *Washington Post*'s Dan Lamothe reported from Syria that even American troops stationed there were appalled at such a betrayal.[128]

Unsurprisingly, CNN managed to shoehorn a Russian angle into the story, contending that the partial withdrawal of U.S. troops was a "gift to Putin and Assad."[129] *USA Today* featured an op-ed by Sen. Tammy Duckworth (D-IL), arguing not only that Trump's relocation of forces betrayed the Kurds, but that any drawdown of U.S. forces in Syria undermined Washington's credibility with allies throughout the Middle East and beyond.[130] *Philadelphia Inquirer* columnist Trudy Rubin asserted that Trump's action warranted impeachment: "In one feckless phone call,

President Trump abandoned our loyal Kurdish allies, green-lit Turkish war crimes, spurred the revival of ISIS, helped the Kremlin and Iran, and sapped U.S. military morale."[131]

A congressional coalition of Democrats and hawkish Republicans moved to rebuke Trump and block his decision to withdraw the troops stationed in northern Syria.[132] The bipartisan coalition ultimately sought to bar any drawdown of U.S. forces in Syria (along with the forces in Afghanistan, Iraq, and virtually everywhere else).[133] This opposition to the withdrawal of troops from Syria was especially strange and hypocritical, since Congress had never authorized the deployment in the first place. Yet the bulk of the news media cheered on the effort.

The question of withdrawal from Syria confirmed that the collusion of pro-interventionist elements in government and the mainstream press was both strong and flagrant. Although the Kurdish issue was the catalyst for the media-congressional campaign to keep U.S. forces in Syria indefinitely, that campaign had begun nearly a year earlier when Trump expressed his intention to reduce the U.S. presence in the country by 2,000 troops. At that time, the *Nation* was one of the few publications— even among the supposedly anti-war left—to express support for Trump's plan.[134] Following the Kurdish brouhaha, the same lopsided media majority created a bloc opposed to even a limited withdrawal.

The media's handling of the Syrian civil war replicated almost all the defects that characterized their performance with respect to the conflicts in the Balkans, Iraq, and Libya. Journalists who lobbied for a full-scale U.S. military intervention in Syria, though, discovered that a war-weary American public was noticeably less responsive to their efforts than had been the case in those earlier episodes. Enough information also leaked out about the true nature of the "moderate" insurgents to make the American public wary of such an entanglement. Invoking the previously reliable terrorist-threat (especially ISIS) card and the Russian-meddling card worked only to a limited extent. Even playing the sympathy-for-the-noble-Kurds card did not generate sufficient public enthusiasm for U.S. involvement in another Middle East war. However, the failure to promote a new U.S. military crusade was not for lack of trying on the part of a sizable contingent in the American press.

Much of that behavior reflected laziness and naiveté on the part of the mainstream media, but another possible cause is even more troubling. The extent of government disinformation and manipulation of the media with respect to the war in Syria became apparent when documents from the Foreign and Commonwealth Office in the UK were leaked to the press in the autumn of 2020.

The Grayzone's Ben Norton provided an extensive account of the propaganda and disinformation campaigns that Western governments had waged.[135] "The leaked files reveal how Western intelligence cutouts played the media like a fiddle, carefully crafting English- and Arabic-language media coverage of the war on Syria to churn out a constant stream of pro-opposition coverage," Norton charged. Details in the documents supported his argument. "More than half of the stringers used by Al Jazeera in Syria were trained in a joint US-UK government program called Basma, which produced hundreds of Syrian opposition media activists. Western government PR firms not only influenced the way the media covered Syria, but as the leaked documents reveal, they produced their own propagandistic pseudo-news for broadcast on major TV networks in the Middle East, including BBC Arabic, Al Jazeera, Al Arabiya, and Orient TV."

The media manipulation by Western governments apparently went further. "One contractor, called InCoStrat, said it was in constant contact with a network of more than 1,600 international journalists and 'influencers,' and used them to push pro-opposition talking points. Another Western government contractor, ARK, crafted a strategy to 're-brand' Syria's Salafi-jihadist armed opposition by 'softening its image.' ARK boasted that it provided opposition propaganda that 'aired almost every day on' major Arabic-language TV networks." Norton pointed out that the firm stated it had "flooded Syria with opposition propaganda." In just six months, ARK reported, "668,600 of its print products were distributed inside Syria, including 'posters, flyers, informative booklets, activity books and other campaign-related materials.'"

Norton concluded that "virtually every major Western corporate media outlet was influenced by the UK government-funded disinformation campaign exposed in the trove of leaked documents, from the

New York Times to the *Washington Post*, CNN to *The Guardian*, the BBC to Buzzfeed."[136]

REPEAT PERFORMANCE:
MORE BIASED, SLOPPY COVERAGE

One of the sadder, more frustrating features of the news media's handling of the conflicts in Libya and Syria is just how little journalists learned from their deeply flawed performances in earlier episodes. Once again, a majority succumbed to corrosive impulses and transformed murky, multidimensional struggles into simplistic, emotionally wrought morality plays. Their analyses lacked not only important historical context but nuance as well. As in the past, most news coverage prodded the American people to support dubious regime-change, nation-building crusades with little thought about the possible adverse consequences if the targeted tyrants were overthrown.

Worse, too many news stories idealized the rebels who were attempting to expel those tyrants. That tendency was especially pronounced in media treatments of the Syrian insurgents. Too many journalists minimized or even ignored the extreme Islamist credentials of several insurgent factions. In reality, most of those groups were not "moderate," even given a very generous definition of the term. They certainly did not advocate Western-style secular democracy. Yet some reporters seemed to go out of their way to deny that reality and conceal the actual ideological pedigrees of the Syrian insurgents Washington was supporting.

Still worse, too many members of the establishment press in both the United States and Europe vilified any colleagues who disputed the sanitized treatment of the Syrian rebels. Iconoclastic British journalist Jonathan Cook's indictment of that behavior had considerable merit. Proponents of the prevailing narrative, he charged, "justify the intimidation and silencing of anyone not entirely convinced that ordinary Syrians might prefer, however reluctantly, their standard-issue dictator, Bashar al-Assad, over the head-chopping, women-stoning, Saudi-financed jihadists of Islamic State and al-Nusra, the al-Qaeda franchise in Syria; or who question whether the Western powers ought to be covertly funding and backing these extremists."[137] The vitriolic attacks on even prominent journalistic mavericks who criticized the Syrian intervention, such as Seymour Hersh and the late Robert Fisk, confirmed Cook's allegations.

In both Libya and Syria, few members of the media held the U.S. and NATO governments accountable in any way for the human tragedies that the Western military interventions helped unleash. Libya and Syria are much worse off today than they were before Washington and its European allies embarked on their regime-change efforts. Qaddafi and Assad were nasty, brutal leaders, to be sure, but that does not justify U.S-led, militarized meddling to try to rectify the situation. The lack of any tangible U.S. security interests at stake in either Libya or Syria made Washington's decisions to intervene—and the media's role as obliging enabler—especially offensive.

In the end, U.S. ministrations did not improve matters in either country; to the contrary, the interventions created chaos and greatly intensified the human suffering. Under Qaddafi, Libya was not engulfed in endless warfare among multiple factions, and brazen, open-air slave markets did not exist. Hundreds of thousands of civilians were not displaced refugees, many desperately trying to flee to safety across the Mediterranean and thousands dying when their overcrowded, unseaworthy boats sank. In Syria, before the United States and its allies sought to unseat Assad, the country was reasonably stable and increasingly modern. The regime-change war destroyed Syria's infrastructure, plunging the country into dire poverty. The fighting also produced more than 500,000 fatalities and an estimated 5 million refugees.

By any reasonable standard, U.S. policy in both countries was a catastrophic failure.[138] But few members of the press have held U.S. officials accountable for the consequences of the policies they adopted. Even when stories accurately describe the extent of the chaos and suffering, the overwhelming majority do not make the connection to Washington's actions. Articles on Libya in the mainstream press attribute the bloodshed and other horrors there to the latest designated villain, Field Marshal Haftar, and to some extent to interference by various Middle East powers. One might conclude that the United States had been little more than an interested observer instead of the primary cause of Libya's destabilization. Mainstream media accounts of the Syrian conflict over the years have been even worse. They attribute virtually all the troubles to Assad and his allies, especially Russia. Among the other outside powers, only Turkey comes in for much criticism, and that perspective has more to do with Ankara's hostility to the Syrian Kurds and the Erdogan government's growing domestic authoritarianism and anti-Americanism than it does to Ankara's meddling in Syria. Once again, precious few news stories acknowledge the extent of Washington's role in destabilizing the country.

The large and theoretically powerful watchdogs in the press were once again asleep—or worse, they cozied up to government advocates of two regime-change crusades. The media outlets that presented more critical accounts of U.S. policy in Libya and Syria are mostly "fringe" publications with modest exposure and less influence. Such iconoclastic outfits as *Consortium News*, Antiwar.com, the Grayzone, and *The American Conservative* produced important and often incisive stories, but their reach was limited. Most Americans never saw those critiques.

The United States confined its interventions to air power and the use of Special Forces. That meant the media could more easily cheer the effort, since pushback from the American public would be minimal. Nevertheless, the flagrant hawkishness in the coverage suggests that at least a sizable portion of the corporate press would have endorsed a decision to send substantial numbers of ground forces if the White House incumbent had opted for that course. Indeed, some members of the Washington press corps were noticeably impatient that the United States wasn't "doing more" in Syria.

Perhaps most sobering, the leaked documents discussed in Ben Norton's Grayzone article indicated that a significant amount of the coverage delivered to American and other audiences was the product of outright manipulation and disinformation by Western governments. Once again, important portions of the media had become willing or inadvertent allies of well-funded, pro-war government operatives.

CHAPTER 7
Toxic Bias Pollutes Russia Coverage

Perhaps the most prominent issue the news media has covered in recent years is Russia's conduct toward the United States. Three features of that coverage are striking and more than a little alarming. One is the pervasiveness and virulence of the hostility directed against nearly every facet of Moscow's policies. A second feature is the willingness of the mainstream media to collaborate with current and former members of the U.S. intelligence community, as well as the Democratic Party, to push the narrative that Russia poses an existential threat to the United States and world peace. Third, this tripartite alliance has fostered a surge of neo-McCarthyism, which insists that gullible or disloyal Americans—including dissident members of the press—are aiding that cause, especially the Kremlin's agenda to undermine America's political system.

The result of such a toxic brew has been the worst media coverage of an important foreign policy issue in decades. It has fostered a dangerous narrative of unrelenting animosity (effectively a new cold war) toward the one country in the international system that has the weaponry to trigger an apocalypse. It has also poisoned public discourse in a way that inflicts serious damage on America's democratic system.

Members of the mainstream press have been major culprits in that destructive process, and the problem began early. A pronounced anti-Russian perspective was evident even before the armed conflict that erupted in 2008 between Russia and the Republic of Georgia, which portrayed itself as a beleaguered U.S. democratic ally and played the "victim card" to the hilt. In covering relations with Russia, most media outlets conveyed an activist, hawkish bias that went beyond their coverage of events in the Balkans, Iraq, Libya, and Syria. Western, especially American, journalists exhibited an intense, nearly universal hostility toward Russian President Vladimir Putin—for understandable reasons. Putin is not an admirable character by any stretch of the imagination. He is a corrupt, autocratic leader who smothered Russia's fragile new democracy, creating a rigged electoral system that assures his hold on power for an indefinite duration. Nor does he hesitate to crush political opponents. However, many leaders around the world engage in corrupt, autocratic, and brutal behavior without attracting the extreme animus that Putin receives from American journalists. For instance, compare the news media's more restrained treatment of China's even more autocratic Xi Jinping to its portrayal of Putin to notice a pronounced difference.

The press's hostility toward both Putin and his country surged when he seized and subsequently annexed Ukraine's Crimean Peninsula in March 2014. Furious Western press accounts slammed the Kremlin's move as an outrageous act of unprovoked aggression, akin to the start of Adolf Hitler's expansionist binge in the late 1930s. A *Wall Street Journal* editorial asserted that Russia's "brazen aggression brings the threat of war to the heart of Europe for the first time since the end of the Cold War. The question now is what President [Barack] Obama and free Europe are going to do about it."[1]

Like many in the press, the *Journal*'s editors assumed that Moscow's actions were just the beginning of a tsunami of aggression. "Vladimir Putin's Russia seized Ukraine's Crimean Peninsula by force on the weekend and now has his sights on the rest of his Slavic neighbor." The pervasive assumption was that additional attempts at territorial expansion would follow the absorption of Crimea, probably beginning with a move to conquer the rest of Ukraine. When Hillary Clinton charged that Putin's actions were "what Hitler did back in the '30s,"[2] media analyses quickly echoed her allegation. In an article for CNN, historian Timothy Snyder asserted that "the seizure of Crimea was meant as a challenge to the European Union. It is meant to prove that European values cannot defend themselves." He concluded that if Putin's aggression was allowed to stand, Europe's post–Cold War democratic state system "is finished."[3]

To this date, the Kremlin has committed no acts of military aggression except in Ukraine, providing additional evidence that Ukraine is a special case in Russian foreign policy. Western warnings in 2014 about vast expansionist goals were both premature and excessive. Most interpretations of the Crimea annexation greatly oversimplified a complex historical and contemporary set of issues regarding that peninsula—and indeed the overall situation in Ukraine.[4] Crimea had been part of Russia beginning in 1782, and it remained so until Soviet dictator Nikita Khrushchev, for reasons that are still not entirely clear, transferred the territory to Ukraine in 1954. Since both Ukraine and Russia were constituent parts of the Soviet Union, the move didn't seem to have much importance at the time. But when the Soviet Union dissolved at the end of 1991, Khrushchev's decision mattered far more. Among other problems, Moscow's crucial Black Sea naval base was now on the territory of a foreign country.

Russian leaders were nervous about that situation, even though the newly independent Ukraine gave Moscow a lease to the base. Russian uneasiness increased when a pro-Western Ukrainian government took power in 2005 following the Orange Revolution and sought membership in NATO. Ukraine's president, Viktor Yushchenko, agitated the Kremlin even more when he indicated that Kyiv might not renew the lease when it expired in 2017. The election of a pro-Russian government in 2010 eased Moscow's concerns. However, its worries returned with a vengeance when the United States and its European allies encouraged anti-government demonstrators in late 2013 and 2014 to oust that elected president, Viktor Yanukovych, before the end of his term and install a new, staunchly pro-Western regime in Kyiv. Putin promptly responded to the so-called Maidan Revolution by orchestrating a snap referendum in Crimea under the watchful eyes of Russian troops. He then had the Russian parliament give its rubber stamp approval to the regional government's "request" to join the Russian Federation.

Unfortunately, all those nuances—especially the role of the Western powers in assisting Ukrainian demonstrators and provoking Moscow

with promises that Ukraine would one day become a NATO member—
were lost or deliberately omitted in the apocalyptic media coverage of
the Crimea annexation.[5] Not only did an array of journalists openly
advocate economic sanctions against Moscow and other components of
a hardline policy, but many of them, especially in the United States,
vilified any person who dared advocate a more cautious policy.

The Kremlin's apparent meddling in the 2016 U.S. presidential election and the subsequent investigations by the FBI and Special Counsel
Robert Mueller into alleged collusion between Donald Trump's presidential campaign and the Putin government greatly intensified the
media's hostility and vitriol. But attributing the emergence and growth
of a new McCarthyism in the United States solely to that development
would be a mistake. Many of the features of the unrelentingly negative
media coverage of Russia and Putin had emerged more than two years
earlier. So, too, had the demonization of the opponents of a hardline
U.S.-NATO approach.

Indeed, some of the nastiest allegations were directed at individuals
who not only had nothing to do with Donald Trump's presidential bid but
were outright critics. Princeton University professor Stephen F. Cohen,
a longtime distinguished scholar of the Soviet Union and its successor
states, was a prominent early target. Cohen's motives were impugned
and his reputation sullied long before the 2016 election because he advocated a less confrontational policy toward Russia. Such terms as "Putin's
American apologist" and "Putin's pal" were among the labels routinely
applied to Cohen.[6]

Analysts who argued that NATO's expansion eastward to Russia's
border had needlessly provoked Moscow, or that Russia's actions in
Ukraine were more defensive than offensive, usually received the same
treatment. Targets included Jeffrey Tayler, columnist for *The Atlantic*;
University of Chicago professor (and dean of the realist school among
U.S. international relations scholars) John J. Mearsheimer; *The American
Conservative* columnists Pat Buchanan and Daniel Larison; *National Interest*
editor Jacob Heilbrunn; and an assortment of journalists with a wide
range of ideological orientations, such as *The Intercept*'s Glenn Greenwald,
Antiwar.com's Justin Raimondo, *Medium* blogger Caitlin Johnstone, and

Boston Globe columnist Stephen Kinzer. Epithets such as "apologists," "stooges," "Russian trolls," "patsies," and "useful idiots" appeared frequently in mainstream media attacks on such maverick foreign policy critics. Those accusations began early, and they proliferated with the onset of the 2014 Ukraine crisis.[7] But Donald Trump and his associates became the principal lightning rods. Even before Trump entered the White House, critics accused him of being intent on appeasing Moscow, because he indicated that he would seek better relations with Putin's government.[8]

TRUMP AND THE MEDIA'S RUSSIA-COLLUSION OBSESSION

The early anti-Russia narrative set the stage for the hyperbole that accompanied the allegations that Moscow had meddled in the U.S. 2016 presidential election to assist Trump's candidacy. Accusations flew: not only had he benefited from Russia's covert political assistance, but he and his campaign staff had actively colluded with that foreign "enemy" power. In other words, Trump's opponents implicitly (and sometimes explicitly) accused him of treason. During previous eras, such an accusation directed against a major party's presidential nominee, much less against the president of the United States, would have been greeted with either stony silence or ridicule in responsible government circles and the news media. When leaders of the ultra-right-wing John Birch Society made a similar accusation in the 1950s that Dwight Eisenhower was an agent of the Soviet Union, no mainstream publication embraced the charge. The allegation seemed too preposterous—even in the middle of the hysteria that Sen. Joseph McCarthy had unleashed with claims of a widespread domestic communist conspiracy.

This time, the response of Trump's opponents and much of the press underscored the extreme political polarization and the extent of hostility toward him. Major political and media figures not only treated the allegation seriously but assumed it was true. Indeed, no allegation against Trump or his advisers seemed too outlandish to consider.[9] Certain Democrats in Congress, such as California Reps. Adam Schiff and

Eric Swalwell and New York Rep. Jerrold Nadler, were especially eager to push the Russia conspiracy narrative. Their role was no small matter, since Schiff was the ranking minority member on the House Intelligence Committee and Nadler had the same status on the House Judiciary Committee. After the Democrats gained control of the House in the 2018 midterm election, the two men became chairmen of those committees and soon launched probes culminating in Trump's impeachment in December 2019.

Some members of the media were at least as enthusiastic as Schiff, Swalwell, and Nadler in pushing the "Trump is a Russian agent" theme. One of the most avid was MSNBC host Rachel Maddow. Writing in February 2019, *New York Post* columnist Kyle Smith noted:

> For two years Maddow built her MSNBC show around an actual conspiracy theory, that Trump was engaged in some kind of illegal collusion with Vladimir Putin, and issued one wild speculation after another: that there was a "continuing operation" involving Putin pulling strings here, that Putin was in a position to blackmail Trump into recalling troops from the Russian border, that a Trump-directed missile attack could have been ordered by Putin. . . . Conclusion: Saying crazy stuff doesn't get you fired from MSNBC.[10]

Collusion allegations, fed by leaks from high-ranking officials in the intelligence agencies and echoed by their allies in Congress (as well as the Obama administration) and the media, produced an FBI investigation, "Crossfire Hurricane," into Trump's campaign in late July 2016. And ultimately, they escalated to the appointment of a special counsel, Robert Mueller, in May 2017 to continue and expand the inquiry. The Russia issue captured more media attention, by a wide margin, than any other issue for the next two years. A pronounced anti-Trump (and broader anti-Russia) bias characterized the coverage.

When Mueller's lengthy investigation failed to uncover credible evidence of collusion between Trump campaign officials and the Russian government, members of the media who had given maximum exposure to that allegation still refused to acknowledge any misconduct (or even mistakes) on their part. CNN correspondent Jake Tapper flatly rebuffed the notion that CNN and most of the mainstream media had gotten anything wrong in their coverage of the Russia-collusion story. He was especially offended at the suggestion that his network had done so. "I'm not sure what you're saying the media got wrong," Tapper responded during an interview. "The media reported the investigation was ongoing. Other than the people in the media on the left, not on this network, I don't know anybody who got anything wrong. We didn't say there was conspiracy. We said that Mueller was investigating conspiracy."[11]

The statement was especially astonishing because CNN itself previously had to retract several stories owing to unsupported assertions and other problems. In one case, three producers were pressured to resign over an erroneous story linking a Trump ally to a Russian bank that was under investigation.[12] Tapper's attempted spin was brazenly disingenuous. Viewers who watched CNN programming for the previous two years or more had witnessed a steady stream of guests, hosts, and in-house analysts who implied, and frequently stated outright, that the conspiracy existed and that Trump himself was likely involved in it. Very few people appeared on camera to dispute that view.

Such sloppiness or malice appeared to be a continuing problem at CNN in its coverage of Trump-Russia issues. In September 2019, the CIA took the unusual step of publicly denouncing a story that chief national security correspondent Jim Sciutto had authored.[13] The article contended that the CIA had pulled a high-level spy out of Russia because President Trump had "repeatedly mishandled classified intelligence and could contribute to exposing the covert source as a spy."[14] The CIA said the story had no validity.

CNN was not alone in practicing such faulty journalism. Before Mueller completed his much-anticipated report in March 2019, Glenn Greenwald documented 10 especially egregious instances in which mainstream media outlets had circulated misinformation regarding Moscow's alleged meddling and the overall Russia-collusion scandal.[15] One was about an anonymous group, PropOrNot, which issued a report declaring that political sites on both the left and right were merely Russian propaganda outlets. It accused more than 200 websites of being "routine peddlers of Russian propaganda during the election season, with combined audiences of at least 15 million Americans." In a

November 2016 story, the *Washington Post* touted the PropOrNot report to claim massive Kremlin infiltration of the internet. Dozens of other outlets then picked up the *Post* story, and it quickly became a media sensation.[16]

Greenwald contended that such credulous treatment by the *Post* and other press outlets reflected highly questionable judgment since "those statistics were provided by a new, anonymous group." PropOrNot "reached these conclusions by classifying long-time, well-known sites— from the Drudge Report to Clinton-critical left-wing websites such as Truthout, Black Agenda Report, Truthdig, and Naked Capitalism, as well as libertarian venues such as Antiwar.com and the Ron Paul Institute—as 'Russian propaganda outlets.'" That shaky editorial judgment, he noted, produced "one of the longest Editor's Note[s] in memory appended to the top of the article (but not until two weeks later, long after the story was mindlessly spread all throughout the media ecosystem)."[17]

The American Conservative's Arthur Bloom observed years later that by uncritically circulating the PropOrNot allegations, the *Post* executed a smear akin to one that would have occurred "if the Bush administration had commissioned a list of news sources that were carrying water for Saddam Hussein in 2006." Such a list "would have looked almost the same as the PropOrNot list, except here it was recast as an effort to defend democratic integrity."[18]

The PropOrNot episode was not the only instance in which *Washington Post* editors seemed a bit too eager to believe negative allegations about Russia despite little or no evidence. A December 2016 story asserted that Russian hackers had invaded the U.S. electricity grid through a Vermont utility, a probe that someday could deprive consumers of heat in winter. The report caused predictable outrage and panic, along with anti-Russia vitriol and threats from U.S. political leaders. But then, Greenwald noted, editor's notes kept diluting the story, "to admit that the malware was found on a laptop not connected to the U.S. electric grid at all—until finally acknowledging, days later, that the whole story was false, since the malware had nothing to do with Russia or with the U.S. electric grid."[19]

On July 27, 2018, CNN broke a major story that Michael Cohen, President Trump's personal attorney, was prepared to tell the Mueller investigation that Trump knew in advance about the infamous Trump Tower meeting in which collaboration with Russian efforts to influence the election allegedly was discussed.[20] "There were, however, two problems with this story," Greenwald emphasized. "First, CNN got caught blatantly lying when its reporters claimed that 'contacted by CNN, one of Cohen's attorneys, Lanny Davis, declined to comment' (in fact, Davis was one of CNN's key sources, if not its only source, for this story), and second, numerous other outlets retracted the story after the source, Davis, admitted it was a lie. CNN, however, to this date has refused to do either."[21]

In addition to the 10 stories that Greenwald singled out for special infamy, he listed 10 others for "dishonorable mention" and made an astute, extremely troubling observation:

> Note that all of these "errors" go only in one direction: namely, exaggerating the grave threat posed by Moscow and the Trump circle's connection to it. It's inevitable that media outlets will make mistakes on complex stories. If that's being done in good faith, one would expect the errors would be roughly 50/50 in terms of the agenda served by the false stories. That is most definitely not the case here. Just as was true in 2002 and 2003, when the media clearly wanted to exaggerate the threat posed by Saddam Hussein and thus all of its "errors" went in that direction, virtually all of its major "errors" in this story are devoted to the same agenda and script.

Despite the dearth of tangible evidence to support allegations of Russian collusion, most media outlets cheered on the FBI investigation and the Mueller probe. Maverick progressive journalist Matt Taibbi could hardly contain his scorn. "The Special Prosecutor literally became a religious figure during the last few years, with votive candles sold in his image and *Saturday Night Live* cast members singing 'All I Want for Christmas Is You' to him featuring the rhymey line: 'Mueller please come through, because the only option is a coup.'"[22]

The massive coverage of the Russia-collusion allegation and the confidence that the Mueller report would confirm all the speculation about Trump's various misdeeds, possibly up to and including treason, reached a decided anti-climax. The report stated, "The investigation did not establish that members of the Trump Campaign conspired or coordinated with the Russian government in its election interference activities."[23] Apparently, Trump's defenders who had asserted that the Russia-collusion scandal was a "giant nothing burger" were not far off the mark.

With rare exceptions, the anti-Trump, anti-Russia media firmly refused to admit error. Instead, they focused on those portions of the Mueller report that declined to exonerate the president of contentions that he may have unlawfully impeded the investigation and thereby committed obstruction of justice. However, even that line of argument proved ineffectual. Although the Mueller commission did not exonerate Trump, neither did it recommend prosecution for obstruction of justice. It left the decision to Attorney General William Barr.

When Barr, a Trump appointee, declined to proceed with a prosecution, the expressions of anger and cynicism flowed throughout the media once more. Accusations flew that Barr himself was nothing more than a sycophant, doing Trump's bidding. The *Bulwark*'s Charles Sykes found it especially damning that Barr was Trump's "handpicked choice" for attorney general—although that is true of every president's appointment of every cabinet official.[24] Jonathan Chait typified the mainstream media's take when he charged that Barr "seems to be covering up something bad for Trump."[25]

At this point, public weariness with the entire set of issues related to alleged collusion with Russia was growing. Dissenters in the journalistic community were not shy about chastising their colleagues who had embraced the Russia-collusion thesis so tenaciously. When the summary of the forthcoming report appeared in late March, Matt Taibbi concluded, "Nobody wants to hear this, but news that Special Prosecutor Robert Mueller is headed home without issuing new charges is a death-blow for the reputation of the American news media."[26] Glenn Greenwald expressed a similar view after the full report appeared, asserting that Mueller "did not merely reject the Trump-Russia conspiracy theories. He obliterated them." Greenwald added, "Several of the media's most breathless and hyped 'bombshells' were dismissed completely by Mueller."[27]

The last stand of the anti-Trump media regarding the collusion allegation occurred when Mueller himself testified before the House Judiciary

Committee. Some journalists still held out hope that he might yet reveal a smoking gun or some heretofore unknown damaging information. Mueller's congressional testimony dashed such expectations. Not only did he fail to provide such a revelation, but he seemed hazy and confused about the investigation and the report that bore his name. David Smith, a writer for the British left-wing paper *The Guardian*, gave a rueful account of Mueller's performance. "Once Wednesday's seven-hour House committee hearing got under way, the welcoming smiles froze on Democratic faces, like a theatre audience realising they bought expensive tickets to the wrong show. It slowly dawned that Mueller was neither going to offer a pugnacious defence of his findings nor bring them into focus for the American public with piercing clarity. Instead the 74-year-old struggled, asking for questions to be repeated, laboriously looking up page references and offering halting, monosyllabic answers."[28]

Even the staunchly anti-Trump *Washington Post* conceded that the hearing had fallen "flat" for those who had hoped that Mueller would recharge the faltering Russia-collusion case. "Many felt blindsided that no one warned them how much Mueller had aged," *Post* reporters Richard Bade and Mike De Bonis stated. "'I was beyond shocked,' one lawmaker said of Mueller's occasional confusion and seeming unfamiliarity with details of the report."[29] Zach Beauchamp, writing in *Vox*, described the testimony succinctly as "a farce and a tragedy."[30]

A few reporters tried to put a more favorable spin on the hearings, but their efforts seemed both transparent and half-hearted.[31] News accounts of Mueller's testimony faded quickly, and many of them implicitly pitied a once highly regarded public servant who no longer seemed capable of fulfilling such a role.

POST-MUELLER: THE MEDIA'S CONTINUING ANTI-TRUMP, ANTI-RUSSIA AGENDA

The massive, heavily one-sided press coverage became harder to defend when evidence emerged that the FBI had committed serious violations of its own procedures and basic requirements of due process in its treatment of suspects connected to the Trump campaign probe. The extent of the agency's abuses became apparent when Justice Department Inspector General Michael Horowitz issued his report on December 9, 2019.[32] Although Horowitz did not endorse the White House's core allegation that the FBI had initiated the Crossfire Hurricane investigation out of political bias, the report identified 17 major instances of improper behavior, including violations of standard procedures and safeguards for the rights of individuals targeted in an investigation.[33]

The most egregious abuses occurred with respect to investigative warrants aimed at Carter Page, a foreign policy adviser to the Trump campaign. Especially disturbing violations included the withholding of exculpatory evidence in warrant applications to the Foreign Intelligence Surveillance Act (FISA) Court. Among the offenses were the failure to disclose that Page was working for the CIA during the period he was making contacts with Russian diplomatic and intelligence officials. In one instance, FBI assistant general counsel Kevin Clinesmith even altered a document to make it appear to state the opposite of its original language about Page's role.[34]

Nevertheless, former FBI director James Comey and other Trump critics were quick to claim that the report exonerated the agency, and the bulk of the mainstream media quickly afforded them opportunities to promote that argument. The *Washington Post* gave Comey a platform to make that claim the day after the report's release. In his op-ed, Comey accused Trump, Barr, and other critics of having smeared him and his colleagues: "The FBI fulfilled its mission—protecting the American people and upholding the U.S. Constitution. Now those who attacked the FBI for two years should admit they were wrong."[35]

Despite the damaging revelations in the inspector general's report, most of the initial accounts in the mainstream media echoed the arguments that Comey and other defenders made. News stories emphasized the rejection of the political bias charge, with that aspect eclipsing all other conclusions that placed the FBI in a less favorable light. NBC News opted for the headline "Internal Justice Watchdog Finds That Russia Probe Was Justified, Not Biased against Trump."[36] PBS's *NewsHour* likewise touted "No Bias in FBI's Russia Probe."[37] Other outlets were at least as flagrant in their spin. *Intelligencer: New York Magazine* asserted, "Inspector General

Finds Russia Investigation Wasn't an FBI Witch Hunt."[38] *Wired* proclaimed, "So Much for the Deep State Plot against Donald Trump."[39]

Even when news stories acknowledged problems with the FBI's behavior, writers and reporters attributed those actions to "errors" and "missteps," not misconduct or abuses.[40] Again, such takes echoed the explanations of Comey and other FBI defenders. In his *Washington Post* op-ed, Comey stated, "The Russia investigation was complicated—not surprisingly, the inspector general found mistakes, 17 of them, things the FBI should have done differently, or better. That's always unfortunate, but human beings make mistakes."[41] Most press reports adopted a similar, benign interpretation.

The following week, the inspector general pushed back on the notion that he had exonerated the FBI. Horowitz clarified that his investigation into the FBI's FISA warrants "did not reach" the conclusion that the bureau was unaffected by political bias during its Russia investigation. In response to questioning from Sen. Josh Hawley (R-MO), Horowitz explained that his investigation left the door open to possible political bias, because his team could not accept the explanations FBI members gave about why there were "so many errors" in their investigation. "We have been very careful," Horowitz told Hawley, "not to reach that conclusion." As reasons for caution, he specifically cited "the alteration of the email, the text messages associated with the individual who did that, and our inability to explain or understand, to get good explanations so that we could understand why this all happened."[42] Such caveats indicated that Horowitz's report was far from an exoneration of the FBI.

Shortly thereafter the media's favorable spin on the FBI's performance became even more difficult to sustain. In mid-December, the FISA Court rebuked the FBI for its actions.[43] Then, in January 2020, the FISA Court retroactively invalidated two of four warrants issued in the Carter Page investigation.[44] That move was virtually unprecedented. So too was the court's next step in early March, when it barred agents involved in the original warrant applications from submitting future surveillance applications.[45]

The FISA Court's measures were stunning, since it was notorious over the years for rubber stamping warrant requests from national security agencies. A 2013 study found that since its creation in 1978, the court granted 33,942 warrants and denied only 12—a rejection rate of 0.03 percent.[46] Although the rate increased slightly in subsequent years, rejections of warrant applications remained rare.[47] Sharp criticism from the FISA Court of a law enforcement or national security agency, much less the imposition of sanctions against that agency's personnel, was only a little less startling than if the Chinese People's Congress had criticized President Xi Jinping and curtailed his powers.

Another blow to the media narrative came in early June 2020 when former deputy attorney general Rod Rosenstein stated in congressional testimony that he would never have signed the FISA warrant renewal application if he had known how unreliable the so-called Steele dossier and other underlying evidence were.[48] On this occasion, his statement received a respectable amount of attention in the mainstream media, including the *Washington Post*, CBS News, and Yahoo News, as well as conservative competitors such as Fox News, *National Review*, and the *Washington Examiner*. Most of them also acknowledged that the admission was the main thrust of Rosenstein's testimony. NBC News, though, went out of its way to spin the testimony with this misleading headline: "Rod Rosenstein Defends Mueller Appointment, Approval of FISA Applications in Russia Probe."[49]

Although increasingly strained, the prevailing media Russia-collusion narrative continued to contend that any problems with the FBI's Crossfire Hurricane investigation were minor and accidental. That narrative suffered another blow in August 2020, though, when former assistant general counsel Kevin Clinesmith pled guilty to altering a crucial document in one of the FISA warrant applications for the continuing surveillance of Carter Page. Mainstream press stories acknowledged the guilty plea but carefully avoided drawing any wider conclusions about the abuses that took place with Crossfire Hurricane. Indeed, some of the accounts asserted that Clinesmith's offense was nothing more than an isolated incident. CNN's treatment was typical:

> Trump kicked off his Friday afternoon briefing with a brief reference to Clinesmith. "That's just the beginning . . . what happened should

never happen again. He is pleading guilty, terrible thing, terrible thing. The fact is they spied on my campaign and they got caught and you'll be hearing more," Trump said. However, the court documents laying out the single charge against Clinesmith don't make any broader allegation of a conspiracy by FBI investigators against Trump, an accusation Trump has frequently made. Instead it shows another FBI official who signed the fourth FISA warrant raising a concern about whether Page was a CIA source and seeking email proof when Clinesmith downplayed the CIA relationship with Page.[50]

A few analyses (almost all in staunchly conservative publications) charged that the forgery episode was part of a larger pattern of FBI abuses during Crossfire Hurricane. Andrew McCarthy's article in *National Review* explicitly concluded that Clinesmith's plea was a "perfect snapshot of Crossfire Hurricane's duplicity."[51] The point was valid; Clinesmith's conduct was merely the most egregious case among numerous episodes of FBI misconduct during that probe, as Horowitz's report had already documented.

Earlier evidence that the foundation of the entire investigation into collusion was flawed and insufficient came to light in May 2020. That's when transcripts of House Intelligence Committee hearings from 2018 into Russian election interference and possible Trump campaign collusion finally were released. The transcripts raised new questions about the official rationale for an investigation into the Trump campaign in the first place. Fox News and other Trump allies highlighted admissions from senior Obama administration officials about the lack of substance in the collusion allegations:

> "I never saw any direct empirical evidence that the Trump campaign or someone in it was plotting/conspiring with the Russians to meddle with the election," former Director of National Intelligence James Clapper testified in 2017. "That's not to say that there weren't concerns about the evidence we were seeing, anecdotal evidence. . . . But I do not recall any instance where I had direct evidence."
>
> Former U.S. Ambassador to the United Nations Samantha Power, according to the transcript of her interview, was asked about the same issue. Power replied: "I am not in possession of anything—I am not in

possession and didn't read or absorb information that came from out of the intelligence community. . . ."

Obama National Security Adviser Susan Rice was asked the same question. "To the best of my recollection, there wasn't anything smoking, but there were some things that gave me pause," she said, according to her transcribed interview, in response to whether she had any evidence of conspiracy. "I don't recall intelligence that I would consider evidence to that effect that I saw . . . conspiracy prior to my departure."

When asked whether she had any evidence of "coordination," Rice replied: "I don't recall any intelligence or evidence to that effect." When asked about collusion, Rice replied: "Same answer."[52]

An even more startling revelation emerged from the hearing transcripts. CrowdStrike, the private cybersecurity firm that first accused Russia of hacking Democratic Party emails and served as a critical source for U.S. intelligence officials in the long Trump-Russia probe, had acknowledged to Congress more than two years earlier that it had no concrete evidence that Russian hackers stole emails from the Democratic National Committee's (DNC) server.

In a *RealClearInvestigations* article, Aaron Maté mused, "CrowdStrike President Shawn Henry's admission under oath . . . raises new questions about whether Special Counsel Robert Mueller, intelligence officials and Democrats misled the public." Maté added, "Henry's recently released testimony does not mean that Russia did not hack the DNC. What it does make clear is that Obama administration officials, the DNC and others have misled the public by presenting as fact information that they knew was uncertain. The fact that the Democratic Party employed the two private firms that generated the core allegations at the heart of Russiagate—Russian email hacking and Trump-Russia collusion—suggests that the federal investigation was compromised from the start."[53]

Former intelligence official Ray McGovern pointed out that the original reliance on CrowdStrike's information and assessment reflected questionable judgment by Mueller and the FBI. "CrowdStrike already had a tarnished reputation for credibility when the DNC and Clinton campaign chose it to do work the FBI should have been doing to investigate how the DNC emails got to *WikiLeaks*. It [CrowdStrike] had asserted that Russians hacked into a Ukrainian artillery app, resulting in heavy losses of howitzers in Ukraine's struggle with separatists supported by Russia. A Voice of America report explained why CrowdStrike was forced to retract that claim."[54]

The bulk of the mainstream media spun the revelations in a very different manner than Fox News, Maté, and McGovern, however. Allegations and innuendos about Trump's supposed subservience to the Russian government persisted in the U.S. and European media despite the accumulating evidence that the belief was erroneous.[55]

House Intelligence Committee chair Adam Schiff delayed release of the transcripts for nearly 18 months despite a 2018 House resolution authorizing their release. That decision raised additional questions about the motivation for keeping such information from the public. Although the reluctant admissions from leading Obama administration officials about a lack of substantive evidence did not prove that the charges were baseless, the admissions certainly did nothing to strengthen the opposing case.

Subsequent Senate hearings in September and October 2020 cast further doubt on the thesis that investigators had enough evidence to justify commencing the Russia-collusion investigation in the first place. The *Wall Street Journal*'s Kimberley A. Strassel provided a blunt assessment. "Chairman Lindsey Graham hauled the former FBI director in front of the Senate Judiciary Committee ostensibly to answer for stunning new details in the bureau's Trump-Russia probe. But the hearing more broadly resurrected the breathtaking arrogance of the swamp. This was the crew that in 2016—based on the thinnest of tips—launched a counterintelligence investigation into a presidential campaign, complete with secret surveillance warrants and informants."[56]

Referring to the salacious dossier that former British intelligence operative Christopher Steele had assembled and promoted, Strassel added, "FBI agent Peter Strzok in 2018 lectured Congress that the bureau had too many 'safeguards' and 'procedures' ever to allow 'improper' behavior. Yet this past week provided evidence the FBI leaders blew through red light after red light. We already knew they based the probe on a dossier that came from a rival campaign. We knew the bureau was warned early on that the dossier was potential Russian disinformation. And now we know it discovered that the man who was the dossier's primary source had been under FBI investigation as a suspected agent for Moscow. The bureau hid all of this from the surveillance court. It even doctored an email to conceal exculpatory information."

Without such misconduct, the investigation into allegations of the Trump campaign's collusion with Russia might well have experienced an early demise. Instead, the FBI's Crossfire Hurricane investigation became a prelude to the longer, more intensive Mueller probe. If the news media had treated the convenient leaks from James Comey and other high-level FBI officials with appropriate caution and skepticism rather than reacting as though they were being given previously undiscovered Biblical texts, the investigation likely would have fizzled quickly. Instead, the investigation and the miasma of suspicions about treason that it generated grew larger. And members of the media did not hold either their sources or themselves accountable for the resulting disinformation.

The drumbeat of allegations from the intelligence bureaucracy and its media allies about Russian activities designed to aid Donald Trump and Trump's indifference to or complicity in those activities did not abate. The accusations and innuendoes persisted even after the tepid outcome of the Mueller investigation, the first failed campaign to oust the president, and growing evidence of the FBI's mishandling of the case. As one set of allegations began to unravel, another set always seemed ready to take its place.

For example, on February 20, 2020, the New York Times broke another "blockbuster" story—this time about a classified intelligence briefing given to the House Intelligence Committee the previous week.[57] Shelby Pierson, a longtime member of the intelligence bureaucracy and (at the time) deputy to Acting Director of National Intelligence (DNI) Joseph Maguire, had delivered the briefing—which immediately leaked to the Times. In a familiar pattern, other outlets quickly picked up and amplified the story, and as usual, the principal sources for the alleged substance of the briefing were both anonymous and unmistakably hostile to Trump and Russia.[58]

Little was surprising or meaningful in the contention that Russia still sought to probe election security measures or that Moscow might attempt to sow more discord in the U.S. political process. As Reuters reporter Jonathan Landay noted, "U.S. officials have long warned that Russia *and other countries* would try to interfere in the 2020 U.S. presidential election campaign."[59] But once again, the accusations emerging from anonymous members of the U.S. intelligence apparatus targeted Russia while barely mentioning other possible foreign actors. That emphasis continued to feed the narrative that Trump was a Russian asset and that Moscow's machinations were the chief threat to U.S. security.

Indeed, the February congressional briefing had a disturbing undertone. The *New York Times* noted the intelligence agencies' assertion that the Russians were making "more creative use of Facebook and other social media. Rather than impersonating Americans as they did in 2016, Russian operatives are working to get Americans to repeat disinformation, the officials said."[60] The implication was that Americans who expressed views on social media that were similar to the Kremlin's were witting or unwitting agents of Russian propaganda. That position impugned either the judgment or loyalty—or both—of those Americans.

Much of the media seemed willing once again to help intelligence officials circulate the "Russians love Trump" narrative. Oddly, the original *New York Times* story was more balanced than most subsequent accounts. Included was a fairly straightforward version of the counterargument made by Trump's congressional allies, which was presented without even inserting a snarky, editorial-style rebuttal:

At the House briefing, Representative Chris Stewart, Republican of Utah . . . was among the Republicans who challenged the conclusion about Russia's support for Mr. Trump. Mr. Stewart insisted that the president had aggressively confronted Moscow, providing anti-tank weapons to Ukraine for its war against Russia-backed separatists and strengthening the NATO alliance with new resources, according to two people briefed on the meeting. Mr. Stewart declined to discuss the briefing but said that Moscow had no reason to support Mr. Trump. He pointed to the president's work to confront Iran, a Russian ally, and encourage European energy independence from Moscow.

A CNN story was even more surprising. It contended that Pierson appeared to have "overstated" the intelligence community's formal assessment about Russia's interference in the 2020 election cycle.[61] Top intelligence officials seemed to be trying to backpedal from Pierson and her assertions. Three of them provided the pertinent information for the CNN story. They specifically disowned her statement that the reason Moscow was engaging in interference was to promote Trump's reelection prospects. They even retreated from Pierson's conclusion that the Russian government had a preference for Trump. "The intelligence doesn't say that," one senior national security official told CNN. "A more reasonable interpretation of the intelligence is not that they have a preference, it's a step short of that. It's more that they understand the President is someone they can work with, he's a dealmaker."

Two aspects of the CNN story were remarkable. One was that the intelligence agencies were willing to scapegoat Pierson and emphasize a more nuanced interpretation of Moscow's probable motives. The other was that CNN was willing to feature the corrections and clarifications in a high-profile article, given that one of its coauthors was outspoken Trump critic and Russia-collusion proponent Jake Tapper. The unexpected balance at CNN was both unusual and refreshing. However, outside of the conservative media ecosystem, few major outlets gave the CNN revelations much additional exposure, which was not the norm for the treatment of CNN stories.

Overall media protectiveness of the intelligence bureaucracy (especially on the Russia issue) had been rising again, even before the *New York Times* article generated a flurry of new allegations. Just the day before that article broke, Trump had reprimanded Maguire and replaced him as acting DNI with Richard Grenell, the U.S. ambassador to Germany. As it turned out, the reason for Trump's displeasure was the congressional briefing, which he had not authorized; the president was especially upset about Pierson's interpretation of the intelligence regarding Russia's election conduct.

It soon became apparent that leaks about the intelligence community's warnings regarding the Russian menace were not entirely partisan. The *Washington Post* published a story (again relying solely on anonymous sources) stating that intelligence agencies had told Democratic presidential candidate Bernie Sanders a few weeks earlier that Moscow was trying to influence primary contests to benefit his candidacy.[62] Outspoken media critic Peter Van Buren noted that both intelligence briefings had remained secret until the nearly simultaneous exclusives in the two papers. He suspected less-than-pure motives. One account appeared in time "to smear Trump for replacing his DNI, and the latter leaked to the *Washington Post* ahead of the Nevada caucuses to try and damage Sanders."[63] Van Buren suggested it was no coincidence that the intelligence agencies regarded both Trump and Sanders as figures who questioned Washington's entrenched foreign policy agenda, albeit from rather different perspectives.

Glenn Greenwald was one of the few other analysts who contended that the supposedly neutral intelligence agencies were in fact pursuing a political and ideological agenda of their own. Referring to the leaked report that Sanders had been briefed about Russian efforts to aid his campaign, Greenwald charged, "It's interference by the CIA and by homeland security and by related agencies in our domestic election, which is infinitely more threatening to our democracy than whatever mischief Russian agencies are primitively doing on Facebook and Twitter." He was especially irritated at the allegations about Russian support of Sanders and the underlying message those agencies were advancing. The "theme or narrative they've settled on," that Russia is looking to help Sanders to make sure that the Democrats nominate the "weakest candidate" against President Trump is "completely moronic," he concluded.[64]

Moronic or not, the revelation of the briefing and the supposed rationale for Moscow's alleged support certainly put Sanders on the defensive. "Unlike Donald Trump, I do not consider Vladimir Putin a good friend. He is an autocratic thug who is attempting to destroy democracy and crush dissent in Russia," Sanders said. "Let's be clear, the Russians want to undermine American democracy by dividing us up and, unlike the current president, I stand firmly against their efforts, and any other foreign power that wants to interfere in our election."[65]

The sight of a presidential candidate who routinely portrayed himself as an advocate of peace endeavoring to be more Catholic than the Pope with respect to hostility toward Russia was indicative of how deeply that theme had imbedded itself in America's politics and the collective American psyche. So too was Sanders's remark about Trump being Putin's "friend."

Accounts like those by Van Buren and Greenwald, questioning either the motives or the conclusions of the two intelligence briefings, were decidedly in the minority. The overall media reaction was reminiscent of the preoccupation with and promotion of the initial Russia-collusion narrative. An article by CNN's Stephen Collinson managed to recap virtually every allegation made about the Trump-Russia connection since the 2016 election, while asserting, "The President's defensive response to a new Russia interference drama, colored by his belief that all such revelations [are] a 'Deep State' assault on his own legitimacy, already appears to be exacerbating the damage caused by Moscow's meddling."[66] Rachel Maddow seemed almost gleeful about the intelligence briefing and the revelations in the *New York Times*. "It is on!" she proclaimed that evening on her MSNBC show. "Russia is running an op to try to help reelect Donald Trump in 2020." She added, "Here we go again."[67]

Media accounts ignored or downplayed an important detail that emerged during the intelligence briefing. Buried in the middle of the Collinson article (and a few other analyses) was a rather surprising admission on Pierson's part. Rep. Will Hurd (R-TX), a former CIA officer, pressed Pierson about what led to her statements that Russia preferred Trump as president. She reportedly responded that neither she nor the other members of the briefing team had the underlying data, they had just the assessment.[68] That omission was curious for such a high-profile congressional briefing—especially one with extensive potential political implications. Collinson and his media colleagues chose not to discuss how members of the House Intelligence Committee were supposed to judge the quality and credibility of the assessment when they had no access to the material on which the assessment was based. But at least Collinson mentioned Hurd's query and the response; most of his journalistic compatriots did not.

In contrast to the February 20 *New York Times* article on the intelligence briefing—which at least briefly presented the arguments of Trump's supporters that his policies toward Russia had been quite hard line—most analyses ignored or glossed over those substantive points. Collinson, for example, summarily dismissed them as "subjective"—as if arms deals to Ukraine, continued NATO expansion, terminating major arms control agreements that Moscow favored, and attacks on Bashar al-Assad and other Russian clients were little more than conjured illusions.[69] Conversely, Trump's friendly but vapid, diplomatic compliments given to Putin during summit sessions (the same kind of rhetorical froth that previous presidents expressed to autocratic leaders over the decades) were deemed definitive evidence that the Trump White House harbored an overly accommodating view of Russia.

The *Washington Post*'s Philip Bump was even more disingenuous. He acknowledged Trump's imposition of sanctions and his encouragement of greater U.S. energy independence and export capabilities but added that, on sanctions, the president "wasn't always a willing partner." Bump acted as if those two items were the Trump administration's only hostile measures toward Moscow, ignoring the Ukraine arms deals and other actions. Moreover, he insisted that the two measures he did acknowledge "are relatively minor compared with the benefits Russia gets from Trump's presidency. Tensions with traditional U.S. allies. A freer hand for Russia in international affairs. Questions about the efficacy of NATO. A distrust of international accountability institutions."[70] Leaving aside the ugly implication that merely questioning the efficacy of NATO constituted illegitimate appeasement of Putin, Bump's analysis was a textbook example of journalistic bias on the issue of Russia.

As in the past, major portions of the media seemed willing to act as public relations personnel for intelligence functionaries who worried that even the temporary appointment of a critic might produce undesired changes. By trashing the Grenell nomination and according prominence to the (apparently preliminary and sketchy) intelligence briefing about Russian plans to influence the 2020 election, journalists helped give the already overhyped fears of the "Russia threat" a new lease on life.

THE MEDIA'S MCCARTHYISM

By early 2020, drive-by smears accusing political or ideological opponents of having unsavory links to Russia had become commonplace. At times, the allegations were so strained as to be almost comical—if it weren't for their ugly echoes of McCarthyism. Senate Majority Leader Mitch McConnell's critics took to calling him "Moscow Mitch."[71] Ironically, they did so even though he had been an ardent hawk during the Cold War and was frequently alarmist about Vladimir Putin's alleged desire to revive the Soviet empire. In August 2018, for example, McConnell said, "I think the Russians are acting like the old Soviet Union."[72] But even such a neo–Cold War stance was not sufficient to shield him from accusations that he did Russia's bidding. To his opponents in the media and elsewhere, McConnell's refusal to endorse new "election security" laws and support the impeachment of President Trump was sufficient to warrant impugning his loyalty to the United States. In July 2019, MSNBC's Joe Scarborough asserted that McConnell's "lack of action" on allegations of Russian election meddling was downright "un-American." He continued his indictment by accusing the majority leader of "aiding and abetting Vladimir Putin's ongoing attempts to subvert American democracy."[73]

When media figures weren't applying the Moscow Mitch label, they were ridiculing McConnell for protesting the smear.[74] They were especially indignant about his accusations that using the term constituted McCarthyism. *Washington Post* columnist Dana Milbank stated, "McCarthyism, by definition, is a type of defamation using indiscriminate allegations based on unsubstantiated charges. But the allegations underlying Moscow Mitch are specific and well-substantiated. He has blocked virtually every meaningful bill to prevent a repeat of Russia's 2016 election interference." How that action automatically constituted disloyal behavior to serve Russia's interests rather than merely reflecting an honest policy disagreement, Milbank did not explain.[75]

On another occasion, Milbank was even more explicit in his allegations of McConnell's alleged Russian servitude, flatly calling the Senate majority leader a "Russian asset." He explained why the label was appropriate: "Russia attacked our country in 2016. It is attacking us today. Its attacks will intensify in 2020. Yet each time we try to raise our defenses to repel the attack, McConnell, the Senate majority leader, blocks us from defending ourselves." Milbank went on: "Let's call this what it is: unpatriotic. The Kentucky Republican is, arguably more than any other American, doing Russian President Vladimir Putin's bidding."[76] His diatribe both exaggerated the significance of Russia's "attacks" and impugned a prominent political leader simply for daring to resist policies that Milbank believed to be important. If that line of argument didn't constitute McCarthyism, it was a great imitation.

The smearing of opponents for allegedly doing the Kremlin's bidding became increasingly common throughout 2020, even in situations where no connection was plausible. A March 3, 2020, exchange between former interim Democratic National Committee chair Donna Brazile and current Republican National Committee chair Ronna McDaniel became extremely heated when McDaniel accused the DNC of rigging the presidential nomination process against Sen. Bernie Sanders. A visibly enraged Brazile exploded, "For people to use Russian talking points to sow division among Americans is stupid," she stated. "So Ronna, go to hell! This is not about—go to hell! I'm tired of it."[77]

Allegations of DNC bias against Sanders were hardly new; they had surfaced repeatedly in the 2016 campaign, and documents leaked to WikiLeaks at the time confirmed many of those charges. To scream that raising similar allegations in the 2020 campaign amounted to "Russian talking points" not only constituted McCarthyism, but it was far-fetched, bizarre McCarthyism. The incident, though, illustrated how prosaic and promiscuous the "Russian tool" smear had become.

THE UKRAINE SEQUEL AND THE MEDIA'S PROMOTION OF IMPEACHMENT

The next press salvo against Trump involved his decision to delay the delivery of economic and military aid to Ukraine. Anti-Trump forces in Congress and the news media claimed that the president would only release the aid if the new government in Kyiv agreed to launch a corruption probe of Trump's rival, Joe Biden. That allegation of an illegal quid pro quo would eventually lead the House of Representatives to vote for two articles of impeachment.

With rare exceptions, the mainstream press echoed the allegations that congressional Democrats made regarding Trump's telephone conversation with Ukraine's president Volodymyr Zelensky about the aid package and other signs of a possible quid pro quo. What was interesting, though, is that complaints about the administration's Ukraine policy—from both Trump's congressional adversaries and the press—soon became much broader. An increasingly prevalent theme in the media was that this episode was more evidence that Trump's policies were pro-Russian and that under his leadership the United States was betraying an ally.

Journalists rushed to back foreign policy establishment figures who criticized the president for failing to adopt a sufficiently confrontational policy toward Moscow. The implication presented by members of the policy bureaucracy—and largely echoed by the journalistic community—was that this president had no right to set the nation's foreign policy agenda. That was especially true if he dared defy the advice of "experts" on Ukraine and Russia and adopted a less interventionist, less intrusive policy.

The point became evident during the 2019 House committee hearings on Trump's alleged attempt to solicit a quid pro quo from Ukraine's president. Strikingly, the testimony by Trump's critics in the diplomatic corps focused not on the president's possible illegal conduct regarding the narrow quid pro quo issue but on their overall disagreement with his policy toward Ukraine—or more accurately, their perception of his Ukraine policy. William Taylor, who served as the interim U.S. ambassador to Kyiv in mid-2019, was quite candid about having a broader focus, stating that his purpose in testifying was "to provide the committees with my views about the strategic importance of Ukraine to the United States, as well as additional information about the incidents in question."[78]

Taylor expressed the dismay he and his colleagues felt when it appeared that the president would withhold or delay military aid to Kyiv unless the Zelensky government investigated the energy firm Burisma, its connections to Hunter and Joe Biden, and possible Ukrainian interference in the 2016 U.S. election. "The Ukrainians were fighting the Russians and counted on not only the training and weaponry [in the aid package], but also the assurance of U.S. support." At that point, Taylor stated, "I realized that one of the key pillars of our strong support for Ukraine was threatened." Such criticism went well beyond whether

Trump's request to Zelensky for an investigation was illegal or improper, as did Taylor's lament that "more Ukrainians would die without U.S. assistance." Those were policy issues, not legal matters.

The ambassador closed with effusive praise for Ukraine, describing its people as implementing "an inclusive, democratic nationalism, not unlike what we in America, in our best moments, feel about our country." Many experts on Ukraine would have been astonished at Taylor's depiction of nationalism in that country as either inclusive or democratic, especially given the influence of such neo-fascist factions as Svoboda and Right Sector. Ukraine was and is a complex place, ideologically and politically, and Ukraine-Russia relations were equally murky and complex. But apparently Taylor did not see it that way. He stressed that Congress "has supported Ukraine with harsh sanctions against Russia for invading and occupying Ukraine. We can be proud of that support and that we stood up to a dictator's aggression against a democratic neighbor."

At times Taylor appeared to be Ukraine's ambassador to the United States rather than the U.S. ambassador to Ukraine. In a subsequent op-ed in the *New York Times*, he elevated Ukraine's importance to stratospheric levels. "Ukraine is defending itself and the West against Russian attack. If Ukraine succeeds, we succeed. The relationship between the United States and Ukraine is key to our national security. . . ." Indeed, he insisted, in "the contest between democracies and autocracies, the contest between freedom and unfreedom, Ukraine is the front line."[79]

Leaving aside the ambassador's painfully biased, oversimplified portrayal of Ukrainian affairs, his testimony raised the question: What did any of his views on such issues have to do with whether President Trump had committed an impeachable offense? Taylor articulated a policy disagreement with the president—his superior and the elected official in charge of U.S. foreign policy with respect to Ukraine and all other countries. Ambassadors are supposed to implement the administration's policy, not oppose or undermine it. But he seemed to take umbrage that the president apparently wanted a Ukraine policy different from what Taylor thought was appropriate.

Similar attitudes emerged from the testimony of former ambassador to Ukraine Marie Yovanovitch (whom Trump had removed from her post earlier that year), Deputy Assistant Secretary of State George P. Kent, and National Security Council staffer Alexander Vindman. Kent, for example, stressed that for the past five years, "we have focused our united efforts across the Atlantic to support Ukraine in its fight for the cause of freedom, and the rebirth of a country free from Russian dominion."[80] Among the establishment foreign policy bromides he voiced was this: "The United States has clear national interests at stake in Ukraine. Ukraine's success is very much in our national interest, in the way we have defined our national interests broadly in Europe for the past 75 years." He neglected to mention that Ukraine was not even an independent country for 47 of those years, much less a "clear national interest" of the United States. His description of the struggle between Ukraine and Russia made even Taylor's one-sided account seem balanced and nuanced.

Kent even described the 2014 Maidan Revolution not by that usual name, but by the laudatory label "Revolution of Dignity," the term used by Ukrainian nationalists. As did Taylor, Kent identified with Ukraine's cause to an unhealthy degree. Also like Taylor, his objections to Trump's Ukraine policy were much broader and deeper than the issue of an alleged political quid pro quo involving the Zelensky government and a possible investigation into Joe Biden's conduct.

As for Yovanovitch, in addition to her anger at being recalled from her ambassadorial post in Kyiv, a major point in her testimony was her belief that Russia would be the biggest beneficiary of the Trump administration's policy toward Ukraine. "We see the potential in Ukraine. Russia, by contrast, sees the risk," she said. "Ukraine is a battleground for great power competition."[81] The potential benefit to Russia of Trump's approach, she argued, was two-fold. Withholding security assistance conveyed to Moscow the message that the United States was not a reliable Ukrainian ally, despite Washington's previous signals. At the same time, allowing corruption to fester in Ukraine—for example, by removing an ambassador (her) dedicated to rooting out such misconduct—also made the nation more vulnerable to Russian influence.

The media portrayals of Taylor, Kent, Yovanovitch, and Vindman were overwhelmingly favorable—often to the point of painting them as heroic figures resisting a president whose policies were designed to undermine an essential U.S. ally and play into Russia's hands.[82] An article in *The Hill* was typical, gushing that Yovanovitch was "a top-notch diplomat, careful, meticulous, whip smart."[83] Whether Trump had actually solicited an illicit quid pro quo became a secondary issue in media analyses; his real crime, according to the mainstream press, was disagreeing with the policy views of such astute professionals.

Articles on the hearings rarely questioned any of the assumptions and conclusions those witnesses voiced. One nearly unanimous assumption was that Russia was committing unprovoked aggression against its neighbor, and that separatist insurgents in Ukraine's eastern Donbas region were nothing more than Moscow's puppets. A balanced treatment regarding the extent of Western support for (if not interference on behalf of) the Maidan Revolution would have raised at least some questions about the "unprovoked" nature of the Russian response.

Even a cursory examination of Ukraine's history, especially the country's internal dynamics from the attainment of independence in 1991 to the 2014 turbulence, also should have led to doubts about the standard narrative surrounding the Maidan Revolution and its aftermath. Such an analysis would have shown a consistent, sharp cleavage between eastern and western Ukraine regarding economics, politics, language, and religion.[84] In every post-independence election, eastern Ukrainians decisively supported pro-Russia parties, while the western regions overwhelmingly backed nationalistic, strongly anti-Russia parties.

An analysis by Vladimir Golstein, professor of Slavic studies at Brown University, emphasized that with the Maidan Revolution "the culture, language, and political thinking of western Ukraine have been imposed on the rest of Ukraine." The goal ostensibly was the unification of the country behind a pro-Western, pro-European Union agenda, but the actual objective, Golstein concluded, "has been to put down and humiliate Ukraine's Russian-speaking population. The radical nationalists of western Ukraine, for whom the rejection of Russia and its culture is an article of faith, intend to force the rest of the country to fit their narrow vision."[85]

Richard Sakwa, professor of Russian and European politics at the University of Kent, concluded that Golstein's assessment was "putting it rather strongly," but he agreed that "the division is real."[86] A bitter division along a geographic, political, economic, and linguistic fault line running through the center of the country was evident before independence, and it grew wider in the years after. Those longstanding fissures raised the question of whether, after the Maidan Revolution brought to power a government utterly dominated by Western-based nationalists, secessionist sentiments in the east might be genuine and not just an artificial Russian creation—as the witnesses in the House committee hearings stated or implied. Unfortunately, almost all such questions and nuances were absent from the media coverage of that testimony and the Ukraine issue overall.

More serious journalistic inquiries also would have cast doubt on the rosy assessment of Ukraine's commitment to liberal democracy, which Taylor, Yovanovitch, and other witnesses presented with almost no caveats. Analysts had amply documented pervasive corruption as well as disturbingly authoritarian developments in the "new Ukraine," including growing anti-Semitism, new restrictions on freedom of expression, and violent incidents perpetrated by ultranationalist and openly fascist factions.[87] Almost none of that troubling context appeared in the witnesses' portrayals of Ukraine or made its way into news stories or opinion pieces about that testimony.

The most debatable point voiced by all four diplomats was the assertion that Ukraine was an essential U.S. ally and any weakening of U.S. support risked unleashing widespread Russian aggression that would endanger the peace of Europe. Given that America was able to protect itself throughout its first two centuries of independence—when Ukraine was part of the Russian empire and the Soviet Union—the contention that it was now somehow an essential U.S. ally was a stretch of logic.

The testimony of Alexander Vindman should have been significantly more pertinent to the central issue of the impeachment hearings. Vindman claimed that he had listened in on Trump's July 25, 2019, telephone call with Zelensky, in which Trump allegedly pressured the Ukrainian leader for the investigation quid pro quo. In his opening statement, though, Vindman emphasized his full agreement with his colleagues and previous witnesses about "the strategic importance of

Ukraine as a bulwark against Russian aggression."[88] In some ways, his identification with Ukraine and its anti-Russia posture was even more pronounced than those of his colleagues. He was born in Ukraine, and his family had left the Soviet Union four decades earlier. Vindman's rhetoric, both in his congressional testimony and in his public statements, exhibited a vehement hostility to Russia and the Russian government. Ukrainian leaders certainly considered him a valuable ally. He admitted that Ukraine's government had offered him the post of defense minister on three separate occasions.[89]

A few conservative critics, both in Congress and the media, suggested that such a close association with Kyiv created an inherent conflict of interest and perhaps even a case of dual loyalty. Fox News host Laura Ingraham raised that possibility explicitly. Vindman's defenders in the press exploded in outrage and excoriated such critics, accusing them of "smearing a war hero," even when most of them merely raised questions about his objectivity and judgment.[90]

ANOTHER "RUSSIAN PLOT": BOUNTY ALLEGATIONS

The predictable House vote for impeachment and the equally predictable Senate vote for acquittal did not spell the end of allegations about Russian attempts to undermine America and Trump's failure to defend his country against such assaults. Another report of evil Russian initiatives surfaced in early summer 2020 and received massive press coverage. The *New York Times* published a story on June 28 charging that Moscow had put a bounty on the lives of American soldiers stationed in Afghanistan.[91] The story was based on information provided by an anonymous source within the intelligence community.

As expected, a furious reaction erupted in Congress and the mainstream media. Although the Kremlin and the Taliban immediately issued denials, members of the press peremptorily dismissed those statements. When the White House insisted that the intelligence agencies had never informed either the president or vice president of such reports, establishment press figures were nearly as scornful of those denials. A mutual back-patting exercise ensued, as major outlets, including the *Washington*

Post, CNN, and the *Wall Street Journal*, rushed to assure readers and viewers that they had "confirmed" or "verified" the reporting in the *New York Times*. What they were confirming or verifying, though, was unclear because they couched their supportive pieces with hedging terms such as "if true." Such terminology signaled that those journalists could not independently confirm the validity of the information in the original story despite creating the impression that they had already done so.[92]

As with so many other inflammatory news accounts about Russian plots directed against the United States, serious doubts about the accuracy of this one developed almost immediately. Just days later, an unnamed intelligence official told CBS reporter Catherine Herridge that the information about alleged bounties was uncorroborated. The source also revealed to Herridge that the National Security Agency (NSA) had concluded that the intelligence collection report did not "match well-established and verifiable Taliban and Haqqani practices" and lacked "sufficient reporting to corroborate any links." The bounty intelligence had been assessed at "low levels" in the National Security Council, but it did not travel farther up the chain of command.

Trump's heated denials that he or any high-level official in his administration had ever received a briefing on the bounty allegation apparently proved to be true. The source confirmed to Herridge that the bounty report was not included in briefings with the president or vice president, both because it was deemed "uncorroborated" and because dissent existed within the intelligence community about its veracity.[93] The Pentagon, which apparently had originated the bounty allegation and tried to sell the intelligence agencies on the theory,[94] soon retreated and issued its own statement about the "unconfirmed" nature of the story.[95]

The sense of déjà vu grew, as though the episode was the second coming of the infamous, uncorroborated, and salacious Steele dossier that had surfaced early in the Russia-collusion episode and served as one important basis for the initial FISA warrants. A number of conservative and anti-war outlets highlighted the multiplying doubts about the bounty charges. They had somewhat different motives for doing so, however. Most conservative critics believed that the scandal was yet another attempt by a hostile news media to discredit President Trump, primarily for partisan reasons. Anti-war types suspected that it was an attempt by both the Pentagon and the top echelons of some intelligence agencies to use the media to generate more animosity toward Russia and to thwart the withdrawal of U.S. troops from Afghanistan, a process that was still in its early stages following the Trump administration's February 29, 2020, peace accord with the Taliban. Congressional Democrats worked closely with neoconservative Republicans such as Rep. Liz Cheney (R–WY) to advance the latter objective.[96]

Whether or not a desire to escalate the new cold war with Russia and keep U.S. troops in Afghanistan motivated the bounty story, both effects came to pass. Congressional hawks immediately called for a delay in further withdrawals while the allegation was investigated. And they made more "Trump is Putin's puppet" assertions. Nancy Pelosi hurled another jibe with that theme. "With him, all roads lead to Putin," Pelosi said. "I don't know what the Russians have on the president, politically, personally, or financially."[97]

Despite the growing cloud of uncertainty about the source or accuracy of the bounty allegation, several high-profile journalists treated it as though it were an established fact. A blatant spin was evident in a *New York Times* article. Under the headline "White House Dismisses Reports of Bounties, But Is Silent on Russia," Michael Crowley and Eric Schmitt wrote, "First President Trump denied knowing about it. Then he called it a possible 'hoax.' Next, the White House attacked the news media. And now an unnamed intelligence official is to blame. The one thing Mr. Trump and his top officials have not done is to address the substance of intelligence reports that Russia paid bounties to Taliban-affiliated fighters to kill American soldiers in Afghanistan, or what they might do in response."[98] The "evidence" they cited for the "intelligence reports" was the earlier story in their own newspaper. They stated further that although the president's aides called the allegations unverified, "many" U.S. intelligence officials deemed them credible. Buried far down in the article was an admission that the intelligence agencies were divided about the report.

Gradually, most of Trump's media critics backed away from their innuendos that he had in fact been briefed about the bounty issue but

had chosen not to act on the intelligence. Their fallback position was that
the information had been included in one of the daily written reports
that the president received. That version at least had plausibility, given
Trump's notoriously lazy inattention to details and his equally notorious
reluctance to read.[99] But it did not change the fact that intelligence personnel giving him verbal briefings did not deem the report sufficiently
credible, much less alarming, to bring it to his attention. Writing in
Consortium News, former intelligence official Ray McGovern reached
a blunt conclusion: "As a preparer and briefer of *The President's Daily
Brief* [PDB] to Presidents Reagan and H.W. Bush, I can attest to the fact
that—based on what has been revealed so far—the Russian bounty story
falls far short of the PDB threshold."[100]

Barbara Boland, national security correspondent for *The American
Conservative* and a veteran journalist on intelligence issues, cited some
"glaring problems" with the bounty charges. One was that the *New York
Times*'s anonymous source stated that the assessment was based "on
interrogations of captured Afghan militants and criminals."[101] Boland
noted that John Kiriakou, a former analyst and case officer for the CIA
who led the team that captured senior al Qaeda member Abu Zubaydah
in 2002, termed the reliance on coercive interrogations "a red flag."
Kiriakou added, "When you capture a prisoner, and you're interrogating
him, the prisoner is going to tell you what he thinks you want to hear."
Boland reminded readers that under "enhanced interrogation" (i.e.,
torture), Khalid Sheik Mohammed, the mastermind of the 9/11 attacks,
made at least 31 confessions, "many of which were completely false."

A second problem Boland saw with the bounty story was identifying
a rational purpose for such a Russian initiative, since Trump's intention
to pull U.S. troops out of Afghanistan was apparent to everyone. Moreover, she emphasized, only eight U.S. military personnel were killed
during the first six months of 2020, and the *New York Times*'s story could
not verify that even one fatality resulted from a paid bounty. If the program existed at all, it was extraordinarily ineffective.

Nevertheless, numerous media accounts breathlessly repeated the
charges as if they were proven. David Sanger and Eric Schmitt asserted
that given the latest incident, "it doesn't require a top-secret clearance

and access to the government's most classified information to see that the list of Russian aggressions in recent weeks rivals some of the worst days of the Cold War."[102] Ray McGovern responded to the Sanger-Schmitt article by impolitely reminding his readers about Sanger's dreadful record during the lead-up to the Iraq War of uncritically repeating unverified leaks from intelligence sources and hyping the danger of Saddam's alleged weapons of mass destruction.[103]

Another prominent journalist who doubled down on the bounty allegation was the *Washington Post*'s Aaron Blake. According to the headline of his July 1, 2020, article, "The only people dismissing the Russia bounties intel: the Taliban, Russia and Trump."[104] Apparently, the NSA's willingness to go public with its doubts and the negative assessments of the allegation by several veteran former intelligence officials did not make an impression on Blake. Despite a perfunctory nod that the intelligence had not yet been confirmed, Blake quoted several of the usual hawks from the president's own party as evidence of how "serious" the situation was.

As time passed, though, the outnumbered media skeptics of the bounty story expressed increasingly vigorous criticisms of the allegation. Analysts David B. Rivkin Jr. and George S. Beebe provided a good summary of the problems with the media's reaction to the bounty allegation. "The initial question to ask in evaluating the veracity of the allegation," they wrote, "is how credible are the sources? Here, the answer: not very." The second question is, "what other information might support or disconfirm the allegations? Here, too, there is reason for skepticism." A crucial third question, they contended, was, "Who benefits from these allegations? The list certainly includes the central Afghan government, which has overseen the interrogations on which the story is based and desperately wants the U.S. military to remain in Afghanistan. . . . Few things could more effectively throw a wrench into the gears of Afghan peace talks than credible reports that the Taliban is working with Russians to kill Americans." The list of possible beneficiaries "also includes Trump's domestic political opponents" who had long sought to tar him with the pro-Russia label. "Notably, the list does not include Russia." Indeed, "as the United States has drawn down its presence,

[Moscow] has backed both a U.S. withdrawal and peace talks with the Taliban. The Kremlin is not looking for ways to impede U.S. departure from a region that Moscow once dominated." None of this, Rivkin and Beebe conceded, proved that the bounty story was false, but "it certainly means that the standard of evidence for validating such allegations should be much higher than our media's barely concealed lust to embrace them would suggest."[105]

Their case for skepticism was warranted. Even the CIA and other agencies that embraced the charges about Russian bounties ascribed only "moderate confidence" to their conclusions. Three levels of confidence— high, moderate, and low—are assigned to intelligence assessments. According to the Office of the Director of National Intelligence, a moderate confidence level means "that the information is credibly sourced and plausible but not of sufficient quality or corroborated sufficiently to warrant a higher level of confidence." The NSA (and possibly others in the intelligence community) designated the reports low confidence, meaning "that the information's credibility and/or plausibility is questionable, or that the information is too fragmented or poorly corroborated to make solid analytic inferences, or that significant concerns or problems with the sources" exist.[106]

Anti-war journalist Caitlin Johnstone offered an especially brutal indictment of the media's performance regarding this installment of the Russian-threat-to-America saga. "All parties involved in spreading this malignant psyop are absolutely vile," she wrote, "but a special disdain should be reserved for the media class who have been entrusted by the public with the essential task of creating an informed populace and holding power to account. How much of an unprincipled whore do you have to be to call yourself a journalist and uncritically parrot the completely unsubstantiated assertions of spooks while protecting their anonymity?"[107]

The media should not have ignored or blithely dismissed the bounty allegation, but far too many members ran enthusiastically with a story based on extremely thin evidence, questionable sourcing, and equally questionable logic. Here again, they seemed to believe the worst about Russia's behavior and Trump's reaction to it because they had long mentally programed themselves to believe such horror stories without doubt or reservation. The assessment by FAIR's Alan MacLeod was devastatingly accurate. With regard to the bounty story, he concluded, "evidence-free claims from nameless spies became fact" in most media accounts.[108] Instead of sober, restrained inquiries from a skeptical, probing press, readers and viewers were treated to another installment of anti-Russia diatribes. That treatment had the effect, whether intended or unintended, of promoting more hawkish policies toward Moscow and undermining the already-belated withdrawal of U.S. troops from Afghanistan.

CONSEQUENCES OF MEDIA HOSTILITY TO RUSSIA

Another noticeable effect of the media's hostility to both Russia and Trump was the gradual shift of many left-of-center journalists to more hawkish views on foreign policy generally. The trend was most obvious in their preferences regarding U.S. policy toward Moscow, but it bled into issues that related just modestly to Russia. For example, the demonization of Russia played a role in media attitudes about Syria policy. Although the animosity within the journalistic community toward Bashar al-Assad was widespread because of his regime's brutality, his status as a Russian client intensified that hostility.

The effect was evident and even more startling with respect to Venezuela and U.S. policy toward the government of Nicolas Maduro. Normally, one would expect liberal and staunchly left-wing journalists to oppose any U.S. attempt to overthrow a Third World government—especially one that was avowedly Marxist. And some of the usual left-wing members of the media did oppose Trump administration moves to back opposition factions in Venezuela led by Juan Guaidó and to openly seek Maduro's overthrow. But others did not, and the root of their surprising receptivity to Washington's machinations was anger at Russia's role in backing Maduro. Their loathing of Russia seemed to eclipse their normal loathing of Donald Trump—so much so that they appeared willing to remain silent about or even support his attempt to help forcibly remove Maduro from power.

MSNBC's Rachel Maddow was one apparent convert to the hawkish cause—a stance that infuriated her anti-war colleagues in the media. The Grayzone's Aaron Maté could barely contain his disgust in a May 2019 article. Maté accused Maddow of being "the loudest voice among the corporate media hack pack doubling down on Russiagate conspiracies." He charged that Maddow had taken "her propaganda to an entirely new level of militaristic cheerleading, launching into a rant that offered de facto encouragement for the current neocon cause-du-jour: regime change in Venezuela. Maddow not only cast Trump as a Russian stooge for daring to discuss—and possibly de-escalate—the Venezuelan crisis with Russian President Vladimir Putin," Maté went on, but she "expressed sympathy for John Bolton and Mike Pompeo, the most militaristic members of the Trump administration."[109]

Maté excoriated Maddow for her views on Russia. In addition to embracing even the most far-fetched Russia-Trump conspiracy theories, he charged, "Maddow has also been a vocal promoter of unhinged propaganda that encourages perilous tensions with Russia, and cultivates pro-war opinion among her base of extremely suggestible liberal viewers." He noted that when "Maddow finally broke her silence on Venezuela, it was on May 3, after Trump held a phone call with Putin to discuss, among other things, lowering the temperature on Venezuela. The diplomatic contact between two world leaders should have been considered routine, but in the feverish world of liberal conspiracism, it was another opportunity for hallucinatory claims of collusion." Maté then detailed a long, rambling Maddow presentation on Venezuela that seemed receptive to a coup against Maduro to "push Russia back." That episode of her show (on May 3, 2019) illustrated just how much hostility to Trump and Russia was driving her perspective on broader foreign policy issues.[110]

FAIR's Adam Johnson blasted the entire roster of MSNBC hosts. Their stance regarding Trump's campaign for a coup against Maduro, he charged, ranged "from silence to support." Documenting the network's coverage of the Venezuela issue, Johnson concluded that it consisted of "five minutes of hand-wringing from Chris Hayes, total silence from all the other primetime personalities, and daytime reporting that echoes

Trump and [Florida Republican Sen. Marco] Rubio's uniform praise for the coup attempt and its primary actors."[111]

THE MEDIA'S MULTIPLE RUSSIA COVERAGE FAILURES

Members of America's news media were tasked with addressing several interlocking issues with respect to the U.S.-Russia relationship. One set was relatively narrow, involving three key questions: Did the Russian government attempt to interfere in the 2016 U.S. election, and if it did, how successful was it? Was such an effort designed to benefit Donald Trump's political prospects, or was it simply aimed at causing dissension and division in American public opinion? And most important, did the Trump campaign collaborate in any interference? The media scrutinized all three questions. Indeed, one could make the case that the degree of attention was excessive and eventually became an obsession. Worse, the scrutiny had a pronounced anti-Trump and anti-Russia bias from the outset.

Media inquiries and the government's efforts (the FBI investigation beginning in the summer of 2016 and the subsequent Mueller probe) uncovered evidence that varied greatly in quality and certainty with respect to the three issues. Fairly strong evidence emerged that the Putin government did seek to meddle in the U.S. election to benefit Russia's national interests and objectives. On this point, journalists should have placed Moscow's effort in the broader context of geopolitical maneuvering by major powers. However, they rarely attempted to provide such context. Meddling in elections and other internal affairs of foreign countries is standard operating procedure throughout the nation-state system, as it has been throughout history. The United States itself has been an especially prolific practitioner. The umbrage that American media and political figures expressed about Russia's conduct regarding the 2016 election might have been more credible if the United States had refrained from engaging in similar conduct. But the historical record shows that Washington has meddled in the political affairs of dozens of countries—including many democracies.[112] Indeed, high-level advisers to Bill Clinton virtually ran Russian President Boris Yeltsin's reelection campaign in 1996.

Likewise, foreign attempts to influence U.S. elections (and American politics generally) are nothing new, and they typically take a variety of forms, both subtle and brazen. Some of the most blatant examples occurred during the 1990s, when influential figures in South Korea and China, almost certainly with the blessing of their respective governments, sought to assist President Bill Clinton's political fortunes.[113] Other countries, especially Washington's major European and East Asian allies, routinely try to nudge U.S. policy debates toward outcomes they prefer, and they work closely with like-minded Americans in Congress, the think tank community, and the media to do so.[114] They spend tens of millions of dollars each year to cultivate favorable treatment, as will be discussed in Chapter 11. This approach may not constitute direct election interference, but it certainly is a relevant factor and some cause for concern.

Foreign leaders were more concerned than normal about the 2016 U.S. election. Officials in allied governments were hardly reticent about their preference for a Hillary Clinton presidency, given candidate Trump's negative comments about Washington's venerable alliances and his demand for greater burden sharing on the part of America's security partners. Evidence emerged that Ukraine's government explicitly sought to damage Trump's prospects and strengthen Clinton's chances.[115] Embarrassing revelations about Trump campaign manager Paul Manafort's relationship with the previous government in Kyiv leaked to the press, forcing him to resign. It is now well established that the information came from Kyiv and that high-level officials were responsible for the leaks.[116] Just as Moscow viewed Trump as friendlier (or at least less hostile) than Clinton to Russia's interests, Kyiv's perspective was the opposite.

Very little of that context appeared in mainstream media accounts about Moscow's activities with respect to U.S. politics. A similar blinkered response emerged following an August 2020 intelligence report about possible foreign interference in the 2020 campaign.[117] The report mentioned that Russia wanted to see Donald Trump reelected, but analysts had also looked at the activities and goals of countries such as China and Iran. The report concluded that both Beijing and Tehran considered Trump "unpredictable" and viewed a victory by Democratic Party nominee Joe Biden as more palatable. However, news stories and opinion pieces in the mainstream media rarely mentioned the latter point, or they spun it as a mere passive "preference" on the part of those governments. In sharp contrast, they insisted that the new analysis was the latest confirmation of Moscow's use of active measures to secure Trump's reelection.[118] Hosts on CNN and MSNBC repeatedly gave platforms to major Democratic Party figures, such as Nancy Pelosi, to emphasize the alleged distinction between Russian and Chinese conduct. On most occasions, the interviewers made clear in both tone and words that they personally agreed with that assessment.[119]

The distinction between "active" Russian measures and a "passive" Chinese preference was factually incorrect. William Evanina, director of the National Counterintelligence and Security Center, issued a statement on the intelligence report. The pertinent passage reads, "China has been expanding its influence efforts ahead of November 2020 to shape the policy environment in the United States, pressure political figures it views as opposed to China's interests, and deflect and counter criticism of China." That assessment certainly indicates something more than a "preference."[120] Yet most mainstream media figures ignored that part of the report. Such indifference irritated *RealityChek* blogger Alan Tonelson. His article in *The American Conservative* made the case that Beijing's tactics to influence U.S. politics and policy were both sophisticated and extensive. He asserted that China's meddling over the years exceeded Russia's "by orders of magnitude" and left Moscow's efforts "in the dust."[121]

CNN's Jim Sciutto was one of the few mainstream anti-Russia journalists who also was unsparing in his criticisms of China's interference in America's political affairs. His 2019 book *The Shadow War* primarily focused on outright espionage. But his discussion of Beijing's moves tended to support Tonelson's case that China's efforts to undermine U.S. policy were far from passive.[122] Such evidence from a staunch Russophobe made attempts by other members of the media to draw a sharp contrast between Russian and Chinese meddling seem strained and unwarranted.

A Russian influence effort undoubtedly existed during the controversial 2016 presidential campaign. However, despite congressional investigations and massive media inquiries, no credible evidence surfaced that the meddling affected the outcome of the U.S. election. Indeed, much of Moscow's campaign seemed both small-scale and amateurish.[123] The $200,000 spent on clumsy propaganda ads on Facebook was a drop in the proverbial ocean of spending by the two major parties and assorted political action committees during that election cycle.

Still, the media persisted in overstating the size, significance, sophistication, and effectiveness of Moscow's conduct. Some articles even circulated overheated statements made by congressional Democrats, comparing the interference to Pearl Harbor or 9/11. Relaying such statements without a cautionary comment was inflammatory and in shockingly bad taste, given the number of Americans who had died in those two attacks. The media hyperbole was indicative of the imbalance—even hysteria—pervading coverage of Russia's election-interference initiatives.

The quality of the coverage of Moscow's motives and objectives was also unimpressive. A Kremlin preference for a Trump presidency over a Clinton one was unsurprising given Clinton's intense hostility toward Russia. When one candidate implies that Russia's head of state is the new Hitler and openly charges that Moscow's behavior in Ukraine was reminiscent of Nazi Germany's expansionist binge at the end of the 1930s, one might well expect the target of such vilification to prefer her opponent. Despite the media's assumption that Putin's regime acted on that preference and meddled decisively in America's politics to help elect Trump, though, it was less clear if that was the dominant, much less sole, motive.

Much of the Russian-generated propaganda seemed more generic than pro-Trump. It highlighted some nasty social and ideological divisions in American society that are much broader and deeper than partisan squabbles during an election campaign. Moscow's messaging highlighted racial, gender, social class, and other grievances. All those pathologies were preexistent, and exacerbating them served a wider purpose than boosting Trump's election prospects. Focusing on such weaknesses is standard operating procedure for one country seeking to weaken another country that it perceives as a rival or enemy. Washington's own arrogant, tone-deaf conduct toward Russia throughout the post–Cold War era (expanding NATO up to Russia's border, undermining Moscow's allies in the Balkans and elsewhere, conducting increasingly provocative military exercises in Eastern Europe and the Black Sea) reinforced the Kremlin's impression that the United States remained an unrelenting adversary. Russian leaders likely deemed efforts to weaken such an adversary a necessary step regardless of which candidate would become the new occupant of the White House.

Again, though, most reporters and analysts paid little attention to the wider geopolitical context—especially the poisonous deterioration in bilateral relations that began long before the 2016 election cycle. Instead, they opted for the simplistic explanation that Russia's election interference was merely a pro-Trump exercise.

The media's performance regarding the third question—whether Trump and his campaign aides colluded with the Russians—was the most defective. Prominent journalists, including most CNN commentators and virtually the entire lineup of hosts on MSNBC, acted as though Trump's guilt was indisputable. The same attitude was evident in opinion columns and even supposedly straight news stories in the *New York Times*, the *Washington Post,* and other newspapers. Such press fixtures were either uninterested in or dismissive of indications that key figures in the FBI and Mueller investigations were flagrantly biased against both Trump and Russia. Even the caustic anti-Trump text and email exchanges between FBI agents (and lovers) Peter Strzok and Lisa Page were dismissed as unimportant.

Such biases should have been considered newsworthy. Strzok made his views clear in his 2020 book, *Compromised: Counterintelligence and the Threat of Donald J. Trump.* The subtitle alone conveyed the magnitude of his hostility. Strzok exaggerated Russia's menace to America's unity and well-being, and he fully subscribed to the more extreme, if not bizarre, versions of the Trump collusion narrative.[124] The man was as far removed from being an objective investigator as one could imagine, and much of his perspective was already apparent in 2017. Yet the mainstream media downplayed both his bias and its possible significance when evaluating Crossfire Hurricane.

The same attitude existed within the Mueller investigative team. Andrew A. Weissmann, the commission's de facto director, was a staunchly partisan Democrat; 13 of the 16 investigators were registered or self-identified Democrats; and at least 6 were significant donors to the party or individual Democratic candidates. Not a single Republican was among the appointees. Nevertheless, most news or opinion articles either ignored that point or contended that political affiliations were irrelevant. The latter argument was especially dubious given that the inquiry was the most sensitive domestic political matter since Watergate.

Media malpractice was evident in other ways. Announcements of "blockbuster" revelations and probable "smoking guns" became commonplace, even though one after another of the hyped disclosures fizzled. Guest analysts and commentators overwhelmingly subscribed to the collusion thesis on all the television networks. Major newspapers and magazines were little better in terms of balance. The president's defenders were woefully outnumbered; only Fox News, the *Wall Street Journal*, *National Review*, and a handful of other outlets offered some dissenting views. Critics of the Russia-collusion thesis had a larger presence on talk radio. But overall, the predetermined "Trump is guilty" conclusion dominated the media narrative.

Almost all of the reporters, pundits, and television hosts clung to that thesis despite the inability of extensive investigations to find confirming evidence. Even when the Mueller report failed to validate the Russia-collusion allegations, few media members backed off, much less apologized for getting such a crucial issue wrong. Instead, they grasped at increasingly scattered straws to sustain the collusion argument. The effort to avoid accountability was disturbing and widespread.

Succumbing to both Russophobia and blind partisanship in their treatment of the Russian election interference and Russia-collusion issues was bad enough. But inflammatory, one-sided coverage has wider and more serious implications than just advancing the preferred narrative of one political party or ideological faction. In this case it helped promote a public image of Russia that contributed to the intensification of a new cold war.

As noted, Moscow had reason to be concerned about Washington's policies long before the 2016 election. The growing suspicion and animosity between the two countries had reached troubling levels even before the United States helped unseat the pro-Russian government in Ukraine and Moscow annexed Crimea. Russian leaders deeply resented NATO's expansion and burgeoning military exercises.[125] The Kremlin fumed at Washington's strategy of weakening Moscow's allies in both the Balkans and the Middle East. All those developments combined to create a profound mistrust of the United States throughout Russia's military and political hierarchy. In a May 2020 interview, Deputy Foreign Minister Sergei Ryabkov stated succinctly, "We have no trust, no confidence whatsoever in America."[126]

Media coverage, though, typically portrayed Russia's countermeasures as unprovoked, naked aggression. That interpretation fit the pattern—already apparent in the coverage of various wars—of viewing complex international issues in stark, melodramatic terms. Too many news reports and opinion pieces equated Moscow's actions with Nazi Germany's behavior. Thus, stories about Trump's alleged collusion portrayed his conduct as not just weak-kneed and insufficiently patriotic but implicitly treasonous. That innuendo reached a crescendo in 2020 with the widespread, unsupported allegations (discussed previously) that the president ignored intelligence warnings that Moscow had placed financial bounties on the lives of American military personnel in Afghanistan.

Smears about disloyalty and serving as "Russian agents" or "Russian assets" were not confined to accusations directed against Trump and his inner circle, however. Anyone who suggested that the Russia threat was overstated or that the United States and its NATO allies shared some of the blame for the deterioration of East-West relations became a target of anti-Russia vitriol in the media. So, too, did analysts who contended that NATO was obsolete and unnecessarily provocative or that a new, more cautious and limited transatlantic security relationship was appropriate. Members of the press stifled debate on policy toward Russia and aided and abetted the onset of both a new McCarthyism and a new cold war. Those developments could produce extremely dangerous consequences for the American people in the future. Once again, journalists had signed on as advocates of an activist, highly confrontational foreign policy.

Many journalists also became cheerleaders for members of the foreign policy bureaucracy and the views they championed. That de facto partnership was especially evident on the issue of U.S. policy toward Ukraine. Several members of the diplomatic corps very publicly went rogue during the events leading up to Trump's impeachment. They seemed determined to thwart the president's supposed desire to chart a U.S. policy course that they believed undermined Ukraine's security and served Russia's interests. What was remarkable was the number of press accounts that blithely accepted the analyses those officials put forth despite the dearth of credible supporting evidence—and even when the analyses the diplomats presented were painfully simplistic and one-sided, usually reflecting intense Russophobia.

A more responsible media would have posed queries about the portrayal of the underlying issues. Thoughtful journalists would have initiated a discussion about the propriety of subordinates contradicting, much less actively seeking to undermine, a president's foreign policy. After all, the Constitution makes the elected president, not unelected ambassadorial appointees or career State Department bureaucrats, the steward of U.S. foreign policy. Yet most media accounts portrayed those subordinates—Ambassadors Yovanovitch and Taylor, Deputy Assistant Secretary of State Kent, and others—as heroes for resisting Trump's perceived policies with respect to Ukraine and Russia.

One final feature of the news media's treatment of the Russia issue in the age of Trump bears noting. In their eagerness to bring down a president they disliked and foster a foreign policy that was unrelentingly hostile to Moscow, some of the most influential members of the press made common cause with leaders of the nation's law enforcement and intelligence agencies. That collaboration violated the media's function as watchdog of government conduct and misconduct, and it fed the ambitions of those powerful, secretive agencies for even greater power and influence. This development has disturbing implications for the health of America's democratic political system.

The sight of retired, high-level intelligence officials routinely appearing as supposedly independent and objective analysts on the major television networks should have created uneasiness about whether the press was being used as a conduit for propaganda by a faction in the intelligence community pushing its own agenda. The concern is not a small one. Those agencies are supposed to execute the republic's foreign policy, not shape it—and especially not shape it to serve parochial ideological or partisan purposes. Yet on Russia policy, and the Russia-collusion allegations in particular, people such as John Brennan, James Clapper, and James Comey appeared to be doing exactly that. They all pushed a hardline policy toward Moscow, and they all had been appointees of the previous Democratic administration. Their comments in interviews echoed those of Adam Schiff and other leading congressional Democrats, who portrayed Trump as a Kremlin stooge or agent and were waging a campaign to impeach him. Having prominent intelligence community figures ratify those allegations gave them greater credibility. The willingness of media outlets to facilitate the campaign of such individuals was inappropriate at best and dangerously corrosive to the integrity of an independent press at worst.

The media's role in intensifying congressional and public hostility toward Russia at times reached extreme levels. Members of the press claimed relatively mundane foreign policy moves by the Trump administration had the covert goal of benefiting Russia. A typical example occurred in June 2020 when the president decided to withdraw 9,500 U.S. troops from Germany—a figure later increased to 11,900. The decision likely reflected Washington's irritation at Berlin's continuing failure to boost its anemic defense spending. Trump and Ambassador Grenell had both warned previously that if Germany persisted in its free-riding behavior, the United States would relocate some or all of the forces stationed in that country. From a military standpoint, such a withdrawal sent a message about burden-sharing, but it had far more symbolic than substantive importance. After all, the United States had deployed more than 300,000 troops to (West) Germany during the Cold War. At the point when Trump made his decision, the total already was down to 34,500.

To some in the media, however, the withdrawal constituted suspicious and dangerous appeasement of Russia. The tone in an analysis by *Politico's* David M. Herszenhorn was typical.[127] Herszenhorn asserted that Trump had "stunned" Germany and the other NATO allies with a unilateral move "seen as a benefit to Russia." Herszenhorn then quoted Retired Lieutenant Gen. Ben Hodges, former commander of U.S. Army Europe, who asserted that Russia would be a main beneficiary of the withdrawal and that a softening of the U.S. military posture was unjustified. "The Kremlin has done nothing to deserve a gift like this," Hodges said. "No change in behavior in Ukraine or Syria or along NATO's eastern flank or in the Black Sea or Georgia. Yet they get a 28 percent reduction in the size of U.S. military capability that was a core part of NATO's deterrence."

Even by the mainstream media's usual standard of opposing any change that might suggest a slightly less confrontational U.S. posture toward Russia, *Politico*'s "news" article constituted both a knee-jerk endorsement of the NATO status quo and unrelenting threat inflation. Warnings about the withdrawal being a "gift to Putin" became more far-fetched when the Pentagon announced that nearly half of the forces being removed from Germany would be redeployed to other NATO members in Europe. The planned redeployment included 1,000 troops who would move to Poland's eastern border with Belarus—a former Soviet republic and Russian client state that served as a military buffer between Russia and NATO.[128] A subsequent statement by Secretary of Defense Mark Esper in October made the "gift" to Russia even less impressive. He indicated that fewer troops (only about 4,500) would be coming home, while a larger percentage would be going to Eastern Europe.[129]

No policy deviation was too minor to become a target for innuendo about an insufficiently uncompromising policy toward Moscow. Critics condemned the Trump administration's April 2020 decision to issue a joint declaration with the Kremlin to mark the date in World War II when Soviet and U.S. forces linked up at the Elbe River, thereby cutting Nazi Germany into two segments. The larger purpose of the declaration was to highlight "nations overcoming their differences in pursuit of a greater cause." The U.S. and Russian governments stressed that a similar standard should apply to efforts to combat COVID-19. That declaration might seem noncontroversial, but opponents of the administration's commemoration decision, including several prominent congressional Democrats, condemned it as "playing into Putin's hands."[130]

At times, the media seemed ready to give any Russia conspiracy theory, no matter how outlandish, its rapt attention. CNN's Wolf Blitzer gave former national security advisor Susan Rice a platform to blame "foreign actors" for the riots and looting that followed the police killing of George Floyd in late May 2020. And Rice left no doubt about which foreign actor was at the top of her list of suspects. The violence, she contended, was "right out of the Russian playbook."[131] Neither at the time nor later was she able to cite any evidence for her accusation. Nevertheless, Rice's comment indicated just how much Russia had become the designated scapegoat for America's domestic troubles—even the country's long-standing racial tensions.

Overstated anti-Russia allegations took on ever-more absurd forms in response to the incident on January 6, 2021, when several hundred pro-Trump demonstrators challenging Joe Biden's victory in the presidential election broke away from a much larger, peaceful protest and stormed the U.S. Capitol. Not only did media personalities shriek that the intrusion was a full-scale insurrection incited by Trump, but they implied or asserted that the move fulfilled Vladimir Putin's dream of seeing America in chaos—and may have been intended to do so.[132]

Media allies gave exposure to allegations from Hillary Clinton, Nancy Pelosi, Chuck Schumer, and other leading Democrats that Trump may have been taking orders from Putin to wage a coup. In one interview, Clinton stated, "I would love to see his phone records to see whether he was talking to Putin the day that the insurgents invaded our Capitol."[133] Pelosi was equally outlandish in her accusations. She conceded that she did not know "what Putin has on him politically, financially, or personally, but what happened last week was a gift to Putin." Nor was it just Trump himself who was doing Putin's bidding; some of his supporters were just as guilty, according to Pelosi. "These people, unbeknownst to them, they are Putin puppets. They were doing Putin's business when they did that at the incitement of an insurrection by the president."[134] Of course, no one presented a scintilla of evidence that Putin was involved in any way with the January 6 events. It was a measure of the extent of anti-Russia hysteria and the tenacity of the Trump–Russia-collusion narrative that such a baseless claim was not derided.

The media's overall performance throughout the past decade regarding the important and sensitive issue of Russia policy does not speak well of journalism's role in the 21st century. There were exceptions, of course. Analysts such as Glenn Greenwald, Matt Taibbi, Caitlin Johnstone, Aaron Maté, Tucker Carlson, and Peter Van Buren refused to be swept along with the crowd and persisted in asking hard questions, scrutinizing allegations, and demanding hard evidence. So did scholars such as Stephen F. Cohen and John J. Mearsheimer. But their restrained assessments were overwhelmed by a tsunami of uncritical accounts (usually based on little or no evidence) that accepted as gospel the anti-Russia and Trump-collusion narratives.

The mission of informing the public is not advanced when journalists create and circulate one-dimensional portraits of a foreign country as a villainous, existential threat, ignoring crucial context and all nuances to do so. Press outlets that collaborate with hawkish advocates and partisan political figures within the government are even worse. They push hostile U.S. policies toward one of the most powerful countries in the international system and denigrate any initiatives that move even modestly in the opposite direction. America's news media repeatedly committed all those offenses with respect to their coverage of Russia policy.

George Beebe, vice president and director of programs at the Center for the National Interest, aptly describes the potential consequences of generating public fear of and hatred toward Russia. He points out that "the safe space in our public discourse for dissenting from American orthodoxy on Russia has grown microscopically thin. When the U.S. government will open a counterintelligence investigation on the presidential nominee of a major American political party because he advocates a rethink of our approach to Russia, only to be cheered on by American media powerhouses that once valued civil liberties, who among us is safe from such a fate? What are the chances that ambitious early- or mid-career professionals inside or outside the U.S. government will critically examine the premises of our Russia policies, knowing that it might invite investigations and professional excommunication? The answer is obvious."[135]

UKRAINE WAR

The long-simmering tensions between Russia and NATO over Ukraine's status surged in late 2021 and early 2022. Vladimir Putin's government took two actions that brought matters to a head. In November 2021, Russia began to deploy forces along multiple locations on the border with Ukraine—deployments that would ultimately reach more than 200,000 troops. The following month, the Kremlin issued a demand for written, binding security guarantees from NATO on a range of issues. Moscow not only wanted the Alliance to officially bar Ukraine from becoming a member but also sought an additional guarantee that no NATO troops or weapons would be deployed on Ukrainian territory. Indeed, Russia sought a commitment that NATO would substantially reduce its military presence in current eastern European members.

Bilateral talks about those demands did ensue. However, although the U.S. side appeared willing to offer informal assurances that Ukraine would not be invited to enter NATO "anytime soon" (a scenario that was highly improbable in any case, given continued French and German opposition), Washington balked at offering a formal guarantee. Russia ended negotiations emphatically on February 24 by launching a multi-pronged invasion of Ukraine with the stated goals of demilitarizing and "de-Nazifying" the country.

The U.S. news media's coverage during the months preceding the Russia-Ukraine war replicated most of the deficiencies in their coverage of previous crises, especially the Persian Gulf War, the Balkan wars, the Iraq War, and Washington's interventions in Libya and Syria. Once again, there was a significant imbalance in on-camera interviews, op-eds, house editorials, and even purportedly straight news stories in favor of hard-line perspectives, although the situation this time was marginally better. A few experts who were advocates of realism and restraint did gain some exposure for their views. Likewise, a handful of media types, like Tucker Carlson and Glenn Greenwald, received attention (albeit usually hostile) in the establishment press for making the case that Washington's actions—especially pushing NATO expansion eastward and establishing a cozy military relationship with Kyiv—had contributed to the onset of a crisis. Nevertheless, the tsunami of media accounts insisting that Washington must maintain solidarity with Kyiv and persist in an uncompromising stance toward Russia swamped more cautious perspectives.

The overall media coverage during the immediate prewar period once again provided very little context regarding the underlying issues. Press accounts conveyed an inadequate picture of the various factors and events that had led to the conflict. Some did acknowledge that NATO's expansion to Russia's border may have contributed to the burgeoning crisis, but the concessions even on that point were limited and grudging. Media treatments of other issues involving important context—such as the tensions that had existed between Russia and Ukraine since the early 1990s regarding the political status of Crimea and the Donbas—were sparse. When they did appear, they rarely deviated from the standard, oversimplified narrative that confirmed maximum Western and Ukrainian virtue and maximum Russian villainy.

As they had with the earlier crises, establishment journalists tended to portray a complex situation as a shallow melodrama, with nearly all blame put on one side. Indeed, experts and pundits who contended that NATO's policies over the previous decades had contributed to the current tensions were frequently smeared as siding with Putin, willingly circulating Russian propaganda and disinformation, or being outright Russian agents.[136] Some of the architects of the new wave of smears were even the same individuals who had used similar tactics in the lead-up to the Iraq War. Max Boot, Jennifer Rubin, and David Frum, for example, were all prominent alumni of that earlier campaign to silence dissenters, and they were now hard at work branding critics of Washington's Russia policy as disloyal.[137] Progressive blogger Caitlin Johnstone observed uneasily, "This latest trend of claiming that opposition to US military posture toward a nuclear superpower constitutes evidence of being a treasonous foreign intelligence operative is a marked uptick in the madness."[138]

Once the Russia-Ukraine war began, the media's performance became even more skewed and defective. The overall message was clear and starkly simplistic: Vladimir Putin was an evil man and now a brutal aggressor. Russia's invasion was an entirely unprovoked assault on a peace-loving neighbor. Ukraine is a bastion of freedom and democracy, and the West, indeed the entire global community, had a moral obligation to come to the country's defense. The invasion was just the opening phase of an expansionist agenda on Moscow's part designed to rebuild the Soviet Union. Putin's new effort was even reminiscent of Adolf Hitler's rampage in the late 1930s, and the democratic powers must halt Russia's aggression in its tracks, or risk repeating the folly of appeasing an aggressor—a policy that had led to World War II. Even if the dire outcome of a world war with nuclear consequences could be avoided, Putin's assault on Ukraine posed an existential threat to democracy, not just in eastern Europe but throughout the international system. Indeed, the Ukraine war was, as President Biden insisted in his March 2022 State of the Union address, nothing less than a crucial struggle between democracy and autocracy.[139]

The unsubtle conclusion in media stories was that the United States must "stand with Ukraine" in the latter's resistance to Russian aggression. The identification of America's interests with Ukraine's was nearly total, and it was infused with righteousness. Smears of and hostility toward dissenters reached toxic levels. The hosts of *The View* lobbied their viewers to insist that the Justice Department investigate (and hopefully charge) Tucker Carlson and former Democratic Rep. Tulsi Gabbard for being Russian agents and committing treason. Host Whoopi Goldberg observed that "they used to arrest people for stuff like this." Pundit Keith Olbermann called on the military to detain Carlson and Gabbard as "Russian assets."[140]

Noticeably missing in the reaction to the Ukraine war was the sense, once so powerful in U.S. foreign policy and general discourse, that America's interests were—and rightfully should be—distinct from the interests and objectives of any foreign country. In his Farewell Address, George Washington admonished his fellow citizens against harboring a "habitual fondness" toward any other nation. He added, in a passage that could have applied perfectly to the attitude of both U.S. officials and most journalists regarding Ukraine: "Sympathy for the favorite Nation, facilitating the illusion of an imaginary common interest, in cases where no real common interest exists, and infusing into one the enmities of the other, betrays the former into a participation in the quarrels and wars of the latter, without adequate inducement or justification."[141]

Biden administration officials and most members of America's political elite did not indicate even a faint receptivity to such detachment. Indeed, their attitude was that no significant daylight should appear between Ukraine's interests and goals and those of the United States. Typical was House Speaker Nancy Pelosi's statement during the visit of a House delegation that she led to Kyiv in early May. "Our commitment is to be there for you until the fight is done," Pelosi promised. "We are on a frontier of freedom and your fight is a fight for everyone. Thank you for your fight for freedom."[142]

Too much media coverage of the Russia-Ukraine war exhibited a similar lack of detachment, balance, or realism. The tendency to elevate Ukraine to heroic status and to ignore or minimize the country's defects was especially pronounced. A typical example was a laudatory April 19, 2022, *New York Times* column by Bret Stephens describing the many reasons why Americans liked Ukrainian leader Volodymyr Zelensky so much. According to Stephens: "We admire Zelensky because he has restored the idea of the free world to its proper place. The free world isn't a cultural expression, as in 'the West'; or a security concept, as in NATO; or an economic description, as in 'the developed world.' Membership in the free world belongs to any country that subscribes to the notion that the power of the state exists first and foremost to protect the rights of the individual. And the responsibility of the free world is to aid and champion any of its members menaced by invasion and tyranny."[143]

The reality with respect to Ukraine was murkier and more troubling. Ukraine has long been one of the more corrupt countries in the international system. Indeed, public frustration at the pervasive financial corruption in President Petro Poroshenko's government was a prominent reason for the victory of Zelensky, a comedian and political novice, in Ukraine's 2019 presidential election. In its annual report published in

January 2022, Transparency International ranked Ukraine 122nd out of 180 countries examined, with a score of 32 on a 1- to 100-point scale. By comparison, Russia, with its notorious level of corruption, ranked just modestly worse, 136th, with a score of 29.[144]

Kyiv's performance with regard to democratic norms and respect for civil liberties was not much better. In Freedom House's 2022 report, Ukraine was listed in the "partly free" category, with a score of 61 out of a possible 100. Other countries in that category included Rodrigo Duterte's Philippines (55), as well as Serbia (62) and Singapore (47)—none known as consistent practitioners of democratic values.[145] Civil liberty abuses in Ukraine became even more extensive after the onset of the war with Russia.[146] Little of that information, though, made its way into mainstream media accounts.

The shallowness of the news media's treatment of the war was most evident with respect to television coverage. American viewers were inundated with images of exploding shells from the invading Russian forces; sights of desperate, tearful refugees (mostly women and children) fleeing the invaders; and shots of other determined Ukrainian civilians arming themselves to defend their country. Because television is a visual medium that always tries to evoke emotions among viewers, such emphasis was to be expected. However, providing a deluge of images of traumatized civilian refugees added little to anyone's understanding of the conflict. It didn't help the media's credibility that some of the material they telecast turned out to be fake.[147]

Even the genuine, emotionally evocative scenes merely emphasized that war is hell, innocent civilians get hurt or killed, and the survivors are terrified. Reasonably intelligent viewers were already aware of all those points. Segments that discussed the larger context of the war were far less frequent. Too often, the raw, emotional images served as a substitute for meaningful contextual analysis.

The Western (especially U.S.) press sometimes served as a willing conduit for outright Ukrainian propaganda. During the early weeks of the war, American news outlets even circulated the story about the "Ghost of Kyiv"—the fighter pilot who supposedly became an ace in a matter of days by shooting down numerous Russian warplanes. That account had all the earmarks of transparent propaganda, and the Ukrainian military ultimately conceded that the story was fictional.[148] In the meantime, however, it had served its purpose well as propaganda for Western audiences. Multiple unfiltered stories from *Ukrayinska Pravda*, *New Voice of Ukraine*, and other Ukrainian media outlets routinely appeared on Yahoo!'s daily news feed—frequently accounting for a third or more of the top dozen stories. Press releases from Ukraine's government also appeared in the Western press, at times without acknowledging that the accuracy of those official accounts could not be confirmed. Moreover, the press published virtually no stories from Russian news sources, creating an even greater sense of imbalance. A similar imbalance was evident on the principal social media platforms.

Solid evidence soon emerged that both Russian and Ukrainian forces were committing war crimes in that tragic conflict—with Russian forces being responsible for the majority of such outrages.[149] During the early months of the war, however, Western media outlets gave minimal coverage to incidents indicating that Ukrainian forces also were guilty of such crimes. One need only compare the number and tone of mainstream news stories about the execution of Russian prisoners of war with the stories on Russian atrocities committed in the city of Bucha. The latter stories were not only far more numerous; they also rarely expressed even the slightest doubt about Russia's guilt. With respect to the execution of Russian POWs, though, the modest number of stories that did appear were decidedly skeptical.[150]

Worse than the emotionalism and double standard in overall coverage of the war was the media's receptivity to some of the most reckless policy options being promoted in some circles. When Rep. Adam Kinzinger (R-IL) contended that NATO should impose a no-fly zone over Ukraine, there was just modest initial pushback from either news personnel or their guest experts on the television networks, despite the obvious and extreme risks of NATO's becoming a full-fledged belligerent in a war with Russia. Fortunately, greater balance did emerge after the Biden administration explicitly ruled out the option as too dangerous, since it likely would necessitate shooting down Russian planes—an action that would lead to a direct U.S.-Russian war, with nuclear implications.[151]

Controversy over the prudence of trying to implement a no-fly zone reflected a lack of consensus about that specific issue within the country's political and policy elites, and it had somewhat of a partisan quality. Most Democrats and their media allies lined up to echo Biden's caution, while Republicans split sharply. Some GOP leaders backed away from proposals for a no-fly zone as too perilous, but more hawkish Republicans (along with a handful of Democrats) continued to lobby for the scheme.

The onset of a more vigorous policy debate regarding the no-fly issue was reminiscent of the greater diversity in media perspectives during the latter stages of the Vietnam War and several other subsequent foreign policy issues during the 1970s and 1980s. On those occasions, America's political establishment had fractured regarding the proper approach to foreign policy challenges. Moreover, as in the case of proposals for a no-fly zone, the split was somewhat partisan in nature. The lack of a consensus among the political and policy elites gave greater room for dissenting views within the news media during the earlier period (see Chapter 2), and that development now applied to the no-fly zone issue.

Less dissent occurred in media coverage of other policies that the Biden administration adopted to support Ukraine's war effort, even though some of those measures were nearly as risky as establishing a no-fly zone. At the top of the list was the decision by the United States and NATO to provide a deluge of weapons, including Stinger anti-aircraft missiles, Javelin anti-tank missiles, Switchblade "kamikaze" drones, and long-range artillery to Ukrainian forces. Similarly, there was widespread media support for the administration's decision to share military intelligence, apparently including targeting information, with Kyiv. When reports leaked that U.S.-supplied intelligence information had enabled Ukraine to shoot down a Russian transport plane carrying hundreds of troops, most accounts ranged from favorable to glowing.[152] A similar reaction was evident with respect to reports that U.S. intelligence sharing had played a role in Ukraine's sinking of Russia's Black Sea fleet's flagship and in Kyiv's unusual success rate in killing top Russian generals.[153]

During the first weeks of the war, political and policy elites appeared to have little opposition to the shipping of weapons, intelligence sharing,

and the other tangible features of U.S. backing for Kyiv's war effort.
Relatively few in the mainstream media warned that such extensive support might ultimately make the United States a de facto belligerent in
the ongoing war, with all the risks entailed in that status. As the weeks
passed, however, some establishment journalists began to assess the risk
of Washington's course more soberly—especially when rumbles from
the Kremlin about the possible need to use tactical nuclear weapons
multiplied. One key sign of a shift in the media narrative took place
when *New York Times* columnist Thomas L. Friedman began to suggest that U.S. officials needed to exercise greater caution.[154] However,
extreme hawks in the media, such as Michael McFaul and Max Boot,
remained thoroughly committed to a confrontational policy, and they
casually dismissed the possibility that U.S. actions might provoke Russia
enough to trigger an escalation to the nuclear level.[155]

The identification of prominent news personnel with Ukraine's overall cause, though, was pervasive. On some occasions, that bias translated
into overt backing for even transparently reckless U.S. policy options. A
notable case involved NBC's chief foreign correspondent Richard Engel,
who questioned in the first week of the war whether the West could just
"watch in silence" while the huge Russian military column continued to
roll toward Kyiv.[156] Both his tone and his words, including the observation that "the U.S./NATO could likely destroy it," implied a belief that
the United States and NATO could not—certainly should not—remain
on the sidelines as the column neared Kyiv, even though airstrikes on the
Russian forces would likely plunge the Alliance into war. Unfortunately,
Engel was not alone in exhibiting such reflexive hawkishness. MSNBC
host Ali Velshi explicitly called for the direct intervention by U.S. and
NATO forces in the Ukraine conflict.[157]

Barely four days into the war, Glenn Greenwald observed: "It is
genuinely hard to overstate how overwhelming the unity and consensus in U.S. political and media circles is. It is as close to a unanimous
and dissent-free discourse as anything in memory, certainly since the
days following 9/11. . . . Every word broadcast on CNN or printed in
The New York Times about the conflict perfectly aligns with the CIA
and Pentagon's messaging."[158] He was exaggerating, but not by much,

and matters improved just modestly as the war dragged on. The small number of experts who offered deeper and more nuanced views of the Russia-Ukraine war, such as retired military officers Daniel Davis and Douglas MacGregor, stood out because of their rarity. So too did the few outlets that featured them. The majority of MacGregor's appearances occurred on one show: *Tucker Carlson Tonight* on Fox News. It was a familiar pattern of largely homogenized, pro-activist messaging that continued the news media's track record on international affairs over the decades.

To the extent that the messaging was divergent, some of it had a partisan hue that did little to elevate the quality of the discussion—with the partial exception of the treatment of the no-fly zone issue. Republican activists and the minority media faction that favored their cause argued that the Biden administration's incompetence and "displays of weakness" (especially the chaotic, humiliating exit from Afghanistan) had emboldened Putin. They noted sneeringly that despite the Democratic Party's four-year-long crusade to portray Donald Trump as Putin's lackey, the Russian dictator had not dared to make such an aggressive move while Trump was in the White House.

Fox News, the *Wall Street Journal*, and other portions of the pro-GOP faction in the press also used the Ukraine war to argue that Biden had given Russia undue leverage by undermining America's energy independence, which they contended was in superb shape when Trump left office. The Biden administration's canceling of oil drilling leases, the termination of the Keystone XL Pipeline, and the White House's overall pro-environmentalist policies became exhibits in the case that Washington had facilitated Putin's aggression.[159] Reversing all of those misguided policies, of course, would supposedly weaken Moscow's war effort. The right-wing press also echoed criticisms that extreme hawks in the GOP directed at the Biden administration's refusal to impose a no-fly zone over Ukraine or transfer fighter planes to Kyiv.[160] The hawkish perspective with the *Journal* and some other conservative publications became sufficiently dominant that they even repudiated Republicans who favored a more cautious policy regarding the war.[161]

The case put forth by Democrats and their much larger contingent of supporters in the press was slightly more sophisticated, but equally self-serving. The focus of the media message was that Biden was handling a very dangerous crisis with great skill and balance. A prominent theme was that the administration had achieved an unprecedented degree of international unity in favor of backing Ukraine and imposing crippling economic sanctions on Moscow.[162] The reality was more ambiguous, and outside the U.S.-dominated West, there was no real consensus in favor of punishing Russia, but such nuance was slow to emerge in the establishment media's coverage.[163]

Emotionalism and close identification with Ukraine and its cause were the overwhelming features of the news media's handling of the Ukraine crisis. It was not enough to denounce the Russian invasion for what it was—an ugly act of aggression. U.S. press coverage went well beyond that standard in its treatment of the war, and the overlap between the dominant media narrative and Washington's official policy was extensive. Stifling dissent, being a catalyst for hatred of another country, and cheerleading for a dangerous military crusade against a nuclear power are not what the American people need from a responsible news media. Unfortunately, for the most part, that is what they received yet again.

CHAPTER 8
Volatile Media Perspectives Regarding China

In the decades since the formation of the People's Republic of China (PRC) in 1949, U.S. news outlets' views of that country have swung wildly. Most times, a herd mentality has been evident, with an overwhelming percentage of news stories portraying China in one particular fashion. Some dissenters have always differed from the dominant narrative, but those mavericks were typically a small minority. During some periods, the prevailing view has been extremely hostile, with nearly all accounts seeing the PRC as both a monstrous oppressor domestically and an existential security threat to the United States. That was the case for more than two decades following the communist revolution, until Richard Nixon's administration suddenly altered U.S. policy in 1971–1972 and Washington no longer treated the PRC as a rogue state.

For the next three decades, the media tended to view China in a more benign fashion. During the 1970s and 1980s, China's image in the American press was that of a useful, de facto diplomatic and even military ally of the United States against the Soviet Union. A considerable number of news stories, editorials, and op-eds also mentioned that the PRC was emerging as a significant U.S. trading partner. When the Cold War ended, the rationale for a strategic partnership no longer applied, but journalistic accounts emphasized the PRC's rising economic importance to America. Not even the Tiananmen Square massacre in 1989 derailed either Washington's cooperative relationship with Beijing or the generally positive view of China in the media for very long.

During George W. Bush's administration, though, the roster of dissenters favoring a more hawkish policy toward Beijing began to grow. An important catalyst for the media's shift was the sense that the PRC was becoming a serious economic competitor to the United States, not just a major trading partner. Although both countries were prospering from the relationship, a growing number of stories appeared stressing the loss of American jobs and the demise of venerable U.S. companies in certain industries. Allegations were also mounting of "unfair" PRC trade practices, including currency manipulation, to make Chinese goods more competitive, and even cases of outright theft of intellectual property.

Negative media accounts were not confined to the economic arena. More analysts began to see the PRC not merely as a worrisome trade competitor but as an emerging military rival. Beijing's surging military budgets and increasingly assertive behavior in the Taiwan Strait and the South China Sea fed those concerns in the media. Uneasiness about the PRC's behavior continued to rise throughout Barack Obama's administration. Nevertheless, a majority of news stories and opinion pieces still presented the U.S.-China relationship as positive and mutually beneficial.

A more noticeable split developed once Donald Trump became president. A hawkish perspective gained strength and challenged the majority pro-cooperation view in the media. The Trump administration's hardline trade policies led to sharp (frequently partisan) debate, with advocates of the status quo condemning the president's apparent willingness to wage a trade war, while economic nationalists saw the firmer stance as long overdue.

However, Beijing's behavior outside the economic arena was what ultimately sparked a surge in both public and media hostility. Two events were especially important catalysts. One was the successful move by President Xi Jinping's regime to greatly dilute Hong Kong's guaranteed political autonomy with the imposition of a new national security law in May 2020. Passage of that law was the culmination of years of ever-greater restraints, a trend that accelerated dramatically when huge pro-democracy demonstrations in Hong Kong began in the spring of 2019. Beijing's crackdown on Hong Kong reinforced already strong condemnations in the American press about Xi's growing domestic repression within the PRC, including squelching even the mildest forms of political dissent.

The other crucial catalyst for the increasingly negative portrayals of the PRC was Beijing's handling of the coronavirus pandemic in the spring of 2020. Complaints erupted throughout the American news media about the communist government's secrecy and duplicity regarding essential information about the spread of the virus. Worse, Chinese officials attempted to shift blame for the pandemic onto the United States. American hostility toward Beijing rose sharply—as confirmed in public opinion polls—and media accounts reflected that shift.

Security hawks and economic nationalists went on the offensive. Proponents of the overall U.S.-China relationship were still active in the policy debates, but many of their news stories and editorials took a cautious, defensive, and at times almost apologetic tone. They sought to prevent fatal damage to the relationship even as they felt compelled to criticize PRC leaders for their conduct regarding both Hong Kong and the coronavirus.

In the aftermath of the pandemic, negative press views of China are reaching their highest levels since the period immediately following the Tiananmen Square massacre. In some ways, the extent of negativity seems greater than at any time since Nixon first visited China in 1972. Certainly, groupthink and a herd mentality throughout the media are less evident. For perhaps the first time since the establishment of the PRC, vigorous debate about how the United States should deal with China seems to be waged between factions of roughly equal strength.

THE EARLY YEARS: PERVASIVE MEDIA HOSTILITY

China's communist revolution in 1949 came as a shock to the American people in general and news outlets in particular. Americans could scarcely believe that Chiang Kai-shek, a leader they regarded as an admirable figure and an important member of the free world, had lost the civil war and been overthrown. Dean Rusk, who served as deputy undersecretary of state for Far Eastern affairs in President Harry Truman's administration, ruefully recalled that the press and public reaction to Chiang's fall from power was akin to "that of a jilted lover."[1]

Even before the United States became a belligerent in World War II, American news publications had lionized Chiang for his resistance to Japanese imperialism. During the war, he emerged as the public's favorite U.S. ally, along with Winston Churchill. The American news media's idealized treatment of Chiang and his policies during World War II rarely wavered. Historian Barbara W. Tuchman observed that journalists covering the Chinese component of the war refrained from reporting atrocities and other disagreeable actions, "even when outside the country and free of censorship."[2]

Tuchman noted that Chiang's government conducted a concerted, extremely sophisticated public relations campaign to foster a heroic image for its leader and that the campaign was highly successful. Correspondents and other observers "concentrated on the admirable aspects and left unmentioned the flaws and failures. An idealized image came through. Generalissimo and Mme. Chiang Kai-shek as 'Man and Wife of the Year' for 1937 gazed at Americans in sad nobility from the cover of *Time*, sober, steady, brave and true."[3] Not coincidentally, *Time's* publisher, Henry Luce, had been born in China to missionary parents. He took a great interest in China's affairs and was a staunch anti-communist and admirer of Chiang. *Time* and other components of Luce's vast magazine empire exerted tremendous influence in shaping American attitudes toward China.

Luce was an important member of the powerful "China Lobby"—Americans who worked diligently to influence American public opinion and U.S. government policy to benefit Chiang.[4] The China Lobby included key politicians, religious leaders, and business executives, as well as prominent journalists and publishers. Chiang's government also employed 10 of its own lobbying and public relations firms to make certain that his government's message was vigorously promoted to U.S. policymakers.[5] The China Lobby was a sophisticated, well-oiled operation. It was so successful that, until the 1970s, those who dared question the policy of strong U.S. support for Chiang risked serious, and possibly fatal, damage to their careers and reputations, especially during the late 1940s and throughout the 1950s.

Once the Cold War erupted, Americans widely viewed Chiang as an important free-world ally against the international communist threat. Congressional and media leaders were not pleased when a communist regime displaced their hero. Even moderate members of the mainstream media, such as the *New York Times* and the *Boston Globe*, criticized the Truman administration, and specifically the State Department, for mishandling the situation and failing to prevent the communist victory in China.

The conservative branch of the news media was decidedly more strident in condemning the administration's policies regarding China. Two prominent right-of-center media platforms during that time, the *Chicago Tribune* and the *Wall Street Journal*, had promoted a markedly more hawkish stance than the administration pursued, warning of the overall threat that international communism posed to the United States and other members of the free world (or at least the anti-communist one). They had voiced concern about the growing strength of communism in China during the years immediately preceding the victory by Mao Zedong's forces in 1949.

The leading conservative papers joined with the Luce magazines to excoriate the Truman administration for its handling of developments in China. The *Chicago Tribune* and, beginning in the early 1950s, the *Washington Times-Herald* were owned by Col. Robert McCormick, a longtime conservative stalwart in the Republican Party.[6] Although partisan politics played a role in the McCormick papers' attacks on the administration's China policy, anti-communist ideology played a substantially larger role. Their critique became more and more pointed and vitriolic.

Once Chiang's regime fell, disputing the dominant conservative narrative that the United States "lost" China became perilous for anyone in the media or government service. According to that narrative, the civil war that had wracked China for years was not the product of internal dynamics or the fatal weaknesses (including widespread corruption and inefficiencies) in Chiang's governing Kuomintang Party. Instead, Chiang's defeat supposedly occurred because of insufficient U.S. economic and military support for his government. In the view of Chiang's American supporters, especially his fans in Congress and the conservative press, the only question was whether that negligence reflected ineptitude on the part of the Truman administration or something more sinister: treason. Increasingly, those critics suspected the latter and gave full throat to their accusations.

The extremely influential Sen. Robert A. Taft (R-OH) spoke on the Senate floor in January 1950, charging that the State Department was "guided by a left-wing group who obviously have wanted to get rid of Chiang and were willing at least to turn China over to the Communists for that purpose."[7] His views did not soften with the passage of time. In an August 1951 interview, the Ohio senator insisted that "we abandoned Chiang Kai-shek" because "the State Department absolutely wanted the Communists to win in China." When a skeptical reporter asked him if he really believed that, Taft replied, "I think Secretary Acheson and the Far Eastern Division of the State Department did."[8]

Taft's criticism was mild compared with the comments of some other critics of the Truman administration's China policy. The leader of the more strident faction was Joseph R. McCarthy, the junior Republican senator from Wisconsin. In a famous speech in Wheeling, West Virginia, barely two months after Chiang's forces fled to Taiwan, McCarthy charged that communists had extensively infiltrated the State Department. China policy became the centerpiece of McCarthy's case, and that of conservative Republicans generally, that traitors had perverted U.S. foreign policy. In subsequent forays, the senator charged that China had been lost because of the machinations of communist sympathizers and agents; he specifically named prominent East Asian policy specialists in the State Department including John Service, John Carter Vincent, and Philip Jessup. He also cited Johns Hopkins University professor Owen Lattimore, a prominent China scholar and occasional adviser to the State Department, who McCarthy charged was the "architect of our Far Eastern policy." Senator Taft followed up his earlier remarks, denouncing the "pro-Communist group in the State Department" who "promoted at every opportunity the Communist cause in China."[9] The conservative contingent in the media amplified the allegations.

Administration officials tried to shield their policy from mounting congressional and public anger. The administration refrained from taking any action that opponents could construe as accommodating Mao's new government. For example, Washington did not follow the example of London and some other Western capitals in establishing diplomatic relations with the PRC. However, the simplest (albeit somewhat unsavory) way to fend off charges of appeasement and possible disloyalty was to quietly discard some of the officials who had urged Washington to distance itself from Chiang and recommended developing a working relationship with Mao and his followers. Acheson later insisted that, despite speculation about the "attack of the primitives, before and during McCarthy's reign," on China policy, it had little effect on the administration's stance.[10] That reflection was self-serving and wishful thinking. The media and congressional onslaught had a significant detrimental impact on policy toward China. The ossification of U.S. policy, based on knee-jerk support of Chiang and unrelenting hostility toward Mao Zedong's communist regime, deepened under Truman's successors, but it began during his administration.

By the 1960s, the dominant media narrative portrayed the PRC as more dangerous and repulsive than the Soviet Union to America's security and way of life. That view penetrated popular culture as well as national policy. A best-selling 1959 novel and subsequent 1962 movie, *The Manchurian Candidate*, was based on the paranoid premise that communist China was able to infiltrate and manipulate America's political system by brainwashing a prisoner of war. In Ian Fleming's book *Goldfinger*, the conspirators behind that arch-nemesis of hero James Bond were Russians. But in the 1964 movie based on the book, the villains were Chinese.

The assumption that China was an existential threat was especially strong among right-wing outlets once Beijing's nuclear ambitions became apparent in the mid-1960s. *National Review*, which was fast becoming the flagship publication of the conservative movement, published two editorials in 1965 warning that the United States could not deter China's communist leaders the way it had deterred the Soviet Union. The second editorial appeared with the headline "Bomb the Bang." *National Review's* editors admonished U.S. officials not to sit passively "like a man who watches and waits while the guillotine is constructed to chop his head off."[11]

Moderate and liberal publications did not go as far as recommending preemptive war against the PRC, but they saw no possibility of peaceful coexistence with Mao Zedong's regime either. The onset of China's bizarre and fanatical Cultural Revolution in 1966 made the notion of a dialogue with that government even more implausible.[12] However, a major policy change was on the horizon, and that development would be the catalyst for a dramatic shift in the media's perception of China.

NIXON'S OPENING TO CHINA WINS PRESS PLAUDITS

President Richard Nixon made an extremely bold and politically risky move to change U.S. policy toward China. In a radio and television address on July 15, 1971, Nixon announced that he would be traveling to the PRC to hold talks with the country's communist rulers. The following February, he did indeed go to China for meetings with Mao Zedong and Premier Zhou Enlai. His visit culminated with the issuance of the Shanghai Communiqué, which began the profound transformation of U.S.-China relations. The language of the communiqué regarding Taiwan became a classic example of nuanced diplomacy. The Chinese side forcefully stated China's claim to Taiwan, but Nixon got his wish that the passage avoid any bombast and invective. The statement of the U.S. position was a masterful stroke of diplomatic obfuscation. It said simply, "The United States acknowledges that all Chinese on either side of the Taiwan Strait maintain there is but one China and that Taiwan is part of China. The United States government does not challenge that position."[13] Contrary to the PRC's wishes—and to allegations from pro-Taiwan elements in the United States—the U.S. side never *endorsed* the position that there was only one China and that Taiwan was part of that country.

Nixon's initiative marked the abandonment of the U.S. campaign to isolate and demonize the PRC. His effort did generate some domestic controversy, but the *New York Times* noted that the president was winning the broad approval of Congress for his new China policy.[14] Perhaps most crucially, the support was firmly bipartisan. A few Senate Democrats, led by hawkish Sen. Henry "Scoop" Jackson (D–WA), did oppose the president's overture to China. A "saddened" Jackson claimed that with the Shanghai Communiqué and the overall shift in U.S. policy, "we are doing the withdrawing and they are doing the staying. That does not strike me as a good horse trade."[15] But most congressional Democrats were at least mildly positive about the president's initiative, and even Jackson eventually came around. Leading figures, including Sen. Ted Kennedy (D–MA) and Senate Majority Leader Mike Mansfield (D–MT), openly supported the president for easing tensions with China.[16]

The bulk of the criticism that emerged came from conservative Republican figures who charged that the embryonic rapprochement with Beijing undercut America's longtime ally Chiang Kai-shek and the Kuomintang Party's rump government on Taiwan. Sen. James Buckley (R–NY) blasted Nixon's trip as a "disastrous adventure" in American diplomacy; he contended the Shanghai Communiqué had done "enormous damage to American credibility."[17] But such influential critics were rare.

Media accounts were mostly favorable as well, although many were still cautious about whether the rapprochement would achieve meaningful, substantive results. Some wariness also remained in media circles about whether communist China could be trusted. Many journalists, though, were enthusiastically supportive. Liberal *New York Times* columnist James Reston stated that the trip to China and the signing of the Shanghai Communiqué was Nixon's finest hour.[18]

An Associated Press sampling of editorial comments in newspapers across the nation found far more support for than criticism of the president's policy.[19] That stance was particularly evident among liberal-leaning publications. The *Boston Globe* stated that "with this good start, it remains to be seen how far the two nations can proceed together on the road to peace." The *Chicago Sun-Times* exuded pleasure: "If all this is not superior to trading insults mixed with myths, we'd like to know what is." The *St. Louis Post-Dispatch* noted that "many Americans may be viewing Communist China in a positive light for the first time." Such a development, the editors concluded, was in itself "a notable advance in international amity and a heartening portent." Those and other papers expressed caution that much additional diplomatic labor was necessary before the bilateral relationship was fully transformed, but they gave the president high marks for his initial foray. Only a handful of right-wing publications expressed outright opposition to the notion of a good U.S. working relationship with the PRC.[20]

PRESS APPROVAL OF DE FACTO ALLIANCE

China observer James Mann, author of *About Face: A History of America's Curious Relationship with China, from Nixon to Clinton*, concluded that after Nixon's rapprochement with Beijing, "China was America's partner in fighting the Cold War: the United States secretly shared intelligence with Chinese officials and helped to arm the People's Liberation Army. For America's policymaking elite, China was considered a special relationship. The United States chided countries like South Korea and Taiwan about human rights abuses, but it refrained from similar criticism of China." While Washington lent prominent official support for Soviet dissidents, "Chinese dissidents were ignored."[21]

Mann contended that although in private some U.S. officials during the 1970s and 1980s were candid about the brutal nature of Washington's strategic partner, their public statements were quite different. The public face of U.S. policy toward Beijing was "colored by romance and sentimentalism, a legacy of the American experience in China dating back to the trader ships and the missionaries. Americans wanted to believe, once again, that they were changing China."[22] Most press coverage exhibited a similar quality. Now that "Red China" was no longer viewed as a grave threat and an ideological bogeyman, some accounts even went to the opposite extreme and ignored or minimized the Beijing regime's ongoing domestic repression.

The media's kid-glove treatment of China built somewhat gradually in the 1970s. Conservatives especially were divided or ambivalent about the new U.S. relationship with Beijing. When longtime anti-communist hawk Sen. Jackson reversed course and called for normalization of relations with China to better combat the Soviet Union, William F. Buckley's *National Review* accused him of "moral blindness," pointing out that the PRC was "a far more totalitarian state than the Soviet Union."[23]

Other right-wing publications featured critics of Washington's growing military assistance to Beijing. Writing in the pages of *Commentary*, a magazine that would soon become a leading voice of neoconservatism, hawkish military analyst Edward Luttwak posed some provocative and unpopular questions to policymakers. "Is it our true purpose to promote the rise of the People's Republic to superpower status?" he asked. "Should we become the artificers of a great power which our grandchildren may have to contend with?"[24] His questions may have even greater pertinence in the 2020s than they did in the late 1970s.

Most American journalists, though, adopted a benign view of the PRC in their coverage during the 1970s and 1980s. Except for the few conservative dissenters, the bulk of the news media in the United States placidly accepted Washington's 180-degree policy turn regarding Beijing. Harry Harding, a prominent scholar on China, stated that during the mid and late 1980s, "American euphoria about developments in China reached its zenith."[25] And the press fully reflected such optimism. That attitude prevailed until China's communist regime committed the Tiananmen Square massacre in June 1989. That atrocity altered press coverage of China substantially even though it had surprisingly little impact on the policy of the U.S. government.

In a 2014 retrospective, the editors of the *New York Times* conceded that the paper's reporters and columnists had been too complacent about the prospects for political reform in the PRC. "Before the violence of June 4, [reporter Nicholas] Kristof and others had been optimistic about the prospect of a more open, more democratic China." Kristof agreed with that assessment. "Looking back at what I wrote 25 years ago, I'd say the tone was right but the timing way too optimistic," Kristof said. "The Communist party indeed has diminishing control over people's lives." But he noted that despite economic and social pluralism, there is "still not a whisker of political pluralism."[26] Given the regime's dramatic tightening of controls under President Xi Jinping, Kristof was still too optimistic in 2014.

The PRC's brutal crackdown on peaceful pro-democracy demonstrators in Tiananmen Square produced an abundance of hostile press accounts in the United States. Security personnel were able to keep American and other foreign reporters well away from the scene of the worst carnage, with one notable exception: *New York Times* reporter Sheryl WuDunn. She managed to disguise herself as a local and get close to the action. Her report provided a searing eyewitness account of the regime's appalling behavior. "Tens of thousands of Chinese troops retook the center of the capital this morning from pro-democracy demonstrators, killing scores of students and workers and wounding hundreds more as they fired submachine guns at crowds of people who tried to resist. . . . Most of the dead had been shot, but some had been run over by armored personnel carriers that forced their way through barricades erected by local residents."[27]

MODERATION IN POST-TIANANMEN SQUARE COVERAGE

The initial press coverage after the crackdown was universally harsh. When information leaked that President George H. W. Bush had sent National Security Advisor Brent Scowcroft on a secret fence-mending mission to Beijing, the media erupted with condemnations. A *Washington Post* editorial contended that the president "should not be making placatory gestures to a blood-stained Chinese government."[28] A short time later, the paper published an op-ed by the recently retired U.S. ambassador to China, Winston Lord. Although a thoroughly moderate member of the U.S. foreign policy establishment, Lord was unsparingly caustic in his assessment of the president's handling of the Tiananmen Square atrocity: "Let us conduct necessary business with the Beijing authorities in workmanlike fashion, not with fawning emissaries."[29]

Yet as widespread as the negative press treatment of the PRC was immediately following the Tiananmen Square bloodletting, the outrage was relatively short-lived. The incident also had surprisingly little impact on U.S. government policy, especially with respect to expanding

U.S.–China economic ties, and that attitude of returning to business as usual subtly influenced the media narrative. Bill Clinton campaigned against the "butchers of Beijing," but once in office, his policy differed little in substance from those of Reagan and Bush. And as bilateral relations gradually returned to normal, media coverage became calmer and focused increasingly on the beneficial economic ties. When the PRC fired missiles into the Taiwan Strait in late 1995 and early 1996 in a futile effort to disrupt Taiwan's first free election and the island's transition to a democratic political system, and the United States sent an aircraft carrier task force to the area in a show of support for Taipei, press reports generally avoided jingoism.[30] So, too, did later media retrospectives about the confrontation.[31]

To be sure, a few dissenters raised their voices throughout the 1990s. Conservative hawks frequently attacked President Clinton's policies toward China. An especially persistent and virulent critic was *Washington Times* defense and national security reporter Bill Gertz. He even impugned the loyalty of Clinton and other administration officials, saying that "highly effective Chinese political influence and intelligence operations against the United States had led the president and his advisers to try to fool the American people into believing that China poses no threat."[32] Among his specific accusations, Gertz charged that the administration had accepted cash payments from the Chinese government and assisted the PRC in improving its nuclear weapons.

The latter allegation came with thin evidence, but the former appeared to have had at least some validity. In 1997, the *Washington Post* reported that Justice Department investigators had discovered evidence, including some based on electronic surveillance, indicating that Chinese officials had tried to steer campaign contributions to the Democratic National Committee and the Clinton campaign.[33] Although only circumstantial evidence ultimately emerged, Mann contended that "the swirl of accusations and news stories about the scandal had an impact. They put Clinton on the defensive concerning China and prompted the administration to hold temporarily in abeyance its plans for a far-reaching improvement in relations with Beijing."[34] Mann's conclusion about the scandal's impact on policy was a bit exaggerated. It had just a modest effect and, outside of right-wing press elements, only a very modest negative impact on the media's perspective.

Gertz's broader complaint was that government and corporate ties to China were endangering America's security. In 2000, Gertz published a book partly based on his *Washington Times* articles. The book, *The China Threat: How the People's Republic Targets America*, was a detailed presentation of the right-wing case for a more confrontational U.S. policy toward the PRC.[35] His worries about the impact of extensive government and corporate ties to Beijing would reemerge with even greater virulence during the second decade of the 21st century.

Most journalists implicitly or explicitly rejected the anti-PRC views of Gertz and his ideological compatriots. Nicholas Kristof was an especially prominent spokesman for a milder, conciliatory China policy. His arguments typified the views of journalists who defended and promoted maximum U.S. engagement with China. Even after Tiananmen Square, he contended that such an approach maximized the likelihood of the PRC becoming less repressive domestically and being a responsible actor internationally.[36] That view continued to guide U.S. foreign policy despite a temporary setback because of the scandal over campaign contributions during the 1996 election.

Moderately favorable and optimistic perspectives regarding China generally characterized the mainstream media coverage throughout the 1990s and into the initial years of George W. Bush's administration. However, some residual pessimism and skepticism remained about prospects for political reform in the PRC. Following Vice President Al Gore's trip to China in 1997, a *New York Times* editorial observed, "Mr. Gore seemed to go out of his way . . . to praise 'a significant advance in democracy' that few others have been able to detect."[37] But *New York Times* columnist Thomas Friedman expressed views more typical of the mainstream media's perspective. "China's going to have a free press," he predicted confidently. "Globalization will drive it."[38] Former *New York Times* and *Washington Post* correspondent Patrick Tyler was more cautious about those prospects but still concluded that vigorous, friendly engagement with the PRC was the best approach. He warned that a more confrontational U.S. policy was counterproductive to U.S. interests and was "profoundly against the interests of a stable international order."[39]

Rising Press Criticism of China during the Bush and Obama Years

A more negative tone began to creep into press treatments of PRC behavior during George W. Bush's administration. In a major campaign address in late 1999, Bush had used the term "strategic competitor" to describe China. The term was midway between friend and enemy. But even such a nuanced relationship got off to a bad start in April 2001, when a PRC fighter plane and a U.S. surveillance aircraft collided near China's coast, killing the Chinese pilot and forcing the damaged American spy plane to land on Hainan Island. Public and press anger at Beijing erupted when Chinese authorities initially refused to release the plane or crew.[40] Although a diplomatic compromise eventually resolved the spat, some U.S. publications continued to vent their fury at the PRC government.

An article by neoconservative writers William Kristol and Robert Kagan in the *Weekly Standard* was especially caustic. The authors described the conciliatory U.S. response as "a national humiliation." Kristol and Kagan saw much wider, dangerous ramifications from such conduct. "As the Chinese understand better than American leaders, President Bush has revealed weakness. And he has revealed fear: fear of the political, strategic, and economic consequences of meeting a Chinese challenge. Having exposed this weakness and fear, the Chinese will try to exploit it again and again, most likely in a future confrontation over Taiwan."[41]

Kristol and Kagan also stressed a theme that would become increasingly visible in right-wing and economic nationalist articles about the U.S.-China relationship. "The Chinese believe, with good reason, that the American business community has a hammerlock on American policy toward China, and that Congress will never dare cut off American business's access to the Chinese market. Congress has a chance to prove that when matters of fundamental national security are at stake, the United States can break this addiction." At the time of the 2001 incident, most portions of the news media expressed relief that sober diplomacy had resolved the crisis without doing serious damage to bilateral ties or escalating to a dangerous military confrontation. Nevertheless, suspicions about China's behavior and motives appeared to tick up a notch.

During Bush's presidency and Barack Obama's, the number of negative articles on Beijing's distressing human rights record also increased. Editorials skewered Obama in 2009 when he refused to meet with Tibet's Dalai Lama, apparently for fear of offending Beijing.[42] Intense pressure in the press contributed to the reversal of that decision the following year.

In addition to the human rights issue, news stories showed greater recognition that economic globalization was not an unalloyed benefit—especially as it pertained to China. Complaints rose about American job losses in certain industries, and a litany of complaints developed about Beijing's "unfair" trade practices.[43] The number of critical stories about double-digit annual increases in the PRC's military budget—much of it used to build new, highly sophisticated weapons—also rose.[44] The primary focus of those weapons systems was especially unsettling. The development of anti-ship missiles and radars seemed focused on "anti-access, area denial" capabilities. The primary purpose also was apparent: making a U.S. intervention to support Taiwan in a crisis prohibitively costly and dangerous.

Still, even publications such as the *Wall Street Journal* that expressed growing concern about the PRC's implicit military challenge to U.S. primacy in the western Pacific defended the extensive and growing bilateral economic ties. Economic nationalists in the media asserted that such a policy was internally contradictory, arguing that massive trade flows contributed to China's economic strength, thereby enabling Beijing to build a more capable military—one that also utilized some of America's best technology.[45] Right-wing journalists such as Bill Gertz were especially alarmed about how the economic ties the Obama administration encouraged seemed to be aiding China's geostrategic challenge to the United States and its allies. Gertz accused the administration of outright appeasement.[46]

Overall, the media perspective on bilateral relations generally avoided the apparent contradiction, as did most foreign policy scholars. Other analyses in the press tried to square the circle, using the term "congagement"—a portmanteau of *containment* and *engagement*—to describe the supposedly optimal policy. Congagement took China's military rise seriously and sought to contain Beijing's geopolitical ambitions while still preserving maximum bilateral economic connections and seeking to find areas of diplomatic and strategic cooperation.[47] That somewhat hazy and ambivalent media treatment persisted through President Obama's time in office, although criticism and warnings from conservative journalists grew more numerous and strident. The trend toward greater criticism among conservatives intensified during Donald Trump's administration.

Even some moderates seemed increasingly uneasy about China's behavior and apparent intentions. Daniel Drezner, an advocate of a balanced policy toward China, conceded that Beijing was adopting a more brass-knuckles style in its foreign policy. Drezner cited an early 2020 episode in which PRC leaders threatened to retaliate economically for comments that an executive with the National Basketball Association's (NBA) Houston Rockets made, expressing support for pro-democracy demonstrators in Hong Kong. Beijing's angry complaints produced an abject apology from league executives. "The NBA incident is only the most visible example," Drezner contended. "The Chinese government has successfully applied similar pressure to U.S. airlines and Hollywood producers. On human rights, Chinese diplomats also have become much more outspoken in recent years, threatening 'countermeasures' in response to any criticism from foreign governments. China has grown much more comfortable with using sticks as well as carrots as part of its economic diplomacy."[48]

American media criticism of China became sharper and more widespread in the late winter and early spring of 2020, just after the NBA brouhaha, when the coronavirus pandemic burst out of China onto the world scene. Even before that episode, though, public opinion in the United States was turning more negative because of the trade disputes, the PRC government's rising authoritarianism at home, its deteriorating human rights record—exemplified in its treatment of the Uighur minority in Xinjiang province—and its heavy-handed attempts to reduce or abolish Hong Kong's political autonomy.

Press coverage reflected growing discontent with Beijing on all those issues. The PRC's attempt in the spring of 2019 to gain the power to extradite Hong Kong residents for trial in mainland courts created great suspicion among American journalists. When pro-democracy demonstrations erupted in Hong Kong in response to Beijing's extradition power play and other grievances, American media accounts across the political spectrum were sympathetic to the demonstrators and hostile to the communist authorities.[49] Conservative columnist George Will typified the reaction of his colleagues. "Just eight years after the Tiananmen massacre," Will wrote in the *National Review,* "there began what was supposed to be half a century of Hong Kong's exceptionalism preserved, after which the city might be gracefully melded with a mellowed mainland. Just 22 years later, this hope has been as refuted as the 1989 hope that the massacre would be followed by a less authoritarian, because more secure, Beijing regime."[50]

In addition to journalistic discontent with the Chinese government's conduct and apparent agenda in Hong Kong, criticism mounted with respect to Xi Jinping's increasingly repressive rule within the PRC itself. There were certainly enough alarming developments to criticize. On March 11, 2018, China's National People's Congress approved an amendment to the constitution to abolish the two-term limit on the presidency, thus allowing Xi to serve in that post indefinitely. That move was just the latest in a series of ominous developments that had occurred since he took office in 2013.

Ending term limits significantly altered China's political system. Deng Xiaoping, the architect of the country's radical economic reforms in the late 1970s, had implemented term limits as a crucial political reform. He and his followers did so to guard against a repeat of the horrid abuses committed during the long, tyrannical rule of Mao Zedong. And the restriction did achieve limited success. China hardly became a democratic state, but within the context of a one-party system, Deng's successors at first served more like chief executive officers; other members of the party elite acted as a board of directors that could, and did, serve as a check on the president's power. Removing the limit on presidential terms meant that an incumbent now had abundant time to accumulate more and more personal power. The threat of strongman rule, with all its potential abuses, had returned.

In truth, Xi was exhibiting alarming behavior even before pushing through the legislation ending term limits. Under the guise of combating corruption (admittedly a very real problem in China), he systematically purged political players who showed signs of independence. His rule had a troubling, hard-line ideological aspect as well. Xi initiated a campaign to revitalize the Communist Party, aiming to renew a commitment to Maoist principles.[51] Even pro-market academics felt the chill of the new political environment, with crackdowns directed against several prominent reformers, including economist Mao Yushi, the head of the Unirule Institute of Economics and the 2012 recipient of the Cato Institute's Milton Friedman Prize for Advancing Liberty.[52] As Xi's stranglehold on power continued, the attack on dissent intensified. Other centers of reform and at least limited political debate, such as Shanghai's Fudan University, were closed or made into robotic instruments of government propaganda.[53]

Official intolerance of dissent soared during the weeks immediately before and after the National People's Congress vote on term limits. Authorities quickly and systematically silenced critics of the constitutional revision. The extent of censorship and other manifestations of repression deepened steadily in the following years. Surveillance of anyone suspected of entertaining views critical of government policies or Xi's leadership became pervasive. The government also instituted a system of "social credits," using massive collections of data to assign scores for "responsible social behavior" to businesses and individuals. Authorities rewarded loyalty to the party with high scores and penalized even mild dissenters and nonconformists. Among the penalties for low social credit scores were greater restrictions on travel and on employment or business opportunities.

Journalists in the United States noticed the growing authoritarianism in China, and criticism of Xi's regimentation policies became more frequent and pointed.[54] The criticism of tightening censorship measures was vocal and emphatic.[55] But discontent with the policies of Xi's regime focused especially on the surveillance and data collection associated with the social credit system. Writing in *The Atlantic*, Anna Mitchell and Larry Diamond denounced the system.[56] "Imagine a society in which you are rated by the government on your trustworthiness. Your 'citizen score' follows you wherever you go. A high score allows you access to faster internet service or a fast-tracked visa to Europe. If you make political posts online without a permit, or question or contradict the government's official narrative on current events, however, your score decreases. To calculate the score, private companies working with your government constantly trawl through vast amounts of your social media and online shopping data." To human rights advocates and other critics, the social credit system was an Orwellian nightmare, and they worried about China gradually exporting it to more liberal societies.

Although Beijing's tightening autocracy generated greater criticism in the American news media, a sizable portion of the corporate media community still held back, regarding good relations—especially profitable economic relations—between the United States and China as a higher priority. The near unanimity of hostility in the media toward Russia—especially after Moscow's annexation of Crimea and apparent meddling in the 2016 U.S. election—was not duplicated with respect to China, despite the far greater degree of repression in the latter country. Even the media's reaction to Beijing's brutal treatment of the Uighurs was not as widespread or vehement as might be expected. Conservative writers who were congenitally hostile to the PRC denounced China's conduct, as did outspoken human rights proponents. But members of the establishment press generally kept their critical accounts restrained, sometimes even tepid.

THE PANDEMIC AND MEDIA CRITICISM OF CHINA

Media negativity toward China's behavior became more widespread and emphatic once the coronavirus crisis erupted in late February and early March of 2020. An increasingly prominent narrative in the United States was that not only did the pandemic originate in China, but Chinese officials withheld key information for weeks that could have enabled other countries to adopt measures to impede the spread of the deadly virus. In late March, more than a month after the crisis began, Secretary of State Mike Pompeo charged that China's government was still withholding important information.[57] The European Union released a report in late April that echoed U.S. allegations that Beijing had spread "disinformation"—even though Chinese officials had protested and warned that the report would make China "very angry."[58]

Conservative outlets, with Fox News commentators leading the charge, were especially harsh in their allegations about Beijing's lack of transparency.[59] But even more centrist publications featured articles accusing China's government of "deceptive practices" and placing primary blame for the pandemic on Xi's regime.[60] Assertions about lack of transparency and outright deception acquired enhanced credibility at the beginning of April when the U.S. intelligence community dismissed Beijing's official statistics about the extent of virus cases as significantly understating the actual number.[61] The conclusion that Beijing had misled the rest of the world about the spread of the virus inside China had already begun to appear in accounts beyond the hard-core conservative media faction.[62] The input from U.S. intelligence agencies both broadened and deepened the media narrative about the Xi government's guilt.

The anti-China agitation on the part of right-wing journalists went well beyond allegations that Beijing had withheld information that might have saved the lives of Americans and other coronavirus victims throughout the world. Conservatives also routinely referred to the coronavirus as the "Wuhan virus" or even the "Chinese virus" in an effort to whip up greater public resentment against Beijing.[63] President Trump himself initially used the latter term before backing away from doing so.[64]

Liberal journalists rejected such labels as not only inaccurate but xenophobic and implicitly racist, and they blasted both Trump and his right-wing media allies for using them.[65] Members of the media taking a softer line on China's responsibility for the onset and spread of the coronavirus were increasingly on the defensive, however. Conservative publications gleefully noted that three consecutive national Harris polls found that more than 50 percent of Americans said they somewhat or strongly agreed with Trump using the term "Chinese virus."[66]

Most of China's conservative adversaries endeavored to draw a sharp distinction between blaming the Chinese people and blaming the Chinese Communist Party. Some media members even used the term "CCP virus" rather than "Chinese virus," in part to neutralize charges of racism. Helen Raleigh, a senior contributor to the *Federalist*, emphasized the importance of placing blame for mishandling the pandemic directly on China's communist rulers, not ordinary Chinese. "It's important that in our quest for justice, we distinguish between the Chinese Communist Party (CCP) and the Chinese people. At fault for the spread of the Wuhan coronavirus is the CCP." She added, "Punishing all Chinese people for the sins of the CCP is unfair and plays into the hands of the CCP's propaganda."[67]

Josh Rogin, a moderately conservative columnist for the *Washington Post*, had earlier promoted a similar view. He stressed the need "to separate the way we talk about the Chinese people from the way we talk about their rulers in Beijing." That approach was not just pertinent with respect to the coronavirus, Rogin emphasized; it was "a crucial point relative to our whole approach toward China. Our beef is not with the Chinese people; our problem is with the CCP—its internal repression, its external aggression, and its malign influence in free and open societies."[68]

Writing in *National Review*, Hoover Institution scholar Michael Auslin also focused on the conduct of the Beijing regime, not the Chinese people. He stated bluntly that "the CCP, which for years has claimed to be a responsible member of the global community, showed its true colors when this crisis hit. It can no longer be denied that Xi's regime is a danger to the world. Justice demands it be held morally culpable for its dangerous and callous behavior."[69] Ian Easton, a research fellow at the 2049 Project and a columnist for the *Taipei Times* proposed that the international community "quarantine" the Chinese government.[70] More moderate commentators echoed the distinction between the Chinese people and the Communist Party. Some even narrowed the blame further, citing Xi Jinping specifically as the true villain.[71]

Journalists trying to promote a conciliatory perspective found it acutely difficult to do so when Beijing conducted a vigorous propaganda campaign to shift the blame for the global pandemic onto the

United States. The Chinese government and state media began to promote the ugly assertion that Washington may have initiated the pandemic as part of a bioweapons program. Stories appeared in China's state media emphasizing the participation of U.S. Army personnel at athletic games in Wuhan in October 2019, just before the first signs of the coronavirus began to appear.[72] A furious Secretary of State Pompeo denounced the Chinese government for making such allegations.[73]

Early on, some right-wing figures in the United States voiced their suspicions that the coronavirus was a bioweapon that Beijing had unleashed on the world. A more restrained version of the China-guilt thesis contended that while it probably had not been a deliberate bioweapons attack, lax containment standards at a virology research lab outside Wuhan may have allowed the release of the virus into the outside world. Most liberal publications quickly dismissed both accusations as crude right-wing conspiracy theories.[74] However, the allegation of a possible lab accident gained new currency in mid-April when evidence emerged that a worker at that lab possibly was the initial victim of the virus and accidentally spread it through his interactions with people in Wuhan.[75] Conservative analyses then reiterated and amplified accusations that this was yet another version of a PRC cover-up regarding its handling of the coronavirus outbreak.

A new round of vitriolic debate in the media ensued. Moderate and liberal journalists seemed determined to obliterate the thesis once and for all, dismissing it as a "fringe theory." Their conservative rivals were equally determined to legitimize, promote, and highlight the theory. As with an expanding number of China issues, though, critics of the lab-origin argument found themselves in a somewhat awkward position. Too often, their case had to rely on evidence provided by the Chinese government. Even when critiques could cite statements and assessments from outside experts, those experts typically had collaborated with colleagues in China and had career incentives to do so again.[76] Disputing Beijing's version of events would be a nearly certain way to be blackballed from future opportunities, and anti-PRC journalists noted such conflicts of interest. Consequently, the lab-origin hypothesis exhibited stubborn staying power.

Both sides remained adamant. On May 3, Secretary Pompeo asserted in a television interview, "I can tell you that there is a significant amount of evidence that this [the coronavirus] came from that laboratory in Wuhan."[77] Media criticism of the theory, though, also received a boost in early May when a leaked assessment from the "Five Eyes" network (the intelligence agencies of the United States, Australia, New Zealand, the United Kingdom, and Canada) stated that the available evidence did not confirm that the Wuhan lab was the source of the virus and that the city's infamous "wet market" still seemed the more likely source. Some publications overstated the definitive nature of the assessment.[78] Intelligence analysts did not debunk the lab leak theory and exonerate the Wuhan lab; they merely concluded that available evidence did not demonstrate that the virus came from the lab.

Conservative publications shot back by emphasizing other damaging, anti-PRC revelations in the Five Eyes dossier. The *New York Post* stated, "A damning dossier leaked from the 'Five Eyes' intelligence alliance claims that China lied to the world about human-to-human transmission of the coronavirus, made whistleblowers disappear and refused to hand over virus samples so the West could make a vaccine. The bombshell 15-page research document also indicated that some of the five intelligence agencies believe that the virus may have been leaked from the Wuhan Institute of Virology."[79]

Both factions were cherry-picking the data, emphasizing the components of the assessment that bolstered their side of the case. What neither side in the media squabble was willing to admit was that no one could say with certainty precisely where or how the virus had begun to spread.

The major legacy media and the social media platforms, however, concluded that the Wuhan lab-leak theory was not only unfounded but simply the latest right-wing conspiracy theory. Prominent Western scientists, many of whom were heavily dependent on the continued good will of the Beijing government, insisted that the natural-origin explanation was beyond dispute. The mainstream news outlets as well as the social media heavyweights then decided that any articles or blog posts to the contrary constituted misinformation and did not deserve a public airing. Facebook and Twitter ordered such posts to be flagged as false or banned entirely. How much hatred of the Trump administration also contributed to those decisions is an intriguing question. Comments from Trump and Pompeo indicating that they believed the lab-leak hypothesis might well be true likely undermined receptivity to the theory on the part of the administration's opponents in the press.

The mainstream media's suppression of debate about the origins of the COVID-19 pandemic and China's possible culpability ultimately proved embarrassing, and the episode became a lesson in the danger of labeling unorthodox views on an issue as misinformation. Advance copies of a long-delayed (now published) article in *Scientific Reports* (part of the prestigious *Nature* family of journals) helped resuscitate the debate in the spring of 2021. The paper makes the case that the lab-leak theory was plausible and that in any case, there was no certainty about COVID-19 origins.[80] The Biden administration's decision in late May to revive the intelligence agencies' inquiry (which the White House had terminated shortly after Biden's inauguration), added fuel to the revived controversy.[81]

Most media outlets that had summarily dismissed lab-leak arguments executed a rapid retreat. Facebook lifted its ban on posts touting the theory as soon as the Biden administration announced the new investigation into COVID-19's origins.[82] The conservative contingent in the media expressed both satisfaction that its perspective on the issue was now acknowledged as legitimate and anger at ideological opponents who had smothered meaningful debate on such an important topic.[83] *Wall Street Journal* columnist Holman W. Jenkins, Jr., asked pointedly, "On what basis was the lab leak theory ruled out for months by the media despite the lack of any evidence or logic for ruling it out?" His answer was unsettling. "We in the press dismissed the lab theory because of an appeal to authority: When anti-Donald Trump spokespeople ridiculed it, that was good enough for us."[84] Unfortunately, a more probable explanation is hard to identify. At the least, the episode reflected acute laziness and sloppy bias on the part of far too many members of the press.

Initially, the ideological split over the lab-leak theory highlighted the growing partisanship of media coverage of China issues. But even the portions of the media that normally were not friendly to the Trump administration and its policies were displeased with Beijing's accusation that the United States rather than China was responsible for the COVID-19 outbreak. That annoyance carried over into other aspects of the PRC's coronavirus policy. As a result, more moderate and occasionally even liberal portions of the press became willing to publish articles highly critical of the Chinese government's overall conduct regarding the pandemic.[85] Writing in *The Atlantic*, Hudson Institute scholar Nadia Schadlow challenged the publication's liberal readers to "consider the possibility that Trump is right about China." She charged that "China, America's most powerful rival, has played a particularly harmful role in the current crisis, which began on its soil. Initially, that country's lack of transparency prevented prompt action that might have contained the virus."[86]

An early March 2020 article published in *Xinhua*, the official Chinese news agency, upset the American press corps even more. A diplomat in the PRC foreign ministry strongly hinted that his country might impose export controls to withhold antibiotics and other life-saving drugs from American consumers. Those controls, he stated, would plunge America "into the mighty sea of coronavirus."[87] Presumably, he could not have made such an inflammatory statement without the approval of senior Chinese leaders.

The implicit threat in the *Xinhua* article focused public and press attention in the United States on how much America depended on China for pharmaceutical ingredients. (By some estimates, the United States gets 80 percent or more of its drug supply from China.)[88] The heightened realization spurred a growing media campaign to reduce such dependence on a less-than-friendly foreign power—and to reduce America's dependence on foreign suppliers generally. Concerns about the potential vulnerability were already evident in 2019, and among a few critics even earlier, but the coronavirus pandemic greatly elevated those concerns. The danger of supply chain disruptions, not to mention Beijing's possible use of its dominance in pharmaceutical sources to gain political or strategic leverage on the United States with respect to other issues, strengthened calls for greater American independence and more geographically diversified supply chains for drugs and other key products, such as semiconductors. That objective was most evident in articles by conservative and economic nationalist analysts,[89] but the sense of alarm was not confined to that portion of the ideological spectrum. Thoroughly establishment publications began to call attention to the vulnerability as well.[90]

Mounting public distrust of China and the anger that distrust fostered about Beijing's handling of the coronavirus made it increasingly difficult for media defenders of close bilateral ties with Beijing to stay the course. Writing in early April 2020, Josh Rogin noted that a recent Harris poll showed "that, outside the Beltway, the coronavirus crisis is actually bringing Americans together on the China issue." But the nature of that growing consensus was very revealing. "Republicans and Democrats now largely agree that the Chinese government bears responsibility for the spread of the pandemic, that it can't be trusted on this or any other issue, and that the U.S. government should maintain a tough position on China on trade and overall, especially if Beijing again falters in its commitments."[91]

A Pew Research Center survey of Americans taken in late April produced similar findings. The results showed that 66 percent of people had negative views of China, including 62 percent of Democrats and Democratic-leaning independents and 72 percent of Republicans and Republican-leaning independents. A mere 26 percent of respondents expressed a favorable attitude toward China. It was the highest percentage of negative views about the PRC recorded since Pew began asking the question in 2005.[92]

National Interest writer Matthew Petti succinctly captured the growing dilemma that progressive political figures and journalists were facing. "The movement will be forced to choose which threat is bigger: China's authoritarian model, or a new Cold War." Trying to occupy a middle ground and still maintain credibility with the American people, he observed, was proving to be increasingly difficult.[93]

Beijing's hypersensitive reaction to criticism did not help either its reputation or its treatment at the hands of U.S. publications. The day after Trump used the "Chinese virus" label, the PRC government announced that it would expel several American reporters, including journalists working for the *New York Times, Wall Street Journal*, and *Washington Post*. Walter Russell Mead, author of an earlier *Wall Street Journal* column titled "China Is the Real Sick Man of Asia," which had angered Chinese authorities, warned that removing the reporters would only "solidify the bipartisan consensus" in the United States that China was a dangerously hostile power.[94]

The surging anti-Beijing sentiment had another troubling aspect beyond its potentially adverse impact on bilateral relations. Just as allegations had become common that anyone who opposed a confrontational policy toward Russia was doing the bidding of Vladimir Putin's government, allegations that some journalists and media outlets were subservient to Beijing grew more frequent. However, in the case of China, the accusations had more substance and plausibility.

In a March 31, 2020, article, J. Arthur Bloom, managing editor of *The American Conservative*, laid out one reason that some media organizations were inhibited from leveling justifiable criticisms of Beijing on an array of issues.[95] "The companies that own the major news networks, NBC, ABC, and CBS, all do significant business in China," he noted. "On the print side, top U.S. newspapers like the *Washington Post* and *New York Times* have been criticized for running paid *China Daily* inserts. What they were paid for these inserts is still unknown." He then delineated some of the other ties that he believed could constitute a conflict of interests for U.S. media firms. "Disney owns ABC and has a park in Shanghai. It also owns ESPN, which was criticized for its coverage of China's retaliation against the NBA earlier this year over one team owner's support of the Hong Kong protests."

Other than its stake in ABC, Disney was relatively uninvolved in news, Bloom conceded, but a key competitor was far more entrenched. Comcast "has a much larger footprint in the U.S. media landscape, between NBC News, CNBC, and MSNBC." The company's role in fostering cultural exchange, he added, "is truly historic: they've brought to millions of American homes a customer service experience akin to a utility provider in a communist country, and have invested billions to bring "Minion Land" and a Harry Potter village to Beijing, with the help of a state-owned investment vehicle."

Bloom then asked a blunt question: "What might the Chinese government do if it were displeased with something that ran on MSNBC? Perhaps they'd have a tense conversation with their partners at 30 Rockefeller Plaza about the forthcoming slate of movie releases in China. Or it might be worse, given their decision to cut off all NBA games to retaliate against one team owner." Bloom described a March 2020 meeting between Comcast executives and the PRC Consul General Huang Ping in New York City. The consul general made a point of discussing China's allegedly splendid response to the coronavirus, as well as U.S. news coverage of the PRC's performance, and expressed the hope that NBC and other U.S. media would "objectively and fairly report China's efforts to control the epidemic."

There should be no doubt, Bloom contended, "that the Chinese government would not view it as objective or fair to question their initial response to the epidemic or their case numbers now." Worse, Comcast and NBC executives seem to have interpreted Huang Ping's comments that way. A few weeks after the meeting, Bloom noted, "NBC News stories appeared saying the only new coronavirus cases in China had come from foreigners, and another one about China asserting its global leadership" battling the pandemic. Perhaps the timing was coincidental, but the stories were decidedly friendly to China's behavior and perspective on the coronavirus issue. They also exhibited a level of credulity that NBC News has rarely displayed with respect to other foreign countries except longstanding, democratic allies of the United States.

In a later article, Bloom documented the extensive financial connections that both the *Washington Post* and the *Wall Street Journal* maintained with a PRC government propaganda entity. "We now have a figure for how much the *Washington Post* and the *Wall Street Journal* have taken from *China Daily*, a state-run newspaper, since 2016. It's $4.6 million, and $6 million, respectively." Bloom pointed out that the Chinese government undoubtedly sought to promote its views on various issues with such large expenditures. "This is more than an order of magnitude greater than the amount Russia is thought to have spent on Facebook advertising prior to the 2016 election."[96]

Bloom was not the only conservative journalist to argue that the vast economic stakes that media outlets or their parent companies had in preserving a friendly relationship with China might compromise the content of their news coverage. Nor was he the only conservative journalist to criticize the mainstream media for being far too solicitous of China about the coronavirus issue. Jarrett Stepman, a regular contributor to the *Daily Signal*, an online publication affiliated with the Heritage Foundation, attacked liberal media outlets for what he viewed as their exceedingly trusting and friendly treatment of China's perspective. They repeated Chinese government statements, he charged, "despite the fact that there's no reason whatsoever to trust the information coming out of an authoritarian communist regime that has repeatedly lied to its own citizens and to the world, sparking the greatest global pandemic in the past century."[97]

Barbara Boland, *The American Conservative*'s national security reporter, openly accused *Bloomberg News* of burying stories critical of China.[98] She specifically cited the editors' decision not to run a follow-up story on the accumulation of massive wealth by members of China's political elite. That decision came after apparent threats from Beijing to terminate Bloomberg's presence in the country. Leta Hong Fincher, the wife of Michael Forsythe, the lead reporter of the earlier story about Chinese corruption, supported Boland's version of the incident. In an *Intercept* article, Hong Fincher stated that "my story shows the lengths that the Bloomberg machine will go to in order to avoid offending Beijing. Bloomberg's company, Bloomberg LP, is so dependent on the vast China market for its business that its lawyers threatened to devastate my family financially if I didn't sign an NDA [non-disclosure agreement] silencing me about how Bloomberg News killed a story critical of Chinese Communist Party leaders." Referring to her husband's follow-up story that Bloomberg had been encouraging, she added, "Bloomberg killed the story at the last minute, and the company fired my husband in November after comments by Bloomberg News editor-in-chief Matt Winkler were leaked. 'If we run the story, we'll be kicked out of China,' Winkler reportedly said on a company call."[99]

The conservative media criticism of China soon extended to international institutions considered sacred by much of America's liberal community—institutions that had close ties with the PRC government. One prominent target was the World Health Organization (WHO). Critics began blasting that organization for being subservient to Beijing. The *Wall Street Journal*'s editorial board stated bluntly that the WHO's "bows to Beijing" had severely damaged the international response to the virus.[100]

Two allegations were especially prominent. First, WHO officials reflexively repeated Beijing's positions about the nature and spread of the virus; WHO statements frequently were so positive about China's performance that they amounted to fawning. Second, the WHO had obediently done Beijing's bidding and excluded Taiwan from participating in collective efforts to stem the spread of the virus, even though Taipei had been remarkably successful in its own containment efforts. As with other coronavirus issues, some of these criticisms began to spread beyond the usual conservative publications into moderate and even left-of-center ones.[101]

Nevertheless, the media reactions to President Trump's April 14, 2020, decision to cut off new funding to the WHO followed ideological and partisan lines, as did the reaction in Congress. Conservative, anti-China portions of the press generally praised the president's action, while most liberals predictably criticized the move as excessive and counterproductive.[102] Notably, few of the latter defended the WHO's relationship with China as part of the rationale for opposing Trump's edict.[103] A few even went to considerable lengths to separate the two issues.[104] Supporters of the funding cutoff, on the other hand, usually stressed the China angle in their attacks on the WHO.[105]

Despite the deepening and broadening criticism directed at China, a significant gap still existed between the now vehemently hostile view of China among conservative portions of the news media and the continuation of a milder view among most moderate and liberal factions. As noted previously, many of those differences existed before the pandemic developed, but the coronavirus exacerbated the cleavage.

Conservative coverage of U.S.-China issues generally became both more extensive and more negative toward Beijing than it had been before the coronavirus outbreak. Beijing's questionable conduct regarding the pandemic, and the generally negative reaction of American public opinion toward that conduct, provided an ideal opening for conservative hawks and their economic nationalist allies to make the case for considering China a duplicitous adversary. There is a fine line between legitimate criticism of the cozy China connections that parent companies of certain major media firms maintained and implicit McCarthyism. Some conservative critics came very close to that line, questioning the integrity and loyalty of their liberal media colleagues who advocated maintaining a cooperative relationship with Beijing.

Establishment journalists and analysts sought to stem, or at least deflect, some of the public hostility toward China. They even tried to turn the coronavirus issue to their advantage in terms of promoting the broader agenda of preserving global cooperation. Rather than defending the Chinese government outright (which was becoming increasingly difficult), they tended to stress two related themes. One was that President Trump was trying to use China as a scapegoat to distract the American people from his own failures to address the pandemic in an expeditious and effective manner—a theme Trump's Democratic Party opponents also embraced enthusiastically.[106] Criticisms included the administration's mixed messages about the seriousness of the virus and the lack of key components, including test kits, masks, and ventilators, needed for a prompt containment and mitigation campaign. Trying to dilute criticism of China was just part of the media campaign to discredit Trump and accuse him of unprincipled blame shifting.

The other theme incorporated that argument in a broader attack on the Trump administration for using an "America First" approach with respect to the global health crisis. Their denunciations cited such incidents as the United States allegedly engaging in ruthless competition with other countries—even longtime allies such as Canada and European Union members—for scarce medical supplies.[107] But references to the administration's hostility toward Beijing and reluctance to cooperate with China frequently featured prominently in the criticisms as well.[108] A front-page story in the April 10, 2020, *New York Times* charged that "President Trump and his leading trade adviser, Peter Navarro, have exploited the pandemic as an opportunity to redouble efforts to force multinational companies to abandon China and shift production to the United States."[109]

More subtle and balanced accounts emphasized the damaging effects taking place because of bilateral quarreling and attempts by both Beijing and Washington to attach blame for the pandemic on the other party.[110] The broader rationale those journalists and their think tank allies pushed was that the coronavirus was an extraordinarily serious threat that required enhanced, not reduced, global cooperation.[111] Indeed, the contention was often that such collaboration was more necessary than ever before and that nationalist policies were dangerous and destructive. The *New York Times* story lamented, "Now, just as the world requires collaboration to defeat the coronavirus—scientists joining forces across borders to create vaccines, and manufacturers coordinating to deliver critical supplies—national interests are winning out."[112]

The assertion that much-enhanced global collaboration was imperative was little more than a new application of the case for globalism that most of those same individuals and news organizations had pushed for decades. The tone of their coverage of the coronavirus outbreak was that it posed both a severe threat to globalism, especially a reasonably open international trading system, and an opportunity to forge tighter, more extensive multilateral cooperation. Preventing a breakdown of the U.S.-China relationship was deemed crucial to preserving the overall globalist agenda.

Johns Hopkins University professor and *Bloomberg News* columnist Hal Brands epitomized that argument, asserting that a "modest multilateralism" was in the best interests of both countries. "The coronavirus reminds us that many clichés about a globalized world are true," Brands insisted. "Pathogens and the pandemics they cause don't care much about geopolitical dividing lines. Economic shocks that begin in one country rarely end there. International organizations are critical to meeting shared challenges. It is hard for even a superpower to remain healthy, physically or economically, in an unhealthy world." Brands conceded that Beijing had politicized the pandemic. But he concluded that the crucial "central axis of any new multilateralism" would need to be "stronger ties between the world's two leading powers," even though the coronavirus had "sharpened the competition between America and China."[113]

China's critics had little patience for the newest edition of pro-globalism arguments. Economic nationalist writer Alan Tonelson, writing for *The American Conservative*, pushed back hard on the April 10, 2020, *New York Times* story, which he accurately described as an implicit editorial rather than a news story. Tonelson contended that "see-no-evil pre-Trump American science and tech collaboration and exchange programs were a one-way street that sent to Beijing cutting edge knowhow crucial both for defense and for national competitiveness. None of that made its way into the *Times*." He charged further that the *New York Times* story was another example of the mainstream media making "no effort to conceal its free-trade, globalist, liberal biases, even if it means throwing in with China."[114]

Despite the pervasive anti-PRC sentiments among conservatives in the media, they split over whether to push to the maximum the growing public anger at Beijing's behavior on the coronavirus and other issues. More pragmatic figures cautioned their right-wing brethren about the risks associated with waging a full-fledged cold war against China. Pat Buchanan fully subscribed to the view that the PRC government was as evil as the USSR had been, and he wondered out loud why anyone had ever thought otherwise. Nevertheless, Buchanan asked, "Is America, in lockdown, with 26 million unemployed and entering a new depression, up for a confrontation and Cold War with China?" He clearly thought not, even arguing that the nations of East Asia, not the United States, should be responsible for preventing China's attempt to establish its hegemony in the South China Sea.[115]

Libertarian publications also promoted the case for caution even as their criticism of Beijing's authoritarianism remained robust. Writing in *Reason*, Daniel Drezner asserted that we face no "China crisis," unless "we cause one by overreacting to Asia's changing political and economic landscape."[116] As American public opinion and media coverage became noticeably more negative toward Beijing, Drezner's comment took on the aura of wishful thinking. Advocating a realistic, balanced policy that avoided both shrill hawkishness and naivete about the nature and conduct of China's government was becoming increasingly challenging.

THE HONG KONG CRACKDOWN

As anger over Beijing's handling of the coronavirus pandemic continued to affect coverage of China issues in the American news media, another PRC action put China's defenders in an even more difficult position. China's leaders had finally had enough of the ongoing pro-democracy demonstrations in Hong Kong. In May 2020, Xi Jinping's government bypassed Hong Kong's legislature and imposed a national security law on the ostensibly autonomous territory. Even before that law went into effect, there was considerable speculation in the media that PRC authorities were using the world's preoccupation with the pandemic as a cover for a move against Hong Kong.[117]

The passage of the national security law effectively negated Hong Kong's autonomous status, which was supposed to last until 2047—50 years after Britain's transfer of the territory to the PRC. Beijing's move also was the latest manifestation of China's regression into virulent authoritarianism under Xi Jinping. PRC officials offered assurances that the security law was merely intended to deal with disruptive demonstrations and other manifestations of subversion and disorder. Foreign Minister Wang Yi stated that the law was aimed only at a "very narrow category of acts that seriously jeopardize national security," such as "treason, secession, sedition or subversion." It would, he emphasized, have "no impact on Hong Kong's high degree of autonomy, the rights and freedoms of Hong Kong residents, or the legitimate rights and interests of foreign investors in Hong Kong."[118]

Comments in the American press were overwhelmingly skeptical, if not scornful, of such assurances, since PRC officials would have the unconstrained authority to decide what constituted treason, secession, sedition, subversion, or legitimate rights.[119] NPR's Emily Feng branded the new law a "power grab" and pointed out that not only would Beijing decide who falls under the provisions of the law, but that the PRC frequently referred to Hong Kong's democracy protests "as the work of 'terrorists.'"[120] The skepticism was thoroughly warranted. Just months later, the authorities arrested dozens of leading democracy advocates.[121]

American anger was bipartisan, and U.S. leaders reacted quickly and harshly. Presumptive Democratic presidential nominee Joe Biden contended that the United States should lead the world in condemning China for its actions. Secretary of State Mike Pompeo condemned the legislation as illicitly undermining Hong Kong's autonomy and freedoms. Just days later, Pompeo issued a report to Congress as required under the 2019 Hong Kong Human Rights and Democracy Act, declaring that Hong Kong no longer was autonomous and, therefore, was no longer entitled "special treatment" on trade and other matters. Instead, the territory would be treated as an ordinary part of the PRC.[122]

Not surprisingly, conservatives in the press were especially categorical in denouncing Beijing's action. The editors of *National Review* not only praised the Trump administration for rescinding Hong Kong's special trade status, but they called for a similarly firm response on other issues:

> We obviously also need a strategy to combat Chinese belligerence elsewhere. Control of Hong Kong is only one step in China's quest to "occupy a central position in the world," as Chinese president Xi Jinping has put it. The Hong Kong security law coincides with increasingly aggressive naval exercises in the South and East China Seas and a sudden military buildup on the Sino–Indian border. The Chinese have also made clear their intention to annex Taiwan, and show no signs of rolling back their programs of industrial espionage and anti-competitive trade practices. The White House must resist China on all fronts.[123]

Fox News contributor Marc Thiessen pointedly condemned the new national security law, arguing that "the Chinese regime is going to be able to ban pro-democracy groups, arrest people for political crimes. They're going to allow the state security service, which is the Chinese secret police that terrorizes people all over mainland China, to operate openly in Hong Kong, which they have not been allowed to do."[124] But even Thiessen and other hawks did not advocate using military measures against China for its subjugation of Hong Kong. They implicitly acknowledged that the United States and other democratic powers could do little except impose sanctions and offer talented residents wanting to leave Hong Kong a refuge in more appreciative countries.

Moderate and liberal commentators were even more candid about the limited options available to the United States and its democratic allies. Most China policy specialists shared their pessimism and sense of constraints.[125] Indeed, many press accounts had already conceded that point the previous year at the height of the pro-democracy demonstrations.[126]

CHINA AND THE 2020 ELECTION CAMPAIGN

It became evident in the spring of 2020 that U.S. policy toward China was going to be a significant issue in the election campaign— especially at the presidential level.[127] Members of the establishment media sought to achieve two goals: first, to contain the damage to U.S.-China relations and the globalist agenda generally that had already taken place, and second, to improve Joe Biden's prospects of being elected president. The *New York Times* launched a salvo that set the tone for defending the status quo regarding China policy. The Republican strategy couldn't be clearer, Jonathan Martin and Maggie Haberman asserted: "the G.O.P. is attempting to divert attention from the administration's heavily crit-icized response to the coronavirus by pinning the blame on China."[128]

Leaving aside the questionable implication that China was not responsible for mishandling the coronavirus outbreak, the Republican Party's negative campaign against China went well beyond that one issue. Moreover, Biden's initial reaction suggested that he and his cam-paign advisers knew that Biden was vulnerable to charges of being soft on the PRC. In mid-April a pro-Biden super PAC, American Bridge, ran a television ad depicting Trump as a stooge for Beijing. Against the backdrop of a fluttering Chinese flag, the narrator intones, "Everyone knew they lied about the virus—China." Yet "President Trump gave China his trust."[129] A subsequent, official Biden campaign ad sought to portray Biden as tougher than Trump toward China. It accused Trump of having "rolled over for the Chinese" during the early stages of the coronavirus outbreak. "Trump praised the Chinese 15 times in January and February as the coronavirus spread across the world."[130]

That approach alienated some of the Democratic Party's usual allies in the media and drew derision from right-of-center outlets. The attempt was reminiscent of John Kerry's 2004 effort to "out hawk" George W. Bush by appearing on stage to accept his party's presidential nomination with a military salute and the statement "John Kerry, reporting for duty." Kerry's attempt fell memorably flat, and Biden's bid to be a newly minted China hawk fared even worse with some progressive media types. The approach created a rift among left-leaning journalists and within the progressive faction generally.[131]

Granted, a few arch-partisans defended the Biden ad. The *Nation*'s Jeet Heer noted with annoyance, "Some political pundits, especially those in the MSNBC resistance liberal camp, loved the ad. 'This is the most devastating political ad I've seen in years,' Joe Scarborough tweeted. 'It reveals the truth about Trump and China, and that truth is ugly.' Scarborough's colleague Joy Reid agreed, tweeting, 'This @JoeBiden ad is going to make @realDonaldTrump very, very angry.'"[132]

But other liberals were disgusted. Heer rejected the reasoning of Scarborough and Reid. In fact, he accused Biden of succumbing to the type of xenophobia that Trump epitomized. Heer was especially upset about the "rolling over for the Chinese" terminology. "The use of the phrase 'the Chinese' is troubling, since it fails to acknowledge the distinction between the Chinese people and the government of the People's Republic of China. For that matter, it [elides] the reality of Chinese people living outside the PRC, in Taiwan, Singapore, and the United States." Heer even accused Biden of dabbling "in 'Yellow Peril' rhetoric."[133] Some moderate Democrats reached a similar conclusion. Writing in *The Atlantic*, Peter Beinart blasted the "utter futility of Biden's China rhetoric." He cautioned that trying to "out-hawk Trump" on China was "pointless, even dangerous."[134]

Beijing's crackdown on Hong Kong, though, made such conciliatory sentiments even more out of step with the trend in American public opinion. Not surprisingly, media accounts, both news stories and opinion pieces, regarding the PRC became increasingly negative and often openly hostile. Nonetheless, advocates of a cooperative relationship between the United States and China did not give up the fight. In a July 22, 2020, *Washington Post* op-ed, Ezra F. Vogel, one of the country's most senior China experts, made an especially pointed argument that U.S. rhetoric toward the PRC was becoming dangerously confrontational.[135] Vogel asserted that U.S. officials were attacking China's Communist Party "without realizing its complexity and diversity. It is no longer the party that exemplifies the communist goals of Stalin or Mao. After Deng Xiaoping came to power in 1978, the party was transformed into an organization to represent the nation. The Party includes people who have been pro-American, including business people, scientists and intellectuals. But when Americans attack the Communist Party as a whole, members—particularly those who would like to see more democratic procedures—rally to support the Party and, by extension, the nation."

Vogel's analysis had a musty, nostalgic quality about it, though; the views and tone sounded like something out of the 1980s and 1990s when American enthusiasm about China's economic and (mostly prospective) political reforms was at its height. He and other proponents of a conciliatory policy toward Beijing constituted a beleaguered contingent as 2020 drew to a close.

A pronounced split in the opinion-shaping community is now apparent, with conservatives advocating a starkly confrontational policy toward China, while moderates and liberals generally embrace a more restrained approach. But even within the latter faction, the trend in media perspectives is toward more extensive criticism of the PRC. Moreover, journalists who expected Joe Biden's administration to reverse Trump's China policy and seek a rapprochement with Beijing were startled when the Biden foreign policy team emphasized hardline views.[136] An early indication of possible continuity with Trump's approach came when Taiwan's de facto ambassador to the United States was invited to attend the inauguration—a first since Washington established diplomatic relations with the PRC.[137] Other gestures and substantive measures quickly followed, including a State Department statement of "rock-solid" U.S. support for Taiwan and the initiation of a new freedom of navigation patrol by the Navy in the South China Sea.[138] Only on the issue of trade relations have any hints of a softer policy appeared—and even those were decidedly limited.

If Beijing's behavior, both domestically and internationally, does not moderate in the coming years, the number and influence of conciliatory analyses in the United States likely will wane further. Indeed, given the tone of American public opinion and the apparent continuation of hardline government policies regarding China, a return to hawkish groupthink in the media, akin to that in the 1950s and 1960s, is no longer out of the question.

CHAPTER 9
Groupthink and Club Membership

Throughout the decades, members of the mainstream media have internalized the conventional wisdom about what constitutes the proper nature and goals of U.S. foreign policy. Commenting in the late 1980s, investigative journalist Mark Hertsgaard concluded, "For all its world-weary cynicism about politics, the U.S. press displayed more often than it cared to admit, a remarkable tendency to believe the basic truth of what its government told it."[1] With the exception of the final years of the Vietnam War and some persistent skepticism during the rest of the 1970s and into the 1980s, Hertzgaard's description accurately reflects the norm from the start of World War II through Barack Obama's administration. The media's willingness—indeed, eagerness—to embrace Washington's official positions on Iraq's phantom weapons of mass destruction, the allegedly benign motives for NATO expansion, and the supposed need for extensive U.S. involvement in Libya, Syria, and Ukraine all confirmed that such pliability was not merely a pre–Vietnam War phenomenon.

On the relatively infrequent occasions when the press wasn't acting as the public relations arm of the national security bureaucracy, it was usually because influential journalists believed that existing U.S. policy was not sufficiently activist and hawkish. The concerted propaganda offensive by pro–interventionist reporters and editors to push the hesitant Clinton administration into the Balkan wars was the most notable example of that phenomenon.

Guardians of the foreign policy status quo typically treat vocal, pro-restraint advocates as heretics. That was true during the most intense period of the Cold War with respect to anyone—even a figure as prominent as George Kennan—who believed that the overall containment policy was being applied too inflexibly. Less politically connected critics were treated more harshly. The victims of McCarthyism are a testament to the extent of such intolerance in the 1950s. And in the 1960s, critics of the Vietnam War were routinely derided as pro-communist or even outright traitors. Until the war effort stumbled and the mission became highly controversial among both political insiders and the American public, the attitude in much of the news media was scarcely less hostile to dissenters within their own ranks.

Discordant views on other issues also were only given significant exposure when America's political and media elites split over a foreign policy issue. Such a split was most evident with respect to the policies of Ronald Reagan's administration in the Third World, especially Africa and Latin America. Policy disputes regarding U.S. aid to the Nicaraguan Contras and Angolan rebel Jonas Savimbi roiled Congress and sparked intense debate throughout the press. The nature of the debate also reflected noticeable ideological and partisan factors—a feature that would occur with greater frequency in subsequent decades.

Much of the intellectual rigidity and lack of tolerance carried over into the post–Cold War era. When partisan divisions were not extensive, the media hostility toward dissidents was as strong as ever, as opponents of U.S. intervention in the Balkans discovered. *New York Times* reporter David Binder, an experienced and heretofore highly regarded analyst of Balkan affairs, found that his articles were no longer welcome in the pages of that paper whenever he strayed from the government's policy line. His employer's policy bias in favor of U.S. military action was simply too strong. Such exclusion would become a familiar pattern for critics (especially early critics) of the Iraq War and subsequent interventions. Previous reputations, however impressive, were not a reliable shield against shunning for foreign policy apostasy.

The treatment meted out to Peter Brock, editor at the *El Paso Herald-Post*, was worse than mere ostracism. Brock not only opposed U.S. policy in the Balkans but debunked much of the media coverage of the ethnic conflicts. For daring to do so, he was subjected to vilification that went well beyond the bounds of normal debate. *Newsday*'s Roy Gutman, a staunch crusader for military intervention in Bosnia on humanitarian grounds, insinuated—with little evidence—that Brock was on the payroll of a Serbian lobbying organization.[2] (Ironically, Gutman would later become a critic of regime-change and so-called humanitarian wars and would suffer similar slings and arrows of outraged criticism from pro-war colleagues.)

Another Brock critic was Charles Lane, who covered Balkan issues for *Newsweek* in the early 1990s and would later become editor of the *New Republic* and a reporter and editorial writer for the *Washington Post*. Lane's denunciation of Brock was exceptionally harsh. In two *New Republic* articles, Lane resorted to a barrage of innuendos to suggest that Brock was a front man for Serbian propagandists.[3] When *Foreign Policy* published Brock's article criticizing the standard narrative of events in Bosnia, Lane's reaction was troubling in other respects as well. According to *Foreign Policy*'s editors Charles William Maynes and Thomas Omestad, Lane sought to determine whether Brock's wife was Serbian (she was not)—a query that Maynes and Omestad found deeply offensive. In a reply to Lane's second *New Republic* piece, they wrote, "In Lane's construct, the ethnic, national or religious background of an author or his or her spouse could serve as a disqualifying factor in international relations reporting in the United States."[4]

Lane, Gutman, and other pro-interventionist journalists seemed outraged that *Foreign Policy* had even published Brock's analysis, although Maynes and Omestad pointed out that the journal was a forum for a wide range of views on international issues. The umbrage that critics displayed was not merely because they believed that the article was poorly researched and badly argued, although they did make such allegations. Their discontent was broader; they were upset that a prestigious journal was willing to countenance the point of view on Balkan affairs that Brock expressed. Lane charged that "this concept of even-handedness is of questionable value in dealing with the starkest moral drama in Europe since 1945."[5] That view ominously foreshadowed the attitude that has become increasingly common during the second and third decades of the 21st century with respect to a growing array of issues.

Lane's phrasing revealed the extreme bias that he and too many of his colleagues harbored. Having convinced himself that the Bosnian conflict was the moral equivalent of the Holocaust, Lane (like other proponents of Western intervention) was utterly intolerant of contrary views. In a moment of candor, he implicitly conceded the point, noting that many reporters in Bosnia had become "emotionally involved" in the story. Lane added, "Serb abuses had led some of us to hope that the West would ride to the rescue."[6] That emotionally wrought herd mentality not only badly skewed the media coverage of the Bosnia conflict; it would produce similarly unbalanced coverage of the Kosovo War, the Libya intervention, the Syrian civil war, and a host of other issues. Moreover, in all those cases, the bias favored U.S. military involvement, not restraint.

The importance of the sense of "club membership" among the governmental and media elites cannot be exaggerated. That was true even during the earliest years of the Cold War. In his epic 1977 *Rolling Stone* exposé of CIA and press collaboration, former *Washington Post* reporter Carl Bernstein cited one especially revealing example. "A few executives—Arthur Hays Sulzberger of the *New York Times* among them—signed secrecy agreements. But such formal understandings were rare: relationships between Agency officials and media executives were usually social—'The P and Q Street axis in Georgetown,' said one source. 'You don't tell [CBS head] William Paley to sign a piece of paper saying he won't fink.'"[7]

Indeed, no such formalities were needed. Leaders of the national security bureaucracies and media poohbahs shared most of the major assumptions about foreign policy. And what was true during the Cold War appears not to have changed all that much since then.

Bernstein noted that CIA officials cited two reasons the agency's working relationship with the *New York Times* was closer and more extensive than with any other newspaper. One reason was quite

logical: the *New York Times* maintained the largest foreign news operation in American daily journalism. The other reason, though, was "the
close personal ties between the men who ran both institutions."[8]

Media figures typically have not only shared most of the same
assumptions, beliefs, and biases as official policymakers about world
affairs and America's proper role in the international system, but they
have also deemed it important that the public be guided to a strong
commitment to those same principles. At times, ideological and partisan
splits have arisen over specific policies, but the orientation of U.S. policy
overall and its most fundamental principles were rarely subjected to
much criticism or debate.

An examination of the educational backgrounds of leading journalists, who play such an important role in shaping public perceptions
about foreign policy, suggests one reason the herd mentality is so strong.
A stunningly disproportionate percentage received their degrees from a
small number of elite universities. (The overwhelming majority graduated from just a few Ivy League universities.) Among the writers at the
New York Times, columnist Thomas L. Friedman attended St. Antony's
College at Oxford University; his colleagues David Sanger and Eric
Schmitt went to Harvard University and Williams College, respectively;
and his former colleague Judith Miller (of Iraq WMD disinformation
infamy) attended Barnard College and Columbia University. Two other
major fixtures at the paper, Ellen Barry and Richard Bernstein, graduated from Yale and Harvard, respectively.

The situation is similar at other high-profile media outlets. At CNN,
Fareed Zakaria and Jim Sciutto are both Yale University alumni, as are
Anderson Cooper (CNN and CBS) and David Martin (CBS). NBC's
Andrea Mitchell went to the University of Pennsylvania; Richard Engel
calls Stanford his alma mater. MSNBC's Mika Brzezinski, in addition to
being the daughter of the late national security heavyweight Zbigniew
Brzezinski, is a proud graduate of Williams College. Her colleague
Rachel Maddow, perhaps the most tenacious and outspoken proponent
of the Russia collusion narrative and related conspiracy theories, went
to Stanford and then Oxford. The *Washington Post* roster has a somewhat
California hue, with both neoconservative columnist Jennifer Rubin

(University of California, Berkeley) and writer John Pomfret (Stanford University) getting their degrees from institutions in that state. But altogether, the *Post* roster of opinion leaders can boast a credible, Ivy League pedigree. The late Fred Hiatt, the editorial page editor who did so much to steer editorials and the op-ed page in a decidedly hawkish direction, graduated from Harvard. And columnist Dana Milbank, who routinely exhibits a fondness for Washington's militarized, globalist foreign policy, is a Yale alumnus.

To be sure, occasional exceptions to the array of elite, mostly northeastern-educated journalists rise to the top. CNN's Jim Clancy attended the University of Denver; ABC's Martha Raddatz went to the University of Utah; CNN's Christiane Amanpour received her degree from the University of Rhode Island; and CBS *60 Minutes* correspondent Scott Pelley graduated from Texas Tech. But those educational backgrounds stand out precisely because they are exceptions.

The strikingly narrow range of educational backgrounds for the large majority of elite journalists has important implications. Those individuals received similar instruction from many of the same professors, and both in the classroom and elsewhere, they interacted predominantly with people going through the same educational immersion and absorbing the same values and biases. That process does not lead to a wide diversity of perspectives about the world and the nature of America's proper role in it. It would be an overstatement to suggest that the media alumni from a few select universities emerged as ideological clones, but the commonality of experiences almost certainly helped promote a commonality of views.

That sameness is reinforced because top-tier journalists overwhelmingly reside and work in two dominant media centers: New York City and Washington, DC. Again, there are exceptions, such as news personnel at the *Los Angeles Times*, the *Atlanta Journal-Constitution*, and CNN headquarters (although not most of the network's on-air talent) in Atlanta. But the Washington–New York City dominance is undeniable. Thus, top journalists largely interact with each other and similar colleagues, along with elites in business and government who also reside in those two metropolitan centers. Such a milieu reinforces already strong pressures toward groupthink on an array of issues, especially foreign policy and national security topics. Most elite journalists occupy an echo chamber in which a small number of often questionable assumptions reverberate. The views those journalists promote too often embody the distortions that can be expected from such an environment.

One recent example was the determination of the mainstream media to dismiss, even ridicule, arguments that the COVID-19 pandemic may have originated with a leak from the Wuhan Institute of Virology. The media's intolerance and hubris forestalled any meaningful debate on that important issue for more than a year.[9] Yet the lab theory was never far-fetched. There was little dispute that the virus appeared first in Wuhan; the proximity of the initial victims to one of the most sophisticated and advanced virology facilities in the world should logically have led to serious consideration of that scenario. The extraordinary vehemence of Chinese officials in deriding the possibility and accusing those who raised questions about the origin of the pandemic having nefarious motives should have reinforced media curiosity and scrutiny.

But as discussed in Chapter 8, the journalists willing to consider that scenario were confined almost entirely to the right-wing minority. Early on, mainstream media outlets accepted the arguments of scientists, many of whom had compromising ties to the Chinese government, that the natural origin thesis was literally indisputable. Not until the spring of 2021, in response to mounting evidence that the lab-leak thesis was quite plausible, did the de facto embargo on debate in the press began to unravel.[10] Here was an issue with crucial potential relevance not only to health policy but to the policy of the United States and other countries toward the People's Republic of China; such rigid groupthink was profoundly unwise. Yet groupthink is a growing phenomenon on multiple issues in the news media.

The herd mentality and underlying biases it embodies is most apparent on traditional foreign policy and national security issues. Much of the anger that the press directed against President Donald Trump was because he expressed heretical views about America's military alliances, free trade, regime-change wars, and other crucial components of the globalist-interventionist orthodoxy that had governed Washington's

approach to world affairs since World War II. In reality, the substance
of Trump's foreign policy did not differ markedly from that of his predecessors (with the partial exception of his trade initiatives), but his
rhetoric frequently was brusque and candidly nationalistic. Journalists
committed to the status quo found such statements unsettling, deeply offensive, ignorant, and intolerable—whether or not corresponding
actions followed.

Media assessments of Trump's foreign policy competence and performance were routinely laced with contempt. The journalistic community's open animosity toward what it considered Trump's underlying
"isolationist" beliefs and goals carried over to vilification of anyone who
appeared to share even roughly similar positions.

A prominent example of a condescending, hostile treatment of
Trump's foreign policy views was the 2020 book *A Very Stable Genius:
Donald J. Trump's Testing of America*, written by *Washington Post* reporters
Philip Rucker and Carol Leonnig.[11] In a prepublication article based on
the book, the authors' reverence for establishment foreign policy and
military professionals oozed from nearly every paragraph.[12] They contended that barely six months into Trump's administration, "Secretary
of Defense Jim Mattis, Director of the National Economic Council Gary
Cohn, and Secretary of State Rex Tillerson had grown alarmed by gap-
ing holes in Trump's knowledge of history, especially the key alliances
forged following World War II. Trump had dismissed allies as worthless,
cozied up to authoritarian regimes in Russia and elsewhere, and advocated withdrawing troops from strategic outposts and active theaters alike."

The journalists implicitly shared the condescending attitude of their
favored protagonists about the commander-in-chief. "Trump organized
his unorthodox worldview under the simplistic banner of 'America First,'"
they wrote, "but Mattis, Tillerson, and Cohn feared his proposals were
rash, barely considered, and a danger to America's superpower standing." Consequently, in July 2017, Mattis invited Trump to the Tank (the
ultra-secure Pentagon room for discussing highly classified matters) "for
what he, Tillerson, and Cohn had carefully organized as a tailored tutori-
al." Much to the dismay of those officials, the session did not go as anticipated. The meeting, Leonnig and Rucker concluded, was "a turning

point in Trump's presidency." Not only were they unable to get him to appreciate America's traditional role and alliances, but "Trump began to tune out and eventually push away the experts who believed their duty was to protect the country by restraining his more dangerous impulses."

More accurately, those experts behaved as though their duty was to prevent the president from making any significant changes to entrenched features of U.S. foreign and national security policies, however questionable those features might be. The authors of *A Very Stable Genius* would have acknowledged that point if they weren't cheerleaders themselves for those same policies. Instead, they favorably noted that the secretary of defense tried to use terms "the impatient president, schooled in real estate, would appreciate to impress upon him the value of U.S. investments abroad." Specifically, Mattis "sought to explain why U.S. troops were deployed in so many regions and why America's safety hinged on a complex web of trade deals, alliances, and bases across the globe."

Leonnig and Rucker gave no indication that they considered even the remote possibility that such assumptions might be disputable. Their undertone of sympathy about the daunting task Mattis and other supposedly sensible advisers faced in trying to educate a know-nothing president pervades their article and book. "For the next 90 minutes, Mattis, Tillerson, and Cohn took turns trying to emphasize their points, pointing to their charts and diagrams. They showed where U.S. personnel were positioned, at military bases, CIA stations, and embassies, and how U.S. deployments fended off the threats of terror cells, nuclear blasts, and destabilizing enemies in places including Afghanistan, Iran, Iraq, the Korea Peninsula, and Syria."

But as various foreign policy critics had already pointed out, all those policies faced pertinent doubts and objections. The war in Afghanistan had dragged on for nearly 16 years at the time of the Tank meeting, and contrary to the continuing flow of optimistic reports from military commanders, there was little credible evidence that the United States was any closer to victory than it had been at the outset. In some respects, victory seemed farther away than ever. Certainly, the Afghanistan strategy should not have been considered an improper subject for reassessment by the president and his advisers. Yet the authors seemed horrified that

Trump demanded an explanation for why the United States hadn't won in Afghanistan. "Trump unleashed his disdain, calling Afghanistan a 'loser war.' That phrase hung in the air and disgusted not only the military leaders at the table but also the men and women in uniform sitting along the back wall behind their principals. They all were sworn to obey their commander in chief's commands, and here he was calling the war they had been fighting a loser war."

The abrupt, abject collapse of the U.S. client regime in Kabul when the United States finally withdrew its troops during Joe Biden's administration made clear that the establishment military hierarchy and its media allies had badly miscalculated the situation. At the least, Trump did not deserve patronizing contempt for disputing their views.

Moreover, the *Washington Post* itself had recently published voluminous documents (the so-called Afghanistan Papers) which showed how U.S. civilian and military officials in the Bush, Obama, and Trump administrations systematically misled Congress and the American people about supposed U.S. progress in that conflict.[13] One might think that two of the paper's other reporters would then adopt a more balanced, restrained perspective on the conduct of the war. Instead, they fawned over the hurt feelings of the advisers who were offended by Trump's candid, accurate assessment. In doing so, Leonnig and Rucker inadvertently underscored their own blind spots and unexamined assumptions about the nature and quality of U.S. foreign policy.

That same myopic approach characterized their assessment of Washington's longstanding policy of trying to isolate North Korea to compel that country to remain nonnuclear. Yet, that approach had produced few, if any, worthwhile results. Pyongyang continued to develop its nuclear arsenal and a reliable ballistic missile fleet in defiance of U.S. and international sanctions. The United States remained committed to defending its South Korean and Japanese allies even as North Korea became increasingly capable of launching a nuclear strike on the American homeland if Washington tried to fulfill those commitments. Thus, the current policy's risk level to the United States is rising, but the justification for treating South Korea and Japan as glorified protectorates became obsolete long ago. Japan is the world's third largest economic power, and South Korea now has a population twice that of North Korea and an economy estimated to be 40 to 50 times larger.[14] To conclude that countries with those advantages could build whatever defenses they deemed necessary to guard against a rogue, poverty-stricken regional power like North Korea was hardly outrageous. Yet Mattis and the other advisers briefing Trump acted as though the United States had no choice but to continue being East Asia's security blanket, and Leonnig and Rucker saw nothing even slightly debatable about that viewpoint.

A smug defense of U.S. policy regarding Iraq, Syria, and Iran was even less justifiable. Washington's approach to Middle East issues had already been a debacle for more than three decades. The United States has persisted in an unproductive standoff with Iran, seeking to get Tehran to capitulate on an array of issues instead of treating the country as an essential geopolitical player in that part of the world. Washington has also persisted in its myopic strategy of automatically siding with Saudi Arabia and other Sunni powers in their regional rivalry with Iran and its Shiite allies. U.S. military meddling in Iraq and Syria (as well as in Libya and Yemen) produced dismal results, destabilizing those countries, generating massive refugee flows and other humanitarian tragedies, and creating conditions for the growth of ISIS and other Islamic extremist movements. A November 2019 Brown University study concluded that Washington's war on terror since the 9/11 attacks had cost the United States $6.4 trillion and led to the deaths of more than 801,000 people.[15] Yet the advisers seeking to "educate" President Trump at the July 2017 briefing appeared to regard existing U.S. policy toward such countries as both inescapable and successful.

Notably, Leonnig and Rucker did not criticize or question those assumptions. They believed that Mattis had made an especially devastating rebuttal to the president's criticism of the continuing lack of financial burden-sharing in NATO. Mattis emphasized that throughout the Cold War, NATO "was not serving only to protect Western Europe. It protected America, too." In fact, that continuing transatlantic security solidarity "'is what keeps us safe,' Mattis said."[16]

The defense secretary's formulation was painfully simplistic even with respect to the Cold War; scholars have shown that the U.S. security shield was far more important to Western Europe than any military contribution the NATO partners made was to U.S. security.[17] In the post–Cold War period, since the alliance has added an assortment of vulnerable mini-states (such as the Baltic republics, Montenegro, and Slovenia), making the case that NATO is what keeps America safe is even more difficult. But nothing in the Leonnig and Rucker article showed any awareness on their part about the controversy among established scholars regarding NATO's relevance and value.[18]

Unfortunately, the uncritical treatment of the conventional wisdom that Trump's advisers spouted throughout the 2017 Pentagon meeting epitomizes the sterile groupthink on foreign policy that continues to dominate the American news media. Army veteran and think tank scholar Danny Sjursen provided a pithy and generally accurate assessment of how the mainstream press habitually reflects the assumptions and values of the U.S. national security apparatus. The media, he contended, "is basically a mouthpiece for the CIA, military-industrial-complex, and broader corporate interests. What we have is the *illusion* of an independent media." Operationally, the result is that "the boundaries of permissible debate are quite narrow, and partisan. In both print and television mediums, hiring and invitations practices act as disciplines unto themselves. . . . Question a sacred cow or touch a political 'third-rail'—American exceptionalism, U.S. empire, Israeli apartheid, or, yes, the Trump-Russia nexus—and one won't be asked back (or invited in the first place)."[19]

The instinctive reaction to Sjursen's argument might be to dismiss it as excessively cynical. But the historical record of media coverage of the Balkan wars, Iraq, Syria, and policy toward Russia supports his analysis. He notes that "even modest defense budget cuts or reallocations, marginal troop reductions in war zones or overseas bases, and dissenting 'free' speech, all threaten U.S. security," according to the conventional wisdom in the news media. "In fact, they're sort of un-American." The outcome, Sjursen concludes, "is a bipartisan hawkish brand of outrage culture."

Most portions of the media embody that attitude as well. Even prominent journalists who deviated from a key component of the dominant interventionist narrative have found themselves exiled from programs and op-ed pages that previously welcomed their perspectives. In September 2020, *The Intercept*'s Glenn Greenwald disclosed in an interview with Megyn Kelly that he had been blacklisted at MSNBC, primarily because he disputed the network's unbridled credulity about Russia's alleged menace and President Trump's collusion with it.

When Kelly asked him how he knew that he was banned, Greenwald responded, "I have tons of friends there. I used to go on all the time. I have producers who tried to book me and they get told, 'No. He's on the no-book list.'"[20] An MSNBC spokesperson denied any official ban. But the last time Greenwald appeared on one of the network's programs on any issue was in December 2016—a rather striking coincidence since the final months of 2016 marked the surge of Russian collusion allegations at MSNBC and similar outlets. Greenwald insisted that two different producers told him he was on the no-book list, and he charged that his situation was not unique. "It's not just me but several liberal-left journalists—including Matt Taibbi and Jeremy Scahill—who used to regularly appear there and stopped once they expressed criticism of MSNBC's Russiagate coverage and skepticism generally about the [Russia menace] narrative."

Journalists and policy experts who had dissented from the drive to war with Iraq recalled similar treatment on CNN, MSNBC, and the other networks. The op-ed pages of top-tier publications now exhibit the same type of imbalance regarding Russia as they did about policy toward Iraq in 2001 and 2002. Being a vocal dissenter from the conventional wisdom in the media about a salient foreign policy topic seems to be a ticket to obscurity—or at least relegation to lesser-known, non-mainstream publications and outlets.

Journalists who previously exhibited healthy wariness of and suspicions about the machinations of the U.S. intelligence agencies are not immune to destructive groupthink. The Russia bogeyman seems especially likely to trigger such a reaction. Former *New York Times* correspondent Tim Weiner, whose book *Legacy of Ashes* recounts the many misdeeds of the CIA, is a graphic example. More than 18 months after the release of the Mueller report, Weiner argued, "Despite the investigation by former special counsel Robert S. Mueller III, despite the work of congressional intelligence committees and inspectors general—and despite impeachment—we still don't know why the president kowtows to Vladimir Putin, broadcasts Russian disinformation, bends foreign policy to suit the Kremlin and brushes off reports of Russians bounty-hunting American soldiers. We still don't know whether Putin has something on him. And we need to know the answers—urgently. Knowing could be devastating. Not knowing is far worse. Not knowing is a threat to a functioning democracy."[21] Weiner failed to acknowledge that there was very little evidence to support such inflammatory allegations and that, therefore, they might be untrue.

Only a pervasive collective mentality based on visceral hatred of Donald Trump combined with intense suspicions about Russia, much of it inherited from the days of the Cold War, could account for the continued credibility of the kind of paranoid theory that Weiner expressed. But an astonishing array of media heavyweights succumbed to that perspective. Commenting on Weiner's argument, George Beebe, a former CIA official and now a scholar at the Center for the National Interest, argues that "the notion that anyone might reasonably believe that America's post–Cold War approach to Russia and other parts of the world has failed and requires rethinking, or that a U.S. president might have cause to question the Intelligence Community's judgments or political leanings, appears not to have occurred to him. That notion also seems to have evaded Andrew Weissmann and Peter Strzok, of Mueller and FBI investigation fame. Each is promoting his own book explaining why he was correct from the start to suspect Trump of treason. But neither reveals any heretofore undiscovered evidence for this suspicion that triggered both the FBI and Mueller Commission investigations. Rather, like Weiner, they regard Trump's refusal to pay homage to conventional American views of the Russian threat as sufficient grounds for questioning his loyalty.'"[22]

THE HUNTER BIDEN LAPTOP EPISODE

Trump-hatred and media groupthink also were evident in an incident during the closing weeks of the 2020 presidential campaign. The *New York Post* published an exclusive article based on files allegedly contained in a computer that former vice president Joe Biden's son, Hunter, had left with a Delaware repair shop but then failed to pick up.[23] Questions about the authenticity of the files were legitimate, including murky aspects about the chain of custody. Nevertheless, the revelations in that article and a subsequent one published the following day[24] raised a variety of important issues. The first story included evidence that Joe Biden was far more involved in his son's questionable dealings with the Ukraine energy company Burisma—including at least one meeting with a Burisma executive—than the elder Biden had contended. That greater involvement raised new questions about the vice president's role in demanding that the Ukraine government fire prosecutor Viktor Shokin.

The second article presented evidence that Hunter Biden had been given a 20 percent stake in a Chinese investment fund at a massive discount from its actual value. Worse, one document asserted that although Hunter's stake was 20 percent, an additional 10 percent was set aside under his supervision "for the big guy." Anthony Bobulinski, Hunter's former business partner, later confirmed that the incriminating email was genuine and said that "the big guy" referred to Joe Biden.[25]

Whether any or all of this was true remained uncertain at the time. Biden's defenders asserted that it was all another Russian disinformation campaign, but the FBI promptly shot down that thesis. Caution was warranted in assuming that the *New York Post* stories were accurate, but the allegations were newsworthy and warranted further investigation by serious journalists.

The reactions of most members of the press, though, were unsettling, if not alarming. While media outlets had routinely circulated minimally sourced allegations on related issues (the sketchy Russian bounties story being a prime example), they showed a distinct lack of curiosity about the Biden computer files allegations and adopted an openly hostile attitude toward the story. Facebook and Twitter took the extraordinary step of blocking access to the *New York Post* articles. Twitter went so far as to temporarily suspend the newspaper's account and that of the White House press secretary (see Chapter 12).

Any journalist who had the temerity to take the *New York Post* stories seriously and suggest that they deserved investigation and discussion faced shrill condemnation. To the extent that coverage occurred at all in the mainstream press, it was utterly dismissive—and it usually labeled contrary assessments as "Russian disinformation." The principal "evidence" for that label was nothing more than the speculation and opinions of former intelligence operatives, most of whom had lengthy anti-Trump track records.[26] The FBI found no evidence of a Russian disinformation campaign regarding the Hunter Biden computer episode—a point that the director of national intelligence confirmed.[27] Nevertheless, establishment media outlets frequently cited the conclusions of the former intelligence operatives and invoked similar arguments to justify ignoring the laptop story.[28]

National Review's David Harsanyi charged that "'Russian disinformation' has become the single laziest, dumbest, and most cynical rationalization for journalistic malpractice and political activism over the last four years. Journalists, after all, are in possession of a highly sophisticated method of bypassing foreign 'disinformation.' It's called 'asking the candidate a question.' Yet, as far as I can tell, they've queried Biden as often about his favorite flavor of ice cream as they have about Hunter's emails."[29] He wasn't wrong.

Unfortunately, major portions of the mainstream media acted as de facto protectors of Joe Biden and his campaign. In the process, they short-circuited meaningful inquiry into the behavior of the Ukrainian and PRC governments. If genuine, the Hunter Biden files indicated that those regimes or their closely allied corporations devoted considerable energy and funds to currying favor with a leading American political player—one who might well become president of the United States and ultimately did so. Such an influence campaign had significant relevance to Washington's current and prospective relations with those countries. Ignoring those implications amounted to an outright abdication of the news media's essential responsibility to monitor the behavior of the U.S. government and its leaders, past and present.

Glenn Greenwald again took his journalist colleagues to task for their negligence and indicated the kinds of questions they should have been asking Joe Biden: "Did Hunter Biden drop that laptop off at that repair shop? Are the emails authentic? Do you deny that they are? Do you claim any have been altered or any of them fabricated? Did you in fact meet with Burisma executives as these emails suggest?" Greenwald concluded that "the reason that they don't answer any questions is because the media has signaled that they don't have to. That journalists will be attacked and vilified simply for asking."[30]

In an October 19, 2020, tweet, Greenwald conceded, "I don't think that the emails—so far—reveal a huge scandal. They so far just establish standard sleaze and DC corruption. The huge scandal to me is the blatant rank-closing and cone of silence—a prohibition—erected *by journalists* around this story to defend Biden." He added, "Is there a single journalist willing to say with a straight face they believe the emails relating to the Bidens are either fabricated or otherwise fraudulently altered, but the Bidens just aren't saying so? There [have] to be some limits to your willingness to go to bat for them."[31]

But Greenwald soon discovered that he was not immune to retaliation for his outspoken, iconoclastic views. Moreover, the growing intolerance for dissent was moving beyond the usual suspects in the mainstream media to infect once-bold alternative sites, including Greenwald's own employer, *The Intercept*. Apparently, believing the Biden story to be a legitimate subject for investigation was a bridge too far for anti-Trump figures at that publication. When Greenwald produced yet another opinion piece in late October 2020, raising concerns about Joe Biden's possible involvement in overseas influence-peddling operations, *The Intercept*'s editors suppressed the article. An angry Greenwald then left *The Intercept* and set up shop at Substack, where Matt Taibbi and other foreign policy dissidents resided. The already thin ranks of publications willing to promote vigorous policy debates, centered largely in the alternative media, grew thinner.

Greenwald's Substack article explaining his departure from *The Intercept* was both poignant and troubling. "The same trends of repression, censorship and ideological homogeneity plaguing the national press generally have engulfed the media outlet I co-founded, culminating in censorship of my own articles." Specifically, the editors "censored an article I wrote this week, refusing to publish it unless I remove all sections critical of Democratic presidential candidate Joe Biden, the candidate vehemently supported by all New-York-based Intercept editors involved in this effort at suppression." He also charged that the editors "demanded that I refrain from exercising a separate contractual right to publish this article with any other publication."[32] The episode was eerily reminiscent of the allegations that surrounded *Newsweek*'s behavior in response to Tareq Haddad's attempt to publish an article critical of the official accounts, which closely hewed to the views of NATO governments, about the Assad regime's alleged use of chemical weapons (see Chapter 6).

The mainstream media's performance with respect to the entire Hunter Biden laptop story was deeply disturbing. Except for Fox News and a handful of conservative and anti-war publications, the legacy press and the new social media platforms simply refused to examine the allegations and pursue further inquiries. Worse, they attempted to stifle what little exposure did occur. The defenses that reporters and publishers raised for such disinterest or intolerance were strained and unconvincing. The simplistic claim that the laptop episode was nothing more than a Russian disinformation initiative was highly implausible given the number of documents involved and, more important, Tony Bobulinski's detailed corroborating testimony and presentation of additional documents.

The decision of most media outlets not to cover this story was indefensible given the behavior of the same outlets with respect to the various "Russian plot" stories over the previous four years. From the revelation of the Steele dossier through the multiple Russia-collusion accusations to the Russian bounties report, the mainstream press provided a deluge of coverage. And it did so even though support for those allegations was far weaker than for the latest assertions about Joe Biden and his family. Such glaringly differential treatment indicates a pervasive partisan and ideological bias in the press. The various Russia horror stories fit the media narrative of a malevolent foreign power and an evil, disloyal U.S. president who dared to question Washington's hoary global commitments. The Biden laptop story, on the other hand, undermined the crusade to rid the nation of the aforementioned evil president and thwart the return of the enlightened policy elite that was entitled to run U.S. foreign policy in perpetuity. Therefore, the first set of stories warranted maximum (indeed, overwhelming) press coverage; the latter story deserved to be buried.

Such a fundamentally corrupt mentality was a betrayal of the media's supposed mission to be the watchdog alerting the public to actual or potential abuses by the governing elite. Even with Biden safely installed in office, establishment media outlets were extraordinarily slow to treat the laptop story seriously, despite mounting evidence that there might be significant substance to it.[33] Conversely, no credible evidence emerged to support allegations that the episode was a Russian disinformation campaign. Notably, the former intelligence officials who had advanced that argument went silent.

The establishment media's reaction to the interview that Hunter Biden gave to *CBS Morning News* in early April 2021 illustrated a continuing campaign to ignore or minimize a story that had potentially serious consequences for U.S. foreign policy and Joe Biden's administration. Hunter Biden's interview to promote his new autobiography focused on his long battles with addiction. When asked about the laptop, he conceded that it might be his—but that he might have been "hacked" or the computer might have been stolen.[34] Leaving aside questions about why he wasn't certain about the possible theft of an expensive machine with sensitive business documents, his concession clearly undermined the media narrative that the episode was entirely fictional and merely a Russian disinformation ploy. Yet most press headlines focused on his comments about addiction. His admission about the laptop rarely received more than passing mentions buried well down in the news stories, although the number of dissident voices criticizing the press on this issue did grow during the spring and summer of 2021.[35]

The news media's handling of difficult and controversial foreign policy developments throughout much of the Cold War and post–Cold War periods were not the institution's finest hour. But with the starkly contrasting treatments of the Trump-Russia allegations and the Biden laptop story, the quality of the mainstream media's performance reached a nadir.

Public confidence in the news media also has reached strikingly low levels, and the mishandling of such issues has contributed to that outcome. Suspicion and cynicism about news coverage among the public is a global phenomenon, but the situation is especially bad in the United States. A Reuters report published in June 2021 confirmed that point.[36] A poll of digital news consumers in 46 countries found that the median figure for "trust in the news" stood at a relatively anemic 44 percent. However, the trust level in the United States regarding the American news media was substantially worse—a dismal 29 percent. The American press ranked dead last in trustworthiness among the 46 countries surveyed.

The media's initial reaction to the Biden administration's overall foreign policy indicates that the problems with groupthink remain as serious as ever. The press expressed audible relief that Trump was no longer president and that America's approach to world affairs would return to normal. But that attitude assumes that Washington's foreign policy was generally in good shape before Trump arrived. Given the number of expensive, dangerous, and pointless military actions undertaken during the previous three decades, no belief could be more erroneous. Likewise, the deteriorating relationships with both Russia and China, which were already in decline during the administrations of George W. Bush and Barack Obama, indicated that U.S. foreign policy was not healthy when Trump entered the Oval Office. The continuing failure or refusal of the news media to recognize that reality does not bode well for worthwhile analysis of U.S. policy going forward.

CHAPTER 10
Harassing Journalistic Dissenters

Whenever U.S. leaders assert that a serious threat, foreign or domestic, exists to the nation's safety, they are highly intolerant of journalists who challenge that assertion. Indeed, they do their best to stifle even mild dissent from press outlets, reporters, or columnists. Challenges to the incumbent president's overall policy or leadership are especially unwelcome, and both liberal and conservative administrations have exhibited an unsettling degree of intolerance. Dovish critics of U.S. foreign policy have more frequently been the targets of harassment, smears, and repression, but outspoken hawks also have suffered such abuses on occasion. Journalists, publishers, broadcasters, and website editors whose views deviate too widely from what the political establishment considers the range of acceptable opinion find themselves and their careers at risk.

Sometimes the government's campaign against troublesome dissidents goes beyond trying to cut off general, iconoclastic foreign policy dissent. Officials instead seek to bar stories that expose specific cases of policy blunders or malfeasance, even if the critics in question did not necessarily oppose the overall thrust of Washington's global policy. Indeed, administrations have even attempted to suppress articles that merely had the potential to cause them embarrassment or political difficulties. Officials invariably portray such moves as necessary to prevent the exposure of classified information that could badly damage the nation's security. All too often, though, those justifications appear to be cynical excuses that conceal far less savory motives.

The track record of censorship, prosecution for espionage or sedition, and other coercive tactics directed against uncooperative journalists is long. Censorship, especially battlefield censorship, was a ubiquitous practice in both the Union and the Confederacy during the Civil War.[1] That pattern resurfaced during both world wars once the United States became a belligerent. As discussed in Chapter 1, although the government preferred to seduce the press and use journalists as propaganda agents during the two world wars, it always kept an iron fist inside its velvet glove.

The Espionage Act of 1917 empowered the postmaster general to deny use of the mail to any publication that, in his sole judgment, advocated insurrection, treason, or resistance to the laws of the United States. Postmaster General Albert Burleson, Woodrow Wilson's appointee and a staunch pro-war loyalist, adopted an extremely broad interpretation of those provisions. He used his new powers to exclude a wide array of newspapers, magazines, and pamphlets that exhibited any hint of pacifist or "isolationist" sentiments. Even if a paper avoided publishing an "illegal idea"—an absurdly vague standard—it could be barred from the mail for betraying, in the words of one postal censor, "an audible undertone of disloyalty" in ostensibly legal comments.[2]

Federal prosecutors during World War I considered the mere circulation of anti-war pamphlets or articles a violation of the Espionage Act. Wilson's administration was notoriously thin-skinned about any criticism of its war effort. Dozens of anti-war pacifists and socialists in the press went to prison during the war, and most of them (along with other critics imprisoned under the Espionage Act)—did not gain their freedom until President Warren Harding took office in March 1921— nearly two and a half years after the Armistice ended the fighting in November 1918.

World War II saw fewer criminal prosecutions, but that outcome reflected the lack of serious press or public opposition to the war, in contrast to the simmering undercurrent of anti-war sentiment that continued even after the United States entered World War I. Following the

Japanese attack on Pearl Harbor, anti-war types were rare. Nevertheless, the government's censorship system was just as pervasive and intolerant as it had been during the "Great War."

Franklin Roosevelt and his advisers did not respect foreign policy dissent in the press any more than Wilson had. Roosevelt believed that articles in the conservative press, especially the *Chicago Tribune* and the *New York Daily News*, that were critical of U.S. allies Britain and the Soviet Union (especially the latter) likely warranted prosecution under the Espionage Act. On one occasion, he fumed that "the tie-in between the attitudes of these papers and the Rome-Berlin broadcasts is something far greater than mere coincidence."[3] His sentiment was not just a case of idle musings or a frustrated outburst to a close friend. He wrote it in a letter to Francis Biddle, the U.S. Attorney General, which suggests he at least flirted with the idea of criminally prosecuting his opponents in the media. Equally disturbing, in May 1940, Roosevelt ignored a Supreme Court decision that barred wiretaps and other electronic surveillance and ordered the FBI to spy on suspected subversives, potentially including members of the press.[4] During the post–Pearl Harbor period, the Roosevelt administration also engaged in some rather unsubtle harassment of the *Tribune*, *Daily News*, and other conservative publications that were critical of how officials were directing the war effort.

As in World War I—and later in both the Cold War and post–Cold War periods—some of the worst enemies of the skeptics in the media were other journalists who held pro-administration views. Indeed, some were shrill advocates of outright suppression. Freda Kirchwey, editor of the *Nation*, charged that the "treason press" in the United States constituted "an integral part of the fascist offensive." Such disloyal publications, she contended, "should be exterminated exactly as if they were enemy machine guns in the Bataan jungle."[5]

The overall level of tolerance toward journalistic dissenters on foreign policy did not improve appreciably after World War II. Before and during the war, right-wing types had been harassed; once Washington's wartime romance with the Soviet Union began to cool, left-wing members of the press found themselves the principal targets. The change began in June 1945, while the fight against Imperial Japan still raged, when FBI agents

raided the office of *Amerasia*, a rather obscure, left-leaning journal spe-
cializing in Asian affairs. The discovery of State Department documents
there led to charges against several journal personnel as well as government employees.[6] *Amerasia*'s editor, Philip J. Jaffe, and one associate eventually received light fines for conspiracy to receive government property
illegally. Whether the government intended to prosecute Jaffe and the
other journalists for espionage may never be known. The government had
obtained the evidence illegally, and that made prosecution a moot point.[7]

The reign of intolerance was furthered with the creation of congressional committees tasked with rooting out "subversion" within the opinion-
shaping sector. Three committees played especially active roles. The best
known was the House Committee on Un-American Activities—or as its
critics altered the name to reflect the body's ugly, arbitrary behavior, the
House Un-American Activities Committee (HUAC). Ironically, HUAC
was not a Cold War creation; it was established in 1938, primarily to deal
with the supposedly serious domestic fascist menace. Even in its early
days, though, HUAC paid a surprising amount of attention to alleged left-
wing subversion. Once the Cold War erupted, the committee became an
implacable nemesis of the political, especially the anti-war, left. HUAC
devoted a disproportionate amount of time to investigating communist
penetration of Hollywood. The scrutiny led to the blacklisting of prominent writers and actors—the so-called Hollywood Ten. But a number of
journalists, including prominent syndicated columnist Heywood Broun,
also came to the committee's hostile attention.[8]

Another stifling investigative body was the Senate Government
Operations Committee's Permanent Subcommittee on Investigations.
Sen. Joseph R. McCarthy (R-WI) held a seat on that subcommittee when
the Republicans were in the minority (1947–1953) and chaired the body
from January 1953 to January 1955 when they narrowly controlled the
Senate. Among other measures during McCarthy's chairmanship, the
subcommittee held extensive hearings on whether the Voice of America
was circulating news stories that undermined U.S. security—or more
accurately, deviated from official U.S. foreign policy.[9] McCarthy focused
on the State Department and other government agencies more than on the
media, but the latter was hardly immune. And as was the case with some

his other allegations, his accusations against the press strained credulity. For example, he regarded *Time* magazine, a staunchly anti-communist, pro-Chiang mouthpiece for the China lobby, as suspiciously left-wing.[10]

One of McCarthy's favorite tactics was to compare material in a targeted newspaper with coverage of a similar issue in the communist *Daily Worker*. The ploy was the ultimate in guilt by association and innuendo: he hauled reporters and editors before his committee to interrogate them about the similarities—while of course ignoring any differences in perspectives. He grilled one editor with particular virulence. James Wechsler of the *New York Post* had joined the Young Communist League in the early 1930s but later emphatically broke with the party. Nevertheless, McCarthy went after him as though he was a dangerous Soviet operative, questioning Wechsler about such things as whether he and his newspaper had published or expressed unflattering opinions about J. Edgar Hoover, the FBI as an agency, or HUAC—as though such actions were in any way unlawful.[11] It hardly seems coincidental that, two years earlier, the *New York Post* had published a multipart series with the headline "Smear Inc.: Joe McCarthy's One-Man Mob."

Media reactions to McCarthy's hearings—and especially his testy exchanges with Wechsler—reflected a growing partisan split. Conservative publications generally found Wechsler's behavior defensive and suspicious. They also explicitly defended McCarthy's right to hold hearings into possible communist subversion of the press. Some centrist and liberal publications portrayed Wechsler's testimony as a needed defense of freedom of the press and considered the committee's hearings as moving into abusive territory.[12] However, the media split demonstrated that McCarthy's supporters were bold and numerous, while Wechsler's defenders were both less numerous and more timid.

The third head of the congressional investigative Hydra was the Senate Committee on Internal Security, which ultraconservative Sen. James Eastland (D–MS) chaired during the mid- and late-1950s. Between 1952 and 1957, the Eastland committee compiled a list of more than 500 suspect journalists. In a series of hearings mainly held during 1955, more than 100 journalists were subpoenaed and interrogated about suspected ties between the Communist Party USA and the newspaper industry.

The committee even delved into alleged communist affiliations of some of the most prominent newspapers in the United States.[13]

In his detailed account of the Eastland committee hearings, Edward Alwood, associate professor of journalism at Quinnipiac University, noted the official rationale was to ask reporters and editors about any involvement they had had with the Communist Party USA. But during the sessions, "the actual questioning went much further. The committee asked about their political interests and personal thoughts and beliefs. Members questioned newspaper editorial policies and hiring practices, areas that were thought to be sacrosanct under the First Amendment."[14]

As has been so often the case, maverick journalists not only had to worry about government harassment, but they had to contend with their own colleagues who aided and abetted the government's efforts. Alwood charged that "the press played an important role in promoting McCarthyism by reporting questionable committee procedures in an uncritical manner, thereby legitimizing them."[15]

As Victor Navasky, longtime editor of the *Nation*, observed, the consequences of the hearings and other probes by the three committees varied from publication to publication. "At papers owned by a conservative like William Randolph Hearst or the Scripps-Howard chain, they conducted their own purges of suspected subversives."[16] Some publications required employees to sign "loyalty oaths" as a condition of continued employment. And in some cases, reporters were fired merely because a witness at one of the hearings had named them as being communists.[17] At a powerful establishment paper like the *New York Times*, the response was more subtle; "reporters were urged to cooperate with congressional investigators," despite objections from some reporters and columnists on staff. Even when no overt purges or blacklists resulted, the chilling impact on foreign policy dissent in the press was palpable. Navasky highlighted the comment of John B. Oakes, the editor of the *New York Times* editorial page: "McCarthyism has a profound effect on us all—on our writing, our speaking and even thinking."[18]

Given the extensive use of intimidation through hostile investigations, Kafkaesque public hearings, and "off the record" phone calls from government officials to private organizations, one would be wrong to assume that the threat of or actual prosecution for violating the Espionage Act, the Internal Security Act of 1950 (the McCarran Act), or other statutes was the only—or even the primary—tool used against journalists who had unorthodox foreign policy views. One would also be wrong to assume that left-wing members of the press were the only victims of harassment throughout the initial decades of the Cold War.

Paul Matzko, author of *The Radio Right: How a Band of Broadcasters Took On the Federal Government and Built the Modern Conservative Movement*, vividly describes how John F. Kennedy's administration used less direct, but equally corrosive, methods in an effort to shut down right-wing radio broadcasts. "Kennedy instructed the Internal Revenue Service (IRS) and the Federal Communications Commission (FCC) to target the offending broadcasters with tax audits and heightened regulatory scrutiny. Within a few years, this censorship campaign had driven conservative broadcasters off hundreds of radio stations; it would be more than a decade before the end of the Fairness Doctrine enabled the resurgence of political talk radio."[19]

Matzko observes that the rise of right-wing radio in the late 1950s and early 1960s "gave most Americans access to radio stations that aired conservative programming all day, every day. During the morning drive, you might listen to a solid hour of attacks on the Kennedy administration's Cuba policy on H. L. Hunt's *Life Line* program. Then you could listen to the Christian Crusade as Billy James Hargis ferreted out supposed communist sympathizers at the highest levels of the federal government." Matzko adds that "throughout the rest of the day, one conservative program after another kept the same basic drumbeat: communists were everywhere, the Kennedy administration was weak, and only conservatism could save America." Although the programs frequently criticized Kennedy's domestic policies, the shrill denunciations of his alleged softness on communism had greater prominence.

Conservative broadcasters urged consumers to boycott goods imported from communist countries—and several major boycotts took place as a result. Many of those same broadcasters "also complicated Kennedy's push for the Nuclear Test Ban Treaty with the USSR in 1963, forcing him to spend political capital on an issue that had seemed like a sure thing before the Radio Right had gotten wind of it. Kennedy quickly concluded that advancing his legislative agenda and winning reelection hinged on undermining these radio critics."

Adopting the recommendations of one of his most powerful supporters, Walter Reuther, head of the United Auto Workers, the president and his brother, Attorney General Robert Kennedy, adopted a two-pronged strategy against their critics. One, they pressured the IRS to conduct intrusive audits of both unfriendly radio stations and individual financial contributors to conservative broadcast programs. Two, they weaponized the so-called Fairness Doctrine to compel radio stations to "balance" conservative programing by airing Kennedy-friendly material. A refusal to provide balanced programming—as defined by Kennedy's appointees on the FCC—would jeopardize the station's FCC license, putting it out of business.

The administration's foreign policy agenda was a key motive for the harassment campaign. According to Matzko, "When Kennedy appointed E. William Henry as FCC chairman in 1963 in the middle of the Nuclear Test Ban Treaty fight, he told Henry, 'It is important that stations be kept fair,' which signaled that Kennedy wanted FCC action to ensure more sympathetic coverage of the administration on the radio." The strategy proved very effective for the test ban issue and beyond. Later in 1963, Henry "issued a new legal requirement, the Cullman Doctrine, which stipulated that radio stations that aired paid personal attacks had to give the targets free response airtime. This led many stations to consider dropping conservative broadcasters who criticized administration officials altogether in order to avoid incurring additional costs for the station."

The White House and the Democratic National Committee then "secretly financed two front organizations to use the threat of Fairness Doctrine complaints to intimidate stations into giving the administration more favorable coverage or even dropping right-wing programming altogether." In one of the first efforts in the fall of 1963, "the Citizens Committee for a Nuclear Test Ban sent demands for free response time to every radio station that aired a conservative criticizing the treaty; indeed, it was a committee-generated complaint that gave Henry the pretext for issuing the Cullman Doctrine."[20] To say the administration's campaign impeded media opposition to the treaty was an understatement.

Matzko warns that the same impulse of government leaders to stifle dissent, especially on foreign policy issues, still exists. He cites a tweet from President Donald Trump:

> In July 2017, NBC reported that Trump had called for a "tenfold" boost in the U.S. nuclear arsenal. Trump, angry about the story, tweeted, "With all of the Fake News coming out of NBC and the Networks, at what point is it appropriate to challenge their License? Bad for country!" This made little sense given that NBC itself does not actually possess a broadcast license—individual stations do—and the Fairness Doctrine is history. But that same impulse, to use executive power to suppress critical coverage of the administration, is precisely what led President Kennedy to order one of the most successful government censorship campaigns in U.S. history."[21]

THE QUEST FOR A DE FACTO OFFICIAL SECRETS ACT

American national security officials and their political allies have always pined for the legal system that exists in Britain for keeping information on defense and foreign policy issues secret. Passed in 1911, Britain's Official Secrets Act gave authorities nearly unlimited authority to prohibit news outlets from publishing any information that the government deemed confidential.[22] The system of information control codified in that statute expanded in World War I with Defense of the Realm regulations that created a comprehensive system of censorship. Although those restraints technically expired when combat ended, most of the restrictions were made permanent in 1920 with parliamentary approval of amendments to the Official Secrets Act. Additional revisions were made in 1989.

The statute does not apply only to top secret defense or intelligence information. Quite the contrary, it also applies to matters of international relations and any information that has been entrusted in confidence to another country. Given such a broad definition, the question is what would *not* be covered. A whistleblower or a journalist who publishes information covered by the act cannot even assert as a defense that the disclosure exposed wrongdoing and was in the public interest. The official commission advising Parliament did propose adding that defense in its September 2020 recommendations: "A statutory public interest defence should be available for anyone—including civilians and journalists—charged with an unauthorised disclosure offence under the Official Secrets Act 1989. If it is found that the disclosure was in the public interest, the defendant would not be guilty of the offence."[23] But other recommendations pointed toward more hardline restrictions. One would remove the requirement that the government prove that a leaked story caused damage to national security. Another would substantially increase the prison terms for individuals convicted of violating the act.

The Official Secrets Act and the supplemental restrictions have chilled press scrutiny of foreign policy mistakes or misdeeds. And the chilling, intimidating impact on both whistleblowers and journalists seems to be the main motive. In one episode in 2003, Katharine Gun, an analyst for the British intelligence agency Government Communications Headquarters, leaked a secret memo exposing plans by the U.S. government to potentially blackmail members of the U.N. Security Council into supporting the Iraq War. She disclosed the memo to reporters at the *Observer*, who then broke the story. The British government responded by filing criminal charges against Gun and threatening to do so against the *Observer* and its reporters. (The incident was later dramatized in a movie starring Keira Knightley.[24]) One key point in the government's reaction was that no one disputed the authenticity of the document or the evidence it revealed about duplicity by the governments of President George W. Bush and British Prime Minister Tony Blair. The Official Secrets Act was being used simply to retaliate for exposing such misconduct.

During the early Cold War, Britain supplemented the Official Secrets Act by revitalizing another measure that could be used against a troublesome press, the so-called D-Notice procedure. D-Notices, issued in the post–World War II period by the government's Defence, Press, and Broadcasting Committee, provided detailed "guidelines" to the media about publishing stories on defense-related issues. Only the most obtuse journalists would fail to understand that violating the "guidelines" was high-risk behavior.

The irony of freedom of the press in Britain today is that the most salacious, inflammatory, and misleading stories are the norm with regard to the entire range of domestic affairs. Indeed, British tabloid journalism has become a global symbol for the degradation of quality journalism. But because of the Official Secrets Act and the other components of an elaborate censorship edifice, the range of press scrutiny or discussion of defense policy and national security issues remains extraordinarily crabbed and restricted.

Members of the U.S. national security bureaucracy have longed to emulate their British cousins and implement the equivalent of the Official Secrets Act and the D–Notice procedure. America's first secretary of defense, James Forrestal, sought to formulate something similar to the D–Notice system. He advocated creating a "security advisory council" of six media representatives to assist him in establishing standards for publishing information relating to national security. He abandoned the scheme when he received pushback even from friendly establishment press organizations. But a succession of administrations have pursued the same goal through systematic, albeit less formal, methods. A British expert on press coverage observed that his country's D–Notice procedure "is, in effect, an institutionalized way of doing what is done in the United States through informal government-press contacts."[25]

Officials in Dwight Eisenhower's administration were especially eager to obtain the kind of protection from press scrutiny that their British counterparts enjoyed. That goal was discussed at some length at a November 1953 meeting of the National Security Council. However, the participants concluded that given the strictures of the First Amendment, getting such a measure through Congress would be difficult. Nevertheless, the council agreed to "have in readiness" revisions to the existing espionage statutes "to correspond generally with the British Official Secrets Acts."[26]

Frustrated by their perceived inability to secure an Official Secrets Act from Congress, U.S. advocates of such restrictions repeatedly have sought to gain through the federal courts an American de facto equivalent. Even that goal suffered a major blow in 1971 when the U.S. Supreme Court issued a decision in *New York Times Co. v. United States*—the so-called Pentagon Papers case.

In that decision, the Supreme Court rejected the Nixon administration's bid for prior restraint—the demand to bar publication of the secret documents or any news story based on the documents that Pentagon official Daniel Ellsberg had leaked to the *New York Times* (and later to the *Washington Post*). The leaked material was embarrassing not only to the Nixon administration but even more so to officials in Lyndon Johnson's administration, because it exposed the flawed logic, puerile justifications, and pervasive deceit undergirding Washington's Vietnam policies. For example, the documents showed that at the time Johnson was castigating Barry Goldwater, his opponent in the 1964 presidential election, for wanting to deepen U.S. military involvement in Vietnam, virtually all of the president's advisers had concluded that a major escalation of Washington's military role would be necessary to prevent a communist victory. Another revelation was that the Saigon government was extremely reluctant to approve the introduction of U.S. combat units and submitted to the Johnson administration's "request" only after intense pressure from U.S. special envoy Maxwell Taylor.

Morton H. Halperin, in his capacity as deputy assistant secretary of defense, had supervisory responsibility for compiling the Pentagon Papers. He later conceded, "Clearly, proposals that the United States send troops in over the objections of the Saigon government would have provoked a major debate within the United States. The administration avoided that controversy by keeping the facts secret."[27]

Undoubtedly, publication of such documents bruised the egos and deflated the reputations of some current and former officials. But that effect was hardly a legitimate reason for keeping the information from Congress and the American people. Halperin's candid assessment underscored the actual, underhanded motive. "The Pentagon Papers reveal a consistent pattern of deception by the administration, centered on withholding from Congress and the public vital information that raises devastating questions about the effectiveness and propriety of administration policies and the credibility of responsible officials. It was not hard to understand why, given the policies and rationales to which the government was committed, the Pentagon Papers had to be kept secret."[28]

For all those reasons, Ellsberg clearly did a great service to the nation in leaking the documents revealing the Johnson administration's blunders and lies, and the *New York Times* did an equally great service in publishing them. The government's contention that disclosing the Pentagon Papers "risked grave and immediate danger to the security of the United States" was little more than a cynical cover story to conceal far more mundane reasons for wanting to keep those documents out of the public arena. Halperin emphasized the key features that the Pentagon Papers did *not* contain. "There was nothing in the nature of weapons or electronic design information, identities of secret agents still in the field, or other material of the sort that could be of great value to foreign governments while of little relevance to public concern. The secrecy of the study could not be justified on such straightforward grounds."[29]

The Supreme Court's rejection of the Justice Department's case for prior restraint to suppress publication of the Pentagon Papers provided an important layer of protection for crucial press freedoms. But the extent of the victory has sometimes been misconstrued or at least overstated. It's important to recall that the ruling was not unanimous; only six of the nine justices endorsed the logic and language in the ruling. The other justices implicitly embraced the government's case and underlying arguments, apparently even with regard to prior restraint.

The ruling also did not decide the question of whether authorities could prosecute journalists once they published a story using the Pentagon Papers or any other classified documents. University of Denver Professor Derigan A. Silver notes that several constitutional scholars have stressed the surprisingly limited nature of the decision. "[David H.] Topol concluded that 'once classified information has reached the media, the government has statutory authorization to prosecute the media.'" Silver also notes that in *New York Times v. United States*, six of the nine justices suggested that the government could prosecute newspapers for publishing classified information even if the government could not enjoin the publication of the Pentagon Papers. Furthermore, "[Benjamin S.] DuVal [Jr.] argued that both the Atomic Energy Act and the Intelligence Identities

Protection Act of 1982 could be read as prohibiting the dissemination of information by 'anyone at all,' while Lawrence P. Gottesman reached a similar conclusion about the Intelligence Identities Protection Act."[30]

The last item mentioned, the Intelligence Identities Protection Act, is a statute enacted in 1982 which prohibits the deliberate revelation of the identities of CIA or other intelligence agents. There is no indication whatever that journalists would be exempt from that prohibition. The ostensible purpose of the law is to prevent the disclosure of information that might endanger the lives of operatives working overseas in hostile environments, a reasonable concern according to analysts.[31] However, the law also has the potential to impede news stories about illegal or unethical activities of U.S. intelligence agencies. It is yet another weapon in the government's arsenal to limit scrutiny of and debate on the nation's national security policies.

In 2005, federal prosecutors sought to use that weapon to compel *New York Times* reporter Judith Miller and several other journalists to identify their sources, whose disclosures had led to the publication of a CIA agent's name. Miller refused and went to jail for 85 days on a contempt charge. Robert Novak, whose syndicated column had outed CIA agent Valerie Plame, also became the target of a lengthy investigation under the Intelligence Identities Protection Act.[32] Although he avoided prosecution, the legal menace for engaging in such disclosures was clear.

The danger became more acute after an important amendment became law in December 2019. The new provision prohibits the outing of "covert agents," regardless of whether the disclosure would present a risk of harm to them. The broader scope eliminated a requirement that, for the law to apply, an intelligence officer or informant had to have recently served or been active overseas. The new language criminalizes such disclosures even after the agent's retirement or death—so long as the intelligence community or the military maintains the classification. As the Reporters Committee for Freedom of the Press points out, the amendment made the law much broader and gave it extensive potential to chill press coverage and discussion of intelligence issues.[33]

Opponents of the Pentagon Papers ruling have sought to erode some of the implicit protections in other ways. A notable case was the prosecution of Samuel Loring Morison. Eisenhower administration officials had once hinted of the possibility of stretching the espionage laws into the operational equivalent of a full-fledged official secrets act. Ronald Reagan's administration sought to do exactly that—unfortunately, with some success.[34] Morison, the grandson of renowned naval historian Samuel Eliot Morison, worked as a civilian analyst of Soviet naval systems for the U.S. Naval Intelligence Support Center. He surreptitiously obtained satellite photographs of a Soviet aircraft carrier under construction at a Black Sea shipyard. He then sent the photographs, along with an analytical memorandum, to *Jane's Defence Weekly*, an authoritative British magazine to which Morison occasionally contributed articles.

The Reagan Justice Department chose to prosecute Morison just as if he had delivered classified material to the KGB or another hostile foreign intelligence service. The administration's rationale was that "foreign agents read that magazine."[35] The legal argument was especially insidious. Morison was not only someone who had leaked information to the press, but he was the author of the resulting article. In other words, he served both as source and reporter. Those points made no difference to federal prosecutors. Roland S. Inlow, who had been the CIA's long-time in-house expert on spy satellites, testified that the grainy images in Morison's magazine article had caused "zero damage" to U.S. security, but the administration was not deterred from pressing the espionage case.[36] Unfortunately, the prosecution succeeded, and Morison received a prison sentence.

The federal district court upheld the Reagan administration's legal theory that the Espionage Act applied to the dissemination of classified information to recipients other than foreign governments—even if those recipients were journalists. That precedent became more entrenched when the Fourth Circuit Court of Appeals upheld Morison's conviction and the U.S. Supreme Court declined to review the ruling in October 1988. The Morison case thus became (and remains) a powerful deterrent to anyone wanting to leak classified information and, potentially, to any member of the press who receives and publishes such material.

The current, ambiguous status of the law with respect to the publication of classified documents is a worrisome, potentially unstable, situation. The Reagan administration threatened on several occasions to prosecute journalists if they disclosed classified material in their stories. Ultimately, officials did not follow through with those threats, but the aggressive underlying mentality was evident and more than a little disturbing.[37] Subsequent administrations, both Republican and Democratic, generally refrained from pursuing the option of post-publication prosecutions, and the prevailing assumption has been that such an attempt would likely run afoul of the courts. The bottom line, though, is that individuals who leak items to the press remain as vulnerable as ever to prosecution for espionage, while members of the press after the Pentagon Papers ruling have enjoyed de facto immunity—so far. Efforts by the administrations of Barack Obama, Donald Trump, and Joe Biden to arrest and prosecute WikiLeaks founder and editor Julian Assange for publishing purloined documents provide a strong indication that such immunity for journalists might be coming to an end.

Even before the Assange case, worries about that danger were rising. Developments during the George W. Bush and Barack Obama administrations indicated that a two-pronged government strategy was emerging to foster post-publication prosecutions. One prong focused on cracking down hard on government employees who leak classified information to the press—even if that information exposed misconduct on the part of agencies involved in national security policy. Indeed, officials seemed willing to pursue and prosecute unauthorized leakers, even if the information revealed atrocities and outright war crimes.

The campaign against such whistleblowers aimed at intimidating anyone else who contemplated engaging in similar behavior. The apparent hope was that the harassment would serve to dry up potential sources for investigative journalists. As part of that strategy, the government put the journalists themselves under surveillance, with the justification that such intrusive action was necessary to identify individuals who broke the law against unauthorized disclosures of classified information.

The other prong was the continuing effort to obtain court decisions approving these ever-widening tactics—that is, to establish the equivalent of the Official Secrets Act. This strategy was not really surprising. U.S. foreign policy mandarins sought to overturn or at least dilute the Pentagon Papers precedent from the outset. Just days after the Supreme Court's decision, Dean Acheson, one of the key architects of Washington's post–World War II foreign policy, called for passage of "a severe Official Secrets Act to prevent irresponsible or corrupt transfer of secret papers from the government to publishers. . . ."[38] During the 1980s and 1990s, hawkish types routinely expressed similar attitudes. Michael A. Ledeen, a special adviser to the secretary of state and later a scholar at the neoconservative American Enterprise Institute, enthusiastically endorsed the British model. Ledeen was especially upset by the publication of Bob Woodward's 1987 book *Veil*, an exposé of CIA dirty tricks around the world. Ledeen stated emphatically that "such a book ought not to have been published," adding that with an American Official Secrets Act, it would not have been.[39]

Attorney General Janet Reno testified before the Senate Select Committee on Intelligence in June 2000 regarding the continuing, annoying problem of leaks. She asserted that "one can reasonably argue that reporters are breaking the law by receiving and publishing classified information," although she stressed that "both Democratic and Republican Administrations have sought to avoid the constitutional and public policy questions that would be posed by subjecting the media to compulsory process or using sensitive techniques against members of the media." Reno added, "While this practice has made our job far more difficult, it represents a policy judgment that takes into account concerns that a free press not be unduly chilled in the exercise of its newsgathering function. For over twenty years, a Department regulation (28 C.F.R. 50.10) has prohibited Department employees from questioning members of the media, or from issuing subpoenas to, or for the telephone toll records of, members of the media without the specific approval of the Attorney General." Her reassurance about exempting the press from such measures, while significant, was less than definitive. "In practice, we have *almost never* issued subpoenas to reporters or used sensitive investigative techniques, such as physical or electronic surveillance or pen-registers, to investigate their contacts." Moreover, she emphasized that "this does not mean that such means are never justified in balancing national security interests against the interests of the press."[40]

In his 2002 study for the Shorenstein Center on the Press, Politics, and Public Policy, Jack Nelson, former Washington bureau chief for the

Los Angeles Times, noted that after the 9/11 attacks, attitudes about plugging leaks and even prosecuting reporters for publishing such material grew stronger and more widespread. "Defense Secretary Donald Rumsfeld called for jail terms for leakers and President George W. Bush joined him in denouncing them. An intelligence official even suggested sending 'SWAT teams into journalists' homes, if necessary to root out reporters' sources."[41]

Rumsfeld was not the only Bush administration official to view enthusiastic investigative reporters as potential threats to national security. In 2006, Sen. Arlen Specter (R–PA), chairman of the Senate Judiciary Committee, held a hearing on "the Department of Justice's Investigation of Journalists Who Publish Classified Information."[42] The testimony of Matthew Friedrich, chief of staff for the Criminal Division at the Department of Justice, did not offer much comfort to defenders of a free press with respect to national security issues. Friedrich contended that many government statutes could be used to prosecute journalists who publish classified information. However, he observed that, as of 2006, it was not Justice Department policy to do so. His comment was even less reassuring than Reno's earlier statement, and it certainly was a slim reed for reporters to rely on.

The position adopted by Attorney General Alberto Gonzales was even more menacing. In a May 21, 2006, interview on ABC TV's *This Week*, Gonzales was asked about the possibility of prosecuting members of the press for publishing classified information. "It depends on the circumstances," he responded. "There are some statutes on the book which, if you read the language carefully, would seem to indicate that that is a possibility." He added ominously that "We [the Justice Department] have an obligation to enforce those laws."[43]

Gonzales noted that in his concurring opinion in the Pentagon Papers case, Justice Byron White stated, "From the face of the statute and the context of the act of which it was a part, it seems undeniable that a newspaper as well as others unconnected with the government are vulnerable to prosecution under 798I [of the Espionage Act] if they communicate or withhold materials covered by that section."[44]

Gonzales indicated that he shared White's sentiment. He also mentioned that the Court of Appeals for the Fourth Circuit "affirmed that the First Amendment does not prevent prosecutions under 798 for unauthorized disclosures of classified information and did so over the objection of various news organizations that appeared in the case as amici to support the defendants' First Amendment arguments." He argued further that "it is the conclusion of legal commentators with respect to section 798 that reporters are not exempt from the reach of this statute if the elements of the statute are otherwise met."[45]

In addition to making the case that the law did not exempt journalists from prosecution under the Espionage Act, Gonzales and other Bush appointees stressed that Congress had spurned efforts to grant members of the press such an exemption. Friedrich noted that Sen. Richard Lugar (R-IN) had introduced legislation to provide a federal shield law to protect reporters. However, after the Judiciary Committee modified Lugar's handiwork, Friedrich stated, the proposed legislation was "very carefully crafted to provide *an exception* if national security is involved."[46]

Such comments suggested that the Bush administration was laying the foundation for prosecuting journalists for publishing articles that included classified information. At a minimum, administration officials were toying with the option. Alberto Gonzales seemed especially enthusiastic about the goal. A British source who sat in on a meeting during the summer of 2005 between the U.S. attorney general and his counterpart in Prime Minister Tony Blair's government relayed the following account: "Gonzales was obsessed with the Official Secrets Act. In particular, he wanted to know exactly how it was used to block newspapers and broadcasters from running news stories derived from official secrets, and how it could be used to criminalize persons who had no formal duty to maintain secrets. He saw it as a panacea for his problems: silence the press. Then you can torture and abuse prisoners and what you will without fear of political repercussions. It was the easy route to dealing with the Guantanamo dilemma. Don't close down Guantanamo. Close down the press. We were appalled by it, but not surprised."[47]

The attitudes expressed by Gonzales were not confined to the executive branch. Sen. Tom Cotton (R-AR) was an especially outspoken proponent of prosecuting the press for disclosing classified information. His enthusiasm for that remedy emerged during the Bush years, well before he was elected to Congress. As an Army lieutenant stationed in Iraq in 2006, Cotton became incensed at a *New York Times* story disclosing the administration's secret program to disrupt the financing of alleged terrorist organizations. In an open letter to the *New York Times*, he accused the paper of having "gravely endangered the lives of my soldiers and all other soldiers and innocent Iraqis here." Cotton asserted that as a Harvard Law School graduate and practicing attorney, he was "well-versed in the espionage laws relevant to this story and others— laws you have plainly violated." He closed with a chilling wish. "I hope that my colleagues at the Department of Justice match the courage of my soldiers here and prosecute you and your newspaper to the fullest extent of the law. By the time we return home, maybe you will be in your rightful place: not at the Pulitzer announcements, but behind bars."[48]

Cotton has given no indication whatsoever that he has changed his views since entering Congress. Nor was he alone at the time in wanting to criminally prosecute journalists for disclosing any classified information that might undercut U.S. policy. Rep. Peter King (R-NY) blasted the *New York Times* for being "treasonous," as did Sen. Jim Bunning (R-KY).[49]

During his 2008 presidential campaign, Democratic Party nominee Barack Obama condemned the Bush administration for excessive secrecy and for taking a menacing posture toward the press on national security matters. During a speech in Washington, DC, he told the audience that the Bush administration "puts forward a false choice between the liberties we cherish and the security we provide."[50] Obama vowed that, as president, he would give U.S. intelligence agencies the tools they needed to defeat terrorists but would do so without undermining the Constitution.

Those words seemed consistent with his actions as a member of the U.S. Senate. As a senator, Obama repeatedly emphasized the need to rein in government surveillance. In 2005, he sponsored a bill to make it harder for federal agents to use special subpoenas, known as national security letters, to obtain business and personal records without a court order. That same year, he joined other congressional Democrats to press for additional civil liberties protections in a vote to extend the

Patriot Act. The law as currently written, he said, "seriously jeopardizes the rights of all Americans and the ideals America stands for."[51]

Obama's election appeared to reduce the threat to the Fourth Amendment and to press freedoms. However, such assumptions about greater transparency and respect for the First Amendment regarding national security issues proved to be an illusion. A May 13, 2014, segment on PBS *Frontline* summarized the shift in Obama's attitude and policies. As president, "Obama has embraced many of the same domestic surveillance programs he once derided as a candidate. For the one-time constitutional law professor, the shift has been particularly striking."[52] The Obama administration actually intensified the harassment of inquisitive journalists and deepened the campaign to criminalize the unauthorized publication of classified materials. (See the following section.) Plenty of trouble had been brewing, though, even before Obama entered the White House.

JULIAN ASSANGE: CATALYST FOR THE GOVERNMENT'S WAR ON A FREE PRESS

The emergence of WikiLeaks, the website that Julian Assange and several colleagues founded in 2006, became the principal catalyst for an intensified campaign to restrict the publication of leaks in the press. Official Washington's hatred of Assange soon bordered on rabid. WikiLeaks published voluminous quantities of leaked documents—in some cases highly classified materials. Those disclosures embarrassed, even discredited, powerful government officials and political factions in the United States and other countries. Among WikiLeaks's revelations was evidence that U.S. personnel were torturing terrorist suspects at the Guantanamo Bay prison as well as at assorted CIA "black sites" in the United States and allied countries.[53] Other leaks provided evidence of U.S. war crimes on the battlefield, notably a brazen killing of civilians, including two Reuters journalists, in Iraq.[54] Some especially spectacular accounts emerged even in the mainstream press because of leaked documents that a young Army private, Chelsea Manning, who had extensive access to incriminating documents, had given to WikiLeaks.

U.S. officials were furious about such incriminating information becoming public. They not only prosecuted Manning for espionage, eventually securing a draconian 35-year prison sentence, but they filed a criminal charge against Assange. The attacks on Assange became a bid for robust censorship powers not seen since the Nixon administration sought to prevent the *New York Times* and *Washington Post* from publishing the Pentagon Papers.

The Manning leaks also highlighted the mainstream media's deference to national security agencies. Originally, Manning offered the files (known as the Iraq War Logs) to both the *Washington Post* and *New York Times*. However, only WikiLeaks decided to publish them, even though the files showed evidence of U.S. war crimes in Iraq and other parts of the Middle East.[55]

The momentum toward censorship had been building for some time, largely in reaction to WikiLeaks, but 2011 was an especially active year on the pro-censorship front. Congress considered one bill that sought to expand the Espionage Act of 1917. The new measure, titled The Securing Human Intelligence and Enforcing Lawful Dissemination Act, explicitly made it a crime to publish classified information concerning the human intelligence activities of the United States or any foreign government. That prohibition included barring the disclosure of the identity of a classified source or informant for any portion of the U.S. intelligence community—not just the identities of covert operatives currently in the field. The three Senate sponsors of the bill, Sens. John Ensign (R-NV), Joseph Lieberman (I-CT), and Scott Brown (R-MA), were all outspoken foreign policy hawks.

Anger at WikiLeaks' disclosures was a prominent motive for the proposed legislation. "The reckless behavior of Wikileaks [sic] has compromised our national security and threatened the safety of our troops overseas, and this bipartisan legislation gives the Department of Justice a tool to prevent something like this from happening again," Senator Brown stated in a press release. "While I strongly support government transparency, certain information must be kept classified in order to protect innocent American lives during this time of war and global terrorism."[56] Once again, a statement from an influential political figure, professing commitment to government transparency, was attached to a substantive measure that sought to achieve the opposite outcome. The provisions that Brown and his cosponsors sought eventually became law in 2019 through amendments to the Intelligence Identities Protection Act (see previous paragraph).

Another proposed measure, the Espionage Statutes Modernization Act,[57] was more comprehensive, and it was particularly pernicious in one area. Introduced by Sen. Ben Cardin (D–MD), the bill sought to make it a crime for anyone with unauthorized possession of any classified information to willfully communicate the information to someone not entitled to receive it. Since a journalist would presumably not be authorized to possess classified documents, publishing any information from such material would be construed as criminal conduct. In 2000, Congress passed a bill similar to the Cardin proposal,[58] but President Bill Clinton vetoed it, expressing his concern that the provision "is overbroad and may unnecessarily chill legitimate activities that are at the heart of a democracy."[59] The much greater public fear that has pervaded the country since the 9/11 attacks increases the likelihood that such a restrictive measure might become law, although, fortunately, the Cardin bill did not do so.

In addition to pushing for new censorship legislation, the government's quest to achieve the functional equivalent of the Official Secrets Act—through the federal courts or unilateral practices under the cover of existing laws—has never abated. To the contrary, the administrations of George W. Bush and Barack Obama markedly stepped up efforts to shield their foreign policies behind a veil of secrecy and to harass journalists who sought to emulate their Pentagon Papers predecessors. Former CIA analyst John Kiriakou, a whistleblower who called attention to some egregious abuses by that agency and paid the price with a 30-month term in federal prison, offered a harsh judgment of Obama's behavior following the prosecution of Chelsea Manning. "President Obama has been unprecedented in his use of the Espionage Act to prosecute those whose whistleblowing he wants to curtail. The purpose of an Espionage Act prosecution, however, is not to punish a person for spying for the enemy, selling secrets for personal gain, or trying to undermine our way of life. It is to ruin the whistleblower personally, professionally and financially. It is meant to send a message to anybody else considering speaking truth to power: challenge us and we will destroy you."[60]

Obama's administration even waged a campaign to harass and intimidate mainstream journalists who used leaked material. On May 13, 2013, stories broke that the Justice Department had seized the records of phone lines used by Associated Press employees.[61] The Associated Press confirmed that the records were from personal home and cell phones of reporters and editors, as well as phones that the Associated Press used in the press quarters of the House of Representatives. The administration's contempt for even the basic requirements of due process was alarming. As CBS reporter Sharyl Attkisson noted, such a seizure was "unheard of." Beyond the abusive display of power that those raids embodied, she was outraged that no advance notice was given about the subpoena. "Advance notice would have given AP the chance to challenge the move in court."[62] Of course, that predictable response likely was the reason the Justice Department did not follow such a procedure.

A coalition of 50 news organizations, including ABC, CNN, the *New York Times*, the *Washington Post*, and the Committee for Freedom of the Press, submitted a letter of protest to Attorney General Eric Holder about the raid. It stated that "none of us can remember an instance where such an overreaching dragnet for newsgathering materials was deployed by the Department [of Justice], particularly without notice to the affected reporters or an opportunity to seek judicial review. The scope of this action calls into question the very integrity of the Department of Justice policies toward the press and its ability to balance, on its own, its police powers against the First Amendment rights of the news media and the public's interest in reporting on all manner of conduct, including matters touching on national security which lie at the heart of this case."[63] Holder summarily rebuffed the protest, and there was no indication that it inhibited in the slightest the Obama administration's crackdown on leaks and news organizations using such information.

In addition to the dragnet raid against the Associated Press, Obama administration officials also conducted electronic surveillance of both *New York Times* journalist James Risen and Fox News correspondent

James Rosen in an effort to identify their sources. The government even named Rosen as an "unindicted co-conspirator" in an espionage case brought against his source.[64] Similarly, the administration asserted that it had the right to prosecute Risen, although it chose not to take that step. These were all ominous warning signals of a government campaign to erase even the limited protections that the Pentagon Papers ruling had provided.

The Obama administration's hostility toward investigative journalists who uncovered material embarrassing to the White House's agenda and reputation on national security extended to revelations that had nothing to do with the Middle East, Russia, and China—Washington's usual foreign policy priorities. Sharyl Attkisson discovered a shocking degree of hostility, bordering on vengeance, from administration officials because of her work on two stories. One was the "Fast and Furious" gun-running scandal. The other was the September 11, 2012, terrorist attack on the U.S. consulate in Benghazi, Libya, that took the lives of Ambassador Christopher Stevens and three other Americans.

Fast and Furious involved a sting operation that the Justice Department and the Bureau of Alcohol, Tobacco, Firearms, and Explosives concocted to infiltrate and weaken Mexican drug cartels. The scheme entailed shipping traceable guns to the drug trafficking gangs and then following the trail to identify and neutralize those organizations and the kingpins who ran them. But Operation Fast and Furious backfired badly. Law enforcement personnel assigned to maintain the traces lost track of where the weapons ultimately ended up. In the end, the cartels simply received more than 1,700 additional weapons at the expense of U.S. taxpayers. Not surprisingly, the Obama administration sought to conceal the nature and extent of the fiasco.[65] Attorney General Holder even defied a congressional subpoena and refused to testify before a House committee investigating the Fast and Furious operation.[66]

Attkisson was one of the reporters who apparently attracted the administration's greatest displeasure for stories she published that exposed how the sting went so badly wrong. That animosity grew when her work on Benghazi became more prominent. "My *Fast and Furious* coverage," Attkisson recalls in her memoir, "bled over into the Benghazi period.

The Obama administration was just as frantic over my reporting on that topic. Just as desperate to learn who was talking to me and what I was learning from them."[67]

She discovered unmistakable signs that her phones had been tapped and her computers compromised, developments that technical experts she called in for assistance confirmed.[68] The operatives who planted the bugs and conducted the computer intrusions apparently concluded that she was using classified information from sources inside the government. Her work on the Benghazi episode seemed to reinforce the administration's campaign of harassment. Attkisson's conclusion was harsh but evidently warranted. She believed that the administration was "going after journalists and sources whom it views as most harmful to its own self-interests."[69]

This was hardly the first time an administration misused national security justifications to conceal more mundane and questionable motives, and it would not be the last. Attkisson astutely concludes, "There are thousands of examples over the decades, but one need look no further than *Fast and Furious* to find government misconduct, bad actors, and false information all wrapped up in one."[70]

The views and actions of Trump administration officials did little to allay the concerns of civil libertarians who worried about possible prosecutions of journalists for espionage. Attorney General Jeff Sessions was evasive when asked at his confirmation hearing whether he would subpoena or prosecute reporters regarding their use of leaked classified information.[71] President Trump reportedly expressed even greater interest than his predecessors in prosecuting journalists who use leaked classified information. In his much-discussed February 2017 Oval Office session with FBI director James B. Comey—during which Trump allegedly asked Comey to end the investigation into the conduct of former national security advisor Michael Flynn—the president reportedly endorsed that approach. "Alone in the Oval Office, Mr. Trump began the discussion by condemning leaks to the news media, saying that Mr. Comey should consider putting reporters in prison for publishing classified information, according to one of Mr. Comey's associates."[72]

The Trump administration showed the same fondness for surveilling targeted journalists that its two immediate predecessors exhibited.

In May and June 2021, news stories broke that the Trump Justice Department had secretly obtained the phone records of multiple reporters working for the *New York Times*, *Washington Post*, and CNN—accounts that the Biden administration subsequently confirmed.[73] The surveillance effort continued for nearly four months in 2017. The principal impetus apparently was articles using leaked information from the FBI and intelligence agencies relevant to the Russia-collusion story. Given Trump's rage about that set of allegations, claims that he had launched a war against journalists he believed were undermining his presidency were entirely credible. The ugly ramification, though, is that conducting such surveillance of "unfriendly" reporters constitutes a serious threat to press freedoms.

Efforts to eviscerate the Pentagon Papers precedent took a major step forward in 2019 when Trump administration officials cajoled the government of Ecuador into expelling Julian Assange from its embassy in London, where he had received sanctuary for nearly seven years. Following the election of a more conservative government in Quito, and Washington's offer of a new multi-million-dollar aid package, Ecuador did so in April of that year. British authorities promptly arrested and jailed Assange for jumping bail on sketchy sexual assault charges in Sweden, and U.S. officials began planning to have him extradited to face espionage charges in the United States. On May 23, 2019, the Justice Department added 17 counts to the 1-count indictment that it had filed years earlier during the Obama administration. Assange's imprisonment in Britain and the onset of a lengthy extradition battle delayed the prospect of a high-profile trial in the United States, but that outcome clearly remained Washington's goal.

The issues at stake went far beyond whether or not Julian Assange was an admirable person—although pro-prosecution factions repeatedly tried to frame the question in that light.[74] His prosecution symbolized a crucial fight over freedom of the press and the ability of journalists to expose government misconduct without fear of criminal prosecution. Unfortunately, a disturbing number of establishment journalists in the United States seemed willing (indeed, eager) to throw him to the government wolves. As allegations of Russian meddling in the U.S. election on behalf of Donald Trump intensified, the increasingly popular trope among centrist and left-of-center members of the media was that Assange was a Kremlin tool.[75] When he was arrested in April 2019, both liberal and establishment Republican-oriented journalists were among the biggest cheerleaders.

The *New York Times*, the *Washington Post*, and other prominent mainstream publications rejected the argument that the government was trying to silence a troublesome journalist. "The case of Mr. Assange," the *New York Times* editorial board stated, "could help draw a sharp line between legitimate journalism and dangerous cybercrime." They desperately tried to make a distinction between WikiLeaks' behavior and the conduct of respectable, establishment publications—like the *New York Times*. The editorial noted the government's allegation that Assange conspired with Chelsea Manning to commit cybercrime and contended that the charge "is far less contentious than had it been, as widely anticipated, for espionage-related crimes. That would have been a direct challenge to the distinction between a journalist exposing abuse of power through leaked materials—something traditional newspapers like The Times do all the time—and a foreign agent seeking to undermine the security of the United States through theft or subterfuge."[76] The argument was a strained, awkward, and unconvincing attempt to disown Assange without exposing the *New York Times* and other legacy publications to increased risk of prosecution for similar conduct.

A *Washington Post* editorial tried even harder to distance itself from Assange.[77] It argued that "Mr. Assange is not a free-press hero. Yes, WikiLeaks acquired and published secret government documents, many of them newsworthy, as shown by their subsequent use in newspaper articles (including in The Post). Contrary to the norms of journalism, however, Mr. Assange sometimes obtained such records unethically. . . . Also unlike real journalists, WikiLeaks dumped material into the public domain without any effort independently to verify its factuality or give named individuals an opportunity to comment."

FAIR's Alan MacLeod cited that *Washington Post* editorial and its characterization of Assange as "no free-press hero" as an example of how secure mainstream publications sought to disown an unpredictable maverick.

Likewise, MacLeod stated, "the *Wall Street Journal* (4/11/19) demanded 'accountability' for Assange, saying, 'His targets always seem to be democratic institutions or governments.'" Other mainstream publications followed suit. "Celebrating his arrest, *The Week* (4/11/19) attacked Assange as a 'delusional, childish narcissist' who undermined the security of every nation. A host of other media outlets across the spectrum (*Washington Post*, 4/12/19; *New York Times*, 4/12/19; London *Times*, 4/7/19) similarly framed him as a 'narcissist,' one with an 'outsized view of his own importance.'"[78]

The attitude of the mainstream press toward Assange had undergone a profound transformation since the early days of WikiLeaks' campaign against government secrecy and misconduct. Although a certain amount of professional jealously was to be expected as the organization published scoop after scoop, Assange had a considerable number of defenders among American progressives. The right-wing press, on the other hand, was intense in its hostility, seeing WikiLeaks and its founder as a threat to U.S. national security. That ideological (and partisan) cast to the media's reaction was unsurprising; most early WikiLeaks disclosures had discomfited George W. Bush's administration, which left-wing figures loathed.

But as the years passed, newer releases revealed possible Obama administration misdeeds, and progressives soon became less and less favorable to Assange. Then in 2016, he committed an apparently unpardonable sin in the eyes of many on the left: WikiLeaks published hacked or leaked information from the Democratic National Committee that exposed political dirty tricks by Hillary Clinton's presidential primary campaign against Bernie Sanders. Assange and WikiLeaks then became anathema to most liberal journalists. In a passage in its April 2019 editorial disavowing Assange as a fellow journalist, the *Washington Post* hinted at its main grievance. The editorial asserted that a "real journalist" would not "have cooperated with a plot by an authoritarian regime's intelligence service to harm one U.S. presidential candidate and benefit another."[79] Never mind that no credible evidence linked Assange or WikiLeaks to a plot to undermine Hillary Clinton's candidacy on behalf of Russia. The *Washington Post*, like most elite, establishment publications, had bought into the Russia-collusion allegation without reservation, and the editors were prepared to dismiss Julian Assange as a bogus journalist.

Former State Department official Peter Van Buren summarized the ideological switch among progressive journalists concisely. "What happens to Assange will be one of the biggest test cases for press freedoms in America ever. At stake? The ability of all journalists to inform the public of things the government wants to withhold. But this has been largely ignored because Assange, once a darling of the progressive activist press, is now regarded as a hero-turned-zero, mostly because of WikiLeaks' role in publishing hacked emails that proved damaging to the Democratic Party and the Hillary Clinton campaign ahead of the 2016 elections."[80]

In fairness, the reverse process occurred with respect to some—although assuredly not all—conservative press outlets. Fox News, *The American Conservative*, and other generally pro-Trump types now decided to portray Assange as a noble whistleblower.[81] A few firmly anti-war publications on the left, such as *The Intercept* and *Truthdig*, continued doing so as well. Yet the pro-Assange faction was divided and diminished, while hawkish media allies of both the Republican and Democratic parties were stronger than ever in their efforts to demonize him and render him irrelevant to future foreign policy debates.

When the formal extradition proceedings began in September 2020, support for Assange in the mainstream press was not much stronger than at the time of his arrest. FAIR's Alan MacLeod noted that Assange's hearing in London should have been the media trial of the century, but "you might not have heard if you're relying solely on corporate media for news."[82] The *New York Times* published "only two bland news articles (9/7/20, 9/16/20)—one of them purely about the technical difficulties in the courtroom—along with a short re-hosted AP [Associated Press] video (9/7/20). There have been no editorials and no commentary on what the case means for journalism."

According to MacLeod, the performance of other major media outlets was about as dismal, and the evidence supported his conclusion. "There was nothing at all from CNN. CBS's two articles (9/7/20, 9/22/20) were copied and pasted from news agencies AP and AFP [Agence France-Presse], respectively. Meanwhile, the entire sum of MSNBC's coverage amounted to one unclear sentence in a mini news roundup article (9/18/20)."

To their credit, several human rights and press freedom organizations were sounding the alarm about Washington's power play. The Electronic Frontier Foundation's Cindy Cohn stated that the case "seems to be a clear attempt to punish Assange for publishing information that the government did not want published, and not merely arising from a single failed attempt at cracking a [computer] password," which had been the original allegation. She concluded that even if the government's case ultimately was confined to charges of illegal computer hacking, "we think that neither journalists nor the rest of us should be breathing a sigh of relief."[83]

A statement from the Knight First Amendment Institute at Columbia University asserted that the Justice Department's case would "treat everyday journalistic practices as part of a criminal conspiracy." The statement continued, "it's very troubling that the indictment sweeps in activities that are not just lawful but essential to press freedom—activities like cultivating sources, protecting sources' identities, and communicating with sources securely."[84]

Trevor Timm, founder of the Freedom of the Press Foundation, told the London court that if the United States successfully prosecuted Assange, it "would criminalise every reporter who received a secret document whether they asked for it or not."[85] The U.S. indictments suggested that Assange alone was encouraging people to illegally disclose classified information by publishing a list of most wanted leaks, but that was simply not correct, Timm said in a written statement. If journalists could be charged with "conspiring" with sources to obtain newsworthy information for publication, that standard would fundamentally alter public discourse. The Justice Department's rationale essentially would "give a carte blanche to those in power to prosecute whomever they want, whenever they want, even foreigners living halfway around the world."[86]

A statement from Amnesty International was especially blunt. "This hearing is the latest worrying salvo in a full-scale assault on the right to freedom of expression. If Julian Assange is prosecuted it could have a chilling effect on media freedom, leading publishers and journalists to self-censor in fear of retaliation," said the organization's Europe director, Nils Muižnieks. "If Julian Assange is extradited it will have far reaching human rights implications, setting a chilling precedent for the protection of those who publish classified information in the public interest."[87]

Unfortunately, such forthright statements on behalf of press freedoms were scarce in the mainstream media, both in the United States and Europe. Nor did the coverage change appreciably even when a key government witness recanted his testimony against Assange in late June 2021. The witness, Sigurdur Thordarson, admitted that he had lied, making false claims in exchange for promises of immunity.[88] Yet coverage of that development in the mainstream press was notable for its absence. The peculiar media blackout produced expressions of outrage among unorthodox, alternative media types. Alan MacLeod fumed, "Such a blatant and juicy piece of important news should have made worldwide headlines. But, instead, as of Friday, July 2, there has been literally zero coverage of it in corporate media; not one word in the *New York Times*, *Washington Post*, CNN, NBC News, Fox News or NPR. A search online for either 'Assange' or 'Thordarson' will elicit zero relevant articles from establishment sources, either US or elsewhere in the Anglosphere."[89]

A report by Media Lens documented the same absence of coverage.[90] Australian journalist John Pilger could scarcely contain his dismay. Citing the Media Lens report, he railed, "Having led the persecution of Julian Assange, the 'free press' is uniformly silent on sensational news that the case against Assange has collapsed. Shame on my fellow journalists."[91]

Beyond the role of Assange and his sources, U.S. and other Western leaders became increasingly alarmed that whistleblowers were becoming emboldened and might leak damaging information to more conventional and respectable media outlets. Their fears were realized in 2013 when Edward Snowden, a contract employee for the National Security Agency, transferred a trove of classified documents to Glenn Greenwald and Laura Poitras at *The Guardian*.[92] Those documents confirmed that, among other abuses, the NSA undermined private computer encryption programs and collected bulk data on Americans' email and other correspondence without obtaining a warrant.[93] Equally appalling, NSA Director James Clapper had lied to Congress and the American people about the program, then managed to avoid prosecution for perjury until the statute of limitations on that offense ran out.[94]

The Justice Department moved quickly, however, to indict Snowden for espionage.[95] But any attempt to do the same with Greenwald and Poitras was much more difficult. Greenwald in particular was a prominent (if controversial) journalist, and going after him risked creating a First Amendment martyr and a media firestorm. It seemed more than coincidental, though, that authorities in countries closely allied with the United States, especially Britain, harassed both journalists—and in one case, Greenwald's romantic partner—with lengthy, menacing interrogations when they traveled internationally.[96]

Ultimately, U.S. leaders focused most of their efforts on apprehending and prosecuting Assange, whom they believed powerful political and media constituencies considered a less respectable player. There apparently was some hesitation about prosecuting even Assange. According to the Associated Press, the Obama administration had conducted a lengthy internal debate about moving aggressively against Assange and WikiLeaks. "A former Justice Department official, who spoke on condition of anonymity to discuss internal discussions, said there was an extensive debate within the government over the feasibility of charging Assange with the publication of stolen, classified materials. But prosecutors grew concerned that such a case would not hold up in court. Even though officials did not agree with Assange's self-characterization as a journalist, the former official said, there was concern that it would be hard to justify charging him with actions that more conventional journalists take."[97]

The Trump administration's legal strategy for prosecuting Assange was bolder and more menacing to press freedoms. Federal officials argued that whatever the relevance of the Pentagon Papers precedent, it did not apply in this case because Assange was not a real journalist engaged in legitimate journalism. Instead, they alleged, he was a coconspirator with Manning and other individuals who illicitly leaked classified information.

Ergo, he committed espionage just as much as they did, and any legal protections that legitimate journalists might enjoy should not extend to his behavior. John Demers, the Justice Department's assistant attorney general for national security stated that thesis explicitly. "Julian Assange is no journalist," Demers said. He engaged in "explicit solicitation of classified information."[98]

Other Trump administration officials amplified the campaign to delegitimize Assange's status as a journalist, thereby justifying his prosecution for espionage. "WikiLeaks walks like a hostile intelligence service and talks like a hostile intelligence service," CIA Director Mike Pompeo said in April 2017 during his first public speech as head of the agency. "Assange and his ilk," Pompeo charged, seek "personal self-aggrandizement through the destruction of Western values."[99]

Some former Obama administration officials seemed sympathetic to the Trump administration's decision to prosecute Assange and the rationale it adopted for that prosecution. "This is just charging a journalist with conspiracy to hack into computer systems, which is no different than breaking into a building or breaking into a classified safe," asserted Mary McCord, a senior Justice Department national security official in the Obama administration. "And that's not First Amendment protected activity."[100]

Associated Press reporters Eric Tucker and Ben Fox concluded that McCord's perspective "is a widely held view in government, even among people generally sympathetic to the mission of the media." The comments of an Obama-era diplomat affirmed their conclusion. WikiLeaks disclosures amounted to a "'deliberate and malicious effort to cause harm to us, to U.S. national security interests, and I think it would be good if there is some accountability at last,' said David Pearce, who was U.S. ambassador to Algeria in 2010 when WikiLeaks released hundreds of thousands of secret diplomatic cables. 'So far there hasn't been any accountability for Mr. Assange.'"[101]

As some worried progressives in the United States and Europe pointed out, endorsing the U.S. government's prosecution of Assange was dangerously misguided.[102] A successful prosecution of Assange and WikiLeaks for espionage would constitute a mortal threat to a free and independent press in the United States. Some of the government's arguments to support the theory that Assange is not a legitimate journalist were paper thin; they appear to be little more than cynical pretexts to secure a major dilution of the Pentagon Papers precedent. One government allegation was that Assange urged Manning to provide more documents after the initial delivery of files. Yet investigative reporters from reputable news outlets routinely use methods similar to those Assange employed, including asking their sources to provide more information when investigating possible government misconduct. As the *New York Times* editorial reluctantly conceded, several of its own journalists do so.

Another argument was that WikiLeaks does not edit leaked material but merely releases it to the public. Other outlets have engaged in similar conduct, though, albeit on a smaller scale, without being considered illegitimate members of the journalistic profession. *BuzzFeed News*, for example, published the unverified, salacious dossier on Trump that former British intelligence agent Christopher Steele compiled.[103] Yet the government did not seek to prosecute that publication, and most mainstream media outlets defended its right to publish the material (although some criticized the actual decision). Unfortunately, many of those media outlets took a very different stance regarding WikiLeaks.

Such attitudes partly reflect resentment that an upstart player has broken several prominent stories. As will be discussed in Chapter 12, legacy publications are less than thrilled about blogs and other online outlets (including social media sites, such as Facebook, Twitter, and Instagram) that sprouted like mushrooms during the first two decades of the 21st century. The *New York Times, Washington Post,* and other mainstream publications also exhibit special resentment toward Assange because he expressed open animosity toward U.S. foreign policy, while those publications generally back Washington's often blundering overseas commitments and initiatives.

The mainstream media's willingness to disown Assange was graphically apparent in the decision made by the Committee to Protect Journalists (CPJ) in December 2019. The CPJ refused to include Assange on its annual list of journalists jailed throughout the world. CPJ Deputy Executive Director Robert Mahoney's attempt to explain the decision was an exercise in painful linguistic contortions. His December 11 blog post on the CPJ website used the unequivocal title, "For the sake of press freedom, Julian Assange must be defended." Much of the substance of the post, though, pointed to the opposite conclusion. "WikiLeaks's practice of dumping huge loads of data on the public without examining the motivations of the leakers can leave it open to manipulation," Mahoney sniffed at one point.[104]

In any case, the CPJ was not about to include him on the list of journalists imprisoned for their activities. "To some, Julian Assange is a warrior for truth and transparency. To others, he is an information bomb-thrower," Mahoney argued. "The question with which CPJ has had to grapple is whether his actions make him a journalist. Each year, we compile a list of journalists imprisoned around the world, based on a set of criteria that have evolved as technology has upended publishing and the news business. After extensive research and consideration, CPJ chose not to list Assange as a journalist, in part because his role has just as often been as a source and because WikiLeaks does not generally perform as a news outlet with an editorial process."[105]

In other words, using an array of rhetorical gymnastics, Mahoney and the CPJ tacitly accepted the logic the U.S. Justice Department used to justify the prosecution of Assange, even as the CPJ officially condemned the prosecution itself. Such a maneuver would never qualify as a profile in courage or an exercise in logic. The bottom line is that the CPJ legitimized the U.S. government's campaign to put Assange outside the boundaries of legitimate journalism.

Kevin Gosztola, managing editor of *Shadowproof.com*, aptly pointed out what was wrong with the CPJ's attempted tightrope act. "Can a laudable press freedom organization claim Assange is not a journalist without aiding the political case brought by prosecutors in President Donald Trump's Justice Department?" Gosztola also highlighted a reason the CPJ seemed so willing to pursue the role it had adopted. "CPJ's Board of Directors is composed of many journalists in the U.S. media establishment, an establishment which clings to the notion that Assange is not a journalist in order to maintain a supposed distinction between his work and their work."[106]

Whatever their motives, journalists who excused or justified efforts to prosecute Julian Assange were tools in the government's campaign to plug leaks and stifle criticism, especially in the national security arena. The intent of national security officials is clearly to suppress embarrassing revelations. Not only has the number of prosecutions against whistleblowers increased over the past decade, but federal officials have resorted to highly questionable tactics against pesky journalists from even established outlets, as the Rosen and Risen episodes confirm. The initiative against Assange was only the boldest one.

Allowing the government to usurp the right to decide who is or is not a "legitimate" journalist is dangerous to the health of the First Amendment.[107] If federal prosecutors prevail and eventually convict Assange of espionage, the implicit protections that the Pentagon Papers ruling afforded the press will be severely diluted. In that case only legacy publications friendly to the national security bureaucracy would be able to count on government restraint—and even that expectation could become quite fragile. Obstreperous online outlets and their writers would routinely find themselves under threat of criminal prosecution if they published a story based on classified information—even if their revelations exposed incompetence, deceit, or criminal behavior on the part of policymakers. At a minimum, an Assange conviction would have a chilling effect on the already insufficient foreign policy dissent in the media; at worst, the government would achieve the de facto, functional equivalent of the Official Secrets Act that officials have long sought.

Assange's defenders around the world reacted with a sense of relief when the British court decided in January 2021 to deny the U.S. extradition request. But the court's reasoning was a cause for disquiet, not relief. The ruling relied heavily on concerns about Assange's fragile physical and mental health and how alleged deficiencies in America's prison system would further endanger his health. The court did not reject the U.S. government's arguments about the key points of law involved in the prospective prosecution of Assange for espionage.[108] In other words, the extradition decision fell far, far short of vindicating press freedoms. Indeed, it was profoundly disappointing in that respect. U.S. prosecutors boasted that they had prevailed on every major substantive legal contention. The U.S. Justice Department gave no indication it would abandon its quest for extradition if a way could be found to meet some of the objections the British court had voiced. And the Biden administration announced in early February 2021 that it would appeal the extradition ruling and continue Washington's attempts to bring Assange back to the United States for trial.[109] In doing so, the new administration implicitly adopted the Trump Justice Department's rationale that Assange is not a legitimate journalist. Worse, the UK High Court approved the U.S. appeal in December 2021, clearing the way for Assange's extradition.

The journalistic community has repeatedly accused Donald Trump of waging war on a free press. Yet many of his actions while in office consisted of rude comments, combined with occasional harassment, such as suspending the White House credentials of press adversaries. That type of petty conduct, obnoxious as it might be, does not constitute a real threat to press freedoms. Spying on journalists is another matter, and prosecuting Julian Assange or other iconoclastic journalists for publishing leaked classified information is a very real and alarming threat. Unfortunately, the Biden administration has continued such menacing practices.

We have witnessed what happens when debate on public issues comes under siege in democratic countries (such as Australia, Hungary, and Poland) that do not have the explicit protections afforded by the First Amendment.[110] But even the First Amendment shield for journalists can be severely weakened in the name of national security if public opposition to government attempts to silence critics and cover up abuses becomes lax. That is why failing to defend Assange and other mavericks and so-called extremists who air Washington's dirty foreign policy laundry is dangerously negligent. The First Amendment is not just for the benefit of the *Washington Post*, *New York Times*, CNN, and other establishment outlets. Its continued health depends on the willingness of those power centers, the rest of the news media, and the general public to defend even the most daring and sometimes outrageous publishers like Julian Assange.

Journalists also need to comprehend that the government's attempt to curb dissent in the media about U.S. foreign policy didn't disappear with the end of the Trump administration. Trump did not create these policies, and his successors, like his predecessors, will have an institutional interest in preserving them.

Vague legislation plays an important role in the campaign to guarantee ideological conformity. Glenn Greenwald points to the potential dangers inherent in the Logan Act, the 18th century federal statute that prohibits private citizens, including members of the press, from conducting diplomacy with foreign governments. Most observers have dismissed the relevance of that law because no one has ever been convicted under its provisions. Greenwald takes a different view.

> This 219-year-old statute is one of the most unconstitutional and dangerous laws in the U.S. Code. Because it has never been used to prosecute anyone, and was only used to obtain an indictment *one time* in its entire history—back in 1803, against someone who wrote [an opinion piece] criticizing U.S. foreign policy toward France—nobody knows what it actually prescribes or allows because there is no binding judicial precedent interpreting what it means. It is precisely because it has never been used to prosecute anyone that there is no judicial clarity about what it means, and that's how the U.S. Government wants it.[111]

In other words, the Logan Act is an amorphous weapon that an ambitious administration could use against foreign policy critics at any time. Journalists could be sent scrambling to defend themselves against criminal prosecution and attempting to get the statute declared unconstitutional for the first time.

Greenwald detects a similar motive for the vague provisions of the Espionage Act. "The [Department of Justice] has never made good on its threats to prosecute any journalist who publishes classified information under the Espionage Act of 1917: they prefer to weaponize the fear of uncertainty regarding the law's scope and application rather than prosecute journalists under it and thus risk a judicial ruling declaring it unconstitutional or inapplicable to journalists." The use of the Espionage Act in that fashion is a textbook example of how a chilling effect induces self-censorship. The Logan Act and the Espionage Act, Greenwald stresses "are exactly the kinds of ambiguous laws that can serve as an abusive pretext in the hands of the FBI, empowering it to investigate anyone it wants."

One important difference between the two laws stands out, however. Although the Logan Act has not yet claimed any victims, the Espionage Act has claimed thousands—including the most recent crop of foreign policy whistleblowers such as John Kiriakou, Chelsea Manning, and Edward Snowden. Moreover, the prosecution of Julian Assange demonstrates that the U.S. government is now positioned to come after troublesome journalists—just as it did during World War I. Members of the U.S. foreign policy apparatus find prying eyes and skeptical voices profoundly threatening to their missions and careers, and they appear ready to take action against their critics.

CHAPTER 11
The Press as a Subsidiary of the National Security State

In addition to the habitual, pronounced media bias in favor of an activist U.S. foreign policy—and often an aggressive, militarized one—elements of the press have actually colluded with government military and intelligence agencies to promote that policy. In some episodes journalists have even become key participants, helping execute Washington's initiatives. Such collusion in the name of patriotism was especially common during the Cold War, but it existed before that period and has continued in the post–Cold War era. The problem of collusion is more than a matter of the press being too credulous and passive with respect to questionable government actions in foreign affairs. An unwillingness to examine official justifications critically is a chronic, serious failing in the journalistic profession. Outright collusion is much worse; it is a malignancy that violates the most fundamental standards of journalistic ethics. Yet the problem has occurred repeatedly, undermining the news media's proper role as public watchdog. Furthermore, the latest episode shows no sign of dissipating.

On some occasions throughout America's history, the collaboration has been truly blatant. Writer Stephen Crane (*The Red Badge of Courage*), who worked as a correspondent during the Spanish-American War for the notoriously jingoistic *New York World*, accepted the surrender of Spanish troops in the Cuban village of Juana Diaz. He turned over jurisdiction of the captured village the next day to a U.S. military officer.[1] Press–government collaboration was usually less flagrant than that, but some later incidents have come close.

As discussed in Chapter 1, during both world wars, many journalists became functionaries in government agencies tasked with censorship or propaganda missions. Frederick Palmer, a former *New York Herald* reporter and Associated Press correspondent, was in charge of censoring information from the battlefield in Europe throughout World War I. The military even gave Palmer a commission as a major in the U.S. Army, thereby emphasizing his status as a government official. Under his guidance, any news dispatches that questioned Washington's war effort even obliquely were ruthlessly sanitized and censored. Battlefield correspondents became little more than mouthpieces for military commanders and Woodrow Wilson's administration back home.

On the propaganda front, the collusion of press and government was equally apparent, and once again, a prominent journalist was in charge. George Creel, who had worked as a reporter and editor for several newspapers in the Rocky Mountain region, directed the Committee on Public Information (CPI). Like Palmer, Creel served loyally as a government agent, recruiting thousands of other journalists to help sell the war to the American people. The scope of the CPI's propaganda campaign was unprecedented in U.S. history. But a good many members of the press were willing to compromise their journalistic integrity to circulate crude propaganda that they knew, or should have known, was outrageously inflammatory fiction.

It is no exaggeration to say that during World War I, an independent press in the United States ceased to exist. Members of the mainstream news media became simply an obedient distribution mechanism for circulating the government's perspective without reservation. They shunned the handful of dissenting colleagues and watched passively even when Wilson's administration prosecuted and imprisoned such dissenters.

World War II followed a similar pattern. Once again, leading journalists became compliant cogs in the national security machine. Broader policies that should have been debated publicly went unexamined in the press, stifled by the efforts of journalists who were mere conduits for the government's propaganda. Two especially important issues received little or no examination by the journalistic community. One was whether modifying the Allied powers' demand that Germany and Japan surrender unconditionally might shorten the horribly destructive and bloody war, thereby saving hundreds of thousands, if not millions, of lives, including the lives of innocent civilians caught up in the fighting and the lives of American troops put at risk in a prolonged war. The other issue that deserved consideration was whether the Soviet Union was a trustworthy, much less a morally tolerable, U.S. ally. Rather than address that troubling question candidly, the media opted to disseminate sanitized, unrealistic accounts of Joseph Stalin's governance and the nature of Soviet society under communist rule.

Expecting reporters and editors to be entirely objective when their country is at war would, of course, be unrealistic. Assuming that war critics and other outspoken iconoclasts would prosper during an armed conflict would also be naïve—unless widespread public disillusionment with the war had already set in. Despite the protections for freedom of the press that the First Amendment affords, the U.S. government would invariably seek reasons and powers to curb dissent in wartime. Nevertheless, the nearly total unwillingness of mainstream journalists to resist censorship incursions and raise even mild doubts about specific policies in the two world wars is disheartening. With few exceptions, they were not just willing but enthusiastic collaborators with government officials to implement some of the most questionable practices.

The media's indiscriminate collusion with the government in World War I especially deserves condemnation. The American people were sharply divided about the need for or wisdom of U.S. entry into the war, and a sizable contingent in the news media opposed that step as well. Influential members of the press should have resisted the Wilson administration's efforts to stifle debate once the United States became a belligerent. Not every criticism of Washington's policy constituted disloyalty or posed a mortal threat to the nation's war effort. Indeed, most of the criticisms did not fit that description. Yet most journalists seemed to accept that apocalyptic scenario. Failing to object as their anti-war media colleagues were silenced—and especially when they were incarcerated—was a betrayal of the watchdog role that a free press is supposed to embody. Instead, most of America's supposedly independent press played the role of the Wilson administration's lapdog.

The media's performance during World War II was not exactly a profile in courage and independence either. After Pearl Harbor, there was almost no opposition among the public to fighting Japan and its allies, and that view was at least as vehement and prevalent in the press as in other sectors of society. The overwhelming majority of journalists genuinely were enthusiastic supporters of the war effort. Given the attack on U.S. soil, the media's collaborative behavior was more understandable and less dishonorable than it had been during World War I. Nonetheless, they should have raised pertinent questions about aspects of U.S. policy.

Unfortunately, the passivity of the press and its reflexive acceptance of Washington's new role as global hegemon did not greatly diminish once the guns fell silent at the end of World War II. Neither did the willingness of too many journalists to collaborate with government agencies when the Cold War between the United States and the Soviet bloc crystalized in the late 1940s. *Washington Post* reporter Carl Bernstein observed that "many journalists who covered World War II were close to people in the Office of Strategic Services, the wartime predecessor of the CIA; more important, they were all on the same side. When the war ended and many OSS officials went into the CIA, it was only natural that these relationships would continue. Meanwhile, the first postwar generation of journalists entered the profession; they shared the same political and professional values as their mentors. 'You had a gang of people who worked together during World War II and never got over it,'" said one Agency official."[2]

Some of those journalists became outright CIA assets. Bernstein's 1977, 25,000-word article in *Rolling Stone* is an extraordinarily detailed account of cooperation between the CIA and members of the press, and it provides key insights into that relationship.[3] In some cases, the "journalists" were actually full-time CIA employees, masquerading as members of the fourth estate. However, Bernstein confirmed that some 400 bona fide American journalists had secretly carried out assignments for the Central Intelligence Agency during the previous 25 years, according to documents on file at CIA headquarters that he had examined. Some of the relationships with the agency were tacit, while others were formal and explicit. He noted that "journalists provided a full range of clandestine services—from simple intelligence gathering to serving as go-betweens with spies in Communist countries. Reporters shared their notebooks with the CIA. Editors shared their staffs."

A December 26, 1977, investigative report in the *New York Times* described the scope of the CIA's global campaign to influence opinion through media manipulation. "In its persistent efforts to shape world opinion, the C.I.A. has been able to call upon" an extensive network "of newspapers, news services, magazines, publishing houses, broadcasting stations and other entities over which it has at various times had some control. A decade ago, when the agency's communications empire was at its peak, [it] embraced more than 500 news and public information organizations and individuals. According to one C.I.A. official, they ranged in importance 'from Radio Free Europe to a third-string guy in Quito who could get something in the local paper.'"[4] The CIA funded these foreign journalistic assets generously.

The *New York Times* report contended that even some agency officials worried about "the potential 'blow-back'—the possibility that the C.I.A. propaganda filtered through these assets, some of it purposely misleading or downright false, might be picked up by American reporters overseas and included in their dispatches to their publications at home."[5] One has to wonder whether U.S. officials regarded that effect as an unavoidable risk or as a collateral benefit. The CIA's charter forbids it from operating inside the United States, so a direct attempt to influence domestic opinion on a policy issue would be out of bounds. A similar restriction theoretically applies to U.S. government–controlled or –funded overseas information operations such as Voice of America and Radio Free Europe/Radio Liberty.

Theory is one thing, reality another. Domestic and foreign information flows do not, indeed cannot, operate in hermetically sealed compartments. Some news stories originally appearing in overseas outlets inevitably find their way back to American outlets. That is a major problem when the U.S. government, through its foreign journalistic hirelings, is deliberately circulating propaganda and disinformation to advance Washington's policy objectives. The blowback effect remains a corrosive threat to the ability of the American people to rely on accurate information when they form their opinions about U.S. foreign policy in general or about specific initiatives.

The troubling connection between U.S. intelligence agencies and America's own press personnel has taken a variety of forms. Bernstein contended that U.S. journalists operating overseas were especially valuable for one aspect of the CIA's mission: recruiting foreign nationals for espionage in their home country. "Many journalists were used by the CIA to assist in this process and they had the reputation of being among the best in the business. The peculiar nature of the job of the foreign correspondent is ideal for such work: he is accorded unusual access by his host country, permitted to travel in areas often off-limits to other Americans, spends much of his time cultivating sources in governments, academic institutions, the military establishment and the scientific communities."[6] Such considerations certainly explain why the intelligence bureaucracy wanted to use members of the press as operatives. Those considerations do not adequately explain, though, why so many journalists were willing to be government pawns.

The roles that cooperative foreign correspondents undertook were extensive and varied, according to Bernstein. "The tasks they performed sometimes consisted of little more than serving as 'eyes and ears' for the CIA; reporting on what they had seen or overheard in an Eastern European factory, at a diplomatic reception in Bonn, on the perimeter of a military base in Portugal." But other functions were more substantive, and some of them corrupted the very heart of journalistic ethics. Such tasks included "planting subtly concocted pieces of misinformation" and "serving up 'black' propaganda to leading foreign journalists at lunch or dinner." Moreover, CIA documents showed that journalists were engaged to perform such tasks "with the consent of the managements of America's leading news organizations."

The roster of collaborators reads like a Who's Who of the news industry. "Among the executives who lent their cooperation to the Agency were William Paley of the Columbia Broadcasting System,

Henry Luce of Time Inc., Arthur Hays Sulzberger of the *New York Times*, Barry Bingham Sr. of the *Louisville Courier-Journal,* and James Copley of the Copley News Service. Other organizations which cooperated with the CIA include the American Broadcasting Company, the National Broadcasting Company, the Associated Press, United Press International, Reuters, Hearst Newspapers, Scripps-Howard, *Newsweek* magazine, the Mutual Broadcasting System, the *Miami Herald* and the old *Saturday Evening Post* and *New York Herald-Tribune.*"

The cozy relationship between the CIA and prominent media organizations was especially pronounced during Allen Dulles's tenure as CIA director throughout Dwight Eisenhower's administration and the first year of John F. Kennedy's presidency.[7] Arthur Schlesinger, Jr., one of Kennedy's top aides, had been extensively involved in CIA and FBI efforts throughout the late 1940s and the 1950s to purge journalism, the entertainment sector, and academia of influence by people suspected of communist affiliations. Schlesinger had originally been recruited by the wartime OSS, so his connection to the national security state was long-standing.[8]

At times, press treatments of the intelligence agencies and their leaders were downright sycophantic. When the reliably pro-interventionist syndicated columnist Henry Taylor published a column that seemed surprisingly critical of the CIA, calling it a "sick elephant," the recently retired Allen Dulles rebuked Taylor and accused him of committing a personal betrayal. The chastised Taylor responded with a long telegram that verged on groveling. He pleaded that nothing he wrote, or ever would write, was meant to be negative about Dulles or the agency. "Certainly you must know that any attack on you by me is inconceivable." He added, "no one has served this country with greater distinction, selflessness, and success than you."[9]

Bernstein emphasized, though, that "by far the most valuable of these associations," according to CIA officials, were "with the *New York Times,* CBS and Time Inc. [the publisher of both *Time* and *Life*]." In fact, the *New York Times* alone "provided cover for about ten CIA operatives" over a nearly two-decade period. "The aid furnished often took two forms: providing jobs and credentials ('journalistic cover' in Agency parlance) for CIA operatives about to be posted in foreign capitals; and lending the Agency the undercover services of reporters already on staff, *including some of the best-known correspondents in the business.*"[10]

CBS News, though, gave the *New York Times* some competition for the designation of the CIA's most useful press asset. Bernstein continued, "CBS was unquestionably the [CIA's] most valuable broadcasting asset. CBS President William Paley and Allen Dulles enjoyed an easy working and social relationship. Over the years, the network provided cover for CIA employees, including at least one well-known foreign correspondent and several stringers." In addition, the network "allowed reports by CBS correspondents to the Washington and New York newsrooms to be routinely monitored by the CIA." And once a year, "CBS correspondents joined the CIA hierarchy for private dinners and briefings."

The extent of the cozy relationships between leading media figures, foreign policy academics, and national security officials during the first two decades of the Cold War was truly impressive. According to Bernstein, Richard Salant, who succeeded Paley as the head of CBS, "served on a super-secret CIA task force which explored methods of beaming American propaganda broadcasts to the People's Republic of China. The other members of the four-man study team were Zbigniew Brzezinski, then a professor at Columbia University; William Griffith, then professor of political science at the Massachusetts Institute of Technology, and John Haves, then vice-president of the Washington Post Company. . . . The principal government officials associated with the project were Cord Meyer of the CIA; McGeorge Bundy, then special assistant to the president for national security; Leonard Marks, then director of the USIA [U.S. Information Agency]; and Bill Moyers, then special assistant to President Lyndon Johnson and [later] a CBS correspondent."

Moyers, of course, became even more prominent in the journalistic world during the next several decades. His career trajectory was a classic example of the revolving door process by which government officials have transitioned from being national security bureaucrats to being highly influential media figures.

CIA officials and the cooperating members of the press seemed oblivious or indifferent to the inherent conflict of interest in serving simultaneously as journalists and government intelligence operatives. Bernstein concluded that "many CIA officials regarded these helpful journalists as operatives; the journalists tended to see themselves as trusted friends of the Agency who performed occasional favors—usually without pay—in the national interest." The comments of Joseph Alsop, one of the nation's leading journalists during the initial post–World War II decades were typical: "I'm proud they asked me and proud to have done it," said Alsop, who had repeatedly undertaken clandestine tasks for the CIA. "The notion that a newspaperman doesn't have a duty to his country is perfect balls."[11]

At a minimum, collaboration between the national security apparatus and the fourth estate creates the impression of a conflict of interest on the part of the latter. Far too often, it created not only the impression but also the reality of such a conflict. Bernstein related that on one occasion, "according to several CIA officials, [C. L.] Sulzberger was given a briefing paper by the Agency which ran almost verbatim under the columnist's byline in the *Times*. 'Cy came out and said, "I'm thinking of doing a piece, can you give me some background?"' a CIA officer said. 'We gave it to Cy as a background piece and Cy gave it to the printers and put his name on it.'"[12]

Another graphic and disturbing episode occurred in 1953 when the CIA and Britain's MI6 plotted to overthrow Iran's democratically elected leader Mohammad Mossadegh and restore the Shah to power. One of the reporters on the scene in Tehran during that turbulent period was Kennett Love, the Middle East correspondent for the *New York Times*. But Love did not merely send dispatches back to his employer; he also sent reports to CIA chief Allen Dulles. Indeed, some of his most important, detailed reports never appeared in the newspaper's pages; they were solely for the eyes of his friends (and possibly his employer) at Langley.

One of Love's accounts was discovered in Dulles's papers. Author and former *Wall Street Journal* reporter Jonathan Kwitny published major portions of that document in his 1984 book *Endless Enemies: The Making of an Unfriendly World*.[13] Love's report to the CIA recounted in great detail the involvement of the agency and the U.S. embassy in the coup that ultimately ousted Mossadegh, including the extent of his personal role during the culminating phase.

> I myself was responsible, in an impromptu sort of way, for speeding the final victory of the royalists. After the radio station fell I went up there to obtain permission to broadcast a dispatch. . . . A half-dozen tanks swarming with cheering soldiers were parked in front of the radio station. I told the tank commander that a lot of people were getting killed trying to storm Dr. Mossadegh's house, and that they, the tank commanders, ought to go down there where they would be of some use instead of sitting idle at the radio station. They declared my suggestion to be a splendid idea. They took their machines in a body to Kokh Avenue and put the three tanks at Dr. Mossadegh's house out of action after a lively duel with armor-piercing, 75-millimeter shells.[14]

Kwitny was scornful of the spectacle of "the Iranian correspondent of the New York Times directing the successful tank attack on the home of the Iranian prime minister, overthrowing the government [and] fixing one-man rule in Iran."[15]

Kwitny's criticism was appropriate. Love always denied that he was a CIA employee, and the *New York Times* likewise denied any knowledge of an official connection between its reporter and the agency. But even if those denials were true, Love's conduct amounted to a distinction without a difference. Even if he was not on the CIA payroll and was merely an eager civilian volunteer, he behaved like an intelligence operative carrying out a covert mission to help overthrow a foreign government that U.S. leaders considered hostile to America's interests. That is not even remotely an appropriate role for a journalist.

When the Senate Intelligence Committee, chaired by Sen. Frank Church (D-ID), conducted its 1976 investigation into the CIA's abuses, the news media took great pains to try to conceal the extent of the fourth estate's ties with the agency. That conduct greatly troubled Carl Bernstein. He noted that "the dimensions of the Agency's involvement with the press became apparent to several members of the panel, as well as to two or three investigators on the staff. But top officials of the CIA, including former directors William Colby and George [H. W.] Bush, persuaded the committee to restrict its inquiry into the matter and to deliberately misrepresent the actual scope of the activities in its final report. The multivolume report contains nine pages in which the use of journalists is discussed in deliberately vague and sometimes misleading terms. It makes no mention of the actual number of journalists who undertook covert tasks for the CIA. Nor does it adequately describe the role played by newspaper and broadcast executives in cooperating with the Agency."[16]

Although leaders of the intelligence community had an obvious and powerful incentive to conceal the extent of the press-government collusion, Bernstein concluded the media was culpable as well. "Contrary to the notion that the CIA insidiously infiltrated the journalistic community," Bernstein wrote, "there is ample evidence that America's leading publishers and news executives allowed themselves and their organizations to become handmaidens to the intelligence services." That was clearly the case from the late 1940s to the late 1970s.

The nature and extent of the relationship during the succeeding decades is less clear. CIA director William Colby supposedly scaled back the ties beginning in 1973, when press reports about them began to appear.[17] The situation following the Church committee investigations and the CIA's own policy changes in the late 1970s is murkier. Colby left the agency in January 1976 and was succeeded by George H. W. Bush. The CIA then announced a new policy regarding its relationship with news media personnel: "Effective immediately, the CIA will not enter into any paid or contractual relationship with any full-time or part-time news correspondent accredited by any U.S. news service, newspaper, periodical, radio or television network or station."[18]

But according to Bernstein, even at the time of the announcement, "the Agency acknowledged that the move would result in termination of less than half of the relationships with the 50 U.S. journalists it said were still affiliated with the Agency." And the "text of the announcement noted that the CIA would continue to 'welcome' the voluntary, unpaid cooperation of journalists. Thus, many relationships were permitted to remain intact."

There is less hard evidence that American journalists in the post–
Cold War era still serve as compliant CIA assets, but it would not be
surprising if they did so. The willingness of mainstream media outlets
to echo the views of that agency and other components of the national
security apparatus on so many issues—including Iraq's fictional weapons of mass destruction, the nature of the contending parties in Syria's
civil war, and the allegedly existential Russian threat—raises justifiable
suspicions.

A growing number of knowledgeable analysts argue that the situation has grown worse, not better, in recent years. Those analysts include
Peter Van Buren at *The American Conservative* on one end of the political
spectrum and Matt Taibbi on the other end.[19] Taibbi wrote recently:

> Billionaire eBay founder Pierre Omidyar launched *The Intercept* in
> February 2014. The outlet was devoted to sifting through Snowden's
> archive of leaked secrets, and its first story described how the NSA and
> CIA frequently made errors using geolocation to identify and assassi-
> nate drone targets. A few months later, former CIA and NSA director
> Michael Hayden admitted, "We kill people based on metadata."
>
> Fast forward seven years. Julian Assange is behind bars, and may
> die there. Snowden is in exile in Russia. Brennan, Clapper, and Hayden
> have been rehabilitated and are all paid contributors to either MSNBC
> or CNN, part of a wave of intelligence officers who've flooded the
> airwaves and op-ed pages in recent years, including the FBI's Asha
> Rangappa, Clint Watts, Josh Campbell, former counterintelligence
> chief Frank Figliuzzi and former deputy director Andrew McCabe,
> the CIA's John Sipher, Phil Mudd, Ned Price, and many others.[20]

In a subsequent interview, Taibbi charged that establishment journalists have worked to shift American public opinion in favor of the intelligence agencies and the foreign policy they promote. A prime example is
the members of the news media who began to see those agencies as part
of a crucial resistance movement against Donald Trump. "Public opinion toward U.S. intelligence agencies has shifted in the past decade in
large part due to a shift in media coverage away from intelligence abuses and more toward actions by members of former President Trump's
administration."[21] Indeed, it is extremely consequential and troubling.

Those journalists have gone from being independent watchdogs monitoring the intelligence apparatus to being promoters of that apparatus.

The extent of collaboration between the news media and the national security agencies seems more extensive than it had been in decades. As Taibbi points out, the parade of former officials on news programs is a long one. Jack Shafer, *Politico*'s senior media writer, describes the increasingly common revolving door between the two entities. "In the old days, America's top spies would complete their tenures at the CIA or one of the other Washington puzzle palaces and segue to more ordinary pursuits. Some wrote their memoirs. One ran for president. Another died a few months after surrendering his post. But today's national-security establishment retiree has a different game plan. . . . After so many years of brawling in the shadows, he yearns for a second, lucrative career in the public eye. He takes a crash course in speaking in soundbites, refreshes his wardrobe and signs a TV news contract. Then, several times a week, waits for a network limousine to shuttle him to the broadcast news studios. . . ." Shafer points out why that development is inherently problematic. "But almost to a one, the TV spooks still identify with their former employers at the CIA, FBI, DEA, DHS, or other security agencies and remain protective of their institutions. This makes nearly every word that comes out of their mouths suspect. Are they telling God's truth or are they shilling for their former bosses?"[22]

Without question, the U.S. government still recruits foreign journalists for propaganda missions in their home countries. Former CIA director Leon Panetta explained candidly that during his tenure the agency worked to influence foreign media outlets ahead of elections as a way to "change attitudes within the country." The preferred method was to "acquire media within a country or within a region that could very well be used for being able to deliver a specific message or work to influence those that may own elements of the media to be able to cooperate, work with you in delivering that message."[23] As former State Department official Peter Van Buren points out, "The CIA has been running such ops to foreign elections continuously since the end of WWII."[24]

The agency's foreign media manipulation goes beyond electioneering activities. As discussed in Chapter 6, the United States and Britain

mounted an extensive joint effort in Syria using an array of Middle
Eastern reporters and columnists.[25] Among the possible effects, one
must ponder how many of those orchestrated "news" stories (designed
for Syrian and other Middle East audiences) found their way back into
American media, impacting the narrative and domestic debate about
the Syrian civil war and what Washington's stance should be toward
that conflict. Given the existence of this latest influence program, the
potential blowback phenomenon is not just a matter of historical interest from the CIA's early decades.

A September 2014 report in *The Intercept* also indicated that the
problem of excessively close ties between the CIA and prominent
American journalists is not merely a historical artifact.[26] *Intercept* reporter Ken Silverstein obtained several hundred pages of CIA documents in
response to two Freedom of Information Act applications. The heavily
redacted documents provided only limited enlightenment; the unre-
dacted portions consisted primarily of correspondence from reporters
and columnists to the agency, while the replies from CIA personnel
were mostly blacked out. As Silverstein noted, "It's impossible to know
precisely how the CIA flacks responded to reporters' queries, because
the emails show only one side of the conversations. The CIA redacted
virtually all of the press handlers' replies other than meager comments
that were made explicitly on the record, citing the CIA Act of 1949,
which exempts the agency from having to disclose 'intelligence sources
and methods' or 'the organization, functions, names, official titles, sala-
ries, or numbers of personnel employed by the Agency.'"

The agency's response was a transparent bureaucratic evasion. As
Silverstein pointed out, "The contents of off-the-record or background
emails from CIA press handlers clearly don't disclose names, titles, or sal-
aries (which can easily be redacted anyway); they may disclose sources
and methods, depending on whether you view manipulation of American
reporters as an intelligence method." Nevertheless, the abundance of the
e-mail exchanges with reporters from the Associated Press, *Washington
Post*, *New York Times*, *Wall Street Journal*, and other outlets confirmed that
very close professional (and sometimes personal) relationships seemed to
exist between those journalists and the CIA. Among those involved in

the email exchanges were Adam Goldman, then at the AP and later at the *Washington Post*; Matt Apuzzo, then at AP, and later at the *New York Times*; Brian Bennett of the *Los Angeles Times*; Siobhan Gorman of the *Wall Street Journal*; Scott Shane of the *New York Times*; and *Washington Post* columnist David Ignatius.

Some of the connections involved speeches and briefings that members of the press delivered to audiences at Langley. Those always present some potential for a conflict of interest, since in providing their assessments of developments in foreign countries the reporters were serving as sources of information for the agency and contributing to its role in formulating U.S. government policy. A potential conflict of interest also existed when the journalists were briefed by CIA analysts, since receipt of such packaged information could skew their published accounts. Nevertheless, there was nothing explicitly inappropriate about such events, as long as members of the press were not receiving financial stipends for their remarks or participation.

Some of the other interactions were cause for greater concern. Silverstein focused much of his attention on the behavior of Ken Dilanian, a national security reporter for the *Los Angeles Times* who later joined the Associated Press. His relationship with the CIA raised some troubling questions. Silverstein charged that numerous emails "show that Dilanian enjoyed a closely collaborative relationship with the agency, explicitly promising positive news coverage and sometimes sending the press office entire story drafts for review prior to publication. In at least one instance, the CIA's reaction appears to have led to significant changes in the story that was eventually published in the *Times*."

The details Silverstein provided from the emails reinforced a worrisome impression. "'I'm working on a story about congressional oversight of drone strikes that can present a good opportunity for you guys,' Dilanian wrote in one email to a CIA press officer, explaining that what he intended to report would be 'reassuring to the public' about such CIA strikes. In another instance, after a series of back-and-forth emails about a pending story on CIA operations in Yemen, he sent a full draft of the unpublished version along with the subject line, 'does this look better?'" Dilanian apparently was signaling that his article would contend that U.S. drone strikes were carefully targeted against terrorists and rarely harmed innocent civilians. Another email showed "that in June 2012, shortly after 26 members of Congress wrote a letter to President Obama saying they were 'deeply concerned' about the drone program, Dilanian approached the agency about a story that he pitched as 'a good opportunity' for the government" to present its view and defuse those congressional concerns. Dilanian added, "Part of what the story will do, if you could help me bring it to fruition, is to quote congressional officials saying that great care is taken to avoid collateral damage and that the reports of widespread civilian casualties are simply wrong." Silverstein commented that "journalists routinely curry favor with government sources (and others) by falsely suggesting that they intend to amplify the official point of view. But the emails show that Dilanian really meant it."

The Dilanian emails appear to show a textbook example of an excessively close relationship between a journalist and a government agency. Clearing stories in advance and currying official cooperation and approval compromise the integrity of the journalist's handiwork. And in at least one case, Dilanian appeared to willingly or unwillingly channel CIA disinformation. Amnesty International and other human rights organizations effectively debunked the government's version of an anti-terrorist drone strike that claimed the strike did not kill innocent civilians.[27] The episode was an important reminder that members of the national security bureaucracy rarely hesitate to exploit journalists or other convenient human tools to advance the bureaucracy's agenda and conceal blunders or crimes.

THE REVOLVING DOOR PROBLEM

As already noted, the revolving door phenomenon has contributed to an unhealthy, if not corrupt, relationship between government and portions of the news media. On a few occasions, journalists have gone on to serve in government policymaking positions. For instance, Heather Nauert, a former ABC News correspondent and a presenter for the Fox News program *Fox and Friends*, served as the acting under secretary of state for public diplomacy and public affairs during the first years of the Trump administration, the fourth highest position in the State Department. President Trump then nominated her to be U.S. ambassador to the United Nations, although intense Senate opposition caused her to withdraw her nomination.

For the most part, however, the revolving door has moved in the opposite direction, with government officials—especially those holding responsible positions in the White House, State Department, Pentagon, and the intelligence community—subsequently becoming significant players in the media. Several examples can be found in the early decades of the Cold War. The initial head of the CIA's foreign propaganda operation was Tom Braden, who subsequently became a syndicated columnist appearing in major newspapers throughout the country. He later became the cohost of the CNN public affairs program *Crossfire*. Another early example, noted previously, was Bill Moyers, who moved from his post as an assistant to Lyndon Johnson directly to his position as a high-profile journalist at CBS.

During the 1990s, Pete Williams, who served as assistant secretary of defense for public affairs during Dick Cheney's tenure as defense secretary in George H. W. Bush's administration, followed a similar career path. Williams was the Pentagon's chief spokesman during both Operation Desert Shield and Operation Desert Storm in 1990–1991. He went on to be a leading correspondent for NBC News. Similarly, George Stephanopoulos served as White House communications director and subsequently as senior adviser to the president during Bill Clinton's first term. He then joined ABC News and became a prominent fixture on several programs.

In Williams's case at NBC, he primarily covered the Supreme Court and other domestic topics, not defense and foreign policy. Consequently, there was little reason to suspect he was serving as a propagandist for his former employer or former colleagues in the Defense Department. Stephanopoulos had a lesser degree of detachment and seemed to support most foreign policy positions that the Clinton and Obama administrations adopted. Nevertheless, there was little evidence of a conflict of interest on his part.

The same cannot be said of all the officials who moved from government service to prominent roles as media correspondents, hosts, "issue experts," and commentators. Jim Sciutto, for example, was an Obama administration political appointee, serving as chief of staff and senior adviser to Gary Locke, Obama's ambassador to China. Locke was also a political appointee, not a professional diplomat, and he was a staunch Democrat, having served as governor of Washington. Sciutto, in his post-government role as CNN's chief national security correspondent, seemed to retain that political bent when he became one of Donald Trump's most vehement and tenacious critics. He also openly embraced hawkish positions on several foreign policy issues, especially U.S. policy toward Russia and Syria. Indeed, foreign policy was the one consideration that seemed to override his fondness for Obama. In his 2019 book, *The Shadow War: Inside Russia's and China's Secret Operations to Defeat America*, Sciutto frequently criticized the Obama administration for not being sufficiently resolute and uncompromising regarding its relationships with both Russia and China.[28]

The most blatant example of an incestuous relationship between the national security elite and the news media involved two high-level former Obama administration officials. James Clapper, former director of the National Security Agency (NSA) and John Brennan, former director of the CIA, quickly became fixtures on television cable news shows, especially on MSNBC. The two men were hardly detached figures confining their observations and analyses to their previous areas of expertise. Instead, they were ideological, even partisan in their opposition to the defense and foreign policies of the Trump administration. Their partisanship was most evident with respect to media coverage of the Russia-collusion issue, but it was broader than that. They lobbied against the Trump administration's policies on topics as diverse as NATO burden-sharing, Washington's stance regarding Ukraine, and whether to continue the military missions in Syria and Afghanistan.

The problem is that networks do little or nothing to inform viewers that these people are editorialists, not detached, relatively neutral analysts. Most viewers likely understand (or soon learn) that prominent individuals such as Clapper and Brennan are partisan ideologues

pontificating on contentious policy debates and political fights. Viewers are less likely to have that same realization when more obscure
but still significant figures are involved. In June 2020, MSNBC hired
former FBI agent Lisa Page as an analyst. People who followed the
Russia-collusion story closely may have remembered that she and her
lover Peter Strzok, the chief of the FBI's counterespionage section,
were staunch anti-Trump partisans (as confirmed in their text and email
exchanges) who pushed that conspiracy theory.[29] But viewers who did
not follow the story in depth likely would not recall her (albeit secondary) role in that episode or her anti-Russia and anti-Trump views.

Viewer and reader caution also is less likely in cases where the
ex-government official is not as flagrantly partisan. CBS News hired
Michael Morrell, former deputy director of the CIA, to join the network
as an on-air commentator. CBS sought to position Morell as an analyst
with exceptional expertise in the intelligence field and without an ideological agenda. However, though he was no longer on the CIA payroll,
Morell consistently pushed the agency's perspective on an assortment
of issues. He was hawkish and hostile to any meaningful changes in
Washington's global interventionist foreign policy, adopting especially
belligerent positions toward Russia and Iran. And at one point, he even
contended that Russia's alleged cyber hacking during the 2016 election
campaign was the "political equivalent" of 9/11.[30]

Morell's history as a government official was troubling for another
reason. He had been outspoken in circulating the CIA's faulty information about Iraq's alleged weapons of mass destruction. Years later,
he apologized for the agency's "mistakes," even while defending its
other dubious practices, including "enhanced interrogation."[31] In any
case, CBS apparently did not regard Morell's history of providing CIA
disinformation (or his continuing defense of torture techniques) as disqualifying him for a role as the network's on-camera expert regarding
intelligence issues and more general national security matters.

Worse than Morrell, who played the role of fellow traveler for the
intelligence bureaucracy and its policy agenda, were the cases in which
supposedly independent commentators (mostly retired military officers)
were actively cooperating with and even taking instructions from the

Pentagon while appearing as guest experts on news programs or publishing op-eds in major newspapers. Such individuals, for example, pushed the weapons systems that military leaders wanted and made the case for policy initiatives that the Pentagon favored.

Contrary to the image they fostered, many of these supposedly independent analysts were nothing of the sort. An April 20, 2008, *New York Times* investigative report concluded, "To the public, these men are members of a familiar fraternity, presented tens of thousands of times on television and radio as 'military analysts' whose long service has equipped them to give authoritative and unfettered judgments about the most pressing issues of the post–Sept. 11 world. Hidden behind that appearance of objectivity, though, is a Pentagon information apparatus that has used those analysts in a campaign to generate favorable news coverage of the administration's wartime performance."[32]

The potential financial conflicts of interest alone are massive. The *New York Times'* report noted that such media commentators "represent more than 150 military contractors either as lobbyists, senior executives, board members or consultants. The companies include defense heavyweights, but also scores of smaller companies, all part of a vast assemblage of contractors scrambling for hundreds of billions in military business generated by the administration's war on terror. It is a furious competition, one in which inside information and easy access to senior officials are highly prized."[33]

As members of a free society, retired military officers have every right to promote their views on foreign policy and other issues. However, not disclosing their connections, especially financial connections to defense firms, to viewers or readers is unethical. As the *New York Times* pointed out, in some cases not even the television networks or publications seemed fully aware of those problematic connections. At a minimum, the media outlets were negligent in not compelling the people they hired to make the appropriate disclosures.

The problem goes deeper. The Pentagon apparently has shown marked intolerance for any deviation from the government's policy message by these analysts, especially under Secretary of Defense Donald Rumsfeld during George W. Bush's administration. A December 24, 2011, *New York*

Times story cited the findings of an internal Department of Defense investigation. The inquiry "confirmed that Mr. Rumsfeld's staff hired a company to track and analyze what the military analysts said during their media appearances. According to the report, four military analysts reported that they were ejected from Mr. Rumsfeld's outreach program 'because they were critical' of the Pentagon."[34] The newspaper also cited comments from two participants in the Pentagon's periodic briefings to key analysts. "One military analyst described the talking points as 'bullet points given for a political purpose.' Another military analyst, the report said, told investigators that the outreach program's intent 'was to move everyone's mouth on TV as a sock puppet.'"[35]

Even the most prominent retired military figures were apparently not immune. One former Pentagon official told investigators that "when Barry McCaffrey, a retired four-star Army general and NBC military analyst, 'started challenging' Mr. Rumsfeld on air, he was told that Mr. Rumsfeld wanted him 'immediately' removed from the invitation list because General McCaffrey was no longer considered a 'team player.'" Pentagon leaders also seemed to be putting pressure on the television networks to reject newly uncooperative analysts. General Wesley Clark told investigators that "CNN officials made him feel as if he was less valued as a commentator because 'he wasn't trusted by the Pentagon.' At one point, he said, a CNN official told him that the White House had asked CNN to 'release you from your contract as a commentator.'"[36]

Which is more unsettling: bullying behavior on the part of a powerful government bureaucracy or the media's timidity about the bullying? That's hard to say. Moreover, although the problem of the Pentagon deploying and guiding an army of friendly advocates in the press was especially flagrant during Rumsfeld's tenure, the problem did not begin with him nor end when he left office. A September 16, 2014, article in the *Nation* made clear that the practice continued during the Obama years. Several retired generals, including Jack Keane, Anthony Zinni, and James Mattis, dominated the television airwaves to push for strong military action against both ISIS and Syria's government. All three men had extensive financial ties with defense contractors; additionally, Keane had connections to the government of the United Arab Emirates, one of the Middle East regimes lobbying hardest for greater U.S. military involvement.[37] Once again, the television programs where the men appeared rarely disclosed those links and their possible effects on the credibility of the analyses the former generals were pushing.

Such episodes should make clear that most of the retired military analysts appearing on television and in newspaper op-ed pages are not truly independent, detached observers, however much they might try to cultivate that persona. They are professional propagandists presenting the Pentagon perspective—and in some cases even the agendas of foreign governments. Indeed, they usually are little more than "sock puppets" for vested interests and ideological factions pushing a militarized U.S. approach to security problems around the world. Viewers and readers need to assess their presentations accordingly.

News consumers have increasingly received a subsidized barrage of laundered government propaganda masquerading as independent analyses. These messages tend to have not only a hawkish slant but also a slant toward preserving the policy and institutional status quo with respect to the U.S. role in the world. That perspective reflects the institutional ties and herd mentality within America's foreign policy and national security institutions. Although the commentators conveying the messages may no longer be formal, active members of the institutions, they continue to advance the underlying institutional missions and viewpoints. Their presence and prominence in the news media helps perpetuate an unsavory collaborative relationship between the media and portions of the foreign policy/national security bureaucracy.

In some cases, the collusion between hawks in government and their counterparts in the press is flagrant; in others, suggestive indications of collaboration merely raise suspicion. Journalist Ben Norton identified the latter pattern with respect to the nature and timing of the June 2020 *New York Times* story on supposed Russian bounties paid to the Taliban to kill American soldiers. By leaking the report at that time, Norton charged, the Pentagon and intelligence agencies "get the best of both worlds: blame the Russian bogeyman, fueling the new cold war, while prolonging the military occupation. It's not a coincidence these dubious Western intelligence agency claims about Russia came just days after a breakthrough in peace talks." Afghanistan's geostrategic location (and trillions of dollars in minerals resources) "is too important to them," he concluded.[38]

Other anti-war journalists have commented on curious cases of coincidental timing. Writing in *MintPress News* at the time of the bounty story, Alan MacLeod contended that the national security state "has a history of using anonymous officials to plant stories that lead to war. In 2003, the country was awash with stories that Saddam Hussein possessed weapons of mass destruction, in 2011 anonymous officials warned of an impending genocide in Libya, while in 2018 officials accused Bashar al-Assad of attacking Douma with chemical weapons, setting the stage for a bombing campaign." He added, "The timing of the [bounties] leak also raised eyebrows. Peace negotiations between the U.S. and the Taliban are ongoing, with President Trump committing to pulling all American troops out of the country. A number of key anti-weapons of mass destruction treaties between the U.S. and Russia are currently expiring, and a scandal such as this one would scupper any chance at peace, escalating a potential arms race that would endanger the world but enrich weapons manufacturers."[39]

In an article with the evocative title "Connecting the Dates," satirical writer Lee Camp noted that all too frequently when peace threatens to break out, prominent news stories appear that shatter those prospects. Although a staunch critic of Donald Trump, he stated that "in certain areas of the world, Trump has threatened to create peace. Sure, he's doing it for his own ego and because he thinks his base wants it, but whatever the reason, he has put forward plans or policies that go against the military industrial complex and the establishment war-hawks." Camp cited three places—Syria, North Korea, and Afghanistan—where Trump embraced such initiatives. "And each time this has happened, he is quickly thwarted, usually with hilarious propaganda. (Well, hilarious to you and me. Apparently believable to people at *The New York Times* and former CIA intern Anderson Cooper.)"[40]

Obviously, critics can take the coincidental-timing thesis too far. But hostile news accounts, usually based on little more than leaks from highly placed anonymous sources, have more than once sabotaged promising

prospects for peace. That certainly has been the case with respect to relations with Russia; and such accounts have had similar effects on policy
regarding Syria, Afghanistan, and the U.S. role in NATO. One needs
to ask if hawkish elements in the Pentagon and the intelligence agencies
manipulate the press or collude with fully willing allies in the press to
promote activist, confrontational policies.

This too-cozy relationship between members of the U.S. national security bureaucracy and the news media creates one serious conflict of interest. A related problem is the willingness of media outlets
and other opinion-shaping entities to have the same type of relationship with foreign governments. As noted in Chapter 8, several media
firms or their parent corporations have extensive financial interests in
the People's Republic of China that would be at risk if news coverage of
that country sufficiently irritated the authorities in Beijing. The issue of
access is crucial, not just in China but in other authoritarian countries. If
journalists want to continue to cover events from places such as Egypt,
Saudi Arabia, Qatar, and the United Arab Emirates, they must strike an
implicit bargain that the coverage will not be unduly negative.

Regimes in those and other countries also seek to influence media
coverage and their overall image in the United States through more
indirect means. One of the most prominent tactics is lucrative foreign
funding of American think tanks that deal with international issues.
Sometimes that government funding is direct, but more often the
money is funneled through grantmaking foundations and other front
groups. A January 2020 report from the Center for International Policy indicated that from 2014 to 2018 the flow of foreign government
money to the top 50 U.S. think tanks amounted to at least $174 mil-
lion.[41] The report's principal author, Ben Freeman, emphasized that
the $174 million figure was a "floor." Given the extensive efforts of
those governments to disguise their contributions, the actual figure
might have exceeded $500 million.[42]

Such contributions create subtle but important pressures on the
recipient organizations to shape their studies and events to benefit the
perspective of their benefactors.[43] One must be skeptical when an organization's position coincides with the interests of its funders: Is that

development merely a coincidence? Consider the uncompromising opposition to any reduction in America's commitment to NATO voiced by organizations such as the Atlantic Council and the German Marshall Fund of the United States, which enjoy generous funding from both U.S. defense-related firms and (directly or indirectly) from European governments. In the case of the Atlantic Council, the inherent conflict of interest is not confined to European policy. The organization receives millions of dollars from the government of Turkey, and the extent of the Atlantic Council's attention to developments involving Ankara's interests—and its friendly treatment of Ankara's positions on those developments—is apparent.[44] Evidence also strongly suggests that Turkey's government channeled money to organizations and individuals close to both Trump's and Hillary Clinton's campaigns in 2016, including Trump aide Michael Flynn. The influence campaign of Recep Tayyip Erdogan's regime seemed more vigorous than ever heading into the 2020 election.[45]

Key East Asian powers have distributed their financial largesse to a similar extent and for the same reasons. The governments of South Korea, Taiwan, and Japan maintain close ties with such think tanks as the Heritage Foundation, the Hudson Institute, the Center for a New American Security, and others that advocate both free trade and strong U.S. diplomatic and military support for those allies. And as in the case of scholars dealing with European and Middle East issues, analysts from the favored think tanks use every opportunity to promote such policies.[46]

The nexus between those think tanks and the mainstream media means that the potential for foreign influence is not confined to turgid reports and studies. Scholars from think tanks beholden to their foreign financial benefactors are frequent guests on television news shows, and their analyses appear often on the op-ed pages of the *New York Times*, *Washington Post*, and other top-tier newspapers. Overwhelmingly, they push for stronger U.S. support for those countries and greater hostility toward their adversaries. Most of the analysts probably believe what they're saying and writing, and they would adopt similar positions even if there were no strong financial incentives to do so. But given the amount of foreign money flowing in—much of it from Washington's client regimes—that factor and its potential for corrupt influence can't be ignored. Foreign funding is, thus, another factor indirectly nudging the American media to advocate a more activist U.S. policy globally and to push for specific policies that might not necessarily be in the best interests of the American people.

Another closely related problem is the direct funding of those same think tanks by defense industry corporations and other components of the military-industrial complex—including agencies in the national security bureaucracy itself. An October 2020 Center for International Policy study, following up on the organization's analysis of foreign funding, conveyed a graphic picture of those relationships.[47] During the previous five years the top 50 think tanks in the United States had received more than $1 billion dollars from defense contractors and the U.S. government in the form of at least 600 separate donations. Far and away, the bulk of that sum went to the RAND Corporation (which has been the Pentagon's de facto research arm for decades). Table 1 lists other think tanks that received generous amounts of cash.

Table 1
Defense industry and government grants to think tanks, 2014–2019

Center for a New American Security	$8,946,000
Atlantic Council	$8,697,000
New America Foundation	$7,283,828
German Marshall Fund of the United States	$6,599,999
Center for Strategic and International Studies	$5,040,000
Council on Foreign Relations	$2,590,000
Brookings Institution	$2,485,000
Heritage Foundation	$1,375,000
Stimson Center	$1,343,753

Source: Ben Freeman, *U.S. Government and Defense Contractor Funding of America's Top 50 Think Tanks*, Foreign Influence Transparency Initiative, Table 2 (Washington: Center for International Policy, October 2020).

What is immediately noticeable is that *all* of the top 10 institutional recipients are renowned advocates of a highly activist U.S. foreign policy, and they specifically embrace an intrusive U.S. military policy. That stance makes them ardent defenders of the foreign policy status quo—especially Washington's global network of military alliances—and vehement opponents of any changes to those institutions that would downsize America's role.

The same Center for International Policy report also lists the top government funders of think tanks. They include the Office of the Secretary of Defense, the Air Force, the Army, the Department of Homeland Security, and the State Department. And the amounts were huge. (See Table 2.)

The defense contractors that provided the most money were Northrop Grumman, Raytheon, Boeing, Lockheed Martin, and Airbus. Because think tanks do not have to disclose contributions in a thorough and transparent fashion, the estimates of funding from defense contractors are inherently conservative. When funding is disclosed, it is typically listed as falling within a wide range (e.g., $25,000 to $100,000). What is known is that financial inputs from defense contractors were far from trivial.

All these funding sources had vested financial and institutional interests in maximizing U.S. military activism around the world. Barbara Boland, national security correspondent for *The American Conservative,*

Table 2
Top U.S. government donors to U.S. think tanks, 2014–2020

Department of Defense (and other national security agencies)	$391,720,000
U.S. Air Force	$281,400,000
U.S. Army	$246,321,000
Department of Homeland Security	$111,192,255
Department of State	$9,090,478

Source: Ben Freeman, *U.S. Government and Defense Contractor Funding of America's Top 50 Think Tanks*, Foreign Influence Transparency Initiative, Table 3 (Washington: Center for International Policy, October 2020).

examined the Center for International Policy report. She stressed, "Disclosure matters because journalists rely on think tanks to provide supposedly non-biased experts to weigh in on complicated policy matters. These think tank experts are frequently hosted on TV panels on CNN or Fox News, or are seen penning op-eds in newspapers or heard on the airwaves of National Public Radio (NPR)."[48] That nexus with the news media is especially problematic. When the volumes of analysis and commentary provided by supposedly independent think tanks are potentially tainted by their sources of funding, even the most diligent press outlets may find it difficult to avoid being channels for government or defense industry propaganda.

RESISTING THE SIREN CALL OF FALSE PATRIOTISM

All of the factors mentioned in this chapter impede the media's ability to play the role of watchdog with respect to defense, foreign policy, and intelligence issues. Even under the best of circumstances, it is not easy for journalists to be detached observers. That is especially true when foreign sources provide information on developments that might impact the security, liberty, and well-being of the United States. Most people, journalists included, identify with one country on the basis of birth or adoption, and they exhibit loyalty to that country, its values, and its actions. It is all too easy for those feelings of nationalism and patriotism to morph into uncritical, even jingoistic, stances.

During both world wars, government officials exploited such factors to enlist the press to support the nation's war effort. Journalists were expected to embrace the government's policies without expressing any doubts, reservations, or questions. The pressure for ideological conformity was intense, but most journalists were willing, indeed eager, collaborators because they believed in the cause being pursued. That attitude persisted into the initial Cold War decades, and once again, distinctions between the government's agenda and the role of an independent press became blurred nearly to the point of erasure. Journalists served as propagandists for official policy and, in a worrisome number of cases, even worked as government operatives to help execute that policy.

Whatever the appeals to patriotism, though, engaging in such collaboration is profoundly damaging to a free, independent press. Journalists cannot promote U.S. foreign or national security policies without becoming hopelessly compromised. Unfortunately, the problem has persisted, although government manipulation efforts may not be as flagrant as they were during the two world wars and much of the Cold War. The Pentagon, the intelligence agencies, and the White House still endeavor to use the news media as propaganda channels, and all too often, they succeed.

CHAPTER 12
A Changing Media Landscape:
The Growth of Social Media

The past 15 years have seen a revolution in how people obtain, circulate, and debate all manner of news. Social media platforms have forced the legacy media—radio, television, and print publications—to compete in ways that equal or even exceed the impact of the internet itself during the previous decade. Facebook, Twitter, Instagram, and other platforms now are ubiquitous in societies throughout the world. Their growing prominence presents opportunities, benefits, problems, and dangers.

The global reach of social media companies is enormous. In late 2020, Twitter had 340 million accounts worldwide, including some 78 million in the United States.[1] The number of Facebook users was even greater—some 2.8 billion globally—which reflects exponential growth; the figure for the third quarter of 2008 was 100 million.[2] Twitter did not even exist before the spring of 2006, or Facebook before the spring of 2004.

Those platforms do far more than augment the reach of legacy media outlets; to a large extent the newcomers have supplanted the older forms of media and become the dominant players. A 2018 Pew Research survey found that approximately two-thirds of U.S. adults (68 percent) get news on social media sites, and about one in five did so "often." Only 32 percent never received news from such sources. The combination of Facebook, Google, and Twitter controlled the information received by huge numbers of Americans, Pew confirmed. "About four-in-ten

Americans (43%) got news on Facebook. The next most commonly used site for news was YouTube (owned by Google), with 21% getting news there, followed by Twitter at 12%."[3]

Financial reports and other evidence indicate that those percentages have grown since the 2018 survey, especially for Twitter. A subsequent Pew survey in January 2021 found that more that 86 percent of Americans obtained news from digital devices and 60 percent did so "often." The percentage of people getting their news on digital devices eclipsed the percentage for television (68 percent) and dwarfed the use of print (32 percent overall and only 10 percent "often"). Moreover, among digital users, 53 percent accessed news from social media sites. An even greater percentage used search engines (primarily Google) for that purpose.[4]

The actual and potential benefits are considerable for expanding the spread of information, creating greater connections among individuals and groups with similar interests, and fostering debate and controversy. A handful of traditional, often stodgy corporate media giants no longer serve as gatekeepers, limiting the public's ability to access diverse sources of information. The information flow has become more fragmented and varied in both viewpoint and quality. On the downside, a handful of high-tech corporations and their leaders have used the explosive growth of social media to acquire enormous power over the most important forms of information. That shift creates the potential for new gatekeepers to limit the exposure of unorthodox views in much the same way that their legacy predecessors were sometimes inclined to do.

The extent of the power that social media corporations have at their disposal was demonstrated in a graphic fashion following the January 6, 2021, storming of the U.S. Capitol by out-of-control supporters of President Donald Trump. The social media powerhouses embraced the narrative that the riot constituted an insurrection and that Trump and some of his backers were responsible. In an extraordinary display of power, Twitter and Facebook moved to terminate Trump's access to their platforms, as well as the accounts of several of his advisers and prominent supporters. Two private companies successfully silenced the president of the United States and other heavyweight officials.

The undertone of intolerance was more than a little troubling. Those social media sites not only barred speech that advocated or seemed to advocate violence, but they targeted websites and posts that dared argue that vote fraud had occurred in the 2020 presidential election—a major theme of Trump's postelection message and the inspiration for the large peaceful rally on January 6 that preceded the attack on the Capitol. Even before the January 6 riot and the subsequent social media crackdown on prominent right-wing figures, YouTube barred all videos continuing to express such arguments.[5] By instituting the ban, social media firms effectively dictated that allegations of fraud were "fake news" and not an appropriate topic for debate. Even anti-Trump advocates of free speech expressed concern about both the intolerance and the extent of the power that the social media firms were able—and clearly determined—to wield.[6]

The growing power of social media is a mixed blessing. Governments face an additional challenge in their efforts to prevent information consumers from receiving stories and images that might prove embarrassing or discrediting to authorities. Regimes worldwide routinely try to enforce secrecy and prevent dissidents from communicating among themselves and coordinating their activities. In those situations, social media platforms can be vehicles for greater transparency. That is not to say the existence of those platforms automatically is antithetical to entrenched governments and their agendas, however. Some incumbent political leaders have become adept at using social media to convey their own viewpoints. Donald Trump, for example, was a prolific user of Twitter; he used it to attack opponents and generate greater support and enthusiasm among his followers. And his tweets, especially the more inflammatory ones, frequently received coverage in the traditional media. That's why the Twitter ban in January 2021 was so significant.

But social media platforms themselves are not immune from government controls. China's communist regime has been all too effective in shutting down, or at least disrupting, potentially troublesome mechanisms for anti-regime commentary. The technique is especially prominent during periods when sensitive domestic or international issues are at the forefront. The crackdown in 2018, when the People's Congress was about to approve a controversial constitutional change removing the limit on the number of presidential terms, was a flagrant example. Two years later, a similar stifling of dissent on social media was evident when Beijing imposed a new national security law and curtailed Hong Kong's political autonomy.

Even when autocratic governments are not trying to curb the information explosion, the growing prominence of social media has some inherent drawbacks. News stories that dispute and sometimes discredit the conventional wisdom and carefully crafted government propaganda do have the opportunity for greater exposure than ever before. However, social media companies supposedly are maintaining neutral platforms, not acting as publishers with responsibility for the truthfulness of the items that appear; that means the potential for "fake news" is considerable. Controversy about fake news has soared in recent years, as some indisputably false stories have circulated widely. And when a story (true or fake) "goes viral," the extent of circulation is magnitudes larger than it would have been in the pre–social media era. That multiplier effect raises questions about how much or how well social media platforms can moderate content to exclude flagrant fraud and other egregiously abusive content without becoming a de facto publisher and incurring the potential legal liabilities of that status.

Although social media may be beneficial on balance, the emergence of these platforms as major news players does not guarantee that efforts to debunk government or special interest group propaganda will be more widespread and effective. Nor does it guarantee the distribution of more critical assessments of U.S. foreign policy initiatives. Sometimes the platforms have merely afforded pro-war propagandists allied with government hawks more opportunities to spread their disinformation. In some cases, those accounts have epitomized the stereotype of fake news.

One example of the latter is the bogus, inflammatory blog that helped shape and increase negative public perceptions of Syrian dictator Bashar al-Assad and generate pressure for U.S. military action. A series of dispatches, "A Gay Girl in Damascus," went viral in the United States and other Western countries in early 2011, just as the Arab Spring surge of reform sentiment sweeping the Middle East reached Syria. The dispatches were supposedly written by a gay 35-year-old Syrian woman, Amina Abdallah Arraf al Omari, who contended that she was being persecuted both for her sexuality and her anti–Assad political beliefs.

In June 2011, though, the poignant, emotionally wrenching accounts were exposed as a hoax. The author was not a lesbian victim of Assad's persecution, but a 40-year-old heterosexual American graduate student named Tom MacMaster. At the time, a growing number of groups were seeking to generate public support for Western intervention on behalf of rebels seeking to overthrow Assad. Whether MacMaster was working with them is uncertain. But he did state openly that he had created the blog and the fictional accounts to call attention to human rights abuses in Syria.[7]

His work certainly had that effect. It painted the Assad regime in the most villainous light, just as public debate in the United States about policy toward Syria was beginning to heat up. When MacMaster created a phony story that Amina had been kidnapped (with the unsubtle implication that Syrian security forces were responsible), the *Washington Post* and numerous other media players gave the story widespread exposure. News of her disappearance became an internet and media sensation. The U.S. State Department even started an investigation. Once the hoax was revealed, chagrined *Washington Post* reporters observed, "The hoax raises difficult questions about the reliance on blogs, tweets, Facebook postings and other Internet communications as they increasingly become a standard way to report on global events. Information from online sources has become particularly important in coverage of the Middle East uprisings, especially in countries that severely restrict foreign media."[8]

Guy Somerset at Antiwar.com criticized the media's credulity in circulating inflammatory accounts without adequate checking. He contended that the MacMaster hoax was reminiscent of a similar false propaganda episode during the era before social media: the "babies pulled from incubators" testimony before Congress on the eve of the Persian Gulf War (see Chapter 3).[9] In that earlier case, a teenage Kuwaiti girl gave a searing, tearful account to Congress of what she had witnessed following Iraq's invasion of Kuwait. She allegedly was a nurse, but she actually was Nayirah al-Sabah, the daughter of Kuwait's ambassador to the United States. Her account of Iraqi troops ripping infants from incubators to leave them to die was likewise a total fabrication. American media outlets eventually debunked her story, but far too late. The powerful impression that her lies created helped inflame American public opinion against Iraq and increase both public and congressional support for military intervention. Quite plausibly, MacMaster's propaganda (and that of other anti-Assad sources) using social media two decades later was designed to accomplish a similar purpose with respect to Syria.

A social media campaign against Iran in January 2020 was only a little more authentic than MacMaster's fictional dispatches. A video of a clip, "Truth from an Iranian," circulated with the hashtag #IraniansDetestSoleimani. The five-minute video featured an Iranian woman supposedly revealing the true attitudes of citizens in that country. Her message was straightforward: Iranians detested their government and especially hated Qasem Soleimani, the military leader the United States had recently assassinated with a drone strike. In less than two weeks, the video was viewed more than 10 million times across the platforms of Facebook, Twitter, and YouTube.[10] Much of the national news media also gave it highly sympathetic coverage.

However, the generic "Iranian woman" turned out to be Saghar Erica Kasraie, who had been a paid lobbyist for a controversial faction in Libya's civil war. That faction, headed by Field Marshal Khalifa Haftar, received strong backing from several countries in the Middle East, including both Egypt and Saudi Arabia—longtime mortal adversaries of Iran's government. The video was part of an ongoing propaganda campaign by one faction in the Middle East power struggle. If not fake news, it certainly was a distorted account whose origins were concealed and misrepresented.

Attempts to combat the fake news problem have created their own difficulties, controversies, and potential for abuse, however. Public and congressional pressure on Facebook and its counterparts to engage in fact-checking to prevent the distribution of fake news is not as simple as the term implies. People scrutinizing the accuracy of information on the media platforms, especially self-anointed or even appointed fact-checkers, are not immune from their own biases; sometimes they do not make even a minimal effort to curb such biases. Some ideological or partisan political activists even use the term "fact-checking" as a smokescreen not only to dispute but to seek to bar analyses that express a different opinion, judgment, or perspective from that of the so-called fact-checker.

Conservatives have been especially vocal in their complaints about biases and censorship on the various media platforms. They charge that pieces that dispute conventional progressive views on a variety of issues are unfairly branded as false or misleading, and then access is restricted or removed entirely. Ninety percent of Republican respondents in an August 2020 Pew Research survey believed that social media organizations deliberately censored views that the companies considered objectionable. Notably, 73 percent of all respondents, and even 59 percent of Democrats, believed the same.[11]

A February 2021 report from New York University's Stern Center for Business and Human Rights purports to show there is no evidence of ideological bias against conservatives in decisions by Twitter and other social media sites to delete posts or suspend accounts.[12] The authors claim that such decisions are made on an even-handed basis for violations of "terms of service." But the study's methodology was deeply flawed and fell far short of validating those definitive conclusions. There wasn't much evidence one way or the other. For example, Twitter could not (or at least did not) provide numerical data for its decisions. Consequently, there was no way to determine (other than relying on the assurances of Twitter management) whether a disproportionate percentage of suspended or banned accounts were right-of-center individuals or organizations. The revelation that a Democratic Party mega-donor funded the study also did not enhance its credibility.[13] Nevertheless, the mainstream media accepted it as definitive and irrefutable.

Complaints about bias are not entirely without merit, though, and right-wing types are not the only people voicing loud objections. Far-left journalists and activists, especially those with a strong anti-war orientation, also contend that their work is subject to an unusual degree of hostile scrutiny by social media platforms. Writers for such outlets as *Consortium News* and Truthdig, among others, have voiced complaints.

The standard response to such objections is that the social media platforms are privately owned, and, therefore, the legal protections that prevent governmental attempts at censorship are not applicable. Making that distinction, however, is problematic. The social media companies have enjoyed a special legal status based on an exception included in amendments to the Communications Decency Act of 1996. That exception, Section 230, shields the companies from libel suits and other legal actions that would create gigantic operational headaches. The benefit is based on the rationale that those sites are platforms and not publishers. But social media companies' definitions of "fake news" have become broader and exhibit (contrary to the New York University study) an increasingly noticeable ideological and political tilt. As a result, a growing number of critics, especially on the political right, are challenging the assumption that these firms are operating as neutral platforms—at least with respect to politics or ideology.

Calls for repeal of the exception, and antitrust suits to inject more competition into the arena, are becoming louder and more widespread.[14] But the issues involved in repealing or even amending Section 230 are extremely complex, as are the possible ramifications.[15] Critics would likely be chagrined if, in a post–Section 230 environment, social media companies exercised even more restrictions on content, lest they be held liable in a successful lawsuit. Likewise, advocates of limited government would hardly be pleased if the replacement for self-policing measures was a new regulatory agency, as the authors of the New York University study and other proponents have urged.

Calls for change have raised other troubling questions as well. In the autumn of 2019, committees in both houses of Congress held hearings in which members, especially Democrats, openly berated the top executives of the principal media companies about their supposed failure to take decisive action against fake news and "hate speech"—a term that seemed even more vague, elastic, and ideologically charged. The implication was not subtle; if the social media companies would not take action on their own to curb the alleged abuses, then governmental power would be brought to bear to resolve the problem. A repeat performance in late 2020 pointed to a similar conclusion.[16]

Some individual members of Congress seek to put maximum pressure on social media platforms to expunge "misinformation," and their ideological intolerance frequently oozes through. Sen. Richard Blumenthal (D-CT), for example, blasted both Twitter's Jack Dorsey and Facebook's Mark Zuckerberg for not doing enough "to block hateful and untrue" content. "Destructive, incendiary misinformation is still a scourge on both your platforms and others," he said and demanded a list of further steps to block misinformation.[17]

Such unsubtle threats did lead Facebook, Twitter, and other entities to become more proactive. But the applicability of those disqualifying labels to some of the targets was questionable. For example, both Facebook and Twitter shut down dozens of accounts that they concluded were Russian bots or propaganda operations sponsored by the Russian government. They did the same with accounts allegedly controlled by the Iranian government. Most of the targets did appear to fit the description ascribed to them, but others seemed to be genuine accounts—some even run by U.S. citizens—whose views merely coincided with the positions of those foreign governments.

Pro-Russia and pro-Iran accounts were not the only targets. In June 2020, Twitter deleted over 170,000 accounts on the grounds that they were instruments of Chinese government propaganda. Again, the standards were rather vague; the term used most often to justify eliminating targeted accounts was that they were "tied to" Beijing's propaganda operations.[18] What "tied to" actually means, Twitter executives did not elaborate. In January 2021, Twitter shut down more than 70,000 accounts because of alleged ties to the QAnon movement that frequently circulates often bizarre conspiracy theories.[19] Once again, the standards used to reach those determinations were vague to the point of being opaque. That kind of decisionmaking has the potential to suppress views that are merely unorthodox or exotic, but neither treasonous nor guilty of inciting violence.

Even if a private business was acting on its own authority, it inevitably limited debate and blurred the crucial distinction between the role of a media platform operator and a publisher. Its actions also raise a valid question of whether restricting or barring accounts runs afoul of prohibitions against censorship. What if a private company is doing the government's bidding, either willingly or under duress? At what point is a private entity simply operating as a de facto government agent?[20] And who determines when that line has been crossed, what standards are used to make the determination, and what the response should be from aggrieved parties and the public? On the last point, should aggrieved parties have recourse to legal action against the government, the company, or both?

The issue of doing the government's bidding gained new salience during the coronavirus pandemic in 2020. Facebook and other media platforms responded to specific requests from the World Health Organization, the U.S. Centers for Disease Control and Prevention, numerous foreign governments, and state governors in the United States to remove articles and videos that disputed the official medical judgments that the various authorities put forth. Failure to do so, government officials and social media executives argued, would needlessly endanger public health.

The unorthodox views that were targeted, including some within the medical community itself, appeared to vary widely in quality and accuracy. Many were based on far-fetched theories and relied on highly dubious evidence. But some minority perspectives attracted adherents with impressive medical and other scientific credentials of their own. Indeed, some dissenting views proved closer to the mark than the mainstream, officially sanctioned analyses. Mainstream versions that did not fare well include the highly influential Imperial College (London) model that forecast approximately 2.2 million deaths in the United States and nearly half a million deaths in Great Britain. Even early on, it was apparent that particular study had missed the mark badly.[21] The wisdom of limiting debate on the pandemic was highly questionable, and given the ubiquitous impact of the decisions by the social media giants, the effect was nearly indistinguishable from what it would have been if the various governments had exercised direct authority and censored non-mainstream views.

Moreover, distinguishing between decisions that the social media giants made of their own volition and decisions made in response to intense government pressure became increasingly difficult. That dilemma became acute in mid-2021. At one point, President Biden even said that Facebook and other social media were "killing people" because the companies were failing to delete misinformation about the safety of COVID-19 vaccines and the threat posed by the Delta variant.[22] The Biden administration's pressure on the social media companies was not subtle. When government officials flagged posts for alleged misinformation and forwarded their conclusions to the people operating those platforms, they were giving far more than a hint or suggestion that the offending post should be removed.[23] As one wag put it, the government "strongly suggesting" something is like Tony Soprano strongly suggesting something. A serious implied threat is always present.

A move by the social media platforms to suppress debate on another significant issue was perhaps even more troubling, despite the absence of governmental pressure. In October 2020, the *New York Post* published a blockbuster story supposedly based on documents gleaned from a laptop computer that Hunter Biden, the son of Democratic Party presidential nominee Joe Biden, had left at a repair shop in 2019.[24] (See the discussion of this incident in Chapter 9.) The most explosive revelation was that Hunter Biden had arranged a 2015 meeting between his father and an executive of the Ukrainian energy company Burisma, where the younger Biden served on the board of directors. Questions about the accuracy of the story were valid, including the chain of custody regarding the computer and the incriminating files. But if true, the incident constituted at least the perception of a serious conflict of interest on the part of Joe Biden. That problem was especially acute since the elder Biden had repeatedly denied he ever had any involvement in his son's business affairs or had even discussed such matters with Hunter. If the computer files were genuine, they indicated that the former vice president had misled the press and the American public.

Although the *New York Post* has a reputation of sometimes engaging in tabloid sensationalism, it has numerous credible reporters in its ranks, is a major news publication, and has more than 230,000 subscribers—the fourth largest subscriber base among U.S. newspapers. In other words, the *New York Post* is not some obscure, fringe website. That status made the move by Facebook and Twitter to curtail the exposure and sharing of the Biden story unusual and alarming. Facebook preemptively limited the spread of the story while sending it to third-party fact-checkers, a move the company said it had taken on various occasions but was not the standard process. Twitter initially allowed the story to surge to the rank of the number 3 trending topic in the United States but then abruptly marked the link as "potentially unsafe" and blocked it.

As *The Intercept*'s Glenn Greenwald observed, Facebook's restrictions were especially unsettling because they embodied flagrant political and ideological bias. "Just two hours after the story was online, Facebook intervened. The company dispatched a life-long Democratic Party operative who now worked for Facebook—Andy Stone, previously a communications operative for Democratic Sen. Barbara Boxer and the Democratic Congressional Campaign Committee, among other D.C. Democratic jobs—to announce that Facebook was 'reducing [the article's] distribution on our platform': in other words, tinkering with its own algorithms to suppress the ability of users to discuss or share the news article."[25]

The *Washington Post* noted that this was "one of the rare occasions they [Facebook and Twitter] have sanctioned a traditional media outlet."[26] When Twitter acted, its suppression efforts went beyond Facebook's. The company banned all users' ability to share the *New York Post* article—not just on their public timeline but on the platform's private direct messaging feature. Twitter went so far as to temporarily lock White House press secretary Kayleigh McEnany's account, as well as the account of the *New York Post* itself. President Trump's campaign account also was temporarily locked, intensifying suspicions of ideological and partisan bias. Twitter's decision to add notices to the offending tweets saying that they violated the company's rules on prohibiting the publication of "hacked materials" did not alleviate those growing suspicions.

Critics blasted the Facebook and Twitter moves as politically motivated censorship. Since leading Twitter and Facebook executives were prominent supporters of Joe Biden and the Democratic Party, conservatives cried foul. Numerous Republicans in Congress, including Sens. Ted Cruz (R-TX) and Josh Hawley (R-MO), issued public statements demanding that company executives answer questions about their actions.

Other members denounced the restrictions as blatant political bias and redoubled calls for drastic reform or abolition of Section 230.[27] Right-wing media outlets, including Fox News and *National Review*, were equally outraged and called for legislative action.

Wall Street Journal columnist Andy Kessler warned the social media giants that they were being reckless with their own futures. Noting that Twitter's actions put its CEO, Jack Dorsey, in a perilous position, Kessler observed, "The timing was especially dumb, as he's set to appear next week, along with Facebook's Mark Zuckerberg and Google's Sundar Pichai, before the Senate Commerce Committee. The topic is Section 230 of the Communications Decency Act, which shields social-media platforms from liability as publishers. Mr. Dorsey just gave his adversaries the fuel to burn his tweet house down."[28]

Clearly, the decisions by Twitter and Facebook regarding the *New York Post*'s exposé had important political effects, but the impact was not limited to that consideration. The newspaper's allegations were relevant to the long-festering issue of U.S. policy toward Ukraine and Russia. Joe Biden was not only vice president during the Obama administration, but he was explicitly in charge of the administration's Ukraine policy. Therefore, new evidence of a possible conflict of interest was extremely pertinent. By limiting access to the *New York Post* story, Twitter and Facebook impeded public consideration of an important and controversial foreign policy issue. That development was no small matter, and it again generated concern about whether the conduct of the social media companies amounts to de facto censorship, even if it does not meet the legal definition.

Glenn Greenwald highlighted some of the most acute dangers flowing from Facebook's and Twitter's actions.[29] "While there is no proof that Biden followed through on any of Hunter's promises to Burisma, there is no reason, at least thus far, to doubt that the emails are genuine. And if they are genuine, they at least add to what is undeniably a relevant and newsworthy story involving influence-peddling relating to Hunter Biden's work in Ukraine and his trading on the name and power of his father, now the front-runner in the 2020 presidential election."

Greenwald also had little patience regarding the rationale for blocking stories based on "hacked materials," which Twitter had invoked.

"That standard, if taken seriously and applied consistently," he contended, "would result in the banning from the platform of huge amounts of the most important and consequential journalism. After all, a large bulk of journalism is enabled by sources providing 'content obtained without authorization' to journalists, who then publish it. Indeed, many of the most celebrated and significant stories of the last several decades—the Pentagon Papers, the WikiLeaks' Collateral Murder video and war logs, the Snowden reporting, the Panama Papers . . . relied upon publication of various forms of 'hacked materials' provided by sources."

Greenwald was not impressed with Facebook's explanation, either. "Facebook's rationale for suppression—that it needs to have its 'fact checking' partners verify the story before allowing it to be spread—poses different but equally alarming dangers. What makes Mark Zuckerberg's social media company competent to 'fact check' the work of other journalists?" And Greenwald asked the crucial question: "Why did Facebook block none of the endless orgy of Russiagate conspiracy theories from major media outlets that were completely unproven if not outright false?" Indeed, "can anyone claim that Facebook's alleged 'fact-checking' process is applied with any remote consistency given how often they failed to suppress sketchily sourced or facially unreliable stories—such as, say, the Steele Dossier and endless articles based on it? Can you even envision the day when an unproven conspiracy theory—leaked by the CIA or FBI to the Washington Post or NBC News—is suppressed pending 'fact-checking' by Facebook?"

Greenwald's last point is especially important. The social media platforms, like so much of the legacy media, seem intent on applying a double standard. Questionable and even far-fetched stories supplied by government officials or friendly political sources are treated with tolerance and even amplified. Conversely, accounts provided by maverick sources or containing content that runs counter to the conventional wisdom on high-profile issues are marginalized, restricted, or excluded. If that process continues, social media platforms will fail to foster greater debate on foreign policy and other important topics. Indeed, they will constrain it further.

Faced with intense congressional and public blowback, Twitter began to execute a limited retreat with respect to its handling of the *New York*

Post article. Jack Dorsey issued a statement admitting that Twitter was wrong to block web links to the article. "Straight blocking of URLs was wrong, and we updated our policy and enforcement to fix," he tweeted. "Our goal is to attempt to add context, and now we have capabilities to do that." Twitter would no longer remove hacked material unless it was "directly shared by hackers or those working with them," the company's lead for legal, public policy, and trust and safety, Vijaya Gadde, said in a subsequent Twitter thread.[30] The insistence on labeling to add context, though, suggested that the surrender was conditional.

As already noted, a crucial underlying issue for social media is whether restrictive policies by private entities regarding types of posts or the expression of certain views constitutes censorship. The traditional definition of the concept would conclude that such practices do not meet that standard. But given the extensive reach of social media platforms, what happens when the private companies that operate the platforms bar certain viewpoints at the explicit or implicit request of federal government or state governments? At what point do private entities become government agents, and when does their restriction of speech become de facto censorship that the First Amendment prohibits? Government censorship by proxy can be just as corrosive and dangerous as direct censorship.

This issue arose on several occasions in 2019 and 2020. The clearest case (noted earlier in this chapter) occurred in April 2020, not with a foreign policy issue but with respect to the coronavirus lockdown that several state governors imposed. Not only did the social media giants bar posts that expressed unorthodox views about treatment options and strategies for dealing with the virus, but Facebook even eliminated posts that announced or promoted demonstrations against the lockdowns.[31] Moreover, the company acknowledged that it did so in response to the requests of certain state governors. The conclusion that the company was acting as an instrument of government policy was hard to avoid.

YouTube removed a widely circulated video about the coronavirus because it violated "community guidelines." The creators of the video argued that the numbers they were collecting and analyzing showed COVID-19 was similar to flu in its mortality rate. Banning such a video, however controversial, was a step too far for Facebook.[32] But a YouTube spokesperson issued a statement saying the video was pulled "because the content contradicted the guidance of the local health authority."[33] Once again, the line between a media company making a content judgment of its own volition and acting as a government instrument was a fine—and increasingly blurry—line.

Journalist Matt Taibbi noted, "At the outset of the crisis, America's biggest internet platforms—Facebook, Twitter, Google, LinkedIn, and Reddit—took an unprecedented step to 'combat fraud and misinformation' by promising extensive cooperation in elevating 'authoritative' news over less reputable sources."[34] Unfortunately, authoritative sources frequently translated into government-approved experts and accounts. Indeed, the joint statement itself emphasized that the platforms were going to provide information "in coordination with government healthcare agencies around the world."[35]

As *The American Conservative* managing editor Arthur Bloom pointed out, the bias in favor of so-called authoritative sources was not confined to the coronavirus issue. Indeed, that bias and the resulting de facto blacklisting of sites that consistently criticize U.S. foreign policy and other behavior "went even further, into the architecture of search engines. My reporting on Google search last year found that one of the 'fringe domain' blacklists included Robert Parry's *Consortium News*. In other words, if Google had been around in the 1980s, Parry's exposes on Iran-Contra would have been excluded from Google News results."[36]

Taibbi expressed concern about a growing flirtation in some political factions (primarily progressive ones) with China's control techniques regarding the internet. He cited one article in *The Atlantic* by two high-profile law professors, Jack Goldsmith and Andrew Keane Woods.[37] Goldsmith and Woods noted that because of "Constitutional and cultural differences," the private sector in the United States, rather than the federal and state governments, has taken the lead in implementing restrictive practices. Nevertheless, they argued, "the trend toward greater surveillance and speech control here, and toward the growing involvement of government, is undeniable and likely inexorable."

Taibbi was appalled that Goldsmith and Woods believed "a Chinese-style system of speech control might not be such a bad thing." In fact, he noted, the two academics argued that "a benefit of the coronavirus was that it was waking us up to 'how technical wizardry, data centralization, and private-public collaboration can do enormous public good.'"[38] He was not misconstruing their argument. Goldsmith and Woods even speculated that Americans could be moved to reconsider their traditional "understanding" of the First and Fourth Amendments, as the "harms from digital speech . . . continue to grow," and "the social costs of a relatively open internet multiply."[39]

The difference between Beijing's control mechanisms with respect to digital content on internet platforms and what American proponents of greater control wanted to see was more a matter of style than substance. As typical in a communist system, China's style was highly centralized, government-run, and brazen. The American counterpart would at least officially remain private, retain the image of being decentralized, and be considerably more subtle. The "requests" and indirect pressure that various governmental units used to stifle criticism of their coronavirus policies on the main media platforms could be a template for dealing with inconvenient criticism of official policy on other issues. So, despite the stylistic differences between the Chinese model and the embryonic American model, the effects could be distressingly similar in terms of limiting public debate and dissent on vital policy issues.

As mentioned earlier, in a growing number of cases, government agencies have asked media platforms to bar specific posts or even entire accounts that supposedly spread disinformation. Such requests from powerful government officials are inherently coercive. Moreover, in the areas of foreign policy and national security, the "requests" frequently amount to outright orders. One menacing development took place in October 2017, with the FBI's first step toward intervening against dissenting views on social media. FBI leaders created a new Foreign Influence Task Force in the bureau's Counterintelligence Division. Next, the FBI defined any effort by countries designated by the Department of Defense as major adversaries (Russia, China, Iran, and North Korea) to influence American public opinion as a threat to U.S. national security.

In February 2020, the FBI defined that threat in more specific terms and indicated that the agency would act against any online media outlet that it determined fell within its ambit. Even before that escalation, the agency had "encouraged" Facebook, Instagram, and Google to remove or restrict ads on the *American Herald Tribune*, an online journal that published opinion pieces critical of U.S. policy toward Iran and the Middle East.[40] Facebook promptly deleted the journal's page, and Instagram eliminated the publication's entire account.

The FBI's allegation that the *American Herald Tribune* was a "foreign" (implying Iranian or Russian) propaganda operation was disputable. The editor was Canadian: Anthony Hall, professor emeritus at the University of Lethbridge in Alberta, Canada; most writers contributing articles were Americans or other Westerners. Worse, the agency's overall rationale for suppressing targeted outlets was chilling. At a conference on election security on February 24, 2020, David K. Porter, assistant section chief of the Foreign Influence Task Force, defined "malign foreign influence activity" as specific "actions by a foreign power to influence U.S. policy, distort political sentiment and public discourse." That definition is neither precise nor substantive.

Porter further described unlawful foreign propaganda as measures "designed to undermine public confidence in the credibility of free and independent news media." Agents of influence who practice that technique, he said, seek to "push consumers to alternative news sources," where "it's much easier to introduce false narratives" and thus "sow doubt and confusion about the true narratives by exploiting the media landscape to introduce conflicting story lines."[41] To say that such an attitude reflects a bias in favor of conventional (and likely pro-government, or at least less negative) sources and outlets would be an understatement. It suggests an official vendetta toward any alternative media that questions government motives or performance.

In addition to pressure from government agencies, establishment think tanks and journalists for legacy outlets also have sought to entice or pressure social media platforms into shunning or smearing critics of the conventional wisdom. In June 2020, NBC News urged Google to bar both *ZeroHedge* and the *Federalist* from generating ad revenue on its platform because of comments in one article accusing much of the media of concealing violence at Black Lives Matter demonstrations. An angry former senior editor of the *Federalist* shot back at the NBC campaign: "Once upon a time, news outlets fought to protect the ideals of free expression. Now, they assign activists masquerading as journalists, and boost Orwellian-sounding outfits (what is the 'NBC News Verification Unit'?), to try to smear and censor those who criticize them."[42]

In this case, the attempt appeared to backfire. NBC's allegations, based on work done by a shadowy British operation, the Center for Countering Digital Hate, proved to be exaggerated. Google soon indicated that it had cautioned the *Federalist* but not barred its ads.[43] The episode also triggered renewed threats from congressional conservatives to pursue antitrust action against Google. Lost in all of the charges and countercharges was the fact that *ZeroHedge* was kicked off the platform, curbing another dissenting voice in the media.

Another brazen example of legacy media–social media collusion was evident in the reaction to the October 14, 2020, *New York Post* story about incriminating emails allegedly found on Hunter Biden's abandoned laptop (discussed earlier in this chapter). *National Review*'s David Harsanyi blasted the naysayers. "Nothing like this has ever happened in modern American journalism. There's been incessant bias, sure. Events and stories have been ignored, of course. There have been loads of smears. We were just subjected to four years of Russian 'collusion' fabulism. But now, most of the institutional media is openly colluding—and pressuring Big Tech—to suppress a story that might damage their chosen presidential candidate. Journalists have become our censors. That's definitely new."[44] Indeed, this development was new and profoundly unhealthy.

U.S. think tanks and foreign governments that fund some of them also are pushing social media corporations to become more restrictive. The analysis and recommendations in an October 2020 report from the German Marshall Fund of the United States were especially troubling.[45] The report targeted two classifications of publications and websites. One is "'Trojan horses,' sites that take on the appearance of news sites and launder disinformation while eschewing the practices of independent journalism (e.g., sourcing, mastheads, verification, corrections)."

These sites, the report contended, "repeatedly publish verifiably false content." The other category covers sites that "fail to gather and present information responsibly."

The ideological bias in the report was evident from the three examples cited: *Breitbart, Daily Wire*, and *Fox*—all leading right-of-center publications. Other conservative examples, including the *Federalist*, also came in for criticism. Two perfunctory comments conceded that left-wing sites were also guilty of "deception," but no specific examples were cited and no detailed accusations were directed at such offenders—as they were at conservative targets.

The report's recommendations were worse than its analysis. A *Wall Street Journal* editorial responding to the report accurately captured its tenor. "Such outlets allegedly 'pose a threat to informed democratic discourse.' Their content reaches readers because it is 'often oppositional to "mainstream media" and so-called elite or conventional wisdom.' The horror! Naturally, the report has a solution: Stop Facebook users from seeing content that rudely challenges elite views."[46] Indeed, the report's authors concluded that "de-amplifying—or adding friction to—the content from a handful of the most dangerous sites could dramatically decrease disinformation online."[47] The *Wall Street Journal* observed sarcastically, "Presumably Facebook can swap-in unimpeachable sources like CNN." Although the *Journal* editorial conceded that there is "genuine misinformation on Facebook," it charged that the ongoing censorship pressure against the company, epitomized by the German Marshall Fund report, "is about controlling political speech. Right-of-center sites have grown in popularity online as alternatives to mainstream news sites that have become relentlessly and almost uniformly left-wing."[48]

In addition to its unsubtle calls for Facebook to act as a de facto censor to exclude or minimize the role of right-wing news sites, the German Marshall Fund report recommended the creation of "a new PBS of the Internet, funded by a fee on online ad revenue." Such a move would give government a direct role in social media and provide a new foothold for the groupthink that already dominates the conventional mainstream media.

Such calls would be worrisome enough coming from a genuine domestic think tank, but much of the funding for the German Marshall Fund of the United States comes from Germany's government and associated front groups. Clearly, Berlin is not pleased about the growing criticism of Germany's defense spending and the escalating debate in the United States about U.S. policy toward NATO. German officials would like to smother such heretical views, and limiting the exposure on Facebook of news sites that feature foreign policy critics (such as Fox News host Tucker Carlson) is one part of that media offensive. Such schemes are the manifestation of an intolerant and coercive mentality, and they should be summarily rejected.

In sum, the most prominent media platforms have displayed arrogant ideological and political biases that advocates of free-wheeling debate should find infuriating.[49] The growing willingness of those platforms to restrict or exclude viewpoints that annoy powerful government agencies or individuals and contradict mainstream policy agendas is even worse, as evidenced by their handling of issues involving the Hunter Biden laptop story, multiple aspects of the COVID-19 pandemic, and the Wuhan lab-leak theory. In all three cases, the social media giants smothered badly needed debate and did a disservice to their users.

Nevertheless, repealing Section 230 or using antitrust measures against social media giants could be a classic case of the cure being worse than the disease. Taking legislative action against even the most arrogant social media gatekeepers, as tempting as that course might be, would likely result in the creation of a regulatory body with oversight functions. That outcome would limit policy debates even more than what is taking place with the current system. One can readily imagine the abuses that would ensue if zealots committed to stamping out "hate speech" or "misinformation" gained control of such a government regulatory apparatus. The arrangements that the social media corporations now operate, however imperfect, still facilitate the exposure of a greater range of ideas and viewpoints than before those platforms existed, and those arrangements provide a better free speech environment than the proposed alternatives.

CONCLUSION
The Media's Obligation to Serve as Foreign Policy Watchdog

The news media's performance regarding U.S. foreign policy has never been especially impressive. Not only is the extent and depth of the coverage usually lacking in comparison to the treatment journalists give to domestic issues, but the degree of oversimplification and bias is worse. Most destructive is a pronounced preference for U.S. foreign policy activism, even outright militarism, which has characterized the vast majority of press accounts over the decades. Some of that behavior reflects inherent nationalism—the belief that one's country is good and that whatever cause it pursues is likely to be worthy. That tacit collective assumption makes most of the American public and the bulk of the journalistic community prone to believe that U.S. foreign policy and national security officials have benign motives. A related assumption is that those officials are giving their fellow Americans honest accounts and not engaging in deception. Evidence that emerged to the contrary, especially since the onset of the Vietnam War, was painful, but it induced somewhat greater skepticism. Unfortunately, much of that skepticism evaporates whenever U.S. leaders contend that the latest adverse development overseas portends a dire threat to the security and liberty of the American people.

Nationalistic pride exists in most countries, but Americans seem to have developed an especially strong version. Most Americans believe that the country's role in the world has been and will remain a crucial force for good. In fact, the dominant narrative since World War II is that the United States has both a strategic and moral imperative to be the global leader. That perspective exists alongside a "can do" spirit, which assumes that the United States will be able to prevail over difficult international challenges even when lesser nations would fail—or even had already failed. American journalists have exhibited such hubris in abundance. Explicitly or implicitly, many of them subscribe to Madeleine Albright's expression of national narcissism that the United States is the "indispensable nation" and that "we see further into the future" than other nations.[1]

Americans generally and members of the media in particular tend to oversimply complex, murky foreign conflicts. Far too often, media outlets have created and promoted artificial melodramas about such conflicts. One faction (nearly always the one favored by the U.S. government) is deemed virtuous and the victim of some terrible outrage perpetrated by an opposing faction or factions. The news media portray the disfavored factions, in turn, not merely as malign impediments to Washington's policy goals and the best interests of the population in the particular country, but as the embodiment of evil. Such a campaign of demonization distorts coverage in multiple ways. Friendly journalists minimize or overlook entirely instances of unsavory behavior on the part of the "virtuous" faction while highlighting, sometimes to the point of caricature, actions of the designated villains. Such binary portrayals were especially flagrant in news stories about the Balkan wars in the 1990s and more recently in stories about Syria's civil war, but they have plagued coverage of other foreign crises as well.

In a related vein, too many journalists have overlooked highly questionable aspects of U.S. policy in terms of prudence or morality. At times, they have ignored or excused atrocities and outright war crimes committed by Washington's allies (such as Saudi Arabia) or clients (such as the Kosovo Liberation Army). Worse, some members of the journalistic community have acted as apologists for atrocities and war crimes that the U.S. government itself has committed. Independent investigative journalist and author James Bovard concludes from his decades-long experience that "most of what passes for journalism is shilling for Leviathan." He adds that it is "impossible to overstate the servility of reporters proud to serve as 'stenographers with amnesia.'"[2] To some extent, that defect applies to the coverage of all policy areas, but it is especially pervasive and virulent with regard to foreign policy and national security issues.

The media bias in favor of not only a highly activist U.S. foreign policy but a highly militarized one is pronounced. Bovard notes that "Obama, like Bush, received unlimited 'benefits of the doubt' whenever he bombed foreign nations." Indeed, that dispensation even applied (albeit to a more limited extent) to Donald Trump's behavior. One of the rare times Trump received favorable words from his enemies in the liberal-dominated media was when he launched a missile attack against Syria in response to the Assad government's alleged use of chemical weapons.[3] He also received at least measured praise in 2020 when he authorized a drone attack that killed the head of Iran's Quds Force.

THE PRESS TOO OFTEN GIVES FOREIGN POLICY LOW PRIORITY

Except when a major war involving large numbers of American troops is raging, the news media tend to give foreign affairs short shrift. If the United States is winning the war, media accounts exhibit strident patriotism, overlaid with celebratory rhetoric. If the war effort turns sour and Americans seem to be suffering serious casualties in an unsuccessful cause, the search for blame begins, both with the American public and the media. The first pattern was evident in the two world wars and the Persian Gulf War. The negative scenario characterized the Korean War, the Vietnam War, and to a lesser but still important extent the Iraq War.

The creation of the all-volunteer military, though, led to one significant change. The scale of most U.S. military interventions in terms of personnel deployed has declined. That means the number of families concerned about the progress (or lack of progress) of an ongoing war has declined as well—fewer families have loved ones directly at risk. And invariably, the number of stories appearing in the media about the war fades as the U.S. military intervention drags on. That clearly was the case with the conflict in Afghanistan, despite a steady trickle of casualties. Indeed, the fundamental factor that rendered that seemingly interminable

war less and less interesting to the media was that the number of casualties was just a trickle—and a trickle of volunteers, not draftees.

It was not until the belated final withdrawal of U.S. troops in the
summer of 2021 culminated in a chaotic debacle reminiscent of the U.S.
departure from South Vietnam more than four decades earlier that the
media paid serious attention. Even then, a stubborn activist bias was
evident, with many accounts admonishing the Biden administration for
not saving the Afghan "allies" who had worked for the U.S. occupation
army and for not (somehow) preventing the Taliban from re-subjugating
Afghanistan's women.[4]

Some analysts make the simplistic argument that restoring the draft
would inhibit U.S. leaders from starting wars because they would have
to worry more about the reaction of a public whose conscripted loved
ones were at risk. However, the existence of a conscript army did not
prevent U.S. engagement in the two world wars, the Korean War, or
Vietnam. And little evidence suggests it would discourage future administrations from launching military interventions—especially ventures
that initially promised to be relatively small-scale. However, the resumption of conscription might amp up media coverage of U.S. wars; conscription would certainly create more opportunities for human interest
stories about beleaguered soldiers from ordinary walks of life, serving
their country and fighting the good fight against Washington's latest
designated enemy.

When media outlets can't run "if it bleeds, it leads" stories, they
are largely indifferent to foreign affairs. Barring an unpopular war,
that blasé attitude is evident even during presidential campaigns—an
egregious case of journalistic malpractice since the president's primary
responsibility under the Constitution is to manage U.S. foreign policy
and be commander in chief of the U.S. military. Those roles dwarf the
executive's constitutional responsibilities in domestic affairs. Yet most
candidates emphasize their views, qualifications, and policy proposals
regarding domestic issues, often largely ignoring questions about their
positions and qualifications on foreign policy. Questions from reporters about a candidate's positions on international issues are notable for
their scarcity.

Journalists not only aided and abetted but became the driving force behind the neglect of foreign policy issues during the 2020 presidential election cycle. The media's lack of interest in foreign affairs reached an early peak during the Democratic Party primaries. In the debate among six candidates held just days before Nevada's presidential caucuses, the five moderators, including NBC heavyweights Chuck Todd and Lester Holt, failed to ask the presidential aspirants even one question on that topic.[5]

Daniel Larison, senior editor at *The American Conservative*, noted that "it is common for presidential debates to skimp on covering these issues, but it has been a long while since there have been no questions about it. If it hadn't been for a question bringing up [Sen. Amy] Klobuchar's inability to name the president of Mexico in a recent interview, there would scarcely have been any mention of the rest of the world."[6] The debate moderators' performance was appalling.

Unfortunately, when it came to foreign policy, the other debates in the 2020 primary season were only marginally better. In the earliest debates, Rep. Tulsi Gabbard (D-HI), a staunch critic of regime-change wars, including those waged by Democratic presidents, forced some discussion of the president's most important role (often by having to pivot from an initial non–foreign policy question).[7] She even pressed media outlets managing the debates to focus one of them exclusively on defense and foreign policy.[8] Not only did those mainstream outlets spurn her proposal, but their coverage of her foreign policy views ranged from negative to rabidly hostile. In any case, she attracted little voter support and was excluded from subsequent debates. Both the quantity and quality of exchanges among the remaining candidates regarding foreign policy and national security plummeted with her departure.

The same dismal media behavior was evident during the two presidential debates between Donald Trump and Joe Biden, and in the sole vice presidential debate between Mike Pence and Kamala Harris. *U.S. News & World Report* senior writer Paul D. Shinkman noted that Afghanistan "was mentioned 23 times during the 2012 vice presidential debate between then-Vice President Joe Biden and Rep. Paul Ryan of Wisconsin. Sen. Kamala Harris of California and Vice President Mike Pence did not reference it once during their face-off last week, a particularly notable absence as this year's debate fell on the 19th anniversary of the beginning of America's longest war."[9] Both candidates' treatment of other defense and foreign policy issues amounted to little more than brief interjections of bumper-sticker clichés.

To its credit, the Trump campaign pressed the Commission on Presidential Debates, as well as NBC News and the moderator it chose for the final presidential debate, White House correspondent Kristen Welker, to focus that debate on foreign policy.[10] The twin rationales seemed reasonable: the first debate had overwhelmingly emphasized domestic policy, and the second debate had been cancelled following Trump's positive COVID-19 diagnosis. Nevertheless, the commission, NBC, and Welker flatly refused, and questions in the final debate heavily featured issues such as health care and the environment that had already been debated at length in the previous encounter.

ACTIVIST BIAS CORRODES MEDIA COVERAGE

The media's failure to pay adequate attention to a crucial set of issues is compounded by the placid willingness of too many major media players to accept the conventional narrative on defense, foreign policy, and national security issues. Most mainstream journalists only bother to ask officials hard questions when they have a strong ideological or partisan motive to do so. Even less often do they seek out information from other sources that might contradict official justifications or the rationales the reporters themselves were inclined to endorse. Such complacent biases have long plagued foreign policy coverage, but the partisan aspect became more evident during the Trump years.

Reporters and commentators showed little restraint in questioning the policies and motives of the White House on an array of issues, including policy toward Russia, relations with traditional U.S. allies, the president's diplomatic outreach to North Korea, and the wisdom of drawing down U.S. troops in Afghanistan. Interestingly, they had exhibited few signs of such aggressiveness regarding U.S. policies during Barack Obama's years in office, even with respect to the administration's dubious interventions in Libya, Yemen, and Syria. Nor did they show much inclination to examine critically the arguments made by individuals and organizations that opposed Trump's initiatives. Indeed, influential journalists aided and abetted dissident administration officials and former members of the national security apparatus in circulating leaks that sought to discredit the Trump administration's policies.

Members of the press thus became de facto guardians of the pre-Trump foreign policy status quo. The press appeared strongly inclined to question or even undermine policies that might lead to a less prominent and intrusive U.S. role in the world but showed no similar willingness to question policies that sought to promote and perpetuate America's role as the "indispensable nation." That mentality seems largely unchanged since Joe Biden took office.

In her 2014 book, *Stonewalled*, former CBS reporter Sharyl Attkisson expressed frustration at the willingness of the press to tamely accept and even promote the policy status quo. She warned her journalist colleagues that "we're losing our mojo" and added, "By 'mojo,' I mean our ability to serve vigorously and effectively as the Fourth Estate. Watchdog to government and other powers that may otherwise overstep their bounds." She concluded with a searing complaint about the trajectory of her profession. "And we're losing it without so much as a whimper. We're voluntarily relinquishing it."[11] Her indictment is doubly valid with respect to media coverage of defense, foreign policy, and national security issues.

Far too often, journalists have allowed not only ideological and partisan biases but careerist incentives to determine their focus and guide their conclusions. The latter factor tends to be underrated, but it plays a crucial role. Fear of losing access and suffering damage to their careers can intimidate reporters, columnists, and editors. Conversely, using that treasured access for career advancement reinforces the incentive to provide "friendly" coverage. The result has been an overly solicitous treatment of most sitting presidents and their policies, especially when Democrats or internationalist Republicans occupy the White House. Media coverage of Ronald Reagan's and George W. Bush's administrations were partial exceptions to that rule (in the latter case, only after the Iraq military mission turned sour). Treatment of the Trump administration's foreign policy is the rare example of a consistently hostile narrative, but that can be attributed to the pervasive assumption that he was a dangerous isolationist who was weakening America's global leadership role.

Going along with the dominant globalist narrative is the easier and safer career path for journalists. The news media, though, must pay a price for its willingness to engage in craven behavior. One example is the extent of public discontent with and even disdain for the quality and integrity of the news-gathering profession. That point was graphically apparent in the results of the annual Gallup survey regarding the honesty and integrity of various professions. The December 2020 poll showed that respondents gave journalists very low marks.[12] Although a few professions (e.g., advertising practitioners, car salespeople, and members of Congress) ranked even lower, members of the press did not fare well, with only 28 percent of respondents giving them positive ratings. And as discussed in Chapter 9, the U.S. press ranked dead last in a 2021 Reuters survey of 46 countries regarding public trust in the news media.[13]

Journalists seem to have thoroughly alienated moderate and conservative news consumers. The overwhelming bulk of the profession's remaining support in the Gallup survey came from respondents identifying as Democrats, and even the 48 percent positive rating from that faction is less than impressive. Only 28 percent of independents approved of the fourth estate's ethics, and a mere 5 percent of Republican respondents gave the press a favorable rating. Among Republicans, just one occupation—members of Congress—received a lower figure, and among independents, only five occupations did so.

According to *RealityChek* blogger Alan Tonelson, those results are both unsurprising and deserved. He cites two prominent reasons for the media's bad reputation. First, the mainstream press "has not only been genuinely terrible when it comes to getting facts and their obvious implications straight, but it's been genuinely terrible in an overwhelmingly pro-globalist vein, including on trade, immigration, and foreign policy issues, and of course on the highest profile of all critics of these views—President Trump." Second, "they're supposed to play such a crucial watchdog role in our democratic republic. Yet their biases have been so flagrant, and even so deliberate, that these news outlets are no longer serving as a source of reliable, trustworthy information, and consequently keep weakening the foundations of accountable government."[14]

That conclusion is hard to argue with, given the media's inadequate—and deteriorating—performance, especially with respect to international policy. And the depressing results of the Gallup and Reuters polls suggest that a large portion of the American public holds a similar negative view.

CAN THE MEDIA BE A RELIABLE FOREIGN POLICY WATCHDOG?

A marked growth in both independence and skepticism is essential for the media to play a decent role as a watchdog of Washington's foreign policy. At the time of the Persian Gulf War, syndicated columnist Colman McCarthy lamented "a media nationalism that joined press and state."[15] A cozy, symbiotic relationship has existed with respect to U.S. foreign policy throughout much of the republic's history, and it is inherently corrosive. An independent press must truly be independent in its assessments of U.S. policies.

Unfortunately, the trend appears to be headed in the opposite direction, toward an even more symbiotic relationship between the media and members of the political and policy elites—all of whom seem firmly committed to perpetuating Washington's current, dominant role in world affairs. That development is especially unfortunate. Now more than ever, we need the press to play its role as diligent watchdog. The elites are increasingly out of touch with geostrategic realities around the world, and journalists need to rouse the public to recognize that problem.

Evidence is mounting that the United States will find it increasingly difficult, dangerous, and unrewarding to preserve its status as global hegemon. The rise of capable competing powers, especially China, makes the financial cost alone prohibitive. The multiple risks involved are becoming more daunting and worrisome as well, as Washington's advantages in terms of both economic and military power continue to shrink. The global system is already multipolar economically—in marked contrast to the situation at the end of World War II when the United States established its hegemonic status. At that time, America accounted for nearly half of the world's economic output; now the figure is barely 20 percent. Washington's military dominance has eroded to a lesser extent, but it is not what it was 75—or even 20—years ago. Yet both Democratic and Republican administrations have expanded the country's security obligations and the roster of U.S. security dependents rather than seeking to shrink them. America's strategic overextension is now a worrisome, perilous reality.

Multiple signs of trouble have already emerged. The United States has betrayed many of its professed values, sacrificed thousands of American lives, and expended more than $6 trillion in waging the so-called War on Terror and propping up cooperative factions in the Middle East and Central Asia.[16] Our attempts to quarantine the power of Russia and China have poisoned relations with both of those important powers and driven them to engage in closer bilateral diplomatic, economic, and military cooperation. Efforts to contain Russia and China simultaneously could prove far more costly in terms of blood and treasure than Washington's misadventures in the Middle East, yet there is strong sentiment within the bipartisan political elite for pursuing that ruinous course. The media's knee-jerk endorsement of the current approach risks the American people being blindsided when Washington's fraying hegemonic strategy ultimately fails.

The technological changes that have transformed the news industry over the past three decades provide some hope for a more serious and widespread watchdog role. A handful of legacy publications and a few commercial television networks can no longer act as stifling information gatekeepers. The rise of online publications and the meteoric assent of social media have created a far more diverse media environment. Foreign policy mavericks can now present their perspectives and judgments without having to appeal to the traditional gatekeepers, who for the most part were thoroughly wedded to the policy status quo. Alternative websites and blogs have proliferated, creating a substantial increase in opportunities to air iconoclastic views.

Nevertheless, the internet and social media are not a panacea guaranteeing a greater diversity of perspectives and more vigorous, wide-ranging policy debates. In some ways, the big tech companies that own most of the social media sites have become the new information gate-keepers. The algorithms that firms such as Google utilize have a major impact on what news stories and analyses are featured most prominently. An analysis that is listed in the first few pages of a Google search is much more likely to be seen and cited and have an impact than one that is buried 30 or 40 pages later. Such stakes create a substantial incentive to direct readers and users toward material that the corporate media power-houses favor and away from pieces that challenge or undermine the pre-ferred narratives.[17] Some evidence indicates that on national security and foreign policy issues (as well as others), readers are indeed steered away from iconoclastic articles and studies and toward more standard fare. At a minimum, the rise of the social media giants does not guarantee that experts who dispute the conventional perspective will have equitable access to the arena of public debate. The new information gatekeepers may turn out to be as limiting as the old gatekeepers, thereby helping enshrine the conventional wisdom about world affairs.

Members of the press who seek to foster greater debate also need to repel government efforts to co-opt portions of the press and turn such obliging factions against media dissenters. That problem was evident during earlier decades. The willingness of some journalists to become cogs in the govern-ment's intelligence and national security machinery during the early years of the Cold War should be ample warning of the danger of such cooption. The behavior by much of the press during the McCarthy era in shunning, purg-ing, and blacklisting colleagues that zealous government operatives branded as disloyal to the country was another warning. Congressional hearings and other manifestations of official displeasure served as triggers for chilling debate, but major media players seemed distressingly eager to comply.

Those experiences should be kept in the forefront because the same danger now shows signs of resurging. Key congressional leaders, such as House Speaker Nancy Pelosi and Senate Intelligence Committee chair Mark Warner (D-VA), have proposed congressional inquiries to expose "extremism," "sedition," and "domestic terrorism." The media must stand firm against becoming a tool in a new round of orchestrated repression of First Amendment rights.

Resistance is also imperative to deter the government from targeting individuals who leak classified documents to the press and prosecuting them under the Espionage Act. Often, such documents expose malfeasance or misconduct on the part of government policymakers, and scrutiny should be at the heart of the mission of a free press. Perhaps even more important, journalists need to maintain solidarity with daring and irreverent media mavericks like Julian Assange to scupper the government's bid to decide who is a "legitimate" journalist. That scheme poses a mortal threat to a free press, and members of the media who collaborate with the government in that campaign betray their profession.

The role of effective watchdog requires cultivating a certain attitude, with skepticism its dominant feature. Too often, members of the press have been willing to accept official accounts and policy justifications at face value. Even when a supposedly dire threat to the nation emerges, enterprising journalists must carefully examine and challenge the government's version of events. Can they identify hidden institutional or ideological agendas? Are officials leaving out important details and overall context? In official statements, lying by omission is more common than lying by commission, but the consequences can be equally destructive. Finally, and probably most difficult, journalists need to brace themselves against the tug of patriotism and national identity when they evaluate the nation's foreign policy. Otherwise, they are vulnerable to undue credulity about the decisions and actions of "their" government in what is admittedly a dangerous world. As hard as the task might be, insightful foreign affairs journalists must strive to be dispassionate observers, not salespeople for government policies—or even for their own pet causes.

The American news media have failed at that mission far more often than they've succeeded with respect to national security and foreign policy. In most cases, the press has been a lapdog for factions that want to spur a hyper-activist, and often militarily aggressive, role for the United States in world affairs. Whether a greater portion of the press can finally become the consistent, vigilant watchdog that the republic needs so badly remains to be seen.

ACKNOWLEDGMENTS

I owe a debt of gratitude to a long list of people for helping make *Unreliable Watchdog* possible. Christopher Preble, Cato's former vice president for defense and foreign policy studies, was the person who initially prodded me to write a sequel to my 1995 book, *The Captive Press: Foreign Policy Crises and the First Amendment*. Chris pointed out that while *The Captive Press* had been well received, including winning an award as an "outstanding academic book" from the College Division of the American Library Association, a tremendous number of important developments in both foreign affairs and the news media had taken place since then. I eventually took his advice, and I am extremely glad that I did.

James Knupp, J. E. Allen, and a series of interns they supervised assisted greatly in the research of this book. Not only did they succeed in tracking down sometimes elusive sources, but they alerted me to important additional information. Sometimes the new material reinforced preliminary conclusions and added to their depth, but on other occasions it led to important modifications. Their input significantly enhanced the quality of the eventual manuscript.

Several colleagues were kind enough to offer insightful observations and suggestions regarding the initial book draft. The critiques of Doug Bandow, Ivan Eland, John Mueller, and Kelley Vlahos were especially helpful. My editor, Jason Kuznicki, thoroughly evaluated the manuscript and did not hesitate to challenge some of my assumptions, priorities, and conclusions. He was a rigorous taskmaster, a trait that I did not always relish at the time. But his diligence helped maximize the book's quality. In retrospect, I am extremely grateful to Jason for his tenacity.

Eleanor O'Connor and the other members of Cato's production and marketing staff have done their usual effective job of keeping the book on schedule and making certain that the distribution to reviewers, critics, and the policy community was as thorough as possible. Once again, Jon Meyers has designed an evocative, attention-getting cover. The team from Publications Professionals LLC, especially Karen Coda and Karen Ingebretsen, did a thorough and constructive job with the copyediting process. Any remaining errors of style or substance are entirely my own.

I have been fortunate for more than three decades to enjoy the enthusiastic support of the Cato Institute's top management for my often-iconoclastic analyses. Chairman Robert A. Levy and the board of directors, President and CEO Peter Goettler, Executive Vice President David Boaz, Vice President Ian Vasquez, and Vice President Gene Healy all remained true to that principled tradition with respect to this book project. *Unreliable Watchdog* epitomizes the Cato Institute's continuing determination to criticize U.S. policy whenever warranted and to offer better alternatives.

I want to express special gratitude to three people who have meant so much to my life and career. My wife, Barbara, has not only been my loving companion for decades, but she is both my strongest supporter and most insistent, constructive critic. Without her influence, this book would not likely have come to fruition in such a timely fashion. My two most important intellectual mentors, Professor David F. Healy and Professor Robert A. Divine, both recently passed away after long, distinguished careers. They taught me never to hesitate to question the conventional wisdom (no matter how entrenched) if the evidence indicates that it is faulty. They also stressed to me how essential it is to speak truth to power, despite the inherent risks. I have endeavored to live up to the ideals that both men embodied. *Unreliable Watchdog* is my latest effort to do so, and I have dedicated the book to those two worthy scholars.

NOTES

INTRODUCTION

1. Seth Ackerman and Jim Naureckas, "Following Washington's Script: The United States Media and Kosovo," in *Degraded Capability: The Media and the Kosovo Crisis*, ed. Philip Hammond and Edward S. Herman (London: Pluto Press, 2000), p. 97.

2. Carl Bernstein, "The CIA and the Media," *Rolling Stone*, January 1, 1977.

3. Peter Van Buren, "You Don't Have to Love Assange to Fear His Prosecution," *The American Conservative*, November 30, 2018.

4. Alan MacLeod, "Media Cheer Assange's Arrest," FAIR, April 18, 2019.

5. Henry Kissinger, *White House Years* (Boston: Little, Brown, 1979), p. 21.

6. Kissinger, *White House Years*, p. 21.

7. Kissinger, *White House Years*, p. 21.

8. U.S. Department of State Archive, Secretary of State Madeleine K. Albright, interview by Matt Lauer, *The Today Show*, NBC, February 19, 1998.

9. Katlyn Marie Carter, "What the 1798 Sedition Act Got Right—and What It Means Today," *Washington Post*, January 14, 2021.

CHAPTER 1

1. *Schenk v. United States*, 29 U.S. 47 (1919), p. 52.

2. The Supreme Court's subsequent decisions in *Brandenburg v. State of Ohio* (1969: https://www.law.cornell.edu/supremecourt/text/395/444) and *New York Times Company v. United States* (the Pentagon Papers case: https://www.law.cornell.edu/supremecourt/text/403/713) greatly narrowed the applicability of

the *Schenk* ruling. However, prosecutions under the Espionage Act remain an ever-present threat to those individuals who leak classified documents and journalists who receive and publish those documents or news stories based on them.

3. Ian C. Freeman, "You Furnish the Pictures and I'll Furnish the War," *Words Matter*, January 25, 2010.

4. Christopher Woolf, "Back in the 1890s, Fake News Helped Start a War," *The World*, Public Radio International, December 8, 2016.

5. Stewart Halsey Ross, *Propaganda for War: How the United States Was Conditioned to Fight the Great War of 1914–1918*, 2nd ed. (Joshua Tree, CA: Progressive Press, 2009), p. 2.

6. Ross, *Propaganda for War*, p. 2.

7. Ross, *Propaganda for War*, p. 3.

8. Phillip Knightley, *The First Casualty, from the Crimea to Vietnam: the War Correspondent as Hero, Propagandist, and Myth Maker* (New York: Harcourt, Brace, Jovanovich, 1975), p. 124.

9. Knightley, *First Casualty*, pp. 127–28.

10. Alan Axelrod, *Selling the Great War: The Making of American Propaganda* (New York: St. Martin's Press, 2009), p. 48.

11. Robert C. Hilderbrand, *Power and the People: Executive Management of Public Opinion in Foreign Affairs, 1897–1921* (Chapel Hill: University of North Carolina Press, 1981), p. 147.

12. Frank Cobb, "The Press and Public Opinion," *New Republic*, December 31, 1919, p. 144.

13. Axelrod, *Selling the Great War*, p. xi.

14. Celia Malone Kingsbury, *For Home and Country: World War I Propaganda on the Home Front* (Lincoln: University of Nebraska Press, 2010), pp. 220–26, 240–47; and Ross, *Propaganda for War*, pp. 236–40, 249–53.

15. Kingsbury, *For Home and Country*, pp. 168–217.

16. David M. Kennedy, *Over Here: The First World War and American Society*, 25th anniversary ed. (New York: Oxford University Press, 2004), p. 51.

17. Douglas M. Charles, *J. Edgar Hoover and the Anti-Interventionists: FBI Political Surveillance and the Rise of the Domestic Security State, 1939–1945* (Columbus: The Ohio State University Press, 2017), pp. 39–87.

18. Charles, *J. Edgar Hoover and the Anti-Interventionists*, pp. 40, 71, 78.

19. Ted Galen Carpenter, *The Captive Press: Foreign Policy Crises and the First Amendment* (Washington: Cato Institute, 1995), p. 39; Richard W. Steele, "Franklin D. Roosevelt and His Foreign Policy Critics," *Political Science Quarterly* 94 (Spring 1979): 15–32; and Wayne S. Cole, *Roosevelt and the Isolationists, 1932–1945* (Lincoln: University of Nebraska Press, 1983), pp. 456–87.

20. Susan Dunn, "The Debate behind U.S. Intervention in World War II," *The Atlantic*, July 8, 2013.

21. Theodore F. Koop, *Weapon of Silence* (Chicago: University of Chicago Press, 1946), p. 148.

22. Knightley, *First Casualty*, pp. 280–83.

23. Quoted in Alan M. Winkler, *The Politics of Propaganda: The Office of War Information, 1942–1945* (New Haven, CT: Yale University Press, 1978), p. 27.

24. Knightley, *First Casualty*, pp. 293–94, 323–27.

25. John Hersey, "Print War, Television War," *Wall Street Journal*, December 3, 1991.

26. "The Peoples of the USSR: The Fighting Great Russians Brought Them All Together," *Life*, March 29, 2943, p. 23; and "Red Leaders: They Are Tough, Loyal, Capable Administrators," *Life*, March 29, 1943, p. 40.

27. Juan Gonzalez and Joseph Torres, *News for All the People: The Epic Story of Race and the American Media* (London: Verso Books, 2012), pp. 274–75.

28. "5 Examples of Japanese Propaganda during World War II," *History Hit*, August 10, 2018.

29. Hannah Miles, "WWII Propaganda: The Influence of Racism," *Artifacts Journal*, Issue 6 (March 2012).

30. Rodger, "All Packed Up and Ready to Go," reprinted in *San Francisco News*, March 6, 1942.

31. "Operation Unthinkable," Wikipedia.

32. Dan D. Nimmo, *Newsgathering in Washington* (New York: Atherton, 1964), p. 227.

33. J. Fred MacDonald, *Television and the Red Menace: The Video Road to Vietnam* (New York: Praeger, 1985), pp. 16–17.

34. MacDonald, *Television and the Red Menace*, p. 86.

35. Carl Bernstein, "The CIA and the Media," *Rolling Stone*, October 20, 1977.

CHAPTER 2

1. William M. Hammond, *Reporting Vietnam: Media and Military at War* (Lawrence: University of Kansas Press, 1998), p. ix.

2. "Military Advisors in Vietnam: 1963," John F. Kennedy Presidential Library, https://www.jfklibrary.org/learn/education/teachers/curricular-resources/high-school-curricular-resources/military-advisors-in-vietnam-1963/.

3. Dwight D. Eisenhower, "The Domino Effect," transcript of speech on April 7, 1954, Speech Vault, Educational Video Group, http://www.speeches-usa.com/Transcripts/dwight_eisenhoer-domino.html.

4. Elisabeth Bumiller, "Records Show Doubts on '64 Vietnam Crisis," *New York Times*, July 14, 2010.

5. Murrey Marder and Chalmers M. Roberts, "U.S. Planned before Tonkin for War on North, Files Show," *Washington Post*, June 14, 1971.

6. James Aronson, *The Press and the Cold War* (Indianapolis, IN: Bobbs-Merrill, 1970), p. 219.

7. Colby Itkowitz, "'The Dragon Lady': How Madame Nhu Helped Escalate the Vietnam War," *Washington Post*, September 26, 2017.

8. Joseph Alsop, "The Crusaders," *Washington Post*, September 23, 1963.

9. Peter Grose, "Vietnam Outlook Bleaker a Year after Diem's Fall," *New York Times*, November 2, 1964.

10. Daniel C. Hallin, *The Uncensored War: The Media and Vietnam* (Berkeley: University of California Press, 1989).

11. David Halberstam, *The Making of a Quagmire* (New York: Random House, 1964), p. 319.

12. Halberstam, *Making of a Quagmire*, p. 315. Such an emphatic endorsement of the war is hard to square with Halberstam's statement eight years later in *The Best and the Brightest* that "in the fall of 1963 I came to the conclusion that [the U.S. intervention] was doomed and that we were on the wrong side of history." David Halberstam, *The Best and the Brightest* (Greenwich, CT: Fawcett, 1972), p. 814.

13. For a discussion of the Saigon press corps and its gradual ideological transformation, see William Prochnau, *Once upon a Distant War: David Halberstam, Neil Sheehan, Peter Arnett—Young War Correspondents and Their Early Vietnam Battles* (New York: Vintage, 1996).

14. Quoted in Phillip Knightley, *The First Casualty, from the Crimea to Vietnam: the War Correspondent as Hero, Propagandist, and Myth Maker* (New York: Harcourt, Brace, Jovanovich, 1975), p. 381.

15. William M. Hammond, *Public Affairs: The Military and the Media, 1962–1968*. (Washington: U.S. Army Center of Military History, 1988), p. 181.

16. J. Fred MacDonald, *Television and the Red Menace: The Video Road to Vietnam* (New York: Praeger, 1985), p. 175.

17. Brian Brooks, "Remembering Vietnam and the 'Five O'Clock Follies,'" *Gateway Journalism Review*, November 12, 2019; Bill Lenderking, "The Five O'Clock Follies," *Vietnam Reflections*, December 2013.

18. Orr Kelly, "In a Military Sense, the War Is about Won," *Washington Star*, November 7, 1967.

19. Quoted in Hammond, *Public Affairs*, p. 336.

20. Hallin, *Uncensored War*, pp. 126, 161–62, 170–71.

21. "Misled. In Every Sense," *New Republic*, February 17, 1968.

22. Ted Galen Carpenter, *The Captive Press: Foreign Policy Crises and the First Amendment* (Washington: Cato Institute, 1995), pp. 146–47.

23. Quoted in Joel Achenbach, "Did the News Media, Led by Walter Cronkite, Lose the War in Vietnam?," *Washington Post*, May 25, 2018.

24. "Final Words: Cronkite's Vietnam Commentary," *All Things Considered*, NPR, July 18, 2009.

25. For discussions of the significance of Cronkite's broadcast, see Achenbach, "Did the News Media"; Mark Bowden, "When Walter Cronkite Pronounced the War a 'Stalemate,'" *New York Times*, February 26, 2018; and Kenneth T. Walsh, "50 Years Ago, Walter Cronkite Changed a Nation," *U.S. News & World Report*, February 27, 2018.

26. Seymour M. Hersh, *Cover-Up* (New York: Random House, 1972).

27. "How Reporter Seymour Hersh Uncovered a Massacre and Changed the Vietnam War Dialogue," CBC Radio, June 14, 2018. Hersh later expanded his analysis into a book-length treatment. See Seymour M. Hersh, *My Lai 4: A Report on the Massacre and Its Aftermath* (New York: Random House, 1970).

28. Hammond, *Reporting Vietnam*, p. 191.

29. Christian G. Appy, *American Reckoning: The Vietnam War and Our National Identity* (New York: Penguin Books, 2015), p. 54.

30. Quoted in Aronson, *The Press and the Cold War*, p. 244.

31. Bill Monroe, "Rusk to John Scali: Whose Side Are You On?," *Washington Journalism Review* (January-February 1991), p. 8.

32. William Beecher, "Raids in Cambodia Go Unprotested," *New York Times*, May 9, 1969.

33. Carpenter, *Captive Press*, pp. 149–50.

34. Appy, *American Reckoning*.

35. Cited in Phillip Knightley, *The First Casualty: The War Correspondent as Hero and Myth-Maker from the Crimea to Iraq* (Baltimore, MD: Johns Hopkins University Press, 2004), p. 410–11.

36. John E. Mueller, "Trends in Popular Support for the Wars in Korea and Vietnam," *American Political Science Review* 64 (March 1971): 18–34.

37. Quoted in Phillip Knightley, *The First Casualty: The War Correspondent as Hero and Myth-Maker from the Crimea to Iraq* (Baltimore, MD: Johns Hopkins University Press, 2004), p. 451.

38. Bill Katovsky, "Introduction," in *Embedded: The Media at War in Iraq, an Oral History*, ed. Bill Katovsky and Timothy Carlson (Guilford, CT: Lyons Books, 2003), p. xii.

39. Lyndon B. Johnson, *Vantage Point: Perspectives of the Presidency, 1963–1969* (New York: Holt, Rinehart and Winston, 1971), p. 384.

40. David Shribman, "Q.&A.: Gen. Maxwell D. Taylor; 'There Are Plenty of Dark Clouds ahead of Us,'" *New York Times*, January 4, 1984.

41. Shribman, "Q.&A.: Gen. Maxwell D. Taylor."

42. Quoted in Katovsky and Carlson, *Embedded*, p. xi.

43. George Shultz, "Address by Secretary Shultz before the Commonwealth Club of California in San Francisco on February 22, 1985," *Department of State Bulletin* 85, no. 2097 (April 1985): 16–21, https://archive.org/stream/departmentofstatb1985unit/departmentofstatb1985unit_djvu.txt.

44. Shultz, "Address by Secretary Shultz," p. 16.

45. Shultz, "Address by Secretary Shultz," p. 17.

46. Shultz, "Address by Secretary Shultz," p. 20.

47. Jeffrey St. Clair and Alexander Cockburn, "How Jimmy Carter and I Started the Mujahideen," *Counterpunch*, January 15, 1998.

48. Robert Pear, "Arming Afghan Guerrillas: A Huge Effort Led by U.S.," *New York Times*, April 18, 1988.

49. Robert Poole et al., "The Reagan Doctrine: Should It Stay or Should It Go?," *Reason*, June 1987.

50. See, for example, Kathleen Howard-Merriam, "Afghan Women: Unsung Heroines," *Christian Science Monitor*, January 17, 1985.

51. Ronald Reagan, "Remarks at the Annual Dinner of the Conservative Political Action Conference," March 1, 1985, American Presidency Project.

52. Ronald Reagan, *An American Life* (New York: Simon and Schuster, 1990), pp. 300, 484, 485.

53. Reagan, *American Life*, p. 480.

54. Joel Brinkley, "Rights Report on Nicaragua Cites Recent Rebel Atrocities," *New York Times*, March 6, 1985; and Paul J. Komyatte, "Contras Human Rights Record Attacked," *Chicago Tribune*, January 10, 1987.

55. Tim Weiner, *Legacy of Ashes: The History of the CIA* (New York: Doubleday, 2007), p. 383.

56. George F. Will, "Our Central America Myopia," *Newsweek*, August 1, 1983.

57. Piero Gleijeses, *Visions of Freedom: Havana, Washington, Pretoria, and the Struggle for Southern Africa, 1976–1991* (Chapel Hill: University of North Carolina Press, 2013), p. 298.

58. William F. Buckley Jr., "Help Savimbi," *National Review*, February 28, 1986, p. 62.

59. Arnaud de Borchgrave and Roger Fontaine, "Savimbi Cites Guerrillas' Gains, Marxist Losses in Angola," *Washington Times*, May 21, 1984.

60. Gleijeses, *Visions of Freedom*, p. 291. Also see Elaine Windrich, *The Cold War Guerrilla: Jonas Savimbi, the U.S. Media, and the Angolan War* (Westport, CT: Greenwood Press, 1992), pp. 52–53.

61. Norman Podhoretz, "Savimbi's Promise," *Washington Post*, January 29, 1986. Also see Windrich, *Cold War Guerrilla*, p. 52.

62. Podhoretz, "Savimbi's Promise."

63. Peter Worthington, "Angola's Unknown War," *National Review*, November 1, 1985, p. 54.

64. Jonas Savimbi, "Don't Sacrifice Angola on the Altar of Socialism," *Wall Street Journal*, June 2, 1986.

65. "The Week," *National Review*, July 4, 1986.

66. Radek Sikorski, "The Mystique of Savimbi," *National Review*, August 18, 1989, pp. 36–37.

67. "A U.S.-Created Monster in Angola," editorial, *Chicago Tribune*, May 11, 1993.

68. Ted Galen Carpenter, *Gullible Superpower: U.S. Support for Bogus Foreign Democratic Movements* (Washington: Cato Institute, 2019), pp. 43–47.

CHAPTER 3

1. Peter Braestrup, *Battle Lines: Report of the Twentieth Century Fund Task Force on the Military and the Media* (New York: Priority, 1985), p. 3.

2. Edward Cody, "U.S. Forces Thwart Journalists' Reports," *Washington Post*, October 26, 1983.

3. Hugh O'Shaughnessy, *Grenada: An Eyewitness Account of the U.S. Invasion and the Caribbean History That Provoked It* (New York: Dodd, Mead, 1984), p. 205. O'Shaughnessy was a British journalist who was in Grenada at the time of the invasion, covering the coup in which a staunchly left-wing government had been overthrown by an even more radical leftist faction.

4. Quoted in O'Shaughnessy, *Grenada*, pp. 205–6.

5. Kevin A. Smith, "The Media at the Tip of the Spear," *Michigan Law Review* 102, no. 6 (2004): 1329.

6. Malcolm W. Browne, "The Military vs. the Press," *New York Times*, March 3, 1991.

7. "Newsweek Is Dropped from Grenada Visits," *New York Times*, October 30, 1983.

8. Phil Gailey, "U.S. Bars Coverage of Grenada; News Groups Protest," *New York Times*, October 27, 1983; and Jonathan Friendly, "Press Voices Criticism of 'Off-the-Record War,'" *New York Times*, November 4, 1984.

9. Ronald Reagan, *An American Life* (New York: Simon and Schuster, 1990), p. 451.

10. Ted Galen Carpenter, *The Captive Press: Foreign Policy Crises and the First Amendment* (Washington: Cato Institute, 1995), pp. 161–62.

11. William Safire, "Essay; Us against Them," *New York Times*, October 30, 1983.

12. Douglas Brinkley, ed., *The Reagan Diaries* (New York: HarperCollins, 2007), p. 192.

13. "*Times* Poll: Bare Majority Backs Grenada News Curbs," *Los Angeles Times*, November 20, 1983.

14. Thomas Griffin, "Truce with the Pentagon," *Time*, February 27, 1984.

15. Rodger, "All Packed Up and Ready to Go," reprinted in *San Francisco News*, March 6, 1942.

16. Jonathan Friendly, "Reporting the News in a Communique War," *New York Times*, October 26, 1983.

17. Reagan, *An American Life*, p. 456.

18. Kendall Breitman, "Poll: Half of Republicans Still Believe WMDs Found in Iraq," *Politico*, January 7, 2015.

19. Chris Kahn, "Despite Report Findings, Almost Half of Americans Think Trump Colluded with Russia: Reuters/Ipsos Poll," Reuters, March 26, 2019.

20. Scott Rasmussen, "Nearly Half of Voters Still Believe Discredited Trump-Russia Collusion Conspiracy Theory," *Just the Polls*, October 15, 2020.

21. Quoted in Mark Hertsgaard, *On Bended Knee: The Press and the Reagan Presidency* (New York: Schocken Books, 1988), p. 233.

22. "The Battle for Grenada," *Newsweek*, November 7, 1983.

23. O'Shaughnessy, *Grenada*, pp. 214–15.

24. *Public Papers of the Presidents of the United States: Ronald Reagan, 1983*, Book 2 (Washington: Government Printing Office, 1985), p. 1731.

25. Christopher Paul and James J. Kim, *Reporters on the Battlefield: The Embedded Press System in Historical Context* (Santa Monica, CA: Rand Corporation, 2004).

26. Bill Katovsky, "Introduction," in *Embedded: The Media at War in Iraq, an Oral History*, ed. Bill Katovsky and Timothy Carlson (Guilford, CT: Lyons Books, 2003), p. xii.

27. "Why the Invasion Was Justified," editorial, *New York Times*, December 21, 1989.

28. Mark Cook and Jeff Cohen, "How Television Sold the Panama Invasion," *Extra!*, January-February 1990.

29. Cook and Cohen, "How Television Sold the Panama Invasion."

30. Cook and Cohen, "How Television Sold the Panama Invasion."

31. For a contemporary analysis, see David R. Henderson, "Do We Need to Go to War for Oil?," Cato Institute Foreign Policy Briefing no. 4, October 24, 1990. Subsequent scholarship significantly strengthened the argument. See Eugene Gholz and Daryl G. Press, "Energy Alarmism: The Myths That Make Americans Worry about Oil," Cato Institute Policy Analysis no. 589, April 5, 2007, especially pp. 11–16; Morris A. Adelman, "The Real Oil Problem," *Regulation* (Spring 2004): 16–21; Jerry Taylor and Peter Van Doren, "An Oil Embargo Won't Work," *Wall Street Journal*, October 10, 2002; and Jerry Taylor and Peter Van Doren, "Driving Bin Laden?," *National Review Online*, March 6, 2006.

32. The administration could have made the valid point that Iraq's take-over extinguished another country (and a fellow UN member at that) as an independent entity—it didn't merely amputate territory—but that point never became a significant line of argument.

33. Stephen Budiansky, "A Messy, Dangerous World," *U.S. News & World Report*, August 13, 1990.

34. John J. Mearsheimer, "A War the United States Can Win—Decisively," *Chicago Tribune*, January 15, 1991.

35. Tom Marks, "Iraq's Not-So-Tough Army," *Wall Street Journal*, August 21, 1990.

36. Carpenter, *Captive Press*, pp. 190–91.

37. Marie Gottschalk, "Operation Desert Cloud: The Media and the Gulf War," *World Policy Journal* (Summer 1992): 460.

38. Vincent Carroll, "The Scarcity of Anti-War Editorial Voices, *Washington Journalism Review*, January-February 1991, p. 14.

39. Gene Ruffini, "Press Fails to Challenge Rush to War," *Washington Journalism Review*, March 1991, p. 21.

40. Mark Hertsgaard, "Following Washington's Lead," *Deadline* 6 (January-February 1991): 4; quoted in Ted Galen Carpenter, *The Captive Press: Foreign Policy Crises and the First Amendment* (Washington: Cato Institute, 1995), p. 189.

41. Reuters, "War in the Gulf: Bush Statement, Excerpts from 2 Statements by Bush on Iraq's Proposal for Ending Conflict," *New York Times*, February 16, 1991.

42. Mark Crispin Miller, "Showdown in Gulf Imagery," *Deadline* 6 (January-February 1991): 9; quoted in Ted Galen Carpenter, *The Captive Press: Foreign Policy Crises and the First Amendment* (Washington: Cato Institute, 1995), p. 190.

43. John R. MacArthur, *Second Front: Censorship and Propaganda in the Gulf War* (New York: Hill and Wang, 1992), p. 67.

44. Jackie Rothenberg, "Human Rights Group Disputes Reports of Iraqi Atrocities in Kuwait," Associated Press, February 6, 1992; and John R. MacArthur, "Remember Nayirah, Witness for Kuwait?," *New York Times*, January 6, 1992.

45. "Deception on Capitol Hill," editorial, *New York Times*, January 15, 1992.

46. Amy Goodman and Juan Gonzalez, "How False Testimony and a Massive U.S. Propaganda Machine Bolstered George H. W. Bush's War in Iraq," *Democracy Now*, December 5, 2018.

47. Phillip Knightley, *The First Casualty, from the Crimea to Vietnam: the War Correspondent as Hero, Propagandist, and Myth Maker* (New York: Harcourt Brace, Jovanovich, 1975), p. 217.

48. Katovsky, "Introduction," in *Embedded*, p. xii.

49. Guy Shields, "Media Gatekeeper and Troubleshooter," in *Embedded: The Media at War in Iraq, an Oral History*, ed. Bill Katovsky and Timothy Carlson (Guilford, CT: Lyons Books, 2003), p. 74.

50. Gottschalk, "Operation Desert Cloud," p. 451.

51. John Mueller, *Policy and Public Opinion in the Gulf War* (Chicago: University of Chicago Press, 1994), pp. 64–72, 115–23.

52. James Gerstenzang and Art Pine, "Bush Sending Troops to Help Somalia's Hungry Millions," *Los Angeles Times*, December 5, 1992.

53. Michael R. Gordon with Thomas L. Friedman, "Details of U.S. Raid in Mogadishu: Success So Near, a Loss So Deep," *New York Times*, October 25, 1993.

54. Richard Falk, "Hard Choices and Tragic Dilemmas," *Nation*, December 20, 1993, p. 761.

55. Carpenter, *Captive Press*, pp. 225–27.

CHAPTER 4

1. For a discussion of the George H. W. Bush administration's initial assessment of these developments and Washington's policy responses, see James A. Baker III with Thomas M. DeFrank, *The Politics of Diplomacy: Revolution, War & Peace, 1989–1992* (New York: G. P. Putnam's Sons, 1995), pp. 634–51.

2. Andy Wilcoxson, "The Exoneration of Milosevic: The ICTY's Surprise Ruling," *Counterpunch*, August 1, 2016.

3. Laura Silber, interview by Peter Brock, February 15, 1993. See Peter Brock, *Media Cleansing: Dirty Reporting—Journalism and Tragedy in Yugoslavia* (Los Angeles: GM Books, 2005), p. 181.

4. Mick Hume, "Nazifying the Serbs: From Bosnia to Kosovo," in *Degraded Capability: The Media and the Kosovo Crisis*, ed. Phillip Hammond and Edward S. Herman (London: Pluto Press, 2000), p. 76.

5. Hume, "Nazifying the Serbs," p. 76.

6. Reuters, "UN Accuses All Sides of Rape," *Washington Post*, January 30, 1993.

7. Peter Brock, "Dateline Yugoslavia: The Partisan Press," *Foreign Policy* 93 (Winter 1993–94): 153–54.

8. Charles Lane, "Brock Crock," *New Republic*, September 5, 1994. Reprinted in http://balkanwitness.glypx.com/brock.htm.

9. Brock, *Media Cleansing*, pp. 246–47.

10. Samantha Power, *The Education of an Idealist: A Memoir* (New York: Dey Street, 2019), p. 65.

11. Power, *Education of an Idealist*, p. 83.

12. Seth Ackerman and Jim Naureckas, "Following Washington's Script: The United States Media and Kosovo," in *Degraded Capability: The Media and the Kosovo Crisis*, ed. Philip Hammond and Edward S. Herman (London: Pluto Press, 2000), p. 99.

13. Power, *Education of an Idealist*, pp. 85–86.

14. Power, *Education of an Idealist*, p. 86.

15. Power, *Education of an Idealist*, p. 95.

16. Power, *Education of an Idealist*, pp. 114, 115.

17. Power, *Education of an Idealist*, pp. 95–96. Emphasis added.

18. See, for example, Power, *Education of an Idealist*, pp. 92, 93, 97, 102. Her accounts are replete with such terms as "Bosnian forces," "Bosnian territory," Bosnian victims," and "my Bosnian friends," when she actually means Bosnian Muslims.

19. "U.S. Media Promotes Biased Coverage of Bosnia," *Project Censored*, April 30, 2010.

20. Charles G. Boyd, "Making Peace with the Guilty: The Truth about Bosnia," *Foreign Affairs* 74, no. 5 (September-October 1995): 22.

21. Brock, *Media Cleansing*, p. 189.

22. Stephen Kinzer, "Where There's War There's Amanpour," *New York Times Magazine*, October 9, 1994.

23. John Kifner, "66 Die as Shell Wrecks Sarajevo Market," *New York Times*, February 6, 1994; Tony Smith, "Shelling of Sarajevo Market Kills 66; More than 200 Wounded," *Washington Post*, February 6, 1994.

24. Brock, *Media Cleansing*, pp. 180–81.

25. "Washington Whispers," *U.S. News & World Report*, March 7, 1994.

26. David Binder, "Anatomy of a Massacre," *Foreign Policy* 97 (Winter 1994–95): 70–78.

27. Radosa Milutinovic, "Former UN Observer Says Markale Market Bombing Caused by Bosnian Army Shelling," Justice Report, September 15, 2015.

28. Roger Cohen, "Shelling Kills Dozens in Sarajevo; U.S. Urges NATO to Strike Serbs," *New York Times*, August 29, 1995.

29. Julian Borger, "Bosnia's Bitter, Flawed Peace Deal, 20 Years On," *The Guardian*, November 10, 2015; Andrew Higgins, "In Bosnia, Entrenched Ethnic Divisions Are a Warning to the World," *New York Times*, November 19, 2018; and Heather A. Conley and Matthew Melino, "Blinking Red Lights: A Resurgence of Ethno-Nationalism and Its Implications for the Future Integrity of Bosnia-Herzegovina," Center for Strategic and International Studies Brief, August 15, 2019.

30. "Bosnia Gets Government after 14-Month Impasse, *Deutsche Welle*, December 23, 2019.

31. "Progress in Bosnia and Herzegovina Hampered by Political Standstill, Corruption, High Representative Tells Security Council," United Nations press release, May 6, 2020.

32. Reuters, "Secessionist Leader Says Serbs Will Undo Bosnia State Institutions," *U.S. News & World Report*, October 14, 2021.

33. Anonymous, Letter to the Editor, *Foreign Policy* 94 (Spring 1994): 162.

34. Anonymous, Letter to the Editor.

35. David Binder, "Foreword," in Peter Brock, *Media Cleansing: Dirty Reporting—Journalism and Tragedy in Yugoslavia* (Los Angeles: GM Books, 2005), p. iii.

36. Binder, "Foreword," p. v.

37. Brock, *Media Cleansing*, p. 76.

38. George Kenney, "The Bosnian Calculation," *New York Times Magazine*, April 23, 1995.

39. "Bosnian War Dead Figure Announced," BBC News, June 21, 2007.

40. Daria Sito Sucic and Matt Robinson, "After Years of Toil, Book Names Bosnian War Dead," Reuters, February 15, 2013.

41. Ted Galen Carpenter, *The Captive Press: Foreign Policy Crises and the First Amendment* (Washington: Cato Institute, 1995), pp. 234–36.

42. Gary Dempsey, "Kosovo Crossfire," *Mediterranean Quarterly* 9, no. 3 (Summer 1998): 96–99.

43. For a discussion of the various causes of the demographic shift in Kosovo's population, see David N. Gibbs, *First Do No Harm: Humanitarian Intervention and the Destruction of Yugoslavia* (Nashville, TN: Vanderbilt University Press, 2009), pp. 175–78.

44. Rajan Menon, *The Conceit of Humanitarian Intervention* (New York: Oxford University Press, 2016), p. 131.

45. For a detailed discussion, see Ted Galen Carpenter, "Cynical Myths and U.S. Military Crusades in the Balkans," *Mediterranean Quarterly* 22, no. 3 (Summer 2011): 10–25.

46. James George Jatras, "NATO's Myths and Bogus Justifications for Intervention," in *NATO's Empty Victory: A Postmortem on the Balkan War*, ed. Ted Galen Carpenter (Washington: Cato Institute, 2000), p. 21.

47. Jatras, "NATO's Myths and Bogus Justifications for Intervention," p. 22.

48. Ackerman and Naureckas, "Following Washington's Script," p. 98.

49. David Binder, "War of Terror by Albanians in Yugoslavia Strains Unity," *New York Times*, November 28, 1982; and David Binder, "Yugoslavs Seek to Quell Strife in Region of Ethnic Albanians," *New York Times*, November 9, 1982.

50. David Binder, "In Yugoslavia, Rising Ethnic Strife Brings Fears of Worse Civil Conflict," *New York Times*, November 1, 1987.

51. Ackerman and Naureckas, "Following Washington's Script," p. 100.

52. Thomas L. Friedman, "Foreign Affairs; More Sticks," *New York Times*, April 6, 1999.

53. Thomas L. Friedman, "Foreign Affairs; Stop the Music," *New York Times*, April 23, 1999.

54. Ackerman and Naureckas, "Following Washington's Script," p. 107.

55. Blaine Harden, "The World: Culture War; What It Would Take to Cleanse Serbia," *New York Times*, May 9, 1999.

56. Hume, "Nazifying the Serbs," pp. 70–71.

57. Hume, "Nazifying the Serbs," p. 72.

58. Carl Cannon, "Turning Point for the President: The Holocaust," *Baltimore Sun*, May 9, 1993. Also see Power, *Education of an Idealist*, p. 55.

59. For a fairly early example of that treatment, see Matt Marshall and Norman Kempster, "'Never Again,' but How to Stop Atrocities? Balkans: Bosnia Bloodletting Brings Back Ugly Memories for Holocaust Survivors. Groping for a Solution, They Say World Must Act," *Los Angeles Times*, January 3, 1993.

60. Steve Coll, "In the Shadow of the Holocaust," *Washington Post Magazine*, September 25, 1994.

61. Brock, *Media Cleansing*, p. 249.

62. Christiane Amanpour, "The Srebrenica Genocide Was a Defining Moment," CNN, October 18, 2019 (first published September 2015, updated in 2019).

63. Hume "Nazifying the Serbs," pp. 72, 73.

64. David Chandler, *From Kosovo to Kabul: Human Rights and International Intervention* (London: Pluto Press, 2002), p. 73.

65. Examples include Frank Csongos, "Yugoslavia: U.S. Defense Secretary Says 100,000 Kosovar Men Missing," Radio Free Europe/Radio Liberty, May 9, 1999; Tim Doggett, "Cohen Fears 100,000 Kosovo Men Killed by Serbs," *Washington Post*, May 16, 1999; and Steven Pearlstein, "NATO Resumes Kosovo Bombing," *Washington Post*, May 17, 1999. Similar credulity was evident among journalists elsewhere in the West. See Phil Davison, "War in the Balkans: '100,000 Albanian Men Are Missing,'" *Independent* (UK), May 16, 1999; and "Thousands of Kosovo men have vanished: Cohen," *CBC News*, May 16, 1999.

66. House of Commons Foreign Affairs Committee, *Foreign Affairs—Fourth Report*, Session 1999–2000, United Kingdom, May 23, 2000.

67. Quoted in George Kenney, "Kosovo: On Means and Ends," *Nation*, December 27, 1999.

68. Quoted in Gibbs, *First Do No Harm*, p. 181.

69. Benjamin Schwarz and Christopher Layne, "The Case against Intervention in Kosovo," *Nation*, April 19, 1999.

70. Ivo Daalder and Michael O'Hanlon, *Winning Ugly: NATO's War to Save Kosovo* (Washington: Brookings Institution, 2000), p. 12.

71. Hume, "Nazifying the Serbs," p. 78.

72. FAIR, "Slanted Sources in NewsHour and Nightline Kosovo Coverage," May 5, 1999.

73. Edward S. Herman and David Peterson, "CNN: Selling NATO's War Globally," in *Degraded Capability: The Media and the Kosovo Crisis*, ed. Philip Hammond and Edward S. Herman (London: Pluto Press, 2000), pp. 114–15.

74. Quoted in Herman and Peterson, "CNN: Selling NATO's War Globally," p. 113.

75. Quoted in Herman and Peterson, "CNN: Selling NATO's War Globally," p. 114.

76. Quoted in Herman and Peterson, "CNN: Selling NATO's War Globally," p. 113.

77. Daniel Williams, "Serbia Yields to NATO Terms," *Washington Post*, June 4, 1999.

78. William M. Arkin, "The Crisis in Kosovo," *Civilian Deaths in the NATO Air Campaign*, Human Rights Watch, February 2000, vol. 12, no. 1 (D).

79. Quoted in Chandler, *From Kosovo to Kabul*, p. 185.

80. James Rupert, "Croatia Accused of Ethnic Cleansing," *Washington Post*, August 9, 1995. Over the following months, the Croatian government resettled ethnic Croats who had been driven out of Bosnia or other regions in homes that were seized from Krajina Serbs. Chris Hedges, "Croatia Resettling Its People in Houses Seized from Serbs," *New York Times*, May 14, 1997.

81. Sarah Helm, "Riddle of Serb Exodus from Krajina," *Independent* (UK), August 27, 1995.

82. For an article making those arguments and epitomizing the "Serbs brought this on themselves" tone, see Roger Cohen, "A Dream in Retreat—A Special Report; Serbs of 'Greater Serbia' Find Suffering and Decay," *New York Times*, September 17, 1995.

83. Charles Krauthammer, "Ethnic Cleansing That's Convenient," *Washington Post*, August 11, 1995.

84. Ted Galen Carpenter, "Kosovo and Macedonia: The West Enhances the Threat," *Mediterranean Quarterly* 13, no. 1 (Winter 2002): 23–25.

85. Morgan Meaker, "Roma in Kosovo: The Justice That Never Came," Al Jazeera, January 26, 2017.

86. Nicholas Wood and David Binder, "Treasured Churches in a Cycle of Revenge," *New York Times*, April 3, 2004.

87. Ted Galen Carpenter, *Gullible Superpower: U.S. Support for Bogus Foreign Democratic Movements* (Washington: Cato Institute, 2019), pp. 86–87.

88. Dick Marty, Rapporteur, *Inhuman Treatment of People and Illicit Trafficking of Human Organs in Kosovo*, Committee on Legal Affairs and Human Rights Report Doc. 12462, Parliamentary Assembly, Council of Europe, January 7, 2011. Also see Ted Galen Carpenter, "Empowering the Body Snatchers: Washington's Appalling Kosovo Policy," *National Interest Online*, December 30, 2010.

89. Zenel Zhinipotoku and Llazar Semini, "Kosovo President, 9 Others Indicted on War Crimes Charges," Associated Press, June 24, 2020.

90. Andrew Gray, "Kosovan President's War Crimes Indictment Puts West in a Bind," *Politico*, June 25, 2020; Keida Kostreci, "After Kosovo President War Crimes Indictment, Kosovo-Serbia Dialogue Uncertain," *Voice of America*, June 26, 2020.

91. Nicholas Burns and Frank Wisner, "A Planned Kosovo-Serbia Meeting at the White House Is Falling Apart. It Was Always a Bad Idea," *Washington Post*, June 24, 2020; Edward P. Joseph, "Anatomy of a Kosovo Summit Catastrophe," *Foreign Policy*, June 24, 2020.

92. Edward S. Herman and Emily Schwartz Greco, "Serb Demonization as Propaganda Coup," Institute for Policy Studies, March 19, 2009.

93. Howard Kurtz, "USA Today Calls Work of Star Reporter Fake," *Washington Post*, March 20, 2004.

94. Brock, *Media Cleansing*, p. 266.

95. Brock, *Media Cleansing*, p. 267.

96. Brock, *Media Cleansing*, p. 267.

CHAPTER 5

1. Authorization for Use of Military Force, Pub. L. 107-40, 115 Stat. 224 (2001), https://www.congress.gov/107/plaws/publ40/PLAW-107publ40.pdf.

2. Barbara Lee, "Why I Opposed the Resolution to Authorize Force," *San Francisco Chronicle*, September 23, 2001.

3. Fiona Harrigan, "Repealing the 2002 AUMF Won't Be Enough to End Forever Wars," *Reason*, June 16, 2021.

4. John Fund, "Who Is Barbara Lee?," *Wall Street Journal*, September 17, 2001.

5. "Who Is Barbara Lee?," editorial, *Washington Times*, September 18, 2001.

6. Robin Toner and Neil A. Lewis, "A Nation Challenged: Congress; House Passes Terrorism Bill Much Like Senate's, but with 5-Year Limit," *New York Times*, October 18, 2001.

7. Robert A. Levy, "The Patriot Act: We Deserve Better," *Liberty*, October 2001 (reprinted as a Cato Commentary, November 1, 2001).

8. Frank Davies, "Patriot Act Is Criticized by Rights Supporters," *Daily Press*, September 8, 2002.

9. Davies, "Patriot Act Is Criticized by Rights Supporters."

10. David Frum and Richard Perle, *An End to Evil: How to Win the War on Terror* (New York: Random House, 2003).

11. Quoted in James Bovard, "Global Undemocratic Revolution," *The American Conservative*, July 1, 2010.

12. David Frum, "Unpatriotic Conservatives," *National Review*, March 25, 2003.

13. Stephen F. Hayes, "Saddam Hussein's American Apologist," *Washington Examiner*, November 19, 2001.

14. Scott Horton, *Enough Already: Time to End the War on Terrorism* (Austin, TX: Libertarian Institute, 2021), pp. 79–71.

15. Patrick E. Tyler and John Tagliabue, "Czechs Confirm Iraqi Agent Met with Terror Ringleader," *New York Times*, October 27, 2001.

16. Judith Miller, *The Story: A Reporter's Journey* (New York: Simon and Schuster, 2015), p. 154.

17. Muhammad Idrees Ahmad, *The Road to Iraq: The Making of a Neoconservative War* (Edinburgh: Edinburgh University Press, 2014), p. 111.

18. David Rose, "Inside Saddam's Terror Regime," *Vanity Fair*, February 1, 2002.

19. Ahmad, *Road to Iraq*, pp. 111–12.

20. Jeffrey Goldberg, "The Great Terror," *New Yorker*, March 25, 2002.

21. Goldberg, "The Great Terror."

22. Aram Roston, *The Man Who Pushed America to War: The Extraordinary Life, Adventures, and Obsessions of Ahmad Chalabi* (New York: Nation Books, 2008), pp. 194–97.

23. Judith Miller, "A Nation Challenged: Secret Sites; Iraqi Talks of Renovations for Chemical and Nuclear Arms," *New York Times*, December 20, 2001.

24. Roston, *Man Who Pushed America to War*, p. 196.

25. James Bamford, "The Man Who Sold the War: Meet John Rendon, Bush's General in the Propaganda War," *Rolling Stone*, November 17, 2005.

26. William Kristol and Robert Kagan, "What to Do about Iraq," *Washington Examiner*, January 21, 2002.

27. Wolf Blitzer, "Search for a Smoking Gun," CNN, January 10, 2003.

28. Bamford, "The Man Who Sold the War." Miller's close personal relationship with Chalabi went back to at the early 1990s. Ahmad, *Road to Iraq*, p. 147.

29. Bamford, "The Man Who Sold the War."

30. Judith Miller, "The Iraq War and Stubborn Myths: Officials Didn't Lie, and I Wasn't Fed a Line," *Wall Street Journal*, April 3, 2015.

31. Veteran Intelligence Professionals for Sanity [Scott Ritter et al.], "Judith Miller's Blame-Shifting Memoir," *Consortium News*, April 7, 2015.

32. Miller, *The Story*, p. xiii.

33. Bob Drogin and John Goetz, "How U.S. Fell under the Spell of 'Curveball,'" *Los Angeles Times*, November 20, 2005. Also see Roston, *Man Who Pushed America to War*; and Ahmad, *Road to Iraq*.

34. Polls replicated in Darren K. Carlson, "Public Convinced Saddam Is a Terrorist," Gallup, March 25, 2003.

35. For an overall assessment of the media's performance during the period leading up to the Iraq War by a prominent establishment figure who reluctantly reaches some rather negative conclusions, see Leslie H. Gelb with Jeanne-Palma Zelmati, "Mission Not Accomplished," *Democracy* 13 (Summer 2009).

36. Walter Pincus and Dana Priest, "Some Iraq Analysts Felt Pressure from Cheney Visits," *Washington Post*, June 5, 2003.

37. "Bush: Saddam Hussein Must Go," CNN, April 6, 2002.

38. Tribune Media Services, "Free Iraq, World from Saddam Hussein," *Greensboro News-Record*, December 10, 2002.

39. David McCormick, "Growing Consensus Is That Saddam Must Go," *Los Angeles Times*, March 2, 2002 (Reprinted in *Deseret News*, March 2, 2002).

40. For a prominent example of that argument from a leading political figure, see Sen. Edward M. Kennedy, "Speech against the Invasion of Iraq," Johns Hopkins University, School of Advanced International Studies, September 27, 2002. Press coverage of the speech was respectful but not overtly favorable. See "Kennedy Counters Bush on Iraq," CNN, September 27, 2002.

41. Colin Powell, "A Policy of Evasion and Deception" (text of U.S. Secretary of State's speech to the United Nations on Iraq), *Washington Post*, February 5, 2003.

42. "Reactions to Powell's Speech at the UN," Democracy in Action: P2004 (website), February 5, 2003.

43. "Rice: Powell Made a 'Compelling' Case," CNN, February 5, 2003.

44. For examples, see "Colin Powell's Compelling Case," *Chicago Tribune*, editorial, February 6, 2003; Philip Gailey, "Arm of Restraint Makes a Compelling Case on Iraq," *St. Petersburg Times*, February 9, 2003; and Michael Tackett, "Persuasive Speech Will Sway Skeptics," *Orlando Sentinel*, February 6, 2003. For a rare dissenting view, see Katrina vanden Heuvel, "Powell Fails to Make Case," *Nation*, February 6, 2003.

45. Quoted in Michael Tackett, "Powell's Credibility Attracts Skeptics," *South Florida Sun-Sentinel*, February 6, 2003.

46. Max Boot, "The Case for American Empire," *Washington Examiner*, October 15, 2001.

47. Pew Research Center, "60% War's Going Very Well—69% We Haven't Won Yet," April 10, 2003.

48. For a very early warning about the danger of ignoring such problems, see Ted Galen Carpenter, "Oust Saddam—And Replace Him with Whom or What?," *Christian Science Monitor*, February 8, 1999.

49. John B. Judis, "Eve of Destruction: What It Was Like to Oppose the Iraq War in 2003," *New Republic*, March 17, 2013.

50. "War with Iraq Is Not in the National Interest," *New York Times*, September 26, 2002.

51. Gelb and Zelmati, "Mission Not Accomplished."

52. The principal foreign policy journals were nearly as bad as the leading news outlets in providing such opportunities. For one of the few exceptions, see John J. Mearsheimer and Stephen Walt, "An Unnecessary War," *Foreign Policy* 134 (January–February 2003): 50–59.

53. Ted Galen Carpenter, "Back Off Tough Iraq Policy," *USA Today*, December 9, 2002.

54. Ted Galen Carpenter, "Overthrow Saddam? Be Careful What You Wish For," United Press International, January 15, 2002; Ted Galen Carpenter, "Faulty Justifications for War with Iraq," *Orange County Register*, February 2, 2003; John Mueller, "What's the Rush?," *Reason*, October 22, 2002; and John Mueller, "Deterring the Egomaniac du Jour," *Reason*, November 1, 2002. For an exceedingly rare anti–Iraq War article in a hawkish, conservative publication, see Doug Bandow, "Don't Start the Second Gulf War," *National Review Online*, August 12, 2002.

55. "In Iraq Crisis, Networks Are Megaphones for Official Views," FAIR, March 18, 2003.

56. "Covering Iraq: American Media vs. the World?," MIT Communications Forum, November 13, 2003.

57. Seth Ashley, "Making the Case for War: A Comparative Analysis of CNN and BBC Coverage of Colin Powell's Presentation to the United Nations Security Council," *Media, War, and Conflict*, July 7, 2014, https://doi.org/10.1177/1750635214541031.

58. "Mission Accomplished: A Look Back at the Media's Fawning Coverage of Bush's Premature Declaration of Victory in Iraq," *Media Matters*, April 27, 2006.

59. "Commander in Chief Lands on USS Lincoln," CNN, May 2, 2003.

60. Gelb and Zelmati, "Mission Not Accomplished."

61. Bill Katovsky, "Introduction," in *Embedded: The Media at War in Iraq, an Oral History*, ed. Bill Katovsky and Timothy Carlson (Guilford, CT: Lyons Books, 2003), pp. xi, xiii.

62. Katovsky, "Introduction," in *Embedded*, pp. xiv–xvi.

63. Katovsky, "Introduction," in *Embedded*, p. xvi.

64. Katovsky, "Introduction," in *Embedded*, p. xix.

65. Peter Maass, "The Toppling: How the Media Inflated the Fall of Saddam's Statue in Firdos Square," *ProPublica*, January 3, 2011.

66. "The Short, Happy War of Howard Kurtz," FAIR, March 20, 2009.

67. Jim Lobe, "Credibility Gap over Iraq WMD Looms Larger," Institute for Policy Studies, June 3, 2003.

68. Judis, "Eve of Destruction."

69. Kenneth M. Pollack, "Spies, Lies, and Weapons: What Went Wrong," *The Atlantic*, January–February 2004.

70. "The Failure to Find Iraqi Weapons," editorial, *New York Times*, September 26, 2003.

71. Pollack, "Spies, Lies, and Weapons."

72. Steven Snyder, "Bush Lied to Me, and I'm Mad as Hell," *Minnesota Daily*, July 21, 2004.

73. Julian Borger, "There Were No Weapons of Mass Destruction in Iraq," *The Guardian*, October 7, 2004.

74. Quoted in Arnaud De Borchgrave, "Commentary: 'Heroes in Error'—Chalabi," United Press International, February 19, 2004.

75. "CIA's Final Report: No WMD Found in Iraq," Associated Press, April 25, 2005.

76. Bryan Burrough, Evgenia Peretz, David Rose, and David Wise, "The Path to War," *Vanity Fair*, May 2004.

77. Seymour M. Hersh, "Torture at Abu Ghraib," *New Yorker*, April 30, 2004.

78. James Bovard, "Why I Write," *Mises Wire*, August 11, 2020.

79. Dexter Filkins, "Defying Threats, Millions of Iraqis Flock to Polls," *New York Times*, January 31, 2005.

80. "NBC News Determines That It Will Call Iraqi Conflict a 'Civil War,'" Associated Press, November 27, 2006.

81. David Folkenflik, "NBC Is Latest to Deem Iraq to Be in Civil War," NPR, November 27, 2006.

82. David Glasner, "The Success of the Surge," *Small Wars Journal*, December 25, 2007.

83. Omar Fadhil, "The Surge Is Working," *Wall Street Journal*, July 13, 2007.

84. Max Boot, "The Surge Is Working," *Los Angeles Times*, September 8, 2007.

85. Tim Grieve, "The Surge Is Working! The Surge Is Working!" *Salon*, September 30, 2007. Also see "The Surge Isn't Working: Pulse on Iraq," Center for American Progress, February 4, 2008.

86. Sam Dagher, "Will 'Armloads' of U.S. Cash Buy Tribal Loyalty?," *Christian Science Monitor*, November 8, 2007. Also see Paul Sperry, "A Surge in Bribes," Antiwar.com, September 16, 2007.

87. "Obama: U.S. to Withdraw Most Iraq Troops by August 2010," CNN, February 27, 2009.

88. Ted Galen Carpenter, "Conservative Hawks Are Incoherent Regarding Iraq Troop Withdrawal," *Cato at Liberty*, November 2, 2011.

89. Jennifer Rubin, "Obama: A Dishonest Withdrawal from Iraq," *Washington Post*, October 23, 2011.

90. Max Boot, "Obama's Tragic Withdrawal," *Wall Street Journal*, October 31, 2011.

91. "Iraq Withdrawal, a Gift to Iran," editorial, *National Review*, October 24, 2011.

92. William J. Bennett, "Obama Risks Iraq for Political Expediency," CNN, October 26, 2011.

93. "From the Editors; The Times and Iraq," editorial, *New York Times*, May 26, 2004.

94. Gary Younge, "Washington Post Apologises for Underplaying WMD Skepticism," *The Guardian*, August 12, 2004; and Jacques Steinberg, "Washington Post Rethinks Its Coverage of War Debate," *New York Times*, August 13, 2004.

95. The *New Republic*'s editors expressed regret for "some of the arguments" that the magazine had endorsed in favor of the Iraq War but denied regretting their overall support for the intervention. They pressured the *Washington Post* to correct a headline that implied the latter. See editor's note June 22, 2004, regarding Howard Kurtz, "New Republic Editors 'Regret' Their Support for the Iraq War," *Washington Post*, June 19, 2004. The clarification suggested just how limited was the *New Republic*'s acknowledgment of error.

96. When a 2014 *New York Times* investigation revealed that, years earlier, occupation forces had found buried caches of obsolete and militarily useless chemical weapons from the 1980s, a few right-wing activists attempted to spin the discovery as vindication of the Bush administration's warnings about Iraq's weapons of mass destruction. That attempt had little credibility, though, since even the Bush administration had not exploited the finding to make such a case. Jessica Schulberg, "No, Chemical Weapons in Iraq Do Not Prove That Bush Was Right to Invade," *New Republic*, October 15, 2014.

97. Michael Rubin, "Iraq Has Voted," *Wall Street Journal*, January 31, 2005.

98. For example, see Vauhini Vara, "Bloggers Share the View from Election Day in Iraq," *Wall Street Journal*, June 30, 2005.

99. Charles Levinson, "Iraq Voters Defy Violence, *Wall Street Journal*, March 10, 2010; and Michael Ledeen "Victory in Iraq," *National Review*, February 9, 2009.

100. Matt Taibbi, "16 Years Later, How the Press That Sold the Iraq War Got Away with It," *Rolling Stone*, March 22, 2019.

101. Judis, "Eve of Destruction."

102. Confidential interview with author, March 7, 2006.

CHAPTER 6

1. Rajan Menon, *The Conceit of Humanitarian Intervention* (New York: Oxford University Press, 2016), p. 112.

2. "Gaddafi's Army Will Kill Half a Million, Warn Libya Rebels," *The Guardian*, March 12, 2011.

3. Quoted in Ross Douthat, "100,000 Libyan Casualties?," *New York Times*, March 24, 2011.

4. Menon, *Conceit of Humanitarian Intervention*, p. 111.

5. David Bromwich, "The Wings of the Hawk," *National Interest* 144 (July/August 2016): 14.

6. Scott Horton, *Enough Already: Time to End the War on Terrorism* (Austin, TX: Libertarian Institute, 2021), p. 162.

7. "At War in Libya," editorial, *New York Times*, March 21, 2011.

8. Hillary Rodham Clinton, *Hard Choices* (New York: Simon and Schuster, 2014), p. 364.

9. Clinton, *Hard Choices*, p. 368.

10. Robert M. Gates, *Duty: Memoirs of a Secretary at War* (New York: Alfred A. Knopf, 2014), p. 518.

11. Edward Cody, "France Pleads for Military Intervention as Gaddafi Forces Attack Libyan Rebels," *Washington Post*, March 17, 2011.

12. Gates, *Duty*, p. 530.

13. Nearly two weeks after passage of the resolution and commencement of the aircraft and missile attacks, President Obama still sought to portray the mission as a limited one to protect innocent civilians. White House, Office of the Press Secretary, "Remarks by the President in Address to the Nation on Libya," National Defense University, March 28, 2011, https://www.whitehouse.gov/the-press-office/2011/03/28/remarks-president-address-nation-libya.

Also see Gates's depiction of his often-uncomfortable testimony before the armed services committees in both the House and Senate. Gates, *Duty*, p. 521.

14. Examples include Conor Friedersdorf, "How Obama Ignored Congress, and Misled America, on War in Libya," *The Atlantic*, September 13, 2012; and Micah Zenko, "The Big Lie about the Libyan War," *Foreign Policy*, March 22, 2016.

15. Nicholas Kristof, "'Thank You, America!'," *New York Times*, August 31, 2011.

16. Ivo H. Daalder and James G. Stavridis, "NATO's Success in Libya," *New York Times*, October 30, 2011.

17. Glenn Greenwald, "Celebrating the Fall of a Dictator," *Salon*, September 1, 2011.

18. Quoted in "Was Libya a Victory for Obama, NATO?," *USA Today*, August 25, 2011.

19. Glenn Greenwald, "State Department Attacks CNN for Doing Basic Journalism, *The Guardian*, September 24, 2012.

20. Missy Ryan and Sudarsan Raghavan, "U.S. Strikes Islamic State Stronghold in Libya, Expanding Campaign against Militant Group," *Washington Post*, August 1, 2016.

21. In her memoirs, Obama administration official Samantha Power explicitly admits that two of the victims were "security officers working for the CIA." Samantha Power, *The Education of an Idealist* (New York: Dey Street, 2019), p. 310.

22. Charles Krauthammer, "How to Do the Benghazi Hearings Right," *Washington Post*, May 14, 2014.

23. Jamelle Bouie, "An Empty Conspiracy," *Slate*, October 12, 2015; and David Horsey, "Raw Politics Drives GOP Probes of Benghazi, Planned Parenthood," *Baltimore Sun*, October 6, 2015.

24. Gabrielle Levy, "GOP Delivers Self-Inflicted Wounds to Benghazi Committee," *U.S. News & World Report*, October 13, 2015.

25. Karen DeYoung, "House Republicans Issue Report on Benghazi Attacks but Find No New Evidence of Wrongdoing by Clinton," *Washington Post*, June 28, 2016.

26. Dan Merica, "Another GOP Congressman Says Benghazi Panel Meant to Hurt Clinton," CNN, October 15, 2015.

27. Christopher S. Chivvis, *Toppling Qaddafi: Libya and the Limits of Liberal Intervention* (New York: Cambridge University Press, 2014), p. 173.

28. Sharyl Attkisson, *Stonewalled: My Fight for Truth against the Forces of Obstruction, Intimidation, and Harassment in Obama's Washington* (New York: HarperCollins, 2014), p. 3.

29. Edith M. Lederer, "UN: Impact of Long Libya War on Civilians Is 'Incalculable," Associated Press, February 17, 2020.

30. Samer Al-Atrush, "What Lies beneath the Nine Years of Turmoil in Libya," Bloomberg, August 26, 2020.

31. Kareem Fahim, "Turkey's Parliament Authorizes Troop Deployment to Libya as Proxy War Escalates," *Washington Post*, January 2, 2020.

32. Julian E. Barnes, "Ex-C.I.A. Asset, Now a Libyan Strongman, Faces Torture Accusations," *New York Times*, February 18, 2020; and David D. Kirkpatrick, "A Police State with an Islamist Twist: Inside Hifter's Libya, *New York Times*, February 20, 2020.

33. Andrew Engel, "A Way Forward in Benghazi," Washington Institute PolicyWatch no. 2088, June 12, 2013, p. 2.

34. Engel, "A Way Forward," p. 1.

35. Engel, "A Way Forward," p. 2.

36. Sara Creta, "As War Drags On, Troubles Mount for Libya's Coast Guards and Migrant Detention Centers," *New Humanitarian*, February 26, 2020.

37. Ruth Sherlock, "Migrants Continue to Die in Attempts to Cross Mediterranean Sea to Europe," NPR, December 29, 2020.

38. David Landler, *Hillary Clinton, Barack Obama, and the Twilight Struggle over American Power* (New York: Random House, 2016), p. 187.

39. Jo Becker and Scott Shane, "Hillary Clinton, 'Smart Power,' and a Dictator's Fall," *New York Times*, February 29, 2016.

40. Daniel Larison, "Clinton's Libyan War and the Delusions of Interventionists," *The American Conservative*, February 29, 2916.

41. Quoted in Conor Friedersdorf, "Hillary Defends Her Failed War in Libya," *The Atlantic*, October 14, 2015, p. 14.

42. Ben Norton, "Media Erase NATO Role in Bringing Slave Markets to Libya," FAIR, November 28, 2017. The resumption of a slave trade appears to have been the culmination of a surge of anti-black racism that soon followed NATO's removal of Qaddafi's regime. See Richard Seymour, "Libya's Spectacular Revolution Has Been Disgraced by Racism," *The Guardian*, August 30, 2011.

43. Norton, "Media Erase NATO Role."

44. Kirkpatrick, "A Police State with an Islamist Twist."

45. Quoted in Daniel Larison, "Power's Pathetic Libyan War Excuse," *The American Conservative*, September 9, 2019.

46. Dexter Filkins, "The Moral Logic of Humanitarian Intervention," *New Yorker*, September 9, 2019.

47. Ted Galen Carpenter and Malou Innocent, *Perilous Partners: The Benefits and Pitfalls of America's Alliances with Authoritarian Regimes* (Washington: Cato Institute, 2015).

48. Horton, *Enough Already*, pp. 181–84. Rubin provided the most detailed justification for that motive. James P. Rubin, "The Real Reason to Intervene in Syria," *Foreign Policy*, June 4, 2012.

49. Ted Galen Carpenter, "Tangled Web: The Syrian Civil War and Its Implications," *Mediterranean Quarterly* 24, no.1 (Winter 2013): 1–11.

50. Clinton, *Hard Choices*, p. 450.

51. Gareth Porter, "A U.S.-Fueled Syrian Sectarian Bloodbath," *Consortium News*, August 31, 2016.

52. Chas W. Freeman, Jr., *America's Continuing Misadventures in the Middle East* (Charlottesville, VA: Just World Books, 2016), p. 114.

53. Stephen Kinzer, "The Media Are Misleading the Public on Syria," *Boston Globe*, February 18, 2016.

54. Kinzer, "The Media Are Misleading the Public." For other accounts of rebel rule in Aleppo, see Marwan Hisham, "Scenes from Aleppo: How Life Has Been Transformed by Rebel Rule," *Vanity Fair*, July 26, 2015; and Eva Bartlett, "Syria War Diary: What Life Is Like under 'Moderate' Rebel Rule," *Global Research*, August 24, 2017.

55. Paul R. Pillar, "Heartstrings and Aleppo," *Lobelog.com*, December 20, 2016.

56. Patrick Cockburn, "There's More Propaganda Than News Coming out of Aleppo This Week," *Independent*, December 16, 2016.

57. Scott Pelley, "Fighting for Life in Syria's Vicious Civil War," transcript, *60 Minutes*, CBS News, December 18, 2016.

58. Scott Pelley, "When Hospitals Become Targets in Syria's Civil War," transcript, *60 Minutes*, CBS News, August 5, 2018.

59. Scott Pelley, "What a Chemical Attack in Syria Looks Like," transcript, *60 Minutes*, CBS News, August 19, 2018.

60. "Syria's White Helmets: 'We Need a No-Fly Zone and Humanitarian Corridors," *News, European Parliament*, June 12, 2016; John Irish, "Enough Red Lines: Time to Act, Syria's White Helmets Tell Macron," Reuters, February 13, 2018; and "Syria's White Helmets Urge No-Fly Zone to End Civilian Exodus," Agence France Presse, February 3, 2020.

61. Ben Swann, "Who Is Funding the Syrian Civil Defense?," *MintPress News*, May 4, 2018.

62. Jessica Donati, "U.S. Relenting, Releases Funding for Syria's 'White Helmets,'" *Wall Street Journal*, June 14, 2018.

63. Quoted in Sondoss Al Asaad, "The White Helmet Myth: A Soft War Propaganda," *Modern Diplomacy*, March 12, 2018.

64. Asaad, "The White Helmet Myth."

65. Swann, "Who Is Funding the Syrian Civil Defense?"

66. Alexandra Larkin and Sophie Lewis, "Netflix's 'The White Helmets' Takes Home the Company's First Oscar Win," CNN, February 27, 2017.

67. Quoted in Robert Parry, "Debate Moderator Distorted Syrian Reality," *Consortium News*, October 11, 2016.

68. Leon Wieseltier, "Aleppo's Fall Is Obama's Failure," *Washington Post*, December 15, 2016.

69. Amnesty International, "Abductions, Torture and Summary Killings at the Hands of Armed Groups," press release, July 5, 2016.

70. Human Rights Watch, *"You Can Still See Their Blood": Executions, Indiscriminate Shootings, and Hostage Taking by Opposition Forces in Latakia Countryside* (New York: Human Rights Watch, 2013).

71. Charles R. Lister, *The Syrian Jihad: Al-Qaeda, the Islamic State, and the Evolution of an Insurgency* (New York: Oxford University Press, 2015), p. 161.

72. Lister, *Syrian Jihad*, p. 131.

73. Mark Hosenball and Phil Stewart, "Kerry Portrait of Syria Rebels at Odds with Intelligence Reports," Reuters, September 5, 2013.

74. Hosenball and Stewart, "Kerry Portrait."

75. Christopher Phillips, *The Battle for Syria: International Rivalry in the New Middle East* (New Haven, CT: Yale University Press, 2016), p. 130.

76. Phillips, *Battle for Syria*, p. 129.

77. Phillips, *Battle for Syria*, pp. 131–32.

78. Phillips, *Battle for Syria*, p. 132.

79. David Enders, "Weeks Spent with Syrian Rebels Reveal a Force of Sunni Muslim Civilians," McClatchy Newspapers, June 25, 2012.

80. Porter, "U.S.-Fueled Sectarian Bloodbath."

81. Karen DeYoung, "Obama Asks for Authorization to Provide Direct Military Training to Syrian Rebels," *Washington Post*, June 26, 2014.

82. Kenneth M. Pollack, "An Army to Defeat Assad," *Foreign Affairs* 93, no. 5 (September–October 2014).

83. Helene Cooper, "Few U.S.-Trained Syrians Still Fight ISIS, Senators Told," *New York Times*, September 16, 2015.

84. Jonah Goldberg, "Team Obama Has Spent $500 M to Train 'Four or Five' Syrian Rebels," *New York Post*, September 18, 2015.

85. James Ball, "Obama Issues Syria a 'Red Line' Warning on Chemical Weapons," *Washington Post*, August 20, 2012.

86. Joby Warrick, "More Than 1,400 Killed in Syrian Chemical Weapons Attack, U.S. Says," *Washington Post*, August 20, 2013.

87. Scott Ritter, "Chemical Weapons Watchdog Is Just an American Lap Dog," *Truthdig*, December 18, 2019.

88. One example was Tucker Reals, "Syria Chemical Weapons Attack Blamed on Assad, but Where's the Evidence?," CBS News, August 30, 2013.

89. Pew Research Center, "Public Opinion Runs against Syrian Airstrikes," September 3, 2013.

90. Ben Rhodes, *The World as It Is: A Memoir of the Obama White House* (New York: Random House, 2019), pp. 216–27. Among the European allies, Germany's Angela Merkel was especially cautious.

91. Rhodes, *The World as It Is*, p. 227.

92. "CIA Fabricated Evidence to Lure US into War with Syria," RT.com, September 9, 2013.

93. Seymour M. Hersh, "The Red Line and the Rat Line," *London Review of Books*, April 17, 2014.

94. Nicholas Kristof, "Trump Was Right to Strike Syria," *New York Times*, April 7, 2017.

95. Matt Lewis, "This seemed like a very different Donald Trump. More serious—and clearly moved emotionally. Frequently invoked the Almighty," Twitter, April 6, 2017, 8:06 p.m., The tweet, now deleted, was quoted in Zack Ford, "Media Fawns over President Trump's Strike on Syria," ThinkProgress, April 7, 2017.

96. Quoted in Jessica Chasmar, "CNN's Fareed Zakaria, 'Donald Trump Became President Last Night," *Washington Times*, April 7, 2017.

97. Quoted in Derek Hawkins, "Brian Williams Is 'Guided by the Beauty of Our Weapons' in Syria Strikes," *Washington Post*, April 7, 2017.

98. Theodore Postol, "MIT Scientist Disputes 'Evidence' of Syria Chemical Weapons Attack," *MintPress News*, April 14, 2017.

99. Michael Gordon, "White House Accepts Reality of Assad's Grip on Power in Syria," *New York Times*, March 31, 2017; and Michelle Nichols, "U.S. Priority on Syria No Longer Focuses on 'Getting Assad Out': Haley," *U.S. News & World Report*, March 30, 2017.

100. Robert Parry, "A New Hole in Syria-Sarin Certainty," *Consortium News*, September 7, 2017.

101. Steve Almasy and Richard Roth, "UN: Syria Responsible for Sarin Attack That Killed Scores," CNN, October 27, 2017.

102. OPCW Technical Secretariat, *Interim Report of the OPCW Fact-Finding Mission in Syria Regarding the Incident of Alleged Use of Toxic Chemicals as a Weapon in Douma, Syrian Arab Republic, on 7 April 2018*, Report no. S/1645/2018, July 6, 2018.

103. OPCW Technical Secretariat, *Report of the Fact-Finding Mission Regarding the Incident of Alleged Use of Toxic Chemicals as a Weapon in Douma, Syrian Arab Republic, on 7 April 2018*, Report no. S/1731/2019, March 1, 2019.

104. WikiLeaks, "OPCW Douma Docs: OPCW-Douma, Release Part 3: First Draft Interim Report, S2018, June 2018," December 14, 2019.

105. Ritter, "Chemical Weapons Watchdog."

106. Scott Ritter, "Bias, Lies & Videotape: Doubts Dog 'Confirmed' Syria Chemical Attacks," *The American Conservative*, June 20, 2019.

107. Peter Hitchens, "Strange News from the OPCW in the Hague," *Peter Hitchens's Blog, Daily Mail*, May 16, 2019.

108. Peter Hitchens, "My Urgent Questions to the Organisation for the Prohibition of Chemical Weapons, *Peter Hitchens's Blog, Daily Mail*, May 29, 2019.

109. Robert Fisk, "The Evidence We Were Never Meant to See about the Douma 'Gas' Attack," *Independent* (UK), May 23, 2019.

110. WikiLeaks, "OPCW Douma Docs: OPCW-Douma, Release Part 3," December 14, 2019; and WikiLeaks, "OPCW Douma Docs: Internal OPCW E-Mail," November 23, 2019; Also see Caitlin Johnstone, "Deluge of New Leaks Further Shreds the Establishment Syria Narrative," CaitlinJohnstone.com, December 15, 2019.

111. See Nikki Carlson, "Tucker Carlson Spreads Disinformation about Attack in Syria," *Media Matters*, November 26, 2019.

112. OPCW Technical Secretariat, *First Report by the OPCW Investigation and Identification Team Pursuant to Paragraph 10 of Decision C-SS-4/Dec.3: "Addressing the Threat from Chemical Weapons Use," Ltamenah (Syrian Arab Republic), 24, 25, and 30 March 2017*, Report no. S/1867/2020, April 8, 2020.

113. Max Blumenthal and Aaron Maté, "Exclusive: OPCW Insiders Slam 'Compromised' New Syria Chemical Weapons Probe," Grayzone, April 28, 2020.

114. See, for example, Jennifer Hansler, "Report Finds Syrian Government Forces Responsible for 2017 Chemical Attack," CNN, April 8, 2020.

115. Bas Spliet, "Time to Pull the Douma 'Gas Attack' Out of the Memory Hole," Antiwar.com, April 15, 2020.

116. See Yves Engler's analysis of the supine behavior of Canada's media regarding the OPCW's conduct. Yves Engler, "Canada Follows U.S. Lead by Ignoring OPCW Scandal," Antiwar.com, December 24, 2019.

117. Engler, "Canada Follows U.S. Lead."

118. Aaron Maté, "U.S. Media Silent on OPCW Syria Leaks," Grayzone, January 2, 2020.

119. Tareq Haddad, "Lies, Newsweek and Control of the Media Narrative: First-Hand Account," Tareqhaddad.com, December 14, 2019.

120. Scott Ritter, "A *Newsweek* Reporter Resigns, A Counter-Narrative Won't Die," *The American Conservative*, December 27, 2019. Regarding the role of the second inspection group, see Jonathan Steele, "OPCW and Douma: Chemical Weapons Watchdog Accused of Evidence-Tampering by Its Own Inspectors," *Counterpunch*, Novembers 15, 2019. Also see WikiLeaks, "OPCW Douma Docs: OPCW-Douma, Release Part 4," December 27, 2019.

121. Tareq Haddad, "I plan on publishing these details in full shortly. However, after asking my editors for comment, as is journalistic practice, I received an email reminding me of confidentiality clauses in my contract. I.e. I was threatened with legal action," Twitter, December 7, 2019, 5:33 a.m.

122. Ritter, "Chemical Weapons Watchdog."

123. Nafeez Ahmed, "Pentagon Report Says West, Gulf States, and Turkey Foresaw Emergence of 'IS,'" Middle East Eye, June 6, 2015.

124. Jay Syrmopoulos, "Media Blacks Out Pentagon Report Exposing U.S. Role in ISIS Creation," MintPress News, June 3, 2015.

125. Ted Galen Carpenter, "A Sober Look at the West's Kurdish Allies," Aspenia Online, November 23, 2017.

126. Human Rights Watch, "Syria: Abuses in Kurdish-Run Enclaves," June 28, 2014; and Roy Gutman, "Have the Syrian Kurds Committed War Crimes?," Nation, February 7, 2017.

127. Peter Wehner, "Trump Betrayed the Kurds. He Just Couldn't Help Himself," The Atlantic, October 15, 2019.

128. Dan Lamothe, "'I Can't Even Look at the Atrocities': U.S. Troops Say Trump's Syria Withdrawal Betrayed an Ally," Washington Post, October 15, 2019.

129. Nick Paton Walsh, "Trump's Betrayal of the Kurds Is a Gift to Putin and Assad," CNN, October 8, 2019.

130. Tammy Duckworth, "With Syria Drawdown, Donald Trump Turns His Back on America's Credibility," USA Today, October 24, 2019.

131. Trudy Rubin, "Trump's Syria Debacle Is Cause for Impeachment," Philadelphia Inquirer, October 14, 2019.

132. Associated Press, "House Overwhelmingly Votes Bipartisan Condemnation of Trump Withdrawal of U.S. Troops from Syria," NBC News, October 16, 2019.

133. Katie Bo Williams, "To Block Trump's Troop Withdrawals, Congress Turns an Old Tactic Upside Down," Defense One, July 14, 2020.

134. John Nichols, "Withdrawing U.S. Troops from Syria Is the Right Thing to Do, Even If Trump Does It," Nation, December 21, 2018.

135. Ben Norton, "Leaked Docs Expose Massive Syria Propaganda Operation Waged by Western Govt Contractors and Media," Grayzone, September 23, 2020.

136. Norton, "Leaked Docs Expose Massive Syria Propaganda Operation."

137. Jonathan Cook, "Establishment Journalists Are Piling on to Smear Robert Fisk Now That He Cannot Answer Back," Brave New Europe, November 30, 2020.

138. Ted Galen Carpenter, Gullible Superpower: U.S. Support for Bogus Foreign Democratic Movements (Washington: Cato Institute, 2019), pp. 161–87, 213–41.

CHAPTER 7

1. "Putin Declares War," editorial, *Wall Street Journal*, March 2, 2014.

2. Philip Rucker, "Hillary Clinton Says Putin's Actions Are Like 'What Hitler Did Back in the '30s,'" *Washington Post*, March 5, 2014.

3. Timothy Snyder, "If Russia Swallows Ukraine, the European System Is Finished," CNN, March 5, 2014.

4. See Richard Sakwa, *Frontline Ukraine: Crisis in the Borderlands* (London: I.B. Taurus, 2013); Samuel Charap and Timothy J. Colton, *Everyone Loses: The Ukraine Crisis and the Ruinous Contest for Post-Soviet Eurasia* (London: Routledge, 2027); John J. Mearsheimer, "Why the Ukraine Crisis Is the West's Fault," *Foreign Affairs* 93, no. 6 (September-October 2014): 77–89; and Ted Galen Carpenter, *Gullible Superpower: U.S. Support for Bogus Foreign Democratic Movements* (Washington: Cato Institute, 2019), pp. 96–98, 106–13, 189–207.

5. For a discussion of Washington's significant, meddlesome role in the Maidan Revolution, see Carpenter, *Gullible Superpower*, pp. 198–205.

6. Cathy Young, "Putin's Pal," *Slate*, July 24, 2014; and Jonathan Chait, "The Nation's Stephen F. Cohen Denies Existence of Ukraine," *Intelligencer: New York Magazine*, August 14, 2014.

7. James Kirchick, "Paleocons for Putin," *Daily Beast*, January 13, 2014, updated April 14, 2017; Brent Scher, "Putin's Patsies," *Washington Free Beacon*, March 4, 2014; Ron Radosh, "The New Apologists for Vladimir Putin—On the Right and the Left," *PJ Media*, March 15, 2014; Seth Mandel, "The Vladimir Putin Fan Club," *Commentary*, May 2014; and Cathy Young, "Putin's Strange Bedfellows, *Boston Globe*, July 29, 2014. Also see the various hit pieces on *Useful Stooges*, whose authors remain anonymous. For example, "Tag: Peter Hitchens, Who Cares?," *Useful Stooges*, posted on Wordpress.com May 5, 2015. Also see Warren Kinsella, "Glen [sic] Greenwald Is Putin's Useful Idiot," *War Room*, December 10, 2016.

8. See Dominic Tierney, "Trump, Putin, and the Art of Appeasement," *The Atlantic*, December 15, 2016.

9. An especially ugly example is the piece by Greg Olear, directed at Dimitri Simes, head of the Center for the National Interest and an adviser to the Trump campaign. Olear accused Simes of literally being a Russian intelligence operative, despite a dearth of evidence. He also accused another Trump adviser, Richard Burt, former U.S. ambassador to Germany, of being a Russian agent. Greg Olear, "Putin's Troika: Three Russian Agents Who Infiltrated the Trump Campaign," *Medium*, January 26, 2019. For Simes's subsequent assessment of the campaign against him, see Dimiti Simes, "The Case for Trump," *National Interest Online*, August 13, 2020.

10. Kyle Smith, "The Real Reason Chris Matthews Was Fired from MSNBC," *New York Post*, March 3, 2019.

11. "CNN's Jake Tapper Doesn't Think the Media 'Got Anything Wrong' while Covering Russia Investigation," Associated Press, April 4, 2019.

12. Michael Grynbaum, "3 CNN Journalists Resign after Retracted Story on Trump Ally," *New York Times*, June 26, 2917.

13. Gregg Re, "CIA Slams CNN's 'Misguided' and 'Simply False' Reporting on Alleged CIA Spy's Extraction from the Kremlin," Fox News, September 9, 2019.

14. Jim Sciutto, "Exclusive: U.S. Extracted Top Spy from Inside Russia in 2017," CNN, September 9, 2019. Sciutto embraced virtually every allegation made about Russian meddling in the 2016 election and beyond, even when the evidence was exceedingly flimsy. See Jim Sciutto, *The Shadow War: Inside Russia's and China's Secret Operations to Defeat America* (New York: HarperCollins, 2019), pp. 185–213.

15. Glenn Greenwald, "Beyond BuzzFeed: The 10 Worst, Most Embarrassing U.S. Media Failures on the Trump-Russia Story," *The Intercept*, January 20, 2019.

16. Craig Timberg, "Russian Propaganda Effort Helped Spread 'Fake News' during Election, Experts Say," *Washington Post*, November 24, 2016.

17. Greenwald, "Beyond BuzzFeed."

18. Arthur Bloom, "They Really Are Lying to You," *The American Conservative*, June 10, 2020.

19. Juliet Eilperin and Adam Antous, "Russian Operation Hacked a Vermont Utility, Showing Risk to U.S. Electric Grid," *Washington Post*, December 31, 2016. See "Editor's Note: An earlier version of this story incorrectly said that Russian hackers had penetrated the U.S. electric grid. Authorities say there is no indication of that so far. The computer at Burlington Electric that was hacked was not attached to the grid."

20. Jim Sciutto, Carl Beinstein, and Marshall Cohen, "Cohen Claims Trump Knew in Advance of 2016 Trump Tower Meeting," CNN, July 27, 2018.

21. Greenwald, "Beyond Buzzfeed."

22. Matt Taibbi, "It's Official: Russiagate Is This Generation's WMD," *Taibbisubstack.com*, March 23, 2019.

23. Robert S. Mueller, *The Mueller Report: The Final Report of the Special Counsel into Donald Trump, Russia and Collusion, with an Introduction by Alan Dershowitz, as Issued by the Department of Justice* (New York: Skyhorse Publishing, 2019), p. 4.

24. Charles Sykes, "Seven Reasons Not to Trust William Barr," *Bulwark*, April 11, 2019.

25. Jonathan Chait, "William Barr Seems to Be Covering Up Something Bad for Trump," *Intelligencer: New York Magazine*, April 4, 2019.

26. Taibbi, "It's Official."

27. Glenn Greenwald, "Robert Mueller Did Not Merely Reject the Trump-Russia Conspiracy Theories. He Obliterated Them," *The Intercept*, April 18, 2019.

28. David Smith, "Did Mueller's Testimony Kill the Trump Impeachment Debate?," *The Guardian*, July 19, 2019.

29. Richard Bade and Mike De Bonis, "Democrats Struggle to Figure Out What to Do Next against Trump after Mueller Testimony Falls Flat," *Washington Post*, July 25, 2019.

30. Zach Beauchamp, "5 Losers and 0 Winners from Mueller's Testimony to the House of Representatives," *Vox*, July 24, 2019.

31. For example, see Nicholas Fandos, "What We Learned from Mueller's 7 Hours on Capitol Hill," *New York Times*, July 24, 2019.

32. Office of the Inspector General, *Review of Four FISA Applications and Other Aspects of the FBI's Crossfire Hurricane Investigation*, Oversight and Review Division 20-012 (Washington: Department of Justice, 2019).

33. Office of the Inspector General, *Review of Four FISA Applications*.

34. Clinesmith entered a guilty plea in August 2020. But his forgery was only the most egregious abuse in the FBI's handling of the Carter Page case. See Andrew C. McCarthy, "Connecting Dots in Clinesmith's Russiagate Guilty Plea," *National Review*, August 14, 2020.

35. James Comey, "The Truth Is Finally Out. The FBI Fulfilled Its Mission," *Washington Post*, December 9, 2019.

36. Ken Dilanian, Pete Williams, and Julia Ainsley, "Internal Justice Watchdog Finds That Russia Probe Was Justified, Not Biased against Trump," NBC News, December 9, 2019.

37. Michael Balsamo and Eric Tucker, "DOJ Inspector General Finds No Bias in FBI's Russia Probe," *NewsHour*, PBS, December 9, 2019.

38. Ed Kilgore, "Inspector General Finds Russia Investigation Wasn't an FBI Witch Hunt," *Intelligencer: New York Magazine*, December 9, 2019.

39. Garrrett M. Graff, "So Much for the Deep State Plot against Donald Trump," *Wired*, December 9, 2019.

40. Examples include Alexander Mallin and Soo Rin Kim, "DOJ Watchdog Finds Russia Investigation Not Improper, Despite Missteps," ABC News, December 9, 2019; Charlie Savage, Adam Goldman, and Katie Brenner, "Report on FBI Inquiry Finds Serious Errors, but Debunks Anti-Trump Plot," *New York Times*, December 9, 2019; Debra J. Saunders, "Justice Department Report Finds Errors, but No Political Bias," *Las Vegas Review-Journal*, April 9, 2019; and

Claire Hansen, "IG Report on Russia Probe Finds No Anti-Trump Bias but Identifies Other Errors," *U.S. News & World Report*, December 9, 2019.

41. Comey, "The Truth Is Finally Out."

42. Tobias Hoonhaut, "Horowitz Pushes Back on Claim That He Exonerated FBI of Political Bias. 'We Did Not Reach that Conclusion,'" *National Review*, December 13, 2019.

43. Katelyn Polantz, Marshall Cohen, and David Shortell, "FISA Court Slams FBI Conduct in Carter Page Surveillance Warrant Application," CNN, December 17, 2019.

44. Tobias Hoonhout, "FISA Court Confirms Two Carter Page Surveillance Applications 'Not Valid,'" *National Review*, January 23, 2020.

45. Charlie Savage, "Court Bans Agents Who Botched Carter Page Surveillance from Seeking Wiretaps," *New York Times*, March 5, 2020.

46. Erica Eichelberger, "FISA Court Has Rejected .03 Percent of All Government Surveillance Requests," *Mother Jones*, June 10, 2013.

47. David Kris, "Don't Read Too Much into the Jump in Rejected FISA Applications," *Lawfare*, April 26, 2018.

48. Mairead McArdle, "Rod Rosenstein Says He Would Not Have Signed Warrant for Page If He Knew Evidence Was Faulty," *National Review*, June 3, 2020.

49. Rebecca Shabad, "Rod Rosenstein Defends Mueller Appointment, Approval of FISA Applications in Russia Probe," NBC News, June 3, 2020.

50. Katelyn Polantz and David Shortell, "Former FBI Lawyer Set to Plead Guilty to Altering E-mail during Russia Investigation," CNN, August 14, 2020.

51. Andrew McCarthy, "Clinesmith's Guilty Plea: The Perfect Snapshot of Crossfire Hurricane's Duplicity," *National Review*, August 24, 2020.

52. Brooke Singman, "House Intel Transcripts Show Top Obama Officials Had No 'Empirical Evidence' of Trump-Russia Collusion," Fox News, May 7, 2020.

53. Aaron Maté, "Hidden over 2 Years: Dem Cyber-Firm's Sworn Testimony It Had No Proof of Russian Hack of DNC," *RealClearInvestigations*, May 13, 2020.

54. Ray McGovern, "Twin Pillars of Russiagate Crumble," Antiwar.com, May 11, 2020.

55. See, for example, Frank Vogl, "What Does Putin Have on Trump?," *Globalist*, April 30, 2020.

56. Kimberley A. Strassel, "The James Comey Election," *Wall Street Journal*, October 1, 2020.

57. Adam Goldman, Julian E. Barnes, Maggie Haberman, and Nicholas Fandos, "Lawmakers Are Warned That Russia Is Meddling to Re-elect President Trump," *New York Times*, February 20, 2020.

58. See Jonathan Landay, "U.S. Intelligence Told Lawmakers of Russian Bid to Boost Trump Re-election, Reuters, February 20, 2020.

59. Landay, "U.S. Intelligence Told Lawmakers." Emphasis added.

60. Goldman, Barnes, Haberman, and Fandos, "Lawmakers Are Warned."

61. Jeremy Diamond, Jake Tapper, and Zachary Cohen, "U.S. Intelligence Briefer Appears to Have Overstated Assessment of 2020 Russian Interference," CNN, February 23, 2020.

62. Shane Harris, Ellen Nakashima, Michael Scherer, and Sean Sullivan, "Bernie Sanders Briefed by U.S. Officials That Russia Is Trying to Help His Presidential Campaign," *Washington Post*, February 21, 2020.

63. Peter Van Buren, "Russiagate II: The Return of the Low Intelligence Zombies," *The American Conservative*, February 24, 2020.

64. "Glenn Greenwald: Interference from the National Intelligence Community Is More Dangerous than Whatever Putin May Be Trying Online," *The Hill*, February 24, 2020.

65. Maggie Miller, "Sanders Says He Was Briefed on Russian Efforts to Help Campaign," *The Hill*, February 21, 2020.

66. Stephen Collinson, "America's Russia Nightmare Is Back," CNN, February 21, 2020.

67. Quoted in Bob Brigham, "Maddow Reports on Russia 'Running an Op to Try to Reelect Donald Trump' in 2020: 'Here We Go Again,'" *Raw Story*, February 20, 2020.

68. Collinson, "America's Russia Nightmare Is Back."

69. Collinson, "America's Russia Nightmare Is Back."

70. Bump, "In One Incident."

71. Jessica Kwong, "Billboard Threatens 'Moscow Mitch' McConnell to Impeach Trump or 'Lose Your Job' as He Faces Kentucky Reelection," Newsweek, November 13, 2019. Four prominent "progressive" organizations—Need to Impeach, Daily Kos, MoveOn, and Public Citizen—sponsored and erected the billboard. The "Moscow Mitch" epithet predated the display and was far more widespread than that one incident, however.

72. Quoted in Joe Gould, "U.S. Senate's Top Republican Likens Russia to 'Old Soviet Union,'" Defense News, August 15, 2018.

73. Morgan Gstalter, "Scarborough Calls McConnell 'Moscow Mitch,' Says Lack of Action on Russian Meddling is 'Un-American,'" The Hill, July 26, 2019.

74. See Lawrence O'Donnell, "The Last Word: 'Moscow Mitch' Angry at Being Called 'Moscow Mitch,'" MSNBC, July 29, 2019; Summer Eldemire, "McConnell Whines about 'Moscow Mitch' Nickname: It's 'Over the Top,'" Daily Beast, September 3, 2019; and Dana Milbank, "Sticks and Stones Break

Bones, but Words Hurt McConnell's Feelings," Washington Post, September 4, 2019.

75. Milbank, "Sticks and Stones."

76. Dana Milbank, "Mitch McConnell Is a Russian Asset," Washington Post, July 26, 2019.

77. Justin Baragona, "Donna Brazile Tells RNC Chairwoman to 'Go to Hell' on Fox News," Daily Beast, March 3, 2020.

78. "Read: Testimony of William Taylor, Acting U.S. Envoy to Ukraine," NPR, November 6, 2019.

79. William B. Taylor, "Yes, Secretary Pompeo, Americans Should Care about Ukraine," New York Times, January 26, 2010.

80. "Read George Kent's Prepared Opening Statement from the Impeachment Hearing," New York Times, November 13, 2019.

81. Adam Edelman, "5 Things We Learned from Marie Yovanovitch's Impeachment Testimony," NBC News, November 15, 2019.

82. For examples, see Jonathan Allen, "Fighting Putin: Taylor Explains Why U.S. Aide [sic] to Ukraine Really Matters," blog, NBC News, November 13, 2019.

83. Jason Crow, "Defending Their Honor as We Hear Their Testimony," The Hill, November 13, 2019.

84. Sakwa, Frontline Ukraine, pp. 10–25.

85. Vladimir Golstein, "Why Everything You've Read about Ukraine Is Wrong," Forbes, May 19, 2014.

86. Sakwa, Frontline Ukraine, p. 25.

87. For an overview of such accounts and the underlying evidence, see Carpenter, Gullible Superpower, pp. 201–3, 208–12.

88. "Read Alexander Vindman's Prepared Opening Statement from the Impeachment Hearing," New York Times, November 19, 2019.

89. Todd Pierce, "U.S. Security Official Vindman Testifies Ukraine Offered Defense Minister Post," Radio Free Europe/Radio Liberty, November 19, 2019.

90. For examples, see Jennifer Rubin, "Slandering an American War Hero Must Have Consequences," Washington Post, October 29, 2019; Jill Filipovic, "Trump Team's Disgusting Smear of Alexander Vindman," CNN, October 29, 2019; and Dartunorro Clark, "'Shameful,' 'Despicable': Republicans and Democrats Decry Attacks on Impeachment Witness Vindman," NBC News, October 29, 2019. The only Republican critics cited in the NBC News article were Mitt Romney and ultra-hawkish, neoconservative Rep. Liz Cheney (R-WY).

91. Charlie Savage, Eric Schmidt, and Michael Schwirtz, "Russia Secretly Offered Afghan Militants Bounties to Kill U.S. Troops, Intelligence Says," New York Times, June 28, 2020.

92. For a detailed list (with links) of such supportive articles and statements, see Caitlin Johnstone, "This Russia-Afghanistan Story Is Western Propaganda at Its Most Vile," CaitlinJohnstone.com, June 28, 2020.

93. Mairead McArdle, "Intel Official: Allegations of Russian Bounties to Taliban 'Uncorroborated,'" *National Review*, June 29, 2020. For a discussion about the unusually public split in the intelligence/national security community about the credibility of the bounty allegations, see Ronald Enzweiler, "Who to Believe on Afghan Intelligence: CIA, NSA, or Pentagon?," Antiwar.com, July 2, 2020.

94. Gareth Porter, "How the Pentagon Failed to Sell Afghan Government's Bunk 'Bountygate' Story to U.S. Intelligence Agencies," Grayzone, July 7, 2020.

95. Jennifer Griffin and Edward DeMarche, "Pentagon Says 'No Corroborating' Evidence to Stand Up NYT Report on Russian Bounties," Fox News, June 30, 2020; and Lolita C. Baldor, "U.S. General Skeptical That Bounties Led to Troop's Deaths," Associated Press, July 7, 2020.

96. Barbara Boland, "House Using Shaky Russian Bounty Story to Keep U.S. Troops in Afghanistan," *The American Conservative*, July 2, 2020.

97. Rishika Dugyala, "Pelosi on Trump: 'With Him, All Roads Lead to Putin,'" *Politico*, June 28, 2020.

98. Michael Crowley and Eric Schmitt, "White House Dismisses Reports of Bounties, but Is Silent on Russia," *New York Times*, July 1, 2020.

99. Carol D. Leonnig, Shane Harris, and Greg Jaffe, "Breaking with Tradition, Trump Skips President's Written Intelligence Report and Relies on Oral Briefing," *Washington Post*, February 9, 2020.

100. Ray McGovern, "Russiagate's Last Gasp," *Consortium News*, June 29, 2020.

101. Barbara Boland, "Three Glaring Problems with the Russian Taliban 'Bounty' Story," *The American Conservative*, July 1, 2020.

102. David E. Sanger and Eric Schmitt, "Trump's New Russia Problem: Unread Intelligence and Missing Strategy," *New York Times*, July 1, 2020.

103. Ray McGovern, "*New York Times* Deploys Heavy Gun to Back 'Intel' on Russian Bounties," Antiwar.com, July 2, 2020.

104. Aaron Blake, "The Only People Dismissing the Russian Bounties Intel: The Taliban, Russia, and Trump," *Washington Post*, July 1, 2020.

105. David B. Rivkin Jr. and George S. Beebe, "Why We Need a Little Skepticism, and More Evidence, on the Russian Bounties," *The Hill*, July 5, 2020. To the extent that there was any corroborating evidence to support the bounty allegations, it consisted of financial transfers from accounts linked to the Russian government to Taliban-linked entities.

The *New York Times* attached great importance to that information. Charlie Savage et al., "Suspicions of Russian Bounties Were Bolstered by Data on Financial Transfers," *New York Times*, June 30, 2020. For a detailed, more skeptical, assessment of the financial connection, see Scott Ritter, "Bountygate: Scapegoating Systemic Military Failure in Afghanistan," *Consortium News*, July 5, 2020.

106. Dave DeCamp, "Memo Raises Fresh Doubts on Russian Bounty Intel, Antiwar.com, July 5, 2020. For an account that minimizes the significance of the doubts expressed in the memo, see Charlie Savage, Eric Schmitt, Rahimi Callimachi, and Adam Goldman, "New Administration Memo Seeks to Foster Doubts about Suspected Russian Bounties," *New York Times*, July 3, 2020.

107. Johnstone, "This Russia-Afghanistan Story."

108. Alan MacLeod, "In 'Russian Bounty' Story, Evidence-Free Claims from Nameless Spies Became Fact," FAIR, July 3, 2020. Also see Hunter DeRensis, "The 'Explosive' Russian Bounty Story Is So Far, a Dud," *Responsible Statecraft*, September 29, 2020.

109. Aaron Maté, "Rachel Maddow Endorses Regime Change in Venezuela to 'Push Russia Back,' Sympathizes with Bolton and Pompeo," Grayzone, May 6, 2019.

110. Rachel Maddow, "Donald Trump Contradicts Top Aides with Reversal after Putin Phone Call," *The Rachel Maddow Show*, MSNBC, May 3, 2019.

111. Adam Johnson, "Action Alert: MSNBC's 'Resistance' to Trump's Venezuela Coup Ranges from Silence to Support," FAIR, February 13, 2019.

112. Ishaan Tharoor, "The Long History of U.S. Interfering with Elections Elsewhere," *Washington Post*, October 13, 2016; and Nina Agrawal, "The U.S. Is No Stanger to Interfering in Elections in Other Countries," *Los Angeles Times*, December 21, 2016.

113. "Campaign Finance Special Report: The Exploits of Charlie Trie," editorial, *Washington Post*, August 3, 1997; and Bob Woodward, "Campaign Finance Special Report: Findings Link Clinton Allies to Chinese Intelligence," *Washington Post*, February 10, 1998.

114. Turkey has long been exceptionally active with its influence campaigns. See Michael Rubin, "Not Just Russia: Don't Let Turkish Money Influence U.S. Elections," *Washington Examiner*, August 26, 2020.

115. Kenneth P. Vogel and David Stern, "Ukrainian Efforts to Sabotage Trump Backfire," *Politico*, January 11, 2017; and Lev Golinkin, "The Full Scope of Ukraine's Impact on 2016 Election Has Yet to be Examined," *Nation*, September 24, 2019.

116. Andrew E. Kramer, "Ukraine Court Rules Manafort Disclosure Caused 'Meddling' in U.S. Elections," *New York Times*, December 12, 2018.

117. William Evanina, "Statement by NCSC Director William Evanina: Election Threat Update for the American Public," press release, Office of the Director of National Intelligence, August 7, 2020.

118. Max Boot, "A Damning New Article Reveals How Trump Enables Russian Election Interference," *Washington Post*, August 8, 2020; Jennifer Rubin, "Russia Is Actively Helping Trump Again," *Washington Post*, August 9, 2020. For a more balanced (and cynical) account, arguing that the intelligence report exaggerated the potential for interference from all three governments, see Caitlin Johnstone, "U.S. Intelligence: If Trump Wins, Russia Did It; If Biden Wins, It Was China and Iran," CaitlinJohnstone.com, August 8, 2020. Also see Dave DeCamp, "Both Sides Have a Foreign Boogeyman to Blame for the 2020 Election," Antiwar.com, August 13, 2020.

119. See the numerous clips featured on *Tucker Carlson Tonight*, Fox News, August 10, 2020. Both the interviewers and their guests also smeared congressional figures such as Sens. Ron Johnson (R-WI) and Ted Cruz (R-TX), who argued that China was the more worrisome political menace, as circulating "Russian talking points." Apparently those two legislators were marked to join "Moscow Mitch" McConnell in the Russophobes' rogues' gallery.

120. Evanina, "Statement by the NCSC Director." Another report indicated that the Chinese consulate in Houston, which the Trump administration ordered closed in July 2020, was not only a center for electronic espionage, but it headed an operation to identify potential recruits for Black Lives Matter demonstrations. The consulate allegedly even supplied videos instructing activists on organizational techniques for such demonstrations. Again, such measures were comparable to Russia's alleged efforts to sow greater social and racial divisions in the United States. "Chinese Consulate in Houston Intervened in U.S. Political Movement," *Radio Free Asia*, August 7, 2020.

121. Alan Tonelson, "China Leaves Russian Meddling in the Dust," *The American Conservative*, August 26, 2020.

122. Sciutto, *Shadow War*, pp. 41–60.

123. For a contrasting view about the sophistication and effectiveness of Moscow's efforts, see Nina Jankowicz, *How to Lose the Information War: Russia, Fake News, and the Future of Conflict* (London: I.B. Taurus, 2020), pp. vi–xvii; 1–19.

124. Peter Strzok, *Compromised: Counterintelligence and the Threat of Donald J. Trump* (Boston: Houghton, Mifflin, Harcourt, 2020).

125. Vladimir Isachenkov for the Associated Press, "Russian General Chafes at 'Provocative' NATO Drills," *San Diego Union Tribune*, June 1, 2020.

126. Jacob Heilbrunn, "Russian Deputy Foreign Minister Sergei Ryabkov: 'We Have No Trust, No Confidence Whatsoever in America,'" *National Interest Online*, May 29, 2020.

127. David M. Herzenhorn, "Trump Orders Large Withdrawal of U.S. Forces from Germany," *Politico*, June 6, 2020.

128. "Poland Says U.S. to Deploy Troops to Eastern Border," *Defense Post*, July 31, 2020; and Ted Galen Carpenter, "Trump's Latest Move in Europe Is a Betrayal of Foreign Policy Realism," *National Interest Online*, August 10, 2020.

129. Meghann Myers, "Esper Hints That the 2nd Cavalry Regiment Could Be Heading Closer to Russia," *Military Times*, October 20, 2020.

130. Jason Ditz, "Critics Lash Joint U.S.-Russia Declaration on Elbe River Anniversary," Antiwar.com, April 26, 2020.

131. Ian Schwartz, "Susan Rice on Violence at Floyd Protests: This Is Right Out of the Russian Playbook," *RealClearPolitics*, June 1, 2020.

132. Julia Davis, "Putin Gleeful after Trumpsters' Violent Insurrection," *Daily Beast*, January 8, 2021.

133. Quoted in Joe Lauria, "Russiagate Ain't Over," *Consortium News*, January 22, 2021.

134. Quoted in Ray McGovern, "Round Up the Usual Suspects; Don't Forget Putin," Antiwar.com, January 21, 2021.

135. George Beebe, "The Stubborn Persistence of the Russia Bogeyman," *National Interest Online*, September 25, 2020.

136. Justin Baragona, "Even Sean Hannity Balks at Tulsi Gabbard's Putin Apologia," *Daily Beast*, February 22, 2022; Carina Kaplan, "The Russia to U.S. Disinformation Pipeline," Inkstick Media, February 25, 2022. For discussions of other examples of such smears, see Caitlin Johnstone, "MSM Pundits Push Idea That Criticizing U.S. Policy on Russia Makes You a Russian Agent," Caitlin Johnstone.com, January 30, 2022.

137. David Frum, "Fox News Abandons the GOP on Russia," *The Atlantic*, January 28, 2022; Jennifer Rubin, "Josh Hawley Seeks to Be Putin's New Favorite Pet," *Washington Post*, February 2, 2022.

138. Johnstone, "MSM Pundits."

139. David Leonhardt and Ian Prasad Philbrick, "Biden for Democracy," *New York Times*, March 1, 2022.

140. Dominic Mastrangelo, "Panel on 'The View' Calls for DOJ to Probe Tucker Carlson over Putin Rhetoric," *The Hill*, March 14, 2022; Kip Jones, "Keith Olbermann Calls for Detaining Tucker Carlson and Tulsi Gabbard: 'They Are Russian Assets,'" Mediaite, March 14, 2022.

141. Text of George Washington's Farewell Address, September 19, 1796.

142. Vanessa Gera, Nicole Winfield, and Lisa Mascaro, "Pelosi, in Surprise Kyiv Trip, Vows Unbending U.S. Support," ABC News, May 1, 2022.

143. Bret Stephens, "Why We Admire Zelensky," *New York Times*, April 19, 2022.

144. Transparency International, 2021 Corruption Perceptions Index.

145. Freedom House, Countries and Territories, Global Freedom Scores.

146. Ted Galen Carpenter, "Risking War for a Corrupt, Increasingly Repressive Ukraine," Antiwar.com, April 26, 2022.

147. Alistair Coleman, "Ukraine Conflict: Further Fake Images Shared Online," BBC, February 25, 2022; Nur Ayoubi, "'Ukraine Girl Confronting a Russian Soldier Is Actually Palestine's Ahed Tamimi," Middle East Eye, February 28, 2022; "Snake Island: Ukraine Says Troops Who Swore at Russian Warship Are Alive," BBC, February 28, 2022.

148. Nicholas Slayton, "Ukrainian Military Confirms That 'the Ghost of Kyiv' Is Made Up," *Task & Purpose*, April 30, 2022.

149. Lexi Lonas, "UN Receiving 'Credible' Information about Ukrainian Troops Torturing Russian Prisoners of War," MSN, May 8, 2022.

150. A CNN headline was typical: "Video *appears* to show execution of Russian *prisoner*" (emphasis added). Yet there was little doubt about the authenticity of the images on the video—and there were multiple victims, not just one prisoner. Nathan Hodge, Eoin McSweeney, and Niamh Kennedy, "Video Appears to Show Execution of Russian Prisoner," CNN, April 8, 2022. CNN viewers and readers were getting a sanitized version of a probable Ukrainian war crime. A similar spin was evident in media coverage of another video showing Russian prisoners being tortured. See Yaron Steinback, "Ukraine to Probe after Videos Show *Alleged* Russian POWs Shot, Abused" (emphasis added), *New York Post*, March 28, 2022.

151. For a concise, expert analysis of the extreme dangers associated with such a scheme, see Sumatra Maitra, "Enforcing a No-Fly Zone in Ukraine Would Be Catastrophic," *National Interest Online*, March 8, 2022.

152. Ken Dilanian, Courtney Kube, Carol E. Lee, and Dan De Luce, "U.S. Intel Helped Ukraine Protect Air Defenses, Shoot Down Russian Plane Carrying Hundreds of Troops," NBC News, April 26, 2022.

153. Shane Harris, Paul Sonne, Dan Lamothe, and Michael Birnbaum, "U.S. Provided Intelligence That Helped Ukraine Sink Russian Warship," *Washington Post*, May 5, 2022; Victor I. Nava, "U.S. Intelligence Helping Ukraine Kill Russian Generals," *Washington Examiner*, May 5, 2022. U.S. officials subsequently disputed the latter report.

154. Thomas L. Friedman, "The War Is Getting More Dangerous for America, and Biden Knows It," *New York Times*, May 6, 2022.

155. Michael McFaul, "The West Shouldn't Back Down in the Face of Putin's Threats," *Washington Post*, April 13, 2022; Max Boot, "Ukraine Can Win. Don't Let Putin Scare Us," *Washington Post*, May 2, 2022.

156. Quoted in David Moye, "NBC Correspondent Appears to Wonder Why U.S. Wouldn't Just Attack Russian Convoy," *HuffPost*, February 28, 2022.

157. Yaol Halon, "MSNBC's Ali Velshi Calls for 'Direct Military' Action from NATO, the West in Ukraine," Fox News, April 3, 2022.

158. Glenn Greenwald, "War Propaganda about Ukraine Becoming More Militaristic, Authoritarian, and Reckless," Substack, February 27, 2022.

159. Andrew Miller, "Rick Perry: Biden Admin. Gave Putin 'Leverage" By Blocking American Pipelines and Drilling," Fox News, February 24, 2022; Dave McCormick, "Biden's Anti-American Energy Policies Embolden Putin, Harm U.S. Workers and Families," Fox Business.com, February 26, 2022.

160. "NATO's Polish MiG-29 Fiasco," editorial, *Wall Street Journal*, March 9, 2022; Hannah Knowles, "More than 40 GOP Senators Urge Biden to Aid 'Transfer of Aircraft' to Ukraine," *Washington Post*, March 10, 2022.

161. Karl Rove, "Republicans Stand Up for Ukraine," *Wall Street Journal*, March 9, 2022.

162. Max Boot, "Thank Goodness Biden, Not Trump, Is President during the Worst European Crisis since 1945," *Washington Post*, March 1, 2022; Mark Landler, Katrin Bennhold, and Matina Stevis-Gridneff, "How the West Marshaled a Stunning Show of Unity against Russia," *New York Times*, March 5, 2022.

163. David Adler, "The West v Russia: Why the Global South Isn't Taking Sides," *The Guardian*, March 10, 2022; Ted Galen Carpenter, "UN Vote Signals Trouble for Washington's Global Coalition against Russia," *National Interest Online*, March 2, 2022; Anthony Faiola and Lesley Wroughton, "Outside the West, Putin Is Less Isolated than You Might Think," *Washington Post*, March 10, 2022; Stephen Kinzer, "These Countries Are Willing to Risk US Ire over Russia-Ukraine," *Responsible Statecraft*, May 2, 2022.

CHAPTER 8

1. Dean Rusk, as told to Richard Rusk, *As I Saw It* (New York: Penguin Books, 1990), p. 158.

2. Barbara W. Tuchman, *Sand against the Wind: Stilwell and the American Experience in China, 1911–1945* (New York: Macmillan, 1971), p. 251.

3. Tuchman, *Sand against the Wind*, pp. 187–88.

4. Ross Y. Koen, *The China Lobby in American Politics* (New York: Macmillan, 1960).

5. Jay Taylor, *The Generalissimo: Chiang Kai-Shek and the Struggle for Modern China* (Cambridge, MA: Belknap Press, 2011), pp. 333–34.

6. Richard Norton Smith, *The Colonel: The Life and Legend of Robert R. McCormick, 1880–1955* (Evanston, IL: Northwestern University Press, 2003).

7. 96 Cong. Rec. 298 (1950) (statement of Sen. Taft).

8. Quoted in James T. Patterson, *Mr. Republican: A Biography of Robert A. Taft* (Boston: Houghton Mifflin, 1972), p. 489.

9. Quoted in Richard P. Stebbins, *The United States in World Affairs, 1950* (New York: Harper & Brothers, 1951), p. 57. For Acheson's reaction to the charges, see Dean Acheson, *Present at the Creation: My Years in the State Department* (New York: W.W. Norton, 1969), p. 364.

10. Acheson, *Present at the Creation*, pp. 365–66.

11. Ted Galen Carpenter, "Blast from the Past: When Hawks Wanted to Bomb a 'Suicidal' China," *National Interest Online*, April 1, 2015.

12. "Trying to Comprehend the Incomprehensible," *New York Times*, November 17, 1968.

13. U.S. Department of State, "Joint U.S.-China Communiqué," Shanghai, February 27, 1972, https://history.state.gov/historicaldocuments/frus1969-76v17/d203.

14. John W. Finney, "Nixon Wins Broad Approval of Congress on China Talks, but Some Criticism Arises," *New York Times*, February 29, 1972.

15. Quoted in Finney, "Nixon Wins Broad Approval."

16. Finney, "Nixon Wins Broad Approval."

17. Quoted in Robert B. Semple Jr., "2 Senate Leaders Will Go to China, Invited by Chou," *New York Times*, March 1, 1972.

18. James Reston, "Washington: Mr. Nixon's Finest Hour," *New York Times*, March 1, 1972.

19. Associated Press, "Editorial Opinions in U.S. on Nixon's Trip," *New York Times*, February 25, 1972.

20. William F. Buckley, Jr., "Nixon Diplomacy Won't Work," *Washington Star*, February 23, 1972.

21. James Mann, *About Face: A History of America's Curious Relationship with China, From Nixon to Clinton*, rev. ed. (New York: Vintage Books, 2000), p. 5.

22. Mann, *About Face*, p. 8.

23. "Jackson on China," *National Review*, August 16, 1974, pp. 907–8.

24. Edward N. Luttwak, "Against the China Card," *Commentary*, October 1978, p. 43.

25. Harry Harding, *A Fragile Relationship: The United States and China since 1972* (Washington: Brookings Institution Press, 1992), p. 169.

26. "It Will Be Incomparably More Difficult to Rule China," *New York Times*, June 3, 2014.

27. Quoted in Edward Timperlake and William C. Triplett II, *Red Dragon Rising: Communist China's Military Threat to America* (Washington: Regnery, 1999), p. 26.

28. "The China Mission," editorial, *Washington Post*, December 11, 1989.

29. Winston Lord, "Misguided Mission," *Washington Post*, December 19, 1989.

30. James Risen, "U.S. Warns China on Taiwan, Sends Warships to Area," *Los Angeles Times*, March 11, 1996.

31. Terry Atlas and William Neikirk, "U.S., China Quietly Worked to Defuse Taiwan Crisis," *Chicago Tribune*, March 31, 1996.

32. Bill Gertz, *Betrayal: How the Clinton Administration Undermined American Security* (Washington: Regnery, 1999), p. 81.

33. "Campaign Finance Special Report: The Exploits of Charlie Trie," editorial, *Washington Post*, August 3, 1997. For a follow-up report, see Bob Woodward, "Campaign Finance Special Report: Findings Link Clinton Allies to Chinese Intelligence," *Washington Post*, February 10, 1998.

34. Mann, *About Face*, p. 351.

35. Bill Gertz, *The China Threat: How the People's Republic Targets America* (Washington: Regnery, 2000).

36. Nicholas D. Kristof and Sheryl WuDunn, *China Wakes: The Struggle for the Soul of a Rising Power* (New York: Vintage Books, 1995).

37. "Newt Gingrich on China," editorial, *New York Times*, April 1, 1997.

38. Thomas L. Friedman, *The Lexus and the Olive Tree* (New York: Anchor Books, 2000), p. 183.

39. Patrick Tyler, *A Great Wall: Six Presidents and China, An Investigative History* (New York: Public Affairs, 1999), p. 426.

40. Neil King Jr., Greg Jaffe, and Charles Hutzler, "China Won't Release Plane, Crew Despite Bush's Intensifying Demands," *Wall Street Journal*, April 3, 2001.

41. William Kristol and Robert Kagan, "A National Humiliation," *Weekly Standard*, April 1, 2001.

42. "No Time for the Dalai Lama," editorial, *Wall Street Journal*, October 6, 2009.

43. Michael Collins, "It's Time to Stand Up to China," *Industry Week*, June 13, 2016.

44. Jane Perlez, "Continuing Buildup, China Boosts Military Spending More than 11 Percent," *New York Times*, March 4, 2012.

45. Kevin L. Kearns and Alan Tonelson, "China's Reagan-esque Trap for Obama," HuffPost, May 25, 2011.

46. Bill Gertz, *Deceiving the Sky: Inside Communist China's Drive for Global Supremacy* (New York: Encounter Books, 2019), pp. 34–41.

47. Helen H. Wang, "America's Smart Congagement Policy in Asia Pacific," *Forbes*, April 29, 2016.

48. Daniel W. Drezner, "There Is No China Crisis," *Reason*, May 2020.

49. "If Bill Allowing Extradition to China Passes, 'Nobody Is Safe,' Says Critic," *NewsHour*, PBS, May 17, 2019; Brandon Hong, "Raining on China's Big

Parade: Hong Kong Protests Give Lie to 'One State, Two Systems,'" *Daily Beast*, October 1, 2019; Bethany Allen-Ebrahiman, "The Depressing Reality behind Hong Kong's Protests," *New Republic*, June 20, 2019; Kristina Olney, "America Must Prevent Another Tiananmen Square and Stand for a Free Hong Kong," *National Review*, August 12, 2019; and Joseph Bosco, "China's Irresponsible Behavior on Virus Shouldn't Overshadow Its Actions in Hong Kong," *The Hill*, March 6, 2020.

50. George Will, "Hong Kong Stands Athwart an Increasingly Nasty Regime," *National Review*, September 19, 2019.

51. Kou Jie, "Xi Calls for Close Study of Report by Mao," *Global Times*, February 29, 2019.

52. Jun Mai, "Chinese Liberal Think Tank Slams Beijing Censors after Website and Media Accounts Shut Down," *South China Morning Post*, January 24, 2017.

53. "Change to Chinese University's Charter Dropping 'Freedom of Thought,' Stirs Debate," Reuters, December 18, 2019; and Emily Feng and Amy Cheng, "Chinese Universities Are Enshrining Communist Party Control in Their Charters," NPR, January 20, 2020.

54. Bradley Thayer and Lianchao Han, "China's Weapon of Mass Surveillance Is a Human Rights Abuse," *The Hill*, May 29, 2019.

55. Tony Lin, "As China Abolishes Two-Term Limit, a Siege on Digital Free Speech," *Columbia Journalism Review*, March 16, 2018.

56. Anna Mitchell and Larry Diamond, "China's Surveillance State Should Scare Everyone," *The Atlantic*, February 2, 2018.

57. David Brunnstrom, "Pompeo Says China Still Withholding Coronavirus Information," Reuters, March 24, 2020.

58. "China Denies Spreading Coronavirus Disinformation following EU Report," Reuters, April 27, 2020.

59. Allyson Chiu, "'China Has Blood on Its Hands'; Fox News Hosts Join Trump in Blame-Shifting," *Washington Post*, March 19, 2020; Louis Casiano, "Coronavirus Is Latest in China's History of Trying to Cover Up Negative Info," Fox News, April 1, 2020; Barnini Chakraborty "China Lied about Coronavirus, Putting World in Jeopardy, U.S. Intelligence Agents Say," Fox News, April 2, 2020.

60. Joseph Bosco, "The Wuhan Virus and Regime Change in Washington," *The Hill*, March 19, 2020.

61. Julian E. Barnes, "C.I.A. Hunts for Authentic Virus Totals in China, Dismissing Government Totals," *New York Times*, April 2, 2020.

62. Adam K. Raymond, "U.S. Intelligence: China Covered Up Extent of Coronavirus Outbreak, *Intelligencer: New York Magazine*, April 1, 2020.

63. David Mastio, "No, Calling the Novel Coronavirus the 'Wuhan Virus' Is Not Racist," *USA Today*, March 11, 2020; Rich Lowry, "Calling the Wuhan

Virus the 'Wuhan Virus' Is Not Racist," *National Review*, March 10, 2020; and Lee Elci, "Elci: 'Wuhan Flu' More Accurately Names Virus and What It Means," *The Day*, March 19, 2020.

64. "Trump Defends Calling Coronavirus the 'Chinese Virus,'" Al Jazeera, March 23, 2020; and Maegan Vazquez, "Trump Says He's Pulling Back from Calling Novel Coronavirus 'China Virus,'" CNN, March 24, 2020.

65. Jill Flipovic, "Trump's Malicious Use of 'Chinese Virus,'" CNN, March 18, 2020; Dylan Scott, "Trump's New Fixation on Using a Racist Term for the Coronavirus Is Dangerous," *Vox*, March 18, 2020; Tim Dickinson, "Racist Trump Defends Using 'Chinese Virus' to Describe Coronavirus Pandemic," *Rolling Stone*, March 18, 2020; and Allyson Chiu, "Trump Has No Qualms about Calling the Coronavirus the 'Chinese Virus.' That's a Dangerous Attitude, Experts Say," *Washington Post*, March 20, 2020.

66. Peter Hasson, "Majority of Americans Agree with Trump's Calling COVID-19 'Chinese Virus,'" *Daily Signal*, April 10, 2020.

67. Helen Raleigh, "Don't Blame All Chinese People for the Actions of Their Evil Government," *Federalist*, April 8, 2020.

68. Josh Rogin, "Don't Blame 'China' for the Coronavirus—Blame the Chinese Communist Party," *Washington Post*, March 19, 2020.

69. Michael Auslin, "Why China Must Be Held Accountable for the Coronavirus Pandemic, *National Review*, March 3, 2020.

70. Ian Easton, "Quarantine China's Government," *Taipei Times*, April 27, 2020.

71. Austin Lowe, "Blame Xi, Not China, for the Impact of the Coronavirus," *The Hill*, March 31, 2020.

72. Henry Austin and Alexander Smith, "Coronavirus: Chinese Official Suggests U.S. Army to Blame for Outbreak," NBC News, March 13, 2020.

73. Laura Kelly, "Pompeo Warns China against Spreading 'Outlandish Rumors' about Coronavirus," *The Hill*, March 16, 2020.

74. Eliza Barclay, "The Conspiracy Theories about the Origins of the Coronavirus, Debunked," *Vox*, March 12, 2020; and Molly Stellino, "Fact Check: Did the Coronavirus Originate in a Chinese Laboratory?," *USA Today*, March 19, 2020.

75. Josh Campbell, Kylie Atwood, and Evan Perez, "U.S. Explores Possibility That Coronavirus Spread Started in Chinese Lab, Not a Market," CNN, April 16, 2020; Harry Kazianis, "What If the Coronavirus Really Did Originate in a Chinese Lab?," *The American Conservative*, April 16, 2020; and Bret Baier, "Sources Believe Coronavirus Outbreak Originated in Wuhan Lab as Part of China's Efforts to Compete with U.S.," Fox News, April 16, 2020.

76. See, for example, Aylin Woodward, "A U.S. Researcher Who Worked with a Wuhan Virology Lab Gives 4 Reasons Why a Coronavirus Leak Would Be Extremely Unlikely," *Business Insider*, May 2, 2020.

77. "This Week," ABC News, May 3, 2020.

78. Alex Marquardt, Kylie Atwood, and Zachary Cohen, "Intel Shared among U.S. Allies Indicates Virus Outbreak More Likely Came from Market, Not a Chinese Lab," CNN, May 5, 2020.

79. Dana Kennedy, "China Lied about Origin of the Coronavirus, Leaked Intelligence Report Says," *New York Post*, May 2, 2020.

80. Sakshi Piplani, Puneet Kumar Singh, David A. Winkler, and Nikolai Petrovsky, "In Silico Comparison of SARS-CoV-2 Spike Protein-ACE2 Binding Affinities across Species and Implications for Virus Origin," *Scientific Reports* 11, no. 13063 (2021), https://doi.org/10.1038/s41598-021-92388-5.

81. Michael D. Shear, Julian E. Barnes, Carl Zimmer, and Benjamin Mueller, "Biden Orders Intelligence Inquiry into Origins of Virus," *New York Times*, May 26, 2021; Shane Harris and Yasmeen Abutaleb, "Coronavirus 'Lab Leak' Theory Jumps from Mocked to Maybe as Biden Orders Intelligence Review," *Washington Post*, May 28, 2021.

82. "Facebook's Lab-Leak About-Face," editorial, *Wall Street Journal*, May 27, 2021.

83. Jonathan Chait, "How the Liberal Media Dismissed the Lab-Leak Theory and Smeared Its Supporters," *Intelligencer: New York Magazine*, May 24, 2021; Holman W. Jenkins, Jr., "Wuhan Lab Theory Is a Media Warning," *Wall Street Journal*, May 28, 2021; and Robby Soave, "The Media's Lab Leak Debacle Shows Why Banning 'Misinformation' Is a Terrible Idea," *Reason*, June 4, 2021.

84. Jenkins, "Wuhan Lab Theory."

85. Patrick Tucker, "Iranian, Russian, Chinese Media Push COVID-19 'Bioweapon' Conspiracies," Defense One, March 10, 2020; and Steven Lee Myers, "China Spins Tale That the U.S. Army Started the Coronavirus Epidemic," *New York Times*, March 13, 2020, updated March 17, 2020.

86. Nadia Schadlow, "Consider the Possibility That Trump Is Right about China," *The Atlantic*, April 5, 2020.

87. Barnini Chakraborty, "China Hints at Denying Americans Life-Saving Coronavirus Drugs," Fox News, March 13, 2020.

88. Some critics question or flatly dispute the 80 percent figure. See Eric Boehm, "Why You Shouldn't Trust Anyone Who Claims 80 Percent of America's Drugs Come from China," *Reason*, April 6, 2020. The actual figure is very hard to calculate and depends on what factors are considered to measure the degree of dependence.

89. Guy Taylor, "'Wake-Up' Call: Chinese Control of U.S. Pharmaceutical Supplies Sparks Growing Concern," *Washington Times*, March 17, 2020; Alan Tonelson, "Not Just China: U.S. Reliance on Foreign Medical Supplies Is Staggering," *The American Conservative*, March 27, 2020; and Rosemary

Gibson, "China's Cartels: Those Who Control the Medicines Control the World," *The American Conservative*, April 2, 2020.

90. Ana Swanson, "Coronavirus Spurs U.S. Efforts to End China's Chokehold on Drugs," *New York Times*, March 11, 2020.

91. Josh Rogin, "The Coronavirus Crisis Is Turning Americans in Both Parties against China," *Washington Post*, April 8, 2020.

92. Kat Devlin, Laura Silver, and Christine Huang, *U.S. Views of China Increasingly Negative Amid Coronavirus Outbreak* (Washington: Pew Research Center, 2020).

93. Matthew Petti, "What Do Progressives Think about China?," *National Interest Online*, April 23, 2020.

94. Walter Russell Mead, "Beijing Escalates the New Cold War," *Wall Street Journal*, March 18, 2020.

95. Arthur Bloom, "China's Long Tentacles Extend Deep into American Media," *The American Conservative*, March 31, 2020. Also see "Major U.S. Media Companies' Business Ties with China," Chinascope, January 27, 2021.

96. Arthur Bloom, "They Really Are Lying to You," *The American Conservative*, June 10, 2020.

97. Jarrett Stepman, "Liberal Media's Double Standard: Censor Trump's Briefings, Air China's Propaganda," *Daily Signal*, April 1, 2020.

98. Barbara Boland, "Bloomberg News Buried Stories Critical of China," *The American Conservative*, April 14, 2020.

99. Leta Hong Fincher, "When Bloomberg News's Reporting on China Was Challenged, Bloomberg Tried to Ruin Me for Speaking Out," *The Intercept*, February 18, 2020.

100. "World Health Disinformation," editorial, *Wall Street Journal*, April 5, 2020. Also see Fred Lucas, "5 Keys to Unlocking Why the World Health Organization Bows to China on COVID-19," *Daily Signal*, April 1, 2020; and Rich Lowry, "Blaming the WHO and China Is Not Scapegoating," *Politico*, April 8, 2020.

101. Javier Hernandez, "Trump Slammed the W.H.O. over Coronavirus. He's Not Alone," *New York Times*, April 8, 2020; Hinnerk Feldwish-Dentrup, "How WHO Became China's Coronavirus Accomplice," *Foreign Policy*, April 2, 2020; and Wilfred Chan, "The WHO Ignores Taiwan. The World Pays the Price," *Nation*, April 3, 2020.

102. Alice Miranda Ollstein, "Trump Halts Funding to World Health Organization," *Politico*, April 14, 2020; Rebecca Falconer, "What They're Saying: Opposition Erupts to Trump's Halting WHO Funding," *Axios*, April 15, 2020; and Matt Stieb, "Trump Cuts Funding to the World Health Organization during a Global Pandemic," *Intelligencer: New York Magazine*, April 14, 2020.

103. For an example of a rare attempt to exonerate Beijing's behavior, see Ethan Paul, "How Biden Can Beat Trump on China," *Responsible Statecraft*, April 15, 2020. For an attempt to fully exonerate the WHO and at least partially exonerate China, see Richard Perez-Pena and Donald G. McNeil Jr., "W.H.O., Now Trump's Scapegoat, Warned about Coronavirus Early and Often," *New York Times*, April 16, 2020. However, a few sharp criticisms of both China and the WHO appeared even in establishment, staunchly pro-globalism publications. See, for example, John West, "Time for China and the WHO to Fess Up," *Globalist*, April 20, 2020.

104. K. Riva Levinson, "The WHO Made Mistakes, but It's China That Must Be Held Accountable," *The Hill*, April 15, 2020.

105. Gordon G. Chang, "Trump Right to Stop Funding World Health Organization over Its Botched Coronavirus Response," Fox News, April 14, 2020; and Salvatore Babones, "Donald Trump Is Right to Dump the WHO," *National Interest Online*, April 15, 2020. Even libertarian, rather than conventionally conservative, publications focused their WHO criticism on the China connection. See Zach Weissmueller, "How China Corrupted the World Health Organization's Response to COVID-19," *Reason*, April 15, 2020; and Christian Britschagi, "The WHO Helped Spread Chinese Lies about COVID-19. Now It's Lecturing People about Drinking During Quarantine," *Reason*, April 15, 2020.

106. Susan E. Rice, "Trump Is Playing the China Card. Who Believes Him?," *New York Times*, May 19, 2020; Laurie Garrett, "Trump Scapegoats China and WHO—and Americans Will Suffer," *Foreign Policy*, May 30, 2020; and Max Boot, "Trump Can't Blame China for His Own Coronavirus Failures," *Washington Post*, May 3, 2020.

107. Anya van Wagtendonk, "U.S. Allies Express Dismay over U.S. Handling of Global Medical Supply Chain," *Vox*, April 4, 2020; and Nahal Toosi, "'Lord of the Flies: PPE Edition': U.S. Cast as Culprit in Global Scrum over Coronavirus Supplies," *Politico*, April 3, 2020.

108. Nahal Toosi, "Trump Aides Pound on China. Health Experts Say: Please Stop," *Politico*, March 13, 2020; and Rachel Maddow, "Trump's Antagonism of China Could Hurt Coronavirus Cooperation," MSNBC, March 30, 2020.

109. Peter S. Goodman, Katie Thomas, Sui-Lee Wee, and Jeffrey Gettleman, "A New Front for Nationalism: The Global Battle against a Virus," *New York Times*, April 10, 2020.

110. Conor Finnegan, "Despite Calls for Global Cooperation, U.S. and China Fight over Leading Coronavirus Response," ABC News, March 31, 2020.

111. Michele Flournoy and Lisa Monaco, "Now's Not the Time for Isolationism," *Politico*, April 8, 2020.

112. Goodman et al., "New Front for Nationalism."

113. Hal Brands, "Modest Multilateralism Is in America's Interest—and China's Too," *Japan Times*, April 26, 2020.

114. Alan Tonelson, "Front Page NYT: 'Nationalism Is Jeopardizing' COVID Fight," *The American Conservative*, April 13, 2020.

115. Patrick J. Buchanan, "Up for a New Cold War—with China," Antiwar.com, April 28, 2020.

116. Drezner, "There Is No China Crisis."

117. Antony Dapiron "The Coronavirus Is Cover for a Crackdown in Hong Kong," *Foreign Policy*, April 22, 2020; and Sean Mantesso, Bang Xiao, and Alan Weedon, "Coronavirus Is Giving Beijing Cover to Extinguish Hong Kong's Democracy, Advocates Say," ABC News (Australia) May 3, 2020.

118. Sarah Zheng, "Two Sessions: National Security Law Will Not Damage Hong Kong's Freedoms, Chinese Foreign Minister Says," *South China Morning Post*, May 24, 2020.

119. Carol Anne Goodwin Jones, "How China's New National Security Law Subverts Hong Kong's Cherished Rule of Law," *Wired*, May 31, 2020.

120. Emily Feng, "4 Takeaways from Beijing's Hong Kong Power Grab," NPR, May 29, 2020.

121. Yanni Chow and Yoyo Chow, "Hong Kong Arrests 53 for Plot to 'Overthrow' Government in Latest Crackdown on Dissent," Reuters, January 5, 2021.

122. Carol Morello, "Pompeo Declares Hong Kong No Longer Autonomous from China," *Washington Post*, May 27, 2020.

123. "The End of Hong Kong?," editorial, *National Review*, May 29, 2020. For a similar perspective in another conservative publication, see Rachel del Guidice, "The End of the Rule of Law in Hong Kong? What China's New Crackdown Could Mean," *Daily Signal*, May 27, 2020.

124. Victor Garcia, "Marc Thiessen: Trump Must Threaten China with 'Brain Drain' and 'Capital Flight' amid Hong Kong Crackdown," Fox News, May 30, 2020.

125. David Wertime, "China's Hong Kong Crackdown Narrows Options for the U.S.," *Politico*, May 29, 2020. Wertime had gathered a number of area specialists for a discussion of those options.

126. Jonah Shepp, "If China Cracks Down on Hong Kong, There's Little Anyone Can Do to Stop It," *Intelligencer: New York Magazine*, August 8, 2019.

127. Doug Bandow, "China to Become a Political Piñata in 2020 Presidential Election," *China-U.S. Focus*, May 5, 2020.

128. Jonathan Martin and Maggie Haberman, "A Key GOP Strategy: Blame China. But Trump Goes Off Message," *New York Times*, April 19, 2020.

129. "New Ad Slams Trump for Putting China First in Coronavirus Crisis," American Bridge, April 17, 2020. Also see Michelle Ye Hee Lee, "Democratic Super PAC Launches $15 Million Ad Blitz Slamming Trump on China and Corona Virus," *Washington Post*, April 17, 2020.

130. Tim Hain, "Biden Ad: Trump Left U.S. Unprepared for Epidemic, 'Rolled Over for the Chinese,'" *RealClearPolitics*, April 19, 2020.

131. Nahal Toosi, "Biden Ad Exposes Rift over China on the Left," *Politico*, April 23, 2020.

132. Jeet Heer, "On China, Biden Falls into Trump's Xenophobia Trap," *Nation*, April 20, 2020.

133. Heer, "On China, Biden Falls into Trump's Xenophobia Trap."

134. Peter Beinart, "The Utter Futility of Biden's China Rhetoric," *The Atlantic*, April 20, 2020.

135. Ezra F. Vogel, "U.S. Policies Are Pushing Our Friends in China toward Anti-American Nationalism," *Washington Post*, July 22, 2020.

136. Dave DeCamp, "Biden Nominees Call for Tough Stance on China during Confirmation Hearings," Antiwar.com, January 19, 2021.

137. Ben Blanchard, "Taiwan-Biden Ties Off to Strong Start with Invite for Top Diplomat," Reuters, January 20, 2021.

138. "U.S. Support for Taiwan 'Rock-Solid' as China Again Sends Warplanes," Al Jazeera, January 24, 2021; and Joseph Choi, "U.S. Carrier Group Enters South China Sea amid Tensions between China, Taiwan," *The Hill*, January 24, 2021.

CHAPTER 9

1. Mark Hertsgaard, *On Bended Knee: The Press and the Reagan Presidency* (New York: Schocken Books, 1988), p. 209.

2. Roy Gutman, letter to the editor, *Foreign Policy* 94 (Spring 1994): 160–61.

3. Charles Lane, "Washington Diarist: War Stories," *New Republic*, January 3, 1994, p. 43; and Charles Lane, "Brock Crock," *New Republic*, September 5, 1994, pp. 18–21.

4. Editor's Note, *Foreign Policy* 97 (Winter 1994–95): 185.

5. Lane, "Washington Diarist."

6. Lane, "Washington Diarist," p. 43.

7. Carl Bernstein, "The CIA and the Media," *Rolling Stone*, January 1, 1977.

8. Bernstein, "The CIA and the Media."

9. Jonathan Chait, "How the Liberal Media Dismissed the Lab-Leak Theory and Smeared Its Supporters," *Intelligencer: New York Magazine*, May 24, 2021; Holman W. Jenkins, Jr., "Wuhan Lab Theory Is a Media Warning," *Wall*

Street Journal, May 28, 2021; and Robby Soave, "The Media's Lab Leak Debacle Shows Why Banning 'Misinformation' Is a Terrible Idea," *Reason*, June 4, 2021.

10. Glenn Kessler, "Timeline: How the Wuhan Lab-Leak Became Credible," *Washington Post*, May 25, 2021; "Facebook's Lab-Leak About-Face," editorial, *Wall Street Journal*, May 27, 2021; Shane Harris and Yasmeen Abutaleb, "Coronavirus 'Lab Leak' Theory Jumps from Mocked to Maybe as Biden Orders Intelligence Review," *Washington Post*, May 28, 2021; and Russ Douthat, "Why the Lab Leak Theory Matters," *New York Times*, May 29, 2021.

11. Philip Rucker and Carol Leonnig, *A Very Stable Genius: Donald J. Trump's Testing of America* (New York: Penguin Books, 2020).

12. Carol Leonnig and Philip Rucker, "'You're a Bunch of Dopes and Babies': Inside Trump's Stunning Tirade against Generals," *Washington Post*, January 17, 2020.

13. Craig Whitlock, Leslie Shapiro, and Armand Emamdjomeh, "The Afghanistan Papers: A Secret History of the War," *Washington Post*, December 9, 2019.

14. Doug Bandow, "South Korea Doesn't Need U.S. Military Babysitting," *Foreign Policy*, October 2, 2020.

15. Amanda Macias, "America Has Spent $6.4 Trillion on Wars in Middle East and Asia since 2001, a New Study Says," CNBC, November 20, 2019.

16. Leonnig and Rucker, "'You're a Bunch of Dopes and Babies.'"

17. Christopher Layne, *Peace of Illusions: American Grand Strategy from 1940 to the Present* (Ithaca, NY: Cornell University Press, 2007).

18. Rajan Menon, *The End of Alliances* (New York: Oxford University Press, 2008); John J. Mearsheimer, *The Great Delusion: Liberal Dreams and International Realities* (New Haven, CT: Yale University Press, 2019); and Ted Galen Carpenter, *NATO: The Dangerous Dinosaur* (Washington: Cato Institute, 2019).

19. Danny Sjursen, "Discredited Russian Bounty Story Exposes Media's Role in Status Quo," Antiwar.com, September 29, 2020.

20. Quoted in Joe Concha, "Glenn Greenwald Tells Megyn Kelly He Has Been 'Formally Banned,' from MSNBC," *The Hill*, September 28, 2020.

21. Tim Weiner, "The Unanswered Question of Our Time: Is Trump an Agent of Russia?," *Washington Post*, September 21, 2020.

22. George Beebe, "The Stubborn Persistence of the Russia Bogeyman," *National Interest Online*, September 25, 2020.

23. Emma-Jo Morris and Gabrielle Fonrouge, "Smoking-Gun Email Reveals How Hunter Biden Introduced Ukrainian Businessman to VP Dad," *New York Post*, October 14, 2020.

24. Emma-Jo Morris and Gabrielle Fonrouge, "Emails Reveal How Hunter Biden Tried to Cash in Big on Behalf of Family with Chinese Firm," *New York Post*, October 15, 2020.

25. Michael Goodwin, "Hunter Biz Partner Confirms Email, Details Joe Biden's Push to Make Millions from China," *New York Post*, October 22, 2020.

26. Natasha Bertrand, "Hunter Biden Story Is Russian Disinfo, Dozens of Former Intel Officials Say," *Politico*, October 19, 2020.

27. Dave DeCamp, "DNI Says Hunter Biden Emails Are Not 'Russian Disinformation,'" Antiwar.com, October 19, 2020; and Devlin Barrett, "FBI Says It Has 'Nothing to Add' to Ratcliffe's Remarks about Hunter Biden, Russian Disinformation," *Washington Post*, October 20, 2020.

28. Alexis Beneviste, "The Anatomy of the New York Post's Dubious Hunter Biden Story," CNN, October 18, 2021; and Judy Woodruff, "Are Trump Allies Peddling Russian Disinformation about the Bidens?," *NewsHour*, PBS, October 16, 2021. Months later, some journalists were still pushing this argument despite the dearth of evidence—an argument Joe Biden also continued to use. See Danya Hajjaji, "As Hunter Biden FBI Probe Rolls On, Laptop Story Resurfaces after U.S. Claims about Russia," *Newsweek*, March 19, 2021; and Tyler Olson, "President Biden Said Hunter Laptop Was Russian Disinformation, but Son Now Says It 'Could' Be His," Fox News, April 2, 2021.

29. David Harsanyi, "The Media's 'Russian Disinformation' Canard," *National Review*, October 20, 2020.

30. Quoted in Charlie Nash, "Glenn Greenwald on Tucker Carlson Calls Adam Schiff 'the Most Pathological Liar in All of American Politics,'" *Mediaite*, October 20, 2020.

31. Quoted in "Glenn Greenwald Calls Out Hypocrites Covering for Biden on Post's Hunter Biden Stories," editorial, *New York Post*, October 20, 2020.

32. Glenn Greenwald, "My Resignation from The Intercept," Substack.com, October 29, 2020.

33. Holman W. Jenkins, Jr., "The Hunter Biden Laptop Is Real," *Wall Street Journal*, July 9, 2021.

34. Jordan Williams, "Hunter Biden Says He Doesn't Know If Delaware Laptop Is His," *The Hill*, April 2, 2021. Also see "Hunter Biden on His Memoir 'Beautiful Things' and His Struggles with Substance Abuse," *Sunday Morning*, CBS News, April 5, 2021.

35. See, for example, Marshall Cohen and Evan Perez, "Hunter Biden Dodges Questions on Laptop Seized by FBI," CNN, April 2, 2021; Jonathan Turley, "Will the Press Ever Cover the Hunter Biden Story Fairly?," *The Hill*, April 3, 2021; "Hunter Biden's Laptop Keeps Damning Joe, but Media Just Ignore It," editorial, *New York Post*, May 31, 2021; Byron York, "The Future of Hunter Biden's Laptop," *Washington Examiner*, July 7, 2021; and Jenkins, "The Hunter Biden Laptop Is Real."

36. Nic Newman, *Reuters Institute Digital News Report 2021*, 10th ed. (Oxford, UK: Reuters Institute for the Study of Journalism, June 2021).

CHAPTER 10

1. Ted Galen Carpenter, *The Captive Press: Foreign Policy Crises and the First Amendment* (Washington: Cato Institute, 1995), pp. 16–18; and Phillip Knightley, *The First Casualty, from the Crimea to Vietnam: the War Correspondent as Hero, Propagandist, and Myth Maker* (New York: Harcourt Brace Jovanovich, 1975), pp. 20–21.

2. Quoted in Walter Karp, *The Politics of War* (New York; Harper and Row, 1979), p. 327.

3. Franklin D. Roosevelt letter to Attorney General Francis Biddle, May 7, 1942, Franklin Roosevelt Papers, Official File 4866, Franklin D. Roosevelt Library, Hyde Park, NY.

4. Edward Alwood, *Dark Days in the Newsroom: McCarthyism Aimed at the Press* (Philadelphia: Temple University Press, 2007), p. 32.

5. Freda Kirchwey, "Curb the Fascist Press," *Nation*, March 28, 1942, pp. 357–58.

6. Alwood, *Dark Days in the Newsroom*, p. 40.

7. Carpenter, *The Captive Press*, pp. 106–7.

8. Alwood, *Dark Days in the Newsroom*, pp. 25–27.

9. Voice of America hearings before the Permanent Subcommittee on Investigations, 83rd Cong., 1st sess., 1953, in *Executive Sessions of the Senate Permanent Subcommittee on Investigations of the Committee on Government Operations*, vol. 1 (Washington: Government Printing Office, 2003), pp. 457–902.

10. Alwood, *Dark Days in the Newsroom*, p. 66.

11. Alwood, *Dark Days in the Newsroom*, pp. 69–71.

12. Alwood, *Dark Days in the Newsroom*, pp. 72–73.

13. Victor Navasky, "Not Just Hollywood Artists and Intellectuals, McCarthy Also Went after 500 U.S. Journalists," *ThePrint*, December 18, 2019.

14. Alwood, *Dark Days in the Newsroom*, p. 1

15. Alwood, *Dark Days in the Newsroom*, p. 6.

16. Navasky, "Not Just Hollywood Artists and Intellectuals."

17. Alwood, *Dark Days in the Newsroom*, p. 57, 59–61.

18. Navasky, "Not Just Hollywood Artists and Intellectuals."

19. Paul Matzko, "How JFK Censored Right-Wing Radio," *Cato Policy Report*, March-April 2020.

20. Matzko, "How JFK Censored Right-Wing Radio."

21. Matzko, "How JFK Censored Right-Wing Radio."

22. Carpenter, *The Captive Press*, pp. 119–25.

23. Owen Bowcott, "Call for UK's 'Antiquated' Official Secrets Act to Be Updated," *The Guardian*, September 1, 2020.

24. Thomas Floyd, "'Official Secrets' Sheds Light on the Story of U.K. Whistleblower Katharine Gun," *Washington Post*, September 5, 2019.

25. Harold Evans, "The Norman Conquest: Freedom of the Press in Britain and America," in *The Media and Foreign Policy*, ed. Simon Serfaty (New York: Free Press, 1991), pp. 193–94.

26. Minutes of the 172nd Meeting of the National Security Council, November 23, 1953, Ann Whitman File, NSC Series, Box 5, Dwight D. Eisenhower Library, Abilene, KS. For this and other examples of Eisenhower administration efforts to restrict press scrutiny of U.S. intelligence activities, see Carpenter, *The Captive Press*, pp. 125–27.

27. Morton H. Halperin and David Hoffman, *Top Secret: National Security and the Right to Know* (Washington: New Republic Books, 1977), p. 9.

28. Halperin and Hoffman, *Top Secret*, p. 10.

29. Halperin and Hoffman, *Top Secret*, p. 10.

30. Derigan A. Silver, "National Security and the Press: The Government's Ability to Prosecute Journalists for the Possession or Publication of National Security Information," *Communication Law and Policy* 13 (2008): 454.

31. Jerry J. Berman and Morton H. Halperin, "The Agents Identities Protection Act," in *The First Amendment and National Security* (Charlottesville, VA: Center for Law and National Security, 1984), pp. 41–55.

32. Atwood, *Dark Days in the Newsroom*, pp. 1–2.

33. Melissa Wasser, "House Expected to Vote on Expanded Intelligence Identities Protection Act," Reporters Committee for Freedom of the Press, December 11, 2019. Also see Charlie Savage, "Expansion of Secrecy Law for Intelligence Operatives Alarms Free Press Advocates," *New York Times*, July 10, 2019.

34. Carpenter, *The Captive Press*, pp. 107–9.

35. Quoted in "Do Loose Lips Sink Ships?," *New Republic*, November 18, 1985.

36. Steven Burkholder, "The Morison Case: The Leaker as 'Spy,'" in *Freedom at Risk: Secrecy, Censorship, and Repression in the 1980s*, ed. Richard O. Curry (Philadelphia, PA: Temple University Press, 1988), p. 118.

37. Quoted in Carpenter, *The Captive Press*, p. 107.

38. Dean Acheson, "The Purloined Papers," *New York Times*, July 7, 1971.

39. Quoted in Carpenter, *The Captive Press*, p. 127.

40. Janet Reno, Attorney General, U.S. Department of Justice, Testimony Concerning Unauthorized Disclosure of Classified Information before the Senate Select Committee on Intelligence, 107th Cong., 1st sess., June 14, 2000, https://fas.org/sgp/othergov/renoleaks.html. Emphasis added.

41. Jack Nelson, "U.S. Government Secrecy and the Current Crackdown on Leaks," Joan Shorenstein Center on the Press, Politics, and Public Policy, Working Paper no. 2003-1, Fall 2002, p. 2.

42. "Examining DOJ's Investigation of Journalists Who Publish Classified Information: Lessons from the Jack Anderson Case," *Hearing before the Senate Committee on the Judiciary*, 109th Cong., 2nd sess. (June 6, 2006) (statements of Matthew Friedrich, Rodney Smolla, Gabriel Schoenfeld, Kevin Anderson, and Mark Feldstein).

43. Quoted in Scott Horton, "State of Exception," *Harper's*, July 2007.

44. Quoted in "Examining DOJ's Investigation of Journalists," *Hearing*.

45. Quoted in "Examining DOJ's Investigation of Journalists," *Hearing*.

46. "Examining DOJ's Investigation of Journalists," *Hearing*. Emphasis added.

47. Quoted in Horton, "State of Exception."

48. The *New York Times* declined to publish the letter, but the conservative blog *Powerline* did so in 2012, and it quickly became a sensation in right-wing circles. For the full text of the letter see Scott Johnson, "A Fateful Letter to the Editor of the Times," *Powerline*, October 23, 2012.

49. Nick Baumann, "The GOP Candidate Who Wants Journos Jailed," *Mother Jones*, November 10, 2011, updated November 4, 2014.

50. Jason M. Breslow, "Obama on Mass Surveillance, Then and Now," *Frontline*, PBS, May 13, 2014.

51. Breslow, "Obama on Mass Surveillance."

52. Breslow, "Obama on Mass Surveillance."

53. Carol Rosenberg and Tom Lasseter, "WikiLeaks Reveal Prison Secrets," *Miami Herald*, April 24, 2011.

54. David Alexander and Phillip Stewart, "Leaked U.S. Video Shows Deaths of Reuters' Staffers in Iraq," Reuters, April 15, 2010.

55. See Pfc. Manning's redacted statement. Also see Alan MacLeod, "Media Cheer Assange's Arrest," FAIR, April 18, 2019.

56. Quoted in "WikiLeaks and the Espionage Act of 1917," Reporters Committee for Freedom of the Press, n.d.

57. Espionage Statutes Modernization Act of 2011, S. 355, 112th Cong. (2011).

58. Intelligence Authorization Act for Fiscal Year 2001, H.R. 4392, 106th Cong. (2000).

59. Quoted in "WikiLeaks and the Espionage Act of 1917."

60. John Kiriakou, "Obama's Abuse of the Espionage Act Is Modern-Day McCarthyism," *The Guardian*, August 6, 2013.

61. See, for example, Charlie Savage and Leslie Kaufman, "Phone Records of Journalists Seized by U.S.," *New York Times*, May 13, 2013.

62. Sharyl Attkisson, *Stonewalled: My Fight for Truth against the Forces of Obstruction, Intimidation, and Harassment in Obama's Washington* (New York: HarperCollins, 2014), p. 299.

63. For the full text of the letter, see Reporters Committee for Freedom of the Press to Eric Holder, Attorney General, May 14, 2013.

64. Tom McCarthy, "James Rosen: Fox News Reporter Targeted as 'Co-Conspirator' in Spying Case," *The Guardian*, May 21, 2013.

65. Ian Tuttle, "El Chapo's Capture Puts 'Operation Fast and Furious' Back in the Headlines," *National Review*, January 22, 2016.

66. Elspeth Reeve, "Obama Allows Holder to Assert Executive Privilege on Fast and Furious," *The Atlantic*, June 20, 2012.

67. Attkisson, *Stonewalled*, p. 301.

68. Attkisson, *Stonewalled:* pp. 1–13.

69. Attkisson, *Stonewalled*, p. 301.

70. Attkisson, *Stonewalled*, p. 313.

71. Peter Sterne, "Sessions 'Not Sure' Whether He Would Prosecute Journalists," *Politico*, January 10, 2017.

72. Michael S. Schmidt, "Comey Memo Says Trump Asked Him to End Flynn Investigation," *New York Times*, May 16, 2017.

73. Devlin Barrett, "Trump Justice Department Secretly Obtained Post Reporters' Phone Records," *Washington Post*, May 7, 2021; and Charlie Savage and Katie Benner, "Trump Administration Secretly Seized Phone Records of Times Reporters," *New York Times*, June 2, 2021.

74. Peter Van Buren, "You Don't Have to Love Assange to Fear His Prosecution," *The American Conservative*, November 30, 2018.

75. Caitlin Johnstone, "Debunking the 'Assange Is a Russian Agent' Smear," *Consortium News*, April 22, 2019.

76. "Curious Eyes Never Run Dry," editorial, *New York Times*, April 11, 2019.

77. "Opinion: Julian Assange Is Not a Free-Press Hero. And He Is Long Overdue for Personal Accountability," editorial, *Washington Post*, April 11, 2019.

78. MacLeod, "Media Cheer Assange's Arrest."

79. "Assange Is Not a Free-Press Hero," *Washington Post*.

80. Van Buren, "You Don't Have to Love Assange."

81. David Weigel and Joby Warrick, "How Julian Assange Evolved from Pariah to Paragon," *Washington Post*, January 4, 2017.

82. Alan MacLeod, "Julian Assange: Press Shows Little Interest in Media 'Trial of the Century,'" FAIR, September 25, 2020.

83. Cindy Cohn, "Julian Assange's Prosecution Is about Much More than Attempting to Hack a Computer Password," Electronic Frontier Foundation, April 19, 2020.

84. Knight Institute, "Comment on the Indictment of Julian Assange," press release, Knight First Amendment Institute at Columbia University, April 11, 2019.

85. Quoted in Bill Goodwin, "Assange Prosecution Would Put Journalists around the World at Risk," *Computer Weekly*, September 10, 2020.

86. Quoted in Goodwin, "Assange Prosecution."

87. Quoted in Amnesty International, "UK: Assange Extradition Hearing Will Be a Key Test for UK and U.S. Justice," press release, September 4, 2020.

88. Amy Goodman, "Attorney: U.S. Case against Julian Assange Falls Apart as Key Witness Says He Lied to Get Immunity," *Democracy Now!*, June 28, 2021.

89. Alan MacLeod, "Key Assange Witness Recants—With Zero Corporate Media Coverage," FAIR, July 2, 2021.

90. "A Remarkable Silence: Media Blackout after Key Witness against Assange Admits Lying," Media Lens, July 1, 2021.

91. Quoted in Caitlin Johnstone, "The Horrifying Rise of Total Mass Media Blackouts on Inconvenient News Stories," *Scoop*, July 4, 2021.

92. Paul Szoldra, "This Is Everything Edward Snowden Revealed in One Year of Unprecedented Top-Secret Leaks," *Business Insider*, September 16, 2016.

93. James Ball, Julian Borger, and Glenn Greenwald, "Revealed: How US and UK Spy Agencies Defeat Internet Privacy and Security," *The Guardian*, September 6, 2013; and Attkisson, *Stonewalled*, pp. 304–5.

94. Jonathan Turley, "James Clapper's Perjury, and Why DC Made Men Don't Get Charged for Lying to Congress," *USA Today*, January 19, 2018. Also see Attkisson, *Stonewalled*, pp. 310–12.

95. Peter Finn and Sari Horwitz, "U.S. Charges Snowden with Espionage," *Washington Post*, June 21, 2013.

96. "Glenn Greenwald's Partner Delayed at Heathrow Airport for Nine Hours," *The Guardian*, August 18, 2013.

97. Eric Tucker and Ben Fox, "Charging Assange Reflects Dramatic Shift in U.S. Approach," Associated Press, April 12, 2019.

98. Quoted in Devlin Barrett, Rachel Weiner, and Matt Zapatosky, "WikiLeaks Founder Julian Assange Charged with Violating Espionage Act," *Washington Post*, May 23, 2019.

99. Quoted in Tucker and Fox, "Charging Assange."

100. Quoted in Tucker and Fox, "Charging Assange."

101. Tucker and Fox, "Charging Assange."

102. Nathan Robinson, "Many Democrats and Liberals Are Cheering Assange's Arrest. That's Foolish," *The Guardian*, April 14, 2019.

103. Ken Bensinger, Miriam Elder, and Mark Schoof, "These Reports Allege Trump Has Deep Ties to Russia," *BuzzFeed News*, June 10, 2017.

104. Robert Mahoney, "For the Sake of Press Freedom, Julian Assange Must Be Defended," Committee to Protect Journalists, December 11, 2019.

105. Mahoney, "For the Sake of Press Freedom."

106. Kevin Gosztola, "Why Did Respected Press Freedom Organization Exclude Assange from Annual List of Jailed Journalists?," *Medium*, December 11, 2019.

107. Jacob Sullum, "The Assange Exception to the First Amendment," *Reason*, April 17, 2019.

108. Caitlin Johnstone, "Assange Extradition Ruling Is a Relief, but It Isn't Justice," *Consortium News*, January 4, 2021.

109. Mark Hosenball, "Biden Administration Plans to Continue to Seek Extradition of WikiLeaks' Assange: Official," Reuters, February 9, 2021.

110. For example, see John Lyons, "AFP Raid on ABC Reveals Investigative Journalism Being Put in Same Category as Criminality," ABC News (Australia), July 14, 2019; International Federation of Journalists, "Hungary: Destruction of Press Freedom under Pretext of COVID-19," press release, June 17, 2021; and Reporters without Borders [RSF], "RSF Declares 'Press Freedom State of Emergency' in Poland," press release, September 13, 2021.

111. Glenn Greenwald, "Rep. Ilhan Omar's Misguided Defense of John Brennan and the Logan Act: A Dangerous and Unconstitutional Law," Substack.com, November 28, 2020. Emphasis in original.

Chapter 11

1. Phillip Knightley, *The First Casualty, from the Crimea to Vietnam: the War Correspondent as Hero, Propagandist, and Myth Maker* (New York: Harcourt, Brace Jovanovich, 1975), pp. 56–58.

2. Carl Bernstein, "The CIA and the Media," *Rolling Stone*, January 1, 1977.

3. Bernstein, "The CIA and the Media."

4. John Crewdson, "Worldwide Propaganda Network Built by the CIA," *New York Times*, December 26, 1977.

5. Crewdson, "Worldwide Propaganda Network."

6. Bernstein, "The CIA and the Media."

7. David Talbot, *The Devil's Chessboard: Allen Dulles, the CIA, and the Rise of America's Secret Government* (New York: HarperCollins, 2015).

8. Talbot, *Devil's Chessboard*, pp. 431–32.

9. Quoted in Talbot, *Devil's Chessboard*, p. 443.

10. Bernstein, "The CIA and the Media." Emphasis added.

11. Quoted in Bernstein, "The CIA and the Media."

12. Quoted in Bernstein, "The CIA and the Media." Bernstein notes that Sulzberger disputed the specifics of that account.

13. Jonathan Kwitny, *Endless Enemies: The Making of an Unfriendly World* (New York: Congdon and Weed, 1984), pp. 160–76.

14. Quoted in Kwitny, *Endless Enemies*, pp. 175–76.

15. Kwitny, *Endless Enemies*, p. 176.

16. Bernstein, "The CIA and the Media."

17. Bernstein, "The CIA and the Media."

18. Bernstein, "The CIA and the Media."

19. Peter Van Buren, "How American Journalists Became a Mouthpiece of the Deep State," *The American Conservative*, May 24, 2021; and Matt Taibbi, "Reporters Once Challenged the Spy State. Now, They're Agents of It," Substack, May 11, 2021.

20. Taibbi, "Reporters Once Challenged the Spy State."

21. "Matt Taibbi: Journalists Have Shifted Public Opinion in Support of Intelligence Agencies," *The Hill*, May 11, 2021.

22. Jack Shafer, "The Spies Who Came in to the TV Studio," *Politico*, February 6, 2018.

23. Quoted in David Shimer, "When the CIA Interferes in Foreign Elections," *Foreign Affairs*, June 21, 2020.

24. Van Buren, "How American Journalists Became a Mouthpiece."

25. Ben Norton, "Leaked Docs Expose Massive Syria Propaganda Operation Waged by Western Govt Contractors and Media," Grayzone, September 23, 2020.

26. Ken Silverstein, "The CIA's Mop-Up Man: L.A. Times Reporter Cleared Stories with Agency before Publication," *The Intercept*, September 4, 2014.

27. Chris Woods, "Bureau Investigation Finds Fresh Evidence of CIA Drone Strikes on Rescuers," Bureau of Investigative Journalism, August 1, 2013.

28. Jim Sciutto, *The Shadow War: Inside Russia's and China's Secret Operations to Defeat America* (New York: HarperCollins, 2019).

29. Paul Callan, "If You Want to Know Whether Strzok Was Biased, Just Look at His Texts," CNN, July 14, 2018.

30. Jessie Hellmann, "Former CIA Chief: Russia's Hacking 'Political Equivalent' of 9/11," *The Hill*, December 12, 2016.

31. Jason Leopold, "A Former CIA Official Apologizes to 'Every American' for Iraq Intelligence Failures," Vice, June 25, 2015.

32. David Barstow, "Behind TV Analysts, Pentagon's Hidden Hand," *New York Times*, April 20, 2008.

33. Barstow, "Behind TV Analysts."

34. David Barstow, "Pentagon Finds No Fault in Ties to TV Analysts," *New York Times*, December 24, 2011.

35. Barstow, "Pentagon Finds No Fault."

36. Barstow, "Pentagon Finds No Fault."

37. Lee Fang, "Who's Paying the Pro-War Pundits?," *Nation*, September 16, 2014.

38. Quoted in Caitlin Johnstone, "This Russia-Afghanistan Story Is Western Propaganda at Its Most Vile," CaitlinJohnstone.com, June 28, 2020.

39. Alan MacLeod, "Afghan Bounty Scandal Comes at Suspiciously Important Time for U.S. Military-Industrial Complex," *MintPress News*, July 1, 2020.

40. Lee Camp, "Connecting the Dates—U.S. Media Used to Stop the 'Threat' of Peace," *Counterpunch*, July 3, 2020.

41. Ben Freeman, *Foreign Funding of Think Tanks in America*, Foreign Influence Transparency Initiative (Washington: Center for International Policy, January 2020). A 2014 investigation also found extensive foreign funding of the leading U.S. think tanks. See Eric Lipton, Brooke Williams, and Nicholas Confessore, "Foreign Powers Buy Influence at Think Tanks," *New York Times*, September 6, 2014. Full disclosure: My employer, the Cato Institute, does not accept money from any government, foreign or domestic. A similar rule applies to Cato Institute scholars, except for reimbursement of expenses for participation in conferences or other events that may have government sponsorship.

42. For an important discussion of the Freeman report, *Foreign Funding of Think Tanks in America*, see Kelley Beaucar Vlahos, "New Report Details $174 Million in Foreign Funding to D.C. Think Tanks," *Responsible Statecraft*, January 29, 2020.

43. Freeman, *Foreign Funding of Think Tanks in America*; and Lipton, Williams, and Confessore, "Foreign Powers Buy Influence at Think Tanks."

44. "Atlantic Council's Turkish Links Cast Shadow over Washington Think Tank Industry," *Ahval News*, August 2020.

45. Michael Rubin, "Not Just Russia: Don't Let Turkish Money Influence U.S. Elections," *Washington Examiner*, August 26, 2020.

46. Eli Clifton, "Taiwan Funding of Think Tanks: Omnipresent and Rarely Discussed," *Responsible Statecraft*, June 17, 2020.

47. Ben Freeman, *U.S. Government and Defense Contractor Funding of America's Top 50 Think Tanks*, Foreign Influence Transparency Initiative (Washington: Center for International Policy, October 2020).

48. Barbara Boland, "Top 50 U.S. Think Tanks Receive over $1B from Gov, Defense Contractors," *The American Conservative*, October 24, 2020.

CHAPTER 12

1. "Twitter by the Numbers: Stats, Demographics & Fun Facts," Omnicore, January 6, 2021.

2. H. Tankovska, "Number of Monthly Active Facebook Users Worldwide as of 4th Quarter 2020," Statista, February 2, 2021.

3. Elisa Shearer and Katrina Eva Matsa, "News Use across Social Media Platforms 2018," Pew Research Center, September 10, 2018.

4. Elisa Shearer, "More than Eight-in-Ten Americans Get News from Digital Devices," Pew Research Center, January 12, 2021.

5. Andrew Hutchinson, "YouTube Will Now Remove Videos Alleging Vote Fraud in the 2020 US Election," SocialMediaToday.com, December 9, 2020.

6. Deena Zaru, "Trump Twitter Ban Raises Concerns over 'Unchecked' Power of Big Tech," ABC News, January 13, 2021.

7. Melissa Bell and Elizabeth Flock, "'A Gay Girl in Damascus' Comes Clean," *Washington Post*, June 12, 2011.

8. Bell and Flock, "'A Gay Girl in Damascus.'"

9. Guy Somerset, "Iraq, Syria, Iran—Some Truths about Social Media Truth," Antiwar.com, January 27, 2020.

10. Somerset, "Iraq, Syria, Iran."

11. Emily Vogels, Andrew Perrin, and Monica Anderson, "Most Americans Think Social Media Sites Censor Political Viewpoints," Pew Research Center, August 19, 2020.

12. Paul M. Barrett and J. Grant Sims, "False Accusations: The Unfounded Claim That Social Media Companies Censor Conservatives," Stern Center for Business and Human Rights, New York University, February 2021.

13. Brian Flood, "Study Dismissing Conservative Concerns about Big Tech Bias Was Funded by Far-Left Biden Mega-Donor," Fox News, February 2, 2021.

14. Dan Paterson, "What Is 'Section 230,' and Why Do Many Lawmakers Want to Repeal It?," CBS News, December 16, 2020.

15. For discussions, see Matthew Feeney and Will Duffield, "Holding Section 230 Hostage, Sen. Graham Demands Platforms EARN IT," *Cato at Liberty*, February 20, 2020; Bobby Allyn, "As Trump Targets Twitter's Legal Shield, Experts Have a Warning," NPR, May 30, 2020; Eric J. Savitz, "Why Repealing Section 230 Could Ruin the Internet," *Barron's*, July 18, 2020; Jason Kelley, "Section 230 Is Good, Actually," Electronic Frontier Foundation, December 3, 2020; and Matthew Feeney, "Biden, Section 230, and the Response to Political Extremism," *Cato at Liberty*, January 29, 2021.

16. Christiano Lima, Steven Overly, Nick Niedzwiadek, and Leah Nyler, "'Censorship Teams' vs. 'Working the Refs': Key Moments from Today's Hearing with Tech CEOs," *Politico*, November 17, 2020.

17. Emilie Munson, "Blumenthal Blasts Twitter, Facebook for 'Baby Steps' to Fight Election Disinformation," *CTPost*, November 17, 2020.

18. Maggie Miller, "Twitter Deletes over 170,000 Accounts Tied to Chinese Propaganda Efforts," *The Hill*, June 11, 2020.

19. Tony Romm and Elizabeth Dwoskin, "Twitter Purges More than 70,000 Accounts Affiliated with QAnon Following Capitol Riot," *Washington Post*, January 11, 2021.

20. Ivan Eland, "Big Tech's Gravest Sin: Working with the Security State," *The American Conservative*, January 30, 2021.

21. "Worst-Case Coronavirus Science," editorial, *Wall Street Journal*, March 27, 2020; and Phillip W. Magness, "How Wrong Were the Models, and Why?," American Institute for Economic Research, April 23, 2020.

22. Lauren Egan, "'They're Killing People': Biden Blames Facebook, Other Social Media for Allowing Covid Misinformation," NBC News, July 16, 2021.

23. Steven Nelson, "White House 'Flagging' Posts for Facebook to Censor over COVID Misinformation," *New York Post*, July 16, 2021.

24. Emma-Jo Morris and Gabrielle Fonrouge, "Smoking-Gun Email Reveals How Hunter Biden Introduced Ukrainian Businessman to VP Dad," *New York Post*, October 14, 2020.

25. Glenn Greenwald, "Facebook and Twitter Cross a Line Far More Dangerous than What They Censor," *The Intercept*, October 15, 2020.

26. Elizabeth Dwoskin, "Facebook and Twitter Take Unusual Step to Limit Spread of New York Post Story," *Washington Post*, October 15, 2020.

27. Jordon Davidson, "Lawmakers Condemn Twitter, Facebook Censorship of New York Post's Biden Corruption Report," *Federalist*, October 14, 2020.

28. Andy Kessler, "No Quick Fix for Social Media Bias," *Wall Street Journal*, October 18, 2020.

29. Greenwald, "Facebook and Twitter Cross a Line."

30. "Twitter CEO: Blocking Links to NY Post Biden Story Was 'Wrong,'" Al Jazeera, October 16, 2020.

31. Elizabeth Culliford, "Facebook Removes Anti-Quarantine Protest Events in Some U.S. States," Reuters, April 20, 2020.

32. Brandy Zadrosny, "YouTube, Facebook Split on Removal of Doctors' Viral Coronavirus Videos," NBC News, April 29, 2020.

33. Veronica Morley, "YouTube Issues Statement on Removal of Controversial Video Interview with Bakersfield Doctors," 23 ABC News, April 27, 2020.

34. Matt Taibbi, "The Inevitable Coronavirus Censorship Crisis Is Here," Substack, April 30, 2020.

35. Catherine Shu and Jonathan Shieber, "Facebook, Reddit, Google, LinkedIn, Microsoft, Twitter, and YouTube Issue Joint Statement on Misinformation," *TechCrunch*, March 16, 2020.

36. Arthur Bloom, "They Really Are Lying to You," *The American Conservative*, June 10, 2020. Also see J. Arthur Bloom, "Revealed: Two More Google Blacklists Designed to Remove 'Fringe Domains' and Op-Eds from Special Search Results," *Daily Caller*, June 11, 2019.

37. Jack Goldsmith and Andrew Keane Woods, "Internet Speech Will Never Go Back to Normal," *The Atlantic*, April 25, 2020.

38. Taibbi, "The Inevitable Coronavirus Censorship Crisis Is Here."

39. Goldsmith and Woods, "Internet Speech Will Never Go Back to Normal."

40. Gareth Porter, "FBI Launches Open Attack on 'Foreign' Alternative Media Outlets Challenging U.S. Foreign Policy," GrayZone, June 5, 2020.

41. Quoted in Porter, "FBI Launches Open Attack."

42. David Harsanyi, "NBC News' Attempt to Demonetize the *Federalist* Is Illiberal Insanity," *National Review*, June 16, 2020.

43. Robby Soave, "NBC Said Google Is Demonetizing *The Federalist* for Spreading Fake News; Google Says the NBC Report Is Fake News," *Reason*, June 17, 2020.

44. David Harsanyi, "The Media's 'Russian Disinformation' Canard," *National Review*, October 20, 2020.

45. Karen Kornbluh, Adrienne Goldstein, and Eli Weiner, "New Study by Digital New Deal Finds Engagement with Deceptive Outlets Higher on Facebook Today than Run-up to 2016 Election," German Marshall Fund of the United States, October 12, 2020.

46. "Facebook's Conservative Emergency," editorial, *Wall Street Journal*, October 14, 2020.

47. Kornbluh, Goldstein, and Weiner, "New Study by Digital New Deal."

48. "Facebook's Conservative Emergency," *Wall Street Journal*.

49. Conservative journalists and organizations have made explicit accusations of flagrant bias. See Rod Dreher, "Google Blacklists Conservative Websites," *The American Conservative*, July 21, 2020.

Conclusion

1. U.S. Department of State Archive, Secretary of State Madeleine K. Albright, interview by Matt Lauer, *The Today Show*, NBC, February 19, 1998.

2. James Bovard, "Why I Write," *Mises Wire*, August 10, 2020.

3. Ted Galen Carpenter, "Liberals Love Trump—When He Embraces Military Intervention," *The American Conservative*, November 27, 2017.

4. Typical accounts include Briana Keiler, "The Moral Injury of Abandoning Afghan Allies," CNN, August 18, 2021; Jill Filipovic, "America

Has Abandoned the Women of Afghanistan," CNN, August 18, 2021; and John McCormack, "Biden's Shameful Betrayal of America's Closest Allies in Afghanistan, *National Review*, September 1, 2021.

5. Jack Hunter, "Woeful Neglect: No Mention of Foreign Policy at Democratic Debate," *Washington Examiner*, February 20, 2020.

6. Daniel Larison, "Foreign Policy? What's That?," *The American Conservative*, February 20, 2020.

7. Veronica Stracqualursi, "Tulsi Gabbard Pushes Anti-War Message in First Democratic Debate," CNN, June 27, 2019; and Nick Corasaniti, "Tulsi Gabbard Criticizes Democrats in Democratic Debate, and Kamala Harris Fires Back," *New York Times*, November 20, 2019.

8. Tess Bonn, "Tulsi Gabbard Calls for Foreign Policy-Focused Debate," *The Hill*, September 26, 2019.

9. Paul D. Shinkman, "Why Foreign Policy Has Been Missing from the 2020 Campaign," *U.S. News & World Report*, October 13, 2020.

10. Morgan Chalfant, "Trump Campaign Demands Change to Final Debate Topics," *The Hill*, October 19, 2020.

11. Sharyl Attkisson, *Stonewalled: My Fight to Truth against the Forces of Obstruction, Intimidation, and Harassment in Obama's Washington* (New York: HarperCollins, 2014), p. 26.

12. Lydia Saad, "U.S. Ethics Ratings Rise for Medical Workers and Teachers," Gallup News, December 22, 2020.

13. Nic Newman, *Reuters Institute Digital News Report 2021*, 10th ed. (Oxford, UK: Reuters Institute for the Study of Journalism, June 2021).

14. Alan Tonelson, "Im-Politic: The Mainstream Media's Approval Rating (Rightly) Keeps Sinking," *RealityChek*, December 24, 2020.

15. Colman McCarthy, "When the Media Danced to Jingo Bells," *Washington Post*, March 17, 1991.

16. Amanda Macias, "America Has Spent $6.4 Trillion on Wars in the Middle East and Asia, a New Study Says," CNBC, November 20, 2019.

17. Kirsten Grind, Sam Schechner, Robert McMillan, and John West, "How Google Interferes with Its Search Algorithms and Changes Your Results," *Wall Street Journal*, November 15, 2019.

INDEX

Note: n designates a numbered note.